Vol. 11 *The Doctrine of the Saints' Perseverance Explained and Confirmed.*

Vol. 12 *Vindiciae Evangelicae: or, the Mystery of the Gospel Vindicated.*
Of the Death of Christ, and of Justification.
A Review of the Annotations of Grotius.

Vol. 13 *The Duty of Pastors and People Distinguished.*
Eshcol: a Cluster of the Fruit of Canaan.
Of Schism; in Three Books.
Nonconformity Vindicated.
Tracts on the Power of the Magistrate, Indulgence, Toleration, etc.

Vol. 14 *Animadversions on 'Fiat Lux'.*
Vindication of Animadversions.
The Church of Rome no safe Guide.
On Union among Protestants.
The State and Fate of Protestantism.

Vol. 15 *Discourse concerning Liturgies.*
Discourse concerning Evangelical Love, Church Peace, and Unity.
Inquiry concerning Evangelical Churches.
Answer to Dr Stillingfleet on the unreasonableness of Separation.
Instruction in the Worship of God.

Vol. 16 *The Nature of a Gospel Church.*
Tracts on Excommunication, Church Censures, Baptism, etc.
On the Divine Original of the Scriptures.
Posthumous Sermons.
Indices.

DIVISION 4 : EXPOSITORY

Vol. 17 *Concerning the Epistle to the Hebrews.*
Concerning the Messiah.
Concerning the Jewish Church.

Vol. 18 *The Sacerdotal Office of Christ.*
A Day of Sacred Rest.
Summary of Observations on Hebrews.

Vol. 19 *Exposition of Hebrews, 1–3:6.*

Vol. 20 *Exposition of Hebrews, 3:7–5:14.*

Vol. 21 *Exposition of Hebrews, 6:1–7:28.*

Vol. 22 *Exposition of Hebrews, 8:1–10:39.*

Vol. 23 *Exposition of Hebrews, 11:1–13:25.*

The Works of John Owen

VOLUME VIII

The Works of JOHN OWEN

EDITED BY

William H. Goold

VOLUME VIII

The Banner of Truth Trust

THE BANNER OF TRUTH TRUST

Head Office
3 Murrayfield Road
Edinburgh, EH12 6EL
UK

North America Office
610 Alexander Spring Road
Carlisle, PA 17015
USA

banneroftruth.org

This edition of *The Works Of John Owen* first published by
Johnstone & Hunter, 1850-53

Reprinted by the Banner of Truth Trust, 1967
Reprinted 1976, 1982, 1991, 1999, 2009, 2019, 2024

VOLUME VIII

*

ISBN
This volume: 978 0 85151 066 8
16-volume set: 978 0 85151 392 8

*

Printed in the USA by
Versa Press Inc.,
East Peoria, IL.

CONTENTS OF VOL. VIII.

SERMON I.

A VISION OF UNCHANGEABLE, FREE MERCY, IN SENDING THE MEANS OF GRACE TO UNDESERVING SINNERS.

SERMON II.

A MEMORIAL OF THE DELIVERANCE OF ESSEX COUNTY, AND COMMITTEE.

SERMON III.

RIGHTEOUS ZEAL ENCOURAGED BY DIVINE PROTECTION.

SERMON IV.

THE STEADFASTNESS OF THE PROMISES, AND THE SINFULNESS OF STAGGERING.

SERMON V.

THE SHAKING AND TRANSLATING OF HEAVEN AND EARTH.

SERMON VI.

THE BRANCH OF THE LORD THE BEAUTY OF ZION; OR, THE GLORY OF THE CHURCH IN ITS RELATION UNTO CHRIST.

SERMON VII.

THE ADVANTAGE OF THE KINGDOM OF CHRIST IN THE SHAKING OF THE KINGDOMS OF THE WORLD.

SERMON VIII.

THE LABOURING SAINT'S DISMISSION TO REST

SERMON IX.

CHRIST'S KINGDOM AND THE MAGISTRATE'S POWER.

SERMON X.

GOD'S WORK IN FOUNDING ZION, AND HIS PEOPLE'S DUTY THEREUPON.

SERMON XI.

GOD'S PRESENCE WITH A PEOPLE THE SPRING OF THEIR PROSPERITY.

SERMON XII.

THE GLORY AND INTEREST OF NATIONS PROFESSING THE GOSPEL.

SERMON XIII.

HOW WE MAY BRING OUR HEARTS TO BEAR REPROOFS.

SERMON XIV.

THE TESTIMONY OF THE CHURCH IS NOT THE ONLY NOR THE CHIEF REASON OF OUR BELIEVING THE SCRIPTURE TO BE THE WORD OF GOD.

SERMON XV.

THE CHAMBER OF IMAGERY IN THE CHURCH OF ROME LAID OPEN.

SERMON XVI.

AN HUMBLE TESTIMONY UNTO THE GOODNESS AND SEVERITY OF GOD IN HIS DEALING WITH SINFUL CHURCHES AND NATIONS.

PREFACE.

THE two following volumes contain, it is believed, the most complete collection of Dr Owen's Sermons which has ever been published.

The first volume (vol. viii.) includes all the Discourses which were published during the lifetime of the author. Among these there will be found his "Humble Testimony to the Goodness and Severity of God;" which—though, from its length, it might rank as a separate treatise—is comprehended in this volume, as it was the substance of some discourses, and is entitled by Owen himself a Discourse. Another valuable sermon, which we have discovered in the "Morning Exercises against Popery, at Southwark," though omitted in every previous collection of his Sermons, and in Russell's edition of his Works, we have not hesitated to include in the present collection, our conviction that it belongs to Owen resting on the high authority of Calamy,[1] who must have had the best opportunities of knowing what sermons, in a publication so important and celebrated as the "Morning Exercises," were the productions of our author. We are strengthened in this conviction by the circumstance, that the Rev. T. H. Horne, also, in the recent admirable edition of the "Morning Exercises," expressly ascribes this sermon to Owen. It is entitled, "The Testimony of the Church not the only nor the chief Reason of our Believing the Scripture to be the Word of God." On the contrary, we have assigned to the subsequent volume, which contains the Posthumous Discourses of our author, a sermon entitled, "Human Power Defeated," though we find it mentioned by Mr Orme in his list of the works which Owen himself committed to the press. Our reason for accounting it posthumous, is not simply that we have not met with it in its original form (for in a few other instances we have been unable to discover copies of original editions), but in the folio volume of Owen's Sermons, published in 1721, and edited so carefully by five Independent ministers, who assure us that the posthumous sermons contained in it were the genuine productions of Owen, "a great part of them having been transcribed from his own copies, and the rest taken from his mouth by a gentleman[2] of honour and known integrity," it is ranked among the posthumous sermons, which had then for the first time been given to the public.

[1] See Calamy's Account of Ministers Ejected, vol. ii. p. 56.
[2] Sir John Hartopp. See vol. ix. p. 18.

The other volume (vol. ix.) embraces all the Posthumous Sermons of our author,—viz., the "Seasonable Words for English Protestants," printed separately in 1690; the posthumous sermons published in 1721; others which issued from the press in 1756, and were prepared from the manuscripts of Sir John Hartopp, which his granddaughter, Mrs Cooke of Stoke Newington, had supplied for the purpose; and, finally, the sermons derived through the same channel, and published in 1760.

An attempt has been made in this edition, by prefatory notes and running annotations, to connect the different sermons (especially in vol. viii.) with the life of Owen, and with the circumstances in which they were originally delivered. Much of the interest and value of a discourse lies in its suitableness to the occasion which called it forth.

There are discourses attributed to Owen on Ps. cxvi. 12, and on 2 Sam. xviii. 20; and said to have been published, the former in 1742, and the latter in 1746. They are not mentioned by Mr Orme. There is a reference to them in Cooke's "Preacher's Assistant;" but after a diligent search, we have failed to recover them.

The merits of Owen as a preacher have not been sufficiently appreciated. In this respect he seems to have stood higher in the estimation of his contemporaries than he has subsequently done. No edition of his Sermons has been published in a form and at a price which placed them within the reach of all classes in the community. Perhaps the value of his other works diverted attention from his minor productions; and his style of careful and elaborate, though often prolix and cumbrous, discussion, was deemed incompatible with the condensation of statement and the vigour of appeal which constitute the main value and charm of a good discourse. From the accounts transmitted to us, however, whether by his various friends and admirers, such as Clarkson, his colleague and successor, or by those even who were quite opposed to him in principle and sentiment, such as Anthony Wood, the ability with which Owen could secure and sustain the attention of an audience must have been great.[1] The effects of his preaching in some instances attest his usefulness in this department of his public labours. John Rogers, in his singular work, "The Heavenly Nymph," records the cases of two individuals, Dorothy Emett and Major Mainwaring, who ascribed their conversion to the preaching of Owen when he was in Dublin. Mr Orme remarks, that the circumstance confutes a saying attributed to Owen, that he never knew an instance of a sinner converted through his instrumentality; though the saying might so far be true, that he himself might be ignorant of the extent of his own usefulness. His congregation in London after the Restoration, though, from the severe measures adopted against Dissent, necessarily small, seems to have been made up of persons altogether superior in character and attainments. Another

[1] See some excellent observations on his character as a pulpit orator, in the "Life of Owen," vol. i. p. 106.

source of evidence as to the popularity and acceptance of our author in preaching the gospel, presents itself in the frequency with which he was called to officiate in this capacity before the House of Commons. He was generally summoned to this duty in connection with some event or crisis of great importance. On examining the journals of the House, we have found that he preached before it on several occasions besides those on which he delivered sermons that were afterwards published. He usually receives the thanks, or "the hearty thanks," of the House, for "his great pains" taken in the discourses preached before them. Nor were such "orders" of the Parliament, that he should be thanked for his services, mere form and indiscriminate courtesy. There is a curious record which we may quote, as showing that the Parliament exercised some measure of discrimination in voting thanks on these occasions:—

"*Die Veneris*, 14 *Martii*, 1650.

"The question being propounded, That thanks be given to the ministers that preached yesterday before the Parliament, and the question being put, 'That that question be now put?' it passed with the negative."

There are no means of ascertaining what ministers actually preached on the occasion here referred to. The ministers who had been appointed to preach were Mr Owen, Mr John Simson, and Mr Leigh; but it is clear from the journals, that Owen sometimes was not in circumstances to fulfil such appointments after they had been made. Perhaps, were all the facts known, it would have been to his credit that he had incurred what wears the aspect of a vote of censure from the House; although we learn, from certain entries elsewhere in its journals, that he was so much of a favourite with Parliament, that they settled "lands of inheritance of the clear value of £100 per annum in Ireland on John Owen, Doctor of Divinity, and his heirs."

His Discourses themselves, however, will best illustrate the position and rank to which he is entitled among the lights and ornaments of the British pulpit. In judging of them, we must remember how often his singular aptitude for the management of affairs drew him into public business, interrupting and disturbing the leisure requisite for elaborate composition. The amount of time and thought expended on more important works might interfere with the care due to the preparation of a single discourse. He himself informs us that his public discourses were frequently delivered under some sudden call to the duty, and at the spur of some great emergency, when brief space was allowed him to prepare them carefully; so that, to use his own similitude, they were often "like Jonah's gourd, the offspring of a night." Although they cannot, therefore, be regarded as models of finished composition and careful preparation, they nevertheless abound in many cardinal excellencies. The doctrine illustrated and urged in them is commonly founded on a sifting and masterly exposition of that portion of Scripture from which the text is selected. So much was it his habit to investigate Scripture, with the view of ascertaining the precise import of its statements, that he often sheds new and striking light on other passages besides the one which it may be the object of the sermon to explain and enforce. Singular tact is evinced in eliciting the general truths or principles raised for consideration by the text. While there are many indications of haste and negligence, it may be safely affirmed, that there is not a paragraph of worthless or frivolous matter which any reader could have wished away, and passages often occur conceived in no common strain of eloquence; while, even amidst the tamest sentences, burning thoughts are found, thrown out freely and at random by the author, as if unconscious of the effect they would produce, or careless whether they produced any effect at all. The depths of Christian experience are admirably unfolded, and the general spirit and tenor of his statements are calculated to tell with power upon the unconverted, and to commend themselves with acceptance to the enlightened conscience. No feature, indeed, in his sermons is more prominent and remarkable,—especially in the sermons delivered towards the close of his life, and which labour under the disadvantage of never having been intended for the press,—than the skill with which he can scrutinize character and motives, till his hearers must have felt as if, in gauging their inward being, the preacher had laid his hand, with intuitive discernment, on the deepest secrets of their bosom. Nor does this result from an affected refinement of metaphysical discussion and analysis; but from the simple adaptation of truth, so as to tell on the wide variety of human character. Among uninspired authors, it is pre-eminently true of Owen, that, by the manifestation of the truth, he commends himself to every man's conscience in the sight of God. At the same time, the highest qualities of thought and a rare knowledge of human nature are often evinced; and on perusing the sermons on Popery, "The Chamber of Imagery," and, "On the Authority of Scripture," the reader will be struck with the powers of sagacious and philosophic analysis displayed in the former, and with the logical point and acumen of the latter,—stamping on them a freshness and value as continued and enduring as the importance of the great controversy itself to which they relate. The more, in short, these Discourses of Owen are studied, it will be found that their chief blemish—if it be a blemish—is the tendency of the author, in the fertility of his resources, to compress within the limits of one sermon what, to minds less affluent, would have furnished precious materials for several sermons; and though some may desiderate in them the minor graces of composition, it would be unwise to forget that, apart from any shapes of elegance and utility into which it may be fashioned by art, sterling gold, in the broad market of the world, will always command a value of its own.

EDITOR.

SERMON I.

A VISION OF UNCHANGEABLE, FREE MERCY, IN SENDING THE MEANS OF GRACE TO UNDESERVING SINNERS:

WHEREIN GOD'S UNCONTROLLABLE ETERNAL PURPOSE, IN SENDING AND CONTINUING THE GOSPEL UNTO THIS NATION, IN THE MIDST OF OPPOSITIONS AND CONTINGENCIES, IS DISCOVERED; HIS DISTINGUISHING MERCY IN THIS GREAT WORK EXALTED, ASSERTED AGAINST OPPOSERS, REPINERS.

WHEREUNTO IS ANNEXED

A SHORT DEFENSATIVE ABOUT CHURCH GOVERNMENT, (WITH A COUNTRY ESSAY FOR THE PRACTICE OF CHURCH GOVERNMENT THERE) TOLERATION, AND PETITIONS ABOUT THESE THINGS.

PREFATORY NOTE.

The occasion on which this sermon was delivered is mentioned in the "Life of Owen," vol. i. p. 34. From the title-page of the original edition of the sermon, Owen appears to have been "minister of the gospel at Coggeshall, in Essex," when it was published. By some inadvertency, Mr Orme, in his valuable memoir of our author, represents him as called to preach this sermon to the House of Commons before he left the parish of Fordham; a statement which can be reconciled with the original title-page only by the supposition that his removal to Coggeshall had occurred in the interval before the publication of the sermon. Asty, however, distinctly informs us that he was settled at Coggeshall when he first preached before the House of Commons.

The sermon was preached on Wednesday the 29th of April 1646; and the time is important, as it was the close of the first civil war. During the previous month, Hopton and Astley, the last generals who kept the field in the interest of Charles I., had been compelled to surrender. "You have now done your work," said Astley to his victors, "and may go to play,—unless you will fall out among yourselves." So truly was the work done, that Oliver Cromwell had returned to his place in Parliament on the 22d of April, and on the following Monday the king left Oxford in disguise, and, after some hesitation of purpose, found his way to the Scots army.

A sufficient interval had hardly elapsed to give Owen an opportunity of exhibiting in his sermon any reflection of these memorable events. It is perhaps more to his credit, that, when summoned from the obscurity of his pastoral duties at Coggeshall to preach the gospel in "the chief place of concourse," and before the rulers of the land, he seizes the opportunity to portray the spiritual destitution which existed in Wales, and large districts of England, and to make an appeal for "help," in a strain of holy fervour and commanding eloquence, that will bear comparison with the best productions of the British pulpit. The reasoning at the outset is somewhat abstract,—not unsuited, perhaps, to an assembly of the leading men in the country; but throughout the discourse there is conspicuous that happy combination of argument and declamation which constitutes genuine oratory. Bogue and Bennett have remarked, "Those who are only acquainted with the general strain of Owen's writings, would not suppose him capable of pouring forth that flood of lucid, glowing, popular eloquence, which is displayed in this sermon."—History of Dissenters, vol. ii. p. 228.

In the "Defensative," or preface to the "Country Essay," etc., Owen assigns reasons on account of which he had not felt himself free to petition Parliament in reference to the establishment of an ecclesiastical polity for England. In the "Country Essay," etc., he condemns very strongly the infliction of civil penalties for religious belief. In the first part of it, he describes a form of church government which commended itself to his judgment. Owen purposely refrained from describing it either as Presbytery or Independency, deeming himself competent to satisfy all men respecting it; "unless such as shall be so simple or malicious as to ask whether this way be that of the Presbyterians or Independents." By his own admission, the scheme proposed in the "Essay" would not exactly agree with either of the two forms of church government which were then competing for national favour and the sanction of the state. There can be no doubt, however, that he was at this time undergoing the change of view which led him in the end to profess Congregationalism. It is simple justice to add, that a comparison of the "Country Essay" with his "Inquiry into Evangelical Churches," published towards the close of his life, effectually redeems his name from any charge of vacillation in regard to his church principles. The peculiar modifications which appear in the Congregationalism of Owen, are conspicuous elements in the first scheme of ecclesiastical polity which he ever broached. See also his "Review of the Nature of Schism," chap. ii. vol. xiii.—Ed.

AMPLISSIMO

SENATUI,

INCLYTISSIMO POPULI ANGLICANI CONVENTUI,

OB

PRISCA ANGLO-BRITANNORUM JURA
STRENUE ET FIDELITER ASSERTA;

LIBERTATEM PATRIAM (NEFARIIS QUORUNDAM MOLITIONIBUS
PÆNE PESSUNDATAM) RECUPERATAM;

JUSTITIAM FORTITER, *ἴσως, ἐπιεικῶς, ἀπροσωπολήπτως*
ADMINISTRATAM;

Ἀρχὴν IN ECCLESIASTICIS *ἀνιεροτυραννικὴν* DISSOLUTAM,

RITUS PONTIFICIOS, NOVITIOS, ANTICHRISTIANOS ABOLITOS;
PRIVILEGIA PLEBIS CHRISTIANÆ POSTLIMINIO RESTITUTA;

POTISSIMUM

PROTECTIONEM DEI O.M. HIS OMNIBUS, ALIISQUE INNUMERIS,
CONSILIO, BELLO, DOMI, FORAS GRATIOSE POTITAM;

TOTO ORBE JURE MERITISSIMO CELEBERRIMO,
TOTI HUIC INSULÆ ÆTERNA MEMORIA RECOLENDO,

VIRIS ILLUSTRIBUS, CLARISSIMIS, SELECTISSIMIS, EX ORDINE COMMUNIUM IN SUPREMA CURIA PARLIAM. CONGREGATIS,

CONCIONEM HANC SACRAM, HUMILEM ILLAM QUIDEM,
IPSORUM TAMEN VOTO JUSSUQUE PRIUS CORAM IPSIS HABITAM,
NUNC LUCE DONATAM,

D.D.C.
JOANNES OWEN.

Die Mercurij, 29 *Aprilis*, 1646.

ORDERED, by the Commons assembled in Parliament, That Mr Jenner and Sir Peter Wentworth do from this House give thanks to Mr Nalton and Mr Owen for the great pains they took in the sermons they preached this day, at the entreaty of this House (it being a day of public humiliation), at Margaret's, Westminster; and to desire them to print their sermons. And it is ordered that none shall presume to print their sermons without licence under their hand-writing.

H. ELSYNGE, *Cler. Parl. D. Com.*

SERMON I.

A VISION OF UNCHANGEABLE, FREE MERCY, IN SENDING THE MEANS OF GRACE TO UNDESERVING SINNERS.

"And a vision appeared to Paul in the night: There stood a man of Macedonia, and prayed him, saying, Come over into Macedonia, and help us."—ACTS xvi. 9.

THE kingdom of Jesus Christ is frequently in the Scripture compared to *growing* things,[1]—small in the beginning and first appearance, but increasing by degrees unto glory and perfection. The shapeless *stone*[2] cut out without hands, having neither form nor desirable beauty given unto it, becomes a great mountain, filling the whole earth, Dan. ii. 35. The small *vine* brought out of Egypt quickly covers the hills with her shadow,—her boughs reach unto the sea, and her branches unto the river, Ps. lxxx. 8. The tender *plant*[3] becomes as the cedars of God; and the grain of mustard-seed to be a tree for the fowls of the air to make their nests in the branches thereof. Mountains are made plains before it, every valley is filled, and the crooked paths made straight, that it may have a passage to its appointed period;—and all this, not only not supported by outward advantages, but in direct opposition to the combined power[4] of this whole creation, as fallen and in subjection to the "god of this world," the head thereof. As Christ was "a tender plant,"[5] seemingly easy to be broken; and "a root out of a dry ground," not easily flourishing, yet liveth for ever;[6] so his people and kingdom,—though as a "lily among thorns,"[7] as "sheep among wolves,"[8] as a "turtle-dove" among a multitude of devourers,[9]—yet stands unshaken, at least unshivered.

[1] "Ecclesia sicut luna defectus habet, et ortus frequentes; sed defectibus suis crevit, &c. Hæc est vera Luna, quæ de fratris sui luce perpetua, lumen sibi immortalitatis et gratiæ mutuatur."—Amb. Hex., lib. iv. cap. 2. Ps. lxviii. 13.

[2] Isa. liv. 11; Zech. iv. 7.

[3] Isa. liii. 2–5.

[4] 1 John iii. 13; Rev. ii. 10; 2 Cor. iv. 4.

[5] Isa. liii. 2.

[6] Heb. vii. 25.

[7] Cant. ii. 2.

[8] Matt. x. 16.

[9] Ps. lxxiv. 19.

The main ground and foundation of all this is laid out, verses 6–9 of this chapter,—containing a rich discovery how all things here below, especially such as concern the gospel and Church of Christ, are carried along through innumerable varieties and a world of contingencies, according to the regular motions and goings forth of a free, eternal, unchangeable decree: as all inferior orbs, notwithstanding the eccentrics and irregularities of their own inhabitants, are orderly carried about by the first Mover.

In verse 6, the planters of the gospel are " forbidden to preach the word in Asia"[1] (that part of it peculiarly so called); and, verse 7, assaying to go with the same message into Bithynia, they are crossed by the Spirit in their attempts; but in my text are called to a place on which their thoughts were not at all fixed:—which calling and which forbidding were both subservient to His free determination " who worketh all things according to the counsel of his own will," Eph. i. 11.

And no doubt but, in the dispensation of the gospel throughout the world, unto this day, there is the like conformity to be found to the pattern of God's eternal decrees; though to the messengers not made known aforehand by *revelation*, but discovered in the *effects*, by the mighty working of Providence.

Amongst other nations, this is the day of England's visitation, "the Day-spring from on high" having visited this people, and " the Sun of righteousness" arising upon us " with healing in his wings;"[2]—a man of England hath prevailed for assistance, and the free grace of God hath wrought us help by the gospel.

Now, in this day three things are to be done, to keep up our spirits unto this duty, of bringing down our souls by humiliation.

First, To take us off the *pride* of our own performances, endeavours, or any adherent worth of our own: "Not for your sakes do I this, saith the Lord God, be it known unto you: be ashamed and confounded for your own ways, O house of Israel,"—O house of England! Ezek. xxxvi. 32.

Secondly, To root out that *atheistical* corruption which *depresses* the thoughts of men, not permitting them, in the highest products of Providence, to look above contingencies and secondary causes;—though God "hath wrought all our works for us," Isa. xxvi. 12; and "known unto him are all his works from the beginning of the world," Acts xv. 18.

Thirdly, To show that the bulk of this people are as yet in the

[1] "Eo ipso tempore, quo ad omnes gentes prædicatio Evangelii mittebatur, quædam loca apostolis adire prohibebatur ab eo, qui 'vult omnes homines salvos fieri.'"—Prosp. Ep. ad Rufin. [cap. xv]. Διὸς δ' ἐτελείετο βουλή.—Hom. i. 5.

[2] Mal. iv. 2.

wilderness, far from their resting-place, like sheep upon the mountains, as once Israel, Jer. l. 6,—as yet wanting help by the gospel.

The *two first* of these will be cleared by discovering how that all revolutions here below—especially every thing that concerns the dispensation of the gospel and kingdom of the Lord Jesus—are carried along according to the eternally fixed purpose of God, free in itself, taking neither rise, growth, cause, nor occasion, from any thing amongst the sons of men.

The *third,* by laying open the helpless condition of gospel-wanting souls, with some particular application; to all which my text directly leads me.

The words in general are the relation of a message from heaven unto Paul, to direct him in the publishing of the gospel,—as to the place and persons wherein and to whom he was to preach. And in them you have these four things:—

1. The *manner* of it; it was by vision,—"A vision appeared."
2. The *time* of it,—"In the night."
3. The *bringer* of it,—"A man of Macedonia."
4. The *matter* of it,—help for the Macedonians, interpreted, verse 18, to be by preaching of the gospel.

A little clearing of the words will make way for observations.

1. For the manner of the delivery of this message,—it was by *vision.* Of all the ways that God used of old to reveal himself unto any in an extraordinary manner,—which were sundry and various, Heb. i. 1,—there was no one so frequent as this of vision. Wherein this did properly consist, and whereby it was distinguished from other ways of the discovery of the secrets of the Lord, I shall not now discuss. In general, visions are revelations of the mind of the Lord concerning some hidden things, present or future, and not otherwise to be known. And they were of two sorts.

(1.) Revelations merely by *word*[1] or some other more internal species,[2] without any outward sensible appearance; which, for the most part, was the Lord's way of proceeding with the prophets;—which transient light, or discovery of things before unknown, they called a vision.[3]

(2.) Revelations accompanied with some sensible *apparitions,* and that either,—

[1.] Of *things;* as usually, among the prophets, rods and pots,[4] wheels and trees,[5] lamps, axes, vessels, rams, goats, and the like, were presented unto them.

[2.] Of *persons;* and those, according to the variety of them, of three sorts.

[1] Isa. i. 1. [2] Amos i. 1. [3] Nahum i. 1; Obad. 1. [4] Jer. i. 11, 13.
[5] Ezek. i. 5–7; Zech. i. 8, iii. 9, 10, &c.; Dan. vii. 8, 9.

1*st*, Of the second person of the Trinity; and this either,—

First, In respect of some glorious *beams* of his *Deity;* as to Isaiah, chapter vi. 1, with John xii. 41;—to Daniel, chapter x. 5, 6,—as afterward to John, Rev. i. 13–15; to which you may add the apparitions of the glory of God not immediately designing the second person, as Ezek. i.

Secondly, With reference to his *humanity* to be assumed; as to Abraham, Gen. xviii. 1, 2;—to Joshua, chapter v. 13–15, &c.

2*dly*, Of angels; as unto Peter, Acts xii. 7;—to the women, Matt. xxviii. 5;—to John, Rev. xxii. 8, &c.

3*dly*, Of men;[1] as in my text.

Now, the several advancements of all these ways in dignity and pre-eminence, according as they clearly make out intellectual verity, or according to the honour and exaltation of that whereof apparition is made, are too fruitless a speculation[2] for this day's exercise.

Our vision is of the latter sort, accompanied with a sensible appearance, and is called ὅραμα. There be two words in the New Testament signifying vision, ὅραμα and ὀπτασία, coming from different verbs, but both signifying *to see*. Some distinguish them, and say that ὀπτασία is a vision,—καθ' ὕπαρ, an appearance to a man awake; ὅραμα,—καθ' ὄναρ, an appearance to a man asleep, called sometimes a dream, Job xxxiii. 15,—like that which was made to Joseph, Matt. ii. 19. But this distinction will not hold, our Saviour calling that vision which his disciples had at his transfiguration, when doubtless they were waking, ὅραμα, Matt. xvii. 9. So that I conceive Paul had his vision waking;—and the night is specified as the time thereof, not to intimate his being asleep, but rather his watchfulness, seeking counsel of God in the night which way he should apply himself in the preaching of the gospel. And such I suppose was that of latter days, whereby God revealed to Zuinglius a strong confirmation of the doctrine of the Lord's supper, from Exod. xii. 11, against the factors for that monstrous figment of transubstantiation.

2. For the second, or time of this vision, I need say no more than what before I intimated.

3. The bringer of the message,—ἀνήρ τις ἦν Μακεδὼν ἑστὼς, he was a man of Macedonia in a vision. The Lord made an appearance unto him as of a man of Macedonia, discovering even to his bodily eyes a man; and to his mind, that he was to be conceived as a man of Macedonia. This was, say some,[3] an angel;—the tutelar angel of the place, say the popish expositors,[4] or the genius of the place, according to the phrase of the heathens, of whom they learned their demonology;—perhaps him, or his antagonist, that not long before ap-

[1] Zech. ii. 1. [2] Vid. Aquin. 2, 2, q. 174, art. 3, 4. Scot. in dist. tert.
[3] Mede, Apost. of Later Times. [4] A Lapide, Sanctius in locum, &c.

peared to Brutus[1] at Philippi. But these are pleasing dreams;—us it may suffice that it was the appearance of a man, the mind of Paul being enlightened to apprehend him as a man[2] of Macedonia; and that with infallible assurance, such as usually accompanieth divine revelations in them to whom they are made, as Jer. xxiii. 28,—for upon it Luke affirmeth, verse 10, they assuredly concluded that the Lord called them into Macedonia.

4. The message itself is a discovery of the *want* of the Macedonians, and the *assistance* they required, which the Lord was willing should be imparted unto them. Their want is not expressed, but included in the assistance desired, and the person unto whom for it they were directed. Had it been to help them in their estates, they should scarcely have been sent to Paul, who, I believe, might for the most part say, with Peter, "Silver and gold have I none;"[3]—or had it been with a complaint that they—who from a province of Greece, in a corner of Europe, had on a sudden been exalted into the empire of the eastern world—were now enslaved to the Roman power and oppression, they might better have gone to the Parthians, then the only state in the world formidable to the Romans. Paul, though a military man, yet fought not with Nero's legions, the then visible devil of the upper world; but with legions of hell, of whom the earth was now to be cleared.[4] It must be a soul-want, if he be intrusted with the supplying of it. And such this was,—help from death, hell, Satan, from the jaws of that devouring lion. Of this the Lord makes them here to speak, what every one in that condition ought to speak,—Help, for the Lord's sake. It was a call to preach the gospel.

The words being opened, we must remember what was said before of their connection with the verses foregoing,—wherein the preachers of the gospel are expressly hindered from above from going to other places, and called hither. Whereof no reason is assigned, but only the will of Him that did employ them; and that no other can be rendered I am farther convinced, by considering the empty conjectures of attempters.

God foresaw that they would *oppose* the gospel, says our Beda. So, say I, might he of all nations in the world, had not he determined to send his effectual grace[5] for the removal of that opposition;

[1] Plutarch. in Vit. Bruti.

[2] Calvin. in locum. "Dicebat se discernere (nescio quo sapore, quem verbis explicare non poterat) quid interesset inter Deum revelantem," &c.—Aug. Confes.

[3] Acts iii. 6.

[4] Plutarch de Defect. Oracu.

Ἑβραῖος κέλεταί με παῖς μακάρεσσιν ἀνάσσων,
Τὸν δὲ δόμον προλιπεῖν καὶ ὁδὸν πάλιν αὖθις ἱκέσθαι.

Respons. Apoll. apud Euseb. Niceph.

[5] "A nullo duro corde resistitur, quia cor ipsum emollit."—Aug., Ezek. xxxvi. 26; Deut. xxx. 6.

besides, he grants the means of grace to despisers, Matt. xi. 21.—They were not *prepared* for the gospel, says Oecumenius. As well, say I, as the Corinthians, whose preparations you may see, 1 Cor. vi. 9–11; or any other nation, as we shall afterward declare: yet to this foolish conjecture adhere the Papists and Arminians.[1]—God would have those places left for to be *converted by John*, says Sedulius; yet the church at Ephesus, the chief city of those parts, was planted by Paul, says Ignatius and Irenæus.[2]—He foresaw a *famine* to come upon those places, says Origen, from which he would deliver his own; and therefore, it seems, left them to the power of the devil. More such fancies[3] might we recount, of men unwilling to submit to the will of God; but upon that, as the sole discriminating cause of these things, we rest, and draw these three observations:—

I. The *rule* whereby all things are dispensed here below,—especially in the making out of the means of grace,—*is the determinate will and counsel of God.* Stay not in Asia, go not into Bithynia, but come to Macedonia. "Even so, Father; for so it seemed good in thy sight."

II. The *sending* of the gospel to any nation, place, or persons, rather than others, as the means of life and salvation, *is of the mere free grace and good pleasure of God.* "Stay not in Asia;" &c.

III. *No men in the world want help, like them that want the gospel.* "Come and help us."

I. Begin we with the first of these: The rule whereby, &c. All events and effects, especially concerning the propagation of the gospel and the Church of Christ, are, in their greatest variety, regulated by the eternal purpose and counsel of God.[4]

All things below in their events are but the *wax*,[5] whereon the eternal *seal* of God's purpose hath left its own impression; and they every way answer unto it. It is not my mind to extend this to the generality of things in the world, nor to show how the creature can by no means deviate from that eternal rule of providence whereby it is guided;—no more than an arrow can avoid the mark, after it hath received the impression of an unerring hand,—or well-ordered wheels not turn according to the motion given them by the master-spring,—or the wheels in Ezekiel's vision[6] move irregularly to the spirit of life that was in them. Nor yet, secondly, how that, on the other

[1] Lapide. Sanctius in loc. Rom. Script. Synd. ar. 1.

[2] Ὑμεῖς μὲν οὖν ἐστε τοιοῦτοι, ὑπὸ τοιῶνδε παιδευτῶν στοιχειωθέντες, Παύλου τοῦ Χριστοφόρου.—Ignat. Epist. ad Eph.; Iren., lib. iii. cap. 3.

[3] "Qui causam quæ sit voluntatis divinæ, aliquid majus eo quærit."—Aug. "Voluntas Dei nullo modo causam habet."—Aquin. p. q. 12, a. 5.

[4] Θεία πάντων ἀρχὴ, δι᾽ ἧς ἃ πάντα καὶ ἔστι, καὶ διαμένει.—Theophrast. apud Picum. de Provid.

[5] "Providentia est ratio ordinis rerum ad finem."—Th. p. q. 22, a. 1, 6.

[6] Ezek. i.

side, doth no way prejudice the liberty of second causes,[1] in their actions, agreeable to the natures they are endued withal. He who made and preserves the fire, and yet hinders not but that it should burn, or act necessarily agreeable to its nature; by his making, preserving, and guiding of men, hindereth not, yea, effectually causeth, that they work freely, agreeable to their nature. Nor yet, thirdly, to clear up what a straight line runs through all the darkness, confusion, and disorder in the world,[2]—how absolutely, in respect of the first fountain and last tendency of things, there is neither deformity, fault, nor deviation, every thing that is amiss consisting in the transgression of a moral rule, which is the sin of the creature,[3] the first cause being free:—as he that causeth a lame man to go, is the cause of his going, but not of his going lame;—or the sun exhaling a smell from the kennel, is the cause of the smell, but not of its noisomeness; for from a garden his beams raise a sweet savour. Nothing is amiss but what goeth off from its own rule; which he cannot do who will do all his pleasure,[4] and knows no other rule.

But omitting these things, I shall tie my discourse to that which I chiefly aimed at in my proposition; viz., to discover how the great variety which we see in the dispensation of the means of grace, proceedeth from, and is regulated by, some eternal purpose of God, unfolded in his word. To make out this, we must lay down three things.

1. The wonderful variety in dispensing of the outward *means* of salvation, in respect of them unto whom they were granted, used by the Lord since the fall;—I say, since the fall, for the grace of *preserving* from sin, and *continuing* with God, had been *general*, universally extended to every creature; but [as] for the grace of *rising* from sin, and *coming* again unto God, *that* is made exceeding *various*, by some distinguishing purpose.

2. That this outward dispensation being presupposed, yet in *effectual working upon particular persons*, there is no less *variety*; for "he hath mercy on whom he will have mercy."

3. Discover the *rules* of this whole administration.

1. For the first, The promise was at first made unto Adam, and by him doubtless conveyed to his issue, and preached to the several generations which his eyes beheld proceeding from his own loins;[5] but yet by the wickedness of the old world, all flesh corrupting their ways, we may easily collect that the knowledge of it quickly departed

[1] Non tantum res, sed rerum modos.

[2] "Videtur ergo quod non sit aliqua deordinatio, deformitas, aut peccatum simpliciter in toto universo, sed tantummodo respectu interiorum causarum, ordinationem superioris causæ volentium, licet non valentium, perturbare."—Brad. de Caus. Dei, lib. i. cap. 34.

[3] Ἡ ἁμαρτία ἐστὶν ἡ ἀνομία.

[4] "Adeo summa justitiæ regula est Dei voluntas, ut quicquid vult, eo ipso quod vult, justum habendum sit."—Aug., Isa. xlvi. 10.

[5] Gen. iii. 15, iv. 26.

from the most;—sin banishing the love of God from their hearts, hindered the knowledge of God from continuing in their minds.[1] After many revivings, by visions, revelations, and covenants, it was at length called in from the wide world, and wholly restrained to the house, family, and seed of Abraham,[2] with whom alone all the means of grace continued for thrice fourteen generations. They alone were in Goshen, and all the world besides in thick darkness;—the dew of heaven was on them as the fleece, when else all the earth was dry. God "showeth his word unto Jacob, his statutes and his judgments unto Israel. He hath not dealt so with any nation," Ps. cxlvii. 19, 20. The prerogative of the Jews was chiefly in this, that to them were committed the oracles of God, Rom. iii. To them pertained "the adoption, and the glory, the covenants, and the giving of the law, and the service of God, and the promises," Rom. ix. 4. But when the fulness[3] of time came, the Son of God being sent in the likeness of sinful flesh, drew all men unto him; and God, who had before winked at the time of their ignorance, then called them every where to repent, commanding the gospel to be preached to the universality of reasonable creatures, and the way of salvation to be proclaimed unto all;—upon which, in few years, the sound of the gospel went out into all nations,[4] and the Sun of righteousness displayed his beams upon the habitable parts of the earth. But yet once more this light, by Satan and his agents, persecutors and seducers, is almost extinguished, as was foretold, 2 Thess. ii.,—remaining but in few places, and burning dim where it was,—the kingdom of the beast being full of darkness, Rev. xvi. 10. Yet God again raiseth up reformers, and by them kindles a light, we hope, never to be put out. But, alas! what a spot of ground doth this shine on, in comparison of the former vast extents and bounds of the Christian world! Now, is all this variety, think you, to be ascribed unto chance, as the philosopher thought the world was made by a casual concurrence of atoms? or hath the idol free-will, with the new goddess contingency, ruled in these dispensations? Truly neither the one nor the other, no more than the fly raised the dust by sitting on the chariot wheel;—but all these things have come to pass according to a certain unerring rule, given them by God's determinate purpose and counsel.

2. Presupposing this variety in the outward means, how is it that thereupon one is taken, another left? The promise is made known to Cain and Abel;—one the first murderer, the other the first mar-

[1] Gen. vi. 5. [2] Gen. v. 24, vi. 18, xii. 1, xviii. 1, 2; Ps. lxxvi. 1, 2; John iv. 22.
[3] Gal. iv. 4; John xii. 32; Acts xvii. 30; Mark xvi. 15; Mal. iii. 4; Prov. viii. 31.
[4] See Tertullian, Lib. ad Jud., reckoning almost all the known nations of the world, and affirming that they all,—that is, some in them,—in his days, submitted to the sceptre of Christ. He lived in the end of the second century.

tyr. Jacob and Esau had the same outward advantages; but the one becomes Israel, the other Edom,—the one inherits the promises, the other sells his right for a mess of pottage. At the preaching of our Saviour, some believed, some blasphemed;—some said he was a good man; others said, nay, but he deceived the people. Have we not the word in its power this day, and do we not see the like various effects,—some continuing in impenitency, others in sincerity closing with Jesus Christ? Now, what shall we say to these things? What guides these wheels? who thus steers his word for the good of souls? Why, this also, as I said before, is from some peculiarly distinguishing purpose of the will of God.

3. To open the third thing proposed, I shall show,—(1.) That all this *variety* is according to God's determinate purpose, and answereth thereunto; (2.) The particular purposes from whence this variety proceedeth.

(1.) Eph. i. 11, "He worketh all things according to the counsel of his own will." As a man may be said to erect a fabric[1] according to the counsel of his will, when he frameth it before in his mind, and maketh all things in event answer his preconceived platform,—all things (especially τὰ πάντα, all those things of which the apostle there treateth, gospel things) have their futurition and manner of being from his eternal purpose:[2]—whence also is the idea in the mind of God of all things, with their circumstances,[3] that shall be; that is, the first mover, continuing itself immovable, giving to every thing a regular motion, according to the impression which from that it doth receive: "For known unto him are all his works from the beginning of the world," Acts xv. 18.

If any *attendants* of actions might free and exempt them from the regular dependence we insist upon, they must be either contingency or sin; but yet for both these we have, besides general rules, clear, particular[4] instances. What seems more contingent and casual than the unadvised slaying of a man with the fall of the head of an axe from the helve, as a man was cutting wood by the way side? Deut. xix. 5; yet God assumes this as his own work, Exod. xxi. 13. The same may be said of free agents and their actions. And for the other, see Acts iv. 27, 28,—in the crucifying of the Son of God's love, —all things came to pass according as his counsel had before determined that it should be done. Now, how in the one of these liberty

[1] Piscat. in loc.

[2] Πάντα δὲ λέγω τὰ οὐκ ἐφ' ἡμῖν, τὰ γὰρ ἐφ' ἡμῖν, οὐ τῆς προνοίας, ἀλλὰ τοῦ ἡμετέρου αὐτεξουσίου.—Damascen. Satis impie.

[3] Matt. x. 29; Job xiv. 5; Prov. xvi. 33, xxi. 1, 30, xix. 21. "Nihil fit nisi omnipotens fieri velit, vel ipse faciendo, vel sinendo ut fiat."—Aug.

[4] Gen. iv. 5–7; 1 Kings xxii. 19–21; 2 Kings v. 18, 19; Ps. lxxvi. 10; Eccles. vii. 26; Isa. vi. 9–11, &c.

is not abridged, the nature of things not changed in the other, sin is not countenanced,[1] belongs not to this discourse. "The counsel of the LORD," then, "standeth for ever, the thoughts of his heart unto all generations," Ps. xxxiii. 11. "His counsel standeth, and he will do all his pleasure," Isa. xlvi. 10. For he is the LORD, and he changeth not, Mal. iii. 6. With him is neither variableness nor shadow of turning, James i. 17. All things that are, come to pass in that unchangeable method in which he hath laid them down from all eternity.

(2.) Let us look peculiarly upon the purposes according to which the dispensations of the gospel, both in *sending* and *withholding* it, do proceed.

[1.] For the *not sending* of the means of grace unto any people, whereby they hear not the joyful sound of the gospel, but have in all ages followed dumb idols, as many do unto this day.

In this chapter of which we treat, the gospel is forbidden to be preached in Asia and Bithynia;—which restraint, the Lord by his providence as yet continues to many parts of the world. Now, the purpose from whence this proceedeth, and whereby it is regulated, you have, Rom. ix. 22, "What if God, willing to show his wrath, and to make his power known, endured with much long-suffering the vessels of wrath fitted to destruction?" compared with Matt. xi. 25, 26, "Thou hast hid these things from the wise and prudent. Even so, Father; for so it seemed good in thy sight;" and with Acts xiv. 16,—he "suffered all nations to walk in their own ways."[2] Now, God's not sending the truth, hath the same design and aim with his sending the efficacy of error; viz., "that they all may be damned" who have it not; "there being no other name under heaven, whereby they may be saved," but only that which is not revealed unto them;—God, in the meantime, being no more the cause[3] of their sins, for which they incur damnation, than the sun is the cause of cold and darkness, which follow the absence thereof: or he is the cause of a man's imprisonment for debt, who will not pay his debt for him, though he be no way obliged so to do. So, then, the not sending of the gospel to any people, is an act regulated by that eternal purpose of God whereby he determineth to advance the glory of his justice, by permitting some men to sin, to continue in their sin, and for sin

[1] "Deus non operatur in malis, quod ei displicet; sed operatur per eos quod ei placet, recipientur vero non pro eo, quod Deus bene usus est ipsorum operibus malis, sed pro eo, quod ipsi male abusi sunt Dei operibus bonis."—Fulgent. ad Monim.

[2] 2 Thess. ii.; Acts iv.

[3] "Liberatur pars hominum, parte pereunte. Sed cur horum sit misertus Deus—illorum non misertus, quæ scientia comprehendere, quæ potest investigare sapientia? Latet discretionis istius ratio, sed non latet ipsa discretio."—Prosp. de Vocat. Gen., [lib. i. cap. 15.]

to send them to their own place;—as a king's not sending a pardon to condemned malefactors is an issue of his purpose that they shall die for their faults. When you see the gospel strangely, and through wonderful varieties and unexpected providences, carried away from a people, know that the spirit which moves in those wheels is that purpose of God which we have recounted.

[2.] To some people, to some nations, the gospel is sent. God calls them to repentance and acknowledgment of the truth,—as in my text, Macedonia: and England, the day wherein we breathe. Now, there is in this a twofold aim. 1. *Peculiar*, towards some in their conversion. 2. *General*, towards all, for conviction. And therefore it is acted according to a twofold purpose, which carries it along, and is fulfilled thereby.

First, His purpose of saving[1] some in and by Jesus Christ, effectually to bring them unto himself, for the praise of his glorious grace. Upon whomsoever the seal of the Lord is stamped, that God knows them, and owns them as his, to them he will cause his gospel to be revealed. Acts xviii. 10, Paul is commanded to abide at Corinth, and to preach there, because God had much people in that city. Though the devil had them in present possession,[2] yet they were God's in his eternal counsel. And such as these they were for whose sake the man of Macedonia is sent on his message. Have you never seen the gospel hover about a nation, now and then about to settle, and anon scared and upon wing again; yet working through difficulties, making plains of mountains and filling valleys, overthrowing armies, putting aliens to flight, and at length taking firm root like the cedars of God? Truly if you have not, you are strangers to the place wherein you live. Now, what is all this but the working of *the purpose* of God to attain its proposed end, of gathering his saints to himself? In the effectual working of grace also for conversion and salvation, whence do you think it takes its rule and determination, in respect of particular objects, that it should be directed to John, not Judas,—Simon Peter, not Simon Magus? Why, only from this discriminating[3] counsel of God from eternity, to bring the one and not the other to himself by Christ. "The Lord added to the church such as should be saved," Acts ii. 47. The purpose of saving is the rule of adding to the church of believers. And Acts xiii. 48, "As many believed as were ordained to eternal life." Their fore-ordain-

[1] Rom. viii. 28, 29; Eph. i. 4; 2 Tim. ii. 19.

[2] Eph. ii. 1, 11.

[3] "Non ob aliud dicit, non vos me elegistis, sed ego vos elegi, nisi quia non elegerunt eum, ut eligeret eos; sed ut eligerent eum, elegit eos. Non quia præscivit eos credituros, sed quia facturus ipse fuerit credentes. Electi sunt itaque ante mundi constitutionem, eâ prædestinatione, quâ Deus ipse sua futura facta prævidit: electi sunt autem de mundo eâ vocatione, quâ Deus id, quod prædestinavit, implevit."—August. de Prædest. Sanctorum. cap. xvi., xvii.

ing to life eternal gives them right to faith and belief. The purpose of God's election is the rule of dispensing saving grace.

Secondly, His purpose of leaving some inexcusable[1] in their sins, for the farther manifestation of his glorious justice, is the rule of dispensing the word unto them. Did you never see the gospel sent or continued to an unthankful people,[2] bringing forth no fruits meet for it? Wherefore it is so sent, see Isa vi. 9, 10;—which prophecy you have fulfilled, John xii. 37–41; in men described, Jude 4, and 1 Pet. ii. 8. But here we must strike sail, the waves swell, and it is no easy task to sail in this gulf. The righteousness of God is a great mountain, easy to be seen; but his judgments are like the great deep: who can search into the bottom thereof? Ps. xxxvi. 6. And so I have, I hope, discovered how all things here below, concerning the promulgation of the gospel, are, in their greatest variety, straightly regulated by the eternal purposes and counsel of God.

The uses of it follow.

Use 1. To discover whence it is that the work of reforming the worship of God, and settling the almost departing gospel, hath so powerfully been carried along in this nation;—that a beautiful fabric is seen to arise in the midst of all oppositions, with the confusion of axes and hammers sounding about it, though the builders have been forced oftentimes, not only with one hand, but with both, to hold the weapons[3] of war;—that although the wheels of our chariots have been knocked off, and they driven heavily, yet the regular motions of the superior wheels of providence have carried on the design towards the resting-place aimed at;—that the ship hath been directed to the port, though the storm had quite puzzled the pilots and mariners:—even from hence, that all this great variety was but to work out one certain fore-appointed end, proceeding in the tracts and paths which were traced out for it from eternity; which, though they have seemed to us a maze or labyrinth, such a world of contingencies and various chances hath the work passed through, yet, indeed, all the passages thereof have been regular and straight, answering the platform laid down for the whole in the counsel of God. Daniel, chap. ix., makes his supplication for the restoration of Jerusalem; verse 23, an angel is sent to tell him, that "at the beginning of his supplication the commandment came forth,"—viz., that it should be accomplished. It was before determined, and is now set on work; but yet what mountains[4] of opposition, what hinderances lay in the way! Cyrus must come to the crown by the death or slaughter of Darius,[5]—his heart be moved to send some to the work: in a short time Cyrus is cut off.

[1] Matt. xi. 21; Acts xiii. 46.
[2] Luke ii. 34; 1 Pet. ii. 7; Ezek. ii. 5; Matt. xxiv. 14; Rom. ix. 22, 23.
[3] Neh. iv. 17. [4] Zech. iv. 7. [5] Scal. de Emend. Temp.

Now, difficulties arise from the following kings:—what their flattering counsellors, what the malignant nations about them conspired, the books of Nehemiah and Ezra sufficiently declare. Whence, verse 25, the angel tells Daniel, that from "the commandment to restore and build Jerusalem unto Messiah the Prince shall be seven weeks, and sixty-two weeks; the street shall be built again, and the wall, in troublesome times;" that is, it shall be seven weeks to the finishing of Jerusalem, and thence to Messiah the Prince sixty-two weeks;—seven weeks, that is, forty-nine years; for so much it was from the decree of Cyrus[1] to the finishing of the wall by Nehemiah: of which time the temple, as the Jews affirmed, was all but three years in building, John ii. 20. During which space, how often did the hearts of the people of God faint in their troubles, as though they should never have seen an end! And therefore, ever and anon they were ready to give over, as Hag. i. 2. But yet we see the decree was fixed, and all those varieties did but orderly work in an exact method for the glorious accomplishment of it.

England's troubles have not yet endured above half the odd years of those reformers' task; yet, good God! how short-breathed are men! What fainting is there! what repining, what grudging against the ways of the Lord! But let me tell you, that as the water in the stream will not go higher than the head of the fountain, no more will the work in hand be carried one step higher or beyond the aim of its fountain, the counsel of God, from whence it hath its rise. And yet, as a river will break through all oppositions, and swell to the height of mountains, to go to the sea from whence it came; so will the stream of the gospel, when it comes out from God, break down all mountains of opposition, and not be hindered from resting in its appointed place. It were an easy thing to recall your minds to some trembling periods of time, when there was trembling in our armies, and trembling in our councils,—trembling to be ashamed, to be repented of,—trembling in the city and in the country; and men were almost at their wits' end for the sorrows and fears of those days: and yet we see how the unchangeable purpose of

[1] I follow in this the vulgar or common account, otherwise there is no part of Scripture chronology so contended about as these weeks of Daniel; most concluding that they are terminated in the death of Christ, happening about the midst of the last week. But about their original, or rise, there is no small debate. Of the four decrees made by the Persian kings about the building of Jerusalem,—viz., 1st, by Cyrus, 2 Chron. xxxvi. 22, 23; 2dly, by Darius, Ezra vi. 8; 3dly, by Artaxerxes, Ezra vii.; of the same to Nehemiah, chap. ii.,—following the account of their reign set down in profane stories, the last only holds exactly. Tertullian ad Jud. begins it from Darius, when this vision appeared to Daniel, whom, it seems, he conceived to be Darius Hystaspes, that followed the Magi, and not Medus, that was before Cyrus; and so with a singular kind of chronology makes up his account.—Vid. Euseb. Demon. Evan., lib. viii. cap. Func. Com. in Chron. Beroald. Chron., lib. iii. cap. 7, 8. Montacut. Apparat.

God hath wrought strongly through all these straits, from one end to another, that nothing might fall to the ground of what he had determined. If a man, in those days, had gone about to persuade us that all our pressures were good omens, that they all wrought together for our good, we could have been ready to cry, with the woman who, when she had recounted her griefs to the physician, and he still replied they were good signs, οἴ μοι ἀγαθῶν ἀπόλλυμαι, "Good signs have undone me,"—These good signs will be our ruin: yet, behold, we hope the contrary. Our day hath been like that mentioned, Zech. xiv. 6, 7, —a day whose light is neither clear nor dark,—a day known only to the Lord, seeming to us to be neither day nor night. But God knew all this while that it was a day,—he saw how it all wrought for the appointed end; and in the evening, in the close, it will be light, so light as to be to us discernible. In the meantime we are like unskilful men, [who] going to the house of some curious artist, so long as he is about his work, despise it as confused; but when it is finished, admire it as excellent:—whilst the passages of providence are on us, all is confusion; but when the fabric is reared, glorious.

Use 2. Learn to look upon the wisdom of God in carrying all things through this wonderful variety, exactly to answer his own eternal purpose;—suffering so many mountains to lie in the way of reforming his churches and settling the gospel, that his Spirit may have the glory, and his people the comfort in their removal. It is a high and noble contemplation, to consider the purposes of God, so far as by the event revealed, and to see what impressions his wisdom and power do leave upon things accomplished here below,—to read in them a temporary history of his eternal counsels. Some men may deem it strange, that his determinate will, which gives rule to these things, and could in a word have reached its own appointment, should carry his people so many journeys in the wilderness, and keep us thus long in so low estate. I say,—not to speak of his own glory, which hath sparkled forth of this flinty opposition,—there be divers things, things of light, for our good, which he hath brought forth out of all that darkness wherewith we have been overclouded. Take a few instances.

(1.) If there had been no difficulties, there had been no deliverances. And did we never find our hearts so enlarged towards God upon such advantages, as to say, Well, this day's temper of spirit was cheaply purchased by yesterday's anguish and fear;—*that* was but a being sick at sea?

(2.) Had there been no tempests and storms, we had not made out for shelter. Did you never run to a tree for shelter in a storm, and find fruit which you expected not? Did you never go to God for safeguard in these times,[1] driven by outward storms, and there find unexpected fruit, the "peaceable fruit of righteousness,"[2] that made you say, Happy tempest, which cast me into such a harbour? It was a storm[3] that occasioned the discovery of the golden mines of India;—hath not a storm driven some to the discovery of the richer mines of the love of God in Christ?

(3.) Had not Esau come against him with four hundred men, Jacob had not been called Israel;—he had not been put to it to try his strength with God, and so to prevail. Who would not purchase with the greatest distress that heavenly comfort which is in the return of prayers? The strength of God's Jacobs in this kingdom had not been known, if the Esaus had not come against them. Some say, this war hath made a discovery of England's strength, what it is able to do. I think so also,—not what armies it can raise against men, but with what armies of prayers and tears it is able to deal with God. Had not the brethren strove in the womb, Rebekah had not asked, "Why am I thus?"—nor received that answer, "The elder shall serve the younger." Had not two sorts of people struggled in the womb of this kingdom, we had not sought, nor received, such gracious answers. Thus do all the various motions of the lower wheels serve for our good, and exactly answer the impression they receive from the master-spring, the eternal purpose of God. Of this hitherto.

II. The sending of the gospel to any one nation rather than another, as the means of life and salvation, is of the *mere free grace and good pleasure of God.*

Now, before I come to make out the absolute independency and freedom of this distinguishing mercy, I shall premise three things.

1. That the not sending of the gospel to any person or people is of God's mere good pleasure,[4] and not of any peculiar distinguishing demerit in that person or people. No man or nation doth "majorem ponere obicem," lay more or greater obstacles against the gospel than another. There is nothing imaginable to lay a block in the passage thereof but only sin. Now, these sins are, or may be, of two sorts;—either, first, Against the gospel itself, which may possibly hinder the receiving of the gospel, but not the sending of it, which it presupposeth: secondly, Against the covenant they are under, and the light they are guided by, before the beams of the gospel shine upon them. Now, in these generally all are equal,[5] all having sinned and

[1] Prov. xviii. 10. [2] Heb. xii. 11.

[3] Pet. Mart. de Relig. Jud. decad. i. lib. 1.

[4] "Qui liberatur, gratiam diligat, qui non liberatur, debitum agnoscat."—Aug. de Bon. Persev., cap. viii. "Ex nequissimis in ipso vitæ exitu gratia invenit quos adoptet, cum tamen multi, etiam qui minus nocentes videantur, doni hujus alieni sunt."—Pros. de Voc. Gen., lib. i. cap. 17.

[5] 1 Cor. i. 25, 26.

come short of the glory of God; and in particular sins against the law and light of nature, no nations have gone farther than they which were soonest enlightened with the word, as afterward will appear: so that the sole cause of this is the good pleasure of God, as our Saviour affirmeth, Matt. xi. 25, 26.

2. That sins against the covenant of works, which men are under before the gospel[1] comes unto them, cannot have any general demerit, that the means of life and salvation by free grace should not be imparted to them. It is true, all nations have deserved to be turned into hell, and a people that have had the truth, and detained it in ungodliness, deserve to be deprived of it;—the first, by virtue of the sanction of the first broken covenant; the other, by sinning against that which they had of the second. But that men in a fallen condition, and not able to rise, should hereby deserve not to be helped up, needeth some distinction to clear it.

There is, then, a twofold demerit and indignity;—one merely negative, or a not deserving to have good done unto us; the other positive, deserving that good should not be done unto us. The first of these is found in all the world, in respect of the dispensation of the gospel. If the Lord should bestow it only on those who do deserve it, he must for ever keep it closed up in the eternal treasure of his own bosom. The second is found directly in none, in respect of that peculiar way which is discovered in the gospel, because they had not sinned against it; which, rightly considered, gives no small lustre to the freedom of grace.

3. That there is a right in the gospel, and a fitness in that gracious dispensation to be made known to all people in the world; that no singular portion of the earth should be any longer a holy land, or any mountain of the world lift up its head above its fellows. And this right hath a double foundation.

(1.) The infinite value and worth of the blood of Christ, giving fulness[2] and fitness to the promises founded thereon to be propounded to all mankind; for through his blood remission of sins is preached to whosoever believes on him, Acts x. 43,—"to every creature," Mark. xvi. 15. God would have a price of that infinite value for sin laid down, as might justly give advantage to proclaim a pardon infinitely to all that will come in and accept of it,—there being in it no defect at all (though intentionally only a ransom for some), but that by it the world might know that he had done whatsoever the Father commanded him, John xiv. 31.

(2.) In that economy and dispensation of the grace of the new covenant, breaking forth in these latter days, whereby all external

[1] Acts xiv. 16, 17, xvii. 30, 31.
[2] Rom. viii. 32; Joel ii. 28; John xvii. 22; Rom. i. 5, xvi. 26.

distinction of places and persons,[1] people and nations, being removed, Jesus Christ taketh all[2] nations to be his inheritance, dispensing to all men the grace of the gospel, bringing salvation, as seemeth best to him, Tit. ii. 11, 12. For being lifted up, he drew all unto him, having redeemed us with his blood, "out of every kindred and tongue, people and nation," Apoc. v. 9. And on these two grounds it is that the gospel hath in itself a right and fitness to be preached to all, even as many as the Lord our God shall call.

These things being premised, I come to the proof of the assertion.

Deut. vii. 7, 8: Moses is very careful in sundry places to get this to take an impression upon their spirits, that it was mere free grace that exalted them into that condition and dignity wherein they stood, by their approach unto God, in the enjoyment of his ordinances;—in this most clearly rendering the cause of God's love in choosing them, mentioned, verse 7, to be only his love. Verse 8, his love towards them is the cause of his love,—his free love eternally determining, his free love actually conferring, those distinguishing mercies upon them. It was not for their righteousness, for they were a stiff-necked people, Deut. ix. 6.

Matt. xi. 25, 26: Our Saviour laying both these things together, the hiding of the mysteries of salvation from some, and revealing them to others, renders the same reason and supreme cause of both, of which no account can be rendered, only the good pleasure of God: "I thank thee, O Father." And if any will proceed higher, and say, Where is the justice of this, that men equally obnoxious should be thus unequally accepted? we say, with Paul, "That he will have mercy on whom he will have mercy, and whom he will he hardeneth. And who art thou, O man, that disputest against God?" "Si tu es homo, et ego homo, audiamus dicentem, O homo, Tu quis?"[3] To send a pardon to some that are condemned, suffering the rest to suffer, hath no injustice. If this will not satisfy, let us say, with the same apostle, Ὢ βάθος, Rom. xi. 33, "O the depth," &c.

Yea, so far is it from truth, that God should dispense and grant his word and means of grace by any other rule, or upon any other motive, than his own will and good pleasure,[4] that we find in Scripture the direct contrary to what we would suppose,—even mercy showed to the more unworthy, and the more worthy passed by; reckoning worthiness and unworthiness by less or greater sin, with

[1] Rom. ix. 13. [2] Eph. iii. 14, 15; Matt. xxviii. 19. [3] August.

[4] "Si hoc voluntatum meritis voluerimus ascribere, ut malos neglexisse gratia, bonos autem elegisse videatur, resistet nobis innumerabilium causa populorum, quibus per tot secula, nulla cœlestis doctrinæ annunciatio corruscavit. Nec meliores fuisse eorum posteros possumus dicere, de quibus scriptum est, 'Gentium populus qui sedebat in tenebris, lucem vidit magnam.'"—*Prosp. de Voc. Gen.*, lib. i. cap. 15.

less or more endeavours. Christ preaches to Chorazin and Bethsaida, which would not repent; and at the same time denies the word to Tyre and Sidon, which would have gotten on sackcloth and ashes, when the other continued delicate despisers, Matt. xi. 21. Ezekiel is sent to them that would not hear him, passing by them that would have hearkened, chap. iii. 5; which is most clear, Rom. ix. 30, 31, "The Gentiles, which followed not after righteousness, have attained to righteousness, even the righteousness which is of faith; but Israel, which followed after the law of righteousness, hath not attained to the law of righteousness." If, in the dispensation of the gospel, the Lord had had any respect to the desert of people, Corinth, that famous place of sinning, had not so soon enjoyed it,—the people whereof, for *worship*, were led away with dumb idols, 1 Cor. xii. 2; and for their *lives*, you have them drawn to the life, 1 Cor. vi. 9–11, "Fornicators, idolaters, adulterers; effeminate, abusers of themselves with mankind, thieves, covetous, drunkards, revilers, extortioners," καί ταῦτά τινες ἦτε, which is to be repeated, ἀπὸ τοῦ κοινοῦ,—"Some of you were fornicators, some idolaters; but ye are sanctified." Seem not these to the eye of flesh goodly qualifications for the gospel of Jesus Christ? Had these men been dealt withal according as they had disposed themselves, not fitter fuel for hell could the justice of God require; but yet ye see to these the gospel comes with the first, "a light shines to them that sit in darkness and in the shadow of death."

If God send or grant the gospel, which is the means of grace, upon any other ground but his mere good pleasure, then it must be an act of remunerative justice.[1] Now, there is no such justice in God towards the creature, but what is founded upon some preceding covenant, or promise of God to the creature,—which is the only foundation of all relation between God and man,—but only those that attend creation and sovereignty. Now, what promise do you find made to, or covenant with, a people as yet without the gospel;—I mean conditional promises, inferring any good to be bestowed on any required performance on their part? Free, absolute promises there are innumerable, that light should shine to them that were in darkness, and those be called God's people which were not his people; but such as depend on any condition on their part to be fulfilled, we find none. God bargains[2] not with the creature about the gospel,

[1] "Si de debito quæratur respectu creaturæ, in Deum cadere non potest, nisi ex aliqua suppositione ipsi Deo voluntaria, quæ non potest esse nisi promisso aut pacto aliquo, ex quibus fidelitatis aut justitiæ debitum oriri solet."—Suarez. de Libert. Div. Vol., disp. 1, sect. 2, num. 5.

[2] "Deus nulla obligatione tenetur, antequam ipse fidem suam astringat, ergo ante promissionem nulla justitia distributiva in Deo reperitur."—Vasq. in q. 21, a. 1, disp. 86.

knowing how unable he is to be merchant for such pearls. If a man had all that goodness which may be found in man without Jesus Christ, they would not in the least measure procure a discovery of him.

I deny not but God may, and perhaps sometimes doth, reveal himself to some in a peculiar and extraordinary manner. Whereunto tends that story in Aquinas,[1] of a corpse taken up in the days of Constantine and Irene, with a plate of gold, and this inscription on it, "Christus nascetur ex virgine, ego credo in illum. O sol sub Irenæ et Constantini temporibus iterum me videbis." But that this should be regular unto men living, *μετὰ λόγου*, in Justin Martyr's phrase,[2] or using their naturals aright (which is impossible they should, the right use of naturals depending on supernaturals), is wide from the word.

If there be any outward motive of granting the gospel unto any, it is some acceptable performances of theirs, holding up to the rule and will of God. Now, this will and rule having no saving revelation but by the gospel, which should thus be procured by acts agreeable unto it, makes up a flat contradiction,—supposing the revelation of the gospel before it be revealed. Doubtless, according to all rules of justice to us made known, it is an easier thing to deserve heaven by obedience now under the covenant of works, than being under that covenant, to do any thing that might cause a new way of salvation, such as the gospel is, to be revealed.

With some observations I descend to application.

[1.] There is the same reason of continuing the gospel unto a people as of sending it; especially if oppositions rise high, apt and able in themselves for its removal. Never nation as yet enjoyed the word that deserved the continuance of the word. God hath always[3] something against a people, to make the continuing of his grace to be of grace, the not removing of his love to be merely of love, and the preaching of the gospel to be a mercy of the gospel, free and undeserved. Though there be work, and labour, and patience for Christ's sake at Ephesus; yet there is somewhat against Ephesus, Rev. ii. 4, 5, for which he might justly remove his candlestick; and if he doth it not, it is of the same mercy that first set it there. As God lays out goodness and grace in the entrance; so patience, long-suffering, and forbearance in the continuance. He bears with our manners, whilst we grieve his Spirit. Look upon the face of this kingdom, and view the body of the people; think of the profaneness, villany, trampling upon the blood of Jesus, ignorance, contempt of God and his ways, despising his ordinances, reviling his servants, branding and defaming the power of godliness, persecuting and tearing one another,—and yet

[1] Aquin. 2, 2, q. 2, art. 7.
[2] Καὶ οἱ μετὰ λόγου βιώσαντες Χριστιανοί εἰσι.—Justin., Apol. ii.
[3] Hos. xi. 8, 9.

hear the joyful sound of the word in every corner; and you will quickly conclude, that you see a great fight of God's love against our sins, and not of our goodness for his love.

[2.] There is the same reason of the reformation and the doctrine of the gospel corrupted with error, and of the worship of God collapsed with superstition, as of the first implantation of the gospel. God, in his just judgment of late ages, had sent upon the western world the efficacy of error, that they should believe lies, because they received not the love of the truth; as he foretold, 2 Thess. ii. Now, whence is it that we see some of the nations thereof as yet suffered to walk in their own ways, others called to repentance,—some wildernesses turned into green pastures for the flock of God, and some places made barren wildernesses for the wickedness of them that dwell therein? How comes it that this island glories in a reformation, and Spain sits still in darkness? Is it because we were better than they, or less engaged in antichristian delusions? Doubtless no. No nation in the world drank deeper of that cup of abomination. It was a proverbial speech amongst all, "England was our good ass" (a beast of burden) for (Antichrist whom they called) the Pope. Nothing but the good pleasure of God and Christ, freely coming to refine us, Mal. iii. 1–4, caused this distinction.

[3.] Though men can do nothing towards the procuring of the gospel, yet men may do much for the expulsion of the gospel. If the husbandmen prove idle or self-seekers, the vineyard will be let to others; and if the people love darkness more than light, the candlestick will be removed. Let England beware! Now this men may do, either upon the first entrance of the gospel, or after some continuance of it. The gospel spreading itself over the earth, finds entertainment, like that of men's seeking plantations amongst barbarous nations; sometimes kept out with hideous outcries at the shore,—sometimes suffered to enter with admiration, and a little after violently assaulted.

1*st*, In the first way, how do we find the Jews putting far from them the word of life, and rejecting the counsel of God *at its first entrance*,—calling for night at the rising of the sun! Hence, Acts xiii. 41, Paul concludes his sermon to them with, "Behold, ye despisers, and wonder, and perish;"—and verse 46, it was necessary the word should be preached to them; but seeing they judged themselves unworthy, they were forsaken;—and verse 51, they shake off the dust of their feet against them,—a common symbol in those days of the highest indignation and deepest curse. The like stubbornness we find in them, Acts xxviii.; whereupon the apostle wholly turned himself to the Gentiles, verse 28. How many nations of Europe, at the beginning of the Reformation, rejected the gospel of God, and procured Christ, with the Gadarenes, to depart as soon as he was entered, will be found at the last day written with the blood of the martyrs of Jesus that suffered amongst them!

2dly, *After some continuance.* So the Church of Laodicea, having for a while enjoyed the word, fell into such a tepid condition,—so little moved with that fire that Christ came to send upon the earth, Rev. iii. 15, 16,—that the Lord was even sick and weary with bearing them. The Church of Rome, famous at the first, yet quickly, by the advantage of outward supportments and glorious fancies, became head of that fatal rebellion against Jesus Christ,[1] which spread itself over most of the churches in the world;—God hereupon sending upon them the "efficacy of error to believe a lie, that they all might be damned that believed not the truth, but had pleasure in unrighteousness," 2 Thess. ii.,—suffering them to retain the empty names of Church and Gospel; which, because they usurp only for their advantage here, to appear glorious, the Lord will use for the advancing of his justice hereafter, to show them inexcusable. O Lord, how was England of late, by thy mercy, delivered from this snare! A captain being chosen for the return of this people into Egypt, O how hath thy grace fought against our backsliding! And let none seek to extenuate this mercy, by catalogues of errors still amongst us: there is more danger of apostasy against Christ, and rebellion against the truth, in one Babylonish error, owned by men pretending to power and jurisdiction over others, than in five hundred scattered amongst inconsiderable, disunited individuals. I would to God we could all speak and think the same things,—that we were all of one mind, even in the most minute differences that are now amongst us. But yet the truth is, the kingdom of Jesus Christ never shakes amongst a people until men, pretending to act with a combined mixed power of heaven and earth, unto which all sheaves must bow or be thrashed, do, by virtue of this trust, set up and impose things or opinions deviating from the rule. As it was in the Papacy, errors owned by mixed associations, civil and ecclesiastical, are for the most part incurable, be they never so absurd and foolish; of which the Lutheran ubiquities and consubstantiation are a tremendous example. These things being presupposed,—

Use 1. *Let no flesh glory in themselves, but let every mouth be stopped;* for we have all sinned and come short of the glory of God. Who hath made the possessors of the gospel to differ from others? or what have they that they have not received? 1 Cor. iv. 7. Why are these things hidden from the great and wise of the world, and revealed to babes and children, but because, O Father, so it pleased

[1] Νῦν δέ ἐστιν ἀποστασία, ἀπέστησαν γὰρ οἱ ἄνθρωποι τῆς ὀρθῆς πίστεως. **Cyrillus Hieros.** Κατήχησις.

thee? Matt. xi. 26. "He hath mercy on whom he will have mercy, and whom he will he hardeneth," Rom. ix. 18. Ah, Lord, if the *glory and pomp of the world* might prevail with thee to send thy gospel, it would supply the room of the cursed Alkoran, and spread itself in the palaces of that strong lion of the east who sets his throne upon the necks of kings; but, alas! Jesus Christ is not there. If *wisdom, learning, pretended gravity, counterfeit holiness, real policy,* were of any value in thine eyes to procure the word of life, it would be as free and glorious at Rome as ever; but, alas! Antichrist hath his throne there. Jesus Christ is not there. If *will-worship and humilities, neglect of the body, macerations, superstitions, beads, and vainly-repeated prayers,* had any efficacy before the Lord, the gospel, perhaps, might be in the cells of some recluses and monks; but, alas! Jesus Christ is not there. If *moral virtues* to an amazement, exact civil honesty and justice, that soul of human society, could have prevailed aught, the heathen worthies in the days of old had had the promises; but, alas! Jesus Christ was far away. Now, if all these be passed by, to whom is the report of the Lord made known? to "whom is his arm revealed?" Why, to a handful of poor sinners amongst the nations formerly counted fierce and barbarous.[1] And what shall we say to these things?—Ὦ βάθος, "O the depth," &c.

Use 2. Let England consider with fear and trembling *the dispensation that it is now under;*—I say, with fear and trembling, for this day is the Lord's day, wherein he will purge us or burn us, according as we shall be found silver or dross:—it is our day, wherein we must mend or end. Let us look to the rock from whence we were hewed, and the hole of the pit from whence we were digged. Was not our father an Amorite, and our mother an Hittite? Are we not the posterity of idolatrous progenitors?[2]—of those who worshipped them who by nature were no gods? How often, also, hath this land forfeited the gospel! God having taken it twice away, who is not forward to seize upon the forfeiture. In the very morning of the gospel, the Sun of righteousness shone upon this land; and they say the first potentate on the earth that owned it was in Britain.[3] But as it was here soon professed, so it was here soon abused; that part of this island which is called England being the first place I read of which was totally bereaved of the gospel,—the sword of the then pagan Saxons fattening the land with the blood of the Christian inhabitants,[4] and in the close wholly subverting the worship of God. Long it was not ere this cloud was blown over; and those men who

1 "Britannorum inaccessa Romanis loca, Christo vero subdita."—Tertul.
2 "Britanniam in Christianam consentire religionem."—Origen. Hom. iv. in Ezek.
3 Niceph., lib. ii. cap. 40. Epist. Eleuth. ad Lucium, an. 169, apud Bar.
4 Anno 469 the Saxons entered.

had been instruments to root out others submitted their own necks to the yoke of the Lord; and, under exceeding variety in civil affairs, enjoyed the word of grace, until, by insensible degrees, like summer unto winter, or light unto darkness, it gives place to antichristian superstition, and left the land in little less than a paganish darkness, drinking deep of the cup of abominations mingled for it by the Roman harlot. And is there mercy yet in God to recover a twice over lost backsliding people? Might not the Lord have said unto us, What shall I do unto thee, O island? How shall I make thee as Admah? how shall I set thee as Zeboim? But his heart is turned within him, his repentings are kindled together: the dry bones shall live, and the fleece shall be wet, though all the earth be dry. God will again water his garden, once more purge his vineyard,—once more of his own accord he will take England upon liking, though he had twice deservedly turned it out of his service. So that, "coming as a refiner's fire, and as fuller's soap, to purify the sons of Levi, to purge them as gold and silver, to offer to the Lord an offering in righteousness," to reform his churches, England, as soon as any, hath the benefit and comfort thereof. Nay, the reformation of England shall be more glorious than of any nation in the world, being carried on neither by might nor power, but only by the Spirit of the Lord of hosts. But is this the utmost period of England's sinning, and God's showing mercy, in continuing and restoring of the gospel? No, truly: we again in our days have made forfeiture of the purity of his worship, by an almost universal treacherous apostasy; from which the free grace and good pleasure of God hath made a great progress again towards a recovery.

There are two sorts of men that I find exceedingly ready to extenuate and lessen the superstition and popish tyranny of the former days, into which we were falling.

(1.) Such as were industriously instrumental in it, whose suffrages had been loud for the choice of a captain to return into Egypt,—men tainted with the errors and loaded with the preferments of the times; with all those who blindly adhere to that faction of men who as yet covertly drive on that design:—to such as these all was nothing, and to them it is no mercy to be delivered. And the truth is, it is a favour to the lamb, and not the wolf, to have him taken out of his mouth; but these men have interest by those things which have no ears, against which there is no contending.

(2.) Such as are disturbed in their optics, or have gotten false glasses,[1] representing all things unto them in dubious colours. Which

[1] "Nunc igitur si nominis odium est, quis nominum reatus? quæ accusatio vocabulorum? nisi aut, barbarum sonat aliqua vox nominis, aut maledicum aut impudicum."—Tertul. Apol. ad Gen., cap. iii.

way soever they look, they can see nothing but errors,—errors of all sizes, sorts, sects, and sexes,—errors and heresies from the beginning to the end; which have deceived some men, not of the worst, and made them think that all before was nothing, in comparison of the present confusion. A great sign they felt it not, or were not troubled at it; as if men should come into a field, and seeing some red weeds and cockle among the corn, should instantly affirm there is no corn there, but all weeds, and that it were much better the hedges were down, and the whole field laid open to the boars of the forest: but the harvest will one day show the truth of these things. But that these apprehensions may not too much prevail, to the vilifying and extenuating of God's mercy, in restoring to us the purity and liberty of the gospel, give me leave, in a few words, to set out the danger of that apostasy from which the good pleasure of God hath given us a deliverance. I shall instance only in a few things. Observe then, that,—

[1.] The darling errors of late years were all of them stones of the old Babel, closing and coupling with that tremendous fabric which the man of sin had erected to dethrone Jesus Christ,—came out of the belly of that Trojan horse, that fatal engine, which was framed to betray the city of God. They were popish errors, such as whereof that apostasy did consist which only is to be looked upon as the great adverse state of the kingdom of the Lord Christ. For a man to be disorderly in a civil state, yea, oftentimes through turbulency to break the peace, is nothing to an under-hand combination with some formidable enemy for the utter subversion of it. Heedless and headless errors may breed disturbance enough, in scattered individuals, unto the people of God; but such as tend to a peace and association "cum ecclesia malignantium," tending to a total subversion of the sacred state, are far more dangerous. Now, such were the innovations of the late hierarchists. In worship, their paintings,[1] crossings, crucifixes, bowings, cringings, altars, tapers, wafers, organs, anthems, litany, rails, images, copes, vestments,—what were they but Roman varnish, an Italian dress for our devotion, to draw on conformity with that enemy of the Lord Jesus? In doctrine, the divinity of Episcopacy, auricular confession, free-will, predestination on faith, yea, works foreseen, "limbus patrum," justification by works, falling from grace, authority of a church, which none knew what it was, canonical obedience, holiness of churches, and the like innumerable,—what were they but helps to Sancta Clara, to make all our articles of religion speak good Roman Catholic? How did their old father of Rome refresh his spirit, to see such chariots as those provided to bring England again unto him! This closing with Popery was the sting in the errors of those days, which cause pining, if not death, in the episcopal pot.

[1] See Canterburian self-conviction. See Ld. Dee. Coll., &c.

[2.] They were such as raked up the ashes of the ancient worthies, whose spirits God stirred up to reform his church, and rendered them contemptible before all, especially those of England, the most whereof died in giving their witness against the blind figment of the real presence,[1] and that abominable blasphemy of the cursed mass. In especial, how did England, heretofore termed ass, turn ape to the pope, having set up a stage, and furnished it with all things necessary for an unbloody sacrifice,[2] ready to set up the abomination of a desolation, and close with the god Maozim [מָעֻזִּים, *Mauzzim*, god of forces, Dan. xi. 38], who hath all their peculiar devotion at Rome?

[3.] They were in the management of men which had divers dangerous and pernicious qualifications: as,—

1*st*, A false repute of learning; I say, a false repute for the greater part, especially of the greatest. And yet, taking advantage of vulgar esteem, they bare out as though they had engrossed a monopoly of it,—though I presume the world was never deceived by more empty pretenders, especially in respect of any solid knowledge in divinity or antiquity; but yet their great preferments had got them a great repute of great deservings,—enough to blind the eyes of poor mortals adoring them at a distance, and to persuade them, that all was not only law, but gospel too, which they broached: and this rendered the infection dangerous.

2*dly*, A great hatred of godliness in the power thereof, or any thing beyond a form, in whomsoever it was found; yea, how many[3] odious appellations were invented for bare profession, to render it contemptible!—especially in the exercise of their jurisdiction, thundering their censures against all appearance of zeal, and closing with all profane impieties; for were a man a drunkard, a swearer, a Sabbath-breaker, an unclean person, so he were no Puritan, and had money,—"patet atri janua ditis," the Episcopal heaven was open for them all. Now, this was a dangerous and destructive qualification, which, I believe, is not professedly found in any party amongst us.

3*dly*, Which was worst of all, they had centred in their bosoms an unfathomable depth of power, civil and ecclesiastical, to stamp their apostatical errors with authority,—giving them not only the countenance of greatness, but the strength of power, violently urging obedience; and to me the sword of error never cuts dangerously but when it is managed with such a hand. This I am sure, that errors in such are not recoverable, without the utmost danger of the civil state.

[1] Coal from the Altar.

[2] Altare Christianum. Antidotum Lincoln. Case of Greg.

[3] Sapientior sis Socrate; doctior Augustino, &c.; Calvinianus si modo dicare clam vel propalam, mox Tartaris, Moscis, Afris, Turcisque sævientibus, et jacebis execratior, &c.

Let now, I beseech you, these and the like things be considered, especially the strong combination that was throughout the[1] papal world for the seducing of this poor nation (that I say nothing how this vial was poured out upon the very throne[2]), and then let us all be ashamed and confounded in ourselves, that we should so undervalue and slight the free mercy of God in breaking such a snare, and setting the gospel at liberty in England. My intent was, having before asserted this restoration of Jerusalem to the good pleasure of God, to have stirred you up to thankfulness unto him, and self-humiliation in consideration of our great undeserving of such mercy; but, alas! as far as I can see, it will scarce pass for a mercy; and unless every man's persuasion may be a Joseph's sheaf, the goodness of God shall scarce be acknowledged. But yet let all the world know, and let the house of England know this day, that we lie unthankfully under as full a dispensation of mercy and grace as ever nation in the world enjoyed, and that without a lively acknowledgment thereof, with our own unworthiness of it, we shall one day know what it is (being taught with briers and thorns) to undervalue the glorious gospel of the Lord Jesus. Good Lord! what would helpless Macedonians give for one enjoyment? O that Wales! O that Ireland! O that France!—where shall I stop? I would offend none, but give me leave to say, O that every, I had almost said, O that any, part of the world had such helps and means of grace as these parts of England have, which will scarce acknowledge any mercy in it! The Lord break the pride of our spirits before it break the staff of our bread and the help of our salvation. O that the bread of heaven and the blood of Christ might be accounted good nourishment, though every one hath not the sauce he desireth! I am persuaded that if every Absalom in the land, that would be a judge for the ending of our differences, were enthroned (he spoke the people's good, though he intended his own power), the case would not be much better than it is. Well, the Lord make England, make this honourable audience, make us all, to know these three things:—

First, That we have received such a blessing, in setting at liberty the truths of the gospel, as is the crown of all other mercies, yea, without which they were not valuable, yea, were to be despised; for success without the gospel is nothing but a prosperous conspiracy against Jesus Christ.

Secondly, That this mercy is of mercy; this love, of free love; and the grace that appeareth, of the eternal, hidden, free grace of God. He hath showed his love unto us because he loved us, and for no other reason in the world;—this people being guilty of blood and murder

[1] Rome's Master-piece. [2] Royal favourite.

of soul and body, adultery, and idolatry, and oppression, with a long catalogue of sins and iniquities.

Thirdly, That the height of rebellion against God is the despising of spiritual gospel mercies. Should Mordecai have trodden the robes under his feet that were brought him from the king, would it not have been severely revenged? Doth the King of heaven lay open the treasures of his wisdom, knowledge, and goodness for us, and we despise them? What shall I say? I had almost said, hell punishes no greater sin: the Lord lay it not to our charge! O that we might be solemnly humbled for it this day, before it be too late!

Use 3. *To discover unto us the freedom of that effectual grace* which is dispensed towards the elect, under and with the preaching of the word; for if the sending of the outward means be of free,[1] undeserved love, surely the working of the Spirit under that dispensation for the saving of souls is no less free; for "who hath made us differ from others? and what have we that we have not received?" O that God should say unto us in our blood, Live;—that he should breathe upon us when we were as dry bones, dead in trespasses and sins! Let us remember, I beseech you, the frame of our hearts and the temper of our spirits, in the days wherein we knew not God and his goodness, but went on in a swift[2] course of rebellion. Can none of you look back upon any particular days or nights, and say, Ah, Lord, that thou shouldst be so patient and so full of forbearance, as not to send me to hell at such an instant! But, O Lord, that thou shouldst go farther, and blot out mine iniquities, for thine own sake, "when I made thee serve with my sins!"—Lord, what shall I say it is? It is the free grace of my God! What expression transcendeth that, I know not.

Use 4. *Of caution.* England received the gospel of mere mercy; let it take heed lest it lose it by justice;—the placer of the candlestick can remove it. The truth is, it will not be removed unless it be abused; and woe to them from whom mercies are taken for being abused,—from whom the gospel is removed for being despised! It had been better for the husbandmen never to have had the vineyard, than to be slain for their ill using of it: there is nothing left to do them good who are forsaken for forsaking the gospel.

The glory of God was of late by many degrees departing from the temple in our land. That was gone to the threshold, yea, to the mount. If now at the return thereof, it find again cause to depart, it will not go by steps, but all at once. This island, or at least the greatest part thereof, as I formerly intimated, hath twice lost the gospel;—once, when the Saxons wrested it from the Britons,—when,

[1] "Non libertate gratiam, sed gratia libertatem consequimur."—Aug.
[2] Ezek. xxxvi. 26; Acts xvi. 14; Phil. i. 29, ii. 13.

if we may believe their own doleful, moaning[1] historian, they were given over to all wickedness, oppression, and villany of life; which doubtless was accompanied with contempt of the word; though for faith and persuasion we do not find that they were corrupted, and do find that they were tenacious enough of antique discipline, as appeared in their following oppositions to the Roman tyranny, as in Beda. Secondly, It was lost in regard of the purity and power thereof, by blind superstition and antichristian impiety, accompanied also with abominable lewdness, oppression, and all manner of sin, in the face of the sun; so that first profaneness working a despising of the gospel, then superstition ushering in profaneness, have in this land showed their power for the extirpation of the gospel. Oh, that we could remember the days of old, that we could "consider the goodness and severity of God;—on them which fell severity, but towards us goodness, if we continue in that goodness; for otherwise even we also shall be cut off!" Yet here we may observe, that though both these times there was a forsaking in the midst of the land, yet there was in it a tenth for to return "as a teil-tree, and as an oak, whose substance is in them when they cast their leaves;" so was the holy seed the substance thereof, Isa. vi. 13. As in the dereliction of the Jews, so of this nation, there was a remnant that quickly took root, and brought forth fruit, both in the one devastation and the other. Though the watcher and the holy one from heaven had called to cut down the tree of this nation, and to scatter its branches from flourishing before him; yet the stump and root was to be left in the earth with a band of iron, that it might spring again. Thus twice did the Lord come seeking fruit of this vine, doing little more than pruning and dressing it, although it brought forth wild grapes; but if he come the third time and find no fruit, the sentence will be, "Cut it down, why cumbereth it the ground?" Now, to prevent this, I shall not follow all those gospel-supplanting sins we find in holy writ, only I desire to cautionate you and us all in three things.

(1.) Take heed of pretending or holding out the gospel for a covert or shadow for other things. God will not have his gospel made a stalking-horse for carnal designs. Put not in that glorious name, where the thing itself is not clearly intended. If in any thing it be, let it have no compeer; if not, let it not be named. If that you aim at be just, it needs no varnish; if it be not, it is the worse for it. Gilded pills lose not their bitterness, and painted faces are thought to have no native beauty. All things in the world should

[1] Gildas de Excid. Britanniæ. "Omnia quæ Deo placebant, et displicebant, æquali lance pendebantur, non igitur admirandum est degeneres tales patriam illam amittere, quam prædicto modo maculabant."—Hist. M.S., apud Foxum.

serve the gospel; and if that be made to serve other things, God will quickly vindicate it into liberty.

From the beginning of these troubles, right honourable, you have held forth religion and the gospel, as whose preservation and restoration was principally in your aims; and I presume malice itself is not able to discover any insincerity in this. The fruits we behold proclaim to all the conformity of your words and hearts. Now, the God of heaven grant that the same mind be in you still, in every particular member of this honourable assembly, in the whole nation, especially in the magistracy and ministry of it;—that we be not like the boatmen,—look one way, and row another;—cry "Gospel," and mean the other thing,—"Lord, Lord," and advance our own ends;—that the Lord may not stir up the staff of his anger and the rod of his indignation against us, as a hypocritical people.

(2.) Take heed of resting upon and trusting to the privilege, however excellent and glorious, of the outward enjoyment of the gospel. When the Jews cried, "The temple of the Lord, the temple of the Lord," the time was at hand that they should be destroyed. Look only upon the grace that did bestow, and the mercy that doth continue it. God will have none of his blessings rob him of his glory; and if we rest at the cistern, he will stop at the fountain.

(3.) Let us all take heed of barrenness under it: "For the earth that drinks in the rain that cometh upon it, and beareth thorns and briers, is rejected, and nigh unto cursing, whose end is to be burned," Heb. vi. 7, 8. Now, what fruits doth it require? Even those reckoned, Gal. v. 22, 23, "The fruit of the Spirit is love, joy, peace, long-suffering, gentleness, goodness, faith, meekness, temperance." O that we had not cause to grieve for a scarcity of these fruits, and the abundant plenty of those works of the flesh recounted, verses 19–21! O that that wisdom which is an eminent fruit of the gospel might flourish amongst us!—it is "first pure, then peaceable, gentle, easy to be entreated;"—that we might have less writing, and more praying!—less envy, and more charity!—that all evil surmisings, which are works of the flesh, might have no toleration in our hearts, but be banished for nonconformity to the golden rule of love and peace! James iii. 17. But ἀπέχω. Come we now to the last proposition.

III. No men in the world want help like them that want the gospel; or, of all distresses, want of the gospel cries the loudest for relief.

Rachel wanted children, and she cries, "Give me children,[1] or I die;"—but that was her impatience; she might have lived, and have had no children; yea, see the justice of God,—she dies so soon as ever

[1] Gen. xxx. 1, xxxv. 18.

she hath children. Hagar[1] wants water for Ishmael, and she will go far from him, that she may not see him die;—a heavy distress; and yet if he had died, it had been but an early paying of that debt which in a few years was to be satisfied. But they that want the gospel may truly cry, Give us the gospel, or we die; and that not temporally with Ishmael, for want of water, but eternally in flames of fire.

A man may want liberty, and yet be happy, as Joseph was; a man may want peace, and yet be happy, as David was; a man may want children, and yet be blessed, as Job was; a man may want plenty, and yet be full of comfort, as Micaiah was;—but he that wants the gospel, wants every thing that should do him good. A throne without the gospel is but the devil's dungeon. Wealth without the gospel is fuel for hell. Advancement without the gospel is but a going high to have the greater fall.

Abraham[2] wanting a child, complains, "What will the Lord do for me, seeing I go childless, and this Eliezer of Damascus must be my heir?" Much more may a man without the means of grace complain, What shall be done unto me, seeing I go gospelless; and all that I have is but a short inheritance for this lump of clay, my body?

When Elisha[3] was minded to do something for the Shunammite who had so kindly entertained him, he asks her whether he should speak for her to the king or the captain of the host. She replies, she dwelt in the midst of her own people, she needeth not those things; but when he finds her to want a child, and tells her of that, she is almost transported. Ah! how many poor souls are there who need not our word to the king or the captain of the host; but yet being gospelless, if you could tell them of that, would be even ravished with joy!

Think of Adam[4] after his fall, before the promise, hiding himself from God, and you have a perfect portraiture of a poor creature without the gospel. Now this appeareth,—

1. *From the description we have of the people that are in this state*[5] *and condition*—without the gospel. They are a people that sit in darkness, yea, in the region and shadow of death, Matt. iv. 16, 17; they are even darkness itself, John i. 5,—within the dominion and dreadful darkness of death. Darkness was one of Egypt's plagues; but yet that was a darkness of the body, a darkness wherein men lived;—but this is a darkness of the soul, a darkness of death; for these men, though they live, yet are they dead. They are fully described,

[1] Gen. xxi. 16. [2] Gen. xv. 2. [3] 2 Kings iv. 13, 14. [4] Gen. iii. 8.

[5] Matt. vi. 23; Luke i. 79; Acts xxvi. 18; Rom. ii. 19; Eph. v. 8; Col. i. 13; 1 Pet. ii. 9.

Eph. ii. 12, "Without Christ, aliens from the commonwealth of Israel, strangers from the covenants of promise, having no hope, and without God in the world." Christless men, and Godless men, and hopeless men,—and what greater distress in the world? Yea, they are called dogs, and unclean beasts. The wrath of God is upon them; they are the people of his curse and indignation. In the extreme north, one day and one night divide the year; but with a people without the gospel it is all night,—the Sun of righteousness shines not upon them; it is night whilst they are here, and they go to eternal night hereafter. What the men of China say concerning themselves and others, that they have two eyes, the men of Europe one, and all the world besides is blind, may be inverted too. The Jews had one eye, sufficient to guide them; they who enjoy the gospel have two eyes; but the men of China, with the rest of the nations that want it, are stark blind, and reserved for the chains of everlasting darkness.

2. *By laying forth what the men that want the gospel do want with it.*

(1.) They want Jesus Christ, for he is revealed only by the gospel. Austin refused to delight in Cicero's "Hortensius," because there was not in it the name[1] of Jesus Christ. Jesus Christ is all, and in all; and where he is wanting there can be no good. Hunger cannot truly be satisfied without manna, the bread of life, which is Jesus Christ;[2]—and what shall a hungry man do that hath no bread? Thirst cannot be quenched without that water or living spring, which is Jesus Christ;—and what shall a thirsty soul do without water? A captive, as we are all, cannot be delivered without redemption,[3] which is Jesus Christ;—and what shall the prisoner do without his ransom? Fools, as we are all, cannot be instructed without wisdom, which is Jesus Christ;—without him we perish in our folly. All building without him is on the sand, which will surely fall. All working without him is in the fire, where it will be consumed. All riches without him have wings, and will away. "Mallem ruere cum Christo, quam regnare cum Cæsare," said Luther. A dungeon with Christ, is a throne; and a throne without Christ, a hell. Nothing so ill, but Christ[4] will compensate. The greatest evil in the world is sin, and the greatest sin was the first; and yet Gregory feared not to cry, "O felix culpa, quæ talem meruit redemptorem!"—"O happy fault, which found such a Redeemer!" All mercies without Christ are bitter; and every cup is sweet that is seasoned but with a drop of his blood;—he truly is "amor et deliciæ humani generis,"—the love and delight of the sons of men,—without whom they must perish eter-

1 Nomen Jesu non erat ibi.
2 John vi. 50; Rev. ii. 17; John iv. 14; Cant. iv. 12.
3 John vii. 37, 38; 1 Cor. i. 30.
4 "Pauca igitur de Christo."—Tertul.

nally; "for there is no other name given unto them, whereby they may be saved, Acts iv. 12. He is the Way;[1] men without him are Cains, wanderers, vagabonds:—he is the Truth; men without him are liars, like the devil, who was so of old:—he is the Life;[2] without him men are dead, dead in trespasses and sins:—he is the Light; without him men are in darkness, and go they know not whither:—he is the Vine; those that are not grafted in him are withered branches, prepared for the fire:—he is the Rock; men not built on him are carried away with a flood:—he is Alpha and Omega, the first and the last, the author and the ender, the founder and the finisher of our salvation. He that hath not him, hath neither beginning of good, nor shall have end of misery. O blessed Jesus! how much better were it not to be, than to be without thee!—never to be born, than not to die in thee! A thousand hells come short of this, eternally to want Jesus Christ, as men do that want the gospel.

(2.) They want all holy communion with God, wherein the only happiness of the soul doth consist. He is the life, light, joy, and blessedness of the soul;—without him the soul in the body is but a dead soul in a living sepulchre. It is true, there be many that say, "Who will show us any good?"[3] but unless the Lord lift up the light of his countenance upon us, we perish for evermore. "Thou hast made us for thyself, O Lord; and our heart is unquiet until it come to thee." You who have tasted how gracious the Lord is, who have had any converse and communion with him in the issues and goings forth of his grace, those delights of his soul with the children of men, would you live—would not life itself, with a confluence of all earthly endearments, be a very hell—without him? Is it not the daily language of your hearts, "Whom have we in heaven but thee? and on earth there is nothing in comparison of thee?" The soul of man is of a vast, boundless comprehension; so that if all created good were centred into one enjoyment, and that bestowed upon one soul, because it must needs be finite and limited, as created, it would give no solid contentment to his affections, nor satisfaction to his desires. In the presence and fruition of God alone there is joy for evermore; at his right hand are rivers of pleasure, the well-springs of life and blessedness. Now, if to be without communion with God in this life, wherein the soul hath so many avocations from the contemplation of its own misery (for earthly things are nothing else), is so unsupportable a calamity; ah! what shall that poor soul do that must want him for eternity?—as all they must do who want the gospel.

[1] John xiv. 6.
[2] John i. 3–5; Eph. iv. 18; John xv. 5; Matt. vii. 26, 27; Matt. xvi. 18.
[3] Ps. iv. 6.

(3.) They want all the ordinances of God,—the joy of our hearts[1] and comfort of our souls. Oh! the sweetness of a Sabbath! the heavenly raptures of prayer!—oh! the glorious communion of saints, which such men are deprived of! If they knew the value of the hidden pearl, and these things were to be purchased, what would such poor souls not part with for them?

(4.) They will at last want heaven and salvation. They shall never come to the presence of God in glory, never inhabit a glorious mansion;—they shall never behold Jesus Christ, but when they shall call for[2] rocks and mountains to fall upon them, to hide them from his presence;—they shall want light in utter darkness, want life under the second death, want[3] refreshment in the midst of flames, want healing under gnawing of conscience, want grace continuing to blaspheme, want glory in full misery;—and, which is the sum of all this, they shall want an end of all this; for "their worm dieth not, neither is their fire quenched."

3. Because being in all this want, they know not that they want any thing, and so never make out for any supply. Laodicea knew much; but yet because she knew not her wants,[4] she had almost as good have known nothing. Gospelless men know not that they are blind, and seek not for eye-salve; they know not that they are dead, and seek not for life. Whatever they call for, not knowing their wants, is but like a man's crying for more weight to press him to death; and therefore, when the Lord comes to any with the gospel, he is "found of them that sought him not, and made manifest to them that asked not after him," Rom. x. 20. This is a seal upon their misery, without God's free mercy, like the stone laid upon the mouth of the cave by Joshua, to keep in the five kings, until they might be brought out to be hanged.[5] All that men do in the world is but seeking to supply their wants;—either their *natural* wants, that nature may be supplied; or their *sinful* wants, that their lusts may be satisfied; or their *spiritual* wants, that their souls may be saved. For the two first, men without the gospel lay out all their strength; but of the last there is amongst them a deep[6] silence. Now this is all one as for men to cry out that their finger bleeds, whilst a sword is run through their hearts, and they perceive it not;—to desire a wart to be cured, whilst they have a plague-sore upon them. And hence perhaps it is that they are said to go to[7] hell "like sheep," Ps. xlix. 14,—very quietly, without dread, as a bird hasting to the

[1] Ps. xlii. 1, 2, xxxiv. 1–4, &c. [2] Rev. vi. 16.
[3] Matt. xxii. 13; Luke xvi. 24; Mark ix. 43, 44; Isa. lxvi. 24.
[4] Rev. iii. 17. [5] Josh. x. 18.
[6] "Ego propero ad inferos, nec est ut aliquid pro me agas."—Advocatus quidam moriens, apud Bel. de arte mor., lib. ii. cap. 10.
[7] לִשְׁאוֹל.

snare, and not knowing that it is for his life, Prov. vii. 23,—and there lie down in utter disappointment and sorrow for evermore.

4. Because all mercies are bitter judgments to men that want the gospel;—all fuel for hell,—aggravations of condemnation;—all cold drink to a man in a fever, pleasant at the entrance, but increasing its torments in the close;—like the book in the Revelation, sweet in the mouth, but bitter in the belly. When God shall come to require his bread and wine, his flax and oil, peace and prosperity, liberty and victories of gospelless men, they will curse the day that ever they enjoyed them. So unspiritual are many men's minds, and so unsavoury their judgments, that they reckon men's happiness by their possessions, and suppose the catalogue of their titles to be a roll of their felicities, calling the proud happy, and advancing in our conceits "them that work wickedness," Mal. iii. 15; but God will one day come in with another reckoning, and make them know that all things without Christ are but as ciphers without a figure,—of no value. In all their banquets, where Christ is not a guest, "their vine is of the vine of Sodom, and of the field of Gomorrah; their grapes are grapes of gall, their clusters are bitter," Deut. xxxii. 32, 33;—their palaces, where Christ is not, are but habitations of ziim and ochim, dragons and unclean beasts;—their prosperity is putting them into full pasture, that they may be fatted for the day of slaughter, the day of consumption decreed for all the bulls of Bashan. The gospel bringing Christ, is the salt that makes all other things savoury.

Use 1. To show us the great privilege and pre-eminence which, by the free grace of God, many parts of this island do enjoy. To us that sat in darkness and in the shadow of death a great light is risen, to guide us into the ways of peace. Let others recount the glories, benefits, profits, outward blessings of this nation; let us look only upon that which alone is valuable in itself, and makes other things so to be,—the gospel of Christ. It is reported of the heralds of our neighbour monarchs, that when one of them had repeated the numerous titles of his master of Spain, the other often repeated, France, France, France! intimating that the dominion which came under that one denomination would counterpoise the long catalogue of kingdoms and dukedoms wherewith the other flourished. Were we to contend with the grand seignior of the east about our enjoyments, we might easily bear down his windy, pompous train of titles with this one,—which "millies repetitum placebit,"—The gospel, the gospel! Upon all the other things you may put the inscription in Daniel, "Mene, mene, tekel,"—they are "weighed in the balances, and found wanting;" but proclaim before those that enjoy the gospel, as Haman before Mordecai, "Lo, thus shall it be done to them whom the Lord will honour!" The fox in the fable had a thousand wiles to save himself from the hunters; but the cat knew " unum magnum," " one great thing" that would surely do it. Earthly supports and contentments are but a thousand failing wiles, which will all vanish in the time of need; the gospel, and Christ in the gospel, is that " unum magnum," that " unum necessarium," which alone will stand us in any stead. In this, this island is as the mountain of the Lord,—exalted above the mountains of the earth. It is true, many other nations partake with us in the same blessing. Not to advance our own enjoyments in some particulars,—wherein perhaps we might justly do it,—but take all these nations with us, and what a molehill are we to the whole earth, overspread with Paganism, Mohammedanism, Antichristianism, with innumerable foolish heresies! And what is England, that it should be amongst the choice branches of the vineyard, the top-boughs of the cedars of God?

Use 2. Shows that such great mercies, if not esteemed, if not improved, if abused, will end in great judgments. Woe be to that nation, that city, that person, that shall be called to an account for despising the gospel! Amos iii. 2, " You only have I known of all the families of the earth." What then? surely some great blessing is coming to that people whom God thus knows, so owns, as to make himself known unto them. No; but, " therefore will I visit upon you all your iniquities." However others may have some ease or mitigation in their punishments, do you expect the utmost of my wrath. Luther said, he thought hell was paved with the bald skulls of friars. I know nothing of that; yet of this sure I am, that none shall have their portion so low in the nethermost hell, none shall drink so deep of the cup of God's indignation, as they who have refused Christ in the gospel. Men will curse the day to all eternity wherein the blessed name of Jesus Christ was made known unto them, if they continue to despise it. He that abuseth the choicest of mercies, shall have judgment without mercy. What can help them who reject the counsel of God for their good? If now England has received more culture from God than other nations, there is more fruit expected from England than other nations. A barren tree in the Lord's vineyard must be cut down for cumbering the ground; the sheep of God must " every one bear twins, and none be barren amongst them," Cant. iv. 2. If, after all God's care and husbandry, his vineyard brings forth wild grapes, he will take away the hedge, break down the wall, and lay it waste. For the present, the vineyard of the Lord of hosts is the house of England; and if it be as earth which, when the rain falls upon it, brings forth nothing but thorns and briers, it is nigh unto cursing, and the end thereof is to be burned, Heb. vi. 8. Men utterly and for ever neglect that ground which they have tried their skill about, and laid out much cost upon, if it bring not forth answerable fruits. Now here give me leave to say, and the Lord avert the evil deserved by it! that England (I mean these cities and those other places which since the beginning of our troubles have enjoyed the gospel in a more free and plentiful manner than heretofore) hath showed itself not much to value it.

(1.) In the time of straits, though the sound of the gospel passed through all our streets, our villages enjoying them who preached peace and brought glad tidings of good things, so that neither we, nor our fathers, nor our fathers' fathers, ever saw the like before us,—though manna fell round about our tents every day; yet, as though all were lost, and we had nothing, manna was loathed as light bread,—the presence of Christ made not recompense for the loss of our swine,—men had rather be again in Egypt, than hazard a pilgrimage in the wilderness. If there be any here that ever entertained thoughts to give up the worship of God to superstition, his churches to tyranny, and the doctrine of the gospel to episcopal corruptions, in the pressing of any troubles, let them now give God the glory, and be ashamed of their own hearts, lest it be bitterness in the end.

(2.) In the time of prosperity, by our fierce contentions about mint and cummin, whilst the weightier things of the gospel have been undervalued, languishing about unprofitable questions, &c.; but I shall not touch this wound, lest it bleed.

Use 3. For exhortation, that every one of us, in whose hand there is any thing, would set in for the help of those parts of this island that as yet sit in darkness, yea, in the shadow of death, and have none to hold out the bread of life to their fainting souls. Doth not Wales cry, and the north cry, yea, and the west cry, Come and help us?—we are yet in a worse bondage than any by your means we have been delivered from;—if you leave us thus, all your protection will but yield us a more free and jovial passage to the chambers of death. Ah! little do the inhabitants of Goshen know, whilst they are contending about the bounds of their pasture, what darkness there is in other places of the land; how their poor starved souls would be glad of the crumbs that fall from our tables! O that God would stir up the hearts,—

(1.) Of ministers, to cast off all by-respects, and to flee to those places where, in all probability, the harvest would be great, and the labourers are few or none at all! I have read of a heretic that swam over a great river in a frost to scatter his errors; the old Jewish, and now popish Pharisees, compass sea and land to make proselytes; the merchants trade not into more countries than the factors of Rome do to gain souls to his holiness. East and west, far and wide, do these locusts spread themselves, not without hazard of their lives as well as the loss of their souls, to scatter their superstitions;—only the preachers of the everlasting gospel seem to have lost their zeal. O that there were the same mind in us that was in Jesus Christ,—who counted it his meat and drink to do his Father's will, in gaining souls!

(2.) Of the magistrates,—I mean, of this honourable assembly,—to turn themselves every lawful way for the help of poor Macedonians. The truth is, in this I could speak more than I intend; for perhaps my zeal and some men's judgments would scarce make good harmony This only I shall say, that if Jesus Christ might be preached, though with some defects in some circumstances, I should rejoice therein. O that you would labour to let all the parts of the kingdom taste of the sweetness of your successes, in carrying to them the gospel of the Lord Jesus; that the doctrine of the gospel might make way for the discipline of the gospel, without which it will be a very skeleton! When manna fell in the wilderness from the hand of the Lord, every one had an equal share. I would there were not now too great an inequality in the scattering of manna, when secondarily in the hand of men; whereby some have all, and others none;—some sheep daily picking the choice flowers of every pasture, others wandering upon the barren mountains, without guide or food. I make no doubt but the best ways for the furtherance of this are known full well unto you; and you therefore have as little need to be petitioned in this as other things. What, then, remains, but that for this, and all other necessary blessings, we all set our hearts and hands to petition the throne of grace?

A SHORT DEFENSATIVE

ABOUT CHURCH GOVERNMENT, TOLERATION, AND PETITIONS ABOUT THESE THINGS.

READER,

THIS, be it what it will, thou hast no cause to thank or blame [1] me for. Had I been mine own, it had not been thine; my submission unto others' judgments being the only cause of submitting this unto thy censure. The substance of it is concerning things now doing, in some whereof I heretofore thought it my wisdom modestly *hæsitare* (or at least not with the most, peremptorily to dictate to others my apprehensions), as wiser [2] men have done in weightier things; and yet this not so much for want of persuasion in my own mind, as out of opinion that we have already had too many needless and fruitless discourses about these matters. Would we could agree to spare perishing paper! [3] and for my own part, had not the opportunity of a few lines in the close of this sermon, and the importunity of not a few friends, urged, I could have slighted all occasions and accusations provoking to publish those thoughts which I shall now impart. The truth is, in things concerning the church (I mean things purely external, of form, order, and the like), so many ways have I been spoken, that I often resolved to speak myself, desiring rather to appear (though conscious to myself of innumerable failings) what indeed I am, than what others incuriously suppose. But yet the many I ever thought unworthy of an apology, and some of satisfaction,—especially those who would make their own judgments a rule for themselves and others, impatient that any should know what they do not, or conceive otherwise than they of what they do, in the meantime, placing almost all religion in that which may be perhaps a hinderance of it,—and being so valued, or rather overvalued,—is certainly the greatest. Nay, would they would make their judgments only so far as they are convinced, and are able to make out their conceptions to others, and not also their impotent desires, to be the rule; that so they might condemn only that which complies not with their minds, and not all that also which they find to thwart their aims and designs! But so it must be. Once more conformity is grown the touchstone (and that not in practice, but opinion) amongst the greatest part of men, however otherwise of different persuasions. Dissent is the only crime; [4] and where that is all that is culpable, it shall be made all that is so. From such as these, who almost hath not suffered? but towards such the best defence is silence. Besides, my judgment commands me to make no known quarrel my own; but rather if it be possible, and as much as in me lieth, live peaceably with all men. Ἱερὸν πόλεμον, I proclaim to none

1 "Laudatur ab his, culpatur ab illis."—[Hor. Sat., lib. i. 2, 11.]

2 See August., Ep. 7, 28, 157, De Orig. Anim.

3 "Deferar in vicum vendentem thus et odores,
Et piper, et quicquid chartis amicitur ineptis."—[Hor. Epist., lib. ii. 1.]
"Occidit miseros crambe repetita magistros."—[Juv.]
"Semper ego auditor tantum?"—[Juv. Sat. i.]

4 "Immortale odium et nunquam sanabile vulnus,
Ardet adhuc, Ombos et Tentyra. Summus utrinque
Inde furor vulgo, quòd numina vicinorum
Odit uterque locus."—Juven., [xv. 35.]
"Græcè scire, aut politè loqui, apud illos hæresis est."—Eras. de Scholiast.

but men whose bowels are full of gall. In this spring of humours, lenitives for our own spirits may perhaps be as necessary as purges for others' brains. Farther, I desire to provoke[1] none; more stings than combs are got at a nest of wasps; even cold stones, smitten together, sparkle out fire: "The wringing of the nose bringeth forth blood." Neither do I conceive it wisdom, in these quarrelsome days, to intrust more of a man's self with others than is very necessary. The heart of man is deceitful; some that have smooth tongues have sharp teeth: such can give titles on the one side and wounds on the other. Any of these considerations would easily have prevailed with me "stultitiâ hac caruisse," had not mine ears been filled, presently after the preaching of the precedent sermon, with sad complaints of some, and false reports of others, neither of the lowest rank of men, as though I had helped to open a gate for that which is now called a Trojan horse; though heretofore counted an engine likelier to batter the walls of Babylon than to betray the towers of Zion. This urged some to be urgent with me for a word or two about church government, according to the former suggestions, undermined, and a toleration of different persuasions, as they said, asserted. Now, truly, to put the accusers to prove the crimination—for so it was, and held forth a grievous crime in their apprehensions (what is really so God will judge)—had been sufficient.[2] But I could not so evade; and therefore, after my sermon was printed to the last sheet, I was forced to set apart a few hours,[3] to give an account of what hath passed from me in both these things, which have been so variously reported; hoping that the reading may not be unuseful to some, as the writing was very necessary to me. And here, at the entrance, I shall desire at the hands of men that shall cast an eye on this heap of good meaning, these few, as I suppose, equitable demands:—

First, Not to prosecute men into odious appellations, and then themselves, who feigned the crime, pronounce the sentence,—like him who said of one brought before him, If he be not guilty, it is fit he should be;—involving themselves in a double guilt, of falsehood and malice; and the aspersed parties in a double misery, of being belied in what they are, and hated for what they are not. If a man be not what such men would have him, it is odds but they will make him what he is not;—if what he really is do not please, and that be not enough to render him odious, he shall sure enough be more. Ithacius will make all Priscillianists who are any thing more devout than himself.[4] If men do but desire to see with their own eyes, presently they are enrolled of this or that sect; every mispersuasion being beforehand, in petitions, sermons, &c., rendered odious and intolerable;—in such a course, innocency itself cannot go long free. Christians deal with one another in earnest, as children in their plays clap another's coat upon their fellow's shoulders, and pretending to beat that, cudgel him they have clothed with it. "What shall be given unto thee, thou false tongue?" If we cannot be more charitable, let us be more ingenuous. Many a man hath been brought to a more favourable opinion of such as are called by dreadful names than formerly, by the experience of false impositions on himself.

Secondly, Not to clothe our differences with expressions fitting them no better than Saul's armour did David; nor make them like a little man in a bombast coat upon stilts, walking about like a giant. Our little differences may be met at every stall, and in too many pulpits, swelled by unbefitting expressions into such a formidable bulk as poor creatures are even startled at their horrid looks and appearance; whilst our own persuasions are set out *ῥήμασι βυσσίνοις*,[5] with silken words

[1] "Noli irritare crabrones. Si lapides teras nonne ignis erumpit?"—Ambros., lib. i. cap. 21; Prov. xxx. 33; Job xiii. 13; Prov. xxv. 18. Vid. Remed. contra Gravam. Nationis Germanicæ. Luth præfat. ad Lib. de Concil. Protest. 34 ministrorum. 4. Conclus. And generally all writers at the beginning of the Reformation.

[2] Si accusasse sufficiet, quis erit innocens?

[3] "Nec nos obniti contrà, nec tendere tantùm
Sufficimus."—[Virg. Æ. v. 21.]

[4] Sulp. Sever. Epist. Hist. Eccles.

[5] Plut. Apophth.

and gorgeous apparel, as if we sent them into the world a-wooing. Hence, whatever it is, it must be temple building,—God's government,—Christ's sceptre, throne, kingdom,—the only way, that for want of which, errors, heresies, sins, spring among us, plagues, judgments, punishments come upon us. To such things as these all pretend, who are very confident they have found out the only way. Such big words as these have made us believe that we are mortal adversaries (I speak of the parties at variance about government),—that one kingdom, communion, heaven cannot hold us. Now, truly, if this course be followed,—so to heighten our differences, by adorning the truth we own with such titles as it doth not merit, and branding the errors we oppose with such marks as in cold blood we cannot think they themselves, but only in their (by us supposed) tendence, do deserve,—I doubt not but that it will be bitterness unto us all in the end. And, query, whether by this means many have not been brought to conceive the kingdom of Jesus Christ, which himself affirms to be within us, to consist in forms, outward order, positive rules, and external government. I design none, but earnestly desire that the two great parties at this day litigant in this kingdom, would seriously consider what is like to be the issue of such proceedings; and whether the mystery of godliness, in the power thereof, be like to be propagated by it. Let not truth be weighed in the balance of our interest. Will not a dram of that turn the scale with some against many arguments? Power is powerful to persuade.

Thirdly, Not to measure men's judgments by their subscribing or refusing to subscribe petitions in these days about church government. For subscribers, would that every one could not see, with what a zealous nescience and implicit judgment many are led! And for refusers, though perhaps they could close with the general words wherewith usually they are expressed, yet there are so many known circumstances restraining those words to particular significations, directing them to by and secondary tendencies, as must needs make some abstain. For mine own part, from subscribing late petitions about church government, I have been withheld by such reasons as these:—

1. I dare not absolutely assert, maintain, and abide by it (as rational men ought to do every clause in any thing owned by their subscription), that the cause of all the evils usually enumerated in such petitions is the want of church government, taking it for any government that ever yet was established amongst men, or in notion otherwise made known unto me; yea, I am confident that more probable causes in this juncture of time might be assigned of them. Neither can any be ignorant how plentifully such evils abounded when church discipline was most severely executed.[1] And, lastly, I am confident that whoever lives to see them suppressed by any outward means (when spiritual weapons shall be judged insufficient), will find it to be, not any thing either included in, or necessarily annexed unto, church discipline that must do it; but some other thing, not unlike that which, in days of yore, when all the world wondered after the beast, suppressed all truth and error, but only what the arch enemy of Jesus Christ was pleased to hold out to be believed. But of this afterward.

2. I dare not affirm that the Parliament hath not established a government already, for the essentials of it; themselves affirming that they have,[2] and their ordinances about rulers, rules, and persons to be ruled (the "requisita" and materials of government), being long since extant. Now, to require a thing to be done by them who affirm that they have already done it, argues either much weakness or supine negligence in ourselves, not to understand what is effected; or a strong imputation on those that have done it, either fraudulently to pretend that which is false, or foolishly to aver what they do not understand. Yet, though I have

1 Vid. catal. hæret. apud Tertul. de præscript. Epiphan. Aug. Vincent.

2 "Ego ancillæ tuæ fidem habui: nonne tu impudens, qui nec mihi ipsi credis?"—Philos. apud Plut. Apophth.

learned to obey, as far as lawfully I may, my judgment is exceedingly far from being enslaved; and according to that, by God's assistance, shall be my practice; which, if it run cross to the prescriptions of authority, it shall cheerfully submit to the censure thereof. In the meantime, all petitioning of any party about this business seems to thwart some declarations of the House of Commons, whereunto I doubt not but they intend for the main inviolably and unalterably to adhere. Add hereunto, that petitioning in this kind was not long since voted breach of privilege, in them who might justly expect as much favour and liberty in petitioning as any of their brethren in the kingdom; and I have more than one reason to suppose that the purpose and design of theirs and others was one and the same.

3. There are no small grounds of supposal that some petitions have not their rise from amongst them by whom they are subscribed, but that the spring and master-wheels giving the first motion to them are distant and unseen; myself having been lately urged to subscription upon this ground, that directions were had for it from above (as we used to speak in the country);—yea, in this I could say more than I intend, aiming at nothing but the quieting of men's spirits, needlessly exasperated; only I cannot but say, that honest men ought to be very cautious how they put themselves upon any engagement that might make any party or faction in the kingdom suppose that their interest, in the least measure, doth run cross to that of the great Council thereof; thereby to strengthen the hands or designs of any, by occasioning an opinion that, upon fresh or new divisions, (which God of his mercy prevent!) we would not adhere constantly to our old principles, walking according to which we have hitherto found protection and safety. And I cannot but be jealous for the honour of our noble Parliament, whose authority is every day undermined, and their regard in the affections of the people shaken, by such dangerous insinuations; as though they could in an hour put an end to all our disturbances, but refuse it. This season, also, for such petitions seems to be very unseasonable, the greatest appearing danger impendent to this kingdom being from the contest about church government; which, by such means as this, is exceedingly heightened, and animosity added to the parties at variance.

4. A particular form of church discipline is usually, in such petitions, either directly expressed or evidently pointed at and directed unto, as that alone which our covenant engageth us to embrace; yea, as though it had long since designed that particular way, and distinguished it from all others, the embracing of it is pressed under the pain of breach of covenant,—a crime abhorred of God and man. Now, truly, to suppose that our covenant did tie us up absolutely to any one formerly-known way of church discipline,—the words formally engaging us into a disquisition out of the word of that which is agreeable to the mind and will of God,—is to me such a childish, ridiculous, selfish conceit, as I believe no knowing men will once entertain, unless prejudice, begotten by their peculiar interest, hath disturbed their intellectuals. For my part, I know no church government in the world already established amongst any sort of men, of the truth and necessity whereof I am convinced in all particulars; especially if I may take their practice to be the best intepreter of their maxims.

Fourthly, Another "postulatum" is, that men would not use an over-zealous speed, upon every small difference, to characterize men (otherwise godly and peaceable) as sectaries; knowing the odiousness of the name,[1] among the vulgar, deservedly or otherwise imposed, and the evil of the thing itself, rightly apprehended, whereunto lighter differences do not amount. Such names as this I know are arbitrary, and generally serve the wills of the greater number. They are commonly sectaries who, "jure aut injuriâ," are oppressed. Nothing was ever

1 "Nunc vero si nominis odium est, quis nominum reatus? quæ accusatio vocabulorum? nisi aut Barbarum sonat aliqua vox nominis, aut maledicum, aut impudicum?"—Tertul. Apol.

persecuted under an esteemed name. Names are in the power of many; things and their causes are known to few. There is none in the world can give an ill title to others, which from some he doth not receive. The same right which in this kind I have towards another, he hath towards me; unless I affirm myself to be infallible, not so him. Those names which men are known by when they are oppressed, they commonly use against others whom they seek to oppress. I would, therefore, that all horrid appellations, as increasers of strife, kindlers of wrath, enemies of charity, food for animosity, were for ever banished from amongst us. Let a spade be called a spade, so we take heed Christ be not called Beelzebub. I know my profession to the greatest part of the world is sectarism, as Christianity; amongst those who profess the name of Christ, to the greatest number I am a sectary, because a Protestant;[1] amongst Protestants, at least the one half account all men of my persuasion Calvinistical, sacramentarian sectaries; amongst these, again, to some I have been a puritanical sectary, an Arian heretic, because anti-prelatical; yea, and amongst these last, not a few account me a sectary because I plead for presbyterial government in churches: and to all these am I thus esteemed, as I am fully convinced, causelessly and erroneously. What they call sectarism, I am persuaded is "ipsissima veritas," the "very truth itself," to which they also ought to submit; that others also, though upon false grounds, are convinced of the truth of their own persuasion, I cannot but believe: and therefore, as I find by experience that the horrid names of heretic, schismatic, sectary, and the like, have never had any influence or force upon my judgment, nor otherwise moved me, unless it were unto retaliation, so I am persuaded it is also with others; for "homines sumus:" forcing them abroad in such liveries doth not at all convince them that they are servants to the master of sects indeed, but only makes them wait an opportunity to cast the like mantle on their traducers. And this usually is the beginning of arming the more against the few with violence, impatient of bearing the burdens which they impose on others' shoulders; by means whereof Christendom hath been made a theatre of blood, and one amongst all, after that by cruelty and villany he had prevailed above the rest, took upon him to be the only dictator in Christian religion. But of this afterward.

Now, by the concession of these, as I hope, not unequitable demands, thus much at least I conceive will be attained, viz., that a peaceable dissent in some smaller things, disputable questions, not absolutely necessary assertions, deserves not any rigid censure, distance of affections, or breach of Christian communion and amity. In such things as these, "veniam petimusque damusque vicissim:" if otherwise, I profess I can hardly bring my mind to comply and close in with them amongst whom almost any thing is lawful but to dissent.

These things being premised, I shall now set down and make public that proposal which heretofore I have tendered, as a means to give some light into a way for the profitable and comfortable practice of church government; drawing out of general notions what is practically applicable, so circumstantiated as of necessity it must be. And herein I shall not alter any thing, or in the least expression go off from that which long since I drew up at the request of a worthy friend, after a discourse about it; and this, not only because it hath already been in the hands of many, but also because my intent is not, either to assert, dispute, or make out any thing farther of my judgment in these things than I have already done (hoping for more leisure so to do than the few hours assigned to the product of this short appendix will permit), but only, by way of a defensative, to evince that the rumours which have been spread by some, and entertained by others too greedily, about this matter, have been exceeding causeless and groundless; so that

1 Acts xxiv. 14, xxviii. 22.—"Hæresis Christianorum." Tertul.,—"Secta Christ." Id.,—"Hæresis catholica, et hæresis sanctissima," Constant. Epist. Chr. Syriac. Tileni Syntagma,—quo probare conatur Calvinianos esse hæreticos, Hun. Calv. Tur. Andrews. Epist. ad Molin.

though my second thoughts have, if I mistake not, much improved some particulars in this essay, yet I cannot be induced, because of the reason before recounted (the only cause of the publication thereof), to make any alteration in it; only I shall present the reader with some few things which gave occasion and rise to this proposal. As,—

(1.) A fervent desire to prevent all farther division and separation,—disunion of minds amongst godly men,—suspicions and jealousies in the people towards their ministers, as aiming at power and unjust domination over them,—fruitless disputes, languishings about unprofitable questions, breaches of charity for trifles, exasperating the minds of men one against another;—all which growing evils, tending to the subversion of Christian love and the power of godliness, with the disturbance of the state, are too much fomented by that sad breach and division which is here attempted to be made up.

(2.) A desire to work and draw the minds of all my brethren (the most, I hope, need it not) to set in for a thorough reformation, and for the obtaining of holy communion,—to keep off indifferently the unworthy from church privileges and profaning of holy things. Whereunto I presumed the discovery of a way whereby this might be effected, without their disturbance in their former station, would be a considerable motive.

(3.) A consideration of the paucity of positive rules in the Scripture for church government, with the great difficulty of reducing them to practice in these present times (both sufficiently evidenced by the endless disputes and irreconcilable differences of godly, precious, and learned men about them), made me conceive that the practice of the apostolical churches, doubtless for a time observed in those immediately succeeding, would be the best external help for the right interpretation of those rules we have, and pattern to draw out a church way by. Now, truly, after my best search and inquiry into the first churches and their constitution, framing an idea and exemplar of them, this poor heap following seems to me as like one of them as any thing that yet I have seen; nothing at all doubting but that if a more skilful hand had the limning of it,[1] the proportions, features, and lines would be very exact, equal and parallel; yea, did not extreme haste now call it from me, so that I have no leisure so much as to transcribe the first draught, I doubt not but by God's assistance it might be so set forth as not to be thought altogether undesirable, if men would but a little lay aside beloved pre-conceptions. But the printer stays for every line; only I must entreat every one that shall cast a candid eye on this unwillingly-exposed embryo and rude abortion, that he would assume in his mind any particular church mentioned in the Scripture, as of Jerusalem, Corinth, Ephesus, or the like; consider the way and state they were then and some ages after, in respect of outward immunities and enjoyments, and tell me whether any rational man can suppose that either there were in those places sundry particular churches, with their distinct, peculiar officers, acting in most pastoral duties severally in them, as distinguished and divided into entire societies, but ruling them in respect of some particulars loyally in combination, considered as distinct bodies; or else that they were such single congregations as that all that power and authority which was in them may seem fitly and conveniently to be intrusted with a small handful of men, combined under one single pastor, with one, two, or perhaps no associated elders. More than this I shall only ask, whether all ordinary power may not, without danger, be asserted to reside in such a church as is here described, reserving all due right and authority to councils and magistrates? Now, for the fountain, seat, and rise of this power, for the just distribution of it between pastors and people, this is no place to dispute; these following lines were intended merely to sedate and bury such contests, and to be what they are entitled,—

[1] Ἀμέραι δ' ἐπίλοιποι μάρτυρες σοφώτατοι.—Pind., Od. i. Olym., 54, 55.

A COUNTRY ESSAY

FOR

THE PRACTICE OF CHURCH GOVERNMENT THERE.

OUR long expectation of some accommodation[1] between the dissenting parties about church government being now almost totally frustrate,—being also persuaded, partly through the apparent fruitlessness of all such undertakings, partly by other reasons not at this time seasonable to be expressed, that all national disputes tending that way will prove birthless tympanies,—we deem it no ungrateful endeavour, waiving all speculative ideas, to give an essay, in such expressions as all our country friends concerned in it may easily apprehend, of what we conceive amongst us may really be reduced to comfortable and useful practice: concealing for a while all arguments for motives and inducements unto this way, with all those rocks and shelves, appearing very hideous in former proposals, which we strive to avoid; until we perceive whether any of our giants in this controversy will not come and look, and so overcome it, that at first dash the whole frame be irrecoverably ruined.

Neither would we have any expect our full sense to each particular imaginable in this business,—it being only a heap of materials, mostwhat unhewed, that we intend, and not a well-compacted fabric;—and if the main be not condemned, we are confident no difference will ensue about particulars, which must have their latitude. However, if it be received as candidly as it is offered, no inconvenience will ensue. Now, that the whole may be better apprehended, and the reasons, if not the necessity, of this undertaking intimated, we shall premise some things concerning the place and persons for whose use is this proposal.

First, For ministers. The place having all this while, through the goodness of God, been preserved in peace and quietness; and by the rich supply of able men sent hither by Parliament, there are in many parishes godly, orthodox, peace-loving pastors.

Secondly, For the people.

1. Very many, as in most other places, extremely ignorant, worldly, profane, scandalously vicious.

[1] The form being given to this essay at the first, I thought not good to alter any thing about it.

2. Scarcely any parish where there are not some visibly appearing, of all ages, sexes, and conditions, fearing God, and walking unblamably with a right foot, as beseemeth the gospel; though in some places they are but like the berries after the shaking of an olive-tree.

3. Amongst these, very few gifted, fitted or qualified for government.

4. Many knowing professors, and such of a long standing, inclined to separation, unless some expedient may be found for comfortable communions; and in this resolution seem to be settled, to a contempt of allurements and threatenings.

5. Seducers everywhere lying in wait to catch and deceive well-meaning souls, any thing discontented with the present administration of church affairs.

6. Upon all which it appears, that comfortable communion is not to be attained within the bounds of respective parishes.

Farther to carry on our intentions, we would desire of authority,—

1. That our divisions may not be allotted out by our committees,—who, without other consideration, have bounded us with the precincts of high constables,—but be left to the prudence of ministers, and other Christians, willingly associating themselves in the work.

2. That men placed in civil authority may not, by virtue of their authority, claim any privilege in things purely ecclesiastical.

In the several parishes let things be thus ordered:—

1. Let every minister continue in his station, taking especial care of all them that live within the precincts of his parish; preaching, exhorting, rebuking, publicly, and from house to house; warning all,—using all appointed means to draw them to Jesus Christ and the faith of the gospel; waiting with all patience on them that oppose themselves, until God give them repentance to the acknowledging of the truth; and in so doing, rest upon the calling he hath already received.

2. Let the respective elders of the several parishes, to be chosen according to the ordinance of Parliament (annually, or otherwise), join with the ministers in all acts of rule and admonition, with those other parts of their charge which the parochial administration doth require.

3. Let all criminal things, tending to the disturbance of that church administration which is amongst them be by the officers orderly delated to such as the civil magistrate shall appoint to take cognizance and determine of such things.

And thus far have we proposed nothing new, nothing not common; neither in that which follows is there any thing so indeed, may it be but rightly apprehended.

For the several combinations of ministers and people:—

1. Let the extremes of the division not be above eight or ten miles distant, and so the middle or centre not more than four or five miles from any part of it,—which is no more than some usually go to

the preaching of the word, and in which space Christians are generally as well known to one another in the country as almost at the next door in cities; but yet this may be regulated according to the number of professors fit for the society intended,—which would not be above five hundred, nor under one hundred.

2. In this division let there be, in the name of Christ and the fear of God, a gathering of professors (visible saints, men and women of good knowledge and upright conversation,—so holding forth their communion with Christ), by their own desire and voluntary consent, into one body,—uniting themselves, by virtue of some promissory engagement or otherwise, to perform all mutual duties, to walk in love and peace, spiritual and church communion, as beseemeth the gospel.

3. Let every one so assembling have liberty, at some of the first meetings, to except against another, whether minister or others, so it be done with a spirit of meekness, and submission of judgment; or to demand such questions for satisfaction as shall be thought fit to be propounded.

4. When some convenient number are thus assembled, let the ministers, if men of approved integrity and abilities, be acknowledged as elders respectively called to teach and rule in the church by virtue of their former mission, and be assumed to be so to this society by virtue of their voluntary consent and election.

5. Let the ministers engage themselves in a special manner to watch over this flock, every one according to his abilities, both in teaching, exhorting, and ruling, so often as occasion shall be administered, for things that contain ecclesiastical rule and church order; acting jointly and as in a classical combination, and putting forth all authority that such classes are intrusted with.

6. If it be judged necessary that any officers be added to them for the purpose before named, let them be chosen by the consent of the multitude.

7. If not, let the ministers have the whole distributed among themselves respectively, according to the difference of their gifts,—reserving to the people their due and just privileges.

8. Let this congregation assemble at the least once in a month, for the celebration of the communion, and other things them concerning; the meeting of the ministers may be appointed by authority, for those of a classis.

9. If any one after his admission be found to walk unworthily, let him, after solemn, repeated admonition, be by joint consent left to his former station.

10. Let any person, in any of the parishes combined as before, that is desirous to be admitted into this society, as is thought fit, be received at any time.

11. If the number in process of time appear to be too great, let it be divided and subdivided, according to conveniency.

12. Any one of the ministers may administer the sacrament, either to some or all of these, in their several parishes or at the common meeting, as opportunity shall serve.

13. Let the rules of admission into this society and fellowship be scriptural, and the things required in the members only such as all godly men affirm to be necessary for every one that will partake of the ordinances with profit and comfort,—special care being taken that none be excluded who have the least breathings of soul in sincerity after Jesus Christ.

Now, beyond these generals for the present we judge it needless to express ourselves, or otherwise to confirm what we have proposed, each assertion almost directly pointing out unto what, in that particular, we do adhere; which being sufficiently confirmed by others, were but a superfluous labour to undertake. Neither shall we trouble you with a catalogue of conveniences,—whereof men are put upon an express annumeration, when otherwise they do not appear,—but commit the consideration of the tendence of the whole to every one's judgment, and conclude with the removal of a few obvious objections; being resolved hereafter, by God's assistance, to endeavour satisfaction about this way unto all,—unless to such as shall be so simple or malicious as to ask whether this way be that of the Presbyterians or Independents.

Obj. 1. By this means parishes will be unchurched.

Ans. 1. If by churches you understand such entire societies of Christians as have all church power, both according to right and exercise, in and amongst themselves, as Independents speak of congregations; then they were never churched by any.

2. If only civil divisions of men that may conveniently be taught by one pastor, and ruled by elders, whereof some may be fit to partake of all the ordinances, some not, as Presbyterians esteem them; then by this way they receive no injury, nor are abridged of any of their privileges.

Obj. 2. This is to erect churches amongst churches, and against churches.

Ans. No such thing; but a mere forming of one church with one presbytery.

Obj. 3. It is against the Parliament's ordinance to assume a power of admitting and excluding of church members not exactly according to their rule, nor subordinate to the supervising of such as are appointed by them.

Ans. 1. For the rules set out by ordinance, we conceive that the church officers are to be interpreters of them, until appeal be made from them, unto which we shall submit; and if it be so determined against us, that any be put on our communion "ipsi viderint,"—we shall labour to deliver our own souls.

2. Though the Parliament forbid any but such authoritatively to be excluded, yet it doth not command that any be admitted but such as desire it; and we shall pray for such a blessing upon the work of our ministry as will either prepare a man for it or persuade them "pro tempore" from it; unless they be stubbornly obstinate, or openly wicked,—against whom we hope for assistance. To objections arising from trouble and inconvenience, we answer, It cost more to redeem their souls.

The God of peace and unity give the increase!

"—— Si quid novisti rectius istis,
Candidus imperti, si non, his utere."
[Hor. Ep., i. 6, 67, 68.]

And this is all which, for the present, I shall assert in this business; and this also is my own vindication. Time and leisure may give me advantage hereafter (if God permit) to deal seriously in this cause. In the meantime, it is not unknown to many, that so much as this was necessary for me to do; and I will not add now any thing that is not necessary.

Now for the other head of the accusation, about toleration of errors, "philosophare volo, sed paucis." Something I shall add of my own present judgment in this matter; but with willing, express submission unto those whom the use and experience of things, with knowledge of foreign parts, skill in the rules of commonwealths, acquaintedness with the affections and spirits of men, have enabled to look punctually into the issues and tendencies of such a toleration. The main prejudice against it arises from the disturbances which it naturally (they say) produceth in civil states. I conceive no sort of men more unfit to judge of this than those whose abilities of learning do properly put them upon the discussing of this, and other controversies, as far as they are purely ecclesiastical,—no men more frequently betraying narrowness of apprehension and weakness in secular affairs. For other consequences, I shall not be much moved with them, until it be clearly determined whether be worse, heretics or hypocrites,—to maintain an error or counterfeit the truth; and whether profession upon compulsion be acceptable to God or man.[1] Laying those aside, let the thing itself be a little considered.

Peace ecclesiastical, quiet among the churches (which without doubt would be shaken by a universal toleration), is that which most men aim at and desire. And truly he that doth not, scarcely deserves the name and privilege of a Christian. Unity in the Scripture

[1] "Hostiæ ab animo libenti accipiuntur."—Tertul.

is so pressed, so commanded, and commended, that not to breathe after it argues a heart acted by another spirit than that which moved the holy penmen thereof. But yet every agreement and consent amongst men professing the name of Christ, is not the unity and peace commended in the Scripture. That which some think to be Christ's order, may perhaps be antichristian confusion; the specious name of unity may be a cloak for tyranny. Learned men have reckoned up a sevenfold unity[1] in the Papacy; all which, notwithstanding, are far enough from that true evangelical unity which we are bound to labour for. Again, that which is good must be sought in a right manner, or it will not be so to us. Peace and quiet is desirable; but there must be good causes and very urgent, to make us build our habitations out of others' ruins, and roll our pillows in their blood. I speak of things ecclesiastical. The historian[2] makes it a part of the oration spoken by Galgacus, the chieftain of the British forces, to stir them up against the Roman insolency, that when they had finished their depopulations, then they said they had peace. The same men have set up bishoprics in the Indies, as their forefathers did colonies here and elsewhere, with fire and sword. I know not how it comes to pass, but so it is, this proceeding with violence in matters of religion hath pleased and displeased all sorts of men, however distinguished by a true or false persuasion, who have enjoyed a vicissitude of the supreme power in any place, in supporting or suppressing of them. "Ure, seca, occide," is the language of men backed with authority: "Quod tibi fieri non vis, alteri ne feceris," say the same men under oppression. To give particular instances, were to lay open that nakedness which I suppose it my duty rather to cover. What, then, you will say; shall every one be suffered to do what he pleaseth?[3] You mean, think or believe what he pleaseth, or that which he is convinced to be a truth. Must all sorts of men and their opinions be tolerated?—These questions are not in one word to be resolved: many proposals are to be confirmed, many notions distinguished and retained, before a positive answer can be given. Take them in their whole latitude, and they may serve all men's turns. A negative universal resolution may tantamount unto,—"The many intrusted with authority, or having that to back them, ought not to tolerate any of different persuasions from them, if they suppose them erroneous." Now truly, for my part, were I in Spain or Italy, a native of those places, and God should be pleased there to reveal

[1] "1. Satanica; 2. Ethnica; 3. Belluina; 4. Iscariotica; 5. Tyrannica; 6. Herodiana; 7. Ventris causa."—Illyricus, de Variis Sectis ap. Papistas.

[2] "Solitudinem ubi faciunt, pacem appellant."—Tacitus Vita Agr. cap. x.

[3] "Humani juris, et naturalis potestatis est, unicuique quod putaverit colere."—Tertul. "Quis imponet mihi necessitatem aut credendi quod nolim, aut quod velim non credendi?"—Lactan.

that truth of his gospel unto me which he hath done in England, I believe those states ought to tolerate me, though they were persuaded that I were the most odious heretic under heaven; and what punishment soever they should impose on me for my profession would be required at their hands;—unless they can convince me that God allows men to slay his servants for professing the gospel, if they believe them to be heretics: and so also excuse the Jews in crucifying his dear Son, because they esteemed him as an impostor. Christ was once crucified amongst thieves: he may be again, in them that are so supposed. I shall therefore summarily set down what I conceive in answer to these questions, premising a few things, if I mistake not, universally granted.

And yet a word or two concerning toleration itself, that some guess may be given at what we aim and intend, must interpose. Much discourse about toleration hath been of late days amongst men; some pleading for it, more against it,—as it always must be. Toleration is the alms of authority; yet men that beg for it, think so much at least their due. Some say it is a sin to grant it; others, that it is no less to deny it. Generally, the pleaders of each side have their interest in the cause. I never knew one contend earnestly for a toleration of dissenters, but was so himself; nor any for their suppression, but were themselves of the persuasion which prevaileth: for if otherwise, this latter would argue a Circumcellion[1] fury, wilfully to seek their own ruin; the former so much charity, and commiseration of the condition of mortality as in these days would procure of the most no other livery but a fool's coat. Who almost would not admire at such new-discovered antipodes as should offer to assert an equal regiment of Trojans and Tyrians,[2]—a like regard and allowance from authority for other sects as for that whereof themselves are a share? Now, amongst these contesters, few (nay, not any) have I found, either on the one side or the other, clearly and distinctly to define what they mean by toleration, or what is the direct purpose, signification, and tendence of non-toleration (a word in its whole extent written only in the forehead of the man of sin),—what bounds, what terriers are to be assigned to the one or to the other,—unto what degrees of longitude[3] or latitude their pole is to be elevated. Some, perhaps, by a toleration understand a universal, uncontrolled licence, "vivendi ut velis," in things concerning religion; that every one may be let

[1] The Circumcelliones, from which this epithet is derived, were fanatics in North Africa, who, in the course of the fourth century, prowled around the huts (circum cellas) of the peasantry, despising labour, and subsisting on alms. They were much under the influence of the Donatists, and often, by their rash demolition of pagan idols, exposed themselves to martyrdom.—Ed.

[2] "Tros, Tyriusque mihi nullo discrimine agetur."—[Virg. Æ., i. 578.]

[3] "Late sibi summovet omne
Vulgus ut in vacuâ regnet Basiliscus arenâ."—[Lucan, i. 9, 725.]

alone, and not so much as discountenanced in doing, speaking, acting, how, what, where, or when he pleaseth, "in agendis et credendis fidei," in all such things as concern the worship of God, articles of belief, or generally any thing commanded in religion; and in the meantime the parties at variance, and litigant about differences, freely to revile, reject, and despise one another, according as their provoked genius shall dispose their minds thereunto. Now truly, though every one of this mind pretends to cry for mercy to be extended unto poor afflicted truth, yet I cannot but be persuaded that such a toleration would prove exceeding pernicious to all sorts of men, and at last end in a dispute, like that recounted by Juvenal between two cities in Egypt, about their differences between their garden and river deities;[1] or like the contest related by Vertomannus in his travels amongst the Mohammedans, about Haly and Homar, the pretended successors to their grand impostor, where every one plied his adversary, "Hastisque clypeisque et saxis grandibus," cleaving their skulls, and making entrance for their arguments by dint of sword: and I wish experience did not sufficiently convince us that the profession of Christianity, where the power of godliness is away, will not prevent these evils: "Tantum religio potuit suadere malorum."

Others there are that press for a non-toleration of any thing that opposes or contradicts the truth in any part, themselves being in their own judgments fully possessed of all,—their tenets being unto them the only form of wholesome words. Moreover (for these things recounted make not the difference, for it is so with all sects of men), the magistrates, or those who are intrusted with all the power over men which, for the preservation of human society, God hath been pleased to make out from himself, are also of the same persuasion with them. These they supplicate that an effectual course may be taken (asserting not only that they are intrusted with power from above so to do, but also that it is their great sin if they do it not) whereby all sectaries and erroneous persons may not only not be countenanced or kept within bounds, and not be forborne in any disturbing, insolent miscarriage; but also, that all that doctrine which is not publicly owned may be sure to be supplanted by the restraint and punishment of the dissenters, whether unto imprisonment, confiscation of goods, or death itself; for they must not cease, nay (if the thing is to be effected), they cannot rationally assign where to stay in punishing, before they come to the period of all, death itself, which is the point and centre wherein all the lines of this sentence meet;[2] wherein, to me, truly there is nothing but "luctus ubique,

[1] "O Sanctas gentes quibus hæc nascantur in hortis
Numina!"—[Sat. xv. 10]

[2] "Inventus, Chrysippe, tui finitor acervi."—[Persi. vi. 80.]

pavor, et plurima mortis imago." I know it is coloured with fair pretences;[1] but "quid ego verba audiam, facta cum video?" It is written with red letters, and the pens of its abettors are dipped in the blood of Christians. Doubtless between these extremes lies the way.

Again, some by a toleration understand a mutual forbearance in communion, though there be great differences in opinion; and this the generality of the clergy (as heretofore they were called) did usually incline unto,—viz., that any men almost might be tolerated, whilst they did not separate. And these lay down this for a ground, that there is a latitude in judgment to be allowed; so that the communion may be held by men of several persuasions, in all things, with an allowance of withdrawing in those particulars wherein there is dissent amongst them: and this the Belgic Remonstrants pressed hard for, before they were cast out by the Synod of Dort.

Others plead for a toleration out of communion; that is, that men renouncing the communion of those whose religion is owned and established by authority, may yet peaceably be suffered to enjoy the ordinances in separation.

Moreover, by communion some understand one thing, some another. Some think that is preserved sufficiently, if the dissenters do acknowledge those from whom they do dissent to be true churches, to enjoy the ordinances of Christ, to have the means of life and salvation in them, closing with them in all substantials of doctrine; but yet, because of some disorders in and amongst them, they dare not be as of them,—but yet only separate from those disorders.

Others, again, think that communion is utterly dissolved if any distinctions of persons be made, more than all acknowledge ought to be, —any differences in the administration of the ordinances,—any divisions in government at all.

Now, all these things, and many more that might be added, must clearly be distinguished and determined by him that would handle his matter at large and exactly, that we may know what he means by those ambiguous words, and in what acceptation he owns them. Until this be done, a man may profess to oppose both toleration and non-toleration without any contradiction at all, because in their several senses they do not always intend the same.

For my part, as on the one side;—if by toleration you mean "potestatem vivendi ut velis" (as the Stoics defined liberty), a universal concession of an unbounded liberty,[2] or rather, bold, unbridled licen-

[1] Ἐχθρὸς γάρ μοι κεῖνος ὁμῶς ἀΐδαο πύλησιν,
Ὅς χ' ἕτερον μὲν κεύθει ἐνὶ φρεσὶν, ἄλλο δὲ βάζει.—[Hom. Il., ix. 312, 313.]

[2] Ἐξουσία αὐτοπραγίας;—[Diog. Laert. in Stoic. Dogm., rendered as above by Cicer. Paradox. Sto. v. 1.]

tiousness, for every one to vent what he pleaseth, and to take what course seems good in his own eyes, in things concerning religion and the worship of God, I cannot give my vote for it;—so, if by non-toleration you mean that which the gloss upon that place, "Hæreticum hominem de vita," intended by adding "supple tolle,"[1] to make up the sense,—as if they were not to be endured in any place who dissent only in not-fundamentals from that which is established, but to be hated "ad furcas et leones," as the Christians of old, or to have their new derided lights extinguished in that light, "qua stantes ardent, qui fixo gutture fumant," in a Nero's bonfire,—into the secrets of them that are thus minded let not my soul descend. "In their anger they will slay a man, and in their self-will they dig down a wall. Cursed be their anger, for it is fierce; and their wrath, for it is cruel." These things, then, being so ambiguous, doubtful, and uncertain, we dare not be too peremptorily dogmatical, nor positively assert but only what is certainly true; as are these following:—

1. That heresies and errors ought not to be tolerated;—that is, men ought not to connive at, or comply with, those ways and opinions which they are convinced to be false, erroneous, contrary to sound doctrine, and that form of wholesome words which is delivered unto us as (next unto Christ) the greatest treasure of our souls,—especially if credibly supposed to shake any fundamentals of the common faith; but with all their strength and abilities, in all lawful ways, upon every just call, to oppose, suppress, and overthrow them,—to root them up and cast them out, that they may not, as noxious weeds and tares, overgrow and choke the good corn, amongst which they are covertly scattered. All predictions of "false Christs, false prophets, false teachers to come," and "to be avoided,"—all cautions to "try spirits, avoid heretics, beware of seducers, keep close to the truth received, —to hate the doctrine of Nicolaitanes, to avoid endless disputes, strife of words, old fables, languishing about unprofitable questions,"—the epithets given to, and descriptions made of, heresies, that they are "pernicious, damnable, cankers, works of the flesh," and the like,—are all incitations and encouragements for the applying of all expedient means for the taking out of the way these stumbling-blocks. Let, then, the Scriptures be searched, and all ways embraced which the gospel holdeth forth, for the discovering, convincing, silencing, reproving, confuting of errors and persons erring, by admonitions, reproofs, mighty Scripture convictions, evidencing of the truth, with fervent prayers to Almighty God, the God of truth, that he would give us one heart and one way; and if these weapons of our warfare do not prevail, we must let them know that one day their disobedience

[1] Tolle de vita.

will be revenged with being cut off, and "cast out as unprofitable branches, fit to be cast into the fire."

2. That any doctrine tending undeniably in its own nature (and not by strained consequences) to the disturbance of the civil state may be suppressed, by all such means as are lawfully to be used for the conservation of the peace and safety of the state. Jesus Christ, though accused of sedition, taught none, practised none. His gospel gives not control to magistracy, righteous laws, or any sort of lawful government established amongst men; and therefore they whose faith is faction, and whose religion is rebellion,—I mean Jesuits and Jesuitical Papists,—some of the articles of whose creeds are directly repugnant to the safety, yea, being, of any commonwealths, wherein themselves and men of their own persuasion do not domineer and rule, may be proceeded against by them who bear not the sword in vain. The like may be said of men seditious, under any pretences whatsoever,—like the Anabaptists at Munster.

3. That such heresies or mispersuasions as are attended with any notorious sin in practice (I mean, not in consequences, but owned by their abettors, and practised accordingly, beyond Epicurus, whose honest life was not corrupted by his foul, dishonest opinion),—like the Nicolaitanes, teaching, as most suppose, promiscuous lust; and the Papists' express abominable idolatry,—may be in their authors more severely punished than such crimes not owned and maintained do singly deserve. To pretend conscience in such a case will not avail; "the works of the flesh are manifest,"—easy to be discerned, known to all. Apologies for such, argue searedness, not tenderness: such "evil communication" as "corrupteth good manners," is not to be tolerated.

4. No pretences whatsoever, nor seeming colour, should countenance men dissenting from what is established, to revile, traduce, deride, or otherwise expose to vulgar contempt, by words or actions, the way owned by authority (if not evidently fallen off from Jehovah to Baal), or fasten bitter, uncharitable appellations on those who act according to that way; that is, the public ministers and ministry, acknowledged, owned, and maintained by the supreme magistrate, where they both are. Here, by the way, I cannot but complain of want of ingenuity and candid charity in those men who, having a comfortable maintenance arising another way, do yet, "ad faciendum populum," continually, in pulpits and other public places, inveigh against that way of maintenance which is allowed by the magistrate, and set apart for those that labour in the word and doctrine; unto whom I wish no farther evil, but only forced patience when their neighbouring tradesmen shall have persuaded the people about them that preachers of the gospel ought to live by the work

of their hands, and so the contribution for their maintenance be subducted.

Such men as these do show of what spirit they are, and what they would do if they were lions; seeing they bark so much, being but snarling dogs. And therefore, truly, if some severe course were used for the restraint of those who in our days strive to get themselves a name, and to build up their repute, by slighting, undervaluing, and, by all uncharitable, malicious ways, rendering odious those from whom they dissent, I should not much intercede for them: these are evil works, fruits of the flesh, evident to all. Now these, and such things as these, are acknowledged by all even-spirited men. Some few I shall now add, I hope not unlike them. As,—

5. That it is a most difficult undertaking to judge of heresies and heretics,—no easy thing to show what heresy is in general;—whether this or that particular error be a heresy or no,—whether it be a heresy in this or that man; especially if such things as stubbornness, and pertinacy upon conviction, with the like, be required to make a man a heretic,—for such things cannot be evidenced or made out, but only (for the most part) by most obscure conjectures, and such as will scarcely satisfy a charitable judgment. Papists, indeed, who have laid it down for a principle, that a contradiction of the doctrine of the church, known to be so, and continued in after admonition, doth infallibly make a man a heretic, are very clear, uniform, and settled in that which they have made the ground, warrant, and foundation of slaying millions of men professing the name of Christ: but for all other Christians, who acknowledge an infallibility in the rule, but no infallibility in any for the discovery of the truth of that rule (though exceeding clear and perspicuous in things necessary),—for them, I say, understanding and keeping close to their own principles, it is a most difficult thing to determine of heresy, with an assurance that they are so out of danger of erring in that determination as to make it a ground of rigorous proceedings against those of whom they have so concluded. Some things, indeed, are so clearly in the Scripture laid down and determined, that to question or deny them bespeaks a spirit self-condemned in that which he doth profess. That twice two makes four, that he that runneth moveth, are not things more evident to reason than many things in the Scripture are to every captivated understanding;—a wilful deviation in such, merits no charity. But generally, errors are about things hard to be understood, not so clearly appearing, and concerning which it is very difficult to pass the sentence of heresy. No judge of heresy since the apostles' days, but hath been obnoxious to error in that judgment; and those who have been forwardest to assume a judicature and power of discerning between truth and error, so as to

have others regulated thereby, have erred most foully. Of old it was generally conceived to be in councils. Now, I should acknowledge myself obliged to any man that would direct me to a council—since that Acts xv.—which I may not be forced from the word to assert that it, in some thing or other, went astray.

Luther feared not to affirm of the first and best of general synods, that he "understood not the Holy Ghost to speak in it;" and that the canons thereof were but plain hay and stubble;[1]—yea, and Beza, that such was the "folly, ignorance, ambition, wickedness of many bishops in the best times, that you would suppose the devil to have been president in their assemblies;"[2] insomuch as Nazianzen complained that he never saw a[3] good end of any, and affirmed that he was resolved never to come at them more. And in truth, the fightings and brawls, diabolical arts of defamation and accusing one another, abominable pride, ambition, and affectation of pre-eminence, which appeared in most of them, did so far prevail, that in the issue they became (as one was entitled) dens of thieves, rather than conventions of humble and meek disciples of Jesus Christ, until at length, the holy dove being departed, an ominous owl overlooked the Lateran fathers; and though with much clamour they destroyed the appearing fowl, yet the foul spirit of darkness and error wrought as effectually in them as ever. But to close this discourse. Ignorance of men's invincible prejudices, of their convictions, strong persuasions, desires, aims, hopes, fears, inducements,—sensibleness of our own infirmities, failings, misapprehensions, darkness, knowing but in part,—should work in us a charitable opinion of poor erring creatures, that do it perhaps with as upright, sincere hearts and affections as some enjoy truth. Austin[4] tells the Manichees, the most paganish heretics that ever were, that they only raged and were high against them who knew not what it was to seek the truth and escape error. With what ardent prayers the knowledge of truth is obtained! And how tender is Salvian[5] in his judgment of the Arians! "They are," saith he, "heretics, but know it not,—heretics to us, but not to themselves; nay, they think themselves so catholic that they judge us to be heretics: what they are to us, that are we to them. They err, but

[1] "Hic prorsus non intelligo Sanctum Spiritum in hoc concilio: hi omnes articuli fænum, stramen, ligna, stipulæ fuerunt."—Luth.

[2] "In optimis illis temporibus, ea fuit nonnullorum episcoporum, partim ambitio, partim futilitas et ignorantia," &c.—Beza, præfat. ad Nov. Testa.

[3] "Ego, si vera scribere oportet, ita animo affectus sum, ut omnia episcoporum concilia fugiam, quoniam nullius concilii finem lætum faustumque vidi: nec quod depulsionem malorum potius quam accessionem et incrementum habuerit."—Greg. Naz. Ep. ad Procop.

[4] "Illi in vos sæviunt, qui nesciunt cum quo labore inveniantur, et quam difficile caveantur errores," &c.—Aug.

[5] "Apud nos sunt hæretici, apud se non sunt: quod ergo illi nobis sunt, hoc nos illis," &c.—Salv. de Prov. &c.

with a good mind; and for this cause God shows patience towards them."

Now, if any should dissent from what I have before asserted concerning this particular, I would entreat him to lay down some notes whereby heresies may infallibly be discerned to be such; and he shall not find me repugning.

6. That great consideration ought to be had of that sovereign dictate of nature, the sum of all moral duties, " Quod tibi fieri non vis, alteri ne feceris;"—"Do not that unto others which you would not have done to you, were you in the same condition with them." In the business in hand, we are supposed by others to be in that estate wherein we suppose those to be of whom we speak; those others being to us what we are to them. Now truly, if none of the former inconveniences and iniquities which we recounted (assertion 2, 3, 4, or the like), do accompany erring persons, it will be something difficult to make it appear how we may, if enjoying authority over them, impose any coercion, restraint, or punishment on them, which we would not acknowledge to be justly laid on us by others (supposing it should be laid) having authority over us, convinced that our persuasion differing from them is false and erroneous. No sort of Christians but are heretics and schismatics to some Christians in authority; and it may be their lot to live under the power and jurisdiction of men so persuaded of them, where they ought to expect that the same measure will be given unto them which, in other places, they have consented to mete out to others.

But men will say, and all men pleading the cause of non-toleration in its full extent do say, That they are heretics and erroneous persons whom we do oppose: we ourselves are orthodox; and no law of nature, no dictate of the Scriptures, requires that we should think it just to render unto them that are orthodox as unto them that are heretics, seducers, and false teachers. Because thieves are punished, shall honest men fear that they shall be so too?—But a thief is a thief in all the world, unto all men: in opinions it is not so.—He is a heretic that is to be punished.—But to whom? in whose judgment? in his own?—no more than we are in ours.—But he is so to them that judge him.—True. Put the case, a Protestant were to be judged by a Papist, as a thousand saints have been: is he not the worst of heretics to his judge? These things turn in a circle: what we are to ourselves, that he is to himself: what he is to us, that we are unto others that may be our judges. But however, you will say, we are in the truth, and therefore ought to go free. Now, truly, this is the same paralogism: who says we are in the truth? others? no, ourselves. Who says erroneous persons (as so supposed) are heretics, or the like? they themselves? no, but we: and those that are to us as we are to them, say no less of us. Let us not suppose that all the world will stoop to us, because we have the truth, as we affirm, but they do not believe. If we make the rule of our proceedings against others to be our conviction that they are erroneous; others will, or may, make theirs of us to be their rule of proceeding against us. We do thus to them, because we so judge of them; will not others, who have the same judgment of us as we of them, do the like unto us? Now here I profess that I do not desire to extend any thing in this discourse to the patronizing of any error whatsoever,—I mean, any thing commonly so esteemed in the reformed churches,—as myself owning any such; much less to the procuring of a licentious immunity for every one in his way; and least of all, to countenance men walking disorderly in any regard, especially in the particulars before recounted;—but only to show how warily, and upon what sure principles, that cannot be retorted on us, we ought to proceed, when any severity is necessarily required, in case of great danger; and how in lesser things, if the unity of faith may in some comfortable measure be kept, then to assert the proposition in its full latitude, urging and pleading for Christian forbearance, even in such manner to be granted as we would desire it from them whom we do forbear; for truly in those disputable things, we must acknowledge ourselves in the same series with other men, unless we can produce express patents for our exemptions. But some, perhaps, will say, that even in such things as these Gamaliel's counsel is not good; better all go on with punishing that can; truth will not be suppressed, but error will. Good God! was not truth oppressed by antichristian tyranny? was not outward force the engine that for many generations kept truth in corners? But of this afterward.

Now, I am mistaken if this principle, that the civil magistrate ought to condemn, suppress, and persecute every one that he is convinced to err, though in smaller things, do not at length, in things of greater importance, make Christendom a very theatre of bloody murders, killing, slaying, imprisoning men round in a compass; until the strongest becomes dictator to the rest, and he alone be supposed to have infallible guidance,—all the rest to be heretics, because overcome and subdued. (When I speak of death and killing in this discourse, I understand not only forcible death itself, but that also which is equivalent thereunto, as banishment, or perpetual imprisonment.) I had almost said, that it is the interest of mortality to consent generally to the persecution of a man maintaining such a destructive opinion.

7. That whatsoever restraint or other punishment may be allowed in case of grosser errors, yet slaying of heretics for simple heresy, as they call it, for my part I cannot close withal; nor shall ever give my

vote to the burning, hanging, or killing of a man, otherwise upright, honest, and peaceable in the state, merely because he misbelieveth any point of Christian faith. Let what pretences you please be produced, or colours flourished, I should be very unwilling to pronounce the sentence of blood in the case of heresy. I do not intend here to dispute; but if any one will, upon Protestant principles and Scripture grounds, undertake to assert it, I promise (if God grant me life) he shall not want a convert or an antagonist. I know the usual pretences: Such a thing is blasphemy.—But search the Scripture, look upon the definitions of divines, and by all men's consent you will find heresy, in what head of religion soever it be, and blasphemy properly so called, to be exceedingly distant. Let a blasphemer undergo the law of blasphemy; but yet I think we cannot be too cautious how we place men in that damnable series calling heaven and earth to witness the contrary. But again: To spread such errors will be destructive to souls.—So are many things, which yet are not punishable with forcible death. Let him that thinks so go kill Pagans and Mohammedans. As such heresy is a canker, but a spiritual one, let it be prevented by spiritual means. Cutting off men's heads is no proper remedy for it. If state physicians think otherwise, I say no more, but that I am not of the college, and what I have already said I submit to better judgments.

8. It may be seriously considered, upon a view of the state and condition of Christians, since their name was known in the world, whether this doctrine of punishing erring persons with death, imprisonment, banishment, and the like, under the name of heretics, hath not been as useful and advantageous for error as truth; nay, whether it hath not appeared the most pernicious invention that ever was broached. In the first, second, and third ages, we hear little of it,—nothing for it,—something against it:—much afterward against it, in Austin and others.[1] Marlinus, the famous French bishop, rejected the communion of a company of his associate bishops, because they had consented, with Maximus the emperor, unto the death of the Priscillianists,—as vile heretics as ever breathed. At the end of the fourth and beginning of the fifth century, when the Arians and orthodox had successively procured the supreme magistrate to join with them, men were killed and dismembered like beasts: banishments, imprisonments, plunderings, especially by the Arians, were as frequent as in new subdued kingdoms. But never was this tragedy so acted to the life, as by the worshippers of images on the one side, and their adversaries on the other:[2] which difference rose about the year 130,

[1] Τοὺς μισοῦντας τὸν Θεὸν, μισεῖν χρὴ καὶ ὑμᾶς, καὶ ἐπὶ τοῖς ἐχθροῖς αὐτοῦ ἐκτήκεσθαι· οὐ μὴν καὶ τύπτειν αὐτοὺς ἢ διώκειν, καθὼς τὰ ἔθνη τὰ μὴ εἰδότα τὸν Κύριον καὶ Θεὸν· ἀλλ' ἐχθροὺς μὲν ἡγεῖσθαι, καὶ χωρίζεσθαι ἀπ' αὐτῶν.—Ignat. Epist. ad Philad.

[2] Theophanes. Histor. Miscel., lib. xxii. cap. 30.

and was carried on with that barbarous outrage on both sides, especially by the Iconolatræ (as the worst were ever best at such proceedings), as is wonderful to consider. Now, excepting only those idolatrous heretics in the last, who were paid home in their own coin for a thousand years together, this doctrine was put in practice against none almost but the martyrs of Jesus. The Roman stories of the killing of heretics, are all martyrologies; thousands slain for heretics now lie under the altar, crying for vengeance, and shall one day sit upon thrones, judging their judges. So that where one man hath suffered for an error, under the name of a heretic, five hundred under the same notion have suffered for truth; a principle would seem more befitting Christians to spare five hundred for the saving of one guiltless person. Truth hath felt more of the teeth of this scorpion than error; and clearly it grew up by degrees, with the whole mystery of iniquity. In the gospel we have nothing like it: the acts of Christ purging the temple, Peter pronouncing the fate of Ananias, and Paul smiting Elymas with blindness, seem to me heterogeneous. The first laws of Constantine speak liberty and freedom.[1] Pecuniary mulcts afterward were added, and general edicts against all sects; and so it is put over into the hands of the Arians, who exceedingly cherished it: yet for a good while pretences must be sought out,—Eustathius of Antioch must be accused of adultery,—Athanasius of sedition, magic, and I know not what,—that a colour might be had for their persecution.[2] The Arian kings in Africa were the first that owned it, γυμνῇ κεφαλῇ, and acted according to their persuasions. Methinks I hear the cries of poor dismembered, mangled creatures, for the faith of the holy Trinity! Next to these, through a few civil constitutions of some weak emperors, it wholly comes to reside in the hands of the pope; kings and princes are made his executioners, and he plays his game to the purpose. Single persons serve not this Bel and dragon, —whole nations[3] must be slaughtered, that he may be drunk with blood. He sends whole armies to crucify Christ afresh,—he gives every one of his soldiers a cross; hence followed cruel sights, bloody battles, wasting of kingdoms, raging against the names, ashes, sepulchres of the dead, with more than heathenish cruelty. Such evil fruits hath this bitter root sent forth, the streams of this fountain have all been blood; so that it cannot be denied but that a judicature of truth, and the contrary assumed, with a forcible backing of the sentence, was the bottom-stone in the foundation and highest in the corner of the tower of Babel: and I believe that upon search it will appear, that error hath not been advanced by any thing in the world so much as by usurping a power for its suppression. In divers con-

1 Euseb. Vit. Const., lib. ii. cap. 27. 2 Socrat. Evag. Rufinus. Sozom.
3 Albigenses, Waldenses, Bohemians.

tests that the pope had with others, the truth was on his side (as in the business of Athanasius and others in the east deposed by the Arians[1]). Now, who would not have thought, that his standing up with all earnestness for the truth would not have been the ruin of the devil's kingdom of darkness, and almost have spoiled the plot of the mystery of iniquity? when the truth is, the largest steps that ever the man of sin took towards his throne was by usurping of power to suppress errors and heresies. It would be a great encouragement to use that way for the extirpation of errors (if any such be, besides the preaching of the gospel, and convictions from thence), which any one could produce and give assurance that it hath not been tried, or been tried and proved ineffectual for the supplantation of truth; and if such a way be not produced, what if both should grow together until harvest?

9. Let us not be too hasty in pressing any opinion arising and divulged with odious consequences of sedition, turbulency, and the like, because tumults and troubles happen in the commonwealth where it is asserted. A coincidence of events is one of the principal causes of error and misjudgings in the world: because errors and tumults arise together, therefore one is the cause of the other, may be an argument "a baculo ad angulum." It is a hard thing to charge them with sedition who protest against it, and none can make it appear that it is "contraria factis" by any of their actions, but only because it is fit they should bear the blame of what happeneth evilly in their days. Upon every disaster in the empire, the noise of old was, "Christianos ad leones."[2] For our part, we ought to remember that we were strangers in Egypt. It is but little more than a hundred years since all mouths were opened and filled with reproaches against that glorious Reformation wherein we rejoice. Was it not the unanimous voice of all the adversaries thereof, that a new religion was brought in, tending to the immediate ruin of all states and commonwealths,—attended with rebellion, the mother of sedition? Have we not frequent apologies of our divines for the confutation of such false, malicious, and putid criminations? It is true, indeed, the light of the gospel breaking out was accompanied with war, and not peace (according to the prediction of our Saviour); whereof the gospel was no more the cause, than John Diazius was of that horrible murder, when his brains were chopped out with an axe by his brother Alphonsus,[3] because he professed the gospel. Hence Luther, the vehemency of whose spirit gave no way to glosses and temporizing excuses, plainly affirms those tumults to be such necessary appendices of the preaching of the gospel, that he should not believe the word of God to be abroad in the world, if he saw it not

[1] Socrat., lib. ii. cap. 11. [2] Arnob. [3] Sleid. Com.

accompanied with tumults; which he had rather partake in, than perish under the wrath of God in an eternal tumult.[1] The truth must go on, though thereby the world should be reduced to its primitive chaos and confusion. Were it not a perpetual course, for men of every persuasion to charge sedition, and the like, upon that which they would have suppressed, knowing that no name is more odious unto them who have power to effect their desire; and did I not find that some, who have had much ado, whilst they were sheep, to keep off that imputation from themselves, within a few years, becoming lions, have laid it home upon others as peaceable as they; I might perhaps be more rigid than now these discoveries will suffer me to be. Far be it from me to apologize for truth itself, if seditious;—only I abhor those false, malicious criminations, whereby God's people in these days wherein we live have exceedingly suffered. It hath pleased God so to order things in this kingdom, that the work of recovering his worship to its purity, and restoring the civil state to its liberty, should be both carried on at the same time by the same persons. Are there none now in this kingdom to whom this reforming is an almost everting of God's worship? And are there none that have asserted that our new religion hath caused all those tumults and bloodshed? And doth not every unprejudiced man see that these are hellish lies and malicious accusations, having indeed neither ground nor colour, but only their coincidence in respect of time? Is any wise man moved with their clamours? Are their aspersions considerable? Are we the only men that have been thus injuriously traduced? Remember the difference between Elijah and Ahab,—what was laid to the charge of Paul; see the apologies of the old Christians, and speak what you find.

Much might here be added concerning the qualifications, carriages, humility, peaceableness, of erring persons; all which ought to be considered, and our proceedings towards them to bo, if not regulated, yet much swayed by such considerations. Some I have known myself, that I dare say the most curious inquirer into their ways, that sees with eyes of flesh, would not be able to discover any thing but mere conviction and tenderness of conscience that causeth them to own the opinions which, different from others, they do embrace. Others, again, so exceeding supercilious, scorning, proud, selfish,—so given to contemning of all others, reviling and undervaluing of their adversaries,—that the blindest pity cannot but see much carnalness and iniquity in their ways. These things, then, deserve to be weighed, all passion and particular interest being set aside. And then, if the

[1] "Ego nisi tumultus istos viderem, verbum Dei in mundo non esse dicerem. Præeligimus temporali tumultu collidi, quam æterno tumultu sub ira Dei conteri." —Luth. de Ser. Arb. cap. xxxii–xxxiv.

die be cast, and we must forward, let us take along with us these two cautions:—

(1.) So to carry ourselves in all our censures, every one in his sphere (ecclesiastical discipline being preserved as pure and unmixed from secular power as possible), that it may appear to all that it is the error which men maintain which is so odious unto us, and not the consequent or their dissent from us, whether by subducting themselves from our power or withdrawing from communion. For if this latter be made the cause of our proceeding against any, there must be one law for them all,—all that will not bow, to the fiery furnace! Recusancy is the fault; and that being the same in all, must have the same punishment,—which would be such an unrighteous inequality as is fit for none but Antichrist to own.

(2.) That nothing be done to any, but that the bound and farthest end of it be seen at the beginning, and not leave way and room for new persecution upon new pretences. "Cedo alteram et alteram,"—one stripe sometimes makes way for another, and how know I that men will stay at thirty-nine? "Principiis obsta."

All these things being considered, I cannot so well close with them who make the least allowance of dissent to be the mother of abominations. Words and hated phrases may easily be heaped up to a great number, to render any thing odious which we have a mind to oppose; but the proving of an imposed evil or absurdity is sometimes a labour too difficult for every undertaker. And so I hope I have said enough to warrant my own hesitancy in this particular. Some might now expect that I should here positively set down what is my judgment concerning errors and erroneous persons dissenting from the truth received and acknowledged by authority, with respect unto their toleration: unto whom I answer, That to consider the power of the magistrate about things of religion, and over consciences;—the several restraints that have been used in this case, or are pleaded for;—the difference between dangerous fundamental errors and others;—the several interests of men, and ways of disengaging;—the extent of communion, and the absolute necessity of a latitude to be allowed in some things;—with such other things as would be requisite for a full handling of the matter in hand,—ask a longer discourse, and more exactness, than the few hours allotted to this appendix can afford. Only for the present I ask, if any will take the pains to inform me,—1. What they mean by a non-toleration? whether only a not countenancing nor holding communion with them; or if crushing and punishing them, then how? to what degree? by what means? where they will undoubtedly bound? 2. What the error is concerning which the inquiry is made? the clear opposition thereof to the word of God? the danger of it? the repugnancy that is in it to peace, quietness, and the power of godliness? 3. What or who are the erring persons? how they walk? in what manner of conversation? what is their behaviour towards others not of their own persuasion? what gospel means have been used for their conviction? what may be supposed to be their prejudices, motives, interests, and the like? And then, if it be worth asking, I shall not be backward to declare my opinion. And truly, without the consideration of these things, and other such circumstances, how a right judgment can be passed in this case, I see not.

And so, hoping the courteous reader will look with a candid eye upon these hasty lines, rather poured out than written; and consider that a day's pains in these times may serve for that which is but for a day's use; the whole is submitted to his judgment by him who professeth his all in this kind to be,—the love of truth and peace.

SERMON II.

EBENEZER:

A MEMORIAL OF THE DELIVERANCE

OF

ESSEX COUNTY, AND COMMITTEE.

IN TWO SERMONS.

PREFATORY NOTE.

THE ancient town of Colchester, which had at an early period in the civil wars declared in favour of the Parliament, was besieged and obliged to surrender to the Royal forces. Lord Fairfax, the general of the Parliamentary army, and a nobleman of high reputation, whom both Milton and Hume unite in praising, after an ineffectual attempt to regain the town by storm, changed his tactics into a rigorous blockade. The Royalists maintained the defence with signal gallantry for nearly eleven weeks, till all their provisions were spent, and they had nothing on which to subsist but horses, dogs, and other animals. At length they surrendered at discretion, when two of their officers, Sir Charles Lucas and Sir George Lisle, suffered military execution on the spot. A fine of £14,000 was imposed on the town.

Owen, at this time pastor of an Independent congregation at Coggeshall, which is not far from Colchester, and which was the head-quarters of Fairfax during the siege, seems to have officiated as chaplain to the Parliamentary general; and on the fall of the town, a day of thanksgiving was observed, when he preached before Fairfax and his victorious army, from Hab. iii. 1–9. A committee of Parliament had been sitting at Colchester when the Royalists seized it, and had been under imprisonment during the siege. They also engaged in the same exercise of thanksgiving for their deliverance at Rumford, on September 28, 1648. Owen preached to them another discourse from the same text. Both discourses were published as one. They take the shape of a running comment upon a very sublime passage of Scripture. The verses are expounded in order, and the author educes from them a series of general principles or observations, which he illustrates with tact and power. Exegetic statements are made the basis of important principles, and relieved by eloquent expressions, and maxims of practical wisdom. Though necessarily brief, some of the appeals interwoven with the details of exposition are specimens of close and urgent dealing with the conscience.

Objection has been taken by Mr Orme to the warlike tone of the preacher in some parts of the discourse. There is certainly but slight reference to the evils and horrors of war. Regret might have been expressed that no course was open to the nation in the pending quarrel with its king, but the stern arbitration of the sword. Still, the objection is hardly just. The audience of Owen consisted of men who, at the call of duty, had been hazarding their lives for the best interests of the nation, and except on the principle that all war is unlawful, the preacher could not be expected to utter sentiments which might have sounded in their ears as a condemnation of their conduct. Moreover, while he could not but allude to military operations, he abstains from all fulsome eulogy of the skill and valour of the conquerors, and ascribes the praise of the victory and deliverance to God; so much so, that he has been charged with committing himself in this discourse to the erroneous principle of inferring the goodness of a cause from the success that may have attended it. Mr Orme conclusively repels the insinuation, by quoting Owen's own explicit disclaimer of the sentiment thus imputed to him:— "A cause is good or bad before it hath success, one way or other; and that which hath not its warrant in itself, can never obtain any from its success. The rule of the goodness of any cause is the eternal law of reason, with the legal rights and interests of men." See Owen's "Reflections on a Slanderous Libel," vol. xvi.—ED.

TO HIS EXCELLENCY,

THOMAS LORD FAIRFAX, &c.

SIR,

ALMIGHTY GOD having made you the instrument of that deliverance and peace which in the county of Essex we do enjoy, next to his own goodness, the remembrance thereof is due unto your name. "Those who honour him he will honour; and those who despise him shall be lightly esteemed," 1 Sam. ii. 30. Part of these ensuing sermons being preached before your excellency, and now by providence called forth to public view, I am emboldened to dedicate them unto your name, as a small mite of that abundant thankfulness, wherein all peace-loving men of this county stand obliged unto you.

It was the custom of former days, in the provinces of the Roman empire, to erect statues and monuments of grateful remembrance[1] to those presidents and governors who, in the administration of their authority, behaved themselves with wisdom, courage, and fidelity; yea, instruments of great deliverances and blessings, through corrupted nature's folly, became the Pagans' deities.

There is scarce a county in this kingdom wherein, and not one from which, your excellency hath not deserved a more lasting monument than ever was erected of Corinthian brass. But if the Lord be pleased that your worth shall dwell only in the praises of his people, it will be your greater glory, that being the place which himself hath chosen to inhabit. Now, for a testification of this is this only intended. Beyond this towards men, God pleading for you, you need nothing but our silence; the issue of the last engagements, whereunto you were called and enforced, answering, yea, outgoing, your former undertakings, giving ample testimony of the continuance of God's presence with you in your army, having stopped the mouths of many gainsayers, and called to the residue in the language of the dumb-speaking Egyptian hieroglyphic, Ὦ γινόμενοι καὶ ἀπογινόμενοι, Θεὸς μισεῖ ἀναίδειαν,[2]—"Men of all sorts know that God hateth impudence."

It was said of the Romans, in the raising of their empire, that they were "sæpe prælio victi, bello nunquam." So naked hath the bow of God been made for your assistance, that you have failed neither in battle nor war.

Truly, had not our eyes beheld the rise and fall of this latter storm, we could not have been persuaded that the former achievements of the army under your conduct could have been paralleled. But He who always enabled them to outdo not only others but themselves, hath in this carried them out to outdo whatever before himself had done by them, that they might show more kindness and faithfulness in the latter end than in the beginning. The weary ox treadeth hard;—dying bites are often desperate;—half-ruined Carthage did more perplex Rome than when it was entire;—hydra's heads in the fable were increased by their loss, and every new stroke begat a new opposition. Such seemed the late tumultuating of the exasperated party in this nation.

1 Lubens meritoque. 2 Plut. de Iside et Osir.

In the many undertakings of the enemy,—all which themselves thought secure, and others esteemed probable,—if they had prevailed in any one, too many reasons present themselves to persuade they would have done so in all. But to none of those worthies which went out under your command to several places in the kingdom, can you say, with Augustus to Varus, upon the slaughter of his legions by Arminius in Germany, "Quintile Vare, redde legiones," God having carried them all on with success and victory.

One especially, in his northern expedition, I cannot pass over with silence, who although he will not, dare not, say of his undertakings, as Cæsar of his Asian war, "Veni, vidi, vici," knowing who works all his works for him; nor shall we say of the enemy's multitude, what Captain Gam did of the French, being sent to spy out their numbers before the battle of Agincourt, that there were of them enough to kill, and enough to take, and enough to run away; yet of him and them both he and we may freely say, "It is nothing with the Lord to help, either with many, or with them that have no power."

The war being divided, and it being impossible your excellency should be in every place of danger, according to your desire, the Lord was pleased to call you out personally unto two of the most hazardous, dangerous, and difficult undertakings;[1] where, besides the travel, labour, watching, heat and cold, by day and night, whereunto you were exposed, even the life of the meanest soldier in your army was not in more imminent danger than oftentimes was your own. And indeed, during your abode at the leaguer amongst us, in this only were our thoughts burdened with you,—that self-preservation was of no more weight in your counsels and undertakings. And I beseech you pardon my boldness, in laying before you this expostulation of many thousands (if we may say to him who hath saved a kingdom what was sometime said unto a king), "Know you not that you are worth ten thousands of us? why should you quench such a light in Israel?"

Sir, I account it among those blessings of Providence wherewith the days of my pilgrimage have been seasoned, that I had the happiness for a short season to attend your excellency, in the service of my master, Jesus Christ; as also, that I have this opportunity, in the name of many, to cast in my χαῖρε into the kingdom's congratulations of your late successes. What thoughts concerning your person my breast is possessed withal, as in their storehouse they yield me delightful refreshment, so they shall not be drawn out, to the disturbance of your self-denial. The goings forth of my heart, in reference to your excellency, shall be chiefly to the Most High, that, being more than conqueror in your spiritual and temporal warfare, you may be long continued for a blessing to this nation, and all the people of God.

Sir,

Your Excellency's

Most humble and devoted Servant,

JOHN OWEN.

COGGESHALL, ESSEX,
Oct. 5, 1648.

[1] Kent, Essex.

TO

THE WORTHY AND HONOURED

SIR WILLIAM MASHAM, SIR WILLIAM ROWE,

WITH THE REST OF THE GENTLEMEN OF THE COMMITTEE LATELY UNDER IMPRISONMENT BY THE ENEMY IN COLCHESTER;

AS ALSO,

TO THE HONOURED

SIR HENRY MILDMAY OF WANSTED, COL. SIR THOMAS HONEYWOOD,

WITH THE REST OF THE GENTLEMEN AND OFFICERS, LATELY ACTING AND ENGAGED AGAINST THE SAME ENEMY.

SIRS,

THE righteous judgments of God having brought a disturbance and noise of war, for our security, unthankfulness, murmuring, and devouring one another, upon our country, those who were intrusted with the power thereof turned their streams into several channels. Troublous times are times of trial.

"Many shall be purified, and made white, and tried; but the wicked shall do wickedly; and none of the wicked shall understand, but the wise shall understand," Dan. xii. 10. Some God called out to suffer, some to do,—leaving "treacherous dealers to deal treacherously."

Of the two first sorts are you. This honour have you received from God, either with patience and constancy to undergo, involuntarily a dangerous restraint; or with resolution and courage voluntarily to undertake a hazardous engagement, to give an example that faith and truth, so shamefully despised in these evil days, have not altogether forsaken the sons of men.

It is not in my thoughts to relate unto yourselves what some of you suffered, and what some of you did,—what difficulties and perplexities you wrestled withal, within and without the walls of your enemies (the birds in the cage and the field having small cause of mutual emulation); for that which remains of these things is only a returnal of praise to Him by whom all your works are wrought.

It cannot be denied but that Providence was eminently exalted in the work of your protection and delivery; yet truly, for my part, I cannot but conceive that it vails to the efficacy of grace, in preventing you from putting forth your hands unto iniquity, in any sinful compliance with the enemies of our peace. The times wherein we live have found the latter more rare than the former. What God wrought in you hath the pre-eminence of what he wrought for you;—as much as to be given up to the sword is a lesser evil than to be given up to a treacherous spirit.

What God hath done for you all, all men know;—what I desire you should do for God, I know no reason why I should make alike public,—the general and particular civilities I have received from all and every one of you advantaging me to make it out in another way. I shall add nothing, then, to what you will meet withal in the following discourse, but only my desire, that you would seriously ponder the second observation, with the deductions from thence. For the rest, I no way fear but that that God who hath so appeared with you, and for you, will so indulge to your spirits the presence and guidance of his grace, in these shaking times, that if any speak evil of you as of evil-doers, they may be ashamed that falsely accuse your good conversation in Christ, and glorify God in the day of visitation.

For these following sermons, one of them was preached at your desire, and is now published upon your request. The first part of the labour I willingly and cheerfully underwent;—the latter, merely in obedience to your commands, being acted in it more by your judgments than mine own. You were persuaded (mean as it was) it might be for the glory of God to have it made public; whereupon my answer was, and is, That for that, not only it, but myself also, should, by his assistance, be ready for the press. The failings and infirmities attending the preaching and publishing of it (which the Lord knows to be very many) are mine;—the inconveniences of publishing such a tractate from so weak a hand, whereof the world is full, must be yours;—the fruit and benefit both of the one and other is His, for whose pardon of infirmities, and removal of inconveniences, shall be, as for you, and all the church of God, the prayer of,

SIRS,

Your most humble and obliged Servant

In the work of the Lord,

JOHN OWEN.

COGGESHALL, *Oct.* 5, 1648.

SERMON II.

A MEMORIAL OF THE DELIVERANCE OF ESSEX COUNTY, AND COMMITTEE.

"A prayer of Habakkuk the prophet upon Shigionoth. O LORD, I have heard thy speech, and was afraid: O LORD, revive thy work in the midst of the years, in the midst of the years make known; in wrath remember mercy. God came from Teman, and the Holy One from mount Paran. Selah. His glory covered the heavens, and the earth was full of his praise. And his brightness was as the light; he had horns coming out of his hand: and there was the hiding of his power. Before him went the pestilence, and burning coals went forth at his feet. He stood, and measured the earth: he beheld, and drove asunder the nations; and the everlasting mountains were scattered, the perpetual hills did bow: his ways are everlasting. I saw the tents of Cushan in affliction: and the curtains of the land of Midian did tremble. Was the LORD displeased against the rivers? was thine anger against the rivers? was thy wrath against the sea, that thou didst ride upon thine horses, and thy chariots of salvation? Thy bow was made quite naked, according to the oaths of the tribes, even thy word. Selah. Thou didst cleave the earth with rivers."—HAB. iii. 1–9.

OF this chapter there are four parts.

First, The title and preface of it, verse 1.

Secondly, The prophet's main request in it, verse 2.

Thirdly, Arguments to sustain his faith in that request, from verse 3 to 17.

Fourthly, A resignation of himself, and the whole issue of his desires unto God, from verse 17 to the end.

We shall treat of them in order.

The prophet[1] having had visions from God, and pre-discoveries of many approaching judgments, in the first and second chapters, in this, by faithful prayer, sets himself to obtain a sure footing and quiet abode in those nation-destroying storms.

Verse 1. "A prayer of Habakkuk the prophet;" that is the title of it. And an excellent prayer it is,—full of arguments to strengthen

[1] The time of this prophecy is conceived to be about the end of Josiah's reign, not long before the first Chaldean invasion.

faith,—acknowledgment of God's sovereignty, power, and righteous judgments,—with resolutions to a contented, joyful, rolling him upon him under all dispensations.

Observation I. *Prayer is the believer's constant, sure retreat in an evil time, in a time of trouble.*

It is the righteous man's wings to the " name of the Lord," which is his " strong tower," Prov. xviii. 10,—a Christian[1] soldier's sure reserve in the day of battle: if all other forces be overthrown, here he will abide by it,—no power under heaven can prevail upon him to give one step backward. Hence that title of Ps. cii., " A prayer of the afflicted, when he is overwhelmed." 'Tis the overwhelmed man's refuge and employment: when " he swooneth with anguish" (as in the original), this fetches him to life again. So also, Ps. lxi. 2, 3. In our greatest distresses let neither unbelief nor self-contrivances jostle us out of this way to the rock of our salvation

II. Observation. *Prophets' discoveries of fearful judgments must be attended with fervent prayers.*

That messenger hath done but half his business who delivers his errand, but returns not an answer. He that brings God's message of *threats* unto his people, must return his people's message of *entreaties* unto him. Some think they have fairly discharged their duty when they have revealed the will of God to man, without labouring to reveal the condition and desires of men unto God. He that is more frequent in the pulpit to his people than he is in his closet for his people, is but a sorry watchman. Moses did not so, Exod. xxxii. 31;—neither did Samuel so, 1 Sam. xii. 23;—neither was it the guise of Jeremiah in his days, chap. xiv. 17. If the beginning of the prophecy be (as it is) " The burden of Habakkuk,"—the close will be (as it is) "The prayer of Habakkuk." Where there is a burden upon the people, there must be a prayer for the people. Woe to them who have denounced desolations, and not poured out supplications! Such men delight in the evil which the prophet puts far from him, Jer. xvii. 16, " I have not desired the woful day, [O Lord], thou knowest."

Now this prayer is " upon Shigionoth;" that is,—1. It is turned to a song; 2. Such a song.

1. That it is a song, penned in metre; and how done so. (1.) To take the deeper impression; (2.) To be the better retained in memory; (3.) To work more upon the affections; (4.) To receive the ingredients of poetical loftiness for adorning the majesty of God with; (5.) The use of songs in the old church; (6.) And for the present; (7.) Their times and seasons, as among the people of God, so all nations of old. Of all, or any of these, being besides my present purpose, I shall not treat.

[1] "Preces et lacrymæ sunt arma ecclesiæ."—Tertul.

2. That it is "upon Shigionoth," a little may be spoken. The word is once in another place (and no more) used, in the title of a song, and that is Ps. vii., "Shiggaion of David;" and it is variously rendered. It seems to be taken from the word שָׁגָה, "erravit," to err, or wander variously, Prov. v. 19. The word is used for delight, to stray with delight: "In her love (תִּשְׁגֶּה) thou shalt err with delight," —we have translated it, "be ravished;" noting affections out of order. The word, then, holds out a delightful wandering and variety;—and this literally, because those two songs, Ps. vii. and Hab. iii., are not tied to any one certain kind of metre, but have various verses, for the more delight; which, though it be not proper to them alone, yet in them the Holy Ghost would have it especially noted.

But now surely the kernel of this shell is sweeter than so. Is not this written also for their instruction who have no skill in Hebrew songs? The true reason of their metre is lost to the most learned. Are not, then, God's variable dispensations towards his held out under these variable tunes,—not all fitted to one string? not all alike pleasant and easy? Are not the several tunes of mercy and judgment in these songs? Is not here affliction and deliverance, desertion and recovery, darkness and light in this variously? Doubtless it is so.

III. Observation. *God often calls his people unto songs upon Shigionoth.*

[1]He keeps them under various dispensations, that so, drawing out all their affections, their hearts may make the sweeter melody unto him. They shall not have all honey, nor all gall;—all judgment, lest they be broken; nor all mercy, lest they be proud. "Thou answeredst them, O LORD our God: thou wast a God that forgavest them, though thou tookest vengeance of their inventions," Ps. xcix. 8. Here is a song upon Shigionoth! They are heard in their prayers, and forgiven;—there is the sweetest of mercies. Vengeance is taken of their inventions, there's a tune of judgment. "By terrible things in righteousness wilt thou answer us, O God of our salvation," Ps. lxv. 5; [which] is a song of the same tune. To be answered in righteousness, what sweeter mercy in the world? Nothing more refreshes the panting soul than an answer of its desires; but to have this answer by terrible things,—that string strikes a humbling, a mournful note. Israel hear of deliverance by Moses,[2] and at the same time have their bondage doubled by Pharaoh,—there's a song upon Shigionoth. Is it not so in our days?—precious mercies and dreadful judgments jointly poured out upon the land? We are clothed by our Father, like Joseph by his, in a party-coloured coat, Gen. xxxvii. 3;—here a piece of unexpected deliverance, and there a piece of deserved cor-

[1] "Graviter in eum decernitur, cui etiam ipsa connectio denegatur."—Prosp. Sent.
[2] Duplicantur lateres quando venit Moses.

rection. At the same hour we may rejoice at the conquest of our enemies, and mourn at the close of our harvest,—victories for his own name's sake, and showers for our sins' sake; both from the same hand at the same time. The cry of every soul is like the cry of the multitude of old and young at the laying the foundation of the second temple: many shouted aloud for joy, and many wept with a loud voice; so that it was a mixed noise, and the several noises could not be distinguished, Ezra iii. 12, 13. A mixed cry is in our spirits, and we know not which is loudest in the day of our visitation. I could instance in sundry particulars, but that every one's observation will save me that easy labour. And this the Lord doth,—

1. To fill[1] all our sails towards himself at once,—to *exercise all our affections*. I have heard that a full wind behind the ship drives her not so fast forward as a side wind, that seems almost so much against her as with her; and the reason, they say, is, because a full wind fills but some of her sails, which keep it from the rest that they are empty; when a side wind fills all her sails, and sets her speedily forward. Which way ever we go in this world, our affections are our sails; and according as they are spread and filled, so we pass on, swifter and slower, whither we are steering. Now, if the Lord should give us a full wind, and continual gale of mercies, it would fill but some of our sails, some of our affections,—joy, delight, and the like; but when he comes with a side wind,—a dispensation that seems almost as much against us as for us,—then he fills all our sails, takes up all our affections, making his works wide and broad enough to entertain them every one;—then are we carried freely and fully towards the haven where we would be. [2] A song upon Shigionoth leaves not one string of our affections untuned. It is a song that reacheth every line of our hearts, to be framed by the grace and Spirit of God. Therein hope, fear, reverence, with humility and repentance, have a share; as well as joy, delight, and love, with thankfulness. Interchangeable dispensations take up all our affections, with all our graces; for they are gracious affections, exercised and seasoned with grace, of which we speak. The stirring of natural affections, as merely such, is but the moving of a dunghill to draw out a stinking steam,—a thing the Lord neither aimeth at nor delighteth in. Their joys are his provocation, and he laugheth in the day of their calamity, when their fear cometh, Prov. i. 26, 27.

2. To *keep them in continual*[3] *dependence upon himself*. He

[1] "Namque bonos non blanda inflant, non aspera frangunt,
Sed fidei invictæ gaudia vera juvant."
Prosp. Epig. in Sent. August.

[2] Ps. cxix. 67; Hos. v. 15; Heb. xii. 10, 11; 1 Pet. i. 6.

[3] "In cælo non in terra mercedem promisit reddendam. Quid alibi poscis, quod alibi dabitur?"—Ambros. Offic., lib. i. cap. 16.

hath promised his own daily bread,—not goods laid up for many years. Many children have been undone by their parents giving them too large a stock to trade for themselves; it has made them spendthrifts, careless, and wanton. Should the Lord intrust his people with a continued stock of mercy, perhaps they would be full, and deny him, and say, "Who is the Lord?" Prov. xxx. 9. Jeshurun did so, Deut. xxxii. 14, 15. Ephraim "was filled according to their pasture, and forgot the Lord," Hos. xiii. 6. Neither, on the other side, will he be always chiding. "His anger shall not burn for ever"—very sore. It is our infirmity at the least, if we say, God hath forgotten to be gracious, and shut up his tender mercies in displeasure, Ps. lxxvii. 9. But laying one thing against another, he keeps the heart of his in an even balance, in a continual dependence upon himself, that they may neither be wanton through mercy, nor discouraged by too much oppression. Our tender Father is therefore neither always feeding nor always correcting. "And it shall come to pass in that day, that the light shall not be clear, nor dark: but it shall be one day which shall be known to the LORD, not day nor night; but it shall come to pass, that at evening time it shall be light," saith the prophet Zechariah, chap. xiv. 6, 7, seeking out God's dispensations towards his, ending in joy and light in the evening.

Use. Labour to have your hearts right tuned for songs on Shigionoth, sweetly to answer all God's dispensations in their choice variety. That instrument will make no music that hath but some strings in tune. If when God strikes with mercy upon the string of joy and gladness, we answer pleasantly; but when he touches upon that of[1] sorrow and humiliation, we suit it not;—we are broken instruments, that make no melody unto God. We must know how to receive good and evil at his hand. "He hath made every thing beautiful in its time," Eccles. iii. 11,—every thing in that whole variety which his wisdom hath produced. A well-tuned heart must have all its strings, all its affections, ready to answer every touch of God's finger, to improve judgments and mercies both at the same time. Sweet harmony ariseth out of some discords. When a soul is in a frame to rejoice with thankful obedience for mercy received, and to be humbled with soul-searching, amending repentance for judgments inflicted at the same time,—then it sings a song on Shigionoth, then it is fit for the days wherein we live. Indeed, both mercies and judgments aim at the same end, and should be received with the same equal temper of mind. A flint is broken between a hammer and a pillow;—an offender is humbled between a prison and a pardon;—a hard heart

[1] "Cum vexamur ac premimur, tum maxime gratias agimus indulgentissimo patri, quod corruptelam nostram non patitur longius procedere: hinc intelligimus nos esse Deo curæ."—Lactan.

may be mollified and a proud spirit humbled between those two. In such a season the several rivulets of our affections flow naturally in the same stream. When hath a gracious soul the soundest joys, but when it hath the deepest sorrows? "Habent et gaudia vulnus." When hath it the humblest meltings, but when it hath the most ravishing joys? Our afflictions, which are naturally at the widest distance, may all swim in the same spiritual channel. Rivulets rising from several heads are carried in one stream to the ocean. As a mixture of several colours make a beautiful complexion for the body; so a mixture of divers affections, under God's various dispensations, gives a comely frame unto the soul. Labour, then, to answer every call, every speaking providence of God, in its right kind, according to the intention thereof; and the Lord reveal his mind unto us, that so we mãy do.

Having passed the title, let us look a little on those parts of the prayer itself that follow.

Verse 2. The beginning of it in verse 2 hath two parts.

1. The *frame* of the prophet's *spirit* in his address to God: "O Jehovah, I have heard thy speech, and was afraid."

2. His *request in this his condition:* "O LORD, revive thy work in the midst of the years, in the midst of the years make known; in wrath remember mercy."

1. In the first you have,—

(1.) Particularly his frame;—he was afraid, or trembled; which he wonderfully sets out, verse 16, "When I heard, my belly trembled; my lips quivered at the voice: rottenness entered into my bones, and I trembled in myself."

(2.) The cause of this fear and trembling;—he "heard the speech of God." If you will ask what speech or report this was that made the prophet himself so exceedingly quake and tremble, I answer, it is particularly that which you have, chap. i. 5–11,—containing a dreadful denunciation of the judgments of God against the people of Israel, to be executed by the proud, cruel, insulting Chaldeans. This voice, this report of God, makes the prophet tremble.

IV. Observation. *An appearance of God in anger and threats against a people, should make his choicest secret ones among them to fear, to quake, and tremble.*

Trembling of man's heart must answer the shaking of God's hand. At the delivery of the law with all its attending threats, so terrible was the sight, that Moses himself (though a mediator then) did "exceedingly fear and quake," Heb. xii. 21. God will be acknowledged in all his goings. If men will not bow before him, he will break them. They who fear not his threatenings, shall feel his inflictings; if his word be esteemed light, his hand will be found heavy.—For,

1. In point of deserving who can say,[1] I have purged my heart, I am clean from sin? None ought to be fearless, unless they be senseless. God's people are so far from being always clear of procuring national judgments, that sometimes[2] judgments have come upon nations for the sins of some of God's people amongst them;—as the plague in the days of David.

2. And in point of[3] suffering, who knows but they may have a deep share? The prophet's book is written within as well as without, with "lamentation, mourning, and woe," Ezek. ii. 10. If "the lion roars, who can but fear?" Amos iii. 8,—fear, to the rooting out of security, not the shaking of faith,—fear, to the pulling down of carnal presidence, not Christian confidence,—fear, to draw out our souls in prayer, not to swallow them up in despair,—fear, to break the arm of flesh, but not to weaken the staff of the promise,—fear, that we may draw nigh to God with reverence, not to run from him with diffidence; in a word, to overthrow faithless presumption, and to increase gracious submission.

2. Here is the prophet's request. And in this there are these two things:—

(1.) The *thing* he desireth: "The reviving God's work, the remembering mercy."

(2.) The *season* he desireth it in: "In the midst of the years."

(1.) For the first,—that which in the beginning of the verse he calls God's work, in the close of it he termeth mercy; and the reviving his work is interpreted to be a remembering mercy. These two expressions, then, are parallel. The reviving of God's work towards his people is a re-acting of mercy, a bringing forth the fruits thereof, and that in the midst of the execution of wrath; as a man in the midst of another, remembering a business of more importance, instantly turneth away, and applieth himself thereunto.

V. Observation. *Acts of mercy are God's proper work towards his people, which he will certainly awake, and keep alive in the saddest times.*

Mercy, you see, is his work, his proper work, as he calleth "judgment his strange act," Isa. xxviii. 21. "He retaineth not his anger for ever, because he delighteth in mercy," Mic. vii. 18. This is his proper work. Though it seem to sleep, he will awake it; though it seem to die, he will revive it. "Can a woman forget her sucking child, that she should not have compassion on the son of her womb? yea, they may forget, yet will I not forget thee. Behold, I have graven

[1] Job xiv. 4, xv. 15, 16; Prov. xvi. 2, xx. 9.

[2] 2 Sam. xxiv. 15; 2 Chron. xxxii. 25.

[3] "Omnes seculi plagæ, nobis in admonitionem, vobis in castigationem à Deo veniunt."—Tertul. Apol., cap. xlii.

thee upon the palms of my hands; thy walls are continually before me," Isa. xlix. 15, 16.

(2.) For the season of this work,—he prays that it may be accomplished " in the midst of the years;" upon which you may see what weight he lays, by his repetition of it in the same verse. It is something doubtful what may be the peculiar sense of these words;—whether " the midst of the years"[1] do not denote the whole time of the people's bondage under the Chaldeans (whence Junius renders the words " interea temporis," noting this manner of expression, "the midst of the years," for a Hebraism), during which space he intercedes for mercy for them; or whether " the midst of the years " do not denote some certain point of time, as the season of their return from captivity, about the midst of the years between their first king and the coming of the Messiah, putting a period to their church and state. Whether of these is more probable is not needful to insist upon: this is certain, that a certain time is pointed at; which will yield us,—

VI. Observation. *The church's mercies and deliverance have their appointed season.*

In the midst of the years it shall be accomplished. As there is a decree bringing forth the wicked's destruction, Zeph. ii. 1, 2; so there is a decree goes forth in its appointed season for the church's deliverance, which cannot be gainsaid, Dan. ix. 23. Every " vision is for its appointed " season and time, Hab. ii. 3; then " it will surely come, it will not tarry." There is a determination upon the weeks and days of the church's sufferings and expectations, Dan. ix. 24, " Seventy weeks are determined upon thy people." As there are three transgressions, and four, of rebels, for which God "will not turn away their punishment," Amos i. 3; so three afflictions, and four, of the people of God, after which he will not shut out their supplications. Hence that confidence of the prophet, Ps. cii. 13, 14, " Thou shalt arise, and have mercy upon Zion: for," saith he, " the time to favour her, yea, the set time, is come." There is a time, yea, a set time, for favour to be showed unto Zion: as a time to break down, so a time to build up,—an acceptable time, a day of salvation. " It came to pass, at the end of four hundred and thirty years, even the selfsame day it came to pass, that all the hosts of the LORD went out of Egypt," Exod. xii. 41. As a woman with child goes not beyond her appointed months, but is pained to be delivered,—no more can the fruitful decree cease from bringing forth the church's deliverance in the season thereof.

1. Because there is an appointed period of the church's humiliation and bearing of her iniquities. Israel shall bear their iniquities

[1] בְּקֶרֶב שָׁנִים, in the inward of years.

in the wilderness; but this is exactly limited to the space of forty years. When their iniquity is pardoned, their warfare is accomplished, Isa. xl. 2. They say some men will give poison that shall work insensibly, and kill at seven years' end. The great Physician of his church knows how to give his sin-sick people potions that shall work by degrees, and at such an appointed season take away all their iniquity: then they can no longer be detained in trouble. God will not continue his course of physic unto them one day beyond health recovered. This is all the fruit of their afflictions, to take away their iniquities, Isa. xxvii. 9; and when that is done, who shall keep bound what God will loose? When sin is taken away from within, trouble must depart from without.

2. Because the church's sorrows are commensurate unto, and do contemporize with, the joys and prosperity of God's enemies and hers. Now, wicked men's prosperity hath assured bounds: "The wickedness of the wicked shall come to an end." There is a time when the "iniquity of the Amorites comes to the full," Gen. xv. 16. It comes up to the brim in the appointed day of slaughter. When their wickedness hath filled the ephah, a talent of lead is laid upon the mouth thereof, and it is carried away on wings, Zech. v. 6–8, swiftly, certainly, irrecoverably. If, then, the church's troubles contemporize, rise and fall with their prosperity, and her deliverance with their destruction, —if the fall of Babylon be the rise of Zion,—if they be the buckets which must go down when the church comes up,—if they be the rod of the church's chastisement,—their ruin being set and appointed, so also must be the church's mercies.

Use. In every distress learn to wait with patience for this appointed time. "He that believeth will not make haste." "Though it tarry, wait for it, it will surely come." He that is infinitely good hath appointed the time; and therefore it is best. He that is infinitely wise hath determined the season; and therefore it is most suitable. He who is infinitely powerful hath set it down; and therefore it shall be accomplished. Wait for it believing, wait for it praying,—wait for it contending. Waiting is not a lazy hope, a sluggish expectation. When Daniel knew the time was come, he prayed the more earnestly, Dan. ix. 2, 3. You will say, perhaps, What need he pray for it, when he knew the time was accomplished? I answer, The more need. Prayer helps the promise to bring forth. Because a woman's time is come, therefore shall she have no midwife? nay, therefore give her one. He that appointed their return, appointed that it should be a fruit of prayer. Wait,[1] contending also in all ways

[1] "Bonum agonem subituri estis, in quo agonothetes Deus vivus est: Christarchos Spiritus Sanctus, corona æternitatis brabium, epithetes Jesus Christus."—Tertul. ad Mar.

wherein you shall be called out; and be not discouraged that you know not the direct season of deliverance. "In the morning sow thy seed, and in the evening withhold not thine hand; for thou knowest not whether shall prosper, either this or that, or whether they both shall be alike good," Eccles. xi. 6.

But proceed we with the prophet's prayer.

From verse 3 to 17, he layeth down several arguments, taken from the majesty, power, providence, and former works of God, for the supporting of his faith to the obtaining of those good things and works of mercy which he was now praying for. We shall look on them, as they lie in our way.

Verse 3. "God came from Teman, the Holy One from mount Paran. Selah. His glory covered the heavens, the earth was full of his praise."

Teman[1] was a city of the Edomites, whose land the people of Israel compassed in the wilderness, when they were stung with fiery serpents, and healed with looking on a brasen serpent, set up to be a type of Christ. Teman is put up for the whole land of Edom; and the prophet makes mention of it for the great deliverance and mercy granted there to the people when they were almost consumed;—that's God's coming from Teman. See Numb. xxi. 5–9. When they were destroyed by fiery serpents, he heals them by a type of Christ,—giving them corporeal, and raising them to a faith of spiritual, salvation.

Paran,[2] the next place mentioned, was a mountain in the land of Ishmael, near which Moses repeated the law; and from thence God carried the people immediately to Canaan;—another eminent act of mercy.

Unto these he addeth the word Selah; as it is a song, a note of elevation in singing; as it respects the matter, not the form, a note of admiration and special observation. Selah,—consider them well, for they were great works indeed. Special mercies must have special observation.

Now, by reason of these actions the prophet affirms that the glory of God covered the heavens, and the earth was full of his praise;—lofty expressions of the advancement of God's glory, and the fulness of his praise amongst his people of the earth, which attended that merciful deliverance and gracious assistance. Nothing is higher or greater than that which covers heaven, and fills earth. God's[3] glory is exceedingly exalted, and his praise increased everywhere, by acts of favour and kindness to his people.

[1] Gen. xxxvi. 15; Jer. xlix. 7; Obad. 9. [2] Deut. i. 1.

[3] "Gloria est frequens de aliquo fama cum laude."—Cic. lib. ii., De Inv. "Consentiens laus bonorum, incorrupta vox bene judicantium de excellente virtute."—Idem. Tusc., lib. iii.

That which I shall choose, from amongst many others that present themselves, a little to insist upon, is, that—

VII. Observation—*Former mercies, with their times and places, are to be had in thankful remembrance unto them who wait for future blessings.*

Faith is to this end separated by them. "Awake, awake, put on strength, O arm of the LORD; awake, as in the ancient days, in the generations of old. Art thou not it that hath cut Rahab, and wounded the dragon? art thou not it which hath dried the sea, the waters of the great deep; that hath made the depths of the sea a way for the ransomed to pass over?" Isa. li. 9, 10. The breaking of Rahab,—that is, Egypt, so called here, and Ps. lxxxvii. 4, lxxxix. 10, for her great strength, which the word signifies,—and the wounding of the dragon, that great and crooked afflicter, Pharaoh, is remembered, and urged for a motive to a new needed deliverance. So Ps. lxxiv. 13, 14, "Thou brakest the heads of leviathan in pieces, and gavest him to be meat to the people inhabiting the wilderness." Leviathan,—the same dragon, oppressing, persecuting Pharaoh,—thou brakest his heads, his counsels, armies, power; and gavest him for meat, that the people for forty years together might be fed, sustained, and nourished with that wonderful mercy. "Out of the eater came forth meat; out of the strong came forth sweetness."

In this reciprocation God walketh with his people. Of free grace he bestoweth mercies and blessings on them; by grace works the returns of remembrance and thankfulness unto himself for them; then showers that down again in new mercies. The countries which send up no vapours, receive down no showers. Remembrance with thankfulness of former mercies is the matter, as it were, which by God's goodness is condensed into following blessings. For,—

1. Mercies have their proper end, when thankfully remembered. What more powerful motive to the obtaining of new, than to hold out that the old were not abused? We are encouraged to cast seed again into that ground whose last crop witnesseth that it was not altogether barren. That sad spot of good Hezekiah, that he rendered not again according to the benefit done unto him, is set down as the opening a door of wrath against himself, Judah, and Jerusalem, 2 Chron. xxxii. 25. On the other side, suitable returns are a door of hope for farther mercies.

2. The remembrance of them strengthens faith, and keeps our hands from hanging down in the time of waiting for blessings. When faith is supported, the promise is engaged, and a mercy at any time more than half obtained. "Faith is the substance of things hoped for," Heb. xi. 1. "God," saith the apostle, "hath delivered us from so great a death, and doth deliver." Now, what conclusion makes he

of this experience?—"In whom we trust that he will yet deliver us," 2 Cor. i. 10. It was a particular mercy with its circumstances, as you may see verse 9, which he made the bottom of his dependence. In the favours of men we cannot do so; they may be weary of helping, or be drawn dry, and grow helpless. Ponds may be exhausted, but the ocean never. The infinite fountains of the Deity cannot be sunk one hair's breadth by everlasting flowing blessings. Now, circumstances of actions, time, place, and the like, ofttimes make deep impressions; mercies should be remembered with them. So doth the apostle again, 2 Tim. iv. 17, 18, "He did deliver me from the mouth of the lion,"—Nero, that lion-like tyrant. And what then? "He shall deliver me from every evil work." David esteemed it very good logic, to argue from the victory God gave him over the lion and the bear, to a confidence of victory over Goliath, 1 Sam. xvii. 37.

Use. The use of this we are led unto, Isa. xliii. 16–18, "Thus saith the LORD, which maketh a way in the sea, and a path in the mighty waters; which bringeth forth the chariot and horse, the army, and the power; They shall lie down together, they shall not rise: they are extinct, they are quenched as tow. Remember ye not the former things, neither consider the things of old." Let former mercies be an anchor of hope in time of present distresses. Where is the God of Marston Moor, and the God of Naseby? is an acceptable expostulation in a gloomy day. O what a catalogue of mercies hath this nation to plead by in a time of trouble! God came from Naseby, and the Holy One from the west. Selah. "His glory covered the heavens, and the earth was full of his praise." He went forth in the north, and in the east he did not withhold his hand. I hope the poor town wherein[1] I live is more enriched with a store-mercy of a few months, than with a full trade of many years. "The snares of death compassed us, and the floods of ungodly men made us afraid," Ps. xviii. 4; but "the LORD thundered in the heavens, the Highest gave his voice; hailstones and coals of fire. Yea, he sent out his arrows, and scattered them; and he shot out lightnings, and discomfited them. He sent from above, he took us, he drew us out of many waters. He delivered us from our strong enemy, and from them which hated us: for they were too strong for us," verses 13, 14, 16, 17. How may we say with the same Psalmist, in any other distress, "O my God, my soul is cast down within me: therefore will I remember thee from the land of Jordan, and of the Hermonites, from the hill Mizar!" Ps. xlii. 6. "Where is the LORD God of Elijah,"—who divides anew the waters of Jordan? 2 Kings ii. 14.

[1] No place in the county so threatened; no place in the county so preserved: small undertakings there blessed; great opposition blasted. Non nobis, Domine, non nobis.

The following verses set forth the glory and power of God, in the accomplishment of that great work of bringing his people into the promised land, with those mighty things he performed in the wilderness.

Verse 4, if I mistake not, sets out his glorious appearance on Mount Sinai; of which the prophet affirms two things:—

1. That "his brightness was as the light."

2. That "he had horns coming out of his hand, and there was the hiding of his power."

1. For the first. Is it not that brightness which appeared when the mountain burned with fire to the midst of heaven, Deut. iv. 11,—a glorious fire in the midst of clouds and thick darkness? The like description you have of God's presence, Ps. xviii. 11, 12, "He made darkness his secret place," and brightness was before him: as the light, the sun, the fountain and cause of it, called "light," Job xxxi. 26. Now, this glorious appearance holds out the kingly power and majesty of God in governing the world, which appeareth but unto few. "The LORD reigneth; let the earth rejoice. Clouds and darkness are round about him. A fire goeth before him; his lightnings enlightened the world," Ps. xcvii. 1–4.

2. "He had horns coming out of his hand." So the words most properly, though by some otherwise rendered. That horns in Scripture are taken for strength and power,[1] needs no proving. The mighty power of God, which he made appear to his people, in that glorious representation of his majesty on Mount Sinai, is by this phrase expressed. There his chariots were seen to be twenty thousand, even many thousands of angels; and the Lord among them in that holy place, Ps. lxviii. 17. There they perceived that "he had horns in his hand;"—an almighty power to do what he pleased. Whence it is added, "And there was the hiding of his power." Though the appearance of it was very great and glorious, yet it was but small to the everlasting hidden depths of his omnipotency. The most glorious appearance of God comes infinitely short of his own eternal majesty as he is in himself;—it is but a discovery that there is the hiding of infinite perfection; or, there his power appeared to us, which was hidden from the rest of the world.

VIII. Observation. *When God is doing great things, he gives glorious manifestations of his excellencies to his secret ones.*

The appearance on Sinai goes before his passage into Canaan: "Surely the Lord GOD will do nothing, but he revealeth his secret unto his servants the prophets," Amos iii. 7. When he is to send Moses for the deliverance of his people, he appears to him in a burning, unconsumed bush, Exod. iii. 2,—a sign manifesting the presence

[1] Deut. xxxiii. 17; Ps. lxxv. 10; Zech. i. 18.

of his power to preserve his church unconsumed in the midst of burning, fiery afflictions. Unto this very end were all the visions that are recorded in the Scripture,—all of them accommodated to the things which God was presently doing. And this he doth,—

1. That they may thereby be prepared to follow him, and serve him in the great works he hath for them to do. Great works are not to be done without great encouragements. If God appears not in light, who can expect he should appear in operation? He that is called to serve Providence in high things, without some especial discovery of God, works in the dark,[1] and knows not whither he goes, nor what he doth. Such a one travels in the wilderness without a directing cloud. Clear shining from God must be at the bottom of deep labouring with God. What is the reason that so many in our days set their hands to the plough, and look back again?—begin to serve Providence in great things, but cannot finish?—give over in the heat of the day? They never had any such revelation of the mind of God upon their spirits, such a discovery of his excellencies, as might serve for a bottom of such undertakings. Men must know that if God hath not appeared to them in brightness, and showed them "the horns in his hand," hid from others, though they think highly of themselves, they'll deny God twice and thrice before the close of the work of this age. If you have no great discoveries, you will wax vain in great undertakings. New workings on old bottoms, are like new wine in old bottles,—both are spoiled and lost. The day is the time of work, and that because of the light thereof;—those who have not light may be spared to go to bed.

2. That they may be the better enabled to give him glory, when they shall see the sweet harmony that is between his manifestations and his operations,—when they can say with the Psalmist, "As we have heard, so have we seen," Ps. xlviii. 8. As he revealeth himself, so he worketh. When his power and mercy answer his appearance in the bush, it is a foundation to a prayer: "The good-will of him that dwelt in the bush bless thee." When a soul shall find God calling him forth to employments, perhaps great and high, yet every way suiting that light and gracious discovery which he hath given of himself, one thing answering another, it sets him in a frame of honouring God aright.

This might be of rich consideration could we attend it. For,—

Use 1. Hence, as I said before, is apostasy from God's work. He appears not unto men;—how can they go upon his employment? Men that have no vision of God, are in the dark, and know not what to do. I speak not of visions beyond the Word; but answers of prayers, gracious applications of providences, with wise consideration

[1] John xii. 35; Rev. xvi. 10.

of times and seasons. Some drop off every day, some hang by the eyelids, and know not what to do: the light of God is not sent forth to lead and guide them, Ps. xliii. 3. Wonder not at the strange backslidings of our days: many acted upon by engagements, and for want of light, know not to the last what they were a-doing.

Use 2. Hence also is the suiting of great light and great work in our days. Let new light be derided whilst men please, he will never serve the will of God in this generation, who sees not beyond the line of foregoing ages.

Use 3. And this, thirdly, may put all those whom God is pleased to employ in his service upon a diligent inquiry into his mind. Can a servant do his master's work without knowing his pleasure? We live for the most part from hand to mouth, and do what comes next;—few are acquainted with the designs of God.

The going forth of the Lord with his people towards their rest, with reference to his harbingers, is described, verse 5.

Verse 5. " Before him went the pestilence, and burning coals went forth at his feet."

" Before him,"—at his face. " The pestilence:" This is often reckoned amongst the weapons wherewith God fighteth with any people to consume them;[1] and as speeding an instrument of destruction it is as any the Lord ever used towards the children of men. " At his feet went forth burning coals;"—a redoubling, say some, of the same stroke,—burning coals for burning diseases. *When one blow will not do the work appointed, God redoubles the stroke of his hand*, Lev. xxvi. 22–25. Or, burning coals, dreadful judgments, mortal weapons, as fire and flames, are often taken in other descriptions of God's dealing with his enemies, Ps. xi. 6, xviii. 8. Prevailing fire is the most dreadful means of destruction, Heb. xii. 29; Isa. xxxiii. 14. In Exod. xxiii. 28, God threateneth to send the hornet upon the Canaanites, before the children of Israel; some stinging judgments, either on their consciences or bodies, or both:—something of the same kind is doubtless here held out. He sent plagues and diseases among them, to weaken and consume them, before his people's entrance. His presence was with Israel; and the pestilence consuming the Canaanites before their entrance is said to be לְפָנָיו,—" at his faces," or appearances, before him, before the entrance of the presence of his holiness. And the following judgments, that quite devoured them, were " the coals going out at his feet," which he sent abroad when he entered their land with his own inheritance, to cast out those " malæ fidei possessores." Sicknesses, diseases, and all sorts of judgments, are wholly at God's disposal. " Affliction cometh not forth of the dust, neither doth trouble spring out of the

[1] Exod. ix. 15; Lev. xxvi. 25; 2 Sam. xxiv. 13; Ezek. xiv. 19; Matt. xxiv. 7.

ground; yet man is born to trouble, as the sons of the burning coal lift up in flying," Job v. 6, 7. When God intends the total destruction of a people, he commonly weakens them by some previous judgments. Let the truth of this be found upon them that hate us, and the interpretation thereof be to the enemies of this nation; but the Lord knows all our hearts may well tremble at what will be the issue of the visitations of the last year.

IX. Observation. *God never wants instruments to execute his anger, and ruin his enemies.*

His treasury of judgments can never be exhausted. If Israel be too weak for the Amorites, he will call in the pestilence and burning diseases to their assistance. What creature hath not this mighty God used against his enemies? An angel destroys Sennacherib's host, Isa. xxxvii. 36, and smites Herod with worms, Acts xii. 23. Heaven above sends down a hell of fire and brimstone on Sodom and Gomorrah, Gen. xix. 24. The stars in their courses fought against Sisera, Judg. v. 20. Devils do his will herein; he sent evil angels among the Egyptians, Ps. lxxviii. 49. Fire consumes persecuting Ahaziah's companies, 2 Kings i. 10, 11. The water drowns Pharaoh and his chariots, Exod. xiv. 28. Earth swallows up Korah, with his fellow-rebels, Numb. xvi. 32. Bears rend the children that mocked Elisha, 2 Kings ii. 24. Lions destroy the strange nations in Samaria, 2 Kings xvii. 25. Frogs, lice, boils, hail, rain, thunder, lightning, destroy the land of Egypt, Exod. viii., ix., x. Locusts are his mighty army to punish Israel, Joel ii. 25. Hailstones destroy the Canaanites, Josh. x. 11. Stones of the wall slay the Syrians, 1 Kings xx. 30. Pestilence and burning diseases are his ordinary messengers. In a word, all creatures serve his providence, and wait his commands for the execution of his righteous judgments. Neither the beasts of the field nor the stones of the earth will be any longer quiet than he causeth them to hold a league with the sons of men.

Use 1. To teach us all to tremble before this mighty God. Who can stand before him,—"qui tot imperat legionibus?" If he will strike, he wants no weapons; if he will fight, he wants no armies. All things serve his will. He saith to one, Come, and it cometh; to another, Go, and it goeth; to a third, Do this, and it doth it. He can make use of ourselves, our friends, our enemies, heaven, earth, fire, water, any thing, for what end he pleaseth. There is no standing before his armies, for they are all things, and himself to make them effectual. There is no flying from his armies, for they are every where, and himself with them. Who would not fear this King of nations? He that contends with him shall find it "as if a man did flee from a lion, and a bear met him; or went into the house, and leaned his hand on the wall, and a serpent bit him," Amos v. 19.

No flying, no hiding, no contending. Worms kill Herod; a fly choked Adrian, &c.

Use 2. To be a bottom of confidence and dependence in an evil day. He that hath God on his side, hath also all things that are seen, and that are not seen. The mountain is full of fiery chariots for Elisha's defence, when outwardly there was no appearance, 2 Kings vi. 17. All things wait their Master's beck, to do him service,—as for the destruction of enemies, so for the deliverance of his. What though we had no army in the time of war? God hath millions, many thousands of angels, Ps. lxviii. 17,—one whereof can destroy so many thousands of men in a night, Isa. xxxvii. 36. He can choose (when few others will appear with him against the mighty, as in our late troubles) "foolish things to confound the wise, and weak things to confound the strong." Sennacherib's angel is yet alive, and the destroyer of Sodom is not dead: and all those things are at our command, if their help may be for our good. "Judah ruleth with God," Hos. xi. 12,—hath a rule by faithful supplications over all those mighty hosts. Make God our friend, and we are not only of the best, but also the strongest side. You that would be on the safest side, be sure to choose that which God is on. Had not this mighty, all-commanding God, been with us, where had we been in the late tumults? So many thousands in Kent, so many in Wales, so many in the north, so many in Essex,—shall they not speed? shall they not divide the prey? is not the day of those factious Independents come? was the language of our very neighbours. The snare is broken, and we are delivered.

The Lord having sent messengers before him into Canaan, stands himself as it were upon the borders, and takes a view of the land.

Verse 6. "He stood, and measured the earth: he beheld, and drove asunder the nations; and the everlasting mountains were scattered, the perpetual hills did bow: his ways are everlasting."

Two things are here considerable:—

1. The Lord's exact foreview of the promised land: "He stood, and measured the earth, and beheld the nations."

2. His operation at that time: "He drove asunder the nations," &c.

1. "He stood and measured:" The prophet here representeth the Lord on the frontier of Canaan, as one taking view of a piece of land, and exactly measuring it out, as intending it for his own; weighing and considering the bounds and limits of it, to see if it will answer the end for which he purposeth it. God's exact notice and knowledge of his people's possession is in those words held out. He views where the lines of every tribe shall run. Nothing happens or is made out to any of God's people, without his own careful providential predis-

position. He views the circuit of the whole, where and how divided, and separated from the dwellings of the unclean, and habitations of the uncircumcised. Fixed bounds, measured limits of habitation is a necessary ingredient to the making up of a national church.

2. What he did, which is two ways expressed: (1.) In reference to the inhabitants; (2.) To the land itself.

(1.) For the inhabitants: He drove them asunder, וַיַּתֵּר "and he made to leap" out of their old channels. Those nations knit and linked together amongst themselves, by leagues and civil society, he separated, disturbed, divided in counsels and arms (as in the case of the Gibeonites[1]), persecuted by the sword, that they suddenly leaped out of their habitations, the residue wandering as no people. God's justly nation-disturbing purposes are the bottom of their deserved ruin.

(2.) For the land: "The everlasting mountains," &c., those strong, firm, lasting mountains of Canaan, not like the mountains of sand in the desert where the people were, but to continue firm to the world's end, as both the words here used, עַד and עוֹלָם, "perpetuity" and "everlasting," do in the Scripture frequently signify. Now, these are said to be scattered, and to bow, because of the destruction of the inhabitants of those lasting hills, being many of them high and mighty ones,[2] like perpetual mountains; they being given in possession to the sons of Israel, even "the chief things of the ancient mountains, and the precious things of the lasting hills," Deut. xxxiii. 15.

X. Observation. *God takes an exact foreview of his people's portion and inheritance.*

Like a careful father, he knows beforehand what he intends to bestow upon them. He views it, measures it, prepares it to the utmost bounds. They shall not have a hair's breadth which he hath not allotted them, nor want the least jot of their designed portion.

Use. Learn to be contented with your lot. He is wise also who took a view of it, and measured it, and found it just commensurate to your good:—had he known that a foot's breadth more had been needful, you would have had it. Had he seen it good, you had had no thorns in your lands, no afflictions in your lives. O how careful, how solicitous are many of God's people! how full of desires!—Oh, that it were with me thus or thus! Possess your souls in patience; as you cannot add to, no more shall any take from your proportion. He took the measure of your wants and his own supplies long since. That which he hath measured out he will cut off for you. He knows how to suit all his children.

XI. Observation. *It is dangerous encroaching, for any of the sons of men, upon God's people's portion, lot, privileges, or inheritance.*

God hath measured it out for them, and he will look that they

[1] Josh. ix. 3. [2] Numb. xiii. 33.

enjoy it. Shall men remove his bounds and land-marks,[1] and be free? will it be safe trespassing upon the lands of the Almighty? will it be easy and cheap? will he not plead his action with power,—especially seeing he hath given them their portion? If he hath given Seir to Edom, what doth he vexing and wasting Jacob? Shall they not possess what the Lord their God gives them to possess? Judg. xi. 24. He hath cautioned all the world, kings and others, in this kind, "Touch not mine anointed, do my prophets no harm," Ps. cv. 14, 15. Touch them not, nor any thing that is theirs: harm them not in any thing I bestow on them. They have nothing but what their Father gives them, and Christ hath bought for them. Will a tender father, think you, contentedly look on, and see a slave snatch away his children's bread? If a man hath engaged himself to give a jewel to a dear friend, will he take it patiently to have an enemy come and snatch it away before his face? God is engaged to his people for all their enjoyments, and will he quietly suffer himself to be robbed, and his people spoiled? Shall others dwell quietly in the land which he hath measured for his own?

Use 1. See whence the great destructions of people and nations in these latter ages have come. Is it not for touching these forbidden things? The holy vessels of the temple at Jerusalem ruined Babylon. Is not the wasting of the western nations at this day from hence, that they have served the whore to deck herself with the spoils of the spouse?—helped to trim her with the portion of God's people, taking away their liberties, ordinances, privileges, lives, to lay at her feet? Doubtless God is pleading with all these kingdoms for their encroaching. They who will not let him be at peace with his, shall have little quiet of their own. The eagle that stole a coal from the altar fired her nest. I know how this hath been abused to countenance the holding of Babylonish wedges. God will preserve to his people his own allowance, not Rome's supplement. This nation hath yet itching fingers, and a hankering mind after the inheritance of God's people. Let them take heed; he hath knocked off their hands a hundred times, and sent them away with bloody fingers. O that we were wise, that we be not quite consumed! Of you I hope better things, and such as accompany salvation; yet give me leave to cautionate you a little.

(1.) As to privileges and liberties of this life. Their liberties and estates are not as other men's, but more exactly measured for their good, and sanctified to them in the blood of Christ. If in these things God hath called you to the defence and protection of his, he will expect a real account. You had better give away a kingdom that belongs to others, than the least of that which God hath made for

[1] Vid. Tertul. ad Scapulam, de persecutione.

his saints. Think not any thing small which God accounts worthy to bestow on his. If he hath meted out liberty for them, and you give them slavery, you will have a sad reckoning.

(2.) In point of ordinances, and Christ-purchased privileges. Here it is dangerous encroaching indeed.[1] God exactly measured Canaan, because it was to be the seat of a national church. If you love your lives, if you love your souls, be tender on this point. Here if you meddle with that which belongs not unto you, were you kings, all your glory would be laid in the dust, 2 Chron. xxvi. 18. Woe to them who cut short the saints of God in the least jot of what he hath allotted to them in spirituals! Is it for any of you, O ye sons of men! to measure out God's children's portion, long since bequeathed them by Christ? Let them alone with what is given them. If God call Israel out of Egypt to serve him, shall Pharaoh assign who, and how they shall go,—first men only, then all, without their cattle? "Nay," says Moses, "we will go as God calls," Exod. x. 26.

Was not one main end of the late tumults to rob God's people of their privileges,—to bring them again under the yoke of superstition? What God brake in war, do not think he will prosper in peace. If you desire to thrive, do not the same, nor any thing like it. Take they any thing of yours that belongs to Cæsar, the civil magistrate, restrain them, keep them within bounds; but if they take only what Christ hath given them,—O touch them not, harm them not! The heap is provided for them, let them take for themselves. Think it not strange that every one should gather his own manna. The Lord forbid that I should ever see the magistrates of England taking away liberties, privileges, ordinances, or ways of worship, from them to whom the Almighty hath made a free grant of them!

(3.) If in taking what God hath measured out for them, they should not all comply with you in the manner and measure of what they take, do them no harm, impoverish not their families, banish them not, slay them not. Alas![2] your judgments, were you kings and emperors, is not a rule to them. They must be tried by their own faith. Are their souls, think you, more precious to you than themselves? You say they take amiss;—they say, No, and appeal to the Word.[3] Should you now smite them? Speak, blood; is that the way of Jesus Christ? Should it be as you affirm, you would be puzzled for your warrant. To run when you are not sent, surely in

[1] "Nero primus in Christianos ferociit, tali dedicatore damnationis nostræ etiam gloriamur, qui enim scit illum, intelligere potest, non nisi aliquod bonum grande à Nerone damnatum."—Tertul. Apol.

[2] "Nova et inaudita est ista prædicatio, quæ verberibus exigit fidem."—Greg., Epist. lii.

[3] Magistrum neminem habemus nisi solum Deum; hic ante te est, nec abscondi potest, sed cui nihil facere possis.

this case is not safe. But what if it should prove, in the close, that they have followed divine directions? Do you not then fight against God, wound Jesus Christ, and prosecute him as an evil-doer? I know the usual colours, the common pleas, that are used for the instigation of authority to the contrary. They are the very same, and no other, that have slain the saints of God this twelve hundred years. Arguments for persecution are dyed in the blood of Christians for a long season;—ever since the dragon gave his power to the false prophet, they have all died as heretics and schismatics. Suppose you saw in one view all the blood of the witnesses of Christ, which had been let out of their veins by vain pretences,—that you heard in one noise the doleful cry of all pastorless churches, dying martyrs, harbourless children of parents inheriting the promise, wilderness-wandering saints, dungeoned believers, wrested out by pretended zeal to peace and truth;—and perhaps it may make your spirits tender as to this point.

Use 2. See the warrantableness of our contests for God's people's rights. It was Jephthah's only argument against the encroaching Ammonites, Judg. xi. By God's assistance they would possess what the Lord their God should give them. If a grant from heaven will not make a firm title, I know not what will. Being called by lawful authority, certainly there is not a more glorious employment than to serve the Lord in helping to uphold the portion he hath given his people. If your hearts be upright, and it is the liberties, the privileges of God's saints, conveyed from the Father, purchased by Christ, you contend for,—go on and prosper, the Lord is with you.

XII. Observation. *The works and labours of God's people are transacted for them in heaven, before they once undertake them.*

The Israelites were now going to Canaan: God doth their work for them beforehand; they did but go up and take possession. Joshua and Caleb tell the people, not only that their enemies' defence was departed from them, but that they were but bread for them, Numb. xiv. 9,—not corn that might be prepared, but bread, ground, made up, baked, ready to eat. Their work was done in heaven. "Known unto God are all his works from the beginning of the world," Acts xv. 18. All that is done here below, is but the writing of a visible copy, for the sons of men to read, out of the eternal lines of his own purpose.

Use. Up and be doing, you that are about the work of the Lord. Your enemies are bread ready to be eaten and yield you refreshment. Do you think if our armies had not walked in a trodden path, they could have made such journeys as they have done of late? Had not God marched before them, and traced out their way from Kent to Essex, from Wales to the north, their carcases had long ere this been cast into the field. Their work was done in heaven before they began it. God was gone over the mulberry-trees, 2 Sam. v. 24. The work might have been done by children, though he was pleased to employ such worthy instruments. They see, I doubt not, their own nothingness in his all-sufficiency. Go on, then; but with this caution, search by all ways and means to find the footsteps of the mighty God going before you.

The trembling condition of the oppressing nations round about, when God appeared so gloriously for his people, is held out, verse 7.

Verse 7. " I saw the tents of Cushan in affliction: the curtains of the land of Midian did tremble."

You have here three things considerable.

1. The mention of two nations, enemies of the church: Cushan and Midian.

2. The state and condition of those nations: the tents of the one in affliction, and the curtains of the other in trembling.

3. The view the prophet had of this,—I saw it, saith he: " I saw," &c.

1. For the first;—these two nations, Cushan and Midian, were the neighbouring people to the Israelites, being in the wilderness when God did such great things for them.

(1.) Cushan; that is, the tent-dwelling Arabians on the south side, towards Ethiopia,—being, as the Ethiopians, of the posterity of Cush (thence called Cushan), the eldest son of scoffing Ham, Gen. x. 6; enemies and opposers of the church (doubtless) all the way down from their profane ancestors.[1] These now beheld the Israelites going to root out their allies and kindred, the Amorites of Canaan, the posterity of Canaan, the younger brother of their progenitor Cush, Gen. x. 6.

(2.) Midian was a people inhabiting the east side of Jordan, on the borders of Moab; so called from their forefather, Midian, the son of Abraham by Keturah, Gen. xxv. 2. These obtained a temporal blessing for a season, from the love borne to their faithful progenitor. In the days of Jacob they were great merchants, Gen. xxxvii. 28. At this time, in less than four hundred years, they were so multiplied, that they had five kings of their nation, Numb. xxxi. 8. Some knowledge of the true God was retained, as it should seem, until now, amongst some of them, being received by tradition from their fathers. Moses' father-in-law was a priest of this country, Exod. ii. 15, 16,—not altogether unacquainted with Jehovah, Exod. xviii.,—and was himself, or his son, persuaded to take up his portion in Canaan, Numb. x. 29, 30. But for the generality of the nation, being not heirs of the promise, they were fallen off to superstition and idolatry. Exceeding enemies they were to the people in the wilderness, vexing

[1] 2 Kings xix. 9; Jer. xiii. 23; Joseph. Antiq.; Isa. xxxvii. 9.

them with their wiles, and provoking them to abominations, that the Lord might consume them, Numb. xxv. 18. None so vile enemies to the church as superstitious apostates. These two nations then set out all manner of opposers;—gross idolaters, as Cushan; and superstitious, envious apostates, as Midian.

2. Their state and condition severally.

(1.) "The tents of Cushan" were in affliction; the tents, the Arabian Ethiopians of Cush, dwelling in tents,—the habitation for the inhabitant, by a hypallage. They were "in affliction, under vanity, under iniquity, the place of vanity,"—so variously are the words rendered, תַּחַת אָוֶן, "under affliction, vanity, or iniquity." Sin and the punishment of it are frequently in the Scripture of the same name, so near is the relation. אָוֶן is properly and most usually iniquity; but that it is here taken for the consequent of it,—a consuming, perplexed, vexed condition,—can be no doubt. The Cushanites, then, were in affliction, full of anguish, fear, dread, vexation, to see what would be the issue of those great and mighty things which God was doing in their borders for his people:[1]—afflicted with Israel's happiness and their own fears; as is the condition of all wicked oppressors.

(2.) "The curtains of the land of Midian," for the Midianites dwelling in curtained tabernacles, by the same figure as before. They trembled,—יִרְגְּזוּן, "moved themselves, were moved;" that is, shaken with fear and trembling, as though they were ready to run from the appearance of the mighty God with his people. The story of it you have in the Book of Numbers,[2] as it was prophetically foretold by Moses concerning other nations, Exod. xv. 14–16, "The people shall hear, and be afraid: sorrow shall take hold on the inhabitants of Palestina. Then the dukes of Edom shall be amazed; the mighty men of Moab," &c. God filled those nations with anguish, sorrow, and amazement, at the protection he granted his people.

3. The prophet's view of all this: "I saw" it, or "I see" it. Though it were eight hundred and seventy years before, supposing him to prophesy about the end of Josiah or beginning of Jehoiakim, yet, taking it under the consideration of faith, he makes it present to his view.

Faith looketh backwards and forwards,—to what God hath done, and to what he hath promised to do. Abraham saw the day of Christ, so many ages after, because he found it by faith in the promise. Habakkuk saw the terrors of Cushan and Midian so many days before, because faith found it recorded among the works of God, to support itself in seeking the like mercies to be renewed. So that

[1] "Tantos invidus habet pœnâ justâ tortores, quantos invidiosus habuerit laudatores."—Prosp. de Vita Contemplativa.

[2] Numb. xxv., xxxi.

this is the sum of this verse: " O Lord, faith makes it evident, and presents it before my view, how in former days, when thou wast doing great things for thy people, thou filledst all thine and their enemies with fear, vexation, trembling, and astonishment."

XIII. Observation. *Faith gives a present subsistence to forepast works as recorded, and future mercies as promised, to support the soul in an evil day.*

I have made the doctrine, by analogy, look both ways, though the words of the text look but one.

The apostle tells us, that " faith is the substance of things hoped for, the evidence of things not seen," Heb. xi. 1.

1. " Of things hoped for." It looks forward to the promises, and so gives the substance of them in present possession, confirming our minds and hearts, that they may have a subsistence, as it were, within us, though not actually made out unto us.

2. It is " the evidence of things not seen." It extends itself not only to things promised, but, taking for its object the whole word of God, it makes evident and present things that are past also. The faith commended, verse 3, is of things long since done,—even the " making of the things that are seen of the things that do not appear." " Abraham saw my day," saith our Saviour, John viii. 56. He saw it as Habakkuk saw the tents of Cushan in affliction;—faith made it present to him; all the ages between him and his promised seed were as nothing to his keen-sighted faith. Hence the apostle puts the mercies of the promise all in one form and rank, as already wrought, though some of them were enjoyed, and some of them in this life cannot be, Rom. viii. 30, " Whom he hath justified, them he hath glorified:" he hath done it for them already, because he hath made them believe it, and that gives it a present subsistence in their spirit. And for forepast works, they are still mentioned by the saints as if they had been done in their days, before their eyes. Elisha calls up to remembrance a former miracle, to the effecting the like, 2 Kings ii. 14.

There be three things in the past or future mercies which faith makes present to the soul, giving, in the substance of them,—(1.) Their love; (2.) Their consolation; (3.) Their use and benefit.

(1.) The *love* of them. The love that was in former works, and the love that is in promised mercies, *that* faith draws out, and really makes ours. The love of every recorded deliverance is given to us by faith. It looks into the good-will, the free grace, the loving-kindness of God, in every work that ever he did for his, and cries, *Yet this is mine:*—this is the kernel of that blessing, and this is mine; for the same good-will, the same kindness he hath towards me also. Were the same outward actings needful, I should have them also. The free love of every mercy is faith's proper object. It makes all Joshua's great victories present to every one of us. The promise that had the love and grace in it, which ran through them all, is given him, Josh. i. 5, "I will be with thee, I will not fail thee, nor forsake thee." Now the apostle tells us that the truth and love of this promise is ours, Heb. iv. 8. Faith may, doth assure itself, that what good-will soever was in all the great mercies which Joshua received upon that promise, is all ours. All the good-will and choice love of, "I will never leave thee nor forsake thee," is mine and thine, if we are believers. He that hath this present, hath all Joshua's victories present. The very glory of the saints in heaven is ours in the love of it. We enjoy that love which gave them glory, and will crown us also in due time.

(2.) In their *comforts* and *refreshments:* "Thou gavest leviathan to be meat to the people in the wilderness," Ps. lxxiv. 14. They fed their souls full of the sweetness of that mercy, the destruction of their oppressing tyrant; we chew the cud upon the blessings of former ages. Who hath not, with joy, delight, and raised affections, gone over the old preservations of the church in former years? How does David run them over with admiration, closing every stop with, "His mercy endureth for ever!" Ps. cxxxvi. And for things to come, as yet in the promise only,—whether general to the whole church, as the calling of the Jews, the coming in of the fulness of the Gentiles, the breaking out of light, beauty, and glory upon the churches and saints, the confusion of nations not subjecting themselves to the standard of the gospel, &c.,—or in particular, farther assurance of love than at present enjoyed, nearer communion with Father and Son, being with Christ, freed from misery and corruption, dwelling with God for ever;—how does faith act over these and the like things in the heart, leaving a savour and relish of their sweetness continually upon the soul? O how sweet are the things of the world to come unto poor believers! Christ leads the soul by faith, not only into the chambers of present enjoyed loves, but also into the fore-prepared everlasting mansions in his Father's house. Thus it gives poor mortal creatures a sweet relish of eternal joys;—brings heaven into a dungeon, glory into a prison, a crown into a cottage, Christ into a slaughter-house. And this arises,—

[1.] From the nature of faith. Though it do not make the thing believed to be (the act cannot create its own object), yet applying it, it makes it the believer's. It is the bond of union between the soul and the thing promised. He that believes in Christ, by that believing receives Christ, John i. 12;—he becomes his. It is a grace uniting its subject and object,—the person believing and the thing believed. There needs no ascending into heaven, or descending; the word of faith makes all things nigh, even within us, Rom. x. 6–8. Some glasses will present things at a great distance very near; faith looking through the glass of the gospel, makes the most remote mercies to be not only in a close distance, but in union. It "is the subsistence of things hoped for;"—that which they have not in themselves, it gives them,—in the full-assured minds of believers.

[2.] From the intendment of all mercies. They are for every believer. All things are theirs,—"world, life, death, things present, things to come," 1 Cor. iii. 22. All promises being made to every believer, and all mercies being the fruit of these promises, they must all belong to every believer. Now, if all these should be kept from us, at that distance wherein they fail in their accomplishment in respect of time, what would they avail us? God, therefore, hath appointed that they shall have a real, though not a natural presence and subsistence at all times, to all believers.

Use 1. See hence what use you make of past mercies, deliverances, blessings, with promised incomings;—carry them about you by faith, that you may use them at need. "Where is the LORD God of Elijah?" "Awake, awake, O arm of the Lord!" &c. "I saw the tents of Cushan." Take store mercies along with you in every trial. Use them, or they will grow rusty, and not pass in heaven. Learn to eat leviathan many years after his death. Forget not your perils;—scatter not away your treasure;—be rich in a heap of mercies,—faith will make you so. The love, the comfort, the benefit, of all former and future blessings are yours, if you know how to use them. Oh, how have we lost our mercies in every hedge and ditch! Have none of us skill to lay up the last eminent deliverance against a rainy day?

Use 2. Learn how to make the poorest and most afflicted condition comfortable and full of joy. Store thy cottage, thy sick-bed, by faith, with all sorts of mercies;—they are the richest furniture in the world. Gather up what is already cast out, and fetch the rest from heaven. Bring the first-fruits of glory into thy bosom. See the Jews called,—the residue of opposers subdued,—the gospel exalted,—Christ enthroned,—all thy sins pardoned,—corruption conquered,—glory enjoyed. Roll thyself in those golden streams every day. Let faith fetch in new and old;—ancient mercies for thy supportment, everlasting mercies for thy consolation. He that hath faith, hath all things.

XIV. Observation. *God's dealing with his enemies in the season of his church's deliverance is of especial consideration.*

"I saw the tents," &c. So did the Israelites behold the Egyptians dead on the shore, Exod. xiv. 30, 31. "The heathen raged, the kingdoms were moved: he uttered his voice, the earth melted. The LORD of hosts is with us; the God of Jacob is our refuge. Selah. Come, behold the works of the LORD, what desolations he hath made in the earth," Ps. xlvi. 6–8. The enemies' undertaking, verse 6,—God's protection to his people, verse 7,—a view of the adversaries' desolation, verse 8,—are all orderly held out.

The Lord tells Moses that he will harden the heart of Pharaoh, that he might show his power; to this very end, that it might be considered, and told to one another, Exod. x. 2, 3. How many psalms have we, that are taken up in setting forth God's breaking, yoking, befooling, terrifying his adversaries at such a season! The remembrance of the slaughter of the first-born of Egypt was an ingredient in the chiefest ordinance the ancient church enjoyed, Exod. xii. The reasons of this are,—

1. Much of the greatness and intenseness of God's love to his own is seen in his enemies' ruin, Isa. xliii. 3, 4, "I gave Egypt for thy ransom, Ethiopia and Seba for thee. Since thou wast precious in my sight, thou hast been honourable, and I have loved thee; therefore will I give men for thee, and people for thy life." When God gives such mighty kingdoms for a small handful, it appears they are precious to him: "Whosoever shall gather together against thee, shall fall for thy sake," Isa. liv. 15. When God will maintain a quarrel with all the world,—swear that he will never have peace with Amalek until he be consumed,—break nations, kings, and kingdoms,—stretch out his hand in judgment round about,—and all to save, preserve, prosper, protect a small handful;—surely he hath endeared affections for them. In the days wherein we live, can we look and see wise men befooled, mighty warriors vanquished, men of might become as children, their persons slain and trodden down in the field,—can we but cry, "Lord, what are we, and what is our house, that thou shouldst do such things for us?" A serious view of what God hath done in this nation of late,—what armies he hath destroyed, what strongholds demolished, what proud, haughty spirits defeated, what consultations made vain,—is enough to make us admire the riches of his love all our days. We may know what esteem a man sets upon a jewel, by the price he gives for it. Surely God values them for whom he hath given the honours, the parts, the polities, the lives of so many tall cedars, as of late he hath done. The loving-kindness of God to his church is seen, as in a glass, in the blood of their persecutors.

2. The manifestation of God's sovereignty, power, and justice, is as dear to him as the manifestation of his mercy. The properties he lays out in destruction are equally glorious with those he lays out in preservation. In the proclamation of his glorious name he omits them not, Exod. xxxiv. 6, 7. In these he triumpheth gloriously when he hath overthrown the horse and his rider in the sea, Exod. xv. 1.

Use. Let not our eyes in the late deliverance be always on the light side of the work, our own mercies;—the dark side of terror and judgment is not without its glory. The folly that was in their counsels, the amazement that was in their armies, the trembling that accompanied all their undertakings, the tympanous products of all their endeavours, do all cry out, "Digitus Dei est hic." Had not God showed infinite wisdom, they had not been so abundantly foolish: had not he been infinite in power, the many thousands of enemies had not been so weak.

In the late engagement in this country, when God stirred us up, with some others in these parts, to make some opposition to the enemy gathering at Chelmsford, what were, think you, the workings of God's providences against them? How came it to pass that we were not swallowed up by them? For,—

1. *They were desirous to ruin us,* if we may judge their desires to answer their interest; or their expressions, with the language of their friends round about us, to answer their desires.

2. *They were able to do it.* They had from the beginning, and so all along, near as many thousands as we had hundreds;—of them very many old, experienced soldiers; with us not three men that had ever seen any fighting.

3. *They were resolved to do it.* Witness their own confessions, and frequent declarations of their purposes, whilst the business was in agitation.

4. *They were provoked to it.* For the first and only considerable opposition was made to them in this place;—first, By hindering their assistance from Colchester; which how much they valued, witness the senseless letter they would have forced the committee to subscribe, to persuade us not to disturb their levies there;—secondly, Suppressing and discouraging all those affected to them and their designs in these parts of the country; restraining some, disarming others, awing all;—thirdly, Hastening the coming of the army, lest their friends should suffer;—fourthly, Encouraging their coming, by declaring that they had friends here: by which, and the like, they were abundantly provoked.

5. *That they were also invited to it,* though by persons somewhat inconsiderable, with promises of a full party of friends to assist them, which they might have had, and a rich booty from their enemies to support them, which they might have found, is too apparent.

Now, being thus advantaged, thus encouraged, thus provoked and resolved, why did they not attempt it, why did they not accomplish their desires? Is it not worth the while to consider how they were restrained?[1] Was not much of God's wisdom seen in mixing a spirit

[1] Gen. xx. 6; Ps. lxxvi. 10.

of giddiness and error in the midst of them, that they knew not well how to determine, nor at all to execute their determinations? Was not his power seen in causing experienced soldiers, as they were, with their multitudes, to be afraid of a poor handful of unskilful men, running together because they were afraid to abide in their houses? Was not his justice exalted in keeping them only for the pit which they had digged for others? Doubtless the hand of God was lifted up. O that we could all learn righteousness, peculiarly amongst ourselves of this place! Is there nothing of God to be discerned in the vexations, birthless consultations, and devices of our observers?—nothing of power in their restraint?—nothing of wisdom in the self-punishment of their anxious thoughts?—nothing of goodness, that after so long waiting for advantage, they begin themselves to think that neither divination nor enchantment will prevail?

XV. Observation. *The measuring out of God's people's portion fills Cushan with affliction and Midian with trembling.*

Their eye is evil, because God is good. Israel's increase is Pharaoh's trouble, Exod. i. 10. When Nehemiah comes to build the walls of Jerusalem, it grieved the enemy exceedingly "that there was come a man to seek the welfare of the children of Israel," Neh. ii. 10. This is the season of that dispensation which you have mentioned, Isa. lxv. 13–15, "Thus saith the Lord God, Behold, my servants shall eat, but ye shall be hungry: behold, my servants shall drink, but ye shall be thirsty: behold, my servants shall rejoice, but ye shall be ashamed: behold, my servants shall sing for joy of heart, but ye shall cry for sorrow of heart, and shall howl for vexation of spirit. And ye shall," &c.

The reasons of this are taken,—1. From their envy; 2. From their carnal fear;—the two principles whereby they are acted in reference to the saints of God.

1. Their envy. They have a devouring envy at them,[1] which at length shall shame them and consume them, Isa. xxvi. 11. They are of their father the devil, and he (through envy) was a "murderer from the beginning," John viii. 44. The portion God measureth out unto his people is in distinguishing mercies, differencing blessings,—in such things as the world hath not, giveth not. Now, this is that which envy takes for its proper object. That others should have enjoyments above them, beyond them, this envious men cannot bear. God accepts Abel, not Cain; presently Cain is wroth, and his countenance falls, Gen. iv. 6. Jacob gets the blessing, and this fills the heart of

[1] "Quis facile potest, quale sit hoc malum, verbis exprimere, quo invidus odio hominis persequitur divinum munus in homine?"—Pros. Vit. Cont. "Invidia est tristitia de bono proximi, prout proprium malum æstimatur et est diminutivum proprii boni."—Aq 22, æ. q. 36, A. 1, c.

Esau with murderous revenge, Gen. xxvii. 41. Upon all God's appearances with the apostles, how were the Jews cut to the heart, vexed, perplexed! God gives distinguishing mercies to his people, such protections, such deliverances;—this Cushan and Midian cannot bear.

2. Their carnal fear. They have all of them that conclusion in their breasts which Haman's wise men and wife made to him, Esth. vi. 13. If they begin to fall before the seed of the Jews, utter ruin will follow. When God begins to own his people, as them in the Acts, chap. v. 24, "they doubt whereunto this will grow;"—their hearts tell them secretly they are usurpers of all they have, and when God owns any, they instantly fear lest for their sakes they should be called to account. When a distinction begins to be made in ordinances, privileges, deliverances, protections, evidently given to some peculiar ones, they tremble within that they are set apart for no good. This picking and choosing of men by the Lord, Ps. iv. 3, they cannot bear with. Such mighty works attend the Israelites! what, thinks Midian, will be the end of this? It is true, their pride calls on them to act openly more of their malice than their fear; but yet this lies at the bottom, like a boasting Atheist's nightly thoughts.[1] The chief priests and Pharisees having gotten the apostles before them,—what big words they use to countenance the business! "Who gave you this power?" Acts iv. 7. But when they are by themselves, they cry, "What shall we do?" and, "Whereunto will this grow?" This lies at the bottom with many at this day;—though they boast, and lift up their mouth to heaven, their hearts do tremble as an aspen leaf.

Use. Learn not to be troubled at the great tumultuating which is amongst many against the ways of God at this day. God is measuring out his children's portion, giving them their bread in season, viewing for them the lot of their inheritance. Men of the world, profane Cushanites, superstitious, apostatical Midianites, will not, cannot be quiet. Vexed they are, envious, and afraid, and will act according to those principles. Cushanites see religion owned, Midianites theirs disclaimed, and both are alike provoked. The Lord convert them, or rebuke them; or the one will have the *armies*, the other their *wiles*. Only judge not their hearts by the outward appearance always. They seem gallant to you;—indeed they are frighted, galled, vexed. I have seen a galled horse, under dressing, leap and curvet as though it had been out of mettle and spirit, when indeed it was pain and smart that made him do it. They pretend to despise us, when they envy us. They look like contemners, but are tremblers. Be not troubled at their outward appearance, they have inward anguish;—they bite others, but are lashed themselves.

[1] Noctu dubitant.

XVI. Observation. *The season of the church's deliverance being come, Cushan and Midian must wax vain, and perish.*

That there is such a season, I told you before. When four hundred and thirty years are expired, Egypt must be destroyed, the Amorites rooted out, and all the nations round made to tremble. When seventy years of captivity expire, Babylon must be ruined, and the Chaldean monarchy quite wasted, that the Jews may return. The church being to be delivered, Haman must be hanged. This you have fully set out, Rev. vi. 12–17. It is the fall of heathenish tyranny, by the prevailing of the gospel, which you have there described. Rome and Constantinople, Pope and Turk, are preserved for a day and an hour wherein they shall fall, and be no more. If the season of enjoying ordinances and privileges be come to this nation, that the tabernacle of God will be here amongst men; woe be to Cushanites! woe be to Midianites!—open opposers, and secret apostates. They shall not be able to be quiet, nor to prevail; God will not let them rest, nor obtain their purposes. The story of Haman must be acted over again; their hearts shall be stirred up to their own ruin, Rev. xx. 8. This is the frame of perishing Babylonians in the day of Zion's restoration. The reasons are:—

1. Because at the deliverance of his people, God will plead with their enemies for their oppressions. "It is the day of the LORD's vengeance, the year of recompenses for the controversy of Zion," Isa. xxxiv. 8. It is the vengeance of the Lord and his temple that lights upon them in that day, Jer. l. 28. "The violence done to me and my flesh be upon Babylon, shall the inhabitant of Zion say; and, My blood upon the inhabitants of Chaldea, shall Jerusalem say," Jer. li. 35. In this day great Babylon must come into remembrance, Rev. xvi. 19, 20.

2. The discerning trial that shall and doth come along with the church's vindication, will cut off all superfluous false professors, so that they also shall perish, Mal. iii. 2, 3 Christ comes with a fan, to send away the chaff in the wings of the wind. Have we not seen this end of many zealots?

3. The Amorites live in Canaan, and must be removed. Oppressors and hypocrites enjoy many rites of the church, which must be taken from them. Rome and her adherents shall not have so much left as the name or title, appearance or show of a church. The outward court, which they have trodden down and defiled, shall be quite left out in the measuring of the temple, Rev. xi. 2.

Use. Bring this observation home to the first from this verse, and it will give you the use of it: proceed we to the next verse.

Verse 8. "Was the LORD displeased against the rivers? was thine anger against the rivers? was thy wrath against the sea, that thou didst ride upon thine horses, and thy chariots of salvation?"

"Was the Lord displeased?" חָרָה "kindled," did he burn?—that is, in wrath. Heat is a great ingredient in the commotion of anger in us, here alluded to, or because the effects of anger are so often compared to fire. "Against the rivers" or floods? Again: "Was thine anger?" אַפֶּךָ "thy nose or face, or thine anger," אַף signifies both. The face[1] is the seat of anger's appearance: fury comes up into the face. "Was thine anger, thy troubling anger" (so the word) "against the sea,"—the Red sea, through which thy people passed; "that thou didst ride upon thy horses, and thy chariots of salvation?" or, "thy chariots were salvation,—'currus salutares,' thy safety-bringing chariots."

The words are an admiring expostulation about the mighty works of the Lord for his people, upon the sea, rivers, and inanimate creatures.

1. The *rivers:*—Jordan and its driving back is doubtless especially intended. The Lord showed his power in disturbing that ancient river in his course, and making his streams run backward. The story of it you have Josh. iii. 15, 16. The people being to enter into Canaan, the Lord divides the waters of that river, making them beneath to sink away, and those above to stand on a heap. This the prophet magnifies, Ps. cxiv. 5, "What ailed thee, O Jordan, that thou wast driven back?" What marvellous, powerful, disturbing thing is happened to thee, that, contrary to thy ancient natural course, thy streams should be frighted, and run back to the springs from whence they came?

2. The *sea:*—that is, the Red sea, which, in like manner, was divided, Exod. xiv. 21; which the prophet also admires in the fore-cited psalm: "The sea saw it, and fled. What ailed thee, O thou sea, that thou fleddest?" What strong, mighty impression of power was on thee, that the multitudes of thy waters should be parted, and thy channel discovered dry to the bottom?

3. "That thou didst ride upon thine horses, and thy chariots of salvation." This you have again, verse 15, "Thou didst walk through the sea with thine horses." These were those clouds and winds which the Lord sent before the Israelites, to the sea and Jordan, to drive them back. "He maketh the clouds his chariot, and walketh upon the wings of the wind," Ps. civ. 3. So Ps. xviii. 10, "He did fly upon the wings of the wind." After the manner of men, God is represented as a mighty conqueror, riding before his armies and making way for them. The power and majesty of God was with and upon those clouds and winds which went before his people, to part those mighty waters, that they might pass dry; and therefore they are called his saving chariots, because by them his people were delivered. Or

[1] "Cætera licet abscondere, et in abdito alere; ira se profert, et in faciem exit." —Senec. de ira.

by horses and chariots here you may understand the angels, who are the host of God. Ps. lxviii. 17, " The chariots of God are twenty thousand, even thousands of angels." They have appeared as horses and chariots of fire, 2 Kings vi. 17. And their ministry, no doubt, the Lord used in these mighty works of drying rivers and dividing seas. Either way, the glorious power and majesty of God, in his delivering instruments, is set forth.

Thus the words severally;—now jointly.

This admiring interrogation includes a negation. " Was the LORD kindled against the rivers? was thy face against the rivers," &c. Was it that the deep had offended the Most High, that, by thine angels, winds, and clouds, thou didst so disturb the floods in their ancient course, and madest naked their hidden channels, until the hoary deep cried out for fear, and lifted up his aged hands to the Almighty, as it were, for pity? verse 10. No, surely, no such thing. All those keep the order by thee unto them appointed; it was all for the salvation and deliverance of thy people. God was not angry with Jordan when he drove it back, nor with the sea when he divided it; but all was effected for Israel's deliverance.

XVII. Observation. *The very senseless creatures are, as it were, sensible of the wrath and power of the Almighty.*

Effects of anger being in and upon the deep, " he utters his voice, and lifts up his hands on high," verse 10. God often in the Scripture sets forth his power and majesty by the trembling of heaven and the shaking of the earth, the vanishing of mountains and the bowing of perpetual hills,—the professed humble subjection of the most eminent parts of the creation. The sea shall fly, as afraid; the rocks, as weak, rend and crumble; the heavens be darkened; the mountains skip like rams, and the little hills like young sheep, Ps. cxiv. 4.

> Τρέμει δ' ὄρη, καὶ γαῖα, καὶ πελώριος
> Βυθὸς θαλάσσης, κὤρέων ὕψος μέγω,
> Ὅταν ἐπιβλέψῃ γοργὸν ὄμμα δεσπότου.
>
> Æsch. apud Justin., Apol. ii.

" The earth shook, the heavens dropped at the presence of God," Ps. lxviii. 8. The almighty Creator holds the whole frame of the building in his own hand, and makes what portion he pleaseth, and when he pleaseth, to tremble, consume, and vanish before him. Though many things are not capable of sense and reason, yet he will make them do such things as sense and reason should prompt the whole subjected creation unto, to teach that part their duty who were endued therewith. A servant is beat, to make a child learn his duty.

Use. See hence the stoutness of sinful hearts,—more stubborn than the mountains, more flinty than the rocks, more senseless than the great deep. Friend, art thou stronger than Horeb? yet that trembled at the presence of this mighty God, whom it never had provoked. Are thy lusts like the streams of Jordan? yet they ran back from his chariots of salvation. Are thy corruptions more firmly seated on thy soul than the mountains on their bases? yet they leaped like frighted sheep before that God against whom they had not sinned. And wilt thou, a small handful of sinful dust, that hast ten thousand times provoked the eyes of his glory, not tremble before him, coming on his horses and chariots of salvation,—his mighty works and powerful word? Shall a lion tremble, and thou not be afraid, who art ready to tremble with a thought of that poor creature? Shall the heavens bow, the deep beg for mercy, and thou be senseless? Shall all creatures quake for the sin of man, and sinful man be secure? Know you not that the time is coming wherein such men will desire the trembling rocks to be a covert to their more affrighted souls?

XVIII. Observation. *No creatures, seas nor floods, greater or lesser waters, shall be able to obstruct or hinder God's people's deliverance, when he hath undertaken it.*

Is the sea against them? it shall be parted. Is Jordan in the way? it shall be driven back. Both sea and Jordan shall tremble before him. Euphrates shall be dried up, to give the kings of the east a passage, Rev. xvi. 12. Waters in the Scriptures are sometimes afflictions, sometimes people and nations. Be they seas (kings and princes), or be they rivers (inferior persons), they shall not be able to oppose. God has decked his house, and made it glorious with the spoils of all opposers. There you have the spoils of Pharaoh, gathered up on the shore of the Red sea, and dedicated in the house of God, Exod. xv. There you have all the armour of Sennacherib's mighty host, with the rest of their spoils, hung up to show, 2 Chron. xxxii. 21. There you have the glory, and throne, and dominion of Nebuchadnezzar, himself being turned into a beast, Dan. iv. 33. There you shall have the carcases of Gog and Magog, with all their mighty hosts, for coming to encamp against the city of God, Ezek. xxxix. There you have the imperial robes of[1] Diocletian and his companion, abdicating themselves from the empire for very madness that they could not prevail against the church. Kings of armies shall fly apace; and she that tarries at home shall divide the spoil, Ps. lxviii. 12. All opposers, though nations and kingdoms, shall perish and be utterly destroyed, Isa. lx. 12, Rev. xix. 18.

God will not exalt any creature unto a pitch of opposition to himself, or to stand in the way of his workings. The very end of all things, in their several stations, is to be serviceable to his purposes towards his own. Obedience in senseless creatures is natural, even against the course of nature, in the season of deliverance. "Sun,

[1] Euseb. Vit. Con. Const. Orat.

stand thou still upon Gibeon; and thou, Moon, in the valley of Ajalon," Josh. x. 12. "Who art thou, O great mountain? before Zerubbabel thou shalt become a plain," Zech. iv. 7. The most mountainous opposers shall be levelled, when the Spirit of God sets in for that purpose. There is a strength in every promise and engagement of God unto his people, that is able to carry the whole frame of heaven and earth before it. If they can believe, all things are possible to them that believe. When the decree is to bring forth the fruit of the promise, it will overturn empires, destroy nations, divide seas, ruin armies, open prisons, break chains and fetters, and bear down all before it; as the wind shut up in the earth will shake the pillars, as it were, of its mighty body, but it will find or make a passage. The least promise of deliverance, if the season thereof be come, though it were shut up under strong and mighty powers, crafty counsels, dungeons, and prisons, like the doors and lasting bars of the earth, the truth and power of God shall make them all to tremble, and give birth to his people's deliverance.

Use 1. Have we seen nothing of this in our days?—no seas divided? no Jordans driven back? no mountains levelled? no hills made to tremble? Whence, then, was the late confusion of armies? casting down of mighty ones? reviving of dead bones? opening of prison doors? bringing out the captives appointed to be slain? Is it not from hence, that nothing can stand against the breaking out of a promise in its appointed season? "Was the LORD displeased with the rivers?" was his anger against the walls and houses, "that he rode upon his horses, and chariots of salvation?"

Use 2. Let faith be strengthened in an evil time. Poor distressed soul, all the difficulty of thy deliverance lies in thine own bosom! If the streams of thy unbelief within be not stronger than all seas of opposition without, all will be easy. O learn to stand still with quietness, between a host of Egyptians and a raging sea, to see the salvation of God! Be quiet in prison, between your friends' bullets and your enemies' swords; God can, God will, make a way. If it were not more hard with us to believe wonders than it is to the promise to effect wonders for us, they would be no wonders, so daily, so continually, would they be wrought.

XIX. Observation. *God can make use of any of his creatures to be chariots of salvation.*

This is the other side of that doctrine which we gathered from verse 5, "Winds and clouds shall obey him." Ravens[1] shall feed Elijah, that will not feed their own young. The sea shall open for Israel, and return upon the Egyptians. And this both in an ordinary

[1] 'Εκβάλλει τοὺς νεοττοὺς ὁ κόραξ.—Arist. Hist. Anima., vi. "Pellunt nidis pullos sicut et Corvi."—Plin. Nat. Hist.

way, as Hos. ii. 21, 22; and in an extraordinary way, as before. So many creatures as God hath made, so many instruments of good hath he for his people. This is farther confirmed, verse 9.

Verse 9. "Thy bow was made quite naked, according to the oaths of the tribes, even thy word. Selah. Thou didst cleave the earth with rivers."

"With nakedness thy bow was made naked." The rest is elliptical, and well supplied in the translation.

The verse hath two parts.

1. A general proposition: "Thy bow was made naked," &c.

2. A particular confirmation of that proposition by instance: "Thou didst cleave the earth with rivers."

1. The proposition holds out two things.

(1.) What God did: "He made his bow quite naked."

(2.) The rule he proceeded by herein: "According to the oaths of the tribes, even his word."

The assertion of this verse is not of some particular act or work, as the former, but a general head or fountain of those particular works which are enumerated in the following verses.

(1.) A *bow* is a weapon of war, an instrument of death; and being ascribed to God, after the manner of men, holds out his strength, power, might, and efficacy, to do whatever he pleaseth. And this is said to be quite naked. When a man goes about to use his bow, he pulls it out of his quiver,[1] and so makes it naked. The exercising of God's power is the making naked of his bow. This he did in all those wonders wherein he stretched out his hand, in bringing his people into the promised land, here pointed at. And it is said that with nakedness it was made naked, because of those very high dispensations and manifestations of his almighty power. This is the making naked of his bow.

(2.) For the *rule* of this, it is "the oaths of the tribes;" or as afterward, "his word,"—the oaths of the tribes, that is, the oaths made to them,—the word he stood engaged to them in. The promise God made by oath unto Abraham, that he would give him the land of Canaan for an inheritance, even to him and his posterity, Gen. xiii. 14–17, is here intimated. This promise was often renewed to him and the following patriarchs. Hence it is called oaths, though but the same promise often renewed: and it had the nature of an oath, because it was made a covenant. Now, it was all for the benefit of the several tribes, in respect of actual possession, and was lastly renewed to them, Exod. iii. 17; hence called "the oaths of the tribes,"

[1] [The gorytus or bow-case; so explained by Grotius, Drusius, &c. Sir J. Chardin states, that the oriental bows were usually carried in a case of cloth or leather attached to the girdle.—Harmer, ii. 513. Vid. Hom. Odys., xxi. 53, 54.]

not which they sware to the Lord, but that which the Lord sware to them. So afterward it is called his word,—" Thy word." This, then, is the purport of this general proposition, " O Lord, according as thou promisedst, and engagedst thyself by covenant to Abraham, Isaac, and Jacob, with their posterity, that thou wouldst give them the land of Canaan to be theirs for an inheritance; so by the dispensation of thy mighty power thou hast fully accomplished it." And this he layeth down for the supportment of faith in a time of trouble.

The words would afford many observations; I shall insist only on one.

XX. Observation. *The Lord will certainly make good all his promises and engagements to his people, though it cost him the making of his bow quite naked,—the manifestation of his power in the utmost dispensations thereof.*

God's workings are squared to his engagements. This is still the close of all gracious issues of providence,—God hath done all according " as he promised," Josh. xxii. 4; 2 Sam. vii. 21. He brought out his people of old with a mighty hand, with temptations, signs, and wonders, and a stretched-out arm; and all because he would keep the oath which he had sworn, and the engagement which he had made to their fathers, Deut. vii. 8. What obstacles soever may lie in the way, he hath done it, he will do it. Take one instance; particular places are too many to be insisted on. It was the purpose of his heart to bring his elect home to himself, from their forlorn condition. This he engageth himself to do, Gen. iii. 15,—assuring Adam of a recovery from the misery he was involved in by Satan's prevalency. This, surely, is no easy work. If the Lord will have it done, he must lay out all his attributes in the demonstration of them to the uttermost. His wisdom and power must bow their shoulders, as it were, in Christ unto it. He was " the power of God, and the wisdom of God;"[1] his engaged love must be carried along through so many secret, mysterious marvels, as the angels themselves " desire to look into,"[2] and shall for ever adore. Though the effecting of it required that which man could not do, and God could not suffer; yet his wisdom will find out a way, that he shall both do it and suffer it who is both God and man. To make good his engagement to his elect, he spared not his only Son: and in him were hid, and by him laid out, " all the treasures of wisdom and knowledge."[3]

Now, this is a precedent of God's proceeding in all other engagements whatsoever. Whatever it cost him, he will spare nothing to make them good to the uttermost. He is our rock, and his work is perfect. A good man, if he want not power, will go through with his serious promises, though he be engaged to his own hurt, Ps. xv. 4. The power of the mighty God is serviceable to his will to the utter-

[1] 1 Cor. i. 24. [2] 1 Pet. i. 12. [3] Col. ii. 3.

most. He cannot will what he cannot do: his will and power are essentially the same. And his power shall not be wanting to execute what his goodness hath moved him to engage unto for his own glory. The reasons of this are,—

1. Deut. xxxii. 4, "He is the Rock, his work is perfect; all his ways are judgment: a God of truth, and without iniquity." Here are many attributes of God to make good this one thing, that his work is perfect,—his αὐτάρκεια, self-sufficiency, perfection, righteousness. I will pitch on one,—he is a God of truth. So he is again called, Ps. xxxi. 5, and in other places. The truth of God in his promises and engagements requires an accomplishment of them, whatever it cost, what power soever is required thereunto. This the saints make their bottom to seek it: "Where are thy loving-kindnesses, which thou swarest in thy truth," Ps. lxxxix. 49. It is impossible but that should come to pass which thou hast sworn in thy truth. No stronger plea than "Remember the word wherein thou hast caused thy servants to put their trust." Jacob says, he is less than all the mercy and all the truth of God, Gen. xxxii. 10. He sees God's truth in all his mercy, by causing all things to come to pass which he hath promised him. It is true, some particular promises have their conditions, whose truth consists not in the relation between the word and the thing, unless the condition intercede. But the great condition under the gospel being only the good of them to whom any engagement is made, we may positively lay down, that God's truth requires the accomplishment of every engagement for his people's good, Rom. viii. 28. It is neither mountain nor hill, king, kingdom, nor nation, hell nor mortality, nor all combined, that can stand in the way to hinder it, Matt. xvi. 18.

2. His people stand in need of all that God hath engaged himself to them for. God's promises are the just measure of his people's wants. Whatever he hath promised, that his people do absolutely want; and whatsoever they want, that he hath promised:—our wants and his promises are every way commensurate. If thou knowest not what thou standest in need of, search the promises and see: whatever God hath said he will do for thee, that thou hast absolute need should be done. Or if thou art not so well acquainted with the promises, search thine own wants: what thou standest absolutely in need of for thy good, that assuredly God hath promised. If, then, this be the case of engagements, they shall all be made good. Think you, will God let his people want that which they have absolute necessity of? By absolute necessity I mean such as is indispensable, as to their present estate and occasions. That may be of necessity in one generation which is not in another, according to the several employments we are called to. Does God call forth his saints "to execute

vengeance upon the heathen, and punishments upon the people; to bind their kings with chains, and their nobles with fetters of iron; to execute upon them the judgment written," as Ps. cxlix. 7–9?—doth he bring them forth to burn the whore, to fight with the beast, and overcome him and his followers?—it is of indispensable necessity that he give them glorious assistance in their undertakings. They shall be assisted, protected, carried on, though it cost him the making of his bow quite naked. According to the several conditions he calls them to, the several issues of providence which he will have them serve in, so want they his appearance in them, with them, for them; and it shall be present. Let them be assured they are in his way, and then, though some prove false and treacherous, some base and cowardly,—though many combine and associate themselves against them in many places, in all places,—though whole kingdoms and mighty armies appear for their ruin,—be they reviled and clamoured by all round about them,—all is one; help they need, and help they shall have, or God will make his bow quite naked.

Use. 1. This day is this doctrine fulfilled before us. God's bow is made quite naked, according to his word. We are less than all the truth he hath showed unto us. Though great working and mighty power hath been required, such as he hath not shown in our days, nor in the days of our fathers; yet the Lord hath not stood at it, for his word's sake, wherein he hath made us to put our trust. I speak of the general mercies we have received. The surrender of Colchester, the particular celebrated this day, though marching in the rear for time, is for the weight in the van,—a mercy of the first magnitude. Essex hath seen more power in a three months' recovery than in the protection of six years. That the mouths of men are stopped, and their faces filled with shame, who made it their trade to revile and threaten the saints of God;—that the adverse strength, which hath lain hid these seven years, should be drawn forth, united, and broken to pieces;—that the people of God, divided, and naturally exasperated through their abuse of peace, should, by the sword of a common enemy and the help of a common friend, have their wrath abated, their counsels united, and their persons set in a hopeful way of closing or forbearance;—that God by their own counsels should shut up men, collected from sundry parts to ruin others, in a city with gates and walls, for their own ruin;—that they should deny peace tendered upon such conditions, because of the exigencies of the time, as might have left them power as well as will for a farther mischief;—that such salvation should go forth in other parts as that the proceedings here should not be interrupted;—that the bitter service which men here underwent should ever and anon be sweetened with refreshing tidings from other places, to keep up their spirits in wet, watching, cold, and loss of blood:—all these, I say, and sundry other such-like things as these, are "the Lord's doing, and marvellous in our eyes."

Especially let us remember how in three things the Lord made his bow quite naked in his late deliverance.

(1.) *In leavening the counsels of the enemy with their own folly.*

(2.) *In ordering all events to his own praise.*

(3.) *By controlling with his mighty power the issue of all undertakings.*

(1.) *In leavening their counsels with their own folly.* God's[1] power and the efficacy of his providence is not more clearly manifested in any thing than in his effectual working in the debates, advices, consultations, and reasonings of his enemies, compassing his ends by their inventions. When God is in none of the thoughts of men by his fear, he is in them all by his providence. The sun is operative with his heat where he reacheth not with his light, and hath an influence on precious minerals in the depths and dark bottoms of rocks and mountains. The all-piercing providence of God dives into the deep counsels of the hearts of the sons of men, and brings out precious gold from thence, where the gracious light of his countenance shines not at all. Men freely advise, debate, use and improve their own reasons, wisdom, interests, not once casting an eye to the Almighty; and yet all this while do his work more than their own. All the counsellings, plottings of Joseph's brethren,—all the transactions of the Jews, Herod, and Pilate, about the death of Christ, with other the like instances, abundantly prove it.[2] Take a few instances wherein God "made his bow quite naked" in the counsels of his and our enemies.

In general, they consult to take arms, wherein God had fully appeared against them,—when, in all probability, their work would have been done without them. Had they not fought, by this time they had been conquerors. One half-year's peace more,—which we desired on any terms, and they would on no terms bear,—in all likelihood had set them where they would be. Their work went on, as if they had hired the kingdom to serve them in catching weather. What with some men's folly, others' treachery, all our divisions,—had not their own counsels set them on fighting,—I think we should suddenly have chosen them and theirs to be umpires of our quarrels. God saw when it was time to deal with them. In their undertaking in our own county, I could give sundry instances how God mixed a perverse

[1] "Quod homines peccant eorum est, quod peccando hoc vel illud agant ex virtute Dei est, tenebras prout visum est dividentis."—Aug., de Præd. "Oportet hæreses esse, sed tamen non ideo bonum hæreses, quia eas esse oportebat, quasi non et malum oportuerit esse; nam et Dominum tradi oportebat, sed væ traditori!"—Tertul., Præf. ad Hær.

[2] Gen. xlv. 7, l. 20; Acts iv. 27, 28.

spirit of folly and error in all their counsels. A part of the magistracy of the county is seized on. Therein their intention towards the residue is clearly discovered; yet not any attempt made to secure them,—which they might easily have accomplished,—although they could not but suppose that there were some gentlemen of public and active spirits left that would be industrious in opposition unto them. Was not the Lord in their counsels also, when they suffered a small, inconsiderable party, in a little village within a few miles of them, to grow into such a body as at length they durst not attempt, when they might have broken their whole endeavour with half a hundred of men? Doubtless, of innumerable such things as these we may say, with the prophet, "The princes of Zoan are become fools, the princes of Noph are deceived; they have also seduced" the people, "even they that are the stay of the tribes thereof. The LORD hath mingled a perverse spirit in the midst thereof; and they have caused" the people "to err in every work thereof, as a drunken man staggereth in his vomit," Isa. xix. 13, 14. Doubtless the wrath of man shall praise the Lord, and the remainder of it will he restrain.

(2.) *In ordering all events to his own praise.* The timing of the enemies' eruptions in several places is that which fills all hearts with wonder, and all mouths with discourse, in these days. From the first to the last they had their season. Had they come together, to the eyes of flesh the whole nation had been swallowed up in that deluge. In particular, let Essex take notice of the goodness of God. The high thoughts and threats of men, which made us for divers weeks fear a massacre, were not suffered to break out into open hostility until the very next day after their strength was broken, in the neighbour county of Kent;—as if the Lord should have said, "I have had you in a chain all this while: though you have showed your teeth, you have not devoured; now go out of my chain,—I have a net ready for you." For the armies coming to our assistance, I cannot see how we needed them many days sooner, or could have wanted them one day longer. Farther, these home-bred eruptions were timely seasoned, to rouse the discontented soldiery and divided nation to be ready to resist the Scottish invasion;—God also being magnified in this, that in this sweet disposal of events unto his glory, the counsels of many of those in whom we thought we might confide ran totally cross to the appearance of God in his providence. What shall we say to these things? If the Lord be for us, who shall be against us? All these things came forth from the Lord of hosts, who is wonderful in counsel, and excellent in operation, Isa. xxviii. 29. Whoso is wise will ponder them, and they shall understand the loving-kindness of the Lord.

(3.) *In controlling mighty actions,*—I mean, giving success to his people in all their undertakings. The commander-in-chief of all the forces in this kingdom, since his sitting down before Colchester, was proffered a pass to go beyond the seas for his security. Whence is it that he hath now the necks of his enemies, and hath given any of them their lives at their entreaty? Greater armies than this have been buried under lesser walls. Did not the number of the besieged at first exceed the number of the besiegers? were not their advantages great? their skill in war, amongst men of their own persuasion, famous and renowned? so that the sitting down before it was judged an action meet only for them who could believe they should see the bow of God made quite naked. It had been possible, doubtless, to reason's eye, that many of those fictions wherewith a faction in the great city fed themselves,—of the many routings, slaughters, and destructions of the army,—might have been true. Some of them, I say; for some were as childish as hellish. In brief, they associated themselves, and were broken in pieces;—high walls, towering imaginations, lofty threats,—all brought down. "So let all thine enemies perish, O LORD: but let them that love him be as the sun when he goeth forth in his might;" and let the land have rest for many years, Judg. v. 31.

Use 2. This will discover unto us the bottom and rise of all God's appearances for his people,—even the engaging of his own free grace. He doth not "make his bow quite naked," according to their deservings, but his own word; not because they of themselves are better than others, but because he loves them more than others. Were God's assistances suited to our walkings, they would be very uneven; but his good-will is constant; so are our deliverances.

Use 3. Be exhorted to thankfulness; not verbal,[1] but real; not the exultation of carnal affections, but the savoury obedience of a sound mind. There are many ingredients in thanksgiving;—suitable and seasonable obedience to answer the will of God in his mercies is doubtless the crown of all. Look, then, under the enjoyment of blessings in general, to close walking with God in the duties of the covenant,—and in particular, to the especial work of this your generation,—and you are in the way to be thankful.

Use 4. Be sedulously careful to prevent that which God hath mightily decried by our late mercies,—viz., mutual animosities, strife, contention, and violence against one another;[2] I mean, of those that fear his name. God hath interposed in our quarrels from heaven. The language of our late deliverance is, Be quiet, "lest a worse thing happen unto you." Our poor brethren of Scotland would not see the hate-

[1] "In beneficio reddendo plus animus, quam census operatur."—Ambr. Offi., lib. i. cap. 32.

[2] Ἡ διαφωνία τῆς νηστείας, τὴν ὁμόνοιαν τῆς πίστεως συνίστησιν.—Iren. Epist. ad Vict. apud Euseb., lib. v. cap. 23. Φιλόνικοί ἐστε ἀδελφοὶ καὶ ζηλωταὶ περὶ μὴ ἀνηκόντων εἰς σωτηρίαν.—Clem. Ep. ad Cor.

fulness of their animosities towards their friends, until God suffered that very thing to be the means to deliver them up to the power of their enemies. The weapons they had formed were used against themselves. Let us learn betimes to agree about our pasture, lest the wolves of the wilderness devour us. Persecution and idolatry have ruined all the states of the Christian world.

2. Of the assertion we have spoken hitherto: come we now to the particular confirmation of it by instance. "Thou didst cleave the earth with rivers,"—cleave the earth, or make channels in the earth, for waters to flow in.

Another most eminent work of almighty power is here set forth,—eminent in itself, and eminent in its typical signification. And the same thing being twice done, hath a plural expression,—"rivers."

(1.) *Eminent of itself.* The bringing of streams of waters from the rock, for the thirsty people in the wilderness, is that which is here celebrated. Now this the Lord did twice:—First, Exod. xvii. 6, when the people were in Rephidim, in the first year after their coming from Egypt, they fainted in their journeys for want of water, and (according to the wonted custom of that rebellious people) complained with murmuring. So they extorted all their mercies; and therefore they were attended with such sore judgments. Whilst the meat was in their mouths, the plague was on their bones. *Mercies extorted by murmurings, unseasoned with loving-kindness, though they may be quails in the mouth, will be plagues in the belly.* Let us take heed lest we repine the Almighty into a full harvest and lean soul, Ps. cvi. 15. Get and keep mercies in God's way, or there is death in the pot.

Forty years after this, when the first whole evil generation was consumed, the children, who were risen up in their fathers' stead, fall a murmuring for water in the wilderness of Zin, and, with a profligacy of rebellion, wish they had been consumed with others in the former plagues, Numb. xx. 4. Here also the Lord gives them water, and that in abundance, verse 11. Now, of this observe,—

[1.] The places from whence this water marvellously issued. They were rocks that, in all probability, never had spring from the creation of the world. Farther, they are observed to be rocks of flint, Ps. cxiv. 8, "Which turned the rock into a standing water, the flint into a fountain of waters:" so Deut. viii. 15. A rock into a pool, and a flint into a stream, is much beyond Samson's riddle of sweetness from the eater.

[2.] The abundance of waters that gushed out,—waters to satisfy that whole congregation, with all their cattle, consisting of some millions. Yea, and not only they, but all the beasts of that wilderness were refreshed thereby also, Isa. xliii. 20, "The beast of the field shall honour me, the dragon and the owl; because I give waters in the wilderness, rivers in the desert, to give drink to my people, my chosen."

The very worst of the sons of men, dragons and owls, fare the better for God's protecting providence towards his own.[1]

And all this was in such abundance, that it was as plentiful as a sea. "He clave the rocks in the wilderness, and gave them drink as out of the great depths. He brought streams also out of the rock, and caused waters to run down like rivers," Ps. lxxviii. 15, 16. So also it is celebrated, Isa. xli. 18, xlviii. 21, Hos. xiii. 5, and in many other places. *Great deliverances call for frequent remembrances.*

Thus were rivers brought out of the rocks, and with or for these rivers God did cleave the earth;—that is, either he provided channels for those streams to run in, that they might not be wasted on the surface of that sandy wilderness, but preserved for the use of his people; or else the streams were so great and strong, that they pierced the earth, and parted channels for themselves. Great rivers of water, brought out of flinty rocks, running into prepared channels, to refresh a sinful, thirsty people, in a barren wilderness, I think, is a remarkable mercy.

(2.) *As it was eminent in itself, so likewise is it exalted in its typical concernment.* Is there nothing but flints in this rock? nothing but water in these streams? nothing but the rod of Moses in the blows given to it? Did the people receive no other refreshment, but only in respect of their bodily thirst? Yes, saith the apostle, "They drank of that spiritual rock which followed them; and that rock was Christ," 1 Cor. x. 4. Was not this rock a sign of that Rock of Ages on which the church is built? Matt. xvi. 18. Did not Moses' smiting hold out his being smitten with the rod of God? Isa. liii. 4, 5. Was not the pouring out of these plentiful streams as the pouring out of his precious blood, in a sea of mercy, abundantly sufficient to refresh the whole fainting church in the wilderness? "Latet Christus in petra;"—"Here is Christ in this rock." Had Rome had wisdom to build on this Rock, though she had not had an infallibility as she vainly now pretends, she might have had an infallibility (if I may so speak), yea, she had never quite failed. Give me leave to take a few observations from hence. As,—

[1.] *Sinners must be brought to great extremities, to make them desire the blood of Jesus;*—weary and thirsty, before rock-water come. Thirst is a continually galling pressure. When a soul gaspeth like a parched land, and is as far from self-refreshment as a man from drawing waters out of a flint, then shall the side of Christ be opened to him. You that are full of your lusts, drunk with the world, here is not a drop for you. If you never come into the wilderness, you shall never have rock-water.

[2.] *Mercy to a convinced sinner seems ofttimes as remote as*

[1] "Vir bonus commune bonum."—Gen xxxi. 3.

rivers from a rock of flint. The truth is, he never came near mercy, who thought not himself far from it. When the Israelites cried, We are ready to die for thirst, then stood they on the ground where rivers were to run.

[3.] *Thirsty souls shall want no water, though it be fetched for them out of a rock.* Panters after the blood of Jesus shall assuredly have refreshment and pardon, through the most unconquerable difficulties. Though grace and mercy seem to be locked up from them, like water in a flint,—whence fire is more natural than water; yet God will not strike the rock of his justice and their flinty hearts together, to make hell-fire sparkle about their ears; but with a rod of mercy on Christ, that abundance of water may be drawn out for their refreshment.

[4.] *The most eminent temporal blessings, and suitable refreshment* (water from a rock for them that are ready to perish), *is but an obscure representation of that love of God, and refreshment of souls, which is in the blood of Jesus.* Carnal things are exceeding short of spiritual,—temporal things of eternal.

[5.] *The blood of Christ is abundantly sufficient for his whole church to refresh themselves,—streams, rivers, a whole sea.*

These, and the like observations, flowing from the typical relation of the blessing intimated, shall not farther be insisted on;—one only I shall take from the historical truth.

XXI. Observation. *God sometimes bringeth plentiful deliverances and mercies for his people from beyond the ken of sense and reason; yea, from above the ordinary reach of much precious faith.*

I mean not what it ought to reach, which is all the omnipotency of God; but what ordinarily it doth, as in this very business it was with Moses. I say, plentiful deliverances, mercies like the waters that gushed out in abundant streams, until the earth was cloven with rivers,—that the people should not only have a taste and away, but drink abundantly, and leave for the beasts of the field,—from beyond the ken of sense and reason, by events which a rationally wise man is no more able to look into, than an eye of flesh is able to see water in a flint; or a man probably suppose that divers millions of creatures should be refreshed with waters out of a rock where there was never any spring from the foundation of the world.

Now, concerning this, observe,—

1. *That God hath done it.*
2. *That he hath promised he will yet do it.*
3. *Why he will so do.*

1. *He hath done it.* I might here tire you with precedents. I could lead you from that mother deliverance, the womb of all others, the redemption that is in the blood of Jesus, down through many dis-

pensations of old and of late, holding out this proposition to the full. One shall suffice me; and if some of you cannot help yourselves with another, you are very senseless.

Look upon Peter's deliverance, Acts xii. The night before he was to be slain, he was kept safe in a prison,—a prison he had neither will nor power to break. He was bound with two chains, beyond his skill to unloose or force asunder. Kept he was by sixteen soldiers, doubtless men of blood and vigilancy, having this to keep them waking, that if Peter escaped with his head, they were to lose theirs. Now, that his deliverance was above sense and reason himself intimates, verse 11, "He hath delivered me from the expectation of the Jews." The wise, subtle Jews, concluded the matter so secure, that, without any doubts or fears, they were in expectation of his execution the next day. That it was also beyond the ready reach of much precious faith, you have an example in those believers who were gathered together in the house of Mary, verse 12, calling her mad who first affirmed it, verse 15, and being astonished when their eyes beheld it, verse 16;—the whole seeming so impossible to carnal Herod, after its accomplishment, that he slays the keepers as false in their hellish trust;—a just recompense for trusty villains.

The time would fail me to speak of Isaac,[1] and Joseph, Gideon, Noah, Daniel, and Job,—all precedents worthy your consideration. View them at your leisure; and you will have leisure, if you intend to live by faith.

2. *He hath said it.* It is a truth abounding in promises and performances. I shall hold out one or two; it will be worth your while to search for others yourselves. He that digs for a mine finds many a piece of gold by the way.

Isa. xli. 14–16, "Fear not, thou worm Jacob, and ye few men of Israel. Behold, I will make thee a new sharp thrashing instrument having teeth: thou shalt thrash the mountains, and beat them small, and shalt make the hills as chaff. Thou shalt fan them," &c. To make a worm a thrashing instrument with teeth, to cause that instrument to beat mountains and hills into chaff, that chaff to be blown away with the wind, that that worm may rejoice in God;—to advance a small handful of despised ones to the ruin of mountainous empires and kingdoms, until they be broken and scattered to nothing,—is a mercy that comes from beyond the ken of an ordinary eye. Ezek. xxxvii. 3, the prophet professeth that the deliverance promised was beyond his apprehension: "Son of man, can these bones live? And I answered, O Lord GOD, thou knowest." The Lord intimates in the following verses that he will provide a means for his church's recovery when it seemeth as remote therefrom as dry bones scattered upon the

[1] Gen. xxii. 14, xxxix., &c.

face of the earth are from a mighty living army. This he calls opening their graves, verses 12, 13.

3. The *reasons of this are,*—

(1.) Because he would have his people wholly wrapt up in his all-sufficiency, not to straiten themselves with what their faith can ken in a promise, much less to what their reason can perceive in appearance. In the application of promises to particular trials and extremities, faith oftentimes is exceedingly disturbed, either in respect of persons, or things, or seasons; but when it will wholly swallow up itself in all-sufficiency, the fountain of all promises, there is no place for fear or disputing. Have your souls in spiritual trials never been driven from all your out-works unto this main fort? Hath not all hold of promises in time of trial given place to temptations, until you have fallen down in all-sufficiency, and there found peace? God accounts a flight to the strong tower of his name to be the most excellent valour. This is faith's first, proper, and most immediate object. To particular promises it is drawn out on particular occasions; here is, or should be, its constant abode, Gen. xvii. 1. And, indeed, the soul will never be prepared to all the will of God, until its whole complacency be taken up in this sufficiency of the Almighty. Here God delights to have the soul give up itself to a contented losing of all its reasonings, even in the infinite unsearchableness of his goodness and power. Therefore will he sometimes send forth such streams of blessings as can flow from no other fountain, that his may know where to lie down in peace. Here he would have us secure our shallow bottoms in this quiet sea, this infinite ocean, whither neither wind nor storm do once approach. Those blustering temptations which rage at the shore, when we were half at land and half at sea,—half upon the bottom of our own reason and half upon the ocean of providence,—reach not at all unto this deep. Oh, if we could in all trials lay ourselves down in these arms of the Almighty, his all-sufficiency in power and goodness! Oh, how much of the haven should we have in our voyage, how much of home in our pilgrimage,—how much of heaven in this wretched earth! Friends, throw away your staves, break the arm of flesh, lie down here quietly in every dispensation, and you shall see the salvation of God. I could lose myself in setting out of this, wherein I could desire you would lose yourselves in every time of trouble. "Hast thou not known, hast thou not heard, that the everlasting God, the LORD, the Creator of the ends of the earth, fainteth not, neither is weary? there is no searching of his understanding. He giveth power to the faint; and to them that have no might he increaseth strength. Even the youths shall faint and be weary, and the young men shall utterly fall: but they that wait upon the LORD shall renew their strength; they shall mount up with wings as eagles;

they shall run, and not be weary; they shall walk, and not faint," Isa. xl. 28-31.

(2.) To convince the unbelieving world itself of his power, providence, and love to them that put their trust in him, that they may be found to cry, "Verily there is a reward for the righteous; verily he is a God that judgeth in the earth," Ps. lviii. 11. When the Egyptian magicians see real miracles, beyond all their juggling pretences, they cry out, "This is the finger of God," Exod. viii. 19. Profane Nebuchadnezzar, beholding the deliverance of those three worthies from the fiery furnace, owns them for the "servants of the most high God," Dan. iii. 26. Daniel being preserved in the lions' den, Darius acknowledgeth the power and kingdom of "the living God," Dan. vi. 26. Glorious appearances of God for his people, beyond the reach of reason, wrest from the world amazement or acknowledgment; and in both God is exalted. He will appear in such distresses, as that he will be seen of his very enemies. They shall not be able, with the Philistines, to question whether it be his hand or a chance happened to them, 1 Sam. vi. 9; but conclude, with the Egyptians, that fly they must, for God fights for his people, Exod. xiv. 25. If God should never give blessings but in such a way as reason might discover their dependence on secondary causes, men would not see his goings, nor acknowledge his operations. But when he mightily makes bare his arm, in events beyond their imaginations, they must vail before him.

Use 1. Consider whether the mercy celebrated this day ought not to be placed in this series of deliverances, brought from beyond the ken of sense and reason, from above the reach of much precious faith. For the latter, I leave it to your own experience;—to the former let me for the present desire your consideration of these five things.

(1.) *By whom you were surprised and put under restraint.* Now these were of two sorts: [1.] The heads and leaders; [2.] The tumultuous multitude.

[1.] *For the first*, some of them being dead, and some under durance, I shall not say any thing. "Nullum cum victis certamen, et æthere cassis." I leave the stream from the flint to your own thoughts.

[2.] *For the multitude*,—an enraged, headless, lawless, godless multitude, gathered out of inns, taverns, alehouses, stables, highways, and the like nurseries of piety and pity. Such as these having got their superiors under their power, governors under their disposal, their restrainers under their restraint, their oppressors, as they thought, under their fury,—what was it that kept in their fury and their revenge, which upon the like occasions and advantages hath almost always been executed? Search your stories,—you will not find many that speak of such a deliverance. For a few governors prevailed on unto durance, by a godless rout, in an insurrection, and yet come off in peace and safety, is surely a work of more than ordinary providence.

(2.) *Consider the season of your surprisal;*—when all the kingdom was in an uproar, and the arm of flesh almost quite withered as to supply,—the north invaded, the south full of insurrections, Wales unsubdued,[1] the great city at least suffering men to lift up their hands against us; so that, to the eye of reason, the issue of the whole was, if not lost, yet exceedingly hazardous, and so your captivity endless. Had they gone on, as was probable they would, whether you had this day been brought out to execution, or thrust into a dungeon, or carried up and down as a pageant, I know not; but much better condition, I am sure, rationally you could not expect.

(3.) *The end of your surprisal.* Amongst others, this was apparently one, to be a reserve for their safety who went on in all ways of ruin. You were kept to preserve them in those ways wherein they perished. Whether could reason reach this or no, that you being in their power, kept on purpose for their rescue if brought to any great strait, with the price of your heads to redeem their own,—that they should be brought to greater distress than ever any before in this kingdom, and you be delivered, without the least help to them in their need? It was beyond your friends' reason, who could not hope it;—it was beyond our enemies' reason, who never feared it: if you believed it, you have the comfort of it.

(4.) *The refusal of granting an exchange for such persons* as they accounted more considerable than yourselves, and whose enlargement might have advantaged the cause they professed to maintain exceedingly more than your restraint,—what doth it but proclaim your intended ruin? This was the way of deliverance which for a long season reason chiefly rested on, the main pillar of all its building; which, when it was cut in two, what could be seen in it but desolation.

(5.) *The straits you were at length reduced to,* between your enemies' swords and your friends' bullets, which, intended for your deliverance, without the safeguard of Providence might have been your ruin, piercing more than once the house wherein you were. Surely it was, then, an eminent work of faith, to "stand still, and see the salvation of God."

The many passages of Providence, evidently working for your preservation, which I have received from some of yourselves, I willingly pass over. What I have already said is sufficient to declare that to reason's eye you were as dead bones upon the earth. For our parts, who were endangered spectators at the best, we were but in the prophet's frame; and to any question about your enlargement, could answer only, The Lord alone knows. And now, behold, the Lord hath

[1] "Idem huic urbi dominandi finis erit, qui parendi fuerit."—Senec. de Rom.

chosen you out to be examples of his loving-kindness, in fetching mercy for you from beyond the ken of reason; yea, from above the reach of much precious faith. He hath brought water for you out of the flint. Reckon your deliverance under this head of operations, and I hope you will not be unthankful.

Use 2. You that have received so great mercy, we that have seen it, and all who have heard the doctrine confirmed, let us learn to live by faith. Live above all things that are seen; subject them to the cross of Christ. Measure your condition by your interest in God's all-sufficiency. Do not in distress calculate what such and such things can effect; but what God hath promised. Reckon upon that, for it shall come to pass. If you could get but this one thing by all your sufferings and dangers, to trust the Lord to the utmost extent of his promises, it would prove a blessed captivity. All carnal fears would then be conquered, all sinful compliances with wicked men removed, &c.

Use 3. Be exhorted to great thankfulness,[1] you that have been made partakers of great deliverances. In great distresses very nature prompts the sons of men to great promises. You have heard the ridiculous story of him who in a storm at sea promised to dedicate a wax candle to the blessed Virgin as big as the mast of his ship, which he was resolved when he came on shore to pay with one of twelve in the pound! Let not the moral of that fable be found in any of you. Come not short of any of your engagements. No greater discovery of a hypocritical frame, than to flatter the Lord in trouble, and to decline upon deliverance, in cold blood. The Lord of heaven give you strength to make good all your resolutions:—as private persons, in all godliness and honesty, following hard after God in every known way of his;—as magistrates, in justice, equity, and faithful serving the kingdom of Christ. Especially, let them never beg in vain for help at your hands, who did not beg help in vain for you at the hands of God.

Use 4. Consider, if there be so much[2] sweetness in a temporal deliverance, oh! what excellency is there in that eternal redemption which we have in the blood of Jesus! If we rejoice for being delivered from them who could have killed the body, what unspeakable rejoicing is there in that mercy whereby we are freed from the wrath to come! Let this possess your thoughts, let this fill your souls,—let this be your haven from all former storms. And here strike I sail, in this to abide with you and all the saints of God for ever.

[1] "Erunt homicidæ, tyranni, fures, adulteri, raptores, sacrilegi, proditores; infra ista omnia, ingratus est."—Senec. Benef., lib. i. "Gratiarum cessat decursus, ubi recursus non fuerit."—Bern. Serm. 50.

[2] "Si tanti vitrum, quanti Margaritum?"—Tertul.

SERMON III.

RIGHTEOUS ZEAL ENCOURAGED

BY

DIVINE PROTECTION:

WITH

A DISCOURSE ABOUT TOLERATION, AND THE DUTY OF THE CIVIL MAGISTRATE ABOUT RELIGION, THEREUNTO ANNEXED.

PREFATORY NOTE.

THE following sermon was preached before the House of Commons on January 31, 1648, which had been appointed as a day of solemn humiliation in connection with the event of the preceding day,—the decapitation of Charles I. Accordingly, no sermon of Owen has excited keener discussion. Because he consented to preach in these circumstances, he is held to have connived at a great crime, and actually invested it with the sanctions of religion. In the opinion of Dr M'Crie (see "Miscellaneous Writings," p. 501), his conduct in this instance was "the greatest blot on his public life," and both his text and the title of his sermon could not fail to be interpreted as encouragement to those who had been accessory to the destruction of the unhappy monarch. On the other hand, some, like Mr Orme, urge that Owen preached by *command;* that no sentiment of the sermon can be construed as approval of the regicide; and that the very passages (see paragraph at the foot of p. 134 and on p. 136) adduced in proof that Owen concurred in it, indicate his desire to keep free and aloof from the expression of any positive opinion on the subject. A bolder line of defence has been instituted, according to which Owen, like Milton, might have regarded the death of Charles as only the appropriate penalty for a long career of violence and duplicity, during which he had made the blood of the best subjects in the realm to flow like water; and that our author, in preaching on this occasion, might have acted under a sense of duty, while discharging a task solemn and painful certainly, but still a task to which he might feel himself bound by higher considerations than mere regard to the authority which enjoined it. The argument to this effect is stated with great point and ability in his "Life," etc., vol. i. p. 40. This much is clear, that after the Restoration he was never called to account for his public appearance on this occasion by a government whose measures of vindictive retaliation against the Puritans are notorious. Asty's explanation of the fact has obvious weight:—"His discourse was so modest and inoffensive, that his friends could make no just exception, nor his enemies take an advantage of his words another day."—Memoirs, p. 8. The only public expression of displeasure at this sermon was given in 1683, about a month before the grave closed over its author. In the school quadrangle of the University,—not too rich in honours to repudiate without serious loss the lustre shed upon it from the name of its great Puritan Vice-Chancellor,—a document containing some positions, extracted from the sermon and denounced as pernicious and damnable, was publicly burned. He suffered in good company; for propositions from the works of Knox, Buchanan, Baxter, and others, were condemned in the same decree, and committed to the same flames. Some reparation for the insult offered in this mean revenge was made, too late to soothe his feelings, had he needed solace under the affront, but tending so far to rescue his memory from unjust reproach, when, in 1710, by an order from the House of Lords, the Oxford decree was burned by the hands of the common hangman.

It is strange, that the appendix to a sermon preached, as some think, in the very consummation of licence and misrule, should be an earnest and able pleading for toleration, in a tone of calmness and moderation rare at any time in controversy, and especially rare in the controversies of that stormy age.

The entire body of the Independents have been blamed for consenting to the death of Charles I., because Owen, the chief ornament of their denomination, was called, in such critical and delicate circumstances, to preach before the House of Commons. Mr Orme successfully disproves the justice of the charge. Whatever offence Owen may thus have committed, to visit it upon the religious body with which he generally acted, is in accordance neither with the principles of justice nor the facts of history.—ED.

Die Mercurii, 31 *Januarii* 1648.

ORDERED by the COMMONS assembled in Parliament, That Mr Allen do give the thanks of this House to Mr Owen for the great pains he took in his sermon preached before the House this day at Margaret's, Westminster; and that he be desired to print his sermon at large; wherein he is to have the like privilege of printing it as others in the like kind usually have had.

HEN. SCOBELL, *Cler. Parl. Dom. Com.*

TO THE RIGHT HONOURABLE

THE COMMONS OF ENGLAND,

ASSEMBLED IN PARLIAMENT.

SIRS,

IT hath always suited the wisdom of God to do great things in difficult seasons. He sets up walls in troublous times, Dan. ix. 25. His builders must hold swords and spears, as well as instruments of labour, Neh. iv. 16. Yea, while sin continueth in its course here (which began in heaven, and, having contemporized with the earth, shall live for ever in hell), great works for God will cause great troubles amongst men. The holy, harmless Reconciler of heaven and earth bids us expect the sword to attend his undertakings for and way of making peace, Matt. x. 34. All the waves in the world arise to their height and roaring from the confronting of the breath of God's Spirit and the vapours of men's corruptions. Hence seasons receive their degrees of difficulty according to the greatness and weight of the works which in them God will accomplish. To their worth and excellency is man's opposition proportioned. This the instruments of his glory in this generation shall continually find true, to their present trouble and future comfort.

As the days approach for the delivery of the decree, to the shaking of heaven and earth,[1] and all the powers of the world, to make way for the establishment of that kingdom which shall not be given to another people (the great expectation of the saints of the Most High before the consummation of all); so tumults, troubles, vexations, and disquietness, must certainly grow and increase among the sons of men.

A dead woman (says the proverb) will not be carried out of her house under four men. Much less will living men of wisdom and power be easily and quietly dispossessed of that share and interest in the things of Christ which long-continued usurpation hath deluded them into an imagination of being their own inheritance. This, then, being shortly to be effected, and the scale being ready to turn against the man of sin, notwithstanding his balancing it, in opposition to the witness of Jesus, with the weight and poise of earthly power; no wonder if heaven, earth, sea, and dry land, be shaken, in their giving place to the things that cannot be moved. God Almighty having called you forth, right honourable, at his entrance to the rolling up of the nation's heavens like a scroll,[2] to serve him in your generation in the high places of Armageddon,[3] you shall be sure not to want experience of that opposition which is raised against the great work of the Lord, which generally swells most against the visible instruments thereof.

And would to God you had only the devoted sons of Babel to contend withal,—

[1] Heb xii. 26, 27; Dan. vii. 27. "Ego nisi tumultus istos viderem, verbum Dei in mundo non esse dicerem."—Luth.

[2] Isa. xxxiv. 4, 5. [3] Rev. xvi. 16.

that the men of this shaking earth were your only antagonists,—that the malignity of the dragon's tail had had no influence on the stars of heaven, to prevail with them to fight in their courses against you![1] But "jacta est alea,"—the providence of God must be served, according to the discovery made of his own unchangeable will, and not the mutable interests and passions of the sons of men. For verily "the Lord of hosts hath purposed to pollute the pride of all glory, and to bring into contempt all the honourable of the earth," Isa. xxiii. 9.

The contradictions of sinners against all that walk in the paths of righteousness and peace, with the supportment which their spirits may receive (as being promised) who pursue those ways, notwithstanding those contradictions, are in part discovered in the ensuing sermon. The foundation of that whole transaction of things which is therein held out, in reference to the present dispensations of Providence,—being nothing but an entrance into the unravelling of the whole web of iniquity, interwoven of civil and ecclesiastical tyranny, in opposition to the kingdom of the Lord Jesus,—I chose not to mention. Neither shall I at present add any thing thereabout, but only my desire that it may be eyed as the granted basis of the following discourse. Only, by your very favourable acceptation of the making out those thoughts,—which were the hasty conception, and, like Jonah's gourd, the child of a night or two (which, with prayer for a rooting in the hearts of them to whom they were delivered, had certainly withered in their own leaves, had they not received warmth and moisture from your commands in general, and the particular desires of many of you, to give them a life of a few days longer),—I am encouraged to the annexing of a few lines, as a free-will offering to attend the following product of obedience.

Now, this shall not be as to the opposition which you do and shall yet farther meet withal; but as to the causes, real or pretended, which are held forth as the bottom of that contradiction wherewith on every side you are encompassed.

The things in reference whereunto your procedence is laden with such criminations as these sad days of recompense have found to be comets portending no less than blood, are first civil, then religious.

For the first, as their being beyond the bounds of my calling gives them sanctuary from being called forth to my consideration; so neither have I the least thoughts with Absalom of a more orderly carrying on of affairs, might my desires have any influence into their disposal. Waiting at the throne of grace, that those whom God hath intrusted with, and enabled for, the transaction of these things, may be directed and supported in their employment, is the utmost of my undertaking herein.

For the other, or religious things, the general interest I have in them as a Christian, being improved by the superadded title of a minister of the gospel (though unworthy the one name and the other), gives me not only such boldness as accrueth from enjoyed favour, but also such a right as will support me to plead concerning them before the most impartial judicature.

And this I shall do (as I said before) merely in reference to those criminations which are laid by conjectural presumptions on your honourable assembly, and made a cause of much of that opposition and contradiction you meet withal. Now, in particular, it is the toleration of all religions, or invented ways of worship,—wherein your constitutions are confidently antedated in many places of the nation; the thing itself, withal, being held out as the most enormous apprehension, and desperate endeavour, for the destruction of truth and godliness, that ever entered the thoughts of men professing the one and the other. The contest hereabout being "adhuc sub judice," and there being no doubt but that the whole matter, commonly phrased as above, hath (like other things) sinful and dangerous ex-

[1] Rev. xii. 4.

tremes, I deemed it not amiss to endeavour the pouring a little cold water upon the common flames which are kindled in the breasts of men about this thing. And who knows whether the words of a weak nothing may not, by the power of the Fountain of beings, give some light into the determination and establishment of a thing of so great concernment and consequence as this is generally conceived to be? What is in this my weak undertaking of the Lord, I shall beg of him that it may be received;—what is of myself, I beg of you that it may be pardoned. That God Almighty would give you to prove all things that come unto you in his way, and to hold fast that which is good, granting you unconquerable assistance in constant perseverance, is the prayer of,

Your devoted Servant

In our dearest Lord,

JOHN OWEN.

COGGESHALL, *Feb.* 28.

SERMON III.

RIGHTEOUS ZEAL ENCOURAGED BY DIVINE PROTECTION.

"Let them return unto thee; but return not thou unto them. And I will make thee unto this people a fenced brasen wall; and they shall fight against thee, but they shall not prevail against thee: for I am with thee to save thee, and to deliver thee, saith the LORD."—JER. xv. 19, 20.

THE words of my text having a full dependence upon, and flowing out from, the main subject-matter of the whole chapter, I must of necessity take a view thereof, and hold out unto you the mind of God contained therein, before I enter upon the part thereof chiefly intended. And this I shall do with very brief observations, that I may not anticipate myself from a full opening and application of the words of my text.

And this the rather are my thoughts led unto, because the whole transaction of things between the Lord and a stubbornly sinful nation, exceedingly accommodated to the carrying on of the controversy he is now pleading with that wherein we live, is set out (as we say) to the life therein.

Of the whole chapter there be these five parts:—

First, *The denunciation of fearful wasting, destroying judgments against Judah and Jerusalem*, verse 3, and so on to verse 10.

Secondly, *The procuring, deserving cause of these overwhelming calamities*, verses 4 and 6.

Thirdly, *The inevitableness of these judgments, and the inexorableness of the Lord as to the accomplishment of all the evils denounced*, verse 1.

Fourthly, *The state and condition of the prophet, with the frame and deportment of his spirit under those bitter dispensations of Providence*, verse 10, and 15–18.

Fifthly, *The answer and appearance of God unto him upon the making out of his complaint*, verses 11–14, and 19–21.

My text lieth in the last part, but yet with such dependence on the former as enforceth to a consideration of them.

First. There is the denunciation of fearful wasting, destroying judgments, to sinful Jerusalem, verse 2, and so onwards, with some interposed ejaculations concerning her inevitable ruin, as verses 5, 6.

Here's death, sword, famine, captivity, verse 2;—banishment, verse 4;—unpitied desolation, verse 5;—redoubled destruction, bereaving, fanning, spoiling, &c., verses 6–9. That universal devastation of the whole people which came upon them in the Babylonish captivity is the thing here intended,—the means of its accomplishment by particular plagues and judgments, in their several kinds (for the greater dread and terror), being at large annumerated,—the faithfulness of God, also, being made hereby to shine more clear in the dispersion of that people;—doing not only for the main what before he had threatened, but in particular executing the judgments recorded, Luke xxi. 24, &c.; Deut. xxviii. 15–57,—fulfilling hereby what he had devised, accomplishing the word he had commanded in the days of old, Lam. ii. 17.

That which hence I shall observe is only from the variety of these particulars, which are held out as the means of the intended desolation.

Observation. *God's treasures of wrath against a sinful people have sundry and various issues for the accomplishment of the appointed end.*

When God walks contrary to a people, it is not always in one path; he hath seven ways to do it, and will do it seven times, Lev. xxvi. 24. He strikes not always with one weapon, nor in one place. As there is with him ποικίλη χάρις, "manifold and various grace," 1 Pet. iv. 10, —love and compassion making out itself in choice variety, suited to our manifold indigencies; so there is ὀργὴ τεθησαυρισμένη, Rom. ii. 5, —stored, treasured wrath, suiting itself in its flowings out to the provocations of stubborn sinners.

The first emblem of God's wrath against man was a "flaming sword turning itself every way," Gen. iii. 24. Not only in one or two, but in all their paths he meeteth them with his flaming sword. As a wild beast in a net,[1] so are sinners under inexorable judgments; the more they strive, the more they are enwrapped and entangled; they shuffle themselves from under one calamity, and fall into another: "As if a man did flee from a lion, and a bear met him; or went into the house, and leaned his hand on the wall, and a serpent bit him," Amos v. 19. Oh! remove this one plague, saith Pharaoh.[2] If he can escape from under this pressure, he thinks he shall be free;—but when he fled from the lion, still the bear met him; and when he went into the house, the serpent bit him. And as the flaming sword turns every way, so God can put it into every thing. To those that

[1] Isa. li. 20. [2] Exod. x. 17.

cry, Give me a king, God can give him in his anger; and from those that cry, Take him away, he can take him away in his wrath, Hos. xiii. 10, 11.

Oh, that this might seal up instruction to our own souls! What variety of calamities have we been exercised withal, for sundry years! What Pharaoh-like spirits have we had under them! Oh, that we were delivered this once, and then all were well! How do we spend all our thoughts to extricate ourselves from our present pressures! If this hedge, this pit were passed, we should have smooth ground to walk on;—not considering that God can fill our safest paths with snares and serpents. Give us peace, give us wealth,—give us as we were, with our own, in quietness. Poor creatures! suppose all these desires were in sincerity, and not, as with the most they are, fair colours of foul and bloody designs; yet if peace were, and wealth were, and former things were, and God were not, what would it avail you? Cannot he poison your peace, and canker your wealth? and when you were escaped out of the field from the lion and the bear, appoint a serpent to bite you, leaning upon the walls of your own house? In vain do you seek to stop the streams, while the fountains are open; turn yourselves whither you will, bring yourselves into what condition you can, nothing but peace and reconciliation with the God of all these judgments can give you rest in the day of visitation. You see what variety of plagues are in his hand. Changing of condition will do no more to the avoiding of them, than a sick man's turning himself from one side of the bed to another; during his turning, he forgets his pain by striving to move,—being laid down again, he finds his condition the same as before.

This is the first thing,—we are under various judgments, from which by ourselves there is no deliverance.

Secondly. The second thing here expressed is, the procuring cause of these various judgments, set down, verse 4, "Because of Manasseh, son of Hezekiah king of Judah, for that which he did in Jerusalem."

The sins of Manasseh filled the ephah of Judah's wickedness, and caused the talent of lead to be laid on the mouth thereof.[1] Oftentimes in the relation of his story doth the Holy Ghost emphatically express this, that for his sin Judah should be destroyed, 2 Kings xxi. 11. Yea, when they had a little reviving under Josiah, and the bowels of the Lord began to work in compassion towards them; yet, as it were remembering the provocation of this Manasseh, he recalls his thoughts of mercy, 2 Kings xxiii. 26, 27. The deposing of divine and human things is oftentimes very opposite.[2] God himself proceeds with them in a diverse dispensation. In the spiritual body the members offend, and the Head is punished: "The iniquity of us all did meet on him,"

[1] Zech. v. 7, 8. [2] "Est quædam æmulatio divinæ rei, et humanæ."—Ter. Apol.

Isa. liii. In the civil politic body the head offends, and the members rue it: Manasseh sins, and Judah must go captive.

Three things present themselves for the vindication of the equity of God's righteous judgments, in the recompensing the sins of the king upon the people.

1. The *concurrence and influence* of the people's power into their rule and government:—they that set him up may justly be called to answer for his miscarriage. The Lord himself had before made the sole bottom of that political administration to be their own wills: "If thou wilt have a king, after the manner of the nations," Deut. xvii. 14; 1 Sam. viii. 7. Though for particulars, himself (according to his supreme sovereignty) placed in many [appointed many of the kings], by peculiar exemption; otherwise his providence was served by their plenary consent, or by such dispensation of things as you have related, 1 Kings xvi. 21, 22, "Then were the people of Israel divided into two parts: half of the people followed Tibni, the son of Ginath, to make him king; and half followed Omri. But the people that followed Omri prevailed against the people that followed Tibni; so Tibni died, and Omri reigned." Now, they who place men in authority to be God's vicegerents, do undertake to God for their deportment in that authority, and therefore may justly bear the sad effects of their sinful miscarriages.

2. Because, for fear of Manasseh's cruelty, or to flatter him in his tyranny for their own advantage, the greatest part of the people had *apostatized* from the ways and worship of Hezekiah, to comply with him in his sin; as at another time "they willingly walked after the commandment," Hos. v. 11. And this is plainly expressed, 2 Kings xxi. 9, "Manasseh seduced the people to do more evil than the nations." When kings turn seducers, they seldom want good store of followers. Now, if the blind lead the blind, both will, and both justly may, fall into the ditch. When kings command unrighteous things, and people suit them with willing compliance, none doubts but the destruction of them both is just and righteous. See verse 6 of this chapter.

3. Because the people, by virtue of their retained sovereignty, did not restrain him in his provoking ways. So Zuinglius, Artic. 42, "Qui non vetat, cum potest, jubet." When Saul would have put Jonathan to death, the people would not suffer him so to do, but delivered Jonathan, that he died not, 1 Sam. xiv. 45. When David proposed the reducing of the ark, his speech to the people was, "If it seem good unto you, let us send abroad to our brethren everywhere, that they may gather themselves to us: and all the congregation said that they would do so: because the thing was right in the eyes of all the people," 1 Chron. xiii. 2, 4. So they bargain with Rehoboam about their subjection, upon condition of a moderate rule, 1 Kings. xii. By

virtue of which power, also, they delivered Jeremiah from the prophets and priests that would have put him to death, Jer. xxvi. 16. And on this ground might they justly feed on the fruit of their own neglected duty. See Bilson on Obed., part iii. page 271.

Be it thus, or otherwise, by what way soever the people had their interest therein, certain it is, that for the sins of Manasseh, one way or other made their own, they were destroyed. And therefore, these things being written for our example, it cannot but be of great concernment to us to know what were those sins which wrapped up the people of God in irrevocable destruction. Now, these the Holy Ghost fully manifesteth in the story of the life and reign of this Manasseh, and they may all be reduced unto two chief heads.

(1.) False worship or superstition: "He built high places, made altars for Baal, and a grove, as did Ahab," 2 Kings xxi. 3.

(2.) Cruelty: "He shed innocent blood very much, till he had filled Jerusalem with blood from one end of it to another," verse 16.

Whether this cruelty be to be ascribed to his tyranny in civil affairs, and so the blood shed is called innocent because not of malefactors; or to his persecution in subordination to his false worship, instituted as before (as the pope and his adherents have devoured whole nations "in ordine ad spiritualia"), is not apparent; but this is from hence and other places most evident, that superstition and persecution, will-worship and tyranny, are inseparable concomitants.[1]

Nebuchadnezzar sets up his great image, and the next news you hear, the saints are in the furnace, Dan. iii. 20. You seldom see a fabric of human-invented worship, but either the foundation or topstone is laid in the blood of God's people. "The wisdom" (religion, or way of worship) "that is from above is first pure, then peaceable, gentle, easy to be entreated, full of mercy and good fruits, without partiality, and without hypocrisy," James iii. 17;—when the other is "earthly, sensual, devilish, bringing along envying, strife, confusion, and every evil work," verse 16. Persecution and blood is the genuine product of all invented worship. I might from hence name and pursue other observations, but I shall only name one, and proceed.

Observation. *When false worship, with injustice by cruelty, have possessed the governors of a nation, and wrapped in the consent of the greatest part of the people who have been acquainted with the mind of God; that people and nation, without unprecedented mercy, is obnoxious to remediless ruin.*

Those two are the Bel and dragon that, what by their actings, what by their deservings, have swallowed that ocean of blood which has flowed from the veins of millions slain upon the face of the earth. Give me the number of the witnesses of Jesus whose souls

[1] See the appendix at the end of this sermon.

under the altar cry for revenge against their false worshipping murderers[1] and the tale of them whose lives have been sacrificed to the insatiable ambition and tyranny of blood-thirsty potentates, with the issues of God's just vengeance on the sons of men for compliance in these two things; and you will have gathered in the whole harvest of blood, leaving but a few straggling gleanings upon other occasions. And if these things have been found in England, and the present administration with sincere humiliation do not run across to unravel this close-woven web of destruction, all thoughts of recovery will quickly be too late. And thus far sin and providence drive on a parallel.

Thirdly. The inevitableness of the desolation threatened, and the inexorableness of God in the execution of it, verse 1, is the third thing considerable: "Though Moses and Samuel stood before me, yet my mind could not be toward this people."

Should I insist upon this, it would draw me out unto Scripture evidences of a nation's travelling in sin beyond the line of God's patience, and so not to be exempted from ruin; but, instead thereof, I shall make it a part of my daily supplications, that they may be to our enemies, if God's enemies, and the interpretation of them to those that hate us.

In brief, the words contain an impossible supposition, and yet a negation of the thing for whose sake it is supposed. Moses and Samuel were men who, in the days of their flesh, offered up strong supplications, and averted many imminent judgments from a sinful people. As if the Lord should say, All that I can do, in such a case as this, I would grant at the intercession of Moses and Samuel, or others interceding in their spirit and zeal; but now the state of things is come to that pass, the time of treaty being expired, the black flag hung out, and the "decree having brought forth," Zeph. ii. 2, that, upon their utmost entreaty, it cannot, it shall not, be reversed.

Observation. *There is a time when sin grows ripe for ruin:* "For three transgressions, and for four, the Lord will not turn away the iniquity of a people," Amos i. 9.

When the sin of the Amorites hath filled the cup of vengeance, they must drink it, Gen. xv. 16. England, under several administrations of civil government, hath fallen twice, yea thrice, into nation-destroying sins. Providence hath once more given it another bottom; if you should stumble (which the Lord avert) at the same block of impiety and cruelty, there is not another sifting to be made, to reserve any grains from the ground. I doubt not but our three transgressions, and four, will end in total desolation. The Lord be your guide;—poor England lieth at stake.

[1] Rev. vi. 9, 10.

Observation. *The greatest difficulty that lieth in bringing of total destruction upon a sinful people, is in the interposition of Moses and Samuel.*

If Moses would but have stood out of the gap, and let the Almighty go, he had broken in upon the whole host of Israel, Exod. xxxii. 9, 10. And let it by the way be observed, of the spirit of Samuel, that when the people of God were most exorbitant, he crieth, "As for me, God forbid that I should sin against the LORD in ceasing to pray for you," 1 Sam. xii. 23. Scarce answered by those who, if their interest be not served, or at least their reason satisfied, will scarce yield a prayer for, yea, pour out curses against, their choicest deliverers. The Lord lay it not to their charge! For us, seeing that praying deliverers are more prevalent than fighting deliverers (it is, Though Moses and Samuel, not Gideon and Samson, stood before me), as some decay, let us gather strength in the Lord, that he may have never the more rest for their giving over, until he establish mount Zion a praise in the earth.

Fourthly. Come we now to the fourth thing in this chapter,—the prophet's state and condition, with the frame and deportment of his heart and spirit under these dispensations. And here we find him expressing two things of himself:—

1. *What he found from others*, verse 10.

2. *What he wrestled withal in his own spirit*, verses 15–18.

1. What he found from others. He telleth you it was cursing and reproach, &c.: "I have neither lent on usury, nor have men lent to me on usury, yet every one of them doth curse me," verse 10.

Now this return may be considered two ways.

(1.) *In itself:* "Every one (saith he) of this people doth curse me."

(2.) *In reference to his deportment:* "I have neither borrowed nor lent on usury, yet they curse me."

(1.) From the first, observe:—

Observation. *Instruments of God's greatest works and glory are oftentimes the chiefest objects of a professing people's cursings and revenges.*

The return which God's labourers meet withal in this generation is in the number of those things whereof there is none new under the sun. Men that, under God, deliver a kingdom, may have the kingdom's curses for their pains.

When Moses had brought the people of Israel out of bondage, by that wonderful and unparalleled deliverance, being forced to appear with the Lord for the destruction of Korah and his associates, who would have seduced the congregation to its utter ruin, he receives at length this reward of all his travail, labour, and pains,—all the congregation gathered themselves against him and Aaron, laying murder and sedition to their charge; telling them they had "killed the people of the LORD," Numb. xvi. 41, 42;—a goodly reward for all their travails. If God's works do not suit with the lusts, prejudices, and interests of men, they will labour to give his instruments the devil's wages. Let not upright hearts sink because they meet with thankless men. "Bona agere, et mala pati, Christianorum est." A man may have the blessing of God and the curse of a professing people at the same time. "Behold, I and the children whom God hath given me, are for signs and for wonders in Israel," Isa. viii. 18. "Cum ab hominibus damnamur, a Deo absolvimur."[1] Man's condemnation and God's absolution do not seldom meet upon the same persons, for the same things. If you labour to do the work of the Lord, pray think it not strange if among men curses be your reward, and detestation your wages.

(2.) *In reference to the prophet's deportment:* "He had neither lent, nor had any lent to him, upon usury." He was free from blame among them,—had no dealings with them in those things which are usually attended with reproaches; as he shows by an instance in usury, a thing that a long time hath *heard very ill.*

Observation. *Men every way blameless, and to be embraced in their own ways, are oftentimes abhorred and laden with curses for following the Lord in his ways.*

"Bonus vir Caius Sejus, sed malus quia Christianus." What precious men should many be, would they let go the work of God in this generation! No advantage against them but in the matter of their God;—and that is enough to have them to the lions, Dan. vi. 5. He that might be honoured for compassing the ends suiting his own worldly interest, and will cheerfully undergo dishonour for going beyond, to suit the design of God, hath surely some impression upon his spirit that is from above.

2. You have the prophet's deportment, and the frame of his spirit during those transactions between the Lord and that sinful people; and this he holds out, in many pathetical complaints, to be fainting, decaying, perplexed, weary of his burden, not knowing how to ease himself, as you may see at large, verses 15–18.

Observation. *In dark and difficult dispensations of providence, God's choicest servants are oftentimes ready to faint under the burden of them.*

How weary was David when he cried out in such a condition, "Oh that I had wings like a dove! for then would I fly away, and be at rest," Ps. lv. 6. Long had he waited for a desired issue of his perplexed state, and had perhaps oftentimes been frustrated of his hope of drawing to a period of his miseries; and now, finding one disappointment to follow on the neck of another, he is weary, and cries,

[1] Tertul. Apol.

What! nothing but this trouble and confusion still? "Oh that I had wings like a dove!"—a ship to sail to a foreign nation (or the like), there to be at peace. In the like strait another time, see what a miserable conclusion he draws of all his being exercised under the hand of God; Ps. lxxiii. 13, "Verily I have cleansed my heart in vain, and washed my hands in innocency." And again, Ps. cxvi. 11, he saith, in the perturbation of his mind, "All men are liars;"—that all the promises, all the encouragements, which in his way he had received from God, should fail of their accomplishment.

It is not with them as it was with that wicked king of Israel, who, being disappointed of peace and deliverance in his own time, cries out, "This evil is of the LORD; what should I wait for the LORD any longer?" 2 Kings vi. 33. The season of deliverance suited not his expectation; therefore he quite throweth off the Lord and his protection:—not unlike many among ourselves, whose desires and expectations being not satisfied in the closing of our distractions, according to the way which themselves had framed for the Lord to walk in, are ready to cast off his cause, his protection, to comply with the enemies of his name, "Si Deus homini non placuerit, Deus non erit." But it may be observed, that deliverance came not to that people until Jehoram was weary of waiting, and then instantly God gives it in. When God hath tired the patience of corrupted men, he will speak peace to them that wait for him. Thus it is not with the saints of God; only, being perplexed in their spirits, dark in their apprehensions, and fainting in their strength, they break out ofttimes into passionate complaints (as Jeremiah for a cottage in the wilderness), but yet for the main holding firm to the Lord.

And the reasons of this quailing are,—

(1.) *The weakness of faith, when the methods of God's proceedings are unfathomable to our apprehensions.* While men see the paths wherein the Lord walketh, they can follow him through some difficulties; but when that is hid from them, though providence so shut up all other ways that it is impossible God should be in them, yet if they cannot discern (so proud are they) how he goeth in that wherein he is, they are ready to faint and give over. God is pleased sometimes to make darkness his pavilion and his secret place. "A fire devours before him, and it is very tempestuous round about him," Ps. l. 3. When once God is attended with fire, darkness, and tempest, because we cannot so easily see him, we are ready to leave him. Now, this the Lord usually doth in the execution of his judgments, "Thy righteousness is like the great mountains; thy judgments are a great deep," Ps. xxxvi. 6. His righteousness, his kindness, is like a great mountain that is easy to be seen,—a man cannot overlook it, unless he wilfully shut his eyes; but his judgments are like the great deep. Who can look into the bottom of the sea, or know what is done in the depths thereof? God's works in their accomplishment are oftentimes so unsuited to the reasons and apprehensions of men, that very many who have been strong in their desires, and great in expectation of them, upon their bringing forth to light, have quite rejected and opposed them as none of his, because distant from what they had framed to themselves. It is evident from the gospel, that the people of the Jews were full of expectation and longing for the great work of the coming of the Messiah just at the season wherein he came; yet being come, because not accommodated to their pre-imaginations, they rejected him, as having neither form nor comeliness in him to be desired, Isa. liii. 2. And the prophet Amos telleth many who desired the day of the Lord, that that day should be darkness to them, and not light, Amos v. 18, 20. So in every generation many desirous of the accomplishment of God's work are shaken off from any share therein, by finding it unsuited to their reasons and expectations.

Now, when the Lord is pleased thus to walk in darkness, many not being able to trace him in his dispensations, are ready to lie down and sink under the burden. David seems to profess that he had nothing at such a time to uphold him but this, that God must be there, or nowhere. I had said (saith he) that it was in vain to walk as I do, but that I should have condemned the generation of thy children, Ps. lxxiii. 15. And truly God never leaves us without so much light, but that we may see clearly where he is not; and so, by recounting particulars, we may be rolled where he is, though his goings there be not so clear. Ask if God be in the counsels of men who seek themselves, and in the ways of those who make it their design to ruin the generation of the just. If you find him there, seek no farther; if not, let that give you light to discern where he makes his abode, that you turn not aside to the flocks of others.

(2.) *A reducing the works of Providence to inbred rules of their own.* But this I cannot pursue.

Be tender toward fainters in difficult seasons. If they leave waiting on the Lord because the evil is of him,—if they cast in their lot with the portion of the ungodly,—they will in the end perish in their gainsaying; but as for such as, what for want of light, what for want of faith, sit down and sigh in darkness, be not too hasty in laying farther burdens on them. When first the confederacy was entered into by the Protestant princes in Germany against Charles V., Luther himself for a season was bewildered, and knew not what to do, until, being instructed in the fundamental laws of the empire, he sat down fully in that undertaking, though the Lord gave it not the desired issue.[1] Our Saviour Christ asks, if, when he comes, he shall

[1] Sleid. Com., lib. viii.

find faith on the earth, Luke xviii. 8. It is his coming with the spirit of judgment and burning, a day of trial and visitation, he there speaks of. Now, what faith shall he want which will not be found in that day? Not the faith of adherence to himself for spiritual life and justification, but of actual closing with him in the things he then doth; that shall be rare,—many shall be staggered and faint in that day.

And thus, by the several heads of this chapter, have I led you through the very state and condition of this nation at this time.

First, *Variety of judgments* are threatened to us, and incumbent on us; as in the first part. Secondly, Of these, *false worship, superstition, tyranny, and cruelty,* lie in the bottom, as their procuring causes; which is the second. Thirdly, These, *if renewed under your hand,* will certainly bring inevitable ruin upon the whole nation; which is the third. Fourthly, All which make many precious hearts, what for want of light, what for want of faith, to fail, and cry out for "the wings of a dove;" which is the fourth.

Fifthly, I come, in the fifth place, to God's direction to you for the future, in this state and condition; which being spread in divers verses, as the Lord gives it to the prophet, I shall meddle with no more of it than is contained in the words which at our entrance I read unto you: "Let them return," &c.

In the words observe four things,—

I. God's *direction* to the prophet, and in him to all that do his work in such a season as this described: "Let them return to thee; return not thou to them."

II. Their *assistance and supportment* in pursuance of that direction: "I will make thee to this people a brasen fenced wall."

III. The *opposition,* with its success and issue, which in that way they should meet withal: "They shall fight against thee, but shall not prevail."

IV. Their *consolation and success* from the presence of the Lord: "For I am with thee to deliver thee," &c.

I. There is God's direction.

Many difficulties in this troublesome season was the prophet intricated withal. The people would not be prevailed with to come up to the mind of God;—they continuing in their stubbornness, the Lord would not be prevailed with to avert the threatened desolation. What now shall he do? To stand out against the bulk of the people suits not his earthly interest;—to couple with them answers not the discharge of his office;—to wait upon them any longer is fruitless;—to give up himself to their ways, comfortless. Hence his complaints, hence his moanings;—better lie down and sink under the burden, than always to swim against the stream of an unreformable multitude. In this strait the Lord comes in with his direction: "Let them return unto thee," &c. Keep thy station, perform thy duty, comply not with the children of backsliding. But whatever be the issue, if there be any closing wrought, let it be by working them off from their ways of folly. All condescension on thy part, where the work of God is to be done, is in opposition to him. If they return, embrace them freely; if not, do thy duty constantly.

That which is spoken immediately to the prophet, I shall hold out to all, acting in the name and authority of God, in this general proposition:—

Observation. *Plausible compliances of men in authority with those against whom they are employed, are treacherous contrivances against the God of heaven, by whom they are employed.*

If God be so provoked that he curseth him who doth his work negligently, what is he by them that do it treacherously?—when he gives a sword into the hands of men, and they thrust it into his own bowels, his glory and honour, those things so dear to him? He that is intrusted with it, and dares not do justice on every one that dares do injustice, is afraid of the creature, but makes very bold with the Creator. Prov. xxv. 2, "It is the glory of God to conceal a thing; but the honour of kings is to search out a matter." That which God aimeth to be glorious in, to manifest his attributes by, is the concealing and covering our iniquities in Christ; but if the magistrate will have glory, if he will not bring upon himself dishonour by dishonouring God, he is to search and find out the transgressions with whose cognizance he is intrusted, and to give unto them condign retribution. If the Lord curse them who come not forth to his help against the mighty, Judges v. 23—what is their due who, being called forth by him, do yet help the mighty against him? For a man to take part with the kingdom's enemies, is no small crime; but for a commission-officer to run from them by whom he is commissionated, to take part with the adversary, is death without mercy. Yet have not some in our days arrived at that stupendous impudence, that when, as private persons, they have declaimed against the enemies of the nation, and by that means got themselves into authority, they have made use of that authority to comply with and uphold those by an opposition to whom they got into their authority?—which is no less than an atheistical attempt to personate the Almighty, unto such iniquities as without his appearance they dare not own. But "he that justifieth the wicked, and he that condemneth the just, even they both are abomination to the LORD," Prov. xvii. 15; and not only to the Lord, but to good men also: "He that saith to the wicked, Thou art righteous; him shall the people curse, nations shall abhor him," Prov. xxiv. 24.

I speak only as to the general (for me, let all particulars find mercy), with a sad remembrance of the late workings of things amongst us, with those vile, sordid compliances, which grew upon the spirits of magistrates and ministers, with those whose garments were dyed with the blood of God's saints and precious ones,—as formerly they were called, for now these names are become terms of reproach. And would this complying went alone; but pretences and accusations must be found out against such as follow with them. When they begin to call darkness light, they will ere long call light darkness; by which means our eyes have seen men of their own accord laying down the weapons wherewith at first they fought against opposers, and taking up them which were used against themselves; as hath happened more than once to penmen, both in our own and our neighbour nation.

Now, this revolting from principles of religion and righteousness, to a compliance with any sinful way or person, is a treacherous opposition to the God of heaven. For,—

It cannot be done but by preferring the creature before the Creator, especially in those things which are the proximate causes of deviation.

Two principal causes I have observed of this crooked walking.

(1.) Fear.

(2.) That desire of perishing things which hath a mixture of covetousness and ambition.

The first maketh men wary what they do against men; the other maketh them weary of doing any thing for God, as whereby their sordid ends are not like to be accomplished.

(1.) Fear. When once magistrates begin to listen after "quid sequitur's," and so to withdraw from doing good for fear of suffering evil, paths of wickedness are quickly returned unto, and the authority of God despised. "Let this man go, and take heed of Cæsar," John xix. 12, did more prevail on Pilate's treacherous heart than all the other clamours of the Jews. Yea, was not the whole Sanhedrim swayed to desperate villany for fear the Romans should come and take away their kingdom? John xi. 48. When men begin once to distrust that God will leave them in the briers, to wrestle it out themselves (for unbelief lieth at the bottom of carnal fear), they quickly turn themselves to contrivances of their own for their own safety, their own prosperity; which commonly is by obliging those unto them by compliances, in an opposition to whom they might oblige the Almighty to their assistance. Surely they conclude he wants either truth or power to support them in his employment.

If a prince should send an ambassador to a foreign state, to treat about peace, or to denounce war; who, when he comes there, distrusting his master's power to make good his undertaking, should comply and wind up his interest with them to whom he was sent, suffering his sovereign's errand to fall to the ground,—would he not be esteemed as arrant a traitor as ever lived? And yet, though this be clipped coin among men, it is put upon the Lord every day as current.

From this principle of carnal fear and unbelief,—trembling for a man that shall die, and the son of man that shall be as grass, forgetting the Lord our maker, Isa. li. 12,—are all those prudential follies which exercise the minds of most men in authority, making them, especially in times of difficulties, to regulate and square all their proceedings by what suits their own safety and particular interests,—counselling, advising, working for themselves, quite forgetting by whom they are intrusted, and whose business they should do.

(2.) A desire of perishing things tempered with covetousness and ambition. Hence was the sparing of the fat cattle and of Agag by Saul, 1 Sam. xv.

When those two qualifications close on any, they are diametrically opposed to that frame which of God is required in them,—viz., "That they should be men fearing God, and hating covetousness." The first will go far, being only a contrivance for safety; but if this latter take hold of any, being a consultation to exalt themselves, it quickly carrieth them beyond all bounds whatsoever. The Lord grant that hereafter there may be no such complaints in this nation, or [that they] may be causeless, as have been heretofore,—viz., that we have poured out our prayers, jeoparded our lives, wasted our estates, spent our blood, to serve the lusts and compass the designs of ambitious, ungodly men!

The many ways whereby these things intrench upon the spirits of men, to bias them from the paths of the Lord, I shall not insist upon; it is enough that I have touched upon the obvious causes of deviation, and manifested them to be treacheries against the God of all authority.

Use. Be exhorted to beware of relapses, with all their causes and inducements, and to be constant to the way of righteousness; and this I shall hold out unto you in two particulars.

1. Labour to recover others, even all that were ever distinguished and called by the name of the Lord, from their late fearful returning to sinful compliances with the enemies of God and the nation. I speak not of men's persons, but of their ways. For three years this people have been eminently sick of the folly of backsliding, and without some special cordial are like to perish in it, as far as I know.

Look upon the estate of this people as they were differenced seven years ago, so for some continuance, and as they are now; and you shall find in how many things we have returned to others, and not one instance to be given of their return to us. That this may be clear, take some particulars.

(1.) In words and expressions;—those are "index animi." Turn them over, and you may find what is in the whole heart. "Out of the abundance of the heart the mouth speaketh." Now, is not that language, are not those very expressions which filled the mouths of the common adversaries only, grown also terms of reproach upon the tongues of men that suffered sometimes under them, and counted it their honour so to do? Hence that common exprobration, A parliament of saints, an army of saints, and such like derisions of God's ways,—now plentiful with them who sat sometimes and took sweet counsel with us. Ah! had it not been more for the honour of God that we had kept our station until others had come to us,—so to have exalted the name and profession of the gospel,—than that we should so return to them as to join with them in making the paths of Christ a reproach? Had it not been better for us, with Judah, to continue "ruling with God, and to be faithful with the saints," Hos. xi. 12, than to stand in the congregation of the mockers, and to sit in the seat of the scornful? What shall we say, when the saints of God "are as signs and wonders [to be spoken against] in Israel?" Isa. viii. 18. O that men would remember how they have left their first station, when themselves use those reproaches unto others which for the same cause themselves formerly bare with comfort! It is bitterness to consider how the gospel is scandalized by this woful return of ministers and people, by casting scriptural expressions by way of scorn on those with whom they were sometimes in the like kind companions of contempt. Surely in this we are returned to them, and not they to us.

(2.) In actions, and those,—

[1.] Of religion. Not only in opinion, but practice also, are we here under a vile return. We are become the lions, and the very same thoughts [are] entertained by us against others as were exercised towards ourselves. Are not others as unworthy to live upon their native soil in our judgments, as we ourselves in the judgments of them formerly over us? Are not groans for liberty, by the warmth of favour, in a few years hatched into attempts for tyranny? And for practice, what hold hath former superstition, in observing days and times, laid upon the many of the people again! Witness the late solemn superstition, and many things of the like nature.

[2.] For civil things, the closing of so many formerly otherwise engaged with the adverse party in the late rebellion, with the lukewarm deportment of others at the same time, is a sufficient demonstration of it. And may not the Lord justly complain of all this? "What iniquity have you seen in me or my ways, that you are gone far from me, and have walked after vanity, and are become vain?" Jer. ii. 5. "Why have you changed your glory for that which doth not profit," verse 11. "Have I been a dry heath or a barren wilderness to you?" Oh, that men should find no more sweetness in following the Lamb under wonderful protections, but that they should thus turn aside into every wilderness! What indignity is this to the ways of God! I could give you many reasons of it; but I have done what I intended,—a little hinted that we are a returning people, that so you might be exhorted to help for a recovery. And how shall that be?

2. By your own keeping close to the paths of righteousness. If you return not, others will look about again. This breach, this evil is of you; within your own walls was the fountain of our backsliding. Would you be the repairers of breaches, the restorers of paths for men to walk in?—do these two things:—

(1.) Turn not to the ways of such as the Lord hath blasted under your eyes. And these may be referred to three heads.

[1.] Oppression; [2.] Self-seeking; [3.] Contrivances for persecution.

[1.] Oppression. How detestable a crime it is in the eyes of the Almighty,—what effects it hath upon men, "making wise men mad!" Eccles. vii. 7,—how frequently it closeth in the calamitous ruin of the oppressors themselves,—are things known to all. Whether it hath not been exercised in this nation, both in general by unnecessary impositions, and in particular by unwarrantable pressures, let the mournful cries of all sorts of people testify. Should you now return to such ways as these, would not the anger of the Lord smoke against you? Make it, I beseech you, your design to relieve the whole, by all means possible, and to relieve particulars, yea, even of the adverse party where too much overborne. O let it be considered by you, that it be not considered upon you! I know the things you are necessitated to are not to be supported by the air. It is only what is unnecessary as to you, or insupportable as to others, that requires your speedy reforming; that so it may be said of you as of Nehemiah, chap. v. 14, 15. And for particulars (pray pardon my folly and boldness), I heartily desire a committee of your honourable House might sit once a-week, to relieve poor men that have been oppressed by men sometimes enjoying parliamentary authority.

[2.] Self-seeking,—when men can be content to lay a nation low, that they may set up themselves upon the heaps and ruins thereof. Have not some sought to advance themselves under that power which, with the lives and blood of the people, they have opposed; seeming to be troubled at former things, not because they were done, but because they were not done by them? But innocent blood will be found a tottering foundation for men to build their honours, greatness, and preferments upon. O return not in this unto any! If men serve themselves of the nation, they must expect that the nation will serve itself upon them. The best security you can possibly have that the people will perform their duty in obedience, is the witness of your own consciences that you have discharged your duty towards them,—in seeking their good by your own trouble, and not your own advantages in their trouble. I doubt not but that in this your practice makes the admonition a commendation; otherwise the word spoken will certainly witness against you.

[3.] Contrivances for persecution. How were the hearts of all men hardened like the nether millstone, and their thoughts did grind blood and revenge against their brethren! What colours, what pretences, had men invented to prepare a way for the rolling of their garments in the tears, yea, blood of Christians! The Lord so keep your spirits from a compliance herein, that withal the bow be not too much bent on the other side,—which is not impossible.

Be there a backsliding upon your spirit to these, or such-like things as these, the Lord will walk contrary to you; and were you "as the signet upon his hand," he would pluck you off.

(2.) Return not to the open enemies of our peace. I could here enlarge myself, to support your spirits in the work mentioned, Job xxix. 14, 15; but I must go on to the following parts of my text. And therefore,—

II. I pass from the direction given to the supportment and assistance promised: "I will make thee to this people a brasen and a fenced wall."

An implied objection, which the prophet might put in, upon his charge to keep so close to the rule of righteousness, is here removed. If I must thus abide by it, to execute whatsoever the Lord calls me out unto, not shrinking nor staggering at the greatest undertakings, what will become of me in the issue? will it not be destructive to stand out against a confirmed people? No, saith the Lord, it shall not be; "I will make thee," &c.

Observation. *God will certainly give prevailing strength and unconquerable defence unto persons constantly discharging the duties of righteousness, especially when undertaken in times of difficulty and opposition.*

The like engagement to this you have made to Ezekiel, chap. iii. 8, 9. Neither was it so to the prophets alone, but to magistrates also. When Joshua undertook the regency of Israel in a difficult time, he takes off his fear and diffidence with this very encouragement, Josh. i. 5. He saith, he will make them a wall,—the best defence against opposition; and that not a weak, tottering wall, that might easily be cast down, but a brasen wall, that must needs be impregnable. What engines can possibly prevail against a wall of brass? And to make it more secure, this brasen wall shall be fenced with all manner of fortifications and ammunition; so that the veriest coward in the world, being behind such a wall, may, without dread or terror, apply himself to that which he findeth to do. God will so secure the instruments of his glory against a backsliding people, in holding up the ways of his truth and righteousness, that all attempts against them shall be vain, and the most timorous spirit may be secure, provided he go not out of the Lord's way; for if they be found beyond the line, the brasen wall, they may easily be surprised. And, indeed, who but a fool would run from the shelter of a brasen wall, to hide himself in a little stubble? And yet so do all who run to their own wisdom, from the most hazardous engagement that any of the ways of God can possibly lead them unto. It is a sure word, and for ever to be rested upon, which the Lord gives in to Asa, 2 Chron. xv. 2, "The Lord is with you, while ye be with him." An unbiassed magistracy shall never want God's continued presence. Very Jeroboam himself receives a promise, upon condition of close walking with God in righteous administrations, of having a house built him like the house of David, 1 Kings xi. 38. What a wall was God to Moses in that great undertaking, of being instrumental for the delivery of Israel from a bondage and slavery of four hundred years' continuance? Pharaoh was against him, whom he had deprived of his sovereignty and dominion over the people. And what a provocation the depriving of sovereignty is unto potentates needs no demonstration: to the corruption of nature which inclines to heights and exaltations, in imitation of the fountain whence it flows, they have also the corruption of state and condition, which hath always inclined to absoluteness and tyranny. All Egypt was against him, as being by him visibly destroyed, wasted, spoiled, robbed, and at length smitten in the apple of the eye, by the loss of their first-born. And if this be not enough, that the king and people whom he opposed were his enemies,—the very people for whose sakes he set himself to oppose the others, they also rise up against him, yea, seek to destroy him. One time they appeal to God for justice against him, Exod. v. 21, "The LORD look upon you, and judge." They appeal to the righteous God to witness that he had not fulfilled what he promised them,—to wit, liberty, safety, and freedom from oppression; but that rather by his means their burdens were increased: and in this they were so confident (like some amongst us), that they appealed unto God for the equity of their complaints. Afterward, being reduced to a strait, such as they could not see how possibly they should be extricated from, without utter ruin (like our present condition in the apprehension of some), they cry out upon him for the whole design of bringing them into the wilderness, and affirm positively, that though they had perished in their former slavery, it had been better for them than to have followed him in this new and dangerous engagement, Exod. xiv. 11, 12;—that generation being, as Calvin observes,[1] so inured to bondage, that they were altogether unfit to bear with the workings and pangs of their approaching liberty. Afterward, do they want drink?—Moses is the cause. Do they want meat?—this Moses would starve them, Exod. xv. 24, xvi. 7. He could not let them alone by the flesh-pots of Egypt; for this they are ready to stone him, Exod. xvii. 3. At this day, have we too much rain, or too short a harvest?—it is laid on the shoulders of the present government. It was no otherwise of old. At length this people came to that height, as, being frightened by the opposition they heard of and framed to themselves in that place whither Moses would carry them, they presently enter into a conspiracy and revolt, consulting to cast off his government, and choose new commanders, and with a violent hand to return to their former condition, Numb. xiv. 4,—an attempt as frequent as fruitless among ourselves. When this would not do, at length, upon the occasion of taking off Korah and his company, they assemble themselves together, and lay, not imprisonment, but murder to his charge; and that of "the people of the Lord," Numb. xvi. 41. Now, what was the issue of all those oppositions? what effect had they? how did the power of Pharaoh, the revenge of Egypt, the backsliding of Israel prevail? Why, God made this one Moses a fenced brasen wall to them all; he was never in the least measure prevailed against;—so long as he was with God, God was with him, no matter who was against him.

One thing only would I commend to your consideration,—viz., that this Moses, thus preserved, thus delivered, thus protected, falling into one deviation, in one thing, from close following the Lord, was taken off from enjoying the closure and fruit of all his labour, Numb. xx. 12. Otherwise he followed the Lord in a difficult season, and did not want unconquerable supportment. Take heed of the smallest turning aside from God. Oh! lose not the fruit of all your labour, for self, for a lust, or any thing that may turn you aside!

Now, the Lord will do this,—

1. Because of *his own engagement.*

2. For *our encouragement.*

1. Because of his own engagement. And that is twofold.

(1.) Of truth and fidelity.

(2.) Of honour and glory.

(1.) His truth and veracity is engaged in it. "Those that honour him, he will honour," 1 Sam. ii. 30. If men honour him with obedience, he will honour them with preservation. "He will be with them, while they are with him," 2 Chron. xv. 2. While they are with him in constancy of duty, he will be with them to keep them in safety. He will never leave them, nor forsake them, Josh. i. 5. "No

[1] In Numb. cap. iv.

weapon that is formed against them shall prosper," Isa. liv. 17. Now, God is never as the waters that fail to any that upon his engagements wait for him; he will not shame the faces of them that put their trust in him. Why should our unbelieving spirits charge that upon the God of truth which we dare not impute to a man that is a worm, a liar? Will a man fail in his engagement unto him who, upon that engagement, undertakes a difficult employment for his sake? The truth is, it is either want of sincerity in our working, or want of faith in dependence, that makes us at any time come short of the utmost tittle that is in any of the Lord's engagements.

[1.] We want sincerity, and do the Lord's work, but with our own aims and ends, like Jehu;—no wonder if we be left to ourselves for our wages and defence.

[2.] We want faith, also, in the Lord's work,—turn to our own counsels for supportment: no marvel if we come short of assistance. "If we will not believe, we shall not be established."

Look to sincerity in working, and faith in dependence; God's truth and fidelity will carry him out to give you unconquerable supportment:—deflexion from these will be your destruction. You that are working on a new bottom, work also on new principles; put not new wine into old bottles, new designs into old hearts.

(2.) He is engaged in point of honour. If they miscarry in his way, what will he do for his great name? Yea, so tender is the Lord herein of his glory, that when he hath been exceedingly provoked to remove men out of his presence, yet because they have been called by his name, and have visibly held forth a following after him, he would not suffer them to be trodden down, lest the enemy should exalt themselves, and say, Where is now their God? They shall not take from him the honour of former deliverances and protections. In such a nation as this, if the Lord now, upon manifold provocations, should give up parliament, people, army, to calamity and ruin, would not the glory of former counsels, successes, deliverances, be utterly lost? would not men say it was not the Lord, but chance that happened to them?

2. For our encouragement. The ways of God are oftentimes attended with so many difficulties, so much opposition, that they must be embraced merely because his; no other motive in the world can suit them to us. I mean, for such as keep them immixed from their own carnal and corrupt interests. Now, because the Lord will not take off the hardship and difficulty of them, lest he should not have the honour of carrying on his work against tumultuating opposition, he secures poor weaklings of comfortable assistance and answerable success, lest his work should be wholly neglected. It is true, the Lord, as our sovereign master, may justly require a close labouring in all his ways without the least sweetening endearments put upon them,

only as they are his, whose we are, who hath a dominion over us. But yet, as a tender father,—in which relation he delights to exercise his will towards his own in Christ,—he pitieth our infirmities, knowing that we are but dust; and therefore, to invite us into the dark, into ways laboursome and toilsome to flesh and blood, he gives us in this security,—that we shall be as a fenced brasen wall to the opposing sons of men.

Use 1. To discover the vanity and folly of all opposition to men called forth of God to his work, and walking in his ways. Would you not think him mad that should strike with his fist, and run with his head against a fenced brasen wall, to cast it down? Is he like to have any success, but the battering of his flesh, and the beating out of his brains? What do the waves obtain by dashing themselves with noise and dread against a rock, but their own beating to pieces? What prevails a man by shooting his arrows against the sky, but a return upon his own head? Nor is the most powerful opposition to the ways of God like to meet with better success. God looks no otherwise upon opposers than you would do upon a man attempting to thrust down a fenced brasen wall with his fingers. Therefore it is said, that in their proudest attempts, strongest assaults, deepest counsels, combinations, and associations, "he laughs them to scorn," derides their folly, contemns their fury, lets them sweat in vain, until their day be come, Ps. ii. How birthless in our own, as well as other generations, have been their swelling conceptions! What, then, is it that prevails upon men to break through so many disappointments against the Lord as they do?—doubtless that of Isa. xxiii. 9, "Surely the LORD of hosts hath purposed it, to stain the pride of all glory, and to bring into contempt all the honourable of the earth." God gives up men unto it, that he may leave no earthly glory or honour without pollution or contempt. And therefore hath opposition in our days been turned upon so many hands, that God might leave no glory without contempt: yet with this difference, that if the Lord will own them, he will recover them from their opposition; as has happened of late to the ministry of one, and will happen ere long to the ministry of another nation. When the Lord hath a little stained the pride of their glory, they shall be brought home again by the spirit of judgment and burning; but if he own them not, they shall perish under the opposition. And when it hath been wheeled about on all sorts of men, the end will be.

Use 2. "Be wise now therefore, O ye [*rulers;*] be instructed, ye judges of the earth; serve the LORD with fear, and rejoice with trembling," Ps. ii. 10, 11. See whence your assistance cometh; see where lie the hills of your salvation, and say, "Asshur shall not save us; we will not ride upon horses; neither will we say any more to the work of our hands, Ye are our gods: for in thee the fatherless findeth mercy," Hos. xiv. 3. It is God alone who is "a sun and shield: his ways do good to the upright in heart." Behold, here is a way to encompass England with a brasen wall: let the rulers of it walk in right ways with upright hearts. Others have been careful to preserve the people to them, and the city to them; oh, be you careful to preserve your God unto you! He alone can make you a fenced wall; if he departs, your wall departs, your shade departs. Give me leave to insist a little on one particular, which I choose out among many others. When God leads out his people to any great things, the angel of his presence is still among them. See at large, Exod. xxiii. 20–22. The angel of the covenant, in whom is the name of God, that hath power of pardoning or retaining transgressions,—Jesus Christ, the angel that redeemeth his out of all their troubles, Gen. xlviii. 16,—he is in the midst of them, and amongst them. And God gives this special caution, if we would have his assistance, that we should beware of him, and obey him, and provoke him not. Would you, then, have God's assistance continued?—take heed of provoking the angel of his presence: provoke him not by slighting of his ways; provoke him not by contemning his ordinances: if you leave him to deal for himself, he will leave you to shift for yourselves. What though his followers are at some difference[1] (the best knowing but in part) about the administration of some things in his kingdom; the envious one having also sown some bitter seeds of persecution, strife, envy, and contention among them?—what though some poor creatures are captivated by Satan, the prince of pride, to a contempt of all his ordinances,—whose souls I hope the Lord will one day free from the snare of the devil;—yet I pray give me leave (it is no time to contest or dispute it) to bear witness in the behalf of my Master to this one truth, that if by your own personal practice and observance, your protection, countenance, authority, laws, you do not assert, maintain, uphold the order of the gospel, and administration of the ordinances of Christ,—notwithstanding the noise and clamours of novel fancies, which, like Jonah's gourd, have sprung up in a night, and will wither in a day,—you will be forsaken by the angel of God's presence, and you will become an astonishment to all the inhabitants of the earth. And herein I do not speak as one hesitating or dubious, but positively assert it, as the known mind of God, and whereof he will not suffer any long to doubt, Ps. ii. 12.

Use 3. "Strengthen ye the weak hands, and confirm the feeble knees. Say to them that are of a fearful heart, Be strong, fear not: behold, your God will come with vengeance, even God with a recompense; he will come and save you," Isa. xxxv. 3, 4. Let the most

[1] See the appendix about Toleration.

weak and fearful, the fainting heart, the trembling spirit, and the doubting mind, know, that full and plenary security, perfect peace, attends the upright in the ways of God. You that are in God's way, do God's work, and take this cordial for all your distempers,—Return not to former provoking ways, and he will make you "a fenced brasen wall."

And so I come to the third thing which I proposed to consider,—

III. The opposition which men cleaving to the Lord in all his ways shall find, with the issue and success of it: "They shall fight against thee; but shall not prevail."

The words may be considered either as a *prediction* depending on God's prescience of what will be; or a *commination* from his just judgment of what shall be.

In the first sense the Lord tells the prophet, from the corruption, apostasy, stubbornness of that people, what would come to pass;—in the second, what, for their sins and provocations, by his just judgment, should come to pass. Time will not allow me to handle the words in both acceptations, wherefore I shall take up the latter only,—viz., that it is a commination of what shall be for the farther misery of that wretched people; they shall judicially be given up to a fighting against him.

Observation. *God oftentimes gives up a sinful people to a fruitless contention and fighting with their only supporters and means of deliverance.*

Jeremiah had laboured with God for them, and with them for God, that, if possible, peace being made, they might be delivered; and, to consummate their sins, they are given up to fight against him.

I cannot now insist upon particular instances; consult the history of the church in all ages,—you shall find it continually upon all occasions verified. From the Israelites opposing Moses, to the Ephraimites' contest with Jephthah, the rejecting of Samuel, and so on, to the kings of the earth giving their power to the beast to wage war with the Lamb, with the inhabitants of the world combining against the witnesses of Christ, is this assertion held out. In following story, no sooner did any plague or judgment break out against the Roman empire, but instantly, "Christianos ad leones;"—their fury must be spent upon them who were the only supporters of it from irrecoverable ruin.

Now the Lord doth this,—

1. *To seal up a sinful people's destruction.* Eli's sons hearkened not, "because the Lord would slay them," 1 Sam. ii. 25. When God intends ruin to a people, they shall walk in ways that tend thereunto. Now, is there a readier way for a man to have a house on his head, than by pulling away the pillars whereby it is supported? If by

Moses standing in the gap the fury of the Lord be turned away, certainly if the people contend to remove him, their desolation sleepeth not. When, therefore, the Lord intends to lay cities waste without inhabitants, and houses without men, to make a land utterly desolate; the way of its accomplishment is by making the hearts of the people fat, and their ears heavy, and shutting their eyes, that they should not see and attend to the means of their recovery, Isa. vi. 10, 11,—so gathering in his peace and mercies from a provoking people, Jer. xvi. 5.

2. *To manifest his own power and sovereignty* in maintaining a small handful, ofttimes a few single persons, a Moses, a Samuel, two witnesses, against the opposing rage of a hardened multitude. If those who undertake his work and business in their several generations should have withal the concurrent obedience and assistance of others whose good is intended, neither would his name be so seen nor his ways so honoured as now, when he bears them up against all opposition. Had not the people of this land been given up (many of them) to fight against the deliverers of the nation, and were it not so with them even at this time, how dark would have been the workings of providence which now, by wrestling through all opposition, are so conspicuous and clear! When, then, a people, or any part of a people, have made themselves unworthy of the good things intended to be accomplished by the instruments of righteousness and peace, the Lord will blow upon their waves, that with rage and fury they shall dash themselves against them; whom he will strengthen with the munition of rocks, not to be prevailed against. So that God's glory and their own ruin lie at the bottom of this close working of providence, in giving up a sinful people to a fruitless contending with their own deliverers, if ever they be delivered.

Obj. But is not a people's contending with the instruments by whom God worketh amongst them, and for them, a sin and provocation to the eyes of his glory? How, then, can the Lord be said to give them up unto it?

Ans. Avoiding all scholastical discourses, as unsuited to the work of this day, I shall briefly give in unto you how this is a sinful thing, yet sinners are given up unto it without the least extenuation of their guilt, or colour for charge on the justice and goodness of God.

(1.) Then, to give up men unto a thing in itself sinful is no more but so to dispose and order things, that sinners may exercise and draw out their sinful principles in such a way. Of this that the Lord doth the Scripture is full of examples, and hath testimonies innumerable. That herein the Holy One of Israel is no ways co-partner with the guilt of the sons of men, will appear by observing the difference of these several agents in these four things:—

[1.] The *principle* by which they work.
[2.] The *rule* by which they proceed.
[3.] The *means* which they use.
[4.] The *end* at which they aim.

[1.] The principle of operation in God is his own sovereign will and good pleasure. He doth whatsoever he pleaseth, Ps. cxv. 3. He saith his purpose shall stand, and he will do all his pleasure, Isa. xlvi. 10. He hath mercy on whom he will have mercy, and whom he will he hardeneth, Rom. ix. 18; giving no account of his matters, Job xxxiii. 13. This our Saviour rendereth the only principle and reason of his hidden operations, "O Father, so it seemed good in thy sight," Matt. xi. 26. His sovereignty in doing what he will with his own, as the potter with his clay, is the rise of his operations; so that whatever he doth, "who will say unto him, What doest thou?" Job ix. 12. "Shall the thing formed say unto him that formed it, Why hast thou made me thus?" Rom. ix. 20. And hence two things will follow:—

1*st*. That what he doth is just and righteous; for so must all acts of supreme and absolute dominion be.

2*dly*. That he can be author of nothing but what hath existence and being itself; for he works as the fountain of beings. This sin hath not. So that though every action, whether good or bad, receives its specification from the working of providence,—and to that is their existence in their several kinds to be ascribed,—yet an evil action, in the evilness of it, depends not upon divine concourse and influence; for good and evil make not sundry kinds of actions, but only a distinction of a subject in respect of its adjuncts and accidents.

But now the principle of operation in man is *nature* vitiated and corrupted;—I say nature, not that he worketh naturally, being a free agent, but that these faculties, will and understanding, which are the principles of operation, are in nature corrupted, and from thence can nothing flow but evil. "An evil tree bringeth forth evil fruit." "Men do not gather figs from thistles." "A bitter fountain sends not forth sweet waters." "Who can bring a clean thing out of an unclean?" If the fountain be poisoned, can the streams be wholesome? What can you expect of light and truth from a mind possessed with vanity and darkness? what from a will averted from the chiefest good, and fixed upon present appearances? what from a heart the figment of whose imagination is only evil?

[2.] Consider the difference in the *rule of operation*. Every thing that works hath a rule to work by;—this is called a law. In that thing which to man is sinful, God worketh as it is a thing only; man, as it is a sinful thing. And how so? Why, every one's sin is his aberration from his rule of operation or working. Ἁμαρτάνειν is "aberrare à scopo:" to sin is not to collime aright at the end proposed. 'Η ἁμαρτία ἐστὶν ἡ ἀνομία is a most exact definition of it. Irregularity is its form, if it may be said to have a form; a privation's form is deformity. Look, then, in any action wherein an agent exorbitates from its rule,—that is sin. Now, what is God's rule in operation? His own infinite, wise will alone. He takes neither motive, rise, nor occasion for any internal acts from any thing without himself; he doth whatever he pleaseth, Ps. cxv. 3; he "worketh all things according to the counsel of his own will," Eph. i. 11;—that is his own law of operation, and the rule of righteousness unto others:—working them agreeably to his own will, which he always must do, he is free from the obliquity of any action. What, now, is the rule of the sons of men? Why, the revealed will of God, "Revealed things belong to us, that we may do them," Deut. xxix. 29. God's revealed will is the rule of our walking, our working; whatever suits not, answers not this, is evil. "Sin is the transgression of the law," 1 John iii. 4. Here, then, comes in the deformity, the obliquity, the ataxy, of any thing. God works, and man worketh; those agents have several rules. God works according to his rule; hence the action is good, as an action;—man deviates from his rule; hence it is sinful, in respect of its qualifications and adjuncts. Man writes fair letters upon a wet paper, and they run all into one blot; not the skill of the scribe, but the defect in the paper, is the cause of the deformity. He that makes a lame horse go, is the cause of his going; but the defect in his joints is the cause of his going lame. The sun exhales a steam from the dunghill; the sun is the cause of the exhalation, but the dunghill of the unwholesome savour. The first cause is the proper cause of a thing's being, but the second of its being evil.

[3.] Consider the *several operations and actings* of God and man; for instance, in a rebellious people's fighting against their helpers under him.

Now, the acts of God herein may be referred to six heads.

1*st.* A continuance of the creature's being and life;—"upholding him by the word of his power," Heb. i. 3, when he might take him off in a moment;—"enduring them with much long-suffering," Rom. ix. 22, when he might cut them off, as he did the opposers of Elijah, with "fire from heaven," 2 Kings i. 12.

2*dly.* A continuance of power of operation to them, when he could make their hands to wither, like Jeroboam's, when they go about to strike, 1 Kings xiii. 4; or their hearts to die within them, like Nabal's, when they intend to be churlish, 1 Sam. xxv. 37. But he raiseth them up, or makes them to stand, that they may oppose, Rom. ix. 17.

3*dly.* Laying before them a suitable object for the drawing forth their corruption unto opposition, giving them such helpers as shall in many things cross their lusts, and exasperate them thereunto,—as Elijah, a man of a fiery zeal, for a lukewarm Ahab.

4thly. Withholding from them that effectual grace by which alone that sin might be avoided,—a not actually keeping them from that sin by the might of his Spirit and grace. That alone is effectual grace which is actual. "He suffers them to walk in their own ways."

And this the Lord may do,—

(1*st.*) In respect of them *judicially,*—they deserve to be forsaken: Ahab is left to fill up the measure of his iniquities,—"Add iniquity to iniquity," Ps. lxix. 27.

(2*dly.*) *In respect of himself, by way of sovereignty,*—doing what he will with his own,—hardening whom he will, Rom. ix. 18.

5thly. He positively sends upon their understandings that which the Scripture sets out under the terms of blindness, darkness, folly, delusion, slumber, a spirit of giddiness, and the like: the places are too many to rehearse. What secret actings in and upon the minds of men,—what disturbing of their advices,—what mingling of corrupt affections with false, carnal reasonings,—what givings up to the power of darkness, in Satan the prince thereof,—this judicial act doth contain, I cannot insist upon. Let it suffice, God will not help them to discern, yea, he will cause that they shall not discern, but hide from their eyes the things that concern their peace, and so give them up to contend with their only helpers.

6thly. Suitably upon the will and affections he hath several acts,—obfirming the one in corruption, and giving up the other to vileness, Rom. i. 24, 26, until the heart become thoroughly hardened, and the conscience seared; not forcing the one, but leaving it to follow the judgment of practical reason,—which being a blind, yea, a blinded guide, whither can it lead a blind follower, but into the ditch?—not defiling the other with infused sensuality, but provoking them to act according to inbred, native corruption, and by suffering frequent vile actings to confirm them in ways of vileness.

Take an instance of the whole: God gives helpers and deliverers to a sinful people; because of their provocations, some or all of them shall not taste of the deliverance by them to be procured. Wherefore, though he sustains their lives in being, whereby they might have opportunity to know his mind and their own peace; yet he gives them a power to contend with their helpers, causing their helpers to act such things as, under consideration of circumstances, shall exceedingly provoke these sinners. Being so exasperated and provoked, the Lord, who is free in all his dispensations, refuseth to make out to them that healing grace whereby they might be kept from a sinful opposition: yea, being justly provoked, and resolved that they should not taste of the plenty to come, he makes them foolish and giddy in their reasonings and counsels,—blinds them in their understandings, that they shall not be able to discern plain and evident things, tending to their own good, but in all their ways shall err like a drunken man in his vomit; whence, that they may not be recovered, because he will destroy them, he gives in hardness and obstinacy upon their hearts and spirits, leaving them to suitable affections, to contend for their own ruin.

Now, what are the ways and methods of sinful man's working in such opposition, would be too long for me to declare; what prejudices are erected, what lusts pursued, what corrupt interests acted and followed,—how self is honoured, what false pretences coined, how God is slighted,—if I should go about to lay open, I must look into the hell of these times, than which nothing can be more loathsome and abominable. Let it suffice, that sinful self, sinful lusts, sinful prejudices, sinful blindness, sinful carnal fears, sinful corrupt interests, sinful fleshly reasonings, sinful passions, and vile affections, do all concur in such a work, are all woven up together in such a web.

[4.] See the *distance of their aims.* God's aim is only the manifestation of his own glory—than which nothing but himself is so infinitely good, nothing so righteous that it should be [his aim]—and this by the way of goodness and severity, Rom. xi. 22;—goodness, in faithfulness and mercy, preserving his who are opposed, whereby his glory is exceedingly advanced;—severity towards the opposers, that, by a sinful, cursed opposition, they may fill up the measure of their iniquities, and receive this at the hand of the Lord, that they lie down in sorrow,—wherein also he is glorious.

God forbid that I should speak this of all that for any time, or under any temptation, may be carried to an opposition, in any kind or degree, to the instruments of God's glory amongst them. Many for a season may do it, and yet belong to God, who shall be recovered in due time. It is only of men given up, forsaken, opposing all the appearances of God with his saints and people in all his ways, of whom I speak.

Now, what are the ends of this generation of fighters against this brasen wall? and how distant from those of the Lord's! "They consult to cast him down from his excellency" whom God will exalt, Ps. lxii. 4. They think not as the Lord, neither doth their heart mean so; but it is in their heart to destroy and to cut off, Isa. x. 7. To satisfy their own corrupt lusts, ambition, avarice, revenge, superstition, contempt of God's people *because* his, hatred of the yoke of the Lord, fleshly interests,—even for these, and such like ends as these, is their undertaking.

Thus, though there be a concurrence of God and man in the same thing, yet, considering the distance of their principles, rules, actings, and ends, it is apparent that man doth sinfully what the Lord doth judicially; which being an answer to the former objection, I return to give in some uses to the point.

Use 1. Let men, constant, sincere, upright in the ways of God, especially in difficult times, know what they are to expect from many, yea, the most of the generation, whose good they intend, and among whom they live;—opposition and fighting are like to be their lot;—and that not only *it will be so* because of men's lusts, corruptions, prejudices, but also *it shall be so* from God's righteous judgments against a stubborn people. *They* harden their hearts that *it may be so*, to compass their ends; and *God* hardens their hearts that *it shall be so*, to bring about his aims. They *will* do it, to execute their revenge upon others; they *shall* do it, to execute God's vengeance upon themselves. This may be for consolation, that in their contending there is nothing but the wrath of man against them whom they oppose (which God will restrain, or cause it to turn to his praise); but there is the wrath of God against themselves,—which who can bear? This, then, let all expect who engage their hearts to God, and follow the Lamb whithersoever he goeth.

Men walking in the sincerity of their hearts are very apt to conceive that all sheaves should bow to theirs,—that all men should cry, "Grace, grace," to their proceedings. Why should any oppose? "Quid meruere?" Alas! the more upright they are, the fitter for the Lord by them to break a gainsaying people. Let men keep close to those ways of God whereto protection is annexed, and let not their hearts fail them because of the people of the land. The storm of their fury will be like the plague of hail in Egypt; it smote only the cattle that were in the field;—those who, upon the word of Moses, drove them into the houses, preserved them alive. If men wander in the field of their own ways, of self-seeking, oppression, ambition, and the like, doubtless the storm will carry them away; but for those who keep house, who keep close to the Lord, though it may have much noise, terror, and dread with it, it shall not come nigh them. And if the Lord, for causes best known, known only to his infinite wisdom, should take off any Josiahs in the opposition, he will certainly effect two things by it.

(1.) To give them rest and peace.

(2.) To further his cause and truth, by drawing out the prayers and appeals of the residue; and this living they valued above their lives.

All you, then, that are the Lord's workmen, be always prepared for a storm. Wonder not that men see not the ways of the Lord, nor the judgments of our God;—many are blinded. Admire not that they will so endlessly engage themselves into fruitless oppositions;—they are hardened. Be not amazed that evidence of truth and righteousness will not affect them;—they are corrupted. But this do; Come, and enter into the chambers of God, and you shall be safe until this whole indignation be overpast. I speak of all them, and only them, who follow the Lord in all his ways with upright hearts and single minds: if the Lord will have you to be a rock and a brasen wall for men to dash themselves against, and to break in pieces, though the service be grievous to flesh and blood, yet it is his, whose you are. Be prepared, the wind blows,—a storm may come.

Use 2. Let men set upon opposition make a diligent inquiry, whether there be no hand in the business but their own? whether their counsels be not leavened with the wrath of God, and their thoughts mixed with a spirit of giddiness, and themselves carried on to their own destruction? Let me see the opposer of the present ways of God, who, upon his opposition is made more humble, more self-denying, more empty of self-wisdom, more fervent in supplications and waiting upon God, than formerly; and I will certainly blot him out of the roll of men judicially hardened. But if therewith men become also proud, selfish, carnally wise, revengeful, furious upon earthly interests, full, impatient; doubtless God is departed, and an evil spirit from the Lord prevaileth on them. O that men would look about them before it be too late; see the Lord disturbing them, before the waves return upon them; know that they may pull down some antics that make a great show of supporting the church, and yet indeed are pargeted posts supported by it! The foundation is on a rock that shall not be prevailed against.

Use 3. See the infinite wisdom and sovereignty of Almighty God, that is able to bring light out of darkness, and to compass his own righteous judgments by the sinful advisings and undertakings of men. Indeed the Lord's sovereignty and dominion over the creature doth not in any thing more exalt itself, than in working in all the reasonings, debates, consultations of men, to bring about his own counsels through their free workings. That men should use, improve their wisdom, freedom, choice, yea, lusts, not once thinking of God; yet all that while do his work more than their own,—"this is the Lord's doing, and it is marvellous in our eyes."

Of the last part of my text I shall not speak at all; neither indeed did I intend.

OF TOLERATION;

AND

THE DUTY OF THE MAGISTRATE ABOUT RELIGION.

THE times are busy, and we must be brief. Prefaces for the most part are at all times needless,—in these, troublesome. Mine shall only be, that ἄνευ προοιμίων καὶ παθῶν, "without either preface or solemnity," I will fall to the business in hand. The thing about which I am to deal is commonly called, Toleration in Religion, or toleration of several religions. The way wherein I shall proceed is not by contest, thereby to give occasion for the reciprocation of a saw of debate with any; but by the laying down of such positive observations, as being either not apprehended or not rightly improved by the most, yet lie at the bottom of the whole difference between men about this business, and tend in themselves to give light unto a righteous and equitable determination of the main thing contended about. And lastly, herein for method I shall first consider the grounds upon which that non-toleration whereunto I cannot consent has been, and is still, endeavoured to be supported; which I shall be necessitated to remove,—

I. By considering the arguments brought from holy writ;

II. From some other general observations. And then in order,—

III. I shall assert the positive truth, as to the substance of the business under contest.

All in these ensuing observations.

I. As to the first of these,—

1. Although the expressions of "toleration," and "non-toleration," wherewith the thing in controversy is vested, do seem to cast the affirmative upon them who plead for a forbearance in things of religion towards dissenting persons, yet the truth is, they are purely upon the negation, and the affirmative lies fully on the other part; and so the weight of proving, which ofttimes is heavy, lies on their shoulders. Though non-toleration sound like a negation, yet punishment (which terms in this matter are ἰσοδυναμοῦντα) is a deep affirmation. And, therefore, it sufficeth not men to say that they have consulted the mind of God, and cannot find that he ever spake to any of his saints or people to establish a toleration of error; and yet this is the first

argument to oppose it produced in the late Testimony of the reverend and learned Assembly of the Church of Scotland.[1] Affirmative precepts must be produced for a non-toleration; that is, the punishing of erring persons. For actings of such high concernment, men do generally desire a better warrant than this,—"There is nothing in the word against them." Clear light is needful for men who walk in paths which lead directly to houses of blood. God hath not spoken of non-toleration, is a certain rule of forbearance; but God hath not spoken of toleration, is no rule of acting in opposition thereunto. What he hath spoken, one way or other, shall be afterward considered. Positive actings must have positive precepts and rules for them, as conscience is its own guide. If, then, you will have persons deviating in their apprehensions from the truth of the gospel civilly punished, you must bring better warrant than this, that God hath not spoken against it; or I shall not walk in your ways, but refrain my foot from your path.

2. That undoubtedly there are very many things under the command of the Lord, so becoming our duty, and within his promise, so made our privilege, which yet, if not performed, or not enjoyed, are not of human cognizance,—as faith itself; yet because the knowledge of the truth is in that rank of things, this also is urged as of weight, by the same learned persons, to the business at hand.

3. Errors, though never so impious, are yet distinguished from peace-disturbing enormities. If opinions in their own nature tend to the disturbance of the public peace, either that public tranquillity is not of God, or God alloweth a penal restraint of those opinions. It is a mistake, to affirm that those who plead for toleration do allow of punishment for offences against the second table,—not against the first. The case is the same both in respect of the one and the other. What offences against the second table are punishable? Doubtless not all, but only such as, by a disorderly eruption, pervert the course of public quiet and society; yea, none but such fall under human cognizance. The warrant of exercising vindictive power amongst men is from the reference of offences to their common tranquillity. "Delicta puniri publicè interest." Where punishment is the debt, "Bonum totius" is the creditor to exact it. And this is allowed as to the offences against the first table. If any of them in their own nature (not some men's apprehensions) are disturbances of public peace, they also are punishable. Only, let not this be measured by disputable consequences, no more than the other are. Let the evidence be in the things themselves, and "Actum est," let who will plead for them. Hence,—

[1] See a "Solemn Testimony against Toleration and the Present Proceedings of Sectaries and their Abettors in England, in reference to Religion and Government," &c.,—a document sanctioned by the General Assembly of the Church of Scotland, Jan. 16, 1649, and published in the course of the same year.—Ed.

Popish religion, warming in its very bowels a fatal engine against all magistracy amongst us, cannot upon our concessions plead for forbearance; it being a known and received maxim, that the gospel of Christ clashes against no righteous ordinance of man.

And let this be spoken to the third argument of the fore-named reverend persons, from the analogy of delinquencies against the first and second table.

4. The plea for the punishment of erring persons from the penal constitution under the Old Testament against idolaters (which in the next place is urged), seems not very firm and convincing. The vast distance that is between idolatry and any errors whatsoever, as merely such, however propagated or maintained with obstinacy, much impaireth the strength of this argumentation.

Idolatry is the yielding unto a creature the service and worship due to the Creator, Rainold. de Idol., lib. ii. cap. 1, sect. 1. " Idololatria est circa omne idolum famulatus et servitus," Tertul. de Pol.;—" The attendance and service of any idol." " Idololatræ dicuntur qui simulacris eam servitutem exhibent, quæ debetur Deo," August., lib. i. de Trinit. cap. 6;—" They are idolaters who give that service to idols which is due unto God." To render glory to the creature as to God is idolatry, say the Papists, Bell., de Eccles. Triumph., lib. ii. cap. 24; Greg. de Valen. de Idol., lib. i. cap. 1;—suitable to the description of it given by the apostle, Rom. i. 25: plainly, that whereunto the sanction under debate was added, as the bond of the law against it (which was the bottom of the commendable proceedings of divers kings of Judah against such), was a voluntary relinquishment of Jehovah revealed unto them, to give the honour due unto him to dunghill idols. Now, though error and ignorance ofttimes lie at the bottom of this abomination, yet error, properly so called, and which under the name of heresy is opposed, is sufficiently differenced therefrom. That common definition of heresy,—that it is an error, or errors, in or about the fundamentals of religion, maintained with stubbornness and pertinacy after conviction (for the main received by most Protestant divines),—will be no way suited unto that which was before given of idolatry, and is as commonly received, being indeed much more clear; as shall be afterward declared. That this latter is proper and suitable to those scriptural descriptions which we have of heresy, I dare not assert; but being received by them who urge the punishment thereof, it may be a sufficient ground of affirming that those things whose definitions are so extremely different are also very distant and discrepant in themselves; and therefore constitutions for the disposal of things concerning the one cannot " eo nomine" include the other. Neither is the inference any stronger, than that a man may be hanged for coveting, because he may be so for murdering.

The penal constitutions of the Judaical polity (for so they were, which yet I urge not) concerning idolaters, must be stretched beyond their limits, if you intend to inwrap heretics within their verge. If heretics be also idolaters, as the Papists (the poor Indians who worship a piece of red cloth, the Egyptians who adored the deities which grew in their own gardens, being not more besotted with this abomination than they who prostrate their souls unto, and lavish their devotion upon, a piece of bread, a little before they prepare it for the draught,—so casting the stumbling-block of their iniquities before the faces of poor Heathens and Jews, causing Averroes to breathe out his soul in this expression of that scandal, " Quoniam Christiani manducant Deum quem adorant, sit anima mea cum Philosophis!) I say, then, the case seems to me to have received so considerable an alteration, that the plea of forbearance is extremely weakened as to my present apprehension. However, for the present I remove such from this debate.

5. The like to this also may be said concerning blasphemy, the law whereof is likewise commonly urged in this cause. The establishment for the punishment of a blasphemer is in Lev. xxiv. 16. Given it was upon the occasion of the blaspheming and cursing of the son of an Egyptian, upon his striving and contending with an Israelite. Being probably, in his own apprehension, wronged by his adversary, he fell to reviling his God. The word here used to express his sin, is נָקַב, signifying also to pierce, and is twice so rendered,—Isa. xxxvi. 6; Hab. iii. 14. Desperate expressions, piercing the honour and glory of the Most High willingly and wilfully, were doubtless his death-deserving crime. It is the same word that Balak used to Balaam, when he would have persuaded him to a deliberate cursing and pouring out of imprecations on the people of God, Numb. xxiii. 13, 14. A resolved piercing of the name and glory of God, with cursed reproaches, is the crime here sentenced to death. The schoolmen tell us, that to complete blasphemy, the perverse affection of the heart, in detestation of the goodness of God, joined with the reproaches of his name, is required.[1] Which, how remote it is from error of any sort (I mean within the compass of them whereof we speak), being a pure misapprehension of the understanding, embraced (though falsely) for the honour of God, I suppose is easily conceived; and so, consequently, that the argument for the death of a person erring, because he came off no easier of old who blasphemed, is " à baculo ad angulum."

If any shall say that blasphemy is of a larger extent and more general acceptation in the Scripture, I shall not deny it; but yet that that kind of blasphemy which was punishable with violent death, was comprehensive of any inferior crime, I suppose cannot be proved.

[1] Thom. 22æ. g. 13, a. 1, ad 1um.

However, blasphemy in the Scripture is never taken in any place, that I can remember, for a man's maintaining his own error; but for his reviling and speaking evil of the truth which he receiveth not: and so Paul before his conversion was a blasphemer.[1] Now, if men to whom forbearance is indulged in by-paths of their own, shall make it their work to cast dirt on the better ways of truth, it is to me very questionable whether they do not offend against that prime dictate of nature for the preservation of human society, "Quod tibi fieri non vis, alteri ne feceris;" and for such I will be no advocate. Neither can, indeed, the law of blasphemy be impartially urged by us in any case of heresy whatsoever. For,—

(1.) The penal sanctions of the laws of God are not in England esteemed of moral equity, and perpetually indispensable; for if so, why do adulterers unmolested behold the violent death of stealers?

(2.) The blasphemer by that law was not allowed his clergy; die he must without mercy, no room being left for the intervention of repentance, as to the removal of his temporal punishment;—when once the witnesses' garments were rent, he was anathema. But in case of any heresy, repentance, yea, recantation, is a sure antidote (at least for once, so it is among the Papists) against all corporeal sufferings.

6. Neither doth that place in Zechariah, chap. xiii. 3, concerning the running through of the false prophet, more prove or approve of the punishment of death to be inflicted for misapprehensions in the matters of religion (and if it proves not that, it proveth nothing; for slaying is the thing expressed, and certainly if proofs be taken from the letter, the letter must be obeyed, or we force the word to serve our hypothesis) than that place of John, x. 1, "He that entereth not by the door is a thief and a robber;" which Bellarmine strongly urgeth to this very purpose, because thieves and robbers are so dealt withal righteously.[2] If such deductions may be allowed, it will be easy to prove "quidlibet ex quolibet," at any time.

If the letter be urged, and the sense of the letter as it lies (indeed[3] the figurative sense of such places is the proper, literal sense of them), let that sense alone be kept to. Let parents, then, pass sentence, condemn, and execute their children, when they turn seducers; and that in any kind whatsoever,—into what seduction soever they shall be engaged, be it most pernicious, or in things of less concernment. The letter allows of none of our distinctions; be they convinced or not convinced, obstinate or not obstinate, all is one—so it must be: thrust through and slain by their parents must they fall to the ground.

[1] Acts xviii. 6, xxvi. 11; 1 Tim. i. 13. [2] Bell. Lib. de Laicis., cap. xxi.
[3] August. de Util. Creden., cap. iii. Thom. pp. q. 1, a. 10. Zanch. de SS. q. 12, cap. 2, reg. 10. Tilen. Syntag. Theol. de Interpret. S. Thes. 8. Whitak. de SS., qu. 5, cap. 2. Armin. Disput. Pri. Thes. 9, 1. Ames. Med. Theol. cap. 34. Thes. 22.

Only observe, his father and his mother that begat him must be made magistrates,—prophets with unclean spirits be turned into heretics:—only "thrusting through," that must be as it is in the letter; yea, though plainly the party of whom it is said, "Thou shalt not live," verse 3, is found alive, verse 6. Surely such an Orleans gloss[1] is scarce sufficient to secure a conscience in slaying heretics. But, when men please, this whole place shall directly point at the discipline of the churches, and their spiritual censures under the gospel,—curing deceivers, and bringing them home to confession and acknowledgment of their folly. See the late Annot. of the Bible.

7. From the asserting of the authority and description of the duty of the magistrate, Rom. xiii., the argument is very easy that is produced for the suppressing by external force of erroneous persons. The paralogism is so foul and notorious in this arguing—"He is to suppress evil deeds; heresy is an evil deed: therefore that also"—that it needs no confutation. That he is to punish all evil deeds was never yet affirmed. Unbelief is a work of the flesh,—so is coveting; one, the root-sin, against the first,—the other against the second table: yet in themselves both exempted from the magistrate's cognizance and jurisdiction. The evil-doers, doubtless, for whose terror and punishment he is appointed, are such as by their deeds disturb that human society the defence and protection whereof is to him committed. That among the number of these are errors, the depravations of men's understandings, hath not yet been proved.

8. The case of the seducer, from Deut. xiii., is urged with more show of reason than any of the others to the business in hand; but yet the extreme discrepancies between the proof and the thing intended to be proved make any argumentation from this place, as to the matter in hand, very intricate, obscure, and difficult. For,—

(1.) The person here spoken of pretends an immediate revelation from heaven: he pretends dreams, and gives signs and wonders, verse 1, and so exempts his spirit from any regular trial. Heretics, for the most part, offer to be tried by the rule that is "in medio," acknowledged of all,—a few distempered enthusiasts excepted.

(2.) His business is to entice from the worship of Jehovah,—not in respect of the manner, but the object, verse 5. All heretics pretend the fear of that great name.

(3.) The accepting and owning idol, dunghill gods in his room, is the thing persuaded to, verse 2 (and those were only stocks and stones); and this in opposition to Jehovah, who had revealed himself by Moses. Heretics worship him, own him, and abhor all thoughts of turning away from following after him, according to their erroneous

[1] *Orleans gloss,*—a very ancient proverbial saying in France, used in ridicule of comments more obscure than the text.—Ménage, Dict. Etymol., sub. v. Glozè.—Ed.

apprehensions. Manichees, Marcionites, Valentinians, and such like names of infidels, I reckon not among heretics; neither will their brain-sick, paganish follies be possibly comprehended under that definition of heresy which is now generally received. Mohammedans are far more rightly termed heretics than they.

(4.) This seducer was to die without mercy. And Ainsworth observes from the rabbins, that this offender alone had traps laid to catch him; and were he but once overheard to whisper his seduction, though never so secretly, there was no expiation of his transgression without his own blood. But now this place is urged for all kind of restraint and punishment whatsoever. Now, where God requires blood, is it allowed to man to commute at an inferior rate? So, I confess, it is urged. But yet what lies at the bottom, in the chambers of their bellies who plead for the power of the magistrate to punish erring persons from those, and such like places as these, is too apparent. Blood is there: swiftly or slowly, they walk to the chambers of death.

(5.) Obstinacy after conviction, turbulency, &c., which are now laid down as the main weights that turn the scale on the side of severity, are here not once mentioned, nor by any thing in the least intimated. If he have done it, yea, but once, openly or secretly, whether he have been convinced of the sinfulness of it or no, be he obstinate or otherwise, it is not once inquired,—die he must, as if he had committed murder, or the like indispensable death-procuring crime. If the punishment, then, of erring persons be urged from this place, all consideration of their conviction, obstinacy, pertinacy, must be laid aside: the text allows them no more plea in this business than our law doth in the case of wilful murder.

(6.) Repentance and recantation will, in the judgment of all, reprieve an erring person from any sentence of any punishment corporeal whatsoever; and many reasons may be given why they should so do. Here is no such allowance. Repent or not repent, recant or not recant, he hath no sacrifice of expiation provided for him,—die he must.

(7.) The law contains the sanction of the third commandment, as the whole was a rule of the Jewish polity in the land of Canaan. This amongst us is generally conceived not binding, as such.

(8.) The formal reason of this law, by some insisted on,—because he sought to turn a man from Jehovah,–

[1.] Is of force only in this case of the object whereunto seduction tends,—viz., strange gods,—and no other.

[2.] Turning from Jehovah respects not any manner of backsliding in respect of the way of worship, but a falling away from him as the object of worship.

Now, there being these and many other discrepancies hindering the cases proposed from running parallel, I profess, for my part, I cannot see how any such evident deductions can possibly be drawn from hence as to be made a bottom of practice and acting in things of so high concernment. What may be allowed from the equity of those and the like constitutions, and deduced by analogy and proportion to the business in hand, I shall afterward declare.

II. The sum of what is usually drawn from holy writ against such forbearance as I suppose may be asserted, and for the punishing heretics with capital punishments, being briefly discussed, I proceed, in the next place, to such other general observations as may serve to the farther clearing of the business in hand; and they are these that follow:—

The forbearance of or opposition unto errors, may be considered with respect either unto civil or spiritual judicature.

First, For the latter, it is either personal or ecclesiastical, properly so called. Personal forbearance of errors, in a spiritual sense, is a moral toleration or approbation of them; so also is ecclesiastical. The warrant for procedence against them on that hand is plain and evident: certainly this way no error is to be forborne. All persons who have any interest and share in truth are obliged, in their several ways and stations, to an opposition unto every error,—an opposition to be carried on by gospel mediums and spiritual weapons. Let them, according as they are called or opportuned, disprove them from the word, "contending earnestly for the faith once delivered unto the saints." Erring persons are usually "bono animo," says Salvian,—very zealous to propagate their false conceptions; and shall the children of truth be backward in her defence? Precepts unto this as a duty, commendations of it, encouragements unto it, are very frequent in the gospel. Alike is this duty incumbent on all churches walking to the rule. The spiritual sword of discipline may be lawfully sheathed in the blood of heresies. No spiritual remedy can be too sharp for a spiritual disease. When the cure is suited to the malady, there is no danger of the application. And this is not denied by any. He that submits himself to any church society, does it "ea lege,"—of being obedient to the authority of Christ in that church in all its censures. "Volenti non fit injuria." Error is offensive, and must be proceeded against. Examples and precepts of this abound in the Scriptures. The blood of many erring persons, I doubt not, will one day have a "quo warranto" granted them against their (as to the particulars in debate) orthodox slayers, who did it to promote the service of God. Let them not fear an after-reckoning who use the discipline of Christ according to his appointment.

This being considered, the occasion of a most frequent paralogism is removed. If errors must be tolerated, say some, then men may do what they please, without control. No means, it seems, must be used to reclaim them. But is gospel conviction no means? Hath the sword of discipline no edge? Is there no means of instruction in the New Testament established, but a prison and a halter? Are the hammer of the word and the sword of the Spirit, which in days of old broke the stubbornest mountains, and overcame the proudest nations, now quite useless? God forbid! Were the churches of Christ established according to his appointment, and the professors of the truth so knit up "in the unity of the Spirit and bond of peace" as they ought to be, and were in the primitive times, I am persuaded those despised instruments would quickly make the proudest heretic to tremble. When the churches walked in sweet communion, giving each other continual account of their affairs, and warning each other of all or any such persons as, either in practice or doctrine, walked not with a right foot (as we have examples in Clem. Epist. ad Corinth.;—the churches of Vienne and Lyons to those of Asia, Euseb.;—of Ignatius to several persons and churches;—of Irenæus to Victor., Euseb.;—Dionysius to Stephen, ibid., and the like), heretics found such cold entertainment as made them ashamed, if not weary, of their chosen wanderings. But this is not my present business.

Secondly, There is an opposition or forbearance in reference to a civil judicature and procedence of things which respecteth errors in a real sense, as to the inflicting or not inflicting of punishment on religious delinquents. And this is the sole thing under debate, viz.,—

Whether persons enjoying civil authority over others,—being intrusted therewithal according to the constitutions of the place and nation where the lot of them both, by providence, is fallen,—are invested with power from above, and commanded in the word of God, to coerce, restrain, punish, confine, imprison, banish, hang, or burn, such of those persons under their jurisdiction as shall not embrace, profess, believe, and practise, that truth and way of worship which is revealed unto them of God? or how far, into what degrees, by what means, in any of these ways, may they proceed?

The general propositions and considerations of the penal laws of God, which were before laid down, have, as I suppose, left this business to a naked debate from the word of truth, without any such prejudices on either part as many take from a misapprehension of the mind of God in them; and therefore, by the reader's patience, I shall venture upon the whole anew, as if no such arguments had ever been proposed for the affirmative of the question in hand, not declining the utmost weight that is in any of them, according to equity and due proportion. And here, first, I shall give in a few things,—

(1.) To the question itself.

(2.) To the manner of handling it.

(1.) To the question itself. For herein I suppose,—

[1.] That the persons enjoying authority do also enjoy the truth; which is to the advantage of the affirmative.

[2.] That their power in civil things is just and unquestionable; which also looks favourably on that side.

[3.] That non-toleration makes out itself in positive infliction of punishment; which is so, or is nothing. Casting men out of protection, exposing them to vulgar violence, is confessedly unworthy of men representing the authority of God, and contrary to the whole end of their trust.

(2.) To the manner of handling this question among persons at variance. And here I cannot but observe,—

[1.] That if I have taken my aim aright, there is no one thing under debate amongst Christians that is agitated with more confidence and mutual animosity of the parties litigant,—each charging other with dreadful inferences,—streams of blood, and dishonour to God, flowing out from their several persuasions; so that ofttimes, instead of a fair dispute, you meet on this subject with a pathetical outcry, as though all religion were utterly contaminated and trampled under foot, if both these contradictory assertions be not embraced. Now, seeing that in itself it is a thing wherein the gospel is exceedingly sparing, if not altogether silent, certainly there must be a farther interest than of judgment alone, or else that very much prejudicated with corrupt affections, or men could not possibly be carried out with so much violence upon supposed self-created consequences, wherewith in this cause they urge one another.

[2.] That generally thus much of private interest appears in the several contesters, that non-toleration is the opinion of the many, and these enjoying the countenance of authority;—toleration, of the oppressed, who always go under the name of the faction, or factions,—the unavoidable livery of the smaller number professing a way of worship by themselves, be it right or wrong. I do not desire to lay forth the usual deportment of men seeking the suppressing of others differing from them, towards those in authority. It is but too clearly made out by daily experience. If they close with them, they are "custodes utriusque tabulæ,"—the church's nursing-fathers, &c.,—what they please; but if they draw back, for want of light or truth to serve them, logs and storks find not worse entertainment from frogs than they from some of them. Such things as these may, nay, ought to be, especially heeded by every one that knows what influence corrupt affections have upon the judgments of men, and would willingly take the pains to wipe his eyes for the discerning of the truth.

These things premised, I assert that,—

Non-toleration,—in the latitude which is for persons in authority enjoying the truth (or supposing they do enjoy it) to punish in an arbitrary way, according to what they shall conceive to be condign, men who will not forsake their own convictions about any head or heads of Christian religion whatsoever, to join with what they hold out, either for belief or worship, after the using of such ways of persuasion as they shall think fit,—is no way warranted in the gospel; nor can any sound proof for such a course be taken from the Old Testament.

The testimonies out of the law, which I can apprehend to have any colour or appearance of strength in them, with the examples approved of God that seem to look this way, I considered at our entrance into this discourse.

I speak of punishing in an arbitrary way; for all instances produced to the purpose in hand, that speak of any punishment, mention nothing under death itself; which yet, at least in the first place, is not aimed at by those that use them in our days, as I suppose. Now, some divines of no small name maintain, that God hath not left the imposition of punishment in any measure to the wills of men.

Some arguments for the proof of the former assertion as laid down I shall in due place make use of; for the present, I desire to commend to the serious pondering of all Christians in general, especially of those in authority, these ensuing considerations:—

1. That it is no privilege of truth to furnish its assertors with this persuasion, that the dissenters from it ought forcibly to be opposed, restrained, punished.

No false religion ever yet in the world did enthrone itself in the minds of men enjoying a civil sovereignty over the persons of others, but it therewithal commanded them, under pain of neglect and contempt of itself, to crush any underling worship that would perk up in inferior consciences.

The old heathens carried their gods into the war (as did the Philistines, 1 Chron. xiv. 12, and the Israelites the ark, with heathenish superstition, 1 Sam. iv. 3), to whom they ascribed the success they obtained; and in requital of their kindness, they forced the dunghill deities of the conquered nations to attend the triumph of their victorious idols; and unless they adopted them into the number of their own gods, all farther worship to them was forbidden. Hence were these inventions among the old Romans, by spells and enchantments, to entice away a deity from any city they besieged (they being as expert at the getting of a devil as Tobias's Raphael, or the present Romanists at his fumigation); by which means they shrived into the honour of having thirty thousand unconquered idols,[1] and deserved worthily that change of their city's epithet from 'Επιτομὴ οἰκουμένης to 'Επιτομὴ δεισιδαιμονίας,—which it justly inheriteth to this very day.

[1] Varro in Augustin. de Civit. Dei.

Rabshakeh's provocation to the example of the gods of the nations, 2 Kings xviii. 33, 34, and the Roman senate's consultation concerning the admitting of Christ to a place among their idols, that he might have been freely worshipped (their consent being prevented by his almighty providence, who will not be enrolled among the vilest works of his most corrupted creatures), do both declare this thing.

Now, not to speak of Cain, who seems to me to have laid the foundation of that cruelty which was afterwards inserted into the church's orthodoxies by the name of Hæreticidium; we find the four famous empires of the world to have drunk in this persuasion to the utmost, of suppressing all by force and violence that consented not to them in their way of worship.

Nebuchadnezzar, the "crown of the golden head," set up a furnace with an image; and a negative answer to that query, "Do you not serve my gods, nor worship my image?" served to cast the servants of the living God into the midst of the fire, Dan. iii.

Daniel's casting into the lions' den, chapter vi., shows that the Persian silver breast and arms did not want iron hands to crush or break the opposers of, or dissenters from, their religious edicts.

And though we find not much of the short-lived founder of the Grecian dominion, yet what was the practice of the branches of that empire, especially in the Syrian and Egyptian sprouts, the books of the Maccabees, Josephus, and others, do abundantly manifest.

For the Romans, though their judgment and practice—which fully and wholly are given over from the dragon to the beast and false prophet—be written in the blood of thousands of Christians, and so not to be questioned; yet, that it may appear that we are not the only men in this generation, that this wisdom of punishing dissenters was not born with us, I shall briefly give in what grounds they proceeded on, and the motives they had to proceed as they did.

(1.) First, then, they enacted it as a law, that no religious worship should be admitted or practised without the consent, decree, and establishment of the senate. Mention is made of a formal law to this purpose in Tertullian, Apol., cap. v., though now we find it not. The foundation of it was doubtless in that of the twelve tables: "Separatim nemo habessit deos, neve novos, sed ne advenas, nisi publicè ascitos, privatim colunto;"—"Let none have gods to himself, neither let any privately worship new or strange deities, unless they be publicly owned and enrolled." And that it was their practice, and in the counsels of the wisest amongst them, appears in that advice given by Mæcenas to Augustus, in Dion Cassius: Τὸ μὲν θεῖον πάντη πάντως αὐτός τε σέβου, κατὰ τὰ πάτρια, καὶ τοὺς ἄλλους τιμᾷν ἀνάγκαζε· τοὺς δὲ δὴ ξενίζοντάς τι περὶ αὐτὸ, καὶ μίσει καὶ κόλαζε, μὴ μόνον τῶν θεῶν ἕνεκα, ὧν καταφρονήσας οὐδ᾽ ἄλλου ἄν τινος προτιμήσειεν, ἀλλ᾽ ὅτι καινά τινα δαιμόνια οἱ τοιοῦτοι ἀντεισφέροντες πολλοὺς ἀναπείθουσιν ἀλλοτριονομεῖν· κἀκ τούτου καὶ συνωμοσίαι καὶ συστάσεις, ἑταιρεῖαί τε γίγνονται, ἅπερ ἥκιστα μοναρχίᾳ συμφέρει·—"Worship," saith he, "the divine power thyself according to the constitutions of thy country, everywhere and at all times; and compel others so to honour it. But hate and punish those who introduce foreign religions; not only for the god's sake,—whom he who contemneth will regard nothing else,—but because such, introducing new deities, do persuade many to transgress (or to change affairs);[1] whence are conjurations, seditions, private societies,—things no way conducing to monarchy," Hist. Rom., lib. lii. 36.

Hence, doubtless, was that opposition which Paul met withal in divers of the Roman territories. Thus, at Athens (though, as I suppose, they enjoyed there their own laws and customs, very suitable, as it should seem, to those of the Romans), preaching Jesus, he was accused to be "a setter forth of strange gods," Acts xvii. For although, as Strabo observeth of the Athenians, that publicly, by the authority of the magistrates, πολλὰ τῶν ξενικῶν ἱερῶν παρεδέξαντο, "they received many things of foreign worships;" yet that none might attempt any such things of themselves is notorious from the case of Socrates, who, as Laertius witnesseth, was condemned as οὓς μὲν νομίζει θεοὺς ἡ πόλις οὐ νομίζοντα, ἕτερα δὲ καινὰ δαιμόνια εἰσηγούμενον,—"one who thought not those to be gods whom the city thought so to be, but brought in certain new deities." Hence, I say, was Paul's opposition, and his haling to Mars-hill. Without doubt, also, this was the bottom of that stir and trouble he met withal about Philippi. It is true, private interest lay in the bottom with the chief opposers; but this legal constitution was that which was plausibly pretended. Acts xvi. 21, "They teach customs which are not lawful for us to receive, neither to observe, being Romans:" οὐκ ἔξεστι Ῥωμαίοις,—"it is not lawful for us Romans" to receive the religion they hold out, because statutes are made amongst us against all religious worship not allowed by public authority. Let Calvin's short annotation on that place be seen. Gallio's refusing to judge between Jews (as he thought) in a Jewish controversy, is no impeachment of this truth; had it been about any Roman establishment, he would quickly have interposed. Now, this law amongst them was doubtless "fundi Christiani calamitas."

This, then, in the first place, was enacted, that no worship should be admitted, no religion exercised, but what received establishment and approbation from them who supposed themselves to be intrusted with authority over men in such things. And this power of the dragon was given over to the beast and false prophet. The antichristian power succeeding in the room of the paganish,—the pope and councils, of the emperors and senate,—it was quickly confirmed that none should be suffered to live in peace who received not his mark and name, Rev. xiii. 16, 17. Whereunto, for my part, I cannot but refer very many of those following imperial constitutions, which were made at first against the opposers of the church's orthodoxism, but were turned against the witnesses of Jesus in the close.

(2.) This being done, they held out the reasons of this establishment. I shall touch only one or two of them, which are still common to them who walk in the same paths with them.

[1.] Now, the first was, That toleration of sundry ways of worship, and several religions, tends to the disturbance of the commonwealth and that civil society which men under the same government do and ought to enjoy. So Cicero tells us, lib. ii., De Leg., "Suosque deos, aut novos, aut alienigenas coli, confusionem habet," &c.;—it brings in confusion of religion and civil society. The same is clearly held out in that counsel of Mæcenas to Augustus before mentioned. "They," saith he, "who introduce new deities, draw many into innovations; whence are conspiracies, seditions, conventicles, no way profitable for the commonwealth."

[2.] The other main reason was, That hereby the gods, whom they owned and worshipped, were dishonoured and provoked to plague them. That this was continually in their mouths and clamours, all the acts at the slaying of the martyrs, the rescripts of emperors, the apologies of the Christians, as Tertullian, Justin Martyr, Arnobius, Minutius Felix, do abundantly testify. All trouble was still ascribed to their impiety. Upon the first breaking out of any judgment, as though the cause of it had been the toleration of Christians, presently the vulgar cry was, "Christianos ad leones." Now, that those causes and reasons have been traduced to all those who have since acted the same things, especially to the emperors' successor at Rome, needs not to be proved. With the power of the dragon, the wisdom also is derived. See that great champion, Cardinal Bellarmine, fighting with these very weapons, Lib. de Laicis, cap. xxi. And indeed, however illustrated, improved, adorned, supported, flourished, and sweetened, they are the sum of all that to this day hath been said in the same case.

(3.) Having made a law, and supported it with such reasons as these, in proceeding to the execution of the penalty of that law as to particular persons (which penalty being, as now, arbitrary, was inflicted unto banishment, imprisonment, mine-digging, torturing in sundry kinds, maiming, death, according to the pleasure of the judges), they always charged upon those persons, not only the denying and opposing their own deities, religion, and worship; but also, that that which they embraced was foolish, absurd, detestable, pernicious, sinful, wicked, ruinous to commonwealths, cities, society, families, honesty, order, and the like. If a man should go about to delineate the Christian religion by the lines and features drawn thereof in the invectives and accusations of their adversaries, he might justly suppose that indeed that was their god which was set up at Rome with this inscription, "DEUS CHRISTIANORUM ONONYCHITES;" being an image with ass's ears, in a gown, claws or talons upon one foot, with a book in his hand. Charged they were that they worshipped an ass's head; which impious folly—first fastened on the Jews by Tacitus, Hist., lib. v. cap. 1, in these words, "Effigiem animalis, quo monstrante errorem sitimque depulerant, penetrali sacravere" (having before set out a feigned direction received by a company of asses), which he had borrowed from Apion, a railing Egyptian of Alexandria[1]—was so ingrafted in their minds that no defensative could be allowed. The[2] sun, the cross, "sacerdotis genitalia," were either really supposed, or impiously imposed on them, as the objects of their worship. The blood and flesh of infants, at Thyestean banquets, was said to be their food and provision; promiscuous lust, with incest, their chiefest refreshment. Such as these it concerned them to have them thought to be, being resolved to use them as if they were so indeed. Hence I am not sometimes without some suspicion, that many of the impure abominations, follies, villanies, which are ascribed unto the primitive heretics, yea, the very Gnostics themselves (upon whom the filth that lies is beyond all possible belief),[3] might be feigned and imposed, as to a great part thereof. For though not the very same, yet things as foolish and opposite to the light of nature, were at the same time charged on the most orthodox.

But you will say, They who charged these things upon the Catholics were Pagans, enemies of God and Christ; but these, who so charged heretics, were Christians themselves. And so say I also, and therefore, for reverence of the name (though perhaps I could), I say no more. But yet this I say, that story which you have in Minutius Felix (or Arnobius, viii. book apologetical), of the meeting of Christians, the drawing away of the light by a dog tied to the candlestick, so to make way for adulteries and incests, I have heard more than once told with no small confidence of Brownists and Puritans. Hath not this very same course been taken in latter ages? Consult the writ-

[1] Joseph. ad. Ap., lib. i.

[2] "Moses novos ritus contrariosque cæteris mortalibus indidit. Profana illic omnia, quæ apud nos sacra; rursum concessa apud illos, quæ nobis incesta. Projectissima ad libidinem gens alienarum concubitum abstinent, inter se nihil illicitum."—Tacitus (de Judæis) Hist., lib. v. "Judæos, impulsore Chresto quotidie tumultuantes Roma expulit," falsely and foolishly.—Suet. Claud., cap. xxv. "Quæsitissimis pœnis afficiebat, quos per flagitia invisos vulgus Christianos apellabat." Tac. An., lib. xv. "Afflicti suppliciis Christiani, genus hominum superstitionis novæ ac maleficæ."—Sueton. in Nerone, cap. xvi.

[3] Epiphan. tom. ii. lib. 1, Hær. 26.

ings of Waldensis and the rest of his companions, about Wickliffe and his followers,—see the occasion of his falling off from Rome in our own chronicles, in Fabian of old, yea, and Daniel of late, to gratify a popish court;—of Eckius, Hosius, Staphylus, Bolsec, Bellarmine, and the rest who have undertaken to pourtray out unto us Luther and Calvin, with their followers;—and you will quickly see that their great design was to put on (as they did upon the head of John Huss at the Council of Constance, when he was led to the stake) the ugly visard of some devilish appearance, that under that form they might fit them for fire and fagot. And herein also is the polity of the dragon derived to the false prophet, and a colour tempered for persecutors to imbrue their hands in the blood of martyrs.

This was the old Roman way, and I thought it not amiss to cautionate those enjoying truth and authority, that, if it be possible, they may not walk in their steps and method. The course accounted so sovereign for the extirpation of error was, as you see, first invented for the extirpation of truth.

2. I desire it may be observed, that the general issue and tendence of unlimited arbitrary persecution, or punishing for conscience' sake (because in all ages, οἱ πλείονες κακοὶ, and the worst of men have sat at the upper end of the world, for the most part more false worshippers having hitherto enjoyed authority over others than followers of the Lamb), hath been pernicious, fatal, and dreadful to the profession and professors of the gospel,—little or not at all serviceable to the truth.

I have heard it averred by a reverend and learned personage, that more blood of heretics hath been shed by wholesome severity, in the maintenance of the truth and opposition unto errors, than hath been shed of the witnesses of Jesus by the sword of persecution, in the hands of heretics and false worshippers;—an assertion, I conceive, under favour, so exceedingly distant from the reality of the thing itself, that I dare take upon me, against any man breathing, that in sundry Christian provinces,—almost in every one of the west,—more lives have been sacrificed to the one idol Hæreticidium, of those that bear witness to the truth, in the belief for which they suffered, than all the heretics, properly so called, that ever were slain in all the provinces of the world by men professing the gospel. And I shall give that worthy divine, or any other of his persuasion, his option among all the chiefest provinces of Europe, to tie me up unto which they please. He that shall consider that above sixty thousand persons were, in six years or little more, cut off in a judicial way, by Duke D'Alva in the Netherlands, in pursuit of the sentence of the inquisition, will conclude that there is "causa facilis" in my hand.

The ancient contest between the Homoousians and the Arians,—the first controversy the churches were agitated withal after they enjoyed a Christian magistrate (and may justly be supposed to be carried on to the advantage of error beyond all that went before it, because of the civil magistrates interesting themselves in the quarrel),—was not carried out to violence and blood before the several persuasions lighted on several dominions and state interests: as between the Goths, Vandals, and the rest of their companions on one side, who were Arians; and the Romans on the other. In all whose bickerings, notwithstanding, the honour of severity did still attend the Arians, especially in Africk, where they persecuted the Catholics with horrible outrage and fury:—five thousand at one time were barbarously exposed to all manner of cruel villany. Some eruptions of passion had been before among emperors themselves; but still with this difference, that they who Arianized carried the bell for zeal against dissenters. Witness Valens, who gave place in persecution to none of his pagan predecessors, killing, burning, slaying, making havoc of all orthodox professors; yea, perhaps that which he did—at least was done by the countenance of his authority—at Alexandria, upon the placing in of Lucius an Arian in the room of Athanasius, thrusting Peter beside the chair, who was rightly placed according to the custom of those times; perhaps, I say, the tumults, rapes, murders, then and there acted, did outgo what before had been done by the Pagans. See Theodoret, Eccles. Hist., lib. iv. cap. 19. It were tedious to pursue the lying, slandering invectives, banishments, deaths, tumults, murders, which attend this council all along, after once they began to invoke the help of the emperors one against another; yet in this space some magistrates, weary with persecuting ways, did not only abstain practically from force and violence,—as most of the orthodox emperors did,—but also enacted laws for the freedom of such as dissented from them. Jovianus, a pious man, grants all peace that will be peaceable; offended only with them who would offer violence to others, Socrates Eccles. Hist., lib. iii. cap. 25. Gratianus makes a law, whereby he granted liberty to all sects, but Manichees, Photinians, and Eunomians, Sozom. Eccles. Hist., lib. vii. cap. 1. Many more the like examples might be produced.

The next difference about the worship of God, to the Arian and its branches, that was controverted in letters of blood, was about images and their worship; in which, though some furious princes—in opposition to that growing idolatry which, by popes, bishops, priests, and especially monks, was in those days violently urged—did mingle some of their blood with their sacrifices; yet not to the tithe almost of what the Iconolatræ, getting uppermost, returned upon them and their adherents.

This, if occasion were, might be easily demonstrated from Paulus Diaconus, and others. After this, about the year 850,—about which time the Iconolatræ having ensnared the west by polity (the posterity of Charles the Great, who had stoutly opposed the worship of images, complying with the popes, the fathers of that worship, for their own ends), and wearied the east by cruelty,—that contest growing towards an end, the whole power of punishing for religion became subservient to the dictates of the pope, the kings of the earth giving their power to the beast; unto which point things had been working all along;—from thence, I say, until the death of Servetus in Geneva, the pursuit of Gentilis, Blandrata, and some other madmen in Helvetia, for the space well-nigh of seven hundred years,—the chiefest season of the reign of Satan and Antichrist,—all punishing for religion was managed by the authority of Rome, and against the poor witnesses of Jesus, prophesying in sackcloth in the several regions of the west. And what streams of blood were poured out, what millions of martyrs slain in that space, is known to all. Hence Bellarmine boasteth that the Albigenses were extinguished by the sword, De Laic. cap. xxii. It is true, there were laws enacted of old by Theodosius, Valentinian, Martian,—as C. De. hæreticis, 1; Manichæis, 1; Arianis, 1; Unicuique, which last provideth for the death of seducers; but yet, truly, though they were made by Catholics, and in the favour of Catholics, considering to what end they were used, I can look upon them no otherwise but as very bottom-stones of the tower of Babel.

This, then, in its latitude proving so pernicious to the profession of the gospel,—having for so long driven the woman into the wilderness and truth into corners,—being the main engine whereby the tower of Babel was built, and that which at this day they cry grace unto, as the foundation-stone of the whole antichristian fabric,[1]—we had need be cautious what use we make (as one terms it well) of the broom of Antichrist, to sweep the church of Christ. Whether that we are in the truth, and they blinded with error of whom we have spoken, be a sufficient plea, we shall see anon. In the meantime we may do well to remember what Louis XII. of France said, yea, swore, concerning the inhabitants of Mirindol, whom, by the instigation of his prelates, he had ordered to be slain, when news was brought him what was their conversation and way of life: "Let them be heretics if you please," saith he, "but assuredly they are better than I and my Catholics." Take heed lest the punished be better than the punishers.

Let me add to this observation only this, that the attempt to suppress any opinions whatsoever by force hath been for the most part fruitless. For either some few particular persons are proceeded against, or else greater multitudes; if some particulars only, the ashes of one hath always proved the seed of many opinionatists. Examples are innumerable; take one, which is boasted of as a pattern of

[1] "Becanus de fide hæreticis servanda."—Bell., De Laicis, &c.

severity, taken from antiquity. About the year 390, Priscillianus, a Manichee, and a Gnostic, by the procurement of Ithacius and Idacius, two bishops, was put to death by Maximus, an usurping emperor, who ruled for a season, having slain Gratianus; as that kind of men would always close with any authority that might serve their own ends. Now, what was the issue thereof? Martinus, a Catholic bishop, renounces their communion who did it; the historian that reports it giving this censure of the whole, "Sic pessimo exemplo sublati sunt homines luce indignissimi;"—though the men (Priscillianus and his companions) were most unworthy to live, yet their sentence of death was most unjust. But no matter for this, was not the heresy suppressed thereby? See what the same historian, who wrote not long after, and was able to testify the event, says of it:[1] "Non solum non repressa est hæresis, sed confirmata, et latius propagata est," &c.;—"The heresy was so far from being suppressed hereby, that it was confirmed and propagated." His followers, who before honoured him as a saint, now adore him as a martyr. The like in all ages hath been the issue of the like endeavours.

But now, if this course be undertaken against multitudes, what is or hath been the usual end of such undertakings? Take some examples of late days. Charles V., the most mighty emperor of Germany, undertakes by violence to extirpate the Lutherans and Calvinists out of the empire. After a tedious war, the death of many thousands, the wasting of the nation, in the close of all himself is driven out of Germany, and the business left much where it began, Sleid. Com. Philip of Spain, will needs force the inquisition upon the Netherlands. What is the issue? After the expense of an ocean of blood, and more coin than would have purchased the country twice over, his posterity is totally deprived of all sovereignty over those parts.

Patrick Hamilton and George Wishart are put to death in Scotland by the procurement of a cardinal; the cardinal is instantly murdered by some desperate young men, and a war raised there about religion, which was never well quieted until, having hunted their queen out of her native kingdom, she had her head chopped off in England.[2] The wars, seditions, tumults, murders, massacres, rapes, burnings, &c., that followed the same attempt in France, cannot be thought of without horror and detestation. Neither knew those things any end, until the present forbearance was granted. Instances might be multiplied, but these things are known to all. If any shall say, All these evils followed the attempting to suppress truth, not error, I shall answer him another time, being loath to do it unless compelled. Only for the present I shall say, that error hath as much right to a forcible defence as truth.

[1] Sulpitius Severus, lib. ii., Eccles. Hist. [2] Hist. of Reformation in Scotland.

3. To stir us up yet farther to a serious consideration of the grounds and reasons which are laid down for the inflicting of punishment upon any for exorbitancies in things of religion (upon what hath been said), the perpetual coincidence of the causes by them held forth who pretend to plead for just severity, with their pretences who have acted unjust persecution, should be well heeded.

The position is laid down in general on both sides, That erring persons are so and so to be dealt withal,—that such is the power and duty of the magistrate in such cases. The definition of heresy is agreed on for the main; only the Papists place the church's determination where others thrust in the heretic's conviction,—a thing much more obscure to bystanders and judges also. The appellations wherewith truth persecuted and error pursued are clothed, still the same. The consequences urged on all sides—of dishonour to God, trouble to the state, and the like—not at all discrepant. The arguments for the one and other for the most part the same. Look what reasons one sect gives for the punishing of another,—the names being changed, are retorted. He blasphemeth to the heretic, who chargeth blasphemy upon him. We use no other arguments, cite no other texts, press no other consequences for the punishing of other heretics, than the Papists, the wisest heretics breathing, do for the punishment of us.

No colour, no pretence, but hath been equally used in all hands. None can say, This is mine. To Luther's objection, that the Church of Christ never burned a heretic, for Huss and Jerome were none; Bellarmine answers, they were heretics to them Catholics, which did suffice, De Laic. cap. xxi. And indeed this vicissitude of things is very pernicious. All Christians almost are heretics to some enjoying authority (as Salvian said the case was between the Homoousians and Arians in his time); and most of those enjoying authority are persuaded it is their duty to suppress them whom they account heretics, and, answerably, have more or less acted according to this persuasion, until, by blood, wars, and horrid devastations of nations, some of them have been wearied. From the first croisade against the Albigenses, through the war of the Hussites under Zisca and the Procopii, those dreadful massacres before recounted, what a stage of blood hath Europe been made on this account! I desire that to this point the declaration of the Netherlands, at the beginning of their troubles (whom Bellarmine affirms to have petitioned for liberty of conscience, as he was writing "De Hæreticidio," the thing being long before granted at Spira, at the convention of the states of the empire, in the year 1526), may be seriously considered.

4. For the necessity of courses of extremity against erroneous persons, for the upholding "the faith once delivered to the saints," and

the keeping the churches in peace, it doth not appear to me to be so urgent as is pretended.

For three hundred years the church had no assistance from any magistrate against heretics; and yet in all that space there was not one long-lived or far-spreading heresy, in comparison of those that followed. As the disease is spiritual, so was the remedy which in those days was applied; and the Lord Jesus Christ made it effectual. The Christians also of those days disclaimed all thoughts of such proceedings. The expressions of the most ancient, as Polycarpus, Ignatius, Irenæus, concerning heretics, are sharp and cutting; their avoiding of them, being admonished, precise and severe; their confutations of them laborious and diligent; their church censures and ejections piercing and sharp; communion amongst the churches close, exact, and carefully preserved, so that a stubborn heretic was thrust out of Christian society;—but for corporeal punishment to be inflicted on them, in their writings not a syllable. Until Augustine was changed from his first resolution and persuasion, by the madness of Donatistical Circumcellions, this doctrine had but poor footing in antiquity. And whether his reasons as to this point be convincing, let any impartial man read his Epistle 50, and determine. What some say,—The Christians would have been of another mind had they enjoyed Christian magistrates,—is so suited to our present frame and temper, but so unworthy of them, that I should wrong them by a defensative. What was their sense of them, in a spiritual way, is clear. John, they say, would not abide in a bath where Cerinthus the heretic, infected with Judaism and Paganism, was; saying, "Let us depart, lest the building fall on us where Cerinthus is," Iren., lib. iii. cap. 3; Euseb. Eccles. Hist., lib. iii. cap. 28. Marcion meeting Polycarpus, and asking him whether he knew him, or acknowledged him, his answer was, "Yea, to be the first-born of the devil," Euseb., lib. iv. cap. 14. Ignatius's epistles are full of the like expressions. Irenæus says, he would have no words with them, lib. iii. cap. 3. Tertullian's books testify for him at large, with what keenness of spirit he pursued the heretics of his days, though before the end of them he had the unhappiness to be almost one himself. Cyprian cries out, "Nulla cum talibus convivia, nulla colloquia, nulla commercia misceantur," Epist. iii. ad Cornel;—"Neither eat, nor talk, nor deal with them." Antonius the hermit leaves testimony when he was dying, "that he never had peaceable conference with them all his days," Vita Anton. inter Oper. Athan. Surely had these men perceived the mind of God for their bodily punishment, they would not have failed to signify their minds therein; but truly their expressions hold out rather the quite contrary. *Τοὺς μισοῦντας τὸν Θεὸν, μισεῖν χρὴ καὶ ὑμᾶς, καὶ ἐπὶ τοῖς ἐχθροῖς αὐτοῦ ἐκτήκεσθαι· οὐ μὴν καὶ τύπτειν αὐτοὺς ἢ διώκειν, καθὼς τὰ ἔθνη τὰ μὴ εἰδότα τὸν Κύριον καὶ Θεὸν, ἀλλ' ἐχθροὺς μὲν ἡγεῖσθαι καὶ χωρίζεσθαι ἀπ' αὐτῶν*, says Ignatius, Epist. ad Philad.;—"Count them enemies, and separate from them who hate God; but for beating or persecuting them, that is proper to the heathen who know not God, nor our Saviour: do not you so." Tertullian in very many places lays down general maxims tending to more liberty than is now pleaded for. One or two places may be pointed at: "Videte ne et hoc ad irreligiositatis elogium concurrat, adimere libertatem religionis, et interdicere optionem divinitatis, ut non liceat mihi colere quem velim, sed cogar colere quem nolim. Nemo se ab invito coli vellet, ne homo quidem," Apol., cap. xxiv. And again to Scapula the governor of Carthage, to dissuade him from the persecution he intended: "Tamen humani juris et naturalis potestatis est unicuique quod putaverit colere, nec alii obest, aut prodest alterius religio: sed nec religionis est cogere religionem, quæ sponte suscipi debeat, non vi; cum et hostiæ ab animo libenti expostulentur: ita et si nos compuleritis ad sacrificandum, nihil præstabitis diis vestris, ab invitis enim sacrificia non desiderabunt." And I desire to know, whether that which he maketh to be the plea of Christians may not also be used by all erring persons: "Quasi non totum quod in nos potestis, nostrum sit arbitrium. Certe si velim, Christianus sum, tunc ergo me damnabis, si damnari velim. Cum vero quod in me potes, nisi velim, non potes, jam meæ voluntatis est quod potes, non tuæ potestatis," Apol., cap. xlix. Hence was that query of Lactantius, "Quis imponet mihi necessitatem aut credendi quod nolim, aut quod velim non credendi?" And long after these, Gregory of Rome, lib. ii. Epist. lii., tells us, "Nova et inaudita est ista prædicatio, quæ verberibus exigit fidem;"—to beat in faith with stripes, was then a new kind of preaching. These and the like were their expressions.

It is true, in the three first centuries many fond, foolish, corrupt opinions were broached by sundry brain-sick men; but they laid little hold of the churches, kept themselves in the breasts of some few disorderly wanderers, and did very little promote the mystery of iniquity: but afterward, when the Roman emperors, and the great men of the earth, under and with them, began to interpose in the things of religion, and were mutually wooed, instigated, and provoked by the parties at variance (as indeed it is a shame to consider, upon all meetings, assemblies, disputes, councils, what running, what flattering, what insinuation at court, were used on all hands), what root did divers heresies take! how far were they propagated! Witness Arianism, which had almost invaded the whole world.

Furthermore, by the ways which were invented, oft from the rule, for the extirpation of errors, when, by the instigation of prelates, the emperors were (to their own ruin) persuaded to them, the man of sin walked to his throne. Those very laws, edicts, and declarations, which were obtained against erring persons, did the bishops of Rome invert and use against all the witnesses of Jesus. The devil durst not be so bold as to employ that his grand agent in his apprenticeship against the saints; but he first suffers him to exercise his hand against heretics, intending to make use of him afterward to another purpose. In most of those contests which the Roman pontiffs had with their fellow-bishops, by which they insensibly advanced their own supremacy, it was the defence of Catholics they undertook; as in the case of Athanasius and others.

Neither did the Christians of old at once step into the persuasion of punishing corporeally in case of religion. Constantine makes a decree at first, Τὴν ἐλευθερίαν θρησκείας οὐκ ἀρνητέαν εἶναι, "that liberty of worship is not to be denied; and therefore the Christians, as others, should have liberty to keep the faith of their religion and heresy," Euseb., Eccles. Hist., lib. x. cap. 5. And in the same edict he saith (how truly I know not, but yet great Constantine said it), "That it is most certain, that this is conducing to the peace of the empire, that free option and choice of religion be left to all." Afterward, when he began a little farther to engage himself in the business of religion, being indeed wearied with the petitions of bishops and their associates for the persecution of one another, what troubles in a few years did he intricate himself withal! Perplexed he was in his spirit to see the untoward revengefulness of that sort of people; insomuch that he writes expressly to them, being assembled in council at Tyre, "That they had neither care of the truth, nor love to peace, nor conscience of scandal, nor would by any means be prevailed on to lay down their malice and animosities," Socrat. Hist., lib. i. cap. 34. At length an Arian priest curries favour with his sister Constantia: she gets him into the esteem of her brother: after some insinuations of his, new edicts, new synods, new recallings, new banishments of other persons, follow one upon the neck of another, Rufin. Eccles. Hist., lib. i. cap. 11. And when this knack was once found out of promoting a sect by imperial favour, it is admirable to consider how those good princes, Constantine and his sons, were abused, misled, enraged, engaged into mutual dissensions, by the lies, flatteries, equivocations of such as called themselves bishops, Rufin., lib. i. cap. 15, 16, &c. As also, how soon, with the many, the whole business of religion was hereupon turned into a matter of external pomp and dominion. But it is beside my purpose to rake into that hell of confusion which by this means brake in upon the churches in succeeding ages. Only for the following imperial edicts and constitutions in the behalf of the catholic faith, and for the punishing of erring persons, I desire to observe,—

(1.) That the emperors were stirred up to them by turbulent priests and aspiring prelates. Let the pope's letters to them witness this. Leo, Epist. lxxv. &c.

(2.) That they were still bottomed upon such and such councils, that were not to be opposed or spoken against, when all of them were spent for the most part about things quite beside and beyond the Scripture (as feastings, and fastings, and bishops' jurisdictions); and some of them were the very ulcers and imposthumations of Christian religion, as those of Nice and Ephesus, both the second; and in general all of them the sea upon which the whore exalted her seat and throne. And these things did those good men, either deceived by the craft of heretics, or wearied by the importunity of the orthodox.

And yet, notwithstanding all this (as I shall afterward declare), I cannot close with that counsel which Themistius, a philosopher, gave to Valens the emperor, and am most abhorrent from the reason of his counsel,—viz., "That he should let all sects alone, because it was for the glory of God to be honoured with diversities of opinions and ways of worship." Yet though this reason be false and impious, the advice itself was well conducing at that time to the peace of the churches, something qualifying the spirit of that heretical emperor, who before had cruelly raged against all orthodox professors of the Deity of Christ, Socrat., lib. iv. cap 27.

5. Lastly, add unto all that hath been said, "Vice coronidis," for the use of such as, enjoying authority, may have misapprehensions of some truths of Christ,—a sad consideration concerning the end and issue which the Lord, in his righteous judgment, hath in all ages given to persecutors and persecution.

Nero (of whom says Tertullian, "Tali dedicatore gaudet sanguis Christianus"), who was the first that employed the sword against our religion, being condemned by the senate to be punished "more majorum," slew himself, with this exprobration of his own sordid villany, "Turpiter vixi, turpius morior," Sueton. in Ner. Domitian, the inheritor of his rage and folly, was murdered in his own house by his servants, Idem in Domit. Trajan, by a resolution of his joints, numbedness of body, and a choking water, perished miserably, Dio Cassius de Traj. This is he whose order not to seek out Christians to punishment, but yet to punish them appearing, you have in his epistle to Pliny, a provincial governor under him, Plin. Epist. xcvii.; which, though commended by Eusebius, Eccles. Hist., lib. iii. cap. 33, yet is canvassed by Tertullian as a foolish, impious, wicked constitution, Apol. cap. ii. Hadrian, perishing with a flux and casting of blood, paid some part of the price of the innocent blood which he had shed, Ælius Spart. in Had. Severus poisoned himself, to put an end to his tormenting pains, Jul. Capitol. Maximinus, with his son yet a child, was torn in pieces of the soldiers, all crying out, "that not a whelp was to be left of so cursed a stock." Decius, having reigned scarce two years, was slain with his children, Euseb., lib. vii. cap. 1. Valerian, being taken by Sapores king of Persia, was carried about in a cage, and being seventy years old, was at length flayed alive, Euseb., lib. vii. cap. 13. Another Valerian, of the same stamp with his brother and kindred, was murdered at Milan. Diocletian being smitten with madness, had his palace consumed with fire from heaven, and perished miserably. The city of Alexandria, in the time of Gallienus, was, for its persecution, so wasted with variety of destroying plagues and judgments, that the whole number of its inhabitants answered not the grey-headed old men that were in it before, Dionys. apud Euseb., lib. vii. cap. 21. What was the end of Julian is known to all. Now, truly, of many of these we might well say, as one of old did, "Quales imperatores." As Trajan, Hadrian, Severus, Julian, what excellent emperors had they been, had they not been persecutors! And all this, says Tertullian, is come to pass that men might learn μὴ θεομαχεῖν. He that desires to see more of this, let him consult Tertul. Apol. et ad Scap.; Euseb. Eccles. Hist., lib. vii. cap. 21; August. de Civit. Dei, lib. xviii. cap. 52; Eutrop., lib. viii. It would be tedious to descend to examples of latter ages, our own and the neighbour nations do so much, too much, abound with them. Let this that hath been spoken suffice to cautionate mortal men how they meddle with the vessels of the sanctuary.

But now may some say, What will be the issue of this discourse? Do you, then, leave every one at liberty in the things of God? Hath the magistrate nothing to do in or about religion? Is he to depose the care thereof? Shall men, exasperated in their spirits by different persuasions, be suffered to devour one another as they please?

III. I have only showed the weakness of those grounds which some men make the bottom of their testimonies against the toleration of any thing but what themselves conceive to be truth; as also, taken away the chief of those arguments upon which such a proceeding against erring persons is bottomed as tends to blood and death. What positively the civil magistrate may, nay, ought to do, in the whole business of religion, comes in the next place to be considered, being the third and last part of our discourse.

Now, my thoughts unto this I shall hold out under these three heads.

1. What is the magistrate's duty as to the truth, and persons professing it.

2. What in reference to the opposers and revilers of it.

3. What in respect of dissenters from it.

1. I shall begin with the first, which to me is much of chiefest importance.

His power, or rather his duty herein, I shall hold out in these ensuing propositions:—

(1.) As all men in general, so magistrates, even as such, are bound to know the mind and will of God in the things which concern his honour and worship. They are bound, I say, to know it. This obligation lies upon all creatures capable of knowing the Creator, answerably to that light which of him they have, and the means of revelation which they do enjoy. He of whom we speak is supposed to have that most sovereign and supreme of all outward teachings, the word of God, with such other helps as are thereby revealed, and therein appointed; so as he is bound to know the will of God in every thing him concerning. Wherein he fails and comes short of the truth, it is his sin;—the defect being not in the manner of the revelation, but in the corruption of his darkened mind. Now, that he is to make this inquiry in reference to his calling, is evident from that of David, 2 Sam. xxiii. 3, "He that ruleth over men must be just, ruling in the fear of God." This fear is only taught by the word. Without a right knowledge of God and his mind, there can be no true fear of him. That command, also, for the Jewish magistrate to study it day and night, and to have the book of the law continually before him, because it was the rule of that civil polity whereof he was, under God, the head and preserver, by analogy confirmeth this truth, Deut. xvii. 18, 19.

(2.) If he desire this wisdom sincerely, and the Lord intend him "as a light of the morning, as a rising sun, a morning without clouds" to his people, doubtless he will reveal himself to him, and teach him his mind; as he did David and Solomon, and other holy men of old. And as to this, I shall only with due reverence cautionate the sons of men that are exalted in government over their brethren, that they take heed of a lifted-up spirit,—the greatest closer of the heart against the truth of God. He hath promised to teach the humble and the lowly in mind; the proud he beholdeth afar off. Is not this the great reason that the rulers believe not on him, and the nobles lay not their necks to the yoke of the Lord, even because their hearts are lifted up within them, and so lie in an unteachable frame before the Lord?

(3.) The truth being revealed to them, and their own hearts made acquainted therewith, after their personal engagements to the practice of the power of godliness, according to the "revelation of God in the face of Jesus Christ," three things are incumbent on him in reference thereunto.

[1.] That, according to the measure of its revelation unto him, he declare, or take care that it be declared, unto others, even all committed to his governing charge. The general equity that is in the obligation of "strengthening others when we are confirmed," desiring them to be like ourselves in all participation of grace from God, —the nature of true zeal for the glory and name of the Lord, are a sufficient warrant for this, yea, demand the performance of this duty. So Jehoshaphat, being instructed in the ways of God, sent princes and priests to teach it in all the cities and towns of Judah, 2 Chron. xvii. 7–9. As also did Hezekiah, 2 Chron. xxx. 6–9. Let this, then, be our first position:—

I. It belongs to the duty of the supreme magistrate, the governor or shepherd of the people, in any nation, being acquainted with the mind of God, to take care that the truth of the gospel be preached to all the people of that nation, according to the way appointed, either ordinary or extraordinary.

I make no doubt but God will quickly reject them from their power who, knowing their Master's will, are negligent herein.

[2.] As he is to declare it, so he is to protect it from all violence whatever. Jesus Christ is the great king of nations, as well as the holy king of saints. His gospel hath a right to be preached in every nation, and to every creature under heaven. Whoever forbids or hinders the free passage of it, is not only sinful and impious towards God, but also injurious towards men. Certainly the magistrate is to protect every one and every thing in their own right, from the violence and injury of unruly men. In the preaching and receiving the gospel there is a right acted, superior to all earthly privileges whatever. In this, then, the magistrate is to protect it, that under him the professors thereof "may lead a quiet and peaceable life, in all godliness and honesty." And for this cause they to whom the sword is committed may with the sword lawfully defend the truth, as the undoubted right and privilege of those who do enjoy it, and of which they cannot be deprived without the greatest injury. Jephthah laid it down as the ground of the equity of the wars he waged against the Ammonites, that they would possess what the Lord their God gave them to possess; the defence whereof he pursued to the subversion of their (at first) invading enemies, Judges xi. 24, 33. It is no new thing to begin in defence, and end in offence. Now, if the truth be given us of the Lord our God to possess, certainly it may be contended for by those who owe protection thereunto. And if this were not so, we may pray, and prevail, for the prosperity of those in authority, and yet, when we have done, not have a right to a quiet and peaceable life. Let this, then, be the second assertion:—

II. The gospel being preached and declared, as of right it ought to be, it is the duty of the magistrate, by the power wherewith he is intrusted, to protect and defend it against all or any persons that, by force or violence, shall seek to hinder the progress or stop the passage of it, under what pretence soever.

And that a neglect of this also will be attended with the anger of the Lord, and the kindling of his wrath, shall not long be doubted of any.

[3.] The protecting, assisting, and supporting of all the professors of it in that profession, and in ways of truth's appointment, for the practice of that which is embraced, and the furtherance of it towards them who as yet embrace it not, is also required. And of this there are sundry parts.

1*st.* That, seeing Christ Jesus hath appointed his disciples to walk in such societies, and requireth of them such kind of worship, as cannot be performed without their meeting together ὁμοθυμαδὸν, "in one place;" that he either provide, or grant being provided, the use of such places under his protection as may, in all or any kind, be suited and fitted for that end and purpose. And the ground of this is,—

(1*st.*) From the right which the gospel of Christ hath to be received amongst men, according to his own appointment; whether that be the appointment of Christ or not, amongst us is no question.

(2*dly.*) Because the magistrate hath the sole power of all public places, and the protection of them is committed to him alone, by virtue of that consent unto government which is among any people. This proved as above.

2*dly.* A protection in the use of those places, and all things exercised in them, answerable to that which he doth and is bound to grant unto men in their own private dwellings and families. The reason why I am protected from all hurt or violence in my family is, because I have a right to dispose of all things in my family, being my own; and so hath not another. It was asserted before that Christians have a right to the ordinances of Christ, and truth a right to be at liberty; and therefore, if any shall invade, disturb, or trouble them in their rights and liberties, he is bound, "ex officio," to give them a protection, "not bearing the sword in vain."

Now, being in my family, in my private house, the assistance of those in authority is due,—

(1*st.*) In respect of them without.

(2*dly.*) In respect of them within.

(1*st.*) For them without, if any one will, against my consent, intrude himself upon my family enjoyments, to share with me, or violently come to take away that is mine, or disturb me in the quiet possession of it, the magistrate takes cognizance of such disturbances, and punisheth them according to equity. Suitably, if any person or persons whatsoever shall with violence put themselves upon the enjoyment of such ordinances as those enjoying the rights of the gospel have obtained to themselves, or shall come in their celebration of them to cause disturbance, certainly that magistrate protects not every one in his undoubted rights, who doth not accommodate the wronged parties with the assistance of his power to the punishment of the transgressors.

(*2dly.*) For house dwellers, servants, or any others, who may break out into such offences and incorrigibleness as the amendment thereof may be beyond what I am intrusted to do to any by law of God or man, shall not the magistrate here also interpose? is not his assistance here abundantly required and always granted?

From parity of reason, is it not as due for their protection who, in the enjoyment of their public religious rights, may receive disturbance, and be under force from some incorrigible by any rule among themselves? For instance,—suppose a person justly excommunicated and ejected any society of Christians, as to any spiritual communion, yet will with outward force and violence put himself upon them in their closest acts of communion; doubtless their rights are here to be by power preserved.

3dly. That whereas the preachers of the gospel are now to be maintained in an ordinary way, and to expect their supportment in a usual course of providence; and seeing that many to whom we have proved that the gospel is to be declared by the care of the magistrate, will not or cannot make such provisions for them as is needful in these last evil days of the world; it is incumbent on those nursing-fathers to provide for them, who, because of their continual labours in the work of the Lord, are disenabled to make provision for themselves. Where churches are settled according to the rule of the gospel, and not too much straitened by reason of want, there may be an alteration as to this proposal. That this engagement lies first upon the churches, was seen of old. Hence that caution or canon of the Council of Chalcedon, cap. vi., Μηδεὶς χειροτονείσθω ἀπολελυμένος, "Let none be ordained at large." "Ne dicatur, mendicat in palæstra infelix clericus," says the scholiast,—"lest he should be driven to beg for want of maintenance."

This being the sum of what, as to this head, I have to assert, I shall give in the proofs of it, and then draw some farther positions.

Reason 1. The bottom of the whole ariseth from that right which the gospel hath to be preached to all nations and people; and that right, paramount to all civil sanctions and constitutions, which every soul hath to receive it in the profession thereof. And all this flows from the donation of the Father unto Jesus Christ, whereby he is made "heir of all things," Heb. i. 2, having the "nations given him for his inheritance, the uttermost parts of the earth for his possession," Ps. ii. 8;—being also "King of kings, and Lord of lords," acting nothing in taking possession of his own but what his sovereignty bears him out in.

Reason 2. All this tends to the apparent good of those committed to his charge, that they may lead their lives in godliness and honesty; which is the very chief end of magistracy committed unto men. This is directly intended; all other things come in by accident, and upon suppositions.

Reason 3. No person living can pretend to the least injury by this, —none is deprived, none wronged.

Reason 4. The precepts given unto them, and the promises made concerning them, do abundantly confirm all that hath been asserted. Ps. ii. 10, 11, they are commanded as kings and judges to serve the Lord, in promoting the kingdom of the Lord Jesus Christ. And it is promised, Isa. xlix. 23, that " they shall be nursing-fathers and nursing-mothers to the church" of Christ, even then when she shall " suck the breasts of kings" (earthly things are the milk of kingly breasts), " when her officers shall be peace, and her exactors righteousness," Isa. lx. 16, 17. This, at least, reacheth to all we have ascribed to them. All is but bowing the knee of magistracy at the name of Jesus.

Hence are these positions:—

III. The providing or granting of places requisite for the performance of that worship which in the gospel is instituted, is the duty of the Christian magistrate.

IV. Protection, as to peace and quietness in the use of the ordinances of the Lord Jesus Christ, from violent disturbers, either from without or within, is also incumbent on him.

V. Supportment and provision, as to earthly things, where regularly failing, is of him required.

And in the neglect of any of these that takes place, which is threatened, Isa. lx. 12, two or three consectaries, added hereunto, shall close this part of the magistrate's power, or rather duty, about the things of religion. As,—

Consect. 1. Positive actings, by way of supportment and assistance, maintenance, allowance of public places, and the like, in the behalf of persons deviating from the truth, in those things wherein they deviate, are contrary to the rule of the word, and duty of them in authority. For,—

Error hath neither right nor promise; nor is any precept given in the behalf thereof.

Consect. 2. The defence and protection of erring persons from violence and injury, in those things wherein they have a right, is no acting of his duty about religious things, but a mere dealing for the preservation of human society, by the defence of persons not acting against the rules thereof.[1]

[1] For this cause the emperors of old still allowed the Novatians the liberty of worship.

Consect. 3. Every particular minute difference among the professors of the truth cannot be proved to come under the cognizance of the magistrate, he being to attend the worship which for the main is acceptable to God in Christ; neither do any testimonies extend his duty any farther. Hence,—

Corollary 1. The present differences about church society and the subject or seat of discipline, which are between those dissenters who are known by the names of Presbyterians and Independents, as they are in themselves (not heightened by the prejudices, lusts, corruptions, and interests of men), hinder not at all, but that the magistrate is bound to the performance of the duties before mentioned unto both parties. And the reasons of this are, because,—

Reason 1. The things wherein they are agreed are clearly as broad as the magistrate's duty can be stretched to cover them.

Reason 2. Neither party, I am persuaded, in their retired thoughts dare avow the main of the worship by their dissenters embraced, to be, as such, rejected of the Lord.

Reason 3. No example in the world can be produced out of the Old Testament, or New, or ecclesiastical history, of a forcible decision of such minute differences. See Socrat. Eccles. Hist., lib. vi. cap. 20.

Corollary 2. All the plea of persons erring in doctrine or worship is not from what the magistrate must do, but from what he may not do.

And this for the first part shall suffice.

2. There is another part of the magistrate's power,—the other side of his sword,—to be exercised towards the opposition of that truth which he hath embraced.

And this hath a twofold object:—

(1.) Things; (2.) Persons.

(1.) Things are of two sorts:—

[1.] Ways of worship.

[2.] Outward appearances, monuments, accommodations, and declarations of those ways.

Of the first I shall speak afterward.

By the second I mean all the outward attendances of any false or erroneous worship, which are either helps to or declarations of the superstition, idolatry, error, or falseness of it; as temples for idolatrous service, crosses, pictures, and the like abused relics of old, unwarranted zeal. Now, concerning these, I affirm,—

1*st*, That the magistrate ought not to make provision of any public places for the practice of any such worship as he is convinced to be an abomination unto the Lord. When I say he ought not to make provision, I understand not only a not actual caring that such be, but also a caring that such may not be. He should not have a negation of acting as to any thing of public concernment. His not opposing here is providing. For instance, he must not allow—that is, it is his duty to oppose—the setting apart of public places under his protection for the service of the mass (as of late in Somerset House), or for any kind of worship in itself disallowed, because not required, and so not accepted. This were to be bound to help forward sin, and that such sin whereof he is convinced;—which is repugnant to the whole revealed will of God. A magistrate, I told you before, is not to act according to what he may do, but what he must do. Now, it cannot be his duty to further sin.

2*dly*. Outward monuments—ways of declaring and holding out false and idolatrous worship—he is to remove; as the Papists' images, altars, pictures, and the like; Turks' mosques; prelates' service-book. Now these are of two sorts:—

(1*st*.) Such things as, in their whole use and nature, serve only for the carrying on of worship in itself wholly false, and merely invented; as altars, images, crosses.

(2*dly*.) Such as are used for the carrying on of worship true in itself, though vilely corrupted; as praying and preaching;—such are those places commonly called churches.

The first are to be abolished; the latter aright used. I speak as to public appearances; for private disquisitions after such things I may be otherwise minded. The reason of this difference is evident to all.

Thus, in days of old, Constantine shut up Pagans' temples, Euseb. de Vita Constant., lib. iv. cap. 23, 24; and demolished some of the most filthy of them, lib. iii. cap. 52. Theodosius utterly cast them to the ground, though not without some blows and bloodshed, Socrat. Eccles. Hist., lib. v. cap. 16. The command of God for the abolishing all monuments of idolatry, Deut. xii. 1–3, with the commendation of those kings of Judah who accordingly performed this duty, 2 Chron. xvii. 6, xxx. 14, are enough to confirm it, and to bottom this position:—

VI. It is the duty of the magistrate not to allow any public places for (in his judgment) false and abominable worship; as also, to demolish all outward appearances and demonstrations of such superstitious, idolatrous, and unacceptable service.

Let Papists, who are idolaters, and Socinians, who are anthropolatræ, plead for themselves.

(2.) Now, for persons there seems something more of difficulty; yet certain clear rules may be proposed concerning them also, to hold out when they and their proceedings come under the cognizance of the civil magistrate, and are obnoxious to the sword which he beareth. And they are these:—

[1.] Such persons as, having embraced any false principles and persuasion in or about things concerning God and his worship, do pursue the upholding or propagating of such principles in a disorderly manner, to the disturbance of civil society, are doubtless under his restraining power, to be acted and put forth in such ways as to other persons running out into the same or the like compass of disorder, upon other grounds, and from the instigation of other lusts. The pretence of disturbance and confusion, upon the bearing with differences in opinion about things commanded in religion, we before rejected, as a colour fitted chiefly for the wearing of persecution. But actual disturbances, indeed, must have actual restraints. For instance, if a man, being persuaded that the power of the magistrate is in Christian religion groundless, unwarrantable, unlawful, should thereupon stir up the people to the abolishing and removal of that power; such stirrings up, and such actings upon that instigation, are as opposite to the gospel of Christ (which opposeth no lawful regimen among the sons of men), so also prejudicial to human society; and therefore to be proceeded against by them who bear not the sword in vain. This case we know happened once in Germany, and may do so again in other places. If such as these suffer, it is "as murderers, or thieves, or evil-doers, or busy-bodies in other men's matters;" which is a shameful thing, no way commendable or praiseworthy, 1 Pet. iv. 15.

[2.] If any persons whatsoever, under any pretence whatsoever, shall offer violence or disturbance to the professors of the true worship of God, so owned, established, and confirmed as above said, in and for the profession of that true, so-owned worship, service, and declaration of the mind of God; such persons are to fear that power which is the minister of God, and a revenger to them that do evil. Let us suppose of them what they suppose, and for their own justification and support in irregular ways bear out of themselves,—that they enjoy the truth, others walking in paths of their own; yet then this practice is contrary to that prime dictate of nature which none can pretend ignorance of, viz., "Do not that to another which thou wouldst not have done unto thyself." If men that would not think it equitable to be so dealt with as they deal with others, supposing themselves in their condition, do yet so deal with them, they are αὐτοκατάκριτοι, and do pronounce sentence against themselves out of their own mouths. This, then, deserveth punishment; and breaking out to the disturbance of public order ought to be punished. We before proved the protection of public places to belong to the magistrate; so that he not only may, but, if he will not be false to Him by whom he is intrusted, he must, put forth his authority for the safe-guarding and revenging of them. Yea, also, and this rule may pass, when some things in the way publicly established are truly offensive. What the ancient Christians thought of the zeal of Audas, a Christian bishop, who would needs demolish a Pagan temple in Persia, I know not; but I am sure his discretion is not much extolled who, by that one fiery act of destroying πυρεῖον,—that is, "a temple of fire" (for the Persians looked upon fire as a god, as the historian observes),—occasioned a cruel persecution of thirty years' continuance, Theod. Eccles. Hist., lib. v. cap. 38.

[3.] When any have entertained any singular opinion in matters of great weight and importance,—such as nearly concern the glory of God, and the minds of Christians, in reverence of his holy name, are most tenderly affected withal, so that without much horror of mind they can scarce hear those errors whereby those grand truths are opposed,—yet those persons who have entertained such uncouth opinions shall not be content so to have done, and also in all lawful ways (as to civil society) endeavoured to propagate the said opinions to others; but, in the pursuit of this their design of opposing truth, shall publicly use such expressions, or perform such acts, as are fit to pour contempt and scorn upon the truth which they do oppose,—reviling it also, or God himself so represented as he is in the truth they abominate, with odious and execrable appellations (as, for instance, the calling the holy Trinity, "Tricipitem Cerberum");—if the question be put, Whether in this case the magistrate be not obliged to vindicate the honour of God by corporeal restraints, in some degrees at least, upon the persons of those men?—truly, for my part, I incline to the affirmative. And the reason hereof is this:—Though men, through the incurable blindness of their minds, falling into error of judgment and misinterpretation of the word, may disbelieve the Deity of Christ, and the Holy Spirit; yet that any pretence from the word, persuasion of conscience, or dictate of religion, should carry them out to reviling, opprobrious speeches of that which of God is held out contrary to their apprehensions, is false and remote from reason itself. For this cause Paul says he was a blasphemer;—not because, being a Jew, he disbelieved the gospel; but because, so disbelieving it, he moreover loaded the truths thereof with contumelious reproaches. Such expressions, indeed, differ not from those piercing words of the holy name of God which he censured to death, Lev. xxiv. 15, but only in this, that there seemeth in that to be a plain opposition unto light, in this not so. The like may be said of a Jew's crucifying a dog.

[4.] There are a sort of persons termed in Scripture ἄτακτοι, 1 Thess. v. 14; ἀγοραῖοι. Acts xvii. 5; ἄτοποι, 2 Thess. iii. 2; ἀνυπότακτοι, 1 Tim. i. 9, and the like,—disorderly, vagabond, wandering, irregular persons, fixed to no calling, abiding in no place, taking no care of their families; that, under a pretence of teaching the truth, without mission, without call, without warrant, uncommanded, undesired, do go up and down, from place to place, creeping into houses, &c. Now, that such ways as these, and persons in these ways, may be judicially inquired into, I no way doubt. The story is famous of Sesostris, king of Egypt, who made a law, that all the subjects of his kingdom should once a-year give an account of their way and manner of living, and if any one were found to spend his time idly, he was certainly punished; and the laws of most nations have provided that their people shall not be wanderers, and whosoever hath not a place of abode and employment is by them a punishable vagabond. And in this, by much experience of the ways, walking, and converse of such persons, I am exceedingly confirmed in. I did as yet never observe any other issue upon such undertakings, but scandal to religion, and trouble to men in their civil relations.

[5.] When men, by the practice of any vice or sin, draw others to a pretended religion; or, by pretence of religion, draw men to any vice or known sin, let them be twice punished,—for their real vice, and pretended religion. The truth is, I have been taught exceedingly to disbelieve all the strange imputations of wickedness and uncleanness that are imposed upon many, to be either the end or the medium of the practice of that communion in religion which they do profess and embrace. I remember that, when I was a boy, all those stories were told me of Brownists and Puritans which afterward I found to have been long before the forgeries of Pagans, and imposed on the primitive Christians. I dare boldly say, I have heard stories of them a hundred times, holding out that very thing, and those deeds of darkness, which Minutius Felix holds out in the tongue of an infidel concerning the Christians of those days; but yet, because sundry venerable persons, to whom antiquity hath given sanctuary from being arraigned on the point of false testimony, have left it upon record of sundry heretics in their days,—as the Gnostics and others,—that they were conjoined into "societates tesserâ pollutionis," and some assert that the like iniquities are not wholly buried, I made the supposition, and hope that, if they depose themselves from common sense and reason, the magistrate will never exalt them to the privilege and exemption of religion.

In these, and such like cases as these, when men shall break forth into disturbance of common order and enormities against the light of nature, beyond all positive command of any pretended religion whatsoever, that the magistrate ought to set hedges of thorns in their ways, sharpened according to their several delinquencies, I suppose no man not abhorred of common sense can once hesitate or doubt. And I am the more inclined to assert a restraint to all such as these, because it may be established to the height without the least prejudice unto the truth, though persons erring should enjoy the place of authority.

3. That which now remaineth in this head to be considered, is

concerning persons maintaining and upholding any great and pernicious errors, but in such ways as are not, by any of the former disorders, to be brought under the cognizance of the civil magistrate, but good, honest, allowable, and peaceable in themselves; not at all to be questioned, but in reference to the things that are carried on in and by those ways,—as communication by discourse and private preaching, and the like.

Now, concerning these, it is generally affirmed, that persons maintaining any error in or against any fundamental article of faith or religion, and that with obstinacy or pertinacy after conviction, ought to be proceeded against by the authority of the civil magistrate, whether unto death or banishment, imprisonment or confiscation of goods.

(1.) Now unto this—supposing what I have written heretofore concerning the incompetency of all and the non-constitution of any judge in this case, with the answers given at the beginning of this treatise to most of the places produced usually for the affirmative—I shall briefly give in my thoughts; reserving the consideration of pressing conformity to the next head to be handled. And,—

[1.] That I cannot but observe, that, in the question itself, there are sundry things gratis assumed; as,—

1*st*. That it is known and confessed what articles in religion are fundamental, and this also to the magistrate; when no one thing among Christians is more questionable, most accounting them so (be they what they will) wherein they differ from others. So that, one way or other, all dissenters shall be hooked in, directly or indirectly, to clash upon fundamentals. In this Papists are secure, who make the church's propositions sufficient to make an article fundamental.

2*dly*. That the persons holding the error are convinced, when perhaps they have been only confuted; between which two there is a wide difference. He that holds the truth may be confuted; but a man cannot be convinced but by the truth. That a man should be said to be convinced of a truth, and yet that truth not shine in upon his understanding to the expelling of the contrary error, to me is strange. To be convinced, is to be overpowered by the evidence of that which before a man knew not. I myself once knew a scholar invited to a dispute with another man about something in controversy in religion. In his own, and in the judgment of all the bystanders, the opposing person was utterly confuted; and yet the scholar, within a few months, was taught of God, and clearly convinced that it was an error which he had maintained, and the truth which he opposed: and then, and not till then, did he cease to wonder that the other person was not convinced by his strong arguments, as before he had thought. May not a Protestant be really worsted in a dispute by a Papist? hath it not so ere now fallen out?—if not, the Jesuits are egregious liars. To say a man is convinced, when, either for want of skill and ability or the like, he cannot maintain his opinion to and against all men, is a mere conceit. The truth is, I am so far from this morose severity of looking upon all erring persons as convinced that have been confuted, that I rather, in charity, incline to believe that no erring person, whilst he continues in his error, is convinced. It will not easily enter into my dull apprehension, how a man can be convinced of an error that is enlightened with a contrary truth, and yet hold that error still. I am loath to charge more corrupt and vile affections upon any than do openly appear. That of Paul, affirming that some men are self-condemned, is quite of another nature. I think a person is said to be convinced, not when there is sufficiency in the means of conviction, but when there is such an efficacy in them as to lay hold upon his understanding.

3dly. That they are obstinate and pertinacious is also a cheap supposal, taken up without the price of a proof. What we call obstinacy, they call constancy; and what we condemn them for as pertinacy, they embrace as perseverance. As the conviction is imposed, not owned, so is this obstinacy. If we may be judges of other men's obstinacy, all will be plain; but if ever they get uppermost, they will be judges of ours. Besides, I know not what good it will do us, or how it will advantage our cause, to suppose men obstinate and convinced before we punish them,—no such qualifications being anywhere in the book of God urged in persons deserving punishment:—if they have committed the crime whereunto the penalty is annexed, be they obstinate or not, they shall be punished.

[2.] But now, supposing all this,—that we are clear in all fundamentals,—that we are convinced that they are convinced, and doubt not but that they are obstinate;—if they keep themselves in the former bounds, what is to be done? I say, besides what we spake at the entrance of this discourse, I shall, as to any ways of corporeal coaction and restraint, oppose some few things.

1*st.* The non-constitution of a judge in case of heresy is a thing civilly criminal. As to spiritual censures, and an ecclesiastical judgment of errors and false doctrines, we find them appointed, and a lawful judge as to the determining concerning them divinely instituted; so that in such ways they may be warrantably proceeded against, Rev. xxii. 15. But now, for any judge that should make disquisition concerning them, or proceed against them, as things criminal, to be punished with civil censures, I conceive the Scripture is silent. And indeed, who should it be? The custom of former ages was, that some persons of one sort should determine of it as to right,—viz., that such or such a thing was heresy, and such or such a one a heretic,—which was the work of priests and prelates; and persons of another sort should "de facto" punish, and determine to be punished, those so adjudged by the former,—and these were, as they called them, the secular magistrates, officers of this world. And indeed, had not the god of this world blinded their eyes, and the God of the spirits of all flesh hardened their hearts, they would not have so given up their power to the man of sin as to be made so sordidly instrumental to his bloody cruelty. We read, Jer. xxvi. 10, 11, that the priests and prophets assemble themselves in judgment, and so pronounce sentence upon the prophet Jeremiah that he should die for a false prophet; verse 12, Jeremiah makes his appeal to the secular magistrate, and all the people; who, taking cognizance of the cause, pronounce sentence in the behalf of the condemned person against the priests and prophets, and deliver him whether they will or not, verse 16. I spare the application of the story: but that princes and magistrates should, without cognizance of the thing or cause, proceed to punishment or censure of it, upon the judgment of the priests condemning such or such a man for a heretic or a false prophet,—blessed be the Lord, we have no warrant. Had this proceeding been regular, Jeremiah had died without mercy for a false prophet, as thousands since, standing before the Lord in his spirit, have done. This course, then, that the civil magistrate should proceed to sentence of corporeal punishment upon others judging of the fault, is vile, sordid, unwarrantable, and exceedingly unworthy of any rational man, much more such as are set over the people of the land. That the same persons must determine of the cause and appoint the punishment is clear.

Now, who must these be?

(1*st.*) Are they the ministers of the gospel?—of all others, they are the most likely to be the most competent judges in spiritual causes. Let it be so; but then, also, they must be the determiners and inflicters of the punishment upon default. Now, let them pour out upon obstinately erring persons all the vengeance that God hath betrusted them withal, "The weapons of our warfare are not carnal, but mighty through God," &c. By this course, admonition, avoiding, rejection, excommunication, will be the utmost that can be inflicted on them; which, for my part, I desire may be exercised to the utmost extent of the rule.

(2*dly.*) Shall the magistrate be made judge of the cause as well as of the person? Is he intrusted to determine what is error, what not,—what heresy, what not,—who is an heretic, who not; and so what punishment is due to such and such errors, according to the degrees wherein they are?

[1*st.*] I desire an institution of this ordinance in the church.

Where is the magistrate intrusted with such a power? where are rules prescribed to him in his proceedings?

[*2dly.*] Is not a judiciary determination concerning truth and error (I mean truths of the gospel) a mere church act? and that church power whereby it is effected? Must not, then, the magistrate, "quâ talis," be a church officer? Will men of this mind tolerate Erastianism?

[*3dly.*] If there be a twofold judicature appointed for the same person, for the same crime, is it not because one crime may in divers respects fall under several considerations? and must not these considerations be preserved immixed, that the formal reason of proceeding in one court may not be of any weight in the other? We proved before, and it is granted of all, that the church is judge in case of heresy and error, as such, to proceed against them, as contrary to the gospel;—their opposition to the faith delivered to the saints is the formal reason upon which that proceedeth to censure. If, now, this be afterward brought under another sentence, of another judicature, must it not be under another consideration? Now, what can this be, but its disturbance of civil society; which, when it doth so,—not in pretence, but really and actually,—none denies it to be the magistrate's duty to interpose with his power.

[*4thly.*] If the magistrate be judge of spiritual offences, and it be left to him to determine and execute judgment, in such proportion as he shall think meet, according to the quality and degrees thereof,—it is a very strange and unlimited arbitrariness over the lives and estates of men: and surely they ought to produce very clear testimonies that they are intrusted from the Lord herewith, or they can have no great quiet in acting.

[*5thly.*] It seems strange to me, that the Lord Jesus Christ should commit this architectonical power in his house unto magistrates, foreseeing of what sort the greatest number of them would be, yea, determining that they should be such, for the trial and affliction of his own. View the times that are past, consult the stories of former ages, take a catalogue of the kings and rulers that have been, since first magistrates outwardly embraced Christian religion in this and other nations where the gospel hath been planted; and ask your own consciences whether these be the men to whom this high trust in the house of God is committed? The truth is, they no sooner left serving the dragon in the persecution of the Pagans, but presently, in a very few years, they gave up their power to the beast, to set up another state in opposition to the Lord Jesus Christ and his gospel; in the supportment whereof the most of them continue labouring till this very day. "Hæ manus Trojam exigent?" What may be added in this case, I refer to another opportunity.

2dly. Gospel constitutions in the case of heresy or error seem not to favour any course of violence,—I mean, of civil penalties. Foretold it is that heresies must be, 1 Cor. xi. 19; but this for the manifesting of those that are approved, not the destroying of those that are not;—I say destroying, I mean with temporal punishment, that I may add this by the way; for,—all the arguments produced for the punishment of heretics, holding out capital censures, and these being the tendence of all beginnings in this kind,—I mention only the greatest, including all other arbitrary penalties, being but steps of walking to the utmost censures. Admonitions, and excommunication upon rejection of admonition, are the highest constitutions (I suppose) against such persons: "Waiting with all patience upon them that oppose themselves, if at any time God will give them repentance to the acknowledgment of the truth." Imprisoning, banishing, slaying, is scarcely a patient waiting. God doth not so wait upon unbelievers. Perhaps those who call for the sword on earth are as unacquainted with their own spirits as those that called for fire from heaven, Luke ix. 54. And perhaps the parable of the tares gives in a positive rule as to this whole business: occasion may be given of handling it at large; for the present I shall not fear to assert, that the answers unto it, borrowed by our divines from Bellarmine, will not endure the trial. We hope that spiritual quiet, and inoffensiveness in the whole mountain of the Lord, which is wrapped up in the womb of many promises, will at length be brought forth to the joy of all the children of Zion.

3dly. Sundry other arguments, taken from the nature of faith, heresy, liberty of conscience, the way of illumination, means of communication of truth, nature of spiritual things, pravitious tendence of the doctrine opposed, if it should be actually embraced by all enjoying authority, and the like, I thought at present to have added; but I am gone already beyond my purposed resting-place.

(2.) Come we, in a few words, to the last thing proposed (wherein I shall be very brief, the main of what I intended being already set down),—the power of the magistrate to compel others to the embracing of that religion and way of worship which he shall establish and set up; which, for the greater advantage, we shall suppose to be the very same, both for the things proposed to be believed and also practised, which God himself hath revealed, and requireth all men everywhere to embrace. What is to be done for the settling and establishing of the profession of the gospel, and the right apprehension of the mind of God therein, contradistinct from all those false and erroneous persuasions which, in these or former days, [are] or have been held forth in opposition thereunto, was before declared;—how it is to be supported, maintained, protected, defended, safe-guarded from all oppositions, disturbances, blasphemings, was then and there set down.

Now, supposing that sundry persons, living under the power, and owning civil obedience to the magistrate, will not consent to sound doctrine, nor receive in some things (fewer or more, less or greater) that form of wholesome words which he holds forth and owns as the mind of Christ in the gospel, nor communicate with him in the worship which, by the authority of those words or that truth, he hath as before established, it is inquired, What is the duty of the magistrate in reference to the bringing of them into that subjection which is due unto, and an acknowledgment of, the truth?

And to this I shall briefly give in my answer in these following positions:—

[1.] In reference unto us in this nation, the greatest difficulty in giving a full return to this question ariseth from the great disorder of the churches of God amongst us. Were the precious distinguished from the vile, churches rightly established, and church discipline [so] exercised that Christians were under some orderly view, and men might be considered in their several capacities wherein they stand, an easy finger would untie the knot of this query. But being in that confusion wherein we are, gathering into any order being the great work in hand, I suppose, under favour, that the time is scarce come for the proposal of this question; but yet something may be given in unto it, though not so clear as the former supposal, being effected, would cause it to be.

[2.] The constant practice of the churches in former ages, in all their meetings for advice and counsel, to consent unto some form of wholesome words, that might be a discriminating "tessera" [symbol] of their communion in doctrine, being used in prime antiquity,—as is manifest in that ancient symbol commonly esteemed apostolical (of the chief heads whereof mention in the like summary is made in the very first writers among them),—having also warrant from the word of God, and being of singular use to hold out unto all other churches of the world our apprehensions of the mind of God in the chief heads of religion, may be considered. If this be done by the authority of the magistrate, —I mean, if such a declaration of the truth wherein the churches by him owned and protected do consent be held out as the confession of that truth which he embraceth,—it will be of singular use unto, yea, indeed, must necessarily precede, any determination of the former question. Of the nature and use of confessions, &c., so much hath of late been learnedly disputed, that I shall not pour out any of mine own conceptions for the present about them in that hasty, tumultuary manner wherein I am enforced to expose this essay.

[3.] Those who dissent from the truth so owned, so established, so decreed, do so either in less matters of small consequence, and about things generally confessed not fundamental; or in great and more weighty heads of doctrine, acts of worship, and the like;—both agreeing in this, that they will not hold communion, either as to all or some parts and duties thereof, with those churches and persons who do embrace the truth so owned, as before, and act accordingly.

1*st*, For the first of these, or such as dissent about things of no great concernment, in comparison of those other things wherein they do agree with them from whom they do dissent, I am bold positively to assert, that, saving and reserving the rules and qualifications set down under the second head, the magistrate hath no warrant from the word of God, nor command, rule, or precept, to enable him to force such persons to submit unto the truth as by him established, in those things wherein they express a conscientious dissent, or to molest them with any civil penalty in case of refusal or non-submission; nor yet did I ever in my life meet with any thing in the shape of reason to prove it, although the great present clamour of this nation is punctually as to this head:—whatever be pretended, this is the Helena about which is the great contest.

What, I pray, will warrant him, then, to proceed? Will the laws against idolatry and blasphemy, with their sanctions towards the persons of blasphemers and idolaters? (For I must ingenuously confess, all that which, in my poor judgment, looks with any appearance of pressing towards Hæreticidium is the everlasting equity of those judicial laws, and the arbitrariness of magistrates from a divine rule in things of the greatest concernment to the glory of God, if free from them; and that [as] these laws, I doubt, will scarcely be accommodated unto any thing under contest now in this age of the world among Christians.)—But shall I say a warrant [may be] taken from hence for the compelling of men sound in so many fundamentals as, were it not for the contest with them, we would acknowledge sufficient for the entertainment of the Lord Jesus in their bosoms, to subject [themselves] to, and close with, the things contrary to their present light and apprehension (though under a promise of being taught of God), or to inflict penalties upon a refusal so to do?—"Credat Apella!"

Shall the examples of extraordinary judgments upon idolaters, false prophets, by sword and fire from heaven, on magicians, apostates, and the like, be here produced? Though such arguments as these have made thousands weep tears of blood, yet the consequence, in reason, cannot but provoke laughter to all men not wholly forsaken of directing principles.

What, then, shall be done? they will say. They have been admonished, rebuked, convinced,—must they now be let alone?

Something as to this I shall add in the close of this discourse;—for the present, let learned Whitaker answer for me. And first, to the first,—of their being confuted: "Possunt quidem controversiæ ad externum forum deferri, et ibi definiri; sed conscientia in eo foro non acquiescit, non enim potest conscientia sedari sine Spiritu sancto." Let controversies (saith he) be determined how you please,—until the conscience be quieted by the Holy Spirit, there will be little peace. Unto which I shall not add any thing, considering what I said before of conviction. And to the latter,—of letting them alone to their own ways, "Ecclesiæ quidem optatius est levibus quibusdam dissensionibus ad tempus agitari, quam in perfida pace acquiescere; non ergo sufficit aliquo modo pacem conservari, nisi illam esse sanctam pacem constiterit," Whit., Con. 4 de Rom. Pont. qu. 1, cap. 1, sect. 2. Better some trouble, than a perfidious, compelled peace. See him handle this more at large, with some excellent conclusions to this purpose, Con. 4 de Rom. Pont. qu. 1, cap. 1, sect. 19, pp. 48 et 50.

For these, then (and under this head I compare all such persons as, keeping in practice within the bounds before laid forth, do so far hold the foundation, as that, neither by believing what is not, nor disbelieving what indeed is, they do take in or keep off any such thing as wherewithal being embraced, or without which being rejected, the life of Christ cannot in any case possibly consist, nor salvation by him be obtained), as the magistrate is not bound by any rule or precept to assist and maintain them in the practice of those things wherein they dissent from the truth; so he is bound to protect them in peace and quietness in the enjoyment of all civil rights and liberties;—nor hath he either warrant or allowance to proceed against them, as to the least penalty, for their dissent in those things they cannot receive. Attempts for uniformity among saints, or such as, for aught we can conclude either from their opinions or practices, may be so, by external force, are purely antichristian.

2dly. Now, for those that stand at a greater distance from the publicly owned and declared truths,—such as before we spake of,—the orderly way of dealing with such is, in the first place, to bring them off from the error of the way which they have embraced; and until that be done, all thoughts of drawing in their assent to that from which at such a distance they stand is vain and bootless. Now, what course is to be taken for the effecting of this? Spiritual ways of healing are known to all,—let them be used; and in case they prove fruitless, for aught that yet I can perceive, the persons of men so erring must be left in the state and condition we described under the second head.

And now, to drive on this business any farther by way of contest, I will not. My intention at the beginning was only positively to assert, and to give in briefly, the scriptural and rational bottoms and proofs of those assertions; wherein I have gone aside, to pull or thrust a line of debate, I have transgressed against my own purpose,—I hope it will be pardoned; though I am heartily desirous any thing which passeth my pen may be brought to the test, and myself reduced where I have gone amiss. Yet my spirit faints within me to think of that way of handling things in controversy which some men, by reciprocation of answers and replies, have wound themselves into. Bolsec,[1] and Staphylus, and Stapleton, seem to live again, and much gall from beneath to be poured into men's ink. O the deep wounds the gospel hath received by the mutual keen invectives of learned men! I hope the Lord will preserve me from being engaged with any man of such a frame of spirit. What hath been asserted may easily be cast up in a few positions;—the intelligent reader will quickly discern what is aimed at, and what I have stood to avow.

If what is proposed be not satisfactory, I humbly offer to the honourable Parliament, that a certain number of learned men, who are differently minded as to this business of toleration, which almost every where is spoken against, may be desired and required to a fair debate of the matter in difference before their own assembly; that so, if it be possible, some light may be given to the determination of this thing, of so great concernment in the judgments of all men, both on the one side and on the other; that so they may "try all things, and hold fast that which is good."

Corol. 1. That magistrates have nothing to do in matters of religion, as some unadvisedly affirm, is exceedingly wide from the truth of the thing itself.

Corol. 2. Corporeal punishments for simple error were found out to help to build the tower of Babel.

Si quid novisti rectius istis,
Candidus imperti; si non, his utere mecum.

[1] BOLSEC was a bitter opponent of Calvin, and wrote with much acrimony against him.—De J. Calv. Hist. Col. 1580. STAPHYLUS was at one time an evangelical theologian of the Lutheran Church, and afterwards became a violent enemy of the Reformation, 1558–1564. STAPLETON was a celebrated Roman Catholic divine, born in Sussex 1535. He left England on the accession of Queen Elizabeth, and was appointed Regius Professor of Divinity in the University of Louvain. He died in 1598. His works were published at Paris in 1620, in four vols. folio.—ED.

SERMON IV.

THE STEADFASTNESS OF THE PROMISES,

AND

THE SINFULNESS OF STAGGERING:

OPENED IN A SERMON PREACHED AT MARGARET'S IN WESTMINSTER, BEFORE THE PARLIAMENT, FEBRUARY 28, 1649,

BEING A DAY SET APART FOR SOLEMN HUMILIATION THROUGHOUT THE NATION.

PREFATORY NOTE.

THE following discourse was preached after Owen's return from Ireland. The expedition of Cromwell had been eminently successful in establishing peace, after the massacres and commotions which had long prevailed in that island. Owen, however, had set his heart upon securing for it higher blessings than outward peace, enforced by the conquering sword of the Protector. It is affecting to note the depth of spiritual concern and anxiety he evinces, that Ireland should enjoy the gospel of Christ, as the only cure for its manifold and inveterate disorders. How humbling, that extensive districts of it should have remained to our day substantially under the same wants and necessities which had a voice so clamant in the ear of Owen! It reads as if the utterance of yesterday, when we find him declaring his heartfelt wish, that "the Irish might enjoy Ireland as long as the moon endureth, so that Jesus Christ might possess the Irish."

Mr Orme holds, apparently on good grounds, that this sermon was really delivered before the House of Commons, not in February 1649, as the title bears, but in February 1650. The epistle dedicatory to the preceding sermon on "Righteous Zeal," etc., has the address and date, "*Coggeshall, Feb.* 28," (undoubtedly 1649), which is the same day on which, by the title of the present sermon, he was preaching at *London*. Some allusions in this sermon are thought to indicate that Owen had been in Ireland; and though, in all the editions of it, the year is said to have been 1649, by the present mode of reckoning it would be 1650. We may add, that in the old collections of Owen's sermons, this one follows the sermon next in the present order, on Heb. xii. 27. On the other hand, Asty affirms that it was preached *before* Owen went to Ireland, and speaks of it as giving rise to his acquaintance with Cromwell. The allusions to Ireland may not be regarded by some as very decisive on the point; and it is singular that the number of the year should differ from the mode of reckoning common to the dates of the other sermons published by Owen about this time. Since authorities differ, we have given the evidence on both sides, and the sermons appear in the order in which, by the dates and titles, they are said to have been preached. Mr Orme seems to us clearly in the right; and, though the matter is not of much importance, we have, under this view, some record in this discourse of the impressions left on the mind of Owen by his visit to Ireland. On the first occasion on which he ever preached before the House of Commons, he entreated that the destitute parts of England and Wales might be supplied with the gospel; and now on his return from his mission to Dublin, as soon as he has the ear of Parliament, he implores, in fervent terms, that the gospel may be sent to Ireland. The fact bespeaks his own heartfelt sense of its value, and shows how wisely he could turn opportunities to account for the advancement of his Master's cause.—ED.

Die Veneris, 1 *Martii*, 1649.

ORDERED by the Parliament, That the thanks of this House be given to Mr Owen for his great pains taken in his sermon preached yesterday before the Parliament, at Margaret's, Westminster (being a day set apart for public humiliation); and that he be desired to print his sermon; and that he have the like privilege in printing as others in like cases have usually had. Ordered, That Sir William Masham do give the thanks of this House to Mr Owen accordingly.

HEN. SCOBELL, *Cler. Parl.*

TO

THE COMMONS OF ENGLAND,

IN PARLIAMENT ASSEMBLED.

SIRS,

THAT God in whose hands your breath is, and whose are all your ways, having caused various seasons to pass over you, and in them all manifested that his works are truth and his ways judgment, calls earnestly by them for that walking before him which is required from them who, with other distinguishing mercies, are interested in the specialty of his protecting providence. As, in a view of present enjoyments, to sacrifice to your net, and burn incense to your drag, as though by them your portion were fat and plenteous, is an exceeding provocation to the eyes of his glory; so, to press to the residue of your desires and expectations by an arm of flesh, the designings and contrivances of carnal reason, with outwardly appearing mediums of their accomplishment, is no less an abomination to him. Though there may be a present sweetness to them that find the life of the hand, yet their latter end will be, to lie down in sorrow. That you might be prevailed on to give glory to God, by steadfastness in believing, committing all your ways to him, with patience in well-doing, to the contempt of the most varnished appearance of carnal policy, was my peculiar aim in this ensuing sermon.

That which added ready willingness to my obedience unto your commands for the preaching and publishing hereof, being a serious proposal for the advancement and propagation of the gospel in another nation, is here again recommended to your thoughts, by

Your most humble Servant

In our common Master,

J. OWEN.

March 8, 1649.

SERMON IV.

THE STEADFASTNESS OF THE PROMISES, AND THE SINFULNESS OF STAGGERING.

"He staggered not at the promise of God through unbelief."—Rom. iv. 20.

In the first chapters of this epistle, the apostle, from Scripture and the constant practice of all sorts of men of all ages, Jews and Gentiles, wise and barbarians, proves all the world, and every individual therein, to "have sinned and come short of the glory of God;"—and not only so, but that it was utterly impossible that, by their own strength, or by virtue of any assistance communicated, or privileges enjoyed, they should ever attain to a righteousness of their own that might be acceptable unto God.

Hereupon he concludes that discourse with these two positive assertions:—

First, That for what is past, "every mouth must be stopped, and all the world become guilty before God," chap. iii. 19.

Secondly, For the future, though they should labour to amend their ways, and improve their assistances and privileges to a better advantage than formerly, "yet by the deeds of the law shall no flesh be justified in the sight of God," verse 20.

Now, it being the main drift of the apostle, in this epistle, and in his whole employment, to manifest that God hath not shut up all the sons of men hopeless and remediless under this condition, he immediately discovers and opens the rich supply which God, in free grace, hath made and provided for the delivery of his own from this calamitous estate, even by the righteousness of faith in Christ; which he unfoldeth, asserteth, proves, and vindicates from objections, to the end of the 3d chapter.

This being a matter of so great weight, as comprising in itself the sum of the gospel wherewith he was intrusted,—the honour and exaltation of Christ, which above all he desired,—the great design of God to be glorious in his saints,—and, in a word, the chief subject of the embassage from Christ to him committed (to wit, that they who neither have, nor by any means can attain, a righteousness of their own, by the utmost of their workings, may yet have that which is complete and unrefusable in Christ, by believing); he therefore strongly confirms it in the 4th chapter, by testimony and example of the Scripture, with the saints that were of old;—thereby also declaring, that though the manifestation of this mystery were now more fully opened by Christ from the bosom of the Father, yet indeed this was the only way for any to appear in the presence of God, ever since sin entered the world.

To make his demonstrations the more evident, he singleth out one for an example who was eminently known, and confessed by all to have been the friend of God,—to have been righteous and justified before him, and thereon to have held sweet communion with him all his days; to wit, Abraham, the father according to the flesh of all those who put in the strongest of all men for a share in righteousness, by the privileges they did enjoy and the works they did perform.

Now, concerning him the apostle proves abundantly, in the beginning of the 4th chapter, that the justification which he found, and the righteousness he attained, was purely that, and no other, which he before described; to wit, a righteousness in the forgiveness of sins through faith in the blood of Christ. Yea, and that all the privileges and exaltations of this Abraham, which made him so signal and eminent among the saints of God as to be called "The father of the faithful," were merely from hence, that this righteousness of grace was freely discovered and fully established unto him;—an enjoyment being granted him in a peculiar manner by faith of that promise wherein the Lord Christ, with the whole spring of the righteousness mentioned, was enwrapped. This the apostle pursues, with sundry and various inferences and conclusions, to the end of verse 17, chap. iv.

Having laid down this, in the next place he gives us a description of that faith of Abraham whereby he became inheritor of those excellent things, from the adjuncts of it;—that as his justification was proposed as an example of God's dealing with us by his grace; so his faith might be laid down as a pattern for us in the receiving that grace.

Now, this he doth from,—

First, The foundation of it, whereon it rested.

Secondly, The matter of it, what he believed.

Thirdly, The manner of it, or how he believed.

First, From the bottom and *foundation* on which it rested,—viz., the omnipotency or all-sufficiency of God, whereby he was able to fulfil whatever he had engaged himself unto by promise, and which he called him to believe, verse 17, "He believed God, who quickeneth the dead, and calleth those things which be not as though they were."

Two great testimonies are here of the power of God.

1. That he "quickeneth the dead:"—able he is to raise up those that are dead to life again.

2. He "calleth things that are not as though they were:"—by his very call or word gives being to those things which before were not, as when he said, "Let there be light, and there was light," Gen. i. 3; by that very word "commanding light to shine out of darkness," 2 Cor. iv. 6.

These demonstrations of God's all-sufficiency he considereth in peculiar reference to what he was to believe; to wit, that "he might be the father of many nations," verse 11,—of the Jews, "according to the flesh,"—of Jews and Gentiles, according to the faith whereof we speak. For the first, "his body being now dead, and Sarah's womb dead," verse 19, he rests on God "as quickening the dead," in believing that he "shall be the father of many nations." For the other, that he should be a father of the Gentiles by faith, the Holy Ghost witnesseth that they "were not a people," Hos. ii. 23. The implanting of them in his stock must be by a power "that calleth things that are not, as though they were,"—giving a new nature and being unto them, which before they had not.

To bottom ourselves upon the all-sufficiency of God, for the accomplishment of such things as are altogether impossible to any thing but that all-sufficiency, is faith indeed, and worthy our imitation. It is also the wisdom of faith to pitch peculiarly on that in God which is accommodated to the difficulties wherewith it is to wrestle. Is Abraham to believe that from his dead body must spring a whole nation?—he rests on God, as "him that quickeneth the dead."

Secondly, His faith is commended from the *matter of it*, or what he did believe; which is said in general to be "the promise of God," verse 20, "He staggered not at the promise of God through unbelief." And particularly, the matter of that promise is pointed at, verses 11, 18,—that he should be "the father of many nations;" that was, his being a "father of many nations," of having "all nations blessed in his seed:"—a matter entangled with a world of difficulties, considering the natural inability of his body and the body of Sarah to be parents of children. But, when God calls for believing, his truth and all-sufficiency being engaged, no difficulty nor seeming impossibilities that the thing to be believed is or may be attended withal, ought to be of any weight with us. He who hath promised is able.

Thirdly, From the *manner* of his believing, which is expressed four ways.

1. "Against hope, he believed in hope," verse 18. Here is a twofold hope mentioned;—one that was against him, the other that was for him.

(1.) He "believed against hope;" that is, when all arguments that might beget hope in him were against him. "Against hope," is against all motives unto hope whatever. All reasons of natural hope were against him. What hope could arise, in or by reason, that two dead bodies should be the source and fountain of many nations? so that against all inducements of a natural hope he believed.

(2.) He "believed in hope;" that is, such hope as arose, as his faith did, from the consideration of God's all-sufficiency. This is an adjunct of his faith,—it was such a faith as had hope adjoined with it. And this believing in hope, when all reasons of hope were away, is the first thing that is set down of the manner of his faith. In a decay of all natural helps, the deadness of all means, an appearance of an utter impossibility that ever the promise should be accomplished, —then to believe with unfeigned hope is a commendable faith.

2. He was "not weak in faith," verse 19, μὴ ἀσθενήσας, "minimè debilis," Beza. He was by "no means weak;" a negation that, by a figure, μείωσις, doth strongly assert the contrary to that which is denied. He was no way weak; that is, he was very strong in faith, as is afterwards expressed, verse 20, He "was strong in faith, giving glory to God." And the apostle tells you wherein this his not weakness did appear: saith he, "He considered not his own body being now dead, when he was about a hundred years old, neither yet the deadness of Sarah's womb," verse 19. It was seen in this, that his faith carried him above the consideration of all impediments that might lie in the way to the accomplishment of the promise.

It is mere weakness of faith that makes a man lie poring on the difficulties and seeming impossibilities that lie upon the promise. We think it our wisdom and our strength to consider, weigh, and look into the bottom of oppositions and temptations that arise against the promise. Perhaps it may be the strength of our fleshly, carnal reason, but certainly it is the weakness of our faith. He that is strong in faith will not so much as debate or consider the things that cast the greatest seeming improbability, yea, impossibility, on the fulfilling of the promise: it will not afford a debate or dispute of the cause, nor any consideration. "Being not weak in faith, he considered not."

3. He was "fully persuaded," verse 21, πληροφορηθεὶς, "persuasionis plenus." This is the third thing that is observed in the manner of his believing. He fully, quietly, resolvedly cast himself on this, that "he who had promised was able to perform it." As a ship at sea (for so the word imports), looking about, and seeing storms and winds arising, sets up all her sails, and with all speed makes to the harbour; Abraham, seeing the storms of doubts and temptations likely to rise against the promise made unto him, with full sail breaks through all, to lie down quietly in God's all-sufficiency.

4. The last is, that "he staggered not," verse 20. This is that which I have chosen to insist on unto you, as a choice part of the commendation of Abraham's faith, which is proposed for our imitation: "He staggered not at the promise of God through unbelief."

The words may be briefly resolved into this doctrinal proposition:—

Observation. *All staggering at the promises of God is from unbelief.*

What is of any difficulty in the text, will be cleared in opening the parts of the observation.

Men are apt to pretend sundry other reasons and causes of their staggering: The promises do not belong unto them,—God intends not their souls in them,—they are not such and such,—and this makes them stagger; when the truth is, it is their unbelief, and that alone, that puts them into this staggering condition. As in other things, so in this, we are apt to have many fair pretences for foul faults. To lay the burden on the right shoulders, I shall demonstrate, by God's assistance, that it is not this, or that, but unbelief alone, that makes us stagger at the promises.

To make this the more plain, I must open these two things:—

I. What is the promise here intended.

II. What it is to stagger at the promise.

I. The promise here mentioned is principally that which Abraham believing, it was said eminently that "it was accounted to him for righteousness." So the apostle tells us, verse 5 of this chapter. When this was, you may see Gen. xv. 6; there it is affirmed, that "he believed the LORD, and it was accounted to him for righteousness." That which God had there spoken to him of, was about "the multiplying of his seed as the stars of heaven, whereas he was yet childless."

The last verse of chapter xiv. leaves Abraham full of earthly glory. He had newly conquered five kings with all their host, was honoured by the king of Sodom, and blessed by the king of Salem; and yet, in the first verse of chapter xv., God, "appearing to him in a vision," in the very entrance, bids him "fear not;"—plainly intimating, that notwithstanding all his outward success and glory, he had still many perplexities upon his spirit, and had need of great consolation and establishment. Abraham was not clear in the accomplishment of former promises about the blessed seed; and so, though he have all outward advancements, yet he cannot rest in them. Until a child of God be clear in the main in the matter of the great promise,—the business of Christ,—the greatest outward successes and advantages will be so far from quieting and settling his mind, that they rather increase his perplexities. They do but occasion him to cry, Here is this and that; here is victory and success; here is wealth and peace;—but here is not Christ.

That this was Abraham's condition appears from verse 2 of that chapter; where God having told him that he was his shield, and his exceeding great reward, he replies, "Lord God, what wilt thou give me, seeing I go childless?" As if he should have said, Lord God, thou toldest me when I was in Haran, now nineteen years ago, that in me and "my seed all the families of the earth should be blessed," Gen. xii. 3,—that the blessed, blessing seed, should be of me: but now I wax old, all appearances grow up against the direct accomplishment of that word; and it was that which, above all, in following thee, I aimed at: if I am disappointed therein, what shall I do? and what will all these things avail me?—what will it benefit me to have a multitude of earthly enjoyments, and leave them in the close to my servant?

I cannot but observe, that this sighing, mournful complaint of Abraham, hath much infirmity, and something of diffidence mixed with it. He shakes in the very bottom of his soul, that improbabilities were growing up, as he thought, to impossibilities against him in the way of promise. Yet hence also mark these two things: First, That he doth not repine in himself, and keep up his burning thoughts in his breast, but sweetly breathes out the burden of his soul into the bosom of his God. "Lord God," saith he, "what wilt thou give me, seeing I go childless?" It is of sincere faith, to unlade our unbelief in the bosom of our God. Secondly, That God takes not his servant at the advantage of his complaining and diffidence; but lets that pass, until having renewed the promise to him, and settled his faith, then he gives in his testimony that he believed God. The Lord overlooks the weakness and causeless wailings of his, takes them at the best, and then gives his witness to them.

This, I say, was the promise whereof we spake,—that he should have a seed of his own, "like the stars that cannot be numbered," Gen. xv. 4, 5. And herein are contained three things.

1. The purely spiritual part of it, that concerned his own soul in Christ. God engaging about his seed, minds him of his own interest in that seed which brings the blessing. Jesus Christ, with his whole mediation, and his whole work of redemption, is in this promise, with the enjoyment of God in covenant, "as a shield, and as an exceeding great reward."

2. The kingdom of Christ, in respect of the propagation and establishment of it, with the multitude of his subjects,—that also is in this promise.

3. The temporal part of it,—multitudes of children to a childless man, and an heir from his own bowels.

Now this promise, in these three branches, takes up your whole interest, comprises all you are to believe for, be you considered either as believers or as rulers. As believers:—so your interest lies in these two things: That your own souls have a share and portion in the Lord Christ; and that the kingdom of the Lord Jesus be exalted and established. As rulers:—That peace and prosperity may be the inheritance of the nation, is in your desires. Look upon this in subordination to the kingdom of Christ, and so all these are in this promise.

To make this more plain, these being the three main things that you aim at, I shall lay before you three promises, suited to these several things, which, or the like, you are to view in all your actings, all staggering at them being from unbelief.

The first thing you are to believe for, is the interest of your own souls in the covenant of grace by Christ. As to this, I shall only point unto that promise of the covenant, Heb. viii. 12, "I will be merciful to their unrighteousness, and their sins and their iniquities will I remember no more."

The second is the establishment of the kingdom of Christ, in despite of all opposition. And for this, amongst innumerable [passages], take that of Isa. lx. 11, "Therefore thy gates shall be open continually; they shall not be shut day nor night; that men may bring unto thee the forces of the Gentiles, and that their kings may be brought: for the nation and kingdom that will not serve thee shall perish."

The quiet and peace of the nation, which ye regard as rulers, as it stands in subordination to the kingdom of Christ, comes also under the promise; for which take that of Jer. xxx. 20, 21.

These being your three main aims, let your eye be fixed on these three, or the like promises; for in the demonstration and the use of the point I shall carry along all three together, desiring that what is instanced in any one may be always extended to both the others.

II. What is it to stagger at the promise? "He staggered not," *οὐ διεκρίθη*, "he disputed not." *Διακρίνομαι* is, properly, to make use of our own judgment and reason in discerning of things, of what sort they be. It is sometimes rendered, "to doubt," Matt. xxi. 21, "If ye have faith" (*καὶ μὴ διακριθῆτε*), "and doubt not:" that is, not use arguings and reasonings in yourselves concerning the promise and things promised. Sometimes it simply denotes to discern a thing as it is:—so the word is used, 1 Cor. xi. 29, *Διακρίνων τὸ σῶμα*, "Discerning the body." In the sense wherein it is here used, as also Matt. xxi. 21, it holds out, as I said, a self-consultation and dispute concerning those contrary things that are proposed to us. So also Acts x. 20, Peter is commanded to obey the vision, *μηδὲν διακρινόμενος*, "nothing doubting." What is that? Why, a not continuing to do what he is said to have done, verse 17, "He doubted in himself what the vision he had seen should mean;" he rolled and disputed it in his own thoughts; he staggered at it.

To stagger, then, at the promise, is to take into consideration the promise itself, and withal, all the difficulties that lie in the way for the accomplishment of it, as to a man's own particular, and then so to dispute it in his thoughts, as not fully to cast it off, nor fully to close with it. For instance, the soul considers the promise of free grace in the blood of Jesus,—looks upon it,—weighs as well as it is able the truth of God, who makes the promise, with those other considerations which might lead the heart to rest firmly upon it; but withal, takes into his thoughts his own unworthiness, sinfulness, unbelief, hypocrisy, and the like,—which, as he supposes, powerfully stave off the efficacy of the promise from him. Hence he knows not what to conclude. If he add a grain of faith, the scale turns on the side of the promise; the like quantity of unbelief makes it turn upon him; and what to do he knows not; let go the promise he cannot, take fast hold he dares not; but here he staggers and wavers to and fro.

Thus the soul comes to be like Paul, in another case, Phil. i. 23. He considered his own advantage on the one side by his dissolution, and the profit of the churches by his abiding in the flesh on the other; and taking in these various thoughts, he cries out he is in a strait;—he staggered, he was betwixt two, and knew not which to choose: or as David, 2 Sam. xxiv. 14, when he had a tender of several corrections made to him, says, "I am in a great strait;"—he sees evil in every one, and knows not which to choose.

A poor creature looking upon the promise sees, as he supposes, in a steadfast closing with the promise, that there lies presumption; on the other hand, certain destruction if he believes not. And now he staggers,—he is in a great strait: arguments arise on both sides, he knows not how to determine them; and so, hanging in suspense, he staggereth. Like a man travelling a journey, and meeting with two several paths that promise both fairly, and he knows not which is his proper way; he guesses, and guesses, and at length cries, Well, I know not which of these ways I should go; but this is certain, if I mistake, I am undone: I'll go in neither, but here I'll sit down, and not move one step in either of them, until some one come that can give me direction. The soul very frequently sits down in this hesitation, and refuses to step one step forward, till God come mightily and lead out the spirit to the promise, or the devil turn it aside to unbelief.

It is as a thing of small weight in the air: the weight that it hath carries it downwards; and the air, with some breath of wind, bears it up again, so that it waves to and fro: sometimes it seems as though it would fall by its own weight; and sometimes again, as though it would mount quite out of sight; but poised between both, it tosseth up and down, without any great gaining either way. The promise draws the soul upward, and the weight of its unbelief sinks it downward. Sometimes the promise attracts so powerfully, you would think the heart quite drawn up into it; and sometimes again unbelief presses down, that you would think it gone for ever;—but neither prevails utterly, the poor creature swags between both. This is to stagger. Like the two disciples going to Emmaus, Luke xxiv. 14, "They talked together of the things that had happened,"—debated the business; and, verse 21, they gave up the result of their thoughts. They "trusted it had been he that should have redeemed Israel." They trusted once; but now, seeing him slain and crucified, they know not what to say to it. What then? do they quite give over all trusting in him? No, they cannot do so, verses 22–24. Certain women had astonished them, and affirmed that he was risen; yea, and others also, going to his grave, found it so. Hereupon they have consultation within themselves, and are sad, verse 17;—that is, they staggered, they were in a staggering condition; much appears for them, something against them, —they know not what to do.

A poor soul, that hath been long perplexed in trouble and anxiety of mind, finds a sweet promise,—Christ in a promise suited to all his wants, coming with mercy to pardon him, with love to embrace him, with blood to purge him,—and is raised up to roll himself in some measure upon this promise. On a sudden, terrors arise, temptations grow strong, new corruptions break out,—Christ in the promise dies to him, Christ in the promise is slain, is in the grave as to him; so that he can only sigh, and say, I trusted for deliverance by Christ, but now all is gone again; I have little or no hope,—Christ in the promise is slain to me. What then? shall he give over? never more inquire after this buried Christ, but sit down in darkness and sorrow? No, he cannot do so: this morning some new arguments of Christ's appearance again upon the soul are made out; Christ is not for ever lost to him. What does he, then? Steadfastly believe he cannot,—totally give over he will not; he staggers,—he is full of self-consultations, and is sad. This it is to stagger at the promise of God.

I come now to prove, that notwithstanding any pretences whatever, all this staggering is from unbelief.

The two disciples, whom we now mentioned, that staggered and disputed between themselves in their journey to Emmaus, thought they had a good reason, and a sufficient appearing cause of all their doubtings. "We hoped," say they, "that it was he that should have redeemed Israel." What do they now stand at? Alas! the "chief priests and rulers have condemned him to death, and crucified him,"

Luke xxiv. 20. And is it possible that deliverance should arise from a crucified man? This makes them stagger. But when our Saviour himself draws nigh to them, and gives them the ground of all this, he tells them it is all from hence,—they are "foolish, and slow of heart to believe," verse 25. Here is the rise of all their doubtings, even their unbelief. Whilst you are slow of heart to believe, do not once think of establishment.

Peter venturing upon the waves at the command of Christ, Matt. xiv., seeing "the wind to grow boisterous," verse 30, he also hath a storm within, and cries out, "Lord, save me!" What was now the cause of Peter's fear and crying out? Why, the wind and sea grew boisterous, and he was ready to sink;—no such thing, but merely unbelief, want of faith, verse 31. "O thou of little faith," saith our Saviour, "wherefore didst thou doubt?" It was not the great wind, but thy little faith that made thee stagger. And in three or four other places, upon several occasions, doth our Saviour lay all the wavering and staggering of his followers as to any promised mercy upon this score, as Matt. vi. 30, viii. 26.

Isa. vii., Ahaz being afraid of the combination of Syria and Ephraim against him, received a promise of deliverance by Isaiah, verse 7. Whereupon the prophet tells him, and all Judah, that "if they will not believe, surely they shall not be established," verse 9. He doth not say, If Damascus and Ephraim be not broken, you shall not be established; no, he doth not stick there. The fear that you will not be established ariseth merely from your unbelief;—that keeps you off from closing with the promise, which would certainly bring you establishment.

And this is the sole reason the apostle gives why the word of promise, being preached, becomes unprofitable, even because of unbelief: it was not "mixed with faith," Heb. iv. 2.

But these things will be more clear under the demonstration of the points, which are two.

1. When a man doubts, hesitates, and disputes, any thing in himself, his reasonings must have their rise, either from something within himself, or from something in the things concerning which he staggereth;—either "certitudo mentis," "the assurance of his mind," or "certitudo entis," the "certainty of the thing itself," is wanting. He that doubteth whether his friend in a far country be alive or not, his staggering ariseth from the uncertainty of the thing itself; when that is made out, he is resolved, as it was with Jacob in the case of Joseph. But he that doubteth whether the needle in the compass, being touched with the loadstone, will turn northward, all the uncertainty is in his own mind.

When men stagger at the promises, this must arise either from within themselves, or some occasion must be administered hereunto from the promise. If from within themselves, that can be nothing but unbelief;—an inbred obstacle to closing with and resting on the promise,—that is unbelief. If, then, we demonstrate that there is nothing in the promise, either as to matter or manner, or any attendancy of it, that should occasion any such staggering, we lay the burden and blame on the right shoulders,—the sin of staggering on unbelief.

Now, that any occasion is not administered, nor cause given, of this staggering from the promise, will appear if we consider seriously whence any such occasion or cause should arise. All the stability of a promise depends upon the qualifications of the promiser to the ends and purposes of the promise. If a man make me a promise to do such and such things for me, and I question whether ever it will be so or not, it must be from a doubt of the want of one of these things in him that makes the promise;—either (1.) of truth; or (2.) of ability to make good his word, because of the difficulty of the thing itself; or (3.) of sincerity to intend me really what he speaks of; or (4.) of constant memory to take the opportunity of doing the thing intended; or (5.) of stableness to be still of the same mind. Now, if there be no want of any of these in him whose promises we speak of, there is then certainly no ground of our staggering, but only from our own unbelief.

Let us now see whether any of these things be wanting to the promises of God; and begin we with the first.

(1.) Is there truth in these promises? If there be the least occasion in the world to suspect the truth of the promises or the veracity of the promiser, then may our staggering at them arise from thence, and not from our own unbelief. On this ground it is that all human faith, that is bottomed merely on the testimony of man, is at best but a probable opinion; for every man is a liar, and possibly may lie in that very thing he is engaged to us in. Though a good man will not do so to save his life, yet it is possible he may be tempted,—he may do so. But now, the author of the promises whereof we speak is truth itself,—the God of truth, who hath taken this as his special attribute, to distinguish him from all others. He is the very God of truth; and holds out this very attribute in a special manner in this very thing, in making of his promise: "He is faithful to forgive us our sins," 1 John i. 9. Whence his word is said not only to be true, but "truth," John xvii. 17,—truth itself. All flesh is as grass, but his word abideth for ever, Isa. xl. 6, 8.

But yet farther, that it may be evident that from hence there can be no occasion of staggering, this God of truth, whose word is truth, hath, in his infinite wisdom, condescended to our weakness, and used all possible means to cause us to apprehend the truth of his promises. The Lord might have left us in the dark,—to have gathered out his mind and will towards us from obscure expressions; and, knowing of what value his kindness is, it might justly be expected that we should do so. Men in misery are glad to lay hold of the least word that drops from him that can relieve them, and to take courage and advantage upon it;—as the servants of Benhadad watched diligently what would fall from the mouth of Ahab concerning their master, then in fear of death, and when he had occasionally called him his brother, they presently laid hold of it, and cry, "Thy brother Benhadad," 1 Kings xx. 33. God might have left us, and yet have manifested much free grace, to have gathered up falling crumbs or occasional droppings of mercy and supply, that we should have rejoiced to have found out one word looking that way. But, to shut up all objections, and to stop for ever the mouth of unbelief, he hath not only spoken plainly, but hath condescended to use all the ways of confirming the truth of what he says and speaks that ever were in use among the sons of men.

There be four ways whereby men seek to obtain credit to what they speak as an undoubted truth, that there may be no occasion of staggering.

[1.] *By often averring and affirming of the same thing.* When a man says the same thing again and again, it is a sign that he speaks the truth, or, at least, that he would be thought so to do; yea, if an honest man do clearly, fully, plainly, often engage himself to us in the same thing, we count it a vile jealousy not to believe the real truth of his intentions. Now, the Lord in his promises often speaks the same things,—he speaks once and twice. There is not any thing that he hath promised us but he hath done it again and again. For instance, as if he should say, "I will be merciful to your sins;" I pray believe me, for "I will pardon your iniquities;" yea, it shall be so,—"I will blot out your transgressions as a cloud."

There is not any want whereunto we are liable, but thus he hath dealt concerning it. As his command is line upon line, so is his promise. And this is one way whereby God causeth the truth of his promises to appear. To take away all colour of staggering, he speaks once, yea twice, if we will hear.

[2.] *The second way of confirming any truth is by an oath.* Though we fear the truth of some men in their assertions, yet when once they come to swear any thing in justice and judgment, there are very few so knownly profligate, and past all sense of God, but that their asseverations do gain credit and pass for truth. Hence the apostle tells us, Heb. vi. 16, that "an oath for confirmation is to men an end of all strife." Though the truth be before ambiguous and doubtful, yet when any interposes with an oath, there is no more contest amongst men. That nothing may be wanting to win our belief to the promises of God, he hath taken this course also,—he hath sworn to their truth, Heb. vi. 13, "When God made promise to Abraham, because he could swear by no greater, he sware by himself." He confirms his promise by an oath. "O felices nos, quorum causâ Deus jurat; O infelices, si nec juranti Deo credimus!" When Christ came, "in whom all the promises of God are yea and amen," to make sure work of the truth of them, he is confirmed in his administration by an oath, Heb. vii. 21. He was made a priest by an oath by him that said, "The Lord sware, and will not repent, Thou art a priest for ever." Now, I pray, what is the cause of this great condescension in the God of heaven, to confirm that word which in itself is truth by an oath? The apostle satisfies us as to the end aimed at, Heb. vi. 17, 18. This was, saith he, the aim of God herein, that his people, seeing him engaged by two such immutable things as his promise and his oath, may be assured that there is an utter impossibility that any one word of his should come short of its truth; or that they firmly resting upon it should be deceived thereby. And this is a second way.

[3.] Another course whereby men confirm the truth of what they speak, *is by entering into covenant to accomplish what they have spoken.* A covenant gives strength to the truth of any engagement. When a man hath but told you he will do such and such things for you, you are full of doubts and fears that he may break with you; but when he hath indented in a covenant, and you can show it under his hand and seal, you look upon that, consider that, and are very secure. Even this way also hath the Lord taken to confirm and establish his truths and promises. That all doubtings and staggerings may be excluded, he hath wrapped them all up in a covenant, and brought himself into a federal engagement, that upon every occasion, and at every temptation, we may draw out his hand and seal, and say to Satan and our own false hearts, See here, behold God engaged in covenant, to make good the word wherein he hath caused me to put my trust; and this is his property, that he is a God keeping covenant. So that having his promise *redoubled*, and that confirmed by an *oath*, all sealed and made sure by an unchangeable *covenant*, what can we require more to assure us of the truth of these things? But yet farther:—

[4.] In things of very great weight and concernment, such as whereon lives and the peace of nations do depend, men use to give hostages for the securing each other of the faith and truth of all their engagements, that they may be mutual pledges of their truth and fidelity. Neither hath the Lord left this way unused to confirm his promise. He hath given us a hostage to secure us of his truth,—one exceedingly dear to him, one always in his bosom, of whose honour he is as careful as of his own. Jesus Christ is the great hostage of his Father's truth, the pledge of his fidelity in his promises. God hath set him forth, and given him to us for this end. "Behold, the LORD himself shall give you a sign" (a sign that he will fulfil his word); "a virgin shall conceive, and bear a son, and shall call his name Immanuel," Isa. vii. 14. That you may be assured of my truth, the virgin's son shall be a hostage of it. "In him are all the promises of God yea and amen." Thus also to his saints he gives the farther hostage of his Spirit, and the first-fruits of glory; that the full accomplishment of all his promises may be contracted in a little, and presented to their view, as the Israelites had the pleasures of Canaan in the clusters of grapes brought from thence.

Now, from all this it is apparent, not only that there is truth in all the promises of God, but also that truth so confirmed, so made out, established, that not the least occasion imaginable is thence administered to staggering or doubting. He that disputes the promises, and knows not how to close with them, must find out another cause of his so doing; as to the truth of the promise, there is no doubt at all, nor place for any.

(2.) But secondly, though there be truth in the promise, yet there may want ability in the promiser to accomplish the thing promised, because of its manifold difficulties. This may be a second cause of staggering, if the thing itself engaged for be not compassable by the ability of the engager. As if a skilful physician should promise a sick man recovery from his disease, though he could rely upon the truth and sincerity of his friend, yet he cannot but question his ability as to this, knowing that to cure the least distemper is not absolutely in his power; but when he promises who is able to perform, then all doubting in this kind is removed. See, then, whether it be so in respect of these promises whereof we speak. When God comes to Abraham to engage himself in that covenant of grace from whence flow all the promises whereof we treat, he lays this down as the bottom of all; "I am," saith he, "God Almighty," Gen. xvii. 1; or "God all-sufficient," very well able to go through with whatever I promise. When difficulties, temptations, and troubles arise, remember who it is that hath promised;—not only he that is true and faithful, but he that is God Almighty, before whom nothing can stand, when he will accomplish his word. And that this was a bottom of great confidence to Abraham, the apostle tells you, Rom. iv. 21, "Being fully persuaded that he who had promised was able also to perform." When God is engaged by his word, his ability is especially to be eyed. The soul is apt to ask, How can this be? It is impossible it should be so to me. But, "he is able that hath promised." And this, Rom. xi. 23, the same apostle holds out to us to fix our faith upon, in reference to that great promise of recalling the Jews, and re-implanting them into the vine. "God," saith he, "is able to graff them in;" though now they seem as dead bones, yet the Lord knows they may live; for he is able to breathe upon them, and make them terrible as an army with banners. Yea, so excellent is this all-sufficiency, this ability of God to accomplish his whole word, that the apostle cautions us that we do not bound it, as though it could go so far only, or so far. Nay, saith he, Eph. iii. 20, he "is able to do exceeding abundantly above all that we ask or think."

When men come to close with the promise indeed, to make a life upon it, they are very ready to question and inquire whether it be possible that ever the word of it should be made good to them. He that sees a little boat swimming at sea, observes no great difficulty in it, looks upon it without any solicitousness of mind at all,—beholds how it tosses up and down, without any fears of its sinking. But now, let this man commit his own life to sea in that bottom,—what inquiries will he make! what a search into the vessel! Is it possible, saith he, this little thing should safeguard my life in the ocean?—It is so with us, in our view of the promises: whilst we consider them at large, as they lie in the word, alas! they are all true,—all yea and amen,—shall be all accomplished; but when we go to venture our souls upon a promise, in an ocean of wrath and temptations, then every blast we think will overturn it; it will not bear us above all these waves. Is it possible we should swim safely upon the plank of a pinnace in the midst of the ocean?

Now, here we are apt to deceive ourselves, and mistake the whole thing in question; which is the bottom of many corrupted reasonings and perplexed thoughts. We inquire whether it can be so to us as the word holds out; when the truth is, the question is not about the nature of the thing, but about the power of God. Place the doubt aright, and it is this: Is God able to accomplish what he hath spoken? —can he heal my backslidings? can he pardon my sins? can he save my soul? Now, that there may be no occasion or colour of staggering upon this point, you see God reveals himself as an all-sufficient God, as one that is able to go through with all his engagements. If you will stagger, you may so do. This is certain, you have no cause to do so from hence,—there is not any promise that ever God entered into but he is able to perform it.

But you will say, Though God be thus able, thus all-sufficient, yet may there not be defects in the means whereby he worketh?—as a man may have a strong arm, able to strike his enemies to the ground, but yet if he strike with a feather or a straw, it will not be done;—

not for want of strength in his arm, but of fitness and suitableness in the instrument whereby he acteth. But,—

[1.] God using instruments, they do not act according to their own virtue, but according to the influence of virtue by him to them communicated. Look to what end soever God is pleased to use any means,—his choosing of them fills them with efficacy to that purpose. Let the way and means of accomplishing what thou expectest by the promise be in themselves never so weak, yet know that, from God's choosing of them to that end, they shall be filled with virtue and efficacy to the accomplishment of it.

[2.] It is expressly affirmed of the great mediums of the promise, that they also are able,—that there is no want of power in them for the accomplishment of the thing promised.

1*st.* There is the *means procuring it,* and that is Jesus Christ:—the promises, as to the good things contained in them, are all purchased by him. And of him the apostle affirms expressly, that "he is able to save them to the uttermost that come to God by him," Heb. vii. 25. No want here, no defect; he is able to do it to the uttermost,—able to save them that are tempted, Heb. ii. 18.

2*dly.* There is the *great means of manifestation,* and that is the word of God. And of this also it is affirmed, that it is able. It hath an all-sufficiency in its kind. Paul tells the elders of Ephesus, that "the word of grace is able to build them up, and to give them an inheritance among all them that are sanctified," Acts xx. 32.

3*dly.* There is *the great means of operation,* and that is the Spirit of grace. He works the mercy of the promise upon the soul. He also is able, exceeding powerful, to effect the end appointed. He hath no bounds nor measure of operation but only his own will, 1 Cor. xii. 11.

Hence, then, it is apparent, in the second place, that there is no occasion for doubting; yea, that all staggering is excluded, from the consideration of the ability of the promiser, and the means whereby he worketh. If thou continuest to stagger, thou must get a better plea than this,—It cannot be, it is impossible. I tell thee, nay, but God is able to accomplish the whole word of his promise.

(3.) There may be want of *sincerity* in promises and engagements; which whilst we do but suspect, we cannot choose but stagger at them. If a man make a promise to me, and I can suppose that he intends not as he says, but hath reserves to himself of another purpose, I must needs doubt as to the accomplishment of what he hath spoken. If the soul may surmise that the Lord intends not him sincerely in his promise, but reserves some other thing in his mind, or that it shall be so to others and not to him, he must needs dispute in himself, stagger, and keep off from believing. This, then, must be demonstrated, in the third place,—that the promises of God, and God in all his promises, are full of sincerity; so that none need fear to cast himself on them: they shall be real unto him. Now, concerning this, observe,—

[1.] *That God's promises are not declarative of his secret purposes and intentions.* When God holds out to any a promise of the pardon of sin, this doth not signify to any singular man that it is the purpose of God that his sin shall be pardoned. For if so, then either all men must be pardoned to whom the word of promise comes,—which is not; or else God fails of his purposes, and comes short of his intendments,—which would render him either impotent, that he could not, or mutable, that he would not, establish them. But "who hath resisted his will?" Rom. ix. 19. He is the Lord, and he changeth not, Mal. iii. 6. So that though every one to whom the promise is held out hath not the fruit of the promise, yet this derogates not at all from the sincerity of God in his promises; for he doth not hold them forth to any such end and purpose as to declare his intentions concerning particular persons.

[2.] *There are some absolute promises, comprehensive of the covenant of grace,* which, as to all those that belong to that covenant, do hold out thus much of the mind of God, that they shall certainly be accomplished in and towards them all. The soul may freely be invited to venture on these promises, with assurance of their efficacy towards him.

[3.] This God principally declares in all his promises of his mind and purpose, that every soul to whom they shall come may freely rest on; to wit, *that faith in the promises, and the accomplishment of the promises, are inseparable.* He that believeth shall enjoy. This is most certain, this God declares of his mind, his heart, towards us,—that as for all the good things he hath spoken of to us, it shall be to us according to our faith. This, I say, the promises of God do signify of his purpose, that the believer of them shall be the enjoyer of them. In them "the righteousness of God is revealed from faith to faith," Rom. i. 17;—from the faith of God revealing, to the faith of man receiving. So that, upon the making out of any promise, you may safely conclude that, upon believing, the mercy, the Christ, the deliverance of this promise is mine. It is true, if a man stand disputing and staggering whether he have any share in a promise, and close not with it by faith, he may come short of it; and yet without the least impeachment of the truth of the promise or sincerity of the promiser,—for God hath not signified by them that men shall enjoy the good things of them whether they believe or not. Thus far the promises of grace are general, and carry a truth to all, that there is an inviolable connection between believing and the enjoyment of the things in them contained. And in this truth is the sincerity of the promiser, which can never be questioned without sin and folly. And this wholly shuts up the spirit from any occasion of staggering. "O ye of little faith! wherefore do ye doubt?" Ah! lest our share be not in this promise,—lest we are not intended in it.—Poor creatures! there is but this one way of keeping you off from it; that is, disputing it in yourselves by unbelief. Here lies the sincerity of God towards thee, that believing, thou shalt not come short of what thou aimest at. Here, then, is no room for staggering. If proclamation be made granting pardon to all such rebels as shall come in by such a season, do men use to stand questioning whether the state bear them any good-will or not? No, saith the poor creature, I will cast myself upon their faith and truth, engaged in their proclamation: whatever I have deserved in particular, I know they will be faithful in their promises. The gospel proclamation is of pardon to all comers in, to all believers: it is not for thee, poor staggerer, to question what is the intendment towards thee in particular, but roll thyself on this, there is an absolute sincerity in the engagement which thou mayest freely rest upon. But,—

(4.) Though all be present, truth, power, sincerity; yet if he that makes the promise should *forget*,—this were a ground of staggering. Pharaoh's butler, without doubt, made large promises to Joseph; and probably spake the truth, according to his present intention. Afterward, standing in the presence of Pharaoh, restored to favour, he had doubtless power enough to have procured the liberty of a poor innocent prisoner. But yet this would not do,—it did not profit Joseph; because, as the text says, he "did not remember Joseph, but forgat him," Gen. xl. 23. This forgetting made all other things useless. But neither hath this the least colour in divine promises. It was Zion's infirmity to say, "The LORD hath forsaken me, and my Lord hath forgotten me," Isa. xlix. 14; for saith the Lord, "Can a woman forget her sucking child, that she should not have compassion on the son of her womb? yea, they may forget, yet will I not forget thee. Behold, I have graven thee upon the palms of my hands; thy walls are continually before me," verses 15, 16.

The causes of forgetfulness are,—

[1.] *Want of love.* The things that men love not, they care not for:—the matters of their love are continually in their thoughts. Now, says God to Zion, Why sayest thou I have forgotten thee? Is it for want of love? Alas! the love of a most tender mother to her sucking child comes infinitely short of my love to thee. My love to thee is more fixed than so, and how shouldst thou be out of my mind? how shouldst thou be forgotten? Infinite love will have infinite thoughtfulness and remembrance.

[2.] *Multiplicity of business.* This with men is a cause of forgetting. I had done, says one, as I promised, but multiplicity of occasions thrust it out of my mind; I pray excuse me.—Alas! though I rule all the world, yet thou art graven upon the palms of my hands; and therefore thy walls are continually before me. See also Ps. lxxvii. 9. Neither, then, is there as to this the least colour given us to stagger at the promise of God.

(5.) But lastly, where all other things concur, yet if the person promising be *changeable*, if he may alter his resolution, a man may justly doubt and debate in himself the accomplishment of any promise made to him. "It is true," may he say, "he now speaks his heart and mind; but who can say he will be of this mind to-morrow? May he not be turned? and then what becomes of the golden mountains that I promised myself upon his engagement?" Wherefore, in the last place, the Lord carefully rejects all sinful surmises concerning the least change or alteration in him, or any of his engagements. He is "the Father of lights, with whom is no variableness, neither shadow of turning," James i. 17,—no shadow, no appearance of any such thing. "I am the LORD," saith he, "I change not; therefore ye sons of Jacob are not consumed," Mal. iii. 6. The Lord knows, that if any thing in us might prevail with him to alter the word that is gone out of his mouth, we should surely perish. We are poor provoking creatures, therefore he lays our not being consumed only on this, even his own unchangeableness. This we may rest upon, "He is in one mind, and who can turn him?"

And in these observations have I given you the first demonstration of the point: all staggering is from our own unbelief.

2. The experience which we have of the mighty workings of God for the accomplishment of all his promises gives light unto this thing. We have found it true, that where he is once engaged, he will certainly go through unto the appointed issue, though it stand him in the laying out of his power and wisdom to the uttermost, Hab. iii. 9, "Thy bow was made quite naked, according to the oaths of the tribes, thy word." If God's oath be passed, and his word engaged, he will surely accomplish it, though it cost him the making of his bow quite naked,—the manifestation of his power to the utmost.

It is true, never did any wait upon God for the accomplishment and fulfilling of a promise, but he found many difficulties fall out between the word and the thing. So was it with Abraham in the business of a son: and so with David in the matter of a kingdom. God will have his promised mercies to fall as the dews upon the parched, gasping earth, or "as the shadow of a great rock in a weary land," Isa. xxxii. 2,—very welcome unto the traveller who hath had the sun beat upon his head in his travel all the day. Zion is a crown of glory in the hand of the Lord, as a royal diadem in the hand of her God, Isa. lxii. 3. The precious stones of a diadem must be cut and polished, before they be set in beauty and glory. God will have ofttimes the precious living stones of Zion to have many a sharp cutting, before they come to be fully fixed in his diadem; but yet in the close, whatever obstacles stand in the way, the promise hath still wrought out its passage;—as a river, all the while it is stopped with a dam, is still working higher and higher, still getting more and more strength, until it bear down all before it, and obtain a free course to its appointed place. Every time opposition lies against the fulfilling of the promise, and so seems to impede it for a season, it gets more and more power, until the appointed hour be come, and then the promise bears down all before it.

Were there any thing imaginable whereof we had not experience that it had been conquered, to open a door for the fulfilling of every word of God, we might possibly, as to the apprehension of that thing, stagger from some other principle than that of unbelief.

What is there in heaven or earth, but God and his ministering spirits, that hath not, one time or other, stood up to its utmost opposition, for the frustrating of the word wherein some or other of the saints of God have put their trust? Devils, in their temptations, baits, subtleties, accusations, and oppositions;—men, in their counsels, reasonings, contrivances, interests, dominions, combinations, armies, multitudes, and the utmost of their endeavours;—the whole frame of nature, in its primitive instituted course,—fire, water, day, night, age, sickness, death, all in their courses have fought against the accomplishment of the promises. And what have they obtained by all their contendings? All disappointed, frustrated, turned back, changed, and served only to make the mercy of the promise more amiable and glorious.

I would willingly illustrate this demonstration with an instance,—that the almighty, all-conquering power that is in the promise, settling all staggering upon its own basis of unbelief, might be the more evident.

I might here mention Abraham, with all the difficulties and appearing impossibilities which the promise unto him did pass through and cast to the ground,—the mercy of it at length arising out of the grave, for he received his son from the dead "in a figure," Heb. xi. 19; or I might speak of Joseph, Moses, or David;—but I shall rather choose a precedent from among the works of God in the days wherein we live, and that in a business concerning which we may set up our Ebenezer, and say, Thus far hath God been a helper.

Look upon the affair of Ireland. The engagement of the great God of revenges against murder and treachery, the interest of the Lord Christ and his kingdom against the man of sin, furnished the undertakers with manifold promises to carry them out to a desired, a blessed issue. Take now a brief view of some mountains of opposition that lie in the way against any success in that place; and hear the Lord saying to every one of them, Who art thou, O great mountain? before my people thou shalt be made a plain, Zech. iv. 7.

Not to mention the strivings and strugglings of two manner of people in the womb of this nation, totally obstructing for a long time the bringing forth of any deliverance for Ireland; nor yet that mighty mountain (which some misnamed a level) that thought at once to have locked an everlasting door upon that expedition; I shall propose some few, of many that have attended it.

(1.) *The silence that hath been in heaven for half an hour, as to this business,*—the great cessation of prayers in the heavens of many churches,—hath been no small mountain in the way of the promise. When God will do good for Zion, he requires that his remembrancers give him no rest, until he do it, Isa. lxii. 7; and yet sometimes, in the close of their supplications, gives them an answer "by terrible things," Ps. lxv. 5. He is sometimes silent to the prayers of his people," Ps. xxviii. 1. Is not then a grant rare, when his people are silent as to prayers? Of how many congregations in this nation may the prayers, tears, and supplications for carrying on of the work of God in Ireland, be written with the lines of emptiness! What a silence hath been in the heaven of many churches for this last half hour! How many that began with the Lord in that work, did never sacrifice at the altar of Jehovah-nissi, nor consider that the Lord hath sworn to have war with such Amalekites as are there "from generation to generation!" Exod. xvii. 15, 16. They have forgotten that Ireland was the first of the nations that laid wait for the blood of God's people desiring to enter into his rest; and therefore "their latter end shall be to perish for ever," Numb. xxiv. 20. Many are as angry as Jonah, not that Babylon is spared, but that it is not spared. Hath not this been held out as a mountain? What will you now do, when such or such, these and those men, of this or that party, look upon you "as the grass upon the house-tops, which withereth afore it groweth up; wherewith the mower filleth not his hand, nor he that bindeth sheaves his bosom;"—that will not so much as say, "The blessing of the LORD be upon you; we bless you in the name of the LORD?" But now, shall the faithlessness of men make the "faith of God of none effect?" Shall the kingdom of Christ suffer because some of those that are his—what through carnal wisdom, what through spiritual folly—refuse to come forth "to his help against the mighty?" No, doubtless! "The Lord sees it, and it displeases him; he sees that there is no man, and wonders that there is no intercessor,"—even marvels that there are no more supplications on this behalf. "Therefore his own arm brought salvation to him; and his own righteousness, it sustained him. He put on righteousness as a breastplate, and an helmet of salvation upon his head; and he put on the garments of vengeance for clothing, and was clad with zeal as a cloak. According to their deeds, accordingly he will repay, fury to his adversaries, recompense to his enemies; to the islands he will repay recompense," Isa. lix. 15–18. Some men's not praying shall not hinder the promises accomplishing. They may sooner discover an idol in themselves than disappoint the living God. *This was a mountain.*

(2.) Our own advices and counsels have often stood in the way of the promises *bringing forth.* This is not a time nor place for narrations; so I shall only say to this in general,—that if the choicest and most rational advices of the army had not been overswayed by the providence of God, in all probability your affairs had been more than ten degrees backward to the condition wherein they are.

(3.) *The visible opposition of the combined enemy* in that nation seemed, as to our strength, unconquerable. The wise man tells us, "A threefold cord is not easily broken." Ireland had a fivefold cord to make strong bands for Zion, twisted together. Never, I think, did such different interests bear with one another for the compassing of one common end.

He that met the lion, the fox, and the ass travelling together, wondered—"quo unâ iter facerent"—whither these ill-matched associates did bend their course; neither did his marvelling cease when he heard they were going a pilgrimage, in a business of devotion.

He that should meet Protestants,—covenanted Protestants, that had sworn, in the presence of the great God to extirpate Popery and Prelacy, as the Scots in Ulster;—others, that counted themselves under no less sacred bond for the maintenance of prelates, service-books, and the like, as the whole party of Ormond's adherents;—joined with a mighty number that had for eight years together sealed their vows to the Romish religion with our blood and their own;—adding to them those that were profound to revolt up and down as suited their own interest, as some in Munster;—all closing with that party which themselves had laboured to render most odious and execrable, as most defiled with innocent blood:—he, I say, that should see all these, after seven years' mutual conflicting and imbruing their hands in each other's blood, to march all one way together, cannot but marvel—"quo unâ iter facerent"—whither they should journey so friendly together. Neither, surely, would his admiration be lessened when he should hear that the first thing they intended and agreed upon was, to cover the innocent blood of forty-one[1] [1641], contrary to that promise, "Behold, the LORD cometh out of his place

[1] Dr Owen refers to the Irish massacre of 1641, when, by the lowest computation, 40,000 Protestants are said to have been slaughtered.—ED.

to punish the inhabitants of the earth for their iniquity: the earth also shall disclose her blood, and shall no more cover her slain," Isa. xxvi. 21; and nextly, to establish Catholic religion, or the kingdom of Babel, in the whole nation, in opposition to the engaged truth, and, in our days, visibly manifested power of the Lord Jesus; with sundry such like things, contrary to their science and conscience, their covenant and light, yea, the trust and honesty, of most of the chief leaders of them. Now, how can the promise stand in the way of this hydra? what says it to this combined opposition?

[1.] Why, first, saith the Lord, "Though hand join in hand, the wicked shall not be unpunished," Prov. xi. 21. Their covering shall be too short and narrow to hide the blood which God will have disclosed.

[2.] And nextly, though they will give their power to the beast, and fight against the Lamb,—consenting in this, who agree in nothing else in the world,—yet they shall be broken in pieces; though they associate themselves, they shall be broken in pieces. If Rezin and the son of Remaliah, Syria and Ephraim, old adversaries, combine together for a new enmity against Judah,—if covenant and Prelacy, Popery and treachery, blood and (as to that) innocency, join hand in hand to stand in the way of the promise,—yet I will not in this join with them, says the Lord. Though they were preserved all distinctly in their several interests for seven years in their mutual conflicts, that they might be scourges to one another, yet if they close to keep off the engagement of God in the word of his promise, not much more than the fourth part of one year shall consume some of them to nothing, and fill the residue with indignation and anguish.

By what means God hath mightily and effectually wrought,—by mixing folly with their counsels, putting fear, terror, and amazedness upon all their undertakings,—to carry on his own purpose, I could easily give considerable instances. That which hath been spoken in general may suffice to bottom us on this, that whilst we are in the way of God, all staggering at the issue is from unbelief; for he can, he will, do more such things as these.

Use 1. My first use shall be as unto temporals; for they also, as I told you, come under the promise, not to be staggered at with the limitations before mentioned. Learn hence, then, to live more by faith in all your actings; believe, and you shall be established. I have, in the days of my pilgrimage, seen this evil under the sun,—many professors of the gospel called out to public actings, have made it their great design to manage all their affairs with wisdom and policy, like the men of the residue of the nations. Living by faith upon the promises hath appeared to them as too low a thing for the condition and employment wherein they now are;—now they must plot, and contrive, and design,—lay down principles of carnal, fleshly wisdom, to be pursued to the uttermost. And what, I pray, hath been the issue of such undertakings?

(1.) First, The power of religion hath totally been devoured by that lean, hungry, never-to-be-satisfied beast of carnal policy;—no signs left that it was ever in their bosoms. Conformity unto Christ in gospel graces is looked on as a mean, contemptible thing. Some of them have fallen to downright atheism,—most of them to wretched formality in the things of God. And then,—

(2.) Secondly, Their plots and undertakings have generally proved tympanous and birthless; vexation and disappointment hath been the portion of the residue of their days. The ceasing to lean upon the Lord, and striving to be wise in our actings, like the men of the world, hath made more Rehoboams than any one thing in this generation.

What now lies at the bottom of all this? *Merely staggering at the promise through unbelief.* What building is that like to be which hath a staggering foundation? When God answers not Saul, he goes to the devil. When the promise will not support us, we go to carnal policy: neither can it otherwise be. Engaged men finding one way to disappoint them, presently betake themselves to another. If men begin once to stagger at the promise, and to conclude, in their fears, that it will not receive accomplishment, that the fountain will be dry, they cannot but think it high time to dig cisterns for themselves. When David says, he shall one day perish by the hand of Saul, whatever God had said to the contrary, his next advice is, Let me go to the Philistines: and what success he had in that undertaking you know. Political diversions from pure dependence on the promise, do always draw after them a long time of entanglements.

Give me leave to give a word of caution against one or two things which men, staggering at the promises through unbelief, do usually in their carnal wisdom run into, for the compassing of the thing aimed at, that they may not be found in your honourable assembly.

[1.] *Take heed of a various management of religion,* of the things of God, to the advantage of the present posture and condition of your affairs. The things of Christ should be as Joseph's sheaf, to which all others should bow. When they are made to cringe, and bend, and put on a flattering countenance, to allure any sort of men into their interest, they are no more the things of Christ. I would it had not been too evident formerly, that men entangled in their affairs, enjoying authority, have, with all industry and diligence, pursued such and such an appearance of religion; not that themselves were so passionately affected with it, but merely for the satisfaction of some in that, whose assistance and compliance they needed for other things.

Oh, let not the things of God be immixed any more with carnal reasonings! His truths are all eternal and unchangeable. Give them at once the sovereignty of your souls, and have not the least thought of making them bend to serve your own ends, though good and righteous. Think not to get the promise like Jacob, by representing yourselves in the things of God for other than you are.

[2.] *Hide no truth of God as to that way of manifestation which to you is committed, for fear it should prove prejudicial to your affairs.* That influence and signature of your power which is due to any truth of God, let it not be withheld by carnal reasonings. I might farther draw out these, and such like things as these;—the warning is, to live upon the faith of that promise, which shall surely be established, without turning aside to needless, crooked paths of your own.

Use 2. Secondly. Be faithful in doing all the work of God whereunto you are engaged, as he is faithful in working all your works whereunto he is engaged. Your work, whereunto (whilst you are in his ways) God is engaged, is your safety and protection: God's work, whereunto you are engaged, is the propagating of the kingdom of Christ, and the setting up of the standard of the gospel. So far as you find God going on with your work, go you on with his. How is it that Jesus Christ is in Ireland only as a *lion staining all his garments with the blood of his enemies;* and none to hold him out as a *lamb sprinkled with his own blood to his friends?* Is it the sovereignty and interest of England that is alone to be there transacted? For my part, I see no farther into the MYSTERY of these things but that I could heartily rejoice, that, innocent blood being expiated, the Irish might enjoy Ireland so long as the moon endureth, so that Jesus Christ might possess the Irish. But God having suffered these sworn vassals of the man of sin to break out into such ways of villany as render them obnoxious unto vengeance, upon such rules of government amongst men as he hath appointed; is there, therefore, nothing to be done but to give a *cup of blood* into their hands? Doubtless the way whereby God will bring the followers after the beast to condign destruction for all their enmity to the Lord Jesus, will be by suffering them to run into such practices against men as shall righteously expose them to vengeance, according to acknowledged principles among the sons of men. But is this all? hath he no farther aim? Is not all this to make way for the Lord Jesus to take possession of his long since promised inheritance? And shall we stop at the first part? Is this to deal fairly with the Lord Jesus?—call him out to the *battle,* and then keep away his *crown?* God hath been faithful in doing great things for you; be faithful in this one,—do your utmost for the preaching of the gospel in Ireland.

Give me leave to add a few motives to this duty.

(1.) *They want it.* No want like theirs who want the gospel. I would there were for the present one gospel preacher for every walled town in the English possession in Ireland. The land mourneth, and the people perish for want of knowledge. Many run to and fro, but it is upon other designs; knowledge is not increased.

(2.) They are sensible of their *wants*, and cry out for *supply.* The tears and cries of the inhabitants of Dublin after the manifestations of Christ are ever in my view. If they were in the dark, and loved to have it so, it might something close a door upon the bowels of our compassion; but they cry out of their darkness, and are ready to follow every one whosoever, to have a candle. If their being gospelless move not our hearts, it is hoped their importunate cries will disquiet our rest, and wrest help as a beggar doth an alms.

(3.) *Seducers and blasphemers* will not be wanting to sow their tares, which those fallowed fields will receive, if there be none to cast in the seed of the word. Some are come over thither already without call, without employments, to no other end but only to vaunt themselves to be God; as they have done in the open streets with detestable pride, atheism, and folly. So that as Ireland was heretofore termed by some in civil things a frippery of bankrupts, for the great number of persons of broken estates that went thither; so, doubtless, in religion it will prove a frippery of monstrous, enormous, contradictious opinions, if the work of preaching the word of truth and soberness be not carried on. And if this be the issue of your present undertakings, will it be acceptable, think you, to the Lord Jesus, that you have used his power and might to make way for such things as his soul abhors?

[1.] Will it be for his honour, that the people whom he hath sought to himself with so high a hand should, at the very entrance of his taking possession, be leavened with those high and heavenly notions which have an open and experimented tendency to earthly, fleshly, dunghill practices? or,—

[2.] Will it be for the credit and honour of your profession of the gospel, that such a *breach should be under your hand?* that it should be as it were by your means? Will it not be a sword, and an arrow, and a maul in the hands of your observers? Who can bear the just scandal that would accrue,—scandal to the magistrates, scandal to the ministers of this generation,—in neglecting such an opportunity of advancing the gospel,—sleeping all the day whilst others sow tares?

[3.] Where will be the hoped, the expected consolation of this great affair, when the testimony and pledge of the peculiar presence of Christ amongst us upon such an issue shall be wanting?

What, then, shall we do? This thing is often spoken of, seldom driven to any close!

1*st*. Pray. "Pray the Lord of the harvest, that he would send out," that he would thrust forth, "labourers into his harvest." The labourers are ready to say, There is a lion in the way, difficulties to be contended withal. And to some men it is hard seeing a call of God through difficulties; when if it would but clothe itself with a few carnal advantages, how apparent is it to them! they can see it through a little cranny. Be earnest, then, with the Master of these labourers, in whose hand is their life and breath, and all their ways, that he would powerfully constrain them to be willing to enter into the fields that are white for the harvest.

2*dly*. Make such provision, that those who will go may be fenced from outward straits and fears, so far as the uncertainty of human affairs in general and the present tumultuating perturbations will admit. And let not, I beseech you, this be the business of an unpursued order. But,—

3*dly*. Let some be appointed (generals die and sink by themselves) to consider this thing, and to hear what sober proposals may be made by any whose hearts God shall stir up to so good a work.

This, I say, is a work wherein God expecteth faithfulness from you: stagger not at his promises nor your own duty. However, by all means possible, in this business I have striven to deliver my own soul.

Once more;—to this of faith, let me stir you up to another work of love, and that in the behalf of many poor perishing creatures, that want all things needful for the sustentation of life. Poor parentless children that lie begging, starving, rotting in the streets, and find no relief; yea, persons of quality, that have lost their dearest relations in your service, seeking for bread, and finding none;—oh, that some thoughts of this also might be seriously committed to them that shall take care for the gospel!

Use 3. I desire now to make more particular application of the doctrine, as to things purely spiritual. Until you know how to believe for your own souls, you will scarcely know how to believe for a nation. Let this, then, teach us to lay the burden and trouble of our lives upon the right shoulder. In our staggerings, our doubtings, our disputes, we are apt to assign this and that reason of them; when the sole reason, indeed, is our unbelief. Were it not for such a cause, or such a cause, I could believe; that is, were there no need of faith. That is, faith must remove the mountains that lie in the way, and then all will be plain. It is not the greatness of sin, nor continuance in sin, nor backsliding into sin, that is the true cause of thy staggering, whatever thou pretendest (the removal of all these is from that promise whose stability and certainty I before laid forth), but solely from thy unbelief, that "root of bitterness" which springs up and troubles thee. It is not the distance of the earth from the sun, nor the sun's withdrawing itself, that makes a dark and gloomy day; but the interposition of clouds and vaporous exhalations. Neither is thy soul beyond the reach of the promise, nor doth God withdraw himself; but the vapours of thy carnal, unbelieving heart do cloud thee. It is said of one place, " Christ could do no great work there." Why so? for want of power in him? Not at all; but merely for want of faith in them;—it was " because of their unbelief." The promise can do no great work upon thy heart, to humble thee, to pardon, to quiet thee. Is it for want of fulness and truth therein? Not at all; but merely for want of faith in thee;—that keeps it off. Men complain, that were it not for such things, and such things, they could believe; when it is their unbelief that casts those rubs in the way. As if a man should cast nails and sharp stones in his own way, and say, Verily I could run, were it not for those nails and stones; when he continues himself to cast them there. You could believe, were it not for these doubts and difficulties, these staggering perplexities; when, alas! they are all from your unbelief.

Use 4. See the sinfulness of all those staggering doubts and perplexities wherewith many poor souls have almost all their thoughts taken up. Such as is the root, such is the fruit. If the tree be evil, so will the fruit be also. Men do not gather grapes from brambles. What is the root that bears this fruit of staggering?—is it not the evil root of unbelief? And can any good come from thence?—are not all the streams of the same nature with the fountain?—if that be bitter, can they be sweet? If the body be full of poison, will not the branches have their venom also? Surely if the mother—unbelief—be the mouth of hell, the daughters—staggerings—are not the gates of heaven.

Of the sin of unbelief I shall not now speak at large. It is, in sum, the universal opposition of the soul unto God. All other sins arise against something or other of his revealed will; only unbelief sets up itself in a direct contradiction to all of him that is known. Hence the weight of condemnation in the gospel is constantly laid on this sin: " He that believeth not, on him the wrath of God abideth; he shall be damned." Now, as every drop of sea-water retains the brackishness and saltness of the whole; so every staggering doubt that is an issue of this unbelief hath in it the unsavouriness and distastefulness unto God that is in the whole.

Farther, to give you a little light into what acceptance our staggering thoughts find with the Lord (according to which must be our esteem of all that is in us), observe that,—

(1.) They grieve him.
(2.) They provoke him.
(3.) They dishonour him.

(1.) Such a frame *grieves* the Lord. Nothing more presses true love than to have an appearance of suspicion. Christ comes to Peter, and asks him, "Simon, son of Jonas, lovest thou me?" John xxi. 15. Peter seems glad of an opportunity to confess him, and his love to him, whom not long since he had denied, and answers readily, "Yea, Lord; thou knowest that I love thee." But when Christ comes with the same question again and again, the Holy Ghost tells us, "Peter was grieved because he said unto him the third time, Lovest thou me?" It exceedingly troubled Peter that his love should come under so many questionings, which he knew to be sincere. The love of Christ to his is infinitely beyond the love of his to him. All our doubtings are nothing but so many questionings of his love. We cry, Lord Jesus, lovest thou us? and again, Lord Jesus, lovest thou us? and that with distrustful hearts and thoughts, that it is not, it cannot be. Speaking of the unbelieving Jews, the Holy Ghost tells us, Jesus was "grieved for the hardness of their hearts," Mark iii. 5. And as it is bitter to him in the root, so also in the fruit. Our staggerings and debates, when we have a word of promise, is a grief to his Holy Spirit, as the unkindest return we can make unto his love.

(2.) It *provokes* him. How can this be, says Zacharias, that I should have a son? This shall be, saith the Lord; and thou thyself, for thy questioning, shalt be a sign of it, "Thou shalt be dumb, and not speak," Luke i. 20. His doubting was a provocation. And our Saviour expresses no less, in that bitter reproof to his disciples upon their wavering, Matt. xvii. 17, "O faithless and perverse generation, how long shall I be with you? how long shall I suffer you?"—that is, in this unbelieving frame. Poor souls are apt to admire the patience of God in other matters,—that he spared them in such and such sins, at such and such times of danger; but his exceeding patience towards them in their carnal reasonings and fleshly objections against believing, this they admire not. Nay, generally they think it should be so, God would not have them one step farther; nay, they could be more steadfast in believing, as they suppose, might it stand with the good-will of God;—when all this while this frame of all others is the greatest provocation to the Lord; he never exercises more forbearance than about this kind of unbelief. When the spies had gone into Canaan, had seen the land, and brought of the good fruit of it,—then to repine, then to question whether God would bring them into it or no, this caused the Lord "to swear in his wrath, that they should not enter into his rest." When God hath brought men to the borders of heaven, discovered to them the riches and excellency of his grace, admitted them to enter as spies into the kingdom of glory,—then to fall a staggering whether he intends them an entrance or no is that which lies heavy on him. The like may be said of all promised mercies and deliverances whatsoever. That this is a provocation, the Lord hath abundantly testified, inasmuch as for it he hath oftentimes snatched sweet morsels from the mouths of men, and turned aside the stream of mercies when it was ready to flow in upon them. "If," saith he, "ye will not believe, surely ye shall not be established," Isa. vii. 9. The very mercy but now promised concerning your deliverance shall be withheld. Oh, stop not success from Ireland by unbelief!

(3.) It *dishonours* God. In the close of this verse it is said, Abraham was "strong in faith" (or staggered not), "giving glory to God." To be established in believing, is to give God the greatest glory possible. Every staggering thought that ariseth from this root of unbelief robs God of his glory.

[1.] It robs him of the glory of his truth: "He that believeth not, hath made him a liar; because he believeth not his record," 1 John v. 10. Let men pretend what they please (as most [pretend?] an end, we give in specious pretences for our unbelief), the bottom of all is, the questioning of the truth of God in our false hearts.

[2.] It robs him of the glory of his fidelity or faithfulness in the discharge of his promises: "If we confess our sins, he is faithful to forgive us our sins," 1 John i. 9. He hath engaged his faithfulness in this business of the forgiveness of iniquities,—he whose right it is; calling that in question, calls the faithfulness of God in question.

[3.] It robs him of the glory of his grace. In a word, if a man should choose to set himself in a universal opposition unto God, he can think of no more compendious way than this. This, then, is the fruit, this the advantage, of all our staggering,—we rob God of glory, and our own souls of mercy.

Use 5. Be ashamed of, and humbled for, all your staggerings at the promises of God, with all your fleshly reasonings and carnal contrivances issuing therefrom. For the most part, we live upon successes, not promises:—unless we see and feel the print of victories, we will not believe; the engagement of God is almost quite forgotten in our affairs. We travel on without Christ, like his mother, and suppose him only to be in the crowd; but we must return to seek him where we left him, or our journeying on will be to no purpose. When Job, after all his complaining, had seen the end of the Lord, he cries out, "Now I abhor myself in dust and ashes." You have seen the end of the Lord in many of his promises,—oh, that it might prevail to make you abhor yourselves in dust and ashes, for all your carnal fears and corrupt reasonings upon your staggerings! When David enjoyed his promised mercy, he especially shames himself for every thought of unbelief that he had whilst he waited for it. "I said," saith he, "in my haste, that all men were liars:" and now he is humbled for it. Is this to be thankful, to forget our provoking thoughts of unbelief when the mercy is enjoyed? The Lord set it home upon your spirits, and give it to receive its due manifestation!

(1.) If there be any counsels, designs, contrivances, on foot amongst us, that are bottomed on our staggering at the promise under which we are, oh, let them be instantly cast down to the ground. Let not any be so foolish as to suppose that unbelief will be a foundation for quiet habitations. You are careful to avoid all ways that might dishonour you as the rulers of so great a nation; oh, be much more careful about such things as will dishonour you as believers! That is your greatest title,—that is your chiefest privilege. Search your own thoughts; and if any contrivance, any compliance, be found springing up, whose seed was sown by staggering at the promise, root them up and cast them out before it be too late.

(2.) Engage your hearts against all such ways for the future. Say unto God, How faithful art thou in all thy ways! how able to perform all thy promises! how hast thou established thy word in heaven and earth! Who would not put their trust in thee? We desire to be ashamed that ever we should admit in our hearts the least staggering at the stability of thy word.

(3.) Act as men bottomed upon unshaken things, that are not at all moved by the greatest appearing oppositions. "He that believeth will not make haste:" be not hasty in your resolves in any distress; wait for the accomplishment of the vision, for it will come. So long as you are in the way of God, and do the work of God, let not so much as your desires be too hasty after appearing strengthenings and assistance. Whence is it that there is amongst us such bleating after the compliance of this or that party of the sons of men,—perhaps priding themselves in our actings upon unbelief, as though we proclaimed, that, without such and such, we cannot be protected in the things of God? Let us, I beseech you, live above those things that are unworthy of the great name that is called upon us.

Oh, that by these and the like ways we might manifest our self-condemnation and abhorrency for all that distrust and staggering at the word of God, which arising from unbelief, hath had such deplorable issues upon all our counsels and undertakings!

SERMON V.

ΟΥΡΑΝΩΝ ΟΥΡΑΝΙΑ:

THE

SHAKING AND TRANSLATING OF HEAVEN AND EARTH:

A SERMON PREACHED TO THE HONOURABLE HOUSE OF COMMONS
IN PARLIAMENT ASSEMBLED, APRIL 19, 1649,

A DAY SET APART FOR EXTRAORDINARY HUMILIATION.

PREFATORY NOTE.

THIS sermon, from Heb. xii. 27, was preached before Parliament on a day set apart for extraordinary humiliation. It was in connection with this sermon that Owen for the first time was introduced to Oliver Cromwell; who, with other officers, listened to it, and afterwards made acquaintance with the preacher, under the circumstances mentioned in the "Life," etc., vol. i. p. 42. Cromwell was preparing to go to Ireland, and procured the appointment of Owen to accompany him, in order that the affairs of Trinity College, Dublin, might be adjusted and placed on a proper footing.—ED.

Die Veneris, April 20, 1649.

ORDERED, by the COMMONS assembled in Parliament, That Sir William Masham do give hearty thanks from this House to Mr Owen for his great pains in his sermon preached before the House yesterday, at Margaret's, Westminster; and that he be desired to print his sermon at large, as he intended to have delivered it if time had not prevented him; wherein he is to have the like liberty of printing thereof as others in like kind usually have had.

HEN. SCOBELL, *Clerc. Parl.*

TO THE RIGHT HONOURABLE,

THE COMMONS OF ENGLAND,

IN PARLIAMENT ASSEMBLED.

SIRS,

ALL that I shall preface to the ensuing discourse is, that seeing the nation's welfare and your own actings are therein concerned (the welfare of the nation and your own prosperity in your present actings being so nearly related, as they are, to the things of the ensuing discourse), I should be bold to press you to a serious consideration of them as now presented unto you, were I not assured—by your ready attention unto, and favourable acceptation of, their delivery—that, being now published by your command, such a request would be altogether needless. The subject-matter of this sermon being of so great weight and importance as it is, it had been very desirable that it had fallen on an abler hand; as also that more space and leisure had been allotted to the preparing of it—first, for so great, judicious, and honourable an audience; and, secondly, for public view—than possibly I could beg from my daily troubles, pressures, and temptations, in the midst of a poor, numerous, provoking people. As the Lord hath brought it forth, that it may be useful to your Honourable Assembly, and the residue of men that wait for the appearance of the Lord Jesus, shall be the sincere endeavour at the throne of grace of

Your most unworthy Servant

In the work of the Lord,

J. OWEN.

COGGESHALL, *May* 1, 1649.

SERMON V.

THE SHAKING AND TRANSLATING OF HEAVEN AND EARTH

"And this word, Yet once more, signifieth the removing of those things that are shaken, as of things that are made, that those things which cannot be shaken may remain."—HEB. xii. 27.

THE main design of the apostle in this scripture to the Hebrews, is to prevail with his countrymen, who had undertaken the profession of the gospel, to abide constant and faithful therein, without any apostasy unto, or mixture with Judaism, which God and themselves had forsaken;—fully manifesting, that in such backsliders the soul of the Lord hath no pleasure, chap. x. 38,—

A task, which whoso undertaketh in any age, shall find exceeding weighty and difficult,—even to persuade professors to hold out and continue in the glory of their profession unto the end, that with patience doing the will of God they "might receive the promise;"[1]—especially if there be "lions in the way,"[2] if opposition or persecution do attend them in their professed subjection to the Lord Jesus. Of all that deformity and dissimilitude to the divine nature which is come upon us by the fall, there is no one part more eminent, or rather no one defect more evident, than inconstancy and unstableness of mind in embracing that which is spiritually good. Man being turned from his unchangeable rest,[3] seeks to quiet and satiate his soul with restless movings towards changeable things.

Now, he who worketh all our works for us and in us, Isa. xxvi. 12, worketh them also by us;[4] and, therefore, that which he will give, he persuades us to have, that at once his bounty and our duty may receive a manifestation in the same thing. Of this nature is perseverance in the faith of Christ;—which, as by him it is promised, and therefore is a grace; so to us it is prescribed, and thereby is a duty.

[1] Chap. x. 36. [2] Prov. xxii. 13, xxvi. 13. [3] Ps. cxvi. 7.
[4] 1 Thess. i. 3; 2 Thess. i. 11; Deut. x. 16, xxx. 6; Ezek. xviii. 31, xxxvi. 26; Acts xi. 18.

"Petamus ut det, quod ut habeamus jubet," Augustine;—"Let us ask him to bestow what he requires us to enjoy." Yea, "Da, Domine, quod jubes, et jube quod vis;"—"Give what thou commandest, and command what thou pleasest."

As a duty it is by the apostle here considered; and therefore pressed on them who by nature were capable, and by grace enabled, for the performance thereof. Pathetical exhortations, then, unto perseverance in the profession of the gospel, bottomed on prevalent scriptural arguments and holy reasonings, are the sum of this epistle.

The arguments the apostle handleth unto the end proposed are of two sorts:—First, *Principal;* Secondly, *Deductive*, or emergencies from the first.

FIRST, His *principal* arguments are drawn from two chief fountains:—1. The *author;* and, 2. The *nature and end of the gospel.*

1. The author of the gospel is either,—

(1.) *Principal and immediate*, which is God the Father, who having at sundry times and in divers manners formerly spoken by the prophets, herein speaketh by his Son, chap. i. 1.

(2.) *Concurrent* and *immediate*, Jesus Christ, this great salvation, being begun to be spoken to us by the Lord, chap. ii. 3. This latter he chiefly considereth, as in and by whom the gospel is differenced from all other dispensations of the mind of God. Concerning him to the end intended he proposeth,—[1.] His *person;* [2.] His *employment.*

[1.] For his person, that thence he may argue to the thing aimed at, he holdeth out,—

1*st.* The *infinite glory of his Deity;* being "the brightness of the Father's glory, and the express image of his person," chap. i. 3.

2*dly.* The *infinite condescension of his love*, in assuming humanity; for, "because the children were partakers of flesh and blood, he also himself took part of the same," chap. ii. 14.

And from the consideration of both these, he presseth the main exhortation which he hath in hand, as you may see, chap. ii. 1, 2, iii. 12, 13, &c.

[2.] The employment of Christ he describeth in his offices, which he handleth,—

1*st.* *Positively*, and very briefly, chapters i., ii., iii.

2*dly.* *Comparatively*, insisting chiefly on his priesthood,—exalting it in sundry weighty particulars above that of Aaron, which yet was the glory of the Jewish worship; and this at large, chapters vi., vii., viii., ix., x. And this being variously advanced and asserted, he layeth as the main foundation, upon which he placeth the weight and stress of the main end pursued, as in the whole epistle is everywhere obvious.

2. The second head of principal arguments he taketh from the gospel itself; which considering as a covenant, he holdeth out two ways.

(1.) *Absolutely*, in its efficacy in respect of,—

[1.] *Justification*. In it God is merciful to unrighteousness, and sins and iniquities he remembers no more, chap. viii. 12;—bringing in perfect remission, that there shall need no more offering for sin, chap. x. 18.

[2.] *Sanctification*. He puts his laws in our hearts, and writes them in our minds, chap. x. 16;—in it purging our consciences by the blood of Christ, chap. ix. 14.

[3.] *Perseverance:* "I will be to them a God, and they shall be to me a people," chap. viii. 10.

All three are also held out in sundry other places.

(2.) *Respectively* to the covenant of works; and in this regard assigns unto it principal qualifications, with many peculiar eminences them attending,—too many now to be named. Now, these are,—

[1.] That it is *new:* "In that he saith, A new covenant, he hath made the first old," chap. viii. 13.

[2.] *Better*. It is a better covenant, and built upon "better promises," chap. vii. 22, viii. 6.

[3.] *Surer*, the Priest thereof being ordained, "not after the law of a carnal commandment, but after the power of an endless life," chap. vii. 16.

[4.] *Unalterable*. So in all the places before named, and sundry others.

All which are made eminent in its peculiar mediator, Jesus Christ; which is the sum of chap. vii.

And still, in the holding out of these things, that they might not forget the end for which they were now drawn forth, and so exactly handled, he interweaves many pathetical entreaties and pressing arguments by way of application, for the confirming and establishing his countrymen in the faith of this glorious gospel; as you may see almost in every chapter.

SECONDLY. His arguments less principal, deduced from the former, being very many, may be referred to these three heads:—

1. The *benefits* by them enjoyed under the gospel.

2. The *example* of others, who by faith and patience obtained the promises, chap. xi.

3. From the *dangerous* and *pernicious consequence* of backsliding; of which only I shall speak. Now this he setteth out three ways.

(1.) From the *nature* of that sin. It is a crucifying to themselves the Son of God afresh, and putting him to open shame, chap. vi. 6; a treading under foot the Son of God, counting the blood of the covenant an unholy thing, and doing despite to the Spirit of grace, chap. x. 29.

(2.) The remediless *punishment* which attends that sin: "There remaineth no more sacrifice for it, but a certain fearful looking for of judgment, and fiery indignation, which shall devour the adversaries," chap. x. 26, 27.

(3.) The *person* against whom peculiarly it is committed, and that is he who is the author, subject, and mediator of the gospel, the Lord Jesus Christ; concerning whom, for the aggravation of this sin, he proposeth two things.

[1.] His goodness and love, and that in his great undertaking to be a Saviour; being "made like unto his brethren in all things, that he might be a merciful and faithful high priest in things pertaining to God, to make reconciliation for the sins of the people," chap. ii. 17. And of this there is a sweet and choice line running through the whole discourse, making the sin of backsliding against so much love and condescension appear exceeding sinful.

[2.] His greatness or power; which he sets out two ways.

1*st.* Absolutely, as he is God, to be "blessed for ever," chap. i.; and, "It is a fearful thing to fall into the hands of the living God," chap. x. 31.

2*dly.* Comparatively, as he is the mediator of the new covenant in reference to Moses. And this he setteth forth, as by many and sundry reasonings in other places of the epistle, so by a double testimony in this 12th chapter, making that inference from them both which you have, verse 25, "See that ye refuse not him that speaketh: for if they escaped not who refused him that spake on earth, much more shall not we escape, if we turn away from him who speaketh from heaven."

Now, the first testimony of his power is taken from a record of what he did heretofore;—the other from a prediction of what he will do hereafter.

The first you have, verse 26, in the first part of it, "His voice then shook the earth;" then,—that is, when the law was delivered by him, as it is described, verses 18–21, foregoing; when the mountain upon which it was delivered, the mediator Moses, into whose hand it was delivered, and the people for whose use it was delivered, did all shake and tremble at the voice, power, and presence of Christ,[1]—who, as it hence appears, is that Jehovah who gave the law, Exod. xx. 2.

The other, in the same verse, is taken from a prediction out of Haggai ii. 6, of what he will do hereafter,—even demonstrate and make evident his power, beyond whatever he before effected: He hath promised, saying, "Yet once more I shake not the earth only, but also heaven."

[1] Exod. xix. 18, 19, xx. 18.

And if any one shall ask, wherein this effect of the mighty power of the Lord Jesus consisteth, and how from thence professors may be prevailed upon to keep close to the obedience of him in his kingdom, —the apostle answers, verse 27, " And this word, Yet once more, signifieth the removing of those things that are shaken, as of things that are made, that those things which cannot be shaken may remain." And thus am I stepped down upon the words of my text, finding them in the close of the arguments drawn from the power of Christ to persuade professors to constancy in the paths of the gospel; and having passed through their coherence, and held out their aim and tendence, their opening and application come now to be considered.

And herein these three things:—I. The apostle's *assertion:* "The things that are shaken shall be removed, as things that are made;" II. The *proof* of this assertion: "This word, Yet once more, signifieth no less;" III. His *inference* from this assertion thus proved: "The things that cannot be shaken must remain."

I. In the first I shall consider,—1. What are the things that are shaken; 2. What is their shaking; 3. What their removal, being shaken.

1. For the first, there is a great variety of judgment amongst interpreters.[1] The foregoing verse tells us it is not only the earth, but the heaven also; but now what heaven and earth this should be is dubious,—is not apparent. So many different apprehensions of the mind of God in these words as have any likeness of truth I must needs recount and remove, that no prejudice may remain from other conceptions against that which from them we shall assert.

(1.) The earth, say some, is the men of the earth, living thereon; and the heavens are the angels, their blessed inhabitants: both shaken or stricken with amazement upon the nativity of Christ and preaching of the gospel. The heavens were shaken, when so great things were accomplished as that "the angels themselves desired to look into them," 1 Pet. i. 12; and the earth was filled with amazement, when, the Holy Ghost being poured out upon the apostles for the preaching of the gospel, men of every nation under heaven were amazed and marvelled at it, Acts ii. 5–7. Thus Rollocus, Piscator, and sundry other famous divines. But,—

[1.] The shaking here intimated by the apostle was then, when he wrote, under the promise, not actually accomplished, as were the things by them recounted; for he holds it forth as an issue of that great power of Christ which he would one day exercise for the farther establishment of his kingdom.

[2.] This that now is to be done must excel that which formerly

[1] "Nescio an facilior hic locus fuisset, si nemo eum exposuisset."—Mald. ad Luc., ii. 34.

was done at the giving of the law; as is clearly intimated in the inference: "Then he shook the earth, but now the heavens also." It is a gradation to a higher demonstration of the power of Christ; which that the things of this interpretation are is not apparent.

[3.] It is marvellous these learned men observed not, that the heavens and the earth shaken, verse 26, are the things to be removed, verse 27. Now, how are angels and men removed by Christ? are they not rather gathered up into one spiritual body and communion?[1] Hence, verse 27, they interpret the shaken things to be Judaical ceremonies, which, verse 26, they had said to be men and angels.

(2.) Others by heaven and earth understand the material parts of the world's fabric, commonly so called; and by their shaking, those portentous signs and prodigies, with earthquakes, which appeared in them at the birth and death of the Lord Jesus. A new star, preternatural darkness, shaking of the earth, opening of graves, rending of rocks, and the like, are to them this shaking of heaven and earth.[2] So Junius, and after him most of ours. But this interpretation is obnoxious to the same exceptions with the former, and also others. For,—

[1.] These things being past before, how can they be held out under a promise?[3]

[2.] How are these shaken things removed? which with their shaking they must certainly be, as in my text.

[3.] This shaking of heaven and earth is ascribed to the power of Christ as mediator, whereunto these signs and prodigies cannot rationally be assigned; but rather to the sovereignty of the Father, bearing witness to the nativity and death of his Son;—so that neither can this conception be fastened on the words.

(3.) The fabric of heaven and earth is by others also intended,—not in respect of the signs and prodigies formerly wrought in them, but of that dissolution, or, as they suppose, alteration, which they shall receive at the last day. So Pareus, Grotius, and many more. Now, though these avoid the rock of holding out as accomplished what is only promised, yet this gloss also is a dress disfiguring the mind of God in the text. For,—

[1.] The things here said to be shaken do stand in a plain opposition to the things that cannot be shaken nor removed; and therefore they are to be removed, that these may be brought in. Now, the things to be brought in are the things of the kingdom of the

[1] Eph. i. 10. Ἀνακεφαλαιώσασθαι, that is, *μίαν κεφαλὴν παρασχεῖν ἀγγέλοις καὶ ἀνθρώποις τὸν Χριστόν· ἀπεσχισμένοι γὰρ ἦσαν οἱ ἄγγελοι καὶ ἄνθρωποι.*—Œcumen. in loc.

[2] Matt. ii. 2, xxvii. 45; Luke xxiii. 44, 45; Matt. xxvii. 51, 52.

[3] Ὃ *γὰρ βλέπει τις, τί καὶ ἐλπίζει,* Rom. viii. 24.

Lord Jesus. What opposition, I pray, does the material fabric of heaven and earth stand in to the kingdom of the Lord Jesus? Doubtless none at all, being the proper seat of that kingdom.

[2.] There will, on this ground, be no bringing in of the kingdom of the Lord Jesus until indeed that kingdom in the sense here insisted on is to cease; that is, after the day of judgment, when the kingdom of grace shall have place no more.

Those are the most material and likely mistakes about the words. I could easily give out, and pluck in again three or four other warping senses; but I hope few in these days of accomplishing will once stumble at them.

(4.) The true mind of the Spirit, by the help of that Spirit of truth, comes next to be unfolded. And first, what are the things that are shaken?

[1.] As the apostle here applies a part of the prophecy of Haggai, so that prophecy, even in the next words, gives light into the meaning of the apostle. Look what heaven and earth the prophet speaks of;—of those, and no other, speaks the apostle. The Spirit of God in the Scripture is his own best interpreter.[1] See, then, the order of the words as they lie in the prophet, Hag. ii. 6, 7, "I will shake heaven and earth: I will shake all nations." God, then, shakes heaven and earth when he shakes all nations; that is, he shakes the heaven and earth of the nations. "I will shake heaven and earth, and I will shake all nations," is a pleonasm for "I will shake the heaven and earth of all nations." These are the things shaken in my text.

The heavens of the nations, what are they?—even their political heights and glory, those forms of government which they have framed for themselves and their own interest, with the grandeur and lustre of their dominions. The nations' earth is the multitudes of their people, their strength and power, whereby their heavens, or political heights, are supported. It is, then, neither the material heavens and earth, nor yet Mosaical ordinances, but the political heights and splendour, the popular multitudes and strength, of the nations of the earth, that are thus to be shaken, as shall be proved.

That the earth, in prophetical descriptions or predictions of things, is frequently, yea, almost always, taken for the people and multitudes of the earth, needs not much proving.[2] One or two instances shall suffice. Rev. xii. 16, "The earth helped the woman" against the flood of the dragon; which that it was the multitudes of earthly people none doubts. Thatan earthquake, or shaking of the earth, are

[1] "Nunquam Pauli sensum ingredieris, nisi Pauli Spiritum imbiberis."—Ber. Ser. de Monte. Τὸ αὐτὸ χρίσμα διδάσκει ὑμᾶς περὶ πάντων, 1 John ii. 27. Ἐν πνεύματι ἁγίῳ νοούμεναι καὶ ἀνοιγόμεναι αἱ γραφαὶ δεικνύουσιν ἡμῖν τὸν Χριστὸν, εἰκότως θυρωρὸς τὸ πνεῦμα τὸ ἅγιον.—Theophylac. in John x.

[2] Ps. lxviii. 8; Hab. ii. 20; Matt. xxiv. 7; 1 Sam. xiv. 25—[Heb.]

popular commotions, is no less evident from Rev. xi. 13, where by an earthquake great Babylon receives a fatal blow. And for the heavens, whether they be the political heights of the nations or the grandeur of potentates, let the Scripture be judge; I mean, when used in this sense of shaking, or establishment, Isa. li. 15, 16, "I am the LORD thy God, that divided the sea, whose waves roared: the LORD of hosts is his name. And I have put my words in thy mouth, and I have covered thee in the shadow of mine hand, that I may plant the heavens, and lay the foundations of the earth, and say unto Zion, Thou art my people." By a repetition of what he hath done, he establisheth his people in expectation of what he will do. And,—

1*st.* He minds them of that wonderful deliverance from an army behind them, and an ocean before them, by his miraculous preparing dry paths for them in the deep: "I am the LORD, that divided the sea, whose waves roared."

2*dly.* Of his gracious acquainting them with his mind, his law, and ordinances at Horeb. "I have put," saith he, "my words in thy mouth."

3*dly.* Of that favourable and singular protection afforded them in the wilderness, when they were encompassed with enemies round about: "I covered thee in the shadow of mine hand."

Now, to what end was all this? Why, saith he, "That I might plant the heavens, and lay the foundations of the earth." What! of these material, visible heavens and earth? Two thousand four hundred and sixty years before, at least, were they planted and established. It is all but [nothing more than] making of "Zion a people," which before was scattered in distinct families. And how is this done? Why, the heavens are planted, or a glorious frame of government and polity is erected amongst them, and the multitudes of their people are disposed into an orderly commonwealth, to be a firm foundation and bottom for the government amongst them. This is the heavens and earth of the nations which is to be shaken in my text.

Isa. xxxiv. 4, "All the host of heaven shall be dissolved, and the heavens shall be rolled together as a scroll: and all their host shall fall down, as the leaf falleth off from the vine." Now, these dissolved, rolled heavens are no other but the power and heights of the opposing nations, their government and tyranny, especially that of Idumea, as both the foregoing and following verses do declare. "The indignation of the LORD," saith he, "is upon the nations, and his fury upon all their armies; he hath delivered them to the slaughter, their slain," &c. Jer. iv. 23–25, "I beheld the earth, and, lo, it was without form and void; and the heavens, and they had no light. I beheld the mountains, and, lo, they trembled, and all the hills moved lightly." Here's heaven and earth shaken, and all in the razing of the political state and commonwealth of the Jews by the Babylonians, as is at large described in the verses following. Ezek. xxxii. 7, "I will cover the heaven, and make the stars thereof dark; I will cover the sun with a cloud, and the moon shall not give her light. All the bright lights of heaven will I make dark over thee, and set darkness upon thy land, saith the Lord GOD." Behold heaven and earth, sun, moon, and stars, all shaken and confounded in the destruction of Egypt,—the thing the prophet treats of, their kingdom and nation being to be ruined.

Not to hold you too long upon what is so plain and evident, you may take it for a rule, that, in the denunciations of the judgments of God, through all the prophets, heaven, sun, moon, stars, and the like appearing beauties and glories of the aspectable heavens, are taken for governments, governors, dominions in political states; as Isa. xiv. 12–15; Jer. xv. 9, li. 25.[1]

Furthermore, to confirm this exposition, St John, in the Revelation, holds constantly to the same manner of expression. Heaven and earth in that book are commonly those which we have described. In particular, this is eminently apparent, chap. vi. 12–15, "And I beheld when he had opened the sixth seal, and, lo, there was a great earthquake; and the sun became black as sackcloth of hair, and the moon became as blood; and the stars of heaven fell unto the earth: and the heavon departed as a scroll when it is rolled together; and every mountain and island were moved out of their places," &c. The destruction and wasting of the Pagan-Romish state, the plagues and commotions of her people, the dethroning her idol-worship, and destruction of persecuting emperors and captains, with the transition of power and sovereignty from one sort to another, is here held out under this grandeur of words,[2] being part of the shaking of heaven and earth in my text.

Add lastly hereunto, that the promises of the restoration of God's people into a glorious condition after all their sufferings, is perpetually, in the Scripture, held out under the same terms, and you have a plentiful demonstration of this point. Isa. lxv. 17, 18, "Behold, I create new heavens and a new earth: and the former shall not be remembered, nor come into mind. But be ye glad and rejoice for ever in that which I create," &c.[3] 2 Pet. iii. 13, "Nevertheless we, according to his promise, look for new heavens and a new earth, wherein dwelleth righteousness." Rev. xxi. 1, "I saw a new heaven and a new earth: for the first heaven and the first earth were passed

[1] Isa. xiii. 13; Ps. lxviii. 8; Joel ii. 10; Rev. viii. 12; Matt. xxiv. 29; Luke xxi. 25; Isa. lx. 20; Obad. 4; Rev. viii. 13, xi. 12, xx. 11.

[2] Euseb. Eccles. Hist., lib. ix., cap. 8, 10, lib. viii. cap. 17; De Vita Constant., lib. i., cap. 50–52.

[3] Isa. lxvi. 22–24.

away; and there was no more sea." The heaven and earth are restored, but the sea,—that shall be no more. Those gatherings together of many waters, rivers from all places,[1] or pretended clergymen from all nations into general councils, which were the sea or many waters on which the whore sat,[2] shall have no place at all in the church's restored condition.

I hope it is now fully cleared what is meant by the things that are shaken,—even the political heights, the splendour and strength of the nations of the earth: the foundation of the whole is laid, and our heap (or building, if your favour will so accept it) will go on apace; for to the analogy hereof shall the residue of the words be interpreted.

2. The second thing considerable is, What is the shaking of these things?

To this the answer is now made brief and facile. Such as are the things shaken, such must their shaking be: spiritual, if spiritual; natural, if natural; civil, if civil. Now, they being declared and proved to be civil things, such also is their shaking.[3] Now, what is a civil shaking of civil constitutions? how are such things done in the world? what are these earthquakes? Truly, the accomplishment hereof is in all nations so under our eyes as that I need not speak one word thereunto.

Neither shall I insist upon the inquiry, when this shaking shall be?

The text is plain, that it must be previous to the bringing in of those things that cannot be moved; that is, the prosperous estate of the kingdom of Christ.[4] Only we may observe, that besides other shakings in particular nations, of less general concernment and importance,[5] this prophecy hath and shall receive a twofold eminent accomplishment, with reference unto a twofold eminent opposition which the kingdom of Christ hath met withal in the world.

(1.) From the Pagan-Roman state, which, at the gospel's first entrance, held in subjection most of the chief provinces of the then known world.[6] What were the bloody endeavours of the heaven and earth of that state for the suppression thereof is known to our children. The issue of the whole in the accomplishment of this promise, shaking those heavens and earth to pieces, I before pointed at from Rev. vi. 12–17, beginning in the plagues of the persecuting emperors, and ending in the ruin of the empire itself. But,—

(2.) The immovable things were not yet in their glory to be brought in. More seed of blood must be sown, that the end of the gospel's year may yield a plentiful harvest. That shaking was only for ven-

[1] Gen. i. 10. [2] Rev. xvii. 1.
[3] Matt. xxiv. 6, 7; Jer. iv. 19; Isa. ix. 5.
[4] Χρονους ἢ καιροὺς, οὓς ὁ πατὴρ ἔθετο ἐν τῇ ἰδίᾳ ἐξουσίᾳ, Acts i. 7.
[5] Σεισμοὶ κατὰ τόπους, Matt. xxiv. 7.
[6] Ἐξῆλθε δόγμα παρὰ Καίσαρος Αὐγούστου, ἀπογράφεσθαι πᾶσαν τὴν οἰκουμένην, Luke ii. 1.

geance upon an old, cursed, and not for the bringing in of a new, blessed state. The vials of God's wrath having crumbled the heavens and earth of pagan Rome into several pieces,[1] and that empire being removed as to its old form, by the craft of Satan it became moulded up again into a papal sovereignty, to exercise all the power of the first beast in persecution of the saints, Rev. xiii. 12. This second pressure, though long and sore, must have an end;—the new-moulded heaven and earth of papal, antichristian Rome, running by a mysterious thread through all the nations of the west, must be shaken also; which when it is accomplished, there shall be no more sea. There is not another beast to arise, nor another state to be formed;—let endeavours be what they will, the Lord Jesus shall reign.[2]

3. What is the *removal* of heaven and earth, being shaken?

The word here translated "removal" is μετάθεσις: whence that is come to pass I dare not positively say. This, doubtless, is a common fault amongst translators, that they will accommodate the words of a text to their own apprehension of the sense and matter thereof. [3]Understanding, as I suppose, that the things here said to be shaken were the Jewish ordinances, they translated their disposition a "removal;" as the truth is they were removed. But the word signifies no such thing. As its natural import, from its rise and composition, is otherwise, so neither in the Scripture nor any profane author doth it ever signify properly a "removal." Translation, or changing, is the only native, genuine import of it:[4] and why it should in this place be haled out of its own sphere, and tortured into a new signification, I know not. Removal is of the matter, translation of the form only. It is not, then, a destruction and total amotion of the great things of the nations; but a change, translation, and a new-moulding of them, that is here intimated. They shall be shuffled together, almost into their primitive confusion, and come out new-moulded, for the interest of the Lord Jesus. All the present states of the world are cemented together by antichristian lime, as I shall show afterward:—unless they be so shaken as to have every cranny searched and brushed, they will be no quiet habitation for the Lord Christ and his people. This, then, is the μετάθεσις of the "heaven and earth" of the nations.

Now, this is evident from that full prediction which you have of the accomplishment hereof, Rev. xvii. 12, the kingdoms of the west "receive power one hour with the beast." Verse 13, in their constitution and government at first received, "they give their power to the beast," and fight against the Lamb. Verse 14, the Lamb with

[1] Τὸ κατέχον, 2 Thess. ii. 6. [2] Rev. xviii. 2; Isa. lx. 12; Ps. ii. 6.
[3] Heb. xi. 5; Jude 4; Gal. i. 6; Heb. vi. 18, vii. 12.
[4] "Mutationem," Trem. "Translationem." Erasm. Ar. Mont.

his faithful and chosen ones overcomes them. There their heaven and earth is shaken. Verse 16, their power is translated, new-moulded, and becomes a power against the beast, in the hand of Jesus Christ.

This, then, is the shaking and removal in my text, which is said to be, "as of things that are made;" that is, by men, through the concurrence of divine Providence for a season (which making you have, Rev. xvii. 12–17);—not like the kingdom of Christ, which, being of a purely divine constitution, shall by no human power receive an end.

The other parts of the text follow briefly.

II. The next thing is the apostle's proof of this assertion. And he tells you, "This word, Once more," the beginning of this sentence he urged from the prophet, "signifies no less."

The words in the prophet are, עוֹד אַחַת מְעַט הִיא, "Yet once it is a little." מְעַט הִיא, "It is a little," is left out by the apostle, as not conducing to the business in hand. Ἔτι ἅπαξ, as he rendereth עוֹד אַחַת, are a sufficient demonstration of the assertion. In themselves they hold out a commutation of things, and, as they stand in conjunction in that place of the prophet, declare that that shaking and commutation must be for the bringing in of the kingdom of the Lord Christ. In brief, being interpreted by the same Spirit whereby they were indited, we know the exposition is true.

III. The last head remaineth under two particulars:—1. What are "the things that cannot be shaken?" 2. What is their remaining?

1. For the first, "the things that cannot be shaken," verse 27, are called "a kingdom that cannot be moved," verse 28,—a kingdom subject to none of those shakings and alterations which other dominions have been tossed to and fro withal. [1]Daniel calls it, a not giving of the kingdom to another people, Dan. ii. 44;—not that œcumenical kingdom which he hath with his Father, as king of nations; but that œconomical kingdom which he hath by dispensation from his Father, as king of saints. Now this may be considered two ways.

(1.) As purely internal and spiritual; which is the rule of his Spirit in the hearts of all his saints. [2]This "cometh not with observation," it is within us, Luke xvii. 20, 21,—consisting in "righteousness, peace, and joy in the Holy Ghost," Rom. xiv. 17.

(2.) As external, and appearing in gospel administrations. [3]So is Christ described as a king in the midst of their kingdom, Rev. i. 14–17, as also chap. iv. and chap. xi. 15. And both these may be again considered two ways.

[1] Ps. ii. 6, cx. 2; Acts ii. 36; Rev. i. 18; 1 Cor. xv. 24–27.
[2] Luke vi. 20; Mark xii. 34, &c.
[3] Ps. xlv. 6, cxlv. 13; Isa. ix. 7; Obad. 21.

[1.] In respect of their essence and being; and so they have been, are, and shall be continued in all ages. He hath built his church upon a rock, " and the gates of hell shall not prevail against it," Matt. xvi. 18.

[2.] In reference to their extent in respect of subjects, with their visible glorious appearance, which is under innumerable promises to be very great in the latter days: " And it shall come to pass in the last days, that the mountain of the LORD'S house shall be established in the top of the mountains, and shall be exalted above the hills, and all nations shall flow unto it," Isa. ii. 2.[1]

These, then, are the things which cannot be shaken; which we may reduce to three heads.

1*st*. The growth of righteousness, peace, and joy in the saints, being filled with light and love from the special presence of Christ; with a wonderful increase of the number of them, multitudes of the elect being to be born in those days,—the residue of the Jews and fulness of the Gentiles meeting in one fold, and there " dwelleth righteousness," 2 Pet. iii. 13.[2]

2*dly*. The administration of gospel ordinances, in power and purity, according to the appointment and unto the acceptation of the Lord Jesus. The temple of God and the altar being measured anew, the outward court, defiled with Gentile worship, is left out, Rev. xi. 1, 2.

3*dly*. The glorious and visible manifestation of those administrations in the eyes of all the world, in peace and quietness,—none making afraid or hurting in the whole mountain of the Lord, Isa. lxv. 25.

For the personal reign of the Lord Jesus on earth, I leave it to them with whose discoveries I am not, and curiosities I would not be, acquainted, Acts iii. 21.

But as for such who from hence do, or for sinister ends pretend to fancy to themselves a terrene kingly state unto each private particular saint,—so making it a bottom " vivendi ut velis," for every one to do that which is good in his own eyes, to the disturbance of all order and authority, civil and spiritual,—as they expressly clash against innumerable promises, so they directly introduce such confusion and disorder as the soul of the Lord Jesus doth exceedingly abhor.

It is only the three things named, with their necessary dependencies, that I do assert.

[1] Isa. xi. 5–10, xix. 18, 19, xxx. 18, 19; Micah iv. 1.

[2] Isa. xlix. 18–22, liv. 1–3, &c., lv. 11, 12, lx. 16, 17; Ezek. xlviii. 35; Amos ix. 11; Rom. xi. 15, &c.; Isa. xlix. 22, 23, lxvi. 21; Mal. iii. 3; Ezek. xliii. 9–11; Rev. xxi. 3; Isa. liv. 11–13, &c.; Zech. xiv. 9–11.

2. And lastly, of these it is said,—they must remain; that is, continue and be firmly established, as the word is often used, Rom. ix. 11.

The words of the text being unfolded, and the mind of the Holy Ghost in them discovered, I shall from them commend to your Christian consideration this following position:—

Observation. The Lord Jesus Christ, by his mighty power, in these latter days, as antichristian tyranny draws to its period, will so far shake and translate the political heights, governments, and strength of the nations, as shall serve for the full bringing in of his own peaceable kingdom;—the nations so shaken becoming thereby a quiet habitation for the people of the Most High.

Though the doctrine be clear from the text, yet it shall receive farther scriptural confirmation, being of great weight and concernment. Dan. ii. 44, "And in the days of these kings shall the God of heaven set up a kingdom, which shall never be destroyed: and the kingdom shall not be left to other people, but it shall break in pieces and consume all these kingdoms, and it shall stand for ever." That this is affirmed of the kingdom of Christ under the gospel, none ever doubted.

Three things are here remarkably intimated of it:—1. The time wherein it shall most eminently be established; and that is, "In the days of these kings," of which Daniel was speaking; 2. The efficacy of its being set up: "It shall break in pieces all these kingdoms;" 3. Its own stability: "It shall never be destroyed."

1. For the first, there is great debate about the principal season of the accomplishing of this prediction;—much hesitation who those kings are in whose days the kingdom of Christ is eminently to be established. In the days when the two legs of the Roman empire shall be divided into ten kingdoms, and those kingdoms have opposed themselves to the power of Christ,—that is, in the days wherein we live,—say some; yea, most of the ancients took this for the Roman empire, and to these the bringing in of the kingdom of Christ is the establishment of it in these days. Others understand the Syrian and Egyptian branches of the Grecian monarchy, and the bringing in of Christ's kingdom to be in his birth, death, and preaching of the gospel; wherein certainly the foundations of it were laid. I will not contend with any mortal hereabout; only I shall oppose one or two things to this latter interpretation. As,—

(1.) The kingdom of Syria was totally destroyed and reduced into a Roman province sixty years before the nativity of Christ; and the Egyptian, thirty;—so that it is impossible that the kingdom of Christ by his birth should be set up in their days.

(2.) It is ascribed to the efficacy of this kingdom, that, being established, it shall break in pieces all those kingdoms: which how can it be, when, at the first setting of it up, they had neither place nor name, nor scarce remembrance?

So that it must needs be the declining, divided Roman empire, shared among sundry nations, that is here intimated: and so, consequently, the kingdom of Christ to be established, is that glorious administration thereof which in these days he will bring in.

2. Be it so or otherwise, this from hence cannot be denied, that the kingdom of Christ will assuredly shake and translate all opposing dominions, until itself be established in and over them all,—ὅπερ ἔδει δεῖξαι,—which is all I intend to prove from this place. The ten-partite empire of the west must give place to the stone cut out of the mountain without hands.

Dan. vii. 27, "The kingdom and dominion, and the greatness of the kingdom under the whole heaven, shall be given to the people of the saints of the Most High, whose kingdom is an everlasting kingdom, and all dominions shall serve and obey him." Hitherto is the end of the matter. Either Antichrist is described in the close of this chapter, or one very like him, St John painting him in the Revelation with all this man's colours; plainly intimating, that though, in the first place, that mad, raging tyrant, Antiochus the Illustrious, was pointed at, yet that another was to rise in his likeness, with his craft and cruelty, that, with the assistance of the ten horns, should plague the saints of the Christians no less than the others had done those of the Jews. Now, what shall be the issue thereof? His dominion with his adherents shall be taken away and consumed, verse 26. And then shall it be given to the people of the Most High, as before; or, they shall enjoy the kingdom of Christ in a peaceable manner, their officers being made peace, and their exactors righteousness.

3. It is clearly evident, from these and other places in that prophecy, that He who is the only potentate will sooner or later shake all the monarchies of the earth, where he will have his name known, that all nations may be suited to the interest of his kingdom; which alone is to endure.

Isa. lx. in many places, indeed throughout, holds out the same. Verse 12, "The nation and kingdom that will not serve thee shall perish;" that is, all the nations of the earth. Not a known nation, but the blood of the saints of Christ is found in the skirts thereof. Now, what shall be the issue when they are so broken?

Verses 17, 18, "I will make thy officers peace, and thine exactors righteousness. Violence shall no more be heard in thy land, wasting nor destruction within thy borders: but thou shalt call thy walls Salvation, and thy gates Praise." See at your leisure to this purpose, Amos ix. 11–15; Jer. xxxi. 23–25; Isa. xxxiii. 20–24.

I shall only add that punctual description which you have of this "whole matter," as Daniel calls it, in the Revelation, with respect unto its accomplishment. Chap. xvii., the Roman harlot having procured the ten kings or kingdoms, into which the last head of the Roman empire sprouted, about the year 450, by the inundation of the northern nations, to join with her, they together make war against the Lamb. Verse 12, "The ten horns which thou sawest" upon the last head of the great beast, the Roman monarchy, "are ten kings, which have received no kingdom as yet,"—to wit, when John saw the vision,—"but receive power as kings one hour with the beast." About four hundred years after this, the pope ascended to his sovereignty, and these western nations grew into distinct dominions about the same time. Verse 13, "These have one mind,"—that is, as to the business in hand, for otherwise they did and do vex one another with perpetual broils and wars,—"and shall give their power and strength unto the beast," or swear to defend the rights of holy church (which is no other than Babylon), and act accordingly. Verse 14, "These shall make war with the Lamb;"—having sworn and undertaken the defence of holy church, or Babylon, they persecuted the poor heretics with fire and sword; that is, the witnesses of the Lamb, and in them the Lamb himself, striving to keep his kingdom out of the world;—"and the Lamb shall overcome them," shaking and translating them into a new mould and frame; "for he is Lord of lords, and King of kings, and they that are with him," whose help and endeavours he will use, "are called, and chosen, and faithful." Verse 16, "The ten horns which thou sawest upon the beast," being now shaken, changed, and translated in mind, interest, and perhaps government, "these shall hate the whore, and shall make her desolate"—are instrumental in the hand of Christ for the ruin of that antichristian state which before they served—"and naked, and shall eat her flesh, and burn her with fire."

Hence, chap. xviii. 2, Babylon, and that whole antichristian state which was supported upon their power and greatness, having lost its props, comes toppling down to the ground: "Babylon the great is fallen, is fallen." And the saints take vengeance on the whore for all her former rage and cruelty: "Double unto her double, according to her works," verse 6. And verse 9, "And the kings of the earth,"—being some of them shaken out of their dominion for refusing to close with the Lamb,—"who have committed fornication, and lived deliciously with her,"—learning and practising false worship of her institution,—"shall bewail her, and lament for her,"—as having received succour from her, her monasteries and shavelings, in their distress, whereunto indeed they were brought for her sake,—"when they shall see the smoke of her burning,"—beholding her darkness, stink, and confusion, in her final desolation.

Now, all this shall be transacted with so much obscurity and darkness, Christ not openly appearing unto carnal eyes, that though "many shall be purified, and made white, and tried, yet the wicked shall do wickedly: and none of the wicked shall understand; but the wise shall understand," Dan. xii. 10. There shall be no such demonstration of the presence of Christ as to open the eyes of hardened men; but at length, having suffered the poor, deceived wretches to drink of the cup prepared for them, he appears himself gloriously, Rev. xix. 13, in a more eminent manner than ever before, to the total destruction of the residue of opposers. And that this will be the utmost close of that dispensation wherein now he walketh, I no way doubt.

The assertion being cleared and proved, the reasons of it come next to be considered. And,—

(1.) It shall be done by the way of recompense and vengeance. It is the great day of the wrath of the Lamb, Rev. vi. 17. "Their land shall be soaked with blood, and their dust made fat with fatness. For it is the day of the LORD'S vengeance, and the year of recompenses for the controversy of Zion," Isa. xxxiv. 7, 8. The day of vengeance is in his heart, when the year of his redeemed is come, Isa. lxiii. 4.[1]

The kings of the earth have given their power to Antichrist, endeavouring to the utmost to keep the kingdom of Christ out of the world. What, I pray, hath been their main business for seven hundred years and upwards,—even almost ever since the man of sin was enthroned? How have they earned the titles, Eldest Son of the Church, The Catholic and Most Christian King, Defender of the Faith, and the like? Hath it not been by the blood of saints? Are there not, in every one of these kingdoms, the slain and the banished ones of Christ to answer for? In particular,—

Hath not the blood of the saints of Jesus[2] (eclipsed by Antichrist and his adherents), Wickliffites and Lollards, cried from the ground for vengeance upon the English "heaven and earth" for a long season? Did not their bodies lie in the streets of France, under the names of Waldenses, Albigenses, and poor men of Lyons? Hath not Germany and the annexed territories her Huss and Hussites, Jerome, and Subutraquians,[3] to answer for? Is not Spain's inquisition enough to

[1] Ps. ii. 4, 5, cxxxvii. 8, 9; Isa. xlvii. 1–3, xlix. 26; Jer. l. 33, 34, li. 24, 25, 34, 35; Zech. xii. 2–4, xiv. 12; Rev. xviii. 6, &c.

[2] Acts; and Mon. Histor. Pap.

[3] Utraquists?—another name for the Calixtines,—adherents of Huss and Jacobellus, who in 1421 exhibited their peculiar creed under four articles:—1. The preaching of the word in the natural tongue; 2. The dispensation of the Lord's

ruin a world, much more a kingdom? Have not all these, and all the kingdoms round about, washed their hands and garments in the blood of thousands of Protestants? and do not the kings of all these nations as yet stand up in the room of their progenitors with the same implacable enmity to the power of the gospel? Show me seven kings that ever yet laboured sincerely to enhance the kingdom of the Lord Jesus, and I dare boldly say, "Octavus quis fuerit, nondum constat." And is there not a cry for all this,—"How long, O Lord, holy and true, dost thou not judge and avenge our blood on them that dwell on the earth?" Rev. vi. 10. Doth not Zion cry, "The violence done to me and my flesh be upon Babylon;" and, My blood upon those heavens of the nations? And will not the Lord avenge his elect, that cry unto him day and night? will he not do it speedily? Will he not call the fowls of heaven to eat the flesh of kings, and captains, and great men of the earth? Rev. xix. 18. Will he not make these heavens like the wood of the vine,—not a pin to be taken off them to hang a garment on in his whole tabernacle? The time shall come wherein the earth shall disclose her slain, and not the simplest heretic (as they were counted) shall have his blood unrevenged: neither shall any atonement be made for this blood, or expiation be allowed, whilst a toe of the image or a bone of the beast is left unbroken.

(2.) A second reason is, That by his own wisdom he may frame such a power as may best conduce to the carrying on of his own kingdom among the sons of men.[1]

He hath promised his church that he will give unto it holy priests and Levites, Isa. lxvi. 20, 21, which shall serve at the great feast of tabernacles, Zech. xiv. 16,—a sufficient demonstration that he will dwell still in his churches by his ordinances, whatsoever some conceive;—so also, that he will "make her civil officers peace, and her exactors righteousness," Isa. lx. 17, 18. They shall be so established that the nations, as nations, may serve it, and the kingdoms of the world shall become the kingdoms of our Lord, Rev. xi. 15.

For the present, the government of the nations (as many of them as are concerned therein) is purely framed for the interest of Antichrist. No kind of government in Europe, or line of governors, so ancient but that the beast is as old as they, and had a great influence into their constitution or establishment, to provide that it might be for his own interest. I believe it will be found a difficult task to

supper to all Christians, the private members of the church as well as the clergy, *sub utrâque specie*, in both kinds,—and hence the name "Utraquists;" 3. The renunciation of secular dignities by the clergy; 4. The introduction of a stricter discipline in regard to the clergy.—Guericke, ii. 439; Gieseler on the Period 1409–1517.—Ed.

[1] Ps. ii. 9–12; Rev. xvii. 14; Matt. xxviii. 20; 1 Cor. xi. 26; Eph. iv. 11–13; 1 Tim. vi. 13, 14; Ps. xlv. 16; Isa. xlix. 7, 23.

name any of the kingdoms of Europe (excepting only that remotest northward) in the setting up and establishment whereof, either as to persons or government, the pope hath not expressly bargained for his own interest, and provided that should have the chiefest place in all the oaths and bonds that were between princes and people. Bellarmine, to prove that the pope had a temporal power indirectly over all kings and nations (if he mean by indirectly, gotten by indirect means, it is actually true as to too many of them),[1] gives sundry instances, in most of the most eminent nations in Europe, how he hath actually exercised such a power for his own interest.[2]

There have been two most famous and remarkable changes of the government of these nations; and into both of them what an influence the pope had, is easily discernible.

The first was between the years 400 and 500 after Christ, when the Roman empire of the west—that which withheld the man of sin from acting his part to the life[3]—was shivered to pieces by many barbarous nations;[4] who, settling themselves in the fruitful soils of Europe, began to plant their heavens, and lay the foundations of their earth, growing up into civil states,—for the most part appointing them to be their kings in peace who had been their leaders in war. This furious inundation settled the Franks in Gaul, the Saxons in England, the West Goths in Spain, the East Goths and Longobards into Italy, and set up the Allemanns in Germany; from some whereof though for divers years the papal world was exceedingly tormented, and Rome itself sacked, yet in the close and making up of their governments, their manners and religion, they all submitted to the usurpation of the man of sin, so that in all their windings up there was a salve for him and his authority.[5]

The second great alteration took up a long space, and was in action about three hundred years,—reckoning it from the translation of the French crown from Childeric IV.[6] unto Pepin and his son Charles by papal authority, unto the conquest of England by the Normans; in which space the line of Charles in France was again by the same authority and the power of Hugh Capet cut off. No state in Europe—the choice patrimony of the beast—that did not receive a signal alteration in this space; nor was there any alteration but that the pope had a hand in every one of them; and, either by pretended collations of right, to pacify the consciences of blood-thirsty potentates

[1] Rev. xviii. 3, Οἱ βασιλεῖς τῆς γῆς μετ' αὐτῆς ἐπόρνευσαν.

[2] Bell. de Rom. Pon., lib. v. cap. 8. [3] 2 Thess. ii. 6, 7. [4] Dan ii. 41.

[5] Οὗτοι μίαν γνώμην ἔχουσι, καὶ τὴν δύναμιν καὶ τὴν ἐξουσίαν ἑαυτῶν τῷ θηρίῳ διαδιδώσουσιν, Rev. xvii. 13.

[6] Childeric III.?—the last of the Merovingian race of French kings,—deposed in A.D. 750 by Pepin, to whom the crown of France, by the sanction of Pope Zachary, was transferred. The date of the Norman Conquest is A.D. 1066.—Ed.

in the undertaking and pursuing their unjust conquests, or foolish *mitred-confirmations of sword-purchases,* he got them all framed to his own end and purpose,—which was to bring all these nations into subjection to his Babylonish usurpations; which their kings finding no way inconsistent with their own designs, did willingly promote, labouring to enforce all consciences into subjection to the Roman see.

Hence it is, as I observed before, that such an interposition was made of the rights of holy church—that is, Babylon, the mother of fornications—in all the ties, oaths, and bonds between princes and people.[1] And for the advancement of the righteous judgments of God, that the sons of men may learn to fear and tremble before him, it may be observed, that that which doth and shall stick upon potentates to their ruin, is not so much their own or any other interest, as the very dregs of this papal, antichristian interest thrust into their oaths and obligations, for no end in the world but to keep the Lord Jesus out of his throne.[2]

This is a second reason why the Lord Jesus, by his mighty power, at the bringing in of his immovable kingdom, "will shake the heavens and the earth of the nations;" even because in their present constitution they are directly framed to the interest of Antichrist, which, by notable advantages at their first moulding, and continued insinuations ever since, hath so rivetted itself into the very fundamentals of them, that no digging or mining, but an earthquake, will cast up the foundation-stones thereof.[3] The Lord Jesus, then, having promised the service of the nations to his church, will so far open their whole frame to the roots, as to pluck out all the cursed seeds of the mystery of iniquity, which, by the craft of Satan and exigencies of state, or methods of advancing the pride and power of some sons of blood, have been sown amongst them.

(3.) A third reason is, because as is their interest, so is their acting. The present power of the nations stands in direct opposition to the bringing in of the kingdom of Christ. Two things there are which confessedly are incumbent on him in this day of his advancement.

[1.] The bringing home of his ancient people to be one fold with the fulness of the Gentiles,—raising up the tabernacle of David, and building it as in days of old, in the accomplishment of innumerable promises,[4] and in answer to millions of prayers put up at the throne of grace for this very glory, in all generations. Now, there be two main hinderances of this work that must be removed. The first whereof is,—

[1] Rev. xiii. 15, 16. [2] Πέμψει αὐτοῖς ὁ Θεὸς ἐνέργειαν πλάνης, 2 Thess. ii. 11.

[3] "Roma sedes Petri, quæ Pastoralis honoris
Facta caput mundo, quicquid non possidet armis,
Relligione tenet."—Prosp., de Ingrat.

[4] John x. 16; Isa. xxxvii. 31; Jer. xxx. 9; Ezek. xxxiv. 23, xxxvii. 24, 25; Hos. iii. 5; Amos ix. 11.

1st, *Real:* the great river Euphrates, the strength and fulness of whose streams doth yet rage so high that there is no passage for the kings of the east to come over. Wherefore this must be dried up, as other waters were for their forefathers in the days of old, Rev. xvi. 12. [1]Doubtless this is spoken in allusion to Abraham's coming over that river into Canaan, when the church of God in his family was there to be erected,—whence he was called the Hebrew (that is, the passenger, to wit, over that river, Gen. xiv. 13);—and then it may well enough denote the Turkish power; which, proud as it is at this day, possessing in peace all those regions of the east, yet God can quickly make it wither and be dried up;—or the deliverance of the Jews from Babylon, when it was taken and destroyed by the drying up of the streams of that river, and so the yoke of her tyranny broken from the church's neck;[2]—and so it can be no other but the power of the Romish Babylon, supported by the kings of the nations, which must therefore be shaken and dried up.

2dly, *Moral,* or the idolatry of the Gentile worshippers.[3] The Jews stick hard as yet at this, that God should abolish any kind of worship which himself had once instituted; but, that he should ever accept any false worship, which he had once strictly prohibited, and nowhere to this day appointed,—to this they will never be reconciled. Now, such is all the invented idolatrous worship which the kings of the earth have sucked in from the cup of fornication held out to them in the hand and by the authority of the Roman whore; this still they cleave close unto, and will not hearken to the angel preaching the everlasting gospel, that men should worship Him who made the heavens, and the earth, and the sea, and the fountains of waters, Rev. xiv. 6, 7,—that is, the God of heaven in Jesus Christ,—in opposition to all their iconolatry,[4] artolatry, hagiolatry, staurolatry, and mass abominations. This, then, must also be removed; and because, as you saw before, it is so rivetted and cemented into and with all the orbs of the nations, heaven and earth, they must be shaken, and brought εἰς μετάθεσιν, before it can be effected.

[2.] The second thing he hath to accomplish is the tremendous, total destruction of Babylon,[5] the man of sin, and all his adherents, that are not obedient to the heavenly call, Rev. xviii. 4.[6] Now, as Samson, intending the destruction of the princes, lords, and residue of the Philistines, who were gathered together in their idol-temple, effected it by pulling away the pillars whereby the building was supported, whereupon the whole frame toppled to the ground;[7] so the

[1] Exod. xiv. 21, 22; Josh. iii. 15, 16; Hab. iii. 8.
[2] Jer. li. 31, 32.
[3] Rev. xi. 2.
[4] Worship of images—bread—saints—the cross.—Ed.
[5] Ps. cxxxvii. 8, 9; Isa. xlvii. 7–9.
[6] Jer. li. 25, 26; Rev. xvii. 1, 2; Zech. ii. 7; Jer. li. 6.
[7] Judges xvi. 28, 29.

Lord, intending the ruin of that mighty power, whose top seems to reach to heaven, will do it by pulling away the pillars and supporters of it, after which it cannot stand one moment. Now, what are the pillars of that fatal building? Are they not the powers of the world, as presently stated and framed? Pull them away, and, alas! what is Antichrist? It is the glory of the kings put upon her that makes men's eyes so dazzle on the Roman harlot. Otherwise she is but like the Egyptian deities, whose silly worshippers through many glorious portals and frontispieces were led to adore the image of an ugly ape.

Add hereunto, that in this mighty work the Lord Jesus Christ will make use of the power of the nations, the horns of them; that is, their strength, Rev. xvii. 16. They must hate the whore, and make her desolate and naked, and eat her flesh, and burn her with fire. Now, whether this can be accomplished or no in their present posture, is easily discernible. Doth not the papal interest lie at the bottom of all, or the most ruling lines of Christendom?[1] Can that be ejected without unbottoming their own dominion? Do they not use the efficacy of the Roman jurisdiction to balance the powers of their adversaries abroad, and to awe their subjects at home? Hath not the pope a considerable strength in every one of their own bosoms? Are not the locusts of their religious orders (all sworn slaves to him) for number sufficient to make an army to fight the greatest emperor in the world? Are not most potentates tied by oath, or other compact, to maintain either the whole or some part of the old power, under the name of rites of holy church, prelates, and the like? And can any expect that such as these should take up the despised quarrel of the saints against that flourishing queen? Doubtless no such fruit will grow on these trees, before they are thoroughly shaken.

(4.) A fourth reason is, that His own people, seeing all earthly things shaken and removing, may be raised up to the laying hold of that durable kingdom that shall not be removed.[2] All carnal interests will doubtless be shaken with that of Babylon. Many of God's people are not yet weaned from the things that are seen:[3]—no sooner is one carnal form shaken out, but they are ready to cleave to another, yea, to warm themselves in the feathered nests of unclean birds. All fleshly dominion within doors, and all civil dominion that opposeth without doors, shall be shaken. Now, these things are so glued also to men's earthly possessions, the talons of the birds of prey having firmly seized on them, that they also must be shaken with them; and therefore from them also will he have us to be loosed, 2 Pet. iii. 12, 13.

And these are some of the reasons of the position laid down, which is so bottomed, so proved, as you have heard. Of the speedy accom-

[1] Petra dedit Petro, Petrus diadema Rudolfo. [2] Heb. xii. 28.
[3] 2 Cor. iv. 18.

plishment of all this I no way doubt. "I believe, and therefore I have spoken." Whether I shall see any farther perfection of this work whilst I am here below, I am no way solicitous; being assured that if I fail of it here, I shall, through the grace of him who loved us, and gave himself for us, meet with the treasures of it otherwhere.

Come we to the uses.

Use 1. The rise of our first use I shall take from that of the prophet, "Who is wise, and he shall understand these things? prudent, and he shall know them? For the ways of the LORD are right, and the just shall walk in them: but the transgressors shall fall therein," Hos. xiv. 9. Labour for this heavenly wisdom and prudence, that we may know these things, and be acquainted with the mind and will of God in the season and generation wherein we live. His way is not so in the dark, nor his footsteps in the deep, but that we may perceive what he is about.

Luke xii. 54–56, our Saviour gives it in as a sure testimony of the Pharisees' hypocrisy, notwithstanding all their pretences, and possession of Moses' chair, that they were wise in earthly things, and had drawn out experiences, by long observation, of what was like to come to pass as to the weather, by considering the ordinary signs of the alterations thereof; but notwithstanding that mighty effectual concurrence of signs in heaven and earth, with the accomplishment of prophecies, all pointing to the instant establishment of the kingdom of God in the coming of the Messiah, not discerning them at all, they come and cry, "If thou be the Christ, give us a sign;" when, without satisfying their sinful curiosity, heaven and earth were full of signs round about them. Men who will not receive God's signs, suppose they should be wonderful proficients in credulity might they have signs of their own fancying. The rich glutton thought that if his way of teaching might have been set up by men rising from the dead, there would have been a world of converts,—more than were made by preaching the word of God.[1] Men suppose that if God from heaven should give in some discriminating prodigy, oh, how abundantly should they be satisfied! The truth is, the same lust and corruption that makes them disbelieve God's signs, moves them to look after signs of their own. For this very thing, then, were the Pharisees branded as hypocrites, that having wisdom in natural things, to calculate and prognosticate from necessary signs, yet in the works of the Lord, though the signs which in his wisdom he was pleased to give were plentiful round about them, they must have some of their own choosing. I pray God none such be found in our day.

1 Chron. xii. 32, it is said of the men of Issachar, that they "had

[1] Ἔχουσι Μωσέα καὶ τοὺς προφήτας. Οὐχὶ πάτερ Ἀβραάμ· ἀλλ' ἐάν τις ἀπὸ νεκρῶν πορευθῇ, Luke xvi. 29, 30.

understanding of the times, to know what Israel ought to do."[1] Israel is in the dark, and knows not what to do, if the times and seasons be not discovered to them. If the mind and will of the Lord in their generation be not made out unto a people, it will be their ruin. Hence it is that the Lord encourageth us to make inquiry after these things, to find out the seasons wherein he will do any great work for his people, knowing that without this we shall be altogether useless in the generation wherein we live, Isa. xlv. 11, "Ask me of THINGS TO COME concerning my sons; and concerning the work of my hands COMMAND ye me." And what is this that the Lord will have his people to inquire of him about? Even the great work of the ruin of Babylon, and restoration of his church; which yet was not to be accomplished for two hundred and forty years. And this he tells you plainly in the following verses: "I have raised him up" (Cyrus) "in righteousness, and I will direct all his ways: he shall build my city, and he shall let go my captives, not for price nor reward, saith the LORD of hosts," verse 13. The Lord is earnest with his people to inquire into the season of the accomplishment of his great intendments for the good of his church, when as yet they are afar off; how much more when they are nigh at hand, even at the doors! "Whoso is wise, and will observe these things, even they shall understand the loving-kindness of the LORD," Ps. cvii. 43. The prophet tells you (Dan. ix. 2) that this was his great study, and at length he understood by books the approach of the time wherein God would deliver his church from Babylonish captivity and pollution. Now, this discovery hath two or three notable products.

(1.) It puts him upon earnest supplications for the accomplishment of their promised deliverance in the appointed season;—wide from that atheistical frame of spirit which would have a predetermination of events and successes to eradicate all care and endeavour to serve that Providence which will produce their accomplishment. A discovery of the approach of any promised and before-fixed work of God should settle our minds to the utmost endeavour of helping the decree to bring forth.

(2.) He finds great acceptation in this his address to the Lord by supplications, for the establishing of that work which he had discovered was nigh at hand. For,—

[1.] An answer is returned him fully to his whole desire in the midst of his supplications, verse 21, "Whiles I was praying, the man Gabriel came," &c.

[2.] The work which he had discovered to be approaching was instantly hastened and gone in hand withal, verse 23, "At the beginning of thy supplications the commandment came forth." Oh, that God

[1] Esther i. 13.

would stir up his saints, in the spirit of Daniel, to consider and understand by books the time that he hath appointed for the deliverance of his people, that, fixing their supplications for the speeding thereof, the commandment may come forth for its full accomplishment!

[3.] Having attained this, the Lord gives him fresh discoveries,—new light of the time for the birth of the Messiah, which he thought not of, prayed not for: "Seventy weeks are determined," &c., verse 24. So delighted is the Lord with his people's diligent inquiry into his ways and walkings towards them, that thereupon he appears unto them, in the revelation of his mind, beyond all that they did expect or desire.

Now, all this have I spoken to stir you up unto that whereunto at the entrance of this use you were exhorted,—that you would labour for that spiritual wisdom and prudence which may acquaint your hearts, at least in some measure, with the mind and will of God concerning his work in the generation wherein you live. And farther to provoke you hereunto, know that you cannot but wander, as in many other, so especially in four sinful things:—1*st*, Sinful cares; 2*dly*, Sinful fears; 3*dly*, Sinful follies; 4*thly*, Sinful negligence.

1*st*. *Sinful cares*,—anxious and dubious thoughts about such things as, perhaps, the Lord intends utterly to destroy, or, at least, render useless. Had it not been the greatest folly in the world for Noah and his sons, when the flood was approaching to sweep away the creatures from the face of the earth, to have been solicitous about flocks and herds that were speedily to be destroyed?[1] Many men's thoughts at this day do even devour them about such things as, if they knew the season, would be contemptible unto them. Wouldst thou labour for honour, if thou knewest that God at this time were labouring to lay all the "honour of the earth in the dust?"[2] Couldst thou set thy heart upon the increase of riches, wert thou acquainted that God intends instantly to make "silver as stones, and cedars as sycamores,"[3]—though not for plenty, yet for value? Would men be so exceedingly solicitous about this or that form of religion, this or that power to suppress such or such a persuasion, if they knew that the Lord would suddenly fill the earth with his knowledge, as the waters cover the sea?[4] Should our spirits sink for fear of this or that persecutor or oppressor, were it discovered unto us that in a short time nothing shall hurt or destroy in the whole mountain of the LORD?[5] Should we tremble at the force and power of this or that growing monarchy giving its power to the beast, had God revealed unto us that he is going to shake it until it be translated? Certain it is, that the root of all the sinful cares, which sometimes

[1] Gen. vi. 13. [2] Isa. xxiii. 9. [3] 1 Kings x. 27.
[4] Hab. ii. 14. [5] Isa. lxv. 25.

are ready to devour the hearts of God's people, is this unacquaintedness with the work and mind of the Lord.

2dly. Sinful fears. Luke xxi. 28, our Saviour having told his disciples of wars, tumults, seditions, famines, earthquakes, &c., which were to come upon the earth, bids them, when they see these things, to "lift up their heads for joy." But how should this be?—rejoice in the midst of so many evils and troubles, in the most whereof they were to have a Benjamin's mess,—a double portion! Yea, saith our Saviour, Rejoice; for I have told you before, that then it is that your deliverance and redemption draweth nigh. It is for them to shake and tremble who are in the dark,—who know not what the Lord is doing. They may be at their wits' end who know no other end of these things; but for you who know the mind of the Lord, what he intendeth and will effect by these things, cast off all sinful fears, and rejoice in him who cometh.

Amongst us in these days new troubles arise,—wars, and rumours of wars, appearances of famine, invasions, conspiracies, revolts, treacheries, sword, blood. Oh, how do men's faces wax pale, and their hearts die within them! Sometimes, with David, they could fly to the Philistines, and wind up their interest with them whom God will destroy. Every new appearance of danger shuffles them off from all their comforts, all their confidence. Hence poor souls are put upon doubling and shifting in the ways of God, in such a frame as God exceedingly abhors. They know not why any mercy is given, nor to what end; and therefore are afraid to own it, lest some sudden alteration should follow, and make it too hot for them to hold it; and all this because they know not the mind of the Lord, nor the judgment of their God. Were they but acquainted with it, so far as it is evidently revealed, they would quickly see all things working together to the appointed end.

3dly. Sinful follies. Toil and labour in vain is, of all follies, the greatest folly;—like the Jews under Julian, building of their temple in the day, God casting it to the ground in the night. When a man labours, toils, wearies and spends himself for the accomplishing of that which shall never come to pass, and that which, if he would but inquire, he might know shall never come to pass, he cannot well want the livery of a brutish man. How many poor creatures that think themselves wiser than those of Teman, and Dedan, and all the children of the east, do spend and consume their days and time in such ways as this, labouring night and day to set up what God will pull down, and what he hath said shall fall! "Come on, let us deal wisely," saith Pharaoh to his Egyptians, Exod. i. 10, to root out and destroy these Israelites. Poor fool! is there any wisdom or counsel against the Most High? I could give instances plenty in these days of men labouring in the dark, not knowing what they are doing, endeavouring with all their strength to accomplish that whereof the Lord hath said, "It shall not prosper;" and all because they discern not the season.

4*thly*. *Sinful negligence.* You are no way able to do the work of God in your generation. It is the commendation of many saints of God, that they were "upright, and served the will of God in their generation." Besides the general duties of the covenant, incumbent on all the saints at all seasons, there are special works of providence which, in sundry generations, the Lord effecteth, concerning which he expects his people should know his mind, and serve him in them. Now, can a servant do his master's work if he know not his will? The Lord requireth that, in the great things which he hath to accomplish in this generation, all his should close with him. What is the reason that some stand in the market-place idle all the day? Some work for a season, and then give over; they know not how to go a step farther, but after a day, a week, a month, or year, are at a stand;—worse than all this, some counterwork the Lord with all their strength,—the most neglect the duty which of them is required. What is the reason of all this? They know in no measure what the Lord is doing, and what he would have them apply themselves unto. The best almost live from hand to mouth, following present appearances to the great neglect of the work which the Lord would have hastened amongst us. All this comes from the same root.

But now, if all these sad and sinful consequences attend this nescience of the mind of God as to the things which he is doing in the days wherein we live, so far as he hath revealed himself and requires us to observe his walkings; by what ways and means may we come to the knowledge thereof, that we be not sinfully bewildered in our own cares, fears, and follies, but that we may follow hard after God, and be upright in our generation?

There be four things whereby we may come to have an insight into the work which the Lord will do and accomplish in our days. (1*st*.) The light which he gives. (2*dly*.) The previous works which he doth. (3*dly*.) The expectation of his saints. (4*thly*.) The fear of his adversaries.

(1*st*.) The *light which he gives.* God doth not use to set his people to work in the dark. They are the "children of light," and they are no "deeds of darkness" which they have to do. However others are blinded, they shall see; yea, he always suits their light to their labour, and gives them a clear discerning of what he is about. The Lord God doth nothing, but he reveals his secrets to his servants. The light of every age is the forerunner of the work of every age.

When Christ was to come in the flesh, John Baptist comes a little before—a new light, a new preacher. And what doth he discover and reveal? Why, he calls them off from resting on legal ceremonies, to the doctrine of faith, repentance, and gospel ordinances;—tells them "the kingdom of God is at hand;"—instructs them in the knowledge of Him who was coming. To what end was all this? Only that the minds of men being enlightened by his preaching, who was a "burning and a shining lamp," they might see what the Lord was doing.

Every age hath its peculiar work, hath its peculiar light. Now what is the light which God manifestly gives in our days? Surely not new doctrines, as some pretend—(indeed old errors, and long since exploded fancies). Plainly, the peculiar light of this generation is that discovery which the Lord hath made to his people of the mystery of civil and ecclesiastical tyranny. The opening, unravelling, and revealing the Antichristian interest, interwoven and coupled together, in civil and spiritual things, into a state opposite to the kingdom of the Lord Jesus, is the great discovery of these days. Who almost is there amongst us now who doth not evidently see, that for many generations the western nations have been juggled into spiritual and civil slavery by the legerdemain of the whore, and the potentates of the earth made drunk with the cup of her abominations?—how the whole earth hath been rolled in confusion, and the saints hurried out of the world, to give way to their combined interest? Hath not God unveiled that harlot, made her naked, and discovered her abominable filthiness? Is it not evident to him that hath but half an eye, that the whole present constitution of the government of the nations is so cemented with antichristian mortar, from the very top to the bottom, that without a thorough shaking they cannot be cleansed? This, then, plainly discovers that the work which the Lord is doing relates to the untwining of this close combination against himself and the kingdom of his dear Son; and he will not leave until he have done it. To what degree in the several nations this shaking shall proceed, I have nothing to determine in particular, the Scripture having not expressed it. This only is certain, it shall not stop, nor receive its period, before the interest of Antichristianity be wholly separated from the power of those nations.

(2*dly.*) The *previous works* he doth. How many of these doth our Saviour give as signs of the destruction of Jerusalem,—and so, consequently, of propagating the gospel more and more to the nations! Matt. xxiv.; Luke xxi. How fearful and dreadful they were in their accomplishment, Josephus the Jewish historian relateth; and how by them the Christians were forewarned, and did by them understand what the Lord was doing, Eusebius and others declare. "When," saith he, "you shall see the abomination of desolation" (the Roman eagles and ensigns) "standing in the holy place," Matt. xxiv. 15,—or

"Jerusalem compassed with armies," as Luke xxi. 20,—then know by that, that "the end thereof is come, and your deliverance at hand."

The works of God are to be sought out of them that have pleasure in them. They are vocal-speaking works; the mind of God is in them. They may be heard, read, and understood: the "rod may be heard, and who hath appointed it." Now, generally, he begins with lesser works, to point out to the sons of men what he is about to accomplish. By these may his will be known, that he may be met in righteousness.

Now, what, I pray, are the works that the Lord is bringing forth upon the earth? what is he doing in our own and the neighbouring nations? Show me the potentate upon the earth that hath a peaceable molehill to build himself a habitation upon. Are not all the controversies, or the most of them, that at this day are disputed in letters of blood among the nations, somewhat of a distinct constitution from those formerly under debate?—those tending merely to the power and splendour of single persons, these to the interest of the many. Is not the hand of the Lord in all this? Are not the shaking of these heavens of the nations from him? Is not the voice of Christ in the midst of all this tumult? And is not the genuine tendence of these things open and visible unto all? What speedy issue all this will be driven to, I know not;—so much is to be done as requires a long space. Though a tower may be pulled down faster than it was set up, yet that which hath been building a thousand years is not like to go down in a thousand days.

(*3dly.*) The *expectation of the saints* is another thing from whence a discovery of the will of God and the work of our generation may be concluded. The secret ways of God's communicating his mind unto his saints, by a fresh favour of accomplishing prophecies and strong workings of the Spirit of supplications, I cannot now insist upon. This I know, they shall not be "led into temptation," but kept from the hour thereof, when it comes upon the whole earth. When God raiseth up the expectation of his people to any thing, he is not unto them as waters that fail; nay, he will assuredly fulfil the desires of the poor.

Just about the time that our Saviour Christ was to be born of a woman, how were all that waited for salvation in Israel raised up to a high expectation of the kingdom of God!—such as that people never had before, and assuredly shall never have again;[1] yea, famous was the waiting of that season through the whole Roman empire. And the Lord, whom they sought, came to his temple. Eminent was their hope, and excellent was the accomplishment.

Whether this will be made a rule to others or no, I know not: this I am assured, that, being bottomed on promises, and built up with

[1] Luke iii. 15.

supplications, it is a ground for them to rest upon. And here I dare appeal to all who with any diligence have inquired into the things of the kingdom of Christ,—that have any savour upon their spirits of the accomplishment of prophecies and promises in the latter days,—who count themselves concerned in the glory of the gospel,—whether this thing of consuming the mystery of iniquity, and vindicating the churches of Christ into the liberties purchased for them by the Lord Jesus, by the shaking and translating all opposing heights and heavens, be not fully in their expectations. Only, the time is in the hand of God, and the rule of our actings with him is his revealed will.

(*4thly.*) Whether *the fears of his adversaries* have not their lines meeting in the same point, themselves can best determine. The whole world was more or less dreaded at the coming of Christ in the flesh. When, also, the signs of his vengeance did first appear to the Pagan world, in calling to an account for the blood of his saints, the kings and captains presently cry out, "The great day of his wrath is come, and who shall be able to stand?" Rev. vi. 17.

I am not of counsel to any of the adherents to the man of sin, or any of those who have given their power unto the beast,—I have not a key to the bosoms of the enemies of Christ,—I am neither their interpreter nor do they allow me to speak in their behalf; yet truly, upon very many probable grounds, I am fully persuaded that, were the thoughts of their hearts disclosed, notwithstanding all their glittering shows, dreadful words, threatening expressions, you shall see them tremble, and dread this very thing, that the whole world as now established will be wrapped up in darkness, at least until that cursed interest which is set up against the Lord Jesus be fully and wholly shaken out from the heavens and earth of the nations.

And thus, without leading you about by chronologies and computations (which yet have their use, well to count a number being wisdom indeed), I have a little discovered unto you some rules whereby you may come to be acquainted with the work of God in the days wherein we live, and also what that work is; which is our first use. The next shall be for direction to guide you what you ought to do, when you know what is the work of your generation.

Use 2. Be exhorted to prepare to meet the Lord, to make his way straight: and this I would press distinctly,—(1.) As to your persons; (2.) As to your employments.

(1.) As to *your persons.* Give the Lord Jesus a throne in your hearts, or it will not at all be to your advantage that he hath a throne and kingdom in the world. Perhaps you will see the plenty of it, but not taste one morsel. Take first that which comes not by observation,—that which is within you, which is "righteousness, and peace, and joy in the Holy Ghost." Take it in its power, and you will be the better enabled to observe it coming in its glory. "Seek first this kingdom of God, and the righteousness thereof, and all these things shall be added unto you." Oh, that it were the will of God to put an end to all that pretended holiness, hypocritical humiliation, self-interested religion, that have been among us, whereby we have flattered God with our lips, whilst our hearts have been far from him! Oh, that it might be the glory of this assembly, above all the assemblies of the world, that every ruler in it might be a sincere subject in the kingdom of the Lord Jesus! Oh, that it might suffice that we have had in our parliament, and among our ministers, so much of the form and so little of the power of godliness; that we have called the world Christ, and lusts Christ, and self Christ, working indeed for them, when we pretended all for Christ! Oh, that I could nourish this one contention in your honourable assembly, that you might strive who should excel in setting up the Lord Jesus in your hearts!

You may be apt to think, that if you can carry on and compass your purposes, then all your enemies will be assuredly disappointed. Do but embrace the Lord Jesus in his kingly power in your bosoms, and "ipso facto" all your enemies are everlastingly disappointed. You are the grains which, in the sifting of the nation, have been kept from falling to the ground. Are you not the residue of all the chariots of England? Oh, that in you might appear the reality of the kingdom of the Lord Jesus, which hath been so long pretended by others!—that sound righteousness, not a pharisaical, rigid, supercilious affectation, not a careless belief and comportment, the issue of novel fancies, might be found upon your spirits!—that you may be thought meet to rejoice with the Lord in his kingdom! Otherwise this day of the Lord which we have described, however desired and longed after, will be "darkness to you, and not light."

(2.) In reference to your *great employments*, whereunto the Lord hath called you. And here I shall briefly hold out unto you one or two things.

[1.] That you would seriously consider why it is that the Lord shakes the heavens and the earth of the nations,—to what end this tendeth, and what is the cause thereof. Is it not from hence, that he may revenge their opposition to the kingdom of his dear Son?—that he may shake out of the midst of them all that antichristian mortar wherewith, from their first chaos, they have been cemented, that so the kingdoms of the earth may become the kingdoms of the Lord Jesus? Is not the controversy of Zion pleaded with them? Are not they called to an account for the transgression of that charge given to all potentates, "Touch not mine anointed?" And what is the aim of the Lord Jesus herein, whose mighty voice shakes them? Is it not to frame and form them for the interest of his own kingdom?—that he may fulfil the word he hath spoken to Zion, "I will make thy officers peace, and thine exactors righteousness?"

Consider, then, I pray, what you have in hand. Wait upon your King, the Lord Christ, to know his mind. If you lay any stone in the whole building that advanceth itself against his sceptre, he will shake all again. Dig you never so deep, build you never so high, it shall be shaken. Nay, that there be no opposition will not suffice:—he hath given light enough to have all things framed for his own advantage. The time is come, yea, the full time is come, that it should be so; and he expects it from you. Say not, in the first place, this or that suits the interest of England; but look what suits the interest of Christ, and assure yourselves that the true interest of any nation is wrapped up therein. More of this in the treatise annexed to my sermon of January 31.[1]

[2.] Be encouraged under all those perplexities and troubles which you are or may be wrapped in. Lift up the hands that hang down, and let the feeble knees be strengthened: "It is but yet a little while, and he that shall come will come, and will not tarry." The more you are for Christ, the more enemies you shall be sure to have; but the Lamb shall overcome. He is come to revenge the blood of his slain upon this generation, and to free the residue from the jaws of the terrible. He is our rock, and his work is perfect. What he hath begun, faster or slower, he will surely accomplish. It is a thing of the utmost imaginable indifferency whether any of our particular persons behold these things here below or not. If otherwise, we shall for the present have "rest with him, and stand in our lot at the end of the days;" but for the work itself, "the decree is gone forth," and it shall not be recalled. Receive strength and refreshment in the Lord.

Use 3. Wonder not, when the heaven is shaken, if you see the stars fall to the ground. We had some who pretended to be church stars, that were merely fixed, to all men's view and by their own confession, in the political heavens. The first shaking of this nation shook them utterly to the ground. If others also tremble like an aspen leaf, and know not which wind to yield unto, or sail backwards and forwards by the same gale, wonder not at that neither. When men lay any other foundation than the immovable corner-stone, at one time or other, sooner or later, assuredly they will be shaken.

Use 4. Let the professing people that are amongst us look well to themselves: "The day is coming that will burn like an oven." Dross will not endure this day: we have many a hypocrite as yet to be uncased. Take heed, you that act high, if a false heart, a defiled heart be amongst you, there shall be no place for it in the mountain of the Lord's house. "The inhabitants of Zion shall be all righteous," Isa.

[1] *Vide* Discourse concerning Toleration, &c.

lx. 21. Many that make a great show now upon the stage, shall be turned off with shame enough. Try and search your hearts; force not the Lord to lay you open to all. The spirit of judgment and burning will try you. Tremble, I pray; for you are entering the most purging, trying furnace that ever the Lord set up on the earth.

Use 5. Be loose from all shaken things:—you see the clouds return after the rain,—one storm in the neck of another. Thus it must be, until Christ hath finished his whole work. "Seeing that all these things must be dissolved, what manner of persons ought we to be in all manner of holy conversation?" Let your eyes be upwards, and your hearts be upwards, and your hands be upwards, that you be not moved at the passing away of shaken things. I could here encourage you by the glorious issue of all these shakings, whose foretaste might be as marrow to your bones, though they should be appointed to consumption before the accomplishment of it; but I must close.

Use 6. See the vanity, folly, madness of such as labour to oppose the bringing in the kingdom of the Lord Jesus. Canst thou hinder the *rain* from descending upon the earth when it is falling? Canst thou stop the *sun* from rising at its appointed hour? Will the *conception* for thee dwell quietly in the womb beyond its month? Surely thou mayest with far more ease turn and stop the current and course of nature than obstruct the bringing in of the kingdom of Christ in righteousness and peace. Whence comes it to pass that so many nations are wasted, destroyed, spoiled, in the days wherein we live?—that God hath taken quietness and peace from the earth? Doubtless from hence, that they will smite themselves against the "stone cut out of the mountain without hands." Shall not "the decree bring forth?" Is it not in vain to fight against the Lord? Some are angry, some troubled, some in the dark, some full of revenge; but the truth is, whether they will hear or forbear, Babylon shall fall, and all the glory of the earth be stained, and the kingdoms become the kingdoms of our Lord Jesus Christ.

SERMON VI.

THE

BRANCH OF THE LORD THE BEAUTY OF ZION;

OR,

THE GLORY OF THE CHURCH IN ITS RELATION UNTO CHRIST.

OPENED IN TWO SERMONS;

ONE PREACHED AT BERWICK, THE OTHER AT EDINBURGH.

PREFATORY NOTE.

All the information which can be given respecting these sermons on Isa. lvi. 7, will be found in the "Life," vol. i. p. 45, and the dedication to Cromwell which is prefixed to them. The first sermon was preached at Berwick, July 21, 1650. The date of the dedication is November 26, 1650. There is no record of Owen's proceedings in Scotland. The decisive battle of Dunbar, September 3, 1650, placed Edinburgh in the hands of Cromwell. The castle for a time held out against him; and as the Presbyterian ministers who had retired to it refused to issue from it on the Sabbath to fill the pulpits in the town, there is every likelihood that Owen found constant employment in preaching the gospel. A celebrated correspondence took place between those ministers, as represented by Dundas, the commandant of the fortress, and Oliver Cromwell. The latter offered them liberty to preach in their respective churches. Not much to their credit, they declined to avail themselves of this permission, on the ground of "the personal persecution" of which they were afraid if they ventured to quit the castle. Cromwell replies with insinuations that they wished "worldly power," and made "worldly mixtures to accomplish the same," and advises them to "trust to the sword of the Spirit, which is the Word of God;" alleging, at the same time, that though they had not listened to his public appeals, "the Lord hath heard us," in the victory of Dunbar. The ministers, in their reply, and in allusion to the practices of Cromwell's officers, "regret that men of mere civil place and employment should usurp the calling and employment of the ministry, particularly in Scotland, contrary to the government and discipline therein established,—to the maintenance whereof you are bound by the Solemn League and Covenant;" and state that they "have not so learned Christ as to hang the equity of their cause upon events." Cromwell, in a long answer, with a postscript of four queries, betraying some temper at the smart rejoinder of the clergy, complains that they make themselves "infallible expositors of the Covenant;" and winds up a reproof to them for calling such successes as that achieved at Dunbar "bare events," with the characteristic words, "The Lord pity you." In one of the postscript queries he has very manifestly the advantage, when he twits the ministers with their inconsistency in "crying down Malignants, and yet 'setting up the head of them,' Charles Stuart.'" It has been thought that the hand of Owen can be traced in the letters of Cromwell; and Hume speaks of them "as the best of Cromwell's wretched compositions." The improvement in the composition may be ascribed to the greater leisure which Cromwell possessed at this time, while waiting the reduction of the castle. The letters are deeply impregnated with all the strongly-marked peculiarities of Cromwell's style of thought,—the perpetual emphasis of a resolute will, expressed in sentences "lumbering," indeed, but, like his own sword, sharp as well as heavy. Owen, we cannot but think, would have been more successful in reply to some of the statements of the ministers, and especially to the charge which they preferred against Cromwell, of suspending the equity of his cause upon his outward success. See Owen's answer to such an accusation in the prefatory note to the third sermon in this volume.—Ed.

TO HIS EXCELLENCY,

THE LORD GENERAL CROMWELL, &c.

My Lord,

It was with thoughts of peace that I embraced my call to this place in time of war. As all peace that is from God is precious to my spirit, so incomparably that between the Father and his elect, which is established and carried on in the blood and grace of Jesus Christ. The ministerial dispensation of this peace being through free grace committed even unto me also, I desire that in every place my *whole* may be, to declare it to the men of God's good pleasure. That this was my chief design, in answer to the call of God upon me, even to pour out a savour of the gospel upon the sons of peace in this place, I hope is manifest to the consciences of all with whom (since my coming hither) in the work of the ministry I have had to do. The enmity between God and us began on our part;—the peace which he hath made begins and ends with himself. This is the way of God with sinners: when he might justly continue their enemy, and fight against them to their eternal ruin, he draws forth love, and beseeches them to be reconciled who have done the wrong, and them to accept of peace who cannot abide the battle. Certainly the bearing forth of this message, which is so "worthy of all acceptation," and ought to be so welcome, cannot but have sweetness enough to season all the pressures and temptations wherewith it is sometimes attended. This it hath been my desire to pursue, and that with the weapons which are not carnal. And though some may be so seasoned with the leaven of contention about carnal things, or at best the tithing of mint and cummin, as to disrelish the weightier things of the gospel, yet the great Owner of the vineyard hath not left me without a comfortable assurance that even this labour in the Lord hath not been in vain.

The following sermons, which I desire to present unto your excellency, were preached, one at Berwick, upon your first advance into Scotland, the other at Edinburgh. My willingness to serve the inheritance of Christ here, even in my absence, caused me to close with the desires that were held out to this purpose. And I do present them to your excellency, not only because the rise of my call to this service, under God, was from you; but also, because in the carrying of it on I have received from you, in the weaknesses and temptations wherewith I am encompassed, that daily spiritual refreshment and support—by inquiry into, and discovery of, the deep and hidden dispensations of God towards his secret ones—which my spirit is taught to value. The carrying on of the interest of the Lord Jesus amongst his saints, in all his ways, which are truth and righteousness—the matter pointed at in this discourse—being the aim of your spirit in your great undertakings, it bears another respect unto you. I am not unacquainted with its meanness, yea, its coming short, in respect of use and fruit, of what the Lord hath since and by others drawn forth; but such as it is, having by Providence stepped first into the world, I wholly commend it to him for an incense who graciously "supplied the seed to the sower;"—beseeching him that we may have joy unspeakable and glorious in the acceptance of that peace which he gives us in the Son of his love, whilst the peace whose desire in the midst of war you continually bear forth to him and to others, is by them rejected to their hurt.

Your Excellency's

Most humble Servant in our dearest Lord,

J. Owen.

Edinburgh, *Nov.* 26, 1650.

SERMON VI.

THE BRANCH OF THE LORD THE BEAUTY OF ZION: OR, THE GLORY OF THE CHURCH IN ITS RELATION UNTO CHRIST.

"For mine house shall be called an house of prayer for all people."
ISA. lvi. 7.

FROM verse 3 of this chapter to verse 8, you have promises and predictions of calling in Gentiles and strangers to the church of God, notwithstanding any objections or hinderances laid in their way by ceremonial and typical constitutions,—they being all to be removed in the cross of Christ, Eph. ii. 13–16; Col. ii. 14;—making way for the accomplishment of that signal promise which is given in the 2d chapter of this prophecy, verses 2, 3, "And it shall come to pass in the last days, that the mountain of the LORD'S house shall be established in the top of the mountains, and shall be exalted above the hills; and all nations shall flow unto it: and many people shall go and say, Come ye, and let us go up," &c.

The words of verse 7 are a recapitulation of the whole, holding out summarily the calling of the Gentiles to the holy mount, or spiritual church of Christ; where also you have a description of the services performed by them upon their coming: "Their burnt-offerings and sacrifices shall be accepted upon mine altar;"—answerable to that eminent prediction of the solemn worship of the called Gentiles, Mal. i. 11, "For from the rising of the sun, even unto the going down of the same, my name shall be great among the Gentiles; and in every place incense shall be offered unto my name, and a pure offering: for my name shall be great among the heathen, saith the LORD of hosts." The spiritual services of the saints of the Gentiles are in each place set forth by those ceremonial ordinances of incense, altar, and sacrifice, as were then most acceptable, from the Lord's own appointment.

Now, this whole promise is once again strengthened, without loss of life or beauty, and comprised in the words of the text. That which before he termed "sacrifice and burnt-offerings," here he calleth "prayer;" and those who before were "the sons of the stranger," are here "all people,"—some, many of all sorts, the whole world, all men, without distinction, the partition wall being broken down.

The thing here spoken of is God's house, described,—First, By its appropriation unto him; it is his peculiar,—"My house." Secondly, By its extent of receipt in respect of others; it is "for all people." Thirdly, By the employment of its inhabitants; that is, prayer,—it "shall be called an house of prayer."

"House" here may be taken two ways.

1. *Properly*, as it was in the type for the material temple at Jerusalem; whereunto these words are applied by our Saviour, Matt. xxi. But that is no farther concerned herein, but as the spiritual holiness of the antitype could not be represented without a ceremonial holiness of the type.

2. *Spiritually*, for the church of Christ to be gathered to him out of all nations; the house wherein "juge sacrificium," a continual spiritual sacrifice, is to be offered to him: this is peculiarly intended.

So, then, observe,—I. *Christ's church of saints, of believers, is God's house.* II. *The church of Christ under the gospel is to be gathered out of all nations.* III. *There are established ordinances and appointed worship for the church of Christ under the gospel.* It is the first that I shall speak unto.

Christ's church of saints, of believers, is God's house.

That his church is of saints and believers will appear in the issue.

By the church of Christ I understand, *primarily*, the whole multitude of them who antecedently are chosen of his Father, and given unto him; consequently, are redeemed, called, and justified in his blood;—the church which he loved, and gave himself for, "that he might sanctify and cleanse it with the washing of water by the word; that he might present it to himself a glorious church, not having spot, or wrinkle, or any such thing; but that it should be holy, and without blemish," Eph. v. 26, 27. And, *secondarily*, also every holy assembly of mount Zion, whereunto the Lord Christ is made beauty and glory,—every particular church of his saints, inasmuch as they partake of the nature of the whole, being purchased by his blood, Acts xx. 28.

That this church belongs unto God, I shall only leave evidenced under the claim whereby he here appropriates it to himself; he calls it his: "*My* house."

That it is his *house*, I shall farther demonstrate. Three things are required to the making of a house:—first, *A foundation;* secondly, *Materials for a superstruction;* thirdly, *An orderly framing of both into a useful building;*—and all these concur to the church of Christ.

First. It hath a foundation. "I have laid the foundation," saith Paul, 1 Cor. iii. 10; and, "Other foundation can no man lay, save that which is laid, which is Jesus Christ," verse 11. That which Paul laid *ministerially*, God himself laid *primarily* and *efficiently*. "Thus saith the Lord God, Behold, I lay in Zion for a foundation a stone, a tried stone, a precious corner-stone, a sure foundation," Isa. xxviii. 16. Now, this foundation is no other but the rock upon which the church is built, Matt. xvi. 18, which makes it impregnable to the gates of hell, communicating strength and permanency continually to every part of the building.

Secondly. A foundation only will not make a house,—there must also be materials for a superstruction. Those you have, 1 Pet. ii. 5. "Ye are," saith he, "lively stones." All God's elect are stones, in due time to be hewed and fitted for this building.

Thirdly. Materials themselves will not serve: they must be fitly framed, and wisely disposed, or they will be a heap, not a house. This, then, is not wanting. Ye "are built upon the foundation of the apostles and prophets, Jesus Christ himself being the chief corner-stone; in whom all the building, fitly framed together, groweth unto an holy temple in the Lord: in whom ye also are builded together for an habitation of God through the Spirit," Eph. ii. 20–22. There is much spiritual and heavenly architecture in these three verses. I shall only touch on some particulars.

1. The foundation of this house, this temple, is laid; and that is Jesus Christ: "Other foundation can no man lay." He is here called "The chief corner-stone," and, "The foundation of the apostles and prophets." It is not, which they were, but which they laid. It is "genitivus efficientis," not "materiæ," that expression holds out,—the persons *working*, not the thing *wrought*.

2. The materials of this building,—elect, believers; said in the former verse to be "fellow-citizens with the saints, and of the household of God." They alone are built on Christ, and thereby have union with him: not one dead, rotten stone in all this building, as shall be declared.

3. The architects or builders are of two sorts.

(1.) Principal: "The Spirit;"—we are "framed for an habitation of God by the Spirit;" he is the principal workman in this fabric,—without him is not one stone laid therein.

(2.) Secondary and instrumental: "The apostles and prophets." And this they were two ways.

[1.] Personally, in their several generations;—this was their work, their labour, to lay the foundation and carry on the building of this house.

[2.] Doctrinally; so they labour in it to this very day;—their doctrine in the Scripture holds out the only foundation, and the only way of building thereon.

4. The manner of the building: it is "fitly framed together," συναρμολογουμένη, closely jointed and knit in together, sweetly closed together with Christ, "the head, from which all the body by joints and bands having nourishment ministered, and knit together, increaseth with the increase of God," Col. ii. 19.

5. What kind of a house it is. It receiveth here a twofold title, "An holy temple," and "An habitation," or tabernacle; because of its allusion to both those holy places of the worship of God, fulfilling the types of them both. Hence it is most evident that this church of Christ is a house, and being appropriated unto God, God's house. To make this the more evident, I shall do these two things:—(1.) Show you what are the chief properties of this house. (2.) Declare what is the relation wherein Jesus Christ stands to this house, having called it all along the church of Christ.

(1.) For the properties, or chief qualities of this house, they are three:—[1.] It is a living house; [2.] It is strong; [3.] It is glorious.

[1.] It is a *living* house: "To whom coming, as unto a living stone, ye also, as living stones, are built up a spiritual house," 1 Pet. ii. 4, 5. Christ, the foundation, is a living stone, and they that are built upon him are living stones. Hence they are said to grow together into a house. Growth is a sign of life, growing from an inward principle. Such as the growth of any thing is, such is its life. The growth of this house is spiritual, so therefore also is its life;—it lives with a spiritual life, a life whose fulness is in its foundation. He hath "life in himself," John v. 26, and they from him: "I am crucified with Christ, nevertheless I live," Gal. ii. 20; yea, it is himself in them,—"yet not I, but Christ liveth in me." It is true, those stones are dead in the rock as well as others; "by nature children of wrath as well as they," Eph. ii. 3; being "dead in trespasses and sins," verse 1. He who hews them out gives them life;—he quickens them when dead in trespasses and sins. There is not one rotten, dead stone in all this building. However some such may, by the advantage of their outward appearance, crowd in, yet they are not of the house itself.

[2.] It is a *strong* house: "The gates of hell cannot prevail against it," Matt. xvi. 18. Though the rain descend, and the floods come, and the winds blow upon this house, yet it will not fall, because it is founded on a rock, Matt. vii. 25. We were all once a house built upon Adam; and when the wind came, and beat upon us, we fell; and the fall of that house was very great. He in his best estate was found to be but sand; now we are built upon a rock that will abide all trials:—the waves may make a noise, and dash themselves against him, but it will be to their own ruin.

But you will say, May not weak and inconsistent materials be built upon a rock, which yet may have never the more strength for their foundation?

It is not so here, for the whole building is framed together in the foundation, Eph. ii. 22; not only on it, but also in it, and so not to be prevailed against, unless the rock itself be overthrown. And it is a living rock that this house is built on,—a rock continually communicating strength unto every stone in the building, that it may be enabled to abide in him. I should proceed too far, should I go to declare the mighty defence and fortification of this house;—what hath been spoken from the foundation is enough to demonstrate it to be a strong house.

[3.] It is a *glorious* house, and that in a threefold respect.

1*st*. It is glorious in respect of inward glory, brought unto it of God in the face of Jesus Christ, being beautiful through the comeliness that he puts upon it. Hence Christ speaking of it says, "How fair art thou, O love, for delights!" Cant. vii. 6; and, "Thou art all fair, my love; there is no spot in thee," chap. iv. 7. And how, I pray, comes that about? Why, Christ washeth it in his own blood, that it might be wholly "a glorious church," Eph. v. 26, 27. And farther, he being "The branch of the Lord and fruit of the earth," is made beauty and glory, excellency and comeliness, thereunto, Isa. iv. 2.

It hath the beauty and glory of justification, which doth not only take away all filthy garments, causing iniquity to pass away, but also gives fair "change of raiment," Zech. iii. 4, 5, even the "garments of salvation," and the "robe of righteousness," Isa. lxi. 10. And then it hath the glory and beauty of sanctification; whence "the King's daughter is all glorious within," Ps. xlv. 13. The comeliness and beauty that is in a sanctified soul is above all the glory of the world. This house is all overlaid with gold within; Christ is unto it "a head of gold," Cant. v. 11. His house is not like Nebuchadnezzar's image, that the head should be of gold, and the members some of them of clay;—they all partake of his nature, and are very glorious therein.

2*dly*. In respect of its outward structure, which it eminently hath in all the peculiar assemblies thereof: "O thou afflicted, and tossed with tempest, and not comforted! behold, I will lay thy stones with fair colours, and thy foundations with sapphires. I will make thy windows of agates and carbuncles, and all thy borders of pleasant stones," Isa. liv. 11, 12. So, also, where it is called the new Jerusalem,—a city, from its laws and polity,—this "city" is said to be of "pure gold,"—not dross and mire,—"the building of the wall of jasper, and the foundations of the wall garnished with all manner of precious stones," Rev. xxi. 18, 19. This is that which the psalmist calls. "The beauty of holiness," Ps. cx. 3. The glory of the ordinances of the gospel is their vigour and purity. There is nothing so glorious as our King on his throne, Christ in his court, this house reigning in the administration of his ordinances:—then "all his garments smell of myrrh, aloes, and cassia, out of the ivory palaces whereby they have made him glad. Kings' daughters are among his honourable women: upon his right hand doth stand the queen in gold of Ophir," Ps. xlv. 8, 9. His goings are seen, the goings of our God and King in the sanctuary, Ps. lxviii. 24, 25, &c. The apostle exalteth the glory of gospel administrations exceedingly above the old tabernacle and temple worship,—which yet was exceeding pompous and glorious. "If," saith he, "the ministration of death, written and engraven in stones, was glorious, so that the children of Israel could not steadfastly behold the face of Moses for the glory of his countenance; which glory was to be done away: how shall not the ministration of the Spirit be rather glorious? For if the ministration of condemnation be glory, much more doth the ministration of righteousness exceed in glory. For even that which was made glorious had no glory in this respect, by reason of the glory that excelleth. For if that which was done away was glorious, much more that which remaineth is glorious," 2 Cor. iii. 7–11. Let men think as meanly as they please of the spiritual service of God amongst his people, all glory that ever yet appeared in the world was but a bubble to it,—all that God ever instituted before came exceeding short of it. He delights in it who beholds the proud afar off.

3dly. It is glorious in respect of the exaltation it hath above and the triumph over all its opposers. To see a house, a palace, hung round about with ensigns, spoils, and banners taken from the enemies that have come against it, is a glorious thing:—thus is this house of God decked: "Kings of armies did flee apace, and she that tarried at home divided the spoil," Ps. lxviii. 12. "She that tarries at home," the mother of the family, the church of God, she "hath all the spoils." The Lord hath affirmed, that not only every one that opposeth, but all that do not serve this house, shall be utterly destroyed, Isa. lx. 12. There you have the spoil of Pharaoh, and all his host, gathered on the shore of the Red sea, and dedicated in this house, Exod. xv. There you have the robes of Nebuchadnezzar, reserved when himself was turned into a beast, Dan. iv. There you have the imperial ornaments of Diocletian and his companion, casting aside their dominion for very madness that they could not prevail against this house. There is the blood of Julian, kept for a monument of vengeance against apostates. There you have the rochets of the prelates of this land, hung up of late, with other garments of their adherents, rolled in blood. There is a place reserved for the remaining spoils of the great whore, when she shall be burned, and made naked, and desolate, Rev. xi. Never any rose, or shall arise, against this house, and go forth unto final prosperity. Let the men of the world take heed how they burden themselves with the foundation-stone of this house;—it will assuredly break them all in pieces.

Thus have I given you a glimpse of this house, with the chief properties of it, which as God assumes as his own, so also peculiarly it belongs unto the Lord Christ; yea, what relation it stands in unto him, or rather he unto it, is the main thing I intend.

(2.) Jesus Christ stands in a twofold relation unto this house:—[1.] In respect of its fabric and building; [2.] In respect of its state and condition.

[1.] In the first regard, Christ relates to this house in a fourfold respect;—as, 1*st.* Its foundation; 2*dly.* Its ark; 3*dly.* Its altar; 4*thly.* Its candlestick.

I shall pass through these, God assisting, in order, and begin with what was first laid down,—his relation to this house, as,—

1*st.* The *foundation* of it. This was in part declared before. He is the stone which the builders rejected, but made of the Lord the head of the corner, Ps. cxviii. 22. He is the lowest in the bottom, to bear up the weight of the building; and the highest in the corner, to couple the whole together. "Other foundation can no man lay but that which is laid, which is Jesus Christ," 1 Cor. iii. 11. He is the rock on which he builds his church, Matt. xvi. 18.

Now there are three things required to a foundation, all which are eminently seen in the Lord Christ, in reference to this house.

(1*st.*) That it be *first* laid in the building. It were a course exceeding preposterous, first to build a house, and then to lay the foundation. Jesus Christ is the first that is laid in this holy fabric, and that in a fourfold respect.

[1*st.*] He is the first in respect of God's eternal purpose. The Lord purposed that "he should have the pre-eminence" in this as well as in all other things, Col. i. 18. He is in that respect "the first-born among many brethren," Rom. viii. 29, the residue of this house being predestinated to be made conformable unto him. "He is before all things: by him all things"—that is, all spiritual things, all the things of this house—"consist: he is the head of the body, the church." This I mean, God purposed that Christ should be the bottom and foundation of this whole building,—that it should be all laid on him. I do not mean that God first intended Christ for a foundation, and then his elect for building (the order of intention and execution is, as to first and last, inverted by all agents); but this I say, God purposing to build his elect into a holy temple, purposed that Jesus Christ should be the foundation.

[2*dly*.] In respect of outward manifestation. God first manifests and declares him, before he laid one stone in this building. Gen. iii. 15, The seed, saith he, of the woman shall bruise the serpent's head:—in that was laid the first stone of this building. Then was the "Lamb slain," ἀπὸ καταβολῆς κόσμου, Rev. xiii. 8, presently "after the foundation of the world:" and thence is grace in him said to be given to the elect, πρὸ χρόνων αἰωνίων, Tit. i. 2, "many ages ago."

[3*dly*.] Because, in order of nature, Christ must be first laid in the heart of every individual stone before they are laid up in this building. If Christ be not in men, they are ἀδόκιμοι, 2 Cor. xiii. 7,—altogether useless for this building. Try them never so often, they must at last be rejected and laid aside.

[4*thly*.] In respect of every particular assembly and little sanctuary of mount Zion. If he be not first laid in the midst of such assemblies, they will prove to be pinnacles of Babel, not towers of Zion. This, therefore, was the way of the saints of old, first to give up themselves to the Lord Christ, and then to one another, by the will of God, 2 Cor. viii. 5.

In these respects Christ the foundation is first laid in this spiritual building,—which is the first property of a foundation.

(2*dly*.) A foundation must be hidden and out of sight unto all those that outwardly look upon the house. They cannot perceive it, though every part of the house doth rest upon it. And this hath occasioned many mistakes in the world. An unwise man coming to a great house, seeing the antics and pictures [figures?] stand crouching under the windows and sides of the house, may haply think that they bear up the weight of the house, when indeed they are for the most part pargeted posts. They bear not the house,—the house bears them. By their bowing, and outward appearance, the man thinks the burden is on them, and supposes that it would be an easy thing, at any time, by taking them away, to demolish the house itself. But when he sets himself to work, he finds these things of no value; there is a foundation in the bottom, which bears up the whole, that he thought not of:—against that he may waste himself, until he be broken in pieces. Men looking upon the church, do find that it is a fair fabric indeed, but cannot imagine how it should stand. A few supporters it seemeth to have in the world, like crouching antics under the windows, that make some show of under-propping it:—here you have a magistrate, there an army, or so. Think the men of the world, "Can we but remove these props, the whole would quickly topple to the ground." Yea, so foolish have I been myself, and so void of understanding before the Lord, as to take a view of some goodly appearing props of this building, and to think, How shall the house be preserved if these should be removed?—they looked unto me like the mariners in Paul's ship, without whose abode therein they could not be saved,—when, lo! suddenly some have been manifested to be pargeted posts, and the very best to be held up by the house, and not to hold it up. On this account the men of the world think it no great matter to demolish the spiritual church of Christ to the ground:—they encourage one another to the work, never thinking of the foundation that lies hidden, against which they dash themselves all to pieces. I say, then, Christ, as the foundation of this house, is hidden to the men of the world,—they see it not, they believe it not. There is nothing more remote from their apprehension than that Christ should be at the bottom of them and their ways, whom they so much despise.

(*3dly.*) The foundation is that which bears up the whole weight of the building. What part of the house soever is not directly poised upon it hath no strength at all. Take a goodly stone, hew it, square it, make it every way fit for your fabric, so that it may seem to be the best of all your materials; yet if you do not lay it upon the foundation, answerable to that which may give it a solid basis, and bear up the weight and poise thereof, it will be useless, cumbersome, and quickly fall to the ground.

Let a man be hewed and squared by the word and ordinances into outward conformity never so exactly, that he seems one of the most beautiful saints in the world; yet if he be not laid rightly by faith upon the foundation, to derive from thence strength, supportment, and vigour, he will quickly fall to the ground. What, then, will become of their building who heap up all sorts of rubbish to make a house for the Lord?

2dly. Christ is the *ark* of this house. The ark in the tabernacle, and afterward in the temple, was the most holy thing in the most holy place. There was nothing in it but the two tables of stone written with the finger of God;—before it was Aaron's rod that budded, with a pot full of manna;—over it was the propitiatory, or mercy-seat, being a plate of gold as long and as broad as the ark, covering it, being shadowed with the cherubims of glory. Now all this glorious fabric did signify, that unless the law with its condemning power were hid in the ark, and covered with the mercy-seat, no person could stand before the Lord. Besides, the law was the old covenant of works, and being renewed unto them chiefly to be subservient to the gospel, and partly, with its appurtenances and carnal administration, to be the tenure of the Israelites' holding the land of Canaan, and this being in the ark, it was said to contain the covenant, and is frequently called "The ark of the covenant." Jesus Christ is the ark of this spiritual house. When the temple was opened in heaven, there was seen in the temple the ark of God's testament, Rev. xi. 19,—Jesus Christ, made conspicuous to all, who lay much hid under the old testament, Rom, iii. 25. God is said to set forth Christ to be ἱλαστήριον, "a propitiation," or mercy-seat; for by that very term is the mercy-seat expressed, Heb. ix. 5. He is, then, the ark and the mercy-seat covering it. He, then, doth these two things:—

(1*st.*) In behalf of this house, and every stone thereof, he hides the law with its condemning power, that nothing from thence shall be laid to their charge. If a man have a suit to be tried in any court, and a powerful friend engage himself that the only evidence which is against him shall not be produced, will it not give him encouragement to proceed? In that great and tremendous trial which is to be above, there is but one principal evidence against us, which gives life to all others; which if it be removed all the rest must fail:—this is the law. Christ, as the ark and mercy-seat, hides this law;—it shall not (I speak in respect to this house) be produced at the day of trial. Will not this be a great encouragement to them to appear at the throne of God? Christ hides the law, as being "the end" of it, Rom. x. 4, "that the righteousness thereof might be fulfilled in us," Rom. viii. 4. He hath so far answered all that the law required, that none from thence can "lay any thing to the charge of God's elect," Rom. viii. 33, 34. Let not poor sinners fear, it will not be with them as with Uzzah:—he touched the ark and died; touch this ark, and live for ever. And,—

(2*dly.*) He is the ark of this house, as containing in himself the new covenant; it is made with him originally, established in him irreversibly,—made out through him in all the grace of it faithfully.

3*dly.* He is the *altar* of this house. There were two altars in the old tabernacle and temple,—an altar for sacrifice and an altar for incense, Exod. xxvii. and xxx. The first was the great brazen altar that stood without the holy place, whereon the burnt-offerings and all sacrifices of blood for remission were offered. The other less, made of shittim-wood, all overlaid with pure gold, and a crown of beaten gold upon it, on which they were to burn pure incense unto the Lord always. And they were both most holy, sanctifying the gifts with legal sanctification that were offered on them, Matt. xxiii. 19. Now, both these doth our Saviour supply in this house. He is the great altar of sacrifice, the altar of offerings for expiation and atonement: "We have an altar, whereof they have no right to eat who serve the tabernacle," Heb. xiii. 10; that is, even He who sanctified the people with his own blood, and suffered without the gate, verse 11. The good-will and soul of Christ offering up himself, through the eternal Spirit, a pure oblation and sacrifice, by one offering to perfect for ever them that are sanctified, is all our altar. He is also the golden altar of incense. Incense is prayer, Ps. cxli. 2, "Let my prayer come before thee as incense." Jesus Christ is the golden altar whereon that incense is offered, Rev. viii. 3, 4, even that altar which is always before God, Rev. ix. 13. As by being the former he makes our persons accepted, so by the latter he makes our duties accepted. And all the living stones of this house are priests to offer sacrifice on these altars. By him, as priests, they have approximation to the holy place;—there they have a share and participation in all the sacrifices that are offered upon or by him.

4th. He is the candlestick of this house. The making, fashioning, and use of the candlestick in the holy place of the tabernacle, you have, Exod. xxv. 31, &c. It was one of the most glorious utensils of that frame, made of pure and beaten gold, with much variety of works,—knops, flowers, and lamps. The use of it was, to bear out light for all the worship of God in that most holy place. The tabernacle was made close, without any window. It was not to receive light from without; it had all its own light from within. It is true, this candlestick, with its seven lamps, did secondarily represent the churches of Christ, which hold out his light among themselves and unto others, Rev. i. 20, "The seven candlesticks thou sawest are the seven churches." Therefore Solomon made "ten candlesticks of pure gold," 1 Kings vii. 49, to set out yet farther the increase and multiplying of the churches of God. Upon this account, also, the two witnesses are said to be "two candlesticks," Rev. xi. 4, and "the two anointed ones that stand before the God of the whole earth," Zech. iv. 3, whence that in the Revelation is taken. There is mention, indeed, of two anointed ones, but of one candlestick;—the Holy Ghost plainly intimating, that though the churches and witnesses of Christ are also candlesticks in a second sense, yet there is one eminent candlestick, which hath light originally in itself, which also it communicates unto all others. And this is that which is mentioned in Zech. iv., which hath the "two olive-trees," or the two anointed churches of Jews and Gentiles, standing by it, receiving light from it to communicate to others: they empty the golden oil out of themselves which they receive from the candlestick. For this candlestick hath "seven lamps," verse 2; which lamps, that burn before the throne, are the "seven Spirits of God," Rev. iv. 5,—seven Spirits, that is, the perfection and completeness of the Spirit of God in all his graces and operations. Now, who hath these seven Spirits? Even he who received not the Spirit "by measure," John iii. 34, being the "stone" upon which are the "seven eyes," Zech. iii. 9. He alone, then, is this candlestick, and all the light which this house hath it is from him.

There are two ways whereby Jesus Christ makes out light to this house:—(1*st.*) By way of doctrinal revelation; (2*dly.*) Of real communication.

(1*st.*) He alone discovers light to all the stones of this building: "No man hath seen God at any time; the only begotten Son, which is in the bosom of the Father, he hath declared him," John i. 18. No saving discovery of God, of his nature, his will, his love, but what is by Christ. The moon and stars give light; but it is only what they receive from the sun. The prophets and apostles held out light; but it was all received from him. They spake by the Spirit of Christ that was in them. "I have received of the Lord that which also I delivered unto you," 1 Cor. xi. 23. The same apostle curses every one that shall bring in any other light into this house, be they angels or men, Gal. i. 8, 9. Christ alone fully knows the mind of God, as being always "in the bosom of the Father," John i. 18; yea, he knows it to the uttermost, being one with his Father, John x. 30. And he is willing to reveal it; for even "for this end came he into the world, that he might bear witness to the truth." And he had ability enough to do it, for "in him were hid all the treasures of wisdom and knowledge," Col. ii. 3. He alone is the author of all light to this his holy habitation. Many attempts have been to set up light in this house, and not from Christ. Some would kindle their traditions, for the doctrine of this house; some their prudentials, for the government of it; some their ceremonials, for the worship of it;—all candles in the sun. Shall men think to compass themselves with sparks, and walk in the light of the fire which themselves have kindled, in the face of the Sun of righteousness? Shall not such men lie down in sorrow? Beloved, take heed of such "ignes fatui,"—foolish, misguiding fires.

(2*dly.*) By way of real communication. He is "the true Light, which lighteth every man," John i. 9. Every one that hath any spiritual light really communicated to him hath it from Christ. It is part of his work to "recover sight to the blind," Luke iv. 18. And therefore he adviseth the church of Laodicea to come to him for eyesalve, that she might see, Rev. iii. 18. At his coming, Zion shines forth, Isa. lx. 1; because his light ariseth upon her, verse 2. The former doctrinal teaching of itself will not suffice: that light may shine in darkness, and the darkness not comprehend it, John i. 5. All the light the sun can give will not make a blind man see: there must be a visive faculty within as well as light without. The stones of this building are by nature all blind,—yea, darkened,—yea, darkness itself. If the Lord Christ do not, by the mighty efficacy of his Spirit, create a visive power within them, as well as reveal the will of his Father to them, they will never spiritually discern the things of God. The natural man discerneth not the things of God, nor indeed can do, 1 Cor. ii. 14. It is true, men, by the help of common gifts, with the use of the former doctrinal revelation, may attain to such a knowledge of the mind of God as may, in a sense, be called illumination, Heb. vi. 4. Far may they go, much may they do, by this light:—they may teach others, and be cast away themselves;—they may dispute for truth, yea, die for truth, and all this while have but the first, common anointing,—see nothing clearly, but men walking like trees. A spiritual insight into the mind of God is not to be obtained without an almighty act of the Spirit of Christ, creating a new power of life and light upon the soul. Some, indeed, think that they have this seeing power in themselves. Do but show them outwardly what is to be seen, and let them alone for the discerning of it. Well, then, let them alone; if ever they are stones of this living house, I am deceived. Thou that art so, know whence is all thy light; and if thou art any thing in the dark, draw nigh to the candlestick from whence all light is. Thence must thy light come, yea, and thence it shall come;—the secrets of the Lord shall make their abode with thee.

And this is the fourfold relation wherein the Lord Christ stands unto this house, as it is a spiritual building.

[2.] In respect of state and condition, Jesus Christ stands in a fivefold relation to this house,—viz., 1*st*, As the owner; 2*dly*, The builder; 3*dly*, The watchman or keeper; 4*thly*, The inhabiter; 5*thly*, The avenger: each of which I shall unfold in order.

1*st*. He is the owner of it. He calls it his: "Upon this rock will I build my church," Matt. xvi. 18. "Moses verily was faithful in all his house, as a servant; but Christ as a Son over his own house, whose house are we," Heb. iii. 5, 6. And that you may see that he doth not own it as his without good right and title, know that in the great economy of grace Jesus Christ hath a threefold right and title to this house.

(1*st*.) Of *inheritance*. He is by his Father "appointed heir of all things," Heb. i. 3. By inheritance he obtains this excellent name, to be Lord of this house. God sends him to the vineyard as the heir, after his servants were refused. And he hath an engagement from his Father, that he shall enjoy his whole inheritance upon demand, Ps. ii. 8. For the Father appointed, "in the fulness of times, to gather together all things in Christ, both which are in heaven, and which are on earth, even in him," Eph. i. 10. So that as Christ is "the first-begotten" of the Father, Heb. i. 6, and "the first-born of every creature," Col. i. 15, the right of heirship is his. But this will not do; for,—

(2*dly*.) When he should come to take possession of this house, he finds that it is *mortgaged*, and that a great debt lies upon it; which he must *pay* to the uttermost farthing, if he ever intend to have it. To the former title there must also be added a right of purchase. He must purchase this house, and pay a great price for it. And what is this price? what is required of him? No less than his dearest blood, Acts xx. 28. Yea, he must make his soul an offering for sin, and charge himself with the whole debt;—all the curse and punishment which this house had in part actually contracted upon itself, and wholly deserved. He must put his shoulders under the burden due to it, and his back to the stripes prepared for it. A hard task! But Jesus Christ being the heir, the right of redemption belonged unto him. It was not for his honour that it should lie unredeemed. Full well he knew that if he did it not, the whole creation was too beggarly to make this purchase. It is true, that nature of ours—which he assumed to pay that by, which he never took—was startled for a while, and would have deprecated this grievous price, crying out, "If it be possible, let this cup pass from me;" but he recollects himself, and says, "I am content to do thy will, O God:" and so, through the eternal Spirit, he offered himself up unto God for a ransom. He likes the house, and will have it to dwell in, whatever it cost him. "Here," saith he, "shall be my habitation, and my dwelling for ever," Ps. cxxxii. "Know ye not," saith the apostle, "that ye are the temple of the Spirit of Christ?" Well, and how come we so to be? "Ye are bought with a price," 1 Cor. vi. 19. They who affirm that he also purchased the unclean sties of the devil, wot not what they say.

(3*dly.*) Unto *purchase* he must also add *conquest.* An unjust usurper had taken possession of this house, and kept it in bondage; —Satan had seized on it, and brought it, through the wrath of God, under his power. He, then, must be conquered, that the Lord Christ may have complete possession of his own house. "For this purpose," then, "was the Son of God manifested, that he might destroy the works of the devil," 1 John iii. 8. And how doth he do it? He overpowers him and destroys him, in that "through death he destroyed him that had the power of death; that is, the devil," Heb. ii. 14. And he spoiled him, having overcome him. He bound the strong man, and then spoiled his goods, Matt. xii. 29. All that darkness, unbelief, sin, and hardness, that he had stuffed this house withal, Christ spoils and scatters them all away. And to make his conquest complete, he triumphs over his enemy, and, like a mighty conqueror, makes an open show of him, to his everlasting shame, Col. ii. 15, "Having spoiled principalities and powers, he made a show of them openly, triumphing over them in his cross;" and by this means strengthens his title to his inheritance.

I might also farther insist on the donation of his Father, and the actual possession he takes of it by his Spirit; but these are sufficient to prove this house to be Christ's. I shall take some observations hence.

Observation 1. [1]Is this the *house* of Christ? is he the *owner* of it?—Let men take heed how they spoil it for themselves. The psalmist makes this a great argument in his pleading against opposers, that they came into the Lord's "inheritance," Ps. lxxix. 1. The title of Christ's *purchase* was not then so clearly known as that of his *inheritance;* and therefore they of old pleaded chiefly by that title. Now he hath proclaimed to all, his other titles also,—the whole right he has to this house,—to his saints. Who, then, shall meddle with it, and go free? Amongst men, every one with all his might will defend his own possession; and shall we think that the Lord Christ will suffer his to be spoiled at an easy rate? Shall not men pay dear for their encroachment? How hath he in our days frustrated all attempts for the persecution of his! "Touch not," saith he, "mine anointed." Men may upon various pretences claim this privilege to such a land, nation, or faction; it will in the end appear to be theirs, and only theirs, who are living stones of this house. Dogs may scramble for their bread, but shall not enjoy it. It is Christ in this house that will make every stone of it a burdensome stone. He hath done it that men may learn μὴ θεομαχεῖν. Do not think it will excuse thee to say thou wast mistaken.

Observation 2. Is Christ the *owner* of this house?—Let the *order* and disposal of it be left to himself. Men are apt to be tampering with his house and household. They will be so kind and careful as to lay out their wisdom and prudence about it;—Thus and thus shall it be; these are parts and members of it. Christ is exceeding jealous of his honour in this particular. He cannot bear it, that men pretending to his glory should think him so wanting in love or wisdom towards his own, as not exactly to dispose of all things that concern the regimen thereof. Men would not be so dealt withal in their own houses as they deal with Christ in his. We have all wisdom enough (as we suppose) to order our own houses;—only the wisdom and love of the Father leaves his to the discretion of others. These thoughts are not from above.

Observation 3. Hath Christ taken *his own house* to himself upon so many *titles*?—Let not men put those buildings on him for his which are not so, which he holds not by these titles. Go to a man that dwells in a stately palace of his own, show him a hog-sty, tell him, "This is your house; here you dwell; this is yours:"—can you put a greater indignity on him? "No," says the man; "that is not

[1] The second of the two sermons under the present text, and latterly printed as one, began at this point, according to a statement in an old edition.—ED.

mine; I dwell in yonder sumptuous palace." And shall we deal thus with the Lord Jesus? He hath bought and adorned his own house:—a glorious house it is. If now men shall hold out to him a sty of swine, a den of unclean beasts, a ruinous heap, whereof the far greatest part are dead stones, and tell him, this is his church, his house,—will it not exceedingly provoke him? will he bear such a reproach? Nay, he will reject such tenders to their ruin.

2dly. Jesus Christ is the *builder* of this house: "This man was counted worthy of more glory than Moses, inasmuch as he who hath builded the house hath more honour than the house," Heb. iii. 3.—"I," saith he, "will build my church," Matt. xvi. 18. This is not a fabric for any workman but Christ. It is true, there are others employed under him; and some so excellent that they may be said to be "wise master-builders," 1 Cor. iii. 10; but yet all the efficacy of their labour in this building is not from themselves, but merely from him by whom they are employed. Except the Lord build this house, they labour in vain that go about to build it.

Now this house receives a twofold building:—(1*st.*) *Spiritual*, of all the stones thereof into one mystical house. Of this I chiefly treat. (2*dly.*) *Ecclesiastical*, of some particular stones into several tabernacles,—which are useful partitions in the great mystical house,—called assemblies and dwelling-places of mount Zion. Both these it hath from Christ alone.

(1*st.*) For the first;—if all the most skilful workmen in the world should go to the pit of nature, by their own strength to hew out stones for this building, they will never, with all their skill and diligence, lay one stone upon it. There is life required to those stones, which none can give but Christ. The Father hath given into his hand alone to give life eternal to whom he will, John xvii. 2. He alone can turn stones into children of Abraham. To him is committed all dispensation of quickening power. He brings us from the dust of death, and no man hath quickened his own soul. With spiritual power, all spiritual life is vested in Christ. If dead stones live, it must be by hearing the voice of the Son of God. Christ's building of his mystical house is his giving life unto dead stones; or rather, being life unto them. Of those who will attempt to build themselves, and draw a principle of spiritual life from the broken cisterns of nature, I shall speak afterward.

(2*dly.*) For the second, or the communion of living stones one with another, and all with Christ, in the order and worship appointed by the gospel, so becoming assemblies and dwelling-places of mount Zion;—this also is of him. This is for his outward solemn worship; and he would never allow that the will of any creature should be the measure of his honour. He sets up the candlesticks; and holds the stars in his hand. Look to the institution of this building,—it is from Christ;—look for directions about this building,—it is wholly from him. From him, his word, his Spirit, is the institution, direction, and perfection of it. From hence, now, take some observations.

Observation 1. Is Christ the *builder* of this house? can he alone fit us for this building? can he alone, and that by his almighty power, put life into dead stones, that they may grow up to be a holy and living habitation unto him?—What, then, becomes of that famous workman, free-will, and a power of believing in ourselves? do not they work effectually in this temple? As it was in Solomon's temple, "there was neither axe, nor hammer, nor any tool of iron heard in the house while it was in building," 1 Kings vi. 7; so in this spiritual house, that iron tool of free-will is not once heard; it comes not nigh the work,—Christ doth all alone. He gives life to whom he pleases. Shall a dead will be thought to have a quickening, life-giving power in it? Shall a spirit of life be spun out of the bowels of nature? Is it the will of man, or the will of God, that draws men unto Christ? and is it his Spirit, or flesh, that unites us to him? Where, then, is this workman employed, that makes all this noise in the world? Even there, where men cry, "Go to, let us build us a city, and a tower whose top may reach unto heaven," Gen. xi. 4,—amongst those who would build a Babel, a tower of their own to get to heaven by. The Lord comes down and scatters all their undertakings. This workman never placed stone in the house of Christ. Nay, it is like the foolish woman, that pulls down her house with both her hands. What free grace sets up, that free will strives to demolish.

Observation 2. See hence a great mistake of many poor creatures, who would fain be stones in this house. What course take they? They hew and square themselves,—strive to cut off this and that rubbish, which (as they suppose) alone hinders them from being fitted to this building; they pare themselves with vows, promises, resolutions, and engagements,—beautify themselves with duties and services; and then, with many perplexing fears, present themselves to the building, never knowing whether they are admitted or no. All this while the great Master-builder stands by, scarcely dealt withal. What, now, is the issue of such attempts? What they build one day, falls down in another. When they have oftentimes in their own thoughts brought the building to such a pass as that they are ready to think it will be well with them, now surely they shall have a share and interest in this living and glorious house; all on a sudden they fall again to the ground, their hopes wither, and they suppose themselves in the world's rubbish again. There is no end of this alternation. Would, now, this poor soul see where its great defect lies? It hath not applied itself aright to the only Builder. Wouldst thou be a stone in this fabric?

Lay thyself before the Lord Jesus; say to him that thou art in thyself altogether unfit for the great building he hath in hand;—that thou hast often attempted to put thyself upon it, but all in vain:—"Now, Lord Jesus, do thou take me into thine own hand. If thou castest me away, I cannot complain,—I must justify thee in all thy ways; but thou callest things that are not as though they were,—thou turnest dead stones into children of Abraham: oh, turn my dead into a living stone!" Fear not; he will in no wise cast thee out.

The vanity of men, attempting to mix their power and wisdom in the heaping up tabernacles for Christ, might be hence discovered; but I forbear.

3*dly*. Jesus Christ is the great *watchman*, or keeper of this house. There are, indeed, other watchmen, and that of God's own appointment, for the use of this house: "Son of man, I have made thee a watchman," Ezek. iii. 17; "I have set watchmen upon thy walls," Isa. lxii. 6, 7; which in a special manner are the pastors of the churches. "They watch," Heb. xiii. 17, as the priests and Levites heretofore kept the watch of the Lord. It cannot be denied but that many who have taken upon them to be these watchmen have watched only for their own advantage, have been very dogs,—yea, dumb dogs, the very worst of dogs, Isa. lvi. 10,—yea, they have been, and oftentimes are, under various pretences, great "smiters and wounders of the spouse of Christ," Cant. v. 7. But yet, were they never so good and true to their trusts, they were never able all to watch and keep this house, had it not another watchman: "Except the Lord keep the city, these watchmen watch in vain," Ps. cxxvii. 1. He that keepeth Israel, who doth neither slumber nor sleep, must keep this house, or it will be destroyed. Christ, then, is that holy one, and that watcher, that came down from heaven, and commanded to cut down the tree and the branches, Dan. iv. 13, 14,—Nebuchadnezzar and his great power,—for meddling with this house. Now, Christ watcheth his house for two ends.

(1*st*.) To see what it wants. 2 Chron. xvi. 9, "The eyes of the LORD run to and fro throughout the whole earth, to show himself strong in its behalf." He looks down from heaven to behold them that fear him, Ps. xiv. He is that stone upon which are "seven eyes," Zech. iii. 9,—a sufficiency, in perfection of wisdom, inspection, and government, for the good of his house. And those seven eyes of his "run to and fro through the whole earth" for this very purpose, Zech. iv. 10. He takes notice of the state and condition of his people, to eye them in their distresses, and to give them timely and suitable deliverance. They may call every spring of their refreshment, Beer-lahai-roi [The well of Him that liveth and seeth me].

(2*dly*.) To see that the son of violence draw not nigh unto it; and if he do, to require it at his hands; to make him eat his own flesh, and drink his own blood, that he may learn to devour no more. Observe, then,—

Observation 1. Whence it is that this house, which seems so often to be nigh to destruction, is yet preserved from ruin. Ofttimes it is brought into a condition that all that look on say, Now it is gone for ever. But still it recovers, and gets up again. The Lord Christ looks on all the while: he knows how far things may proceed for trial. When it comes to that pass that, if pressures and troubles should continue, the house will be overborne indeed, then he puts in, rebukes the winds and waves, and makes all things still again. Like a father who looks upon his child in a difficult and dangerous business,—knows that he can relieve him when he pleases, but would willingly see him try his strength and cunning,—lets him alone until perhaps the child thinks himself quite lost, and wonders his father doth not help him; but when the condition comes to be such that, without help, he will be lost indeed, instantly the father puts in his hand and saves him. So deals the Lord Jesus with his house,—lets it oftentimes strive and wrestle with great oppositions, to draw out and exercise all the graces thereof; but yet all this while he looketh on, and when danger is nigh indeed, he is not far off.

Observation 2. Let all the enemies of the church know, that there is one who hath an *eye* over them in all their counsels and undertakings. Whilst they are digging deep, he looks on and laughs them to scorn. How perplexed was the king of Syria when he found that the prophet was acquainted with all his designs, and made them known to the king of Israel! It cannot but be a matter of perplexity to the enemies of this house, when they shall find that the great Friend and Protector thereof is continually present in all their advisoes. Let them not wonder at their birthless undertakings; the eye of Christ is still upon them.

Observation 3. Let the saints see their *privilege;*—whoever they are, in what condition soever, the eye of Christ is upon them. He watches over them for good, and knows their souls in adversity. When no eye sees them, he looks on them; they cannot be cast out of his care, nor hid from his sight. There are many poor souls who go heavily all the day long,—that mourn in their spirits unknown, unregarded, unpitied;—the eye of Christ is on them for good continually; they cannot be thrown out of his watchful care.

4thly. Christ is the *indweller* of this house. He hath not *built* it and *framed* it for no use. It is for a habitation for himself. He hath chosen Zion; he hath desired it for his habitation. "This is my rest," saith he; " here will I dwell," Ps. cxxxii. 13, 14. This house is built up to be an habitation unto him, Eph. ii. 22. He is the

"King of saints," and this house is his court. It is true, for his human nature, "the heaven must receive him, until the time of the restitution of all things," Acts iii. 21; but yet, he dwelleth in this house three ways:—

(1*st.*) By his Spirit. Christ dwells in this house, and every stone of it, by his Spirit, "Know ye not that Christ is in you, except ye be reprobates?" 2 Cor. xiii. 5.—"Christ in you;" that is, the Spirit of Christ, Christ by his Spirit. So the Holy Ghost expounds it, Rom. viii. 9, "If the Spirit of God dwell in you:" which, verse 10, is, "If Christ be in you." Christ and his Spirit, as to indwelling, are all one; for he dwells in us by his Spirit. "The love of God is shed abroad in our hearts by the Holy Ghost, that is given unto us," Rom. v. 5. There is not only the "love of God," a grace of the Spirit, "shed abroad" in us, but there is also the "Holy Spirit given unto us." This is fully asserted, Rom. viii. 11, "The Spirit of him that raised up Jesus, dwells in you;" as also, 2 Tim. i. 14, "Keep the good thing committed to thee by the Holy Ghost which dwelleth in us." Hence the saints are said to be "temples of the Holy Ghost." Jesus Christ doth not build temples merely for graces, created graces; he dwells in them himself,—he dwells in them by his Spirit. And this is a glorious privilege of this house, that Jesus Christ in a mystical and wonderful manner should dwell in it, and every stone of it. Hereby all believers come to be not one personal, but one mystical Christ, 1 Cor. xii. 12. However we are distanced in respect of his human nature, yet mystically we are one,—one body, one mystical Christ,—because we have one Spirit dwelling in us and him. If a man were never so tall, so that his head should reach the stars, and his feet stand upon the ground, yet, having but one soul, he is but one man still. Though Christ in his human nature be exceedingly distanced from us, yet there being one and the same Spirit in him and us, we are one mystical Christ. Yet observe,—

Observation 1. Though Christ be united unto the persons of the saints by the indwelling of the Spirit, yet the saints have not that which is called *personal* union with him, nor with the Spirit. Personal union is by a person of the Deity assuming the nature of man into one personality with itself, that having of its own no personal subsistence. Things are here clean otherwise: Christ doth not assume the saints into a personal subsistence with himself, but dwells in their persons by his Spirit.

Observation 2. That the operations of the indwelling Spirit of Christ, and all his manifestations, are *voluntary.* He worketh as he will, and revealeth what he will, even where he dwells. He doth not work in us naturally, but voluntarily, unto what proportion he pleaseth; therefore, though he dwell equally in all saints in respect of truth and reality, yet he doth not in respect of working and efficacy.

(2*dly.*) *By his graces.* Christ dwelleth in this house, and in all the stones thereof, by his graces. He " dwells in our hearts by faith," Eph. iii. 17. He dwells in us by his word " in all wisdom," Col. iii. 16. All the graces we are made partakers of, we receive from his fulness, and by them he inhabits in us. They are indeed the ornaments of the living stones of this house, to make them meet and fit for such an indweller as the Lord Christ. Christ will not dwell in a soul whose mind is darkness, his will stubbornness, and his affections carnal and sensual. He puts light, and life, and love upon the soul, that it may be meet for him to dwell in. Christ dwells in all the world by his power and presence, but he dwells only in his saints by his Spirit and grace.

(3*dly.*) *By his ordinances.* Where two or three of his are assembled together, there is he in the midst of them. The ordinances of Christ are the great ornaments of his kingly court; by them he is glorious in all the assemblies of mount Zion. Some would fain cast out this indwelling of Christ from among his saints;—in due time he will thoroughly rebuke them. Some, again, would thrust him out into the world; but he will make men know that his ordinances are given unto his. It is true, the benefit of some of them extends to the world; but the right and enjoyment of them is the privilege of his saints. Thus Christ dwells in his house. Hence, observe,—

Observation 1. The intimacy of the Lord Jesus with his saints, and the delight he takes in them. He dwelleth with them, he dwelleth in them,—he takes them to the nearest union with himself possible: he in them, they in him, that they may be one. He hath made many an admirable change with us. He took our sin, and gives us his righteousness; he took our nature, and gives us his Spirit. Neither is it a bare indwelling,—he thereby holds with us all acts of the choicest communion. " If," saith he, " any man hear my voice, and open to me, I will come in to him." And what then ? " I will sup with him, and he with me," Rev. iii. 20.

(1.) *I will sup with him;"*—I will delight and satisfy myself with him. Jesus Christ takes abundance of delight and contentment in the hearts of his saints. When they are faithful, when they are fruitful, he is marvellously refreshed with it. Hence is that prayer of the spouse, "Awake, O north wind; and come, thou south; blow upon my garden, that the spices thereof may flow out. Let my Beloved come into his garden, and eat his pleasant fruits," Cant. iv. 16. She would have the spices, the graces she hath received, breathed on by a fresh gale of the Spirit, that they might yield a sweet savour. And why so? That her Beloved may have something for his entertainment,—that he may come and sup, and eat of his pleasant fruits. A poor soul, that hath received Christ, hath not any desire so fervent as that it may have something for the entertainment of him; that he who filled it when it was hungry may not (as it were) be sent away empty. And the Lord Jesus is exceedingly taken with those refreshments. "The King is held in the galleries," Cant. vii. 5. He is detained, yea, bound with delight;—he knows not how to pass away. Therefore "he rests in his love," Zeph. iii. 17. He is exceedingly satiated in the delight he takes in his saints. Neither is this all, that when Christ comes he will sup with us, (though this be a great deal; for what are we, that we should entertain our Lord?) but also,—

(2.) *The saints sup with him:* he provides choice refreshments for them also. When Christ comes in unto us, he will entertain a soul bounteously. He provides love for us. When the Spirit of Christ is bestowed on us, he sheds abroad the love of God in our hearts, Rom. v. 5. He sheds it abroad,—pours it out abundantly. Friends, love is a choice dainty:—he that knows it not is a stranger to all spiritual banquets:—it is a choice dish in the feast of fat things that Christ prepareth. He provides "righteousness, and peace, and joy in the Holy Ghost," for us. *That* [is] his kingdom, Rom. xiv. 17; and this kingdom of his is *within us.* Of such precious things as these doth Christ provide a supper for them with whom he dwells. If Christ be in you, more or less, you shall not want this entertainment. We are, indeed, sometimes like mad guests, that when meat is set on the table, cast it all down, without tasting a morsel. When Christ hath prepared sweet and precious dainties for us, we cast them on the ground; we throw away our peace, our joy, by folly and unbelief: but this makes not the truth of God of none effect.

Observation 2. Doth Christ dwell in us by his Spirit?—should we not be careful lest we grieve that Spirit of his? The Spirit of Christ is very tender. Did the saints continually consider this, that Christ dwells in them,—that he is grieved and troubled at all their unbelief, unruly passions, worldly desires, foolish imaginations,—surely they could not but be much more watchful over themselves than generally they are. He is refreshed when we walk with him, and hold fellowship with him. To turn aside from him, to hold fellowship with the world or flesh,—this grieves him and burdens him. Oh, "grieve not the Spirit of God, whereby you are sealed to the day of redemption." And let me tell you, if you do, though he will not utterly depart from you, nor take his kindness away for evermore, yet he will do that which shall make your heart ache, your joints tremble, and break all your bones in pieces. For,—

(1.) He will depart from you as to all *sense of his presence,* that you shall have neither joy, nor comfort, nor peace. He will hide his face, and make you believe (as we say) that he is gone utterly from you. And this he will do, not for a day, or a night, or so, but for a great while together. You shall go to seek him, and you shall not find him; yea, beg and cry, and have no answer. Now all the world for one smile from Christ, for one impression of his presence upon my heart,—and all in vain. When the Spirit of Christ was thus departed from David, upon his miscarriage, as to the sense and joy of it, how doth he cry out, "Make me to hear the voice of joy and gladness, that the bones which thou hast broken may rejoice!" Ps. li. 8. If thou valuest the presence of Christ at no greater rate but to jeopard it upon every occasion, thou mayest haply go without the comfort of it all thy days. Examine yourselves,—is it not so with some of you? Have you not lost the sense of the presence of Christ by your folly and uneven walking? Perhaps you value it not much, but go on as Samson with his hair cut, and think to do as at other times; but if the Philistines set upon thee, it will be sorrow and trouble; in every assault thou wilt find thyself a lost man;—sooner or later it will be bitterness to thee.

(2.) He will depart as to the *efficacy of his working in thee,* and leave thee so weak that thou shalt not be able to walk with God. His Spirit is "a Spirit of grace and supplications." He will so withdraw it that thou shalt find thy heart in a poor condition, as to those things. To be cold in prayer, dead in hearing, estranged from meditation, slight in all duties,—this shall be thy portion;—a frame that a tender soul would tremble to think of. Ah, how many poor creatures are come to this state in these days, by their neglect and contempt of Christ dwelling in them! They have lost their first love, their first life; their graces are ready to die, and their whole soul is asleep, in a heartless, lifeless, zealless frame. They shall be saved, but "yet as through fire."

(3.) He will depart *as to assurance of what is to come,* as well as to a sense of what is present. It is the indwelling Spirit of Christ that gives assurance: hereby are we "sealed to the day of redemption." He "beareth witness with our spirits that we are the children of God." Upon our grieving him, he will withdraw as to this also. We shall be bewildered, and in the dark, not knowing what will become of our souls to eternity. For if Christ by his Spirit do not speak peace, who shall?

Observation 3. Doth he dwell in us by his grace?

(1.) Let us *first know whence all graces are,* that in a want or weakness of them we may know whither to go for a supply. "Of his fulness we receive, and grace for grace." All supplies of graces are from Christ. "Lord, increase our faith," say the apostles. Not only faith originally is from him, but all increases of it also. "I believe;

help thou my unbelief," says the poor man. We wrestle and struggle with a little grace, a little faith, a little love, a little joy; and are contented if we can keep our heads above water, that we be not quite sunk and lost. How sweet would it be with us, if, upon a serious consideration from whence all these graces flow, we would apply ourselves to draw out farther degrees and heightenings of them, whereby he might dwell more plentifully in us, and we might always converse with him in his gracious train of attendants! How this may be done in particular, is not my business now to show.

(2.) Learn to *tender* [make much of] *the graces of Christ*, as those which hold out his presence to us. Let us tender them in our own hearts, and prize them in whomsoever they are. They are pledges of the indwelling of Christ. Certainly, if men valued Christ, they would more value his graces. Many pretend to love him, to honour him, yea, with Peter, to be ready to die with him, or for him; but what evil surmises have they of the graces of Christ appearing in others! how do they call them hypocrisy, humour, folly, pride, singularity, with other terms of a later invention! I cannot so easily believe that any one can love the Lord Jesus and hate the appearances of him in others. Where is any thing of Christ, there is also Christ.

5thly. Jesus Christ is the great avenger of this house, and of all the injuries or wrongs that are done unto it. "All," saith he, "that devour Israel shall offend," Jer. ii. 3. He will not hold him guiltless that rises up against it. See Isa. lix. 15–18. He takes upon him the avenging of his house, as his own proper work: "Shall he not avenge his elect? He will do it speedily." See also Isa. lxiii. 2–6. How dreadful is he in the execution of his revenging judgments against the enemies thereof! So also is he described, Rev. xix. 13–15. He hath promised to make the stones of this house heavy stones; they shall burden all that touch them, Zech. xii. 3. He comes forth of "the myrtle-trees in the bottom" (his lowly people in a low condition) with the "red horse" following him, Zech. i. 8. Upon this account he fearfully broke the old Roman-pagan empire, Rev. vi. 12–17; and will as fearfully destroy the antichristian Roman power, with all its adherents, Rev. xvii.–xix. Sooner or later he will call to an account every instrument of persecution in the world. Hence he is said to be a lion in the behalf of this house, that treads down all before him, Micah v. 8. Jacob says of him in Judah, "He is a lion, as an old lion; who shall rouse him up?" Gen. xlix. 9. Suppose any do rouse him up: how then? "He will not lie down until he eat of the prey, and drink the blood of the slain," Numb. xxiii. 24. Many poor creatures have, by their opposition to his house, roused up this lion: and what hath been the issue? What attempts have been to cause him to lie down again!—All in vain. If he be once roused up, he will not couch down until he eat and drink the blood of the slain. But suppose great opposition be made unto him,—will he not give over? Not at all. He will be as a lion that cometh upon his prey, if a multitude of shepherds be called forth against him, he will not be afraid at their voice, nor abase himself at their noise, Isa. xxxi. 4. In brief, sooner or later, temporally or eternally, he will avenge all the injuries and destroy all the enemies of his holy dwelling, 2 Thess. i. 6–10.

And these are some of the relations wherein the Lord Christ stands unto this house of God, being made thereby unto it beauty and glory, comeliness and excellency. The carrying on of this building, by the union of all the stones thereof to the foundation, and their cementing one to another by faith, love, and order, I shall not now treat of, nor of the following points of the text.

The general uses of what hath been said are three; the heads whereof I shall name.

Use 1. See the eminent privilege of them which are indeed stones of this house, which is living, strong, and glorious,—which is so nearly related to the Lord Christ. There is more of duty, dignity, and safety, in this thing, than can easily be expressed. To do service unto Christ as his, to have the honour of being his, and to be safeguarded as his, are great privileges. Let them who have any sense of these things farther draw out these particulars, from what hath been spoken.

Use 2. Learn hence the vanity of resting upon outward church privileges, if we are not withal interested in this spiritual estate. Where men are living stones indeed, they lie in beauty and order in the assemblies;—where they are otherwise, where assemblies are made up of dead rubbish, and yet cry, "The house of the Lord, the house of the Lord,"—the Lord Jesus abhors those assemblies; he stands not in these relations unto them.

Use 3. See hence the ruin of persecution that hath appeared in the world in various forms. It hath put on all manner of colours and pretences, and prevailed with all sorts of persons at one time or other to close with it. What hath been the issue? what is like to be? The house, indeed, hath been battered sometimes; but they who have come against it have been broken all to pieces. Shall the residue of men who, under new pretences or old ones new painted, drive on the same design,—shall they prosper? Thou, O Lord Jesus, in thine anger wilt cut them off. The Lord open the eyes of the sons of men, that they may not hope any more to separate between Christ and his saints, between whom there are so many everlasting relations!

Μόνῳ σοφῷ Θεῷ, διὰ Ἰησοῦ Χριστοῦ, ᾧ ἡ δόξα εἰς τοὺς αἰῶνας. Ἀμήν.

SERMON VII.

THE

ADVANTAGE OF THE KINGDOM OF CHRIST

IN THE

SHAKING OF THE KINGDOMS OF THE WORLD;

OR,

PROVIDENTIAL ALTERATIONS IN THEIR SUBSERVIENCY TO CHRIST'S EXALTATION.

PREFATORY NOTE.

The battle of Worcester, "the crowning mercy," as Cromwell termed it, which effectually reduced Britain under his control, was fought on the 3d of September 1651, the anniversary of his victory at Dunbar. On the 24th of October following, a day of thanksgiving was observed for this success, and "sundry other mercies." On this occasion Owen, by this time Dean of Christ Church College, Oxford, preached before the House of Commons the following sermon. "It contains," says Mr Orme, "many free and eloquent passages, especially on the danger of human governments interfering with the principles and rights of the kingdom of Christ; and on the abomination and extent of the antichristian apostasy." He refers, in illustration, to the passage which occurs on page 322.—Ed.

Tuesday, October 28, 1651.

Ordered by the Parliament, That the thanks of this House be given to Mr Owen, Dean of Christ Church in Oxford, for his great pains taken in his sermon preached before the Parliament, at Margaret's, Westminster, on Friday the 24th of October (being a day set apart for public thanksgiving); and that he be desired to print his sermon; and that he have the like privilege in printing the same as others in like case have usually had; and that the Lord-General do give him the thanks of this House, and desire him to print his sermon accordingly.

Hen. Scobell, *Cler. Parl.*

TO THE

SUPREME AUTHORITY OF THE NATION,

THE COMMONS ASSEMBLED IN PARLIAMENT.

RIGHT HONOURABLE,

OF all the times which the Holy One of Israel hath caused to pass over the nations of the world, there hath not any from the days of old been so filled with eminent discoveries of his presence, power, and providence, in disposing of all affairs here below according to the counsel of his own will, as the season wherein he hath made you a spectacle unto men and angels, being the instrument in his hand to perform all his pleasure. Neither in this season hath he, upon any opportunity, so gloriously laid hold upon his own strength and goodness, to manifest the *fixedness of his eye* on those who are as the *apple* of it, as in that mighty deliverance the high praises whereof, according to his good hand upon you, you lately rendered unto him.

The more beauty and desirableness any design against the Lord Christ is clothed withal, the more power and subtlety it is supported with, the greater is the brightness of his coming for its wasting and desolation. With what deceivableness of unrighteousness and lies in hypocrisy the late grand attempt of those in Scotland, with their adherents (which also was of the former, and is gone into destruction), was carried on, is in some measure now made naked, to the loathing of its abominations. In digging deep to lay a foundation for blood and revenge,—in covering private and sordid ends with a pretence of things public and glorious,—in limning a face of religion upon a worldly stock,—in concealing distant aims and bloody animosities to compass one common end, that a theatre might be provided to act several parts upon,—in pleading a necessity from an oath of God unto most desperate undertakings against God, and such like things as these, perhaps it gives not place to any which former ages have been acquainted withal. Now, to reject all the claims of the authors and abettors thereof to any commission from above, to divest them of all pretences to religion and zeal thereof, to disappoint them in their expected associations, and to make all their strength to become as tow that hath smelt the fire, hath been His work alone who takes to himself his great power to carry on the interest of his kingdom against all opposers. Under the shadow of this mercy—composed of as many branches of wisdom, power, goodness, and faithfulness, as any outward dispensation hath brought forth since the name of Christian was known—do you now sit in council, and the residue of the nation in peace. What obligations from the Lord, what cords of love are upon us! The returnal and improvement of all his dealings with us, which he requireth and expecteth from us, I have pointed you unto in the following sermon For the present I shall only add, that as whatever there hath been of beauty, glory, or advantage unto the people of God, in the late transactions, hath been eminently of undeserved grace; so the dreadful vengeance which the Lord hath executed against the men of his enmity and warfare hath been most righteously procured, by their clothing cursed designs of revenge, persecution, bondage in soul and body, spoil and rapine, with the most glorious pretences of zeal, covenant, reformation, and such like things,— which never came into their hearts. Therefore, that the God of all our mercies and deliverances would for ever keep alive in your hearts a faithful acknowledgment of his grace, and a practical detestation of those ways which are such a provocation to the eyes of his glory, shall be the constant prayer of

Your most humble Servant

In our dearest Lord,

J. Owen.

From my Study, Ch. Ch., Oxon.,
Nov. 7.

SERMON VII.

THE ADVANTAGE OF THE KINGDOM OF CHRIST IN THE SHAKING OF THE KINGDOMS OF THE WORLD.

"And all the trees of the field shall know that I the LORD have brought down the high tree, have exalted the low tree, have dried up the green tree, and have made the dry tree to flourish: I the LORD have spoken, and have done it.—EZEK. xvii. 24.

ALTHOUGH all the works of God's providence—which are great, and sought out of all that have pleasure in them, Ps. cxi. 2—have such a stamp and impress of his own image on them, his wisdom, goodness, power, love, that they declare their author, and reveal from heaven his kindness and wrath towards the children of men;[1] yet such are the prejudices, lusts, inordinacy of affections, and interest of many, that it hath always been a long and difficult task to convince them of his presence in them, when it hath been most uncontrollably evident. The Egyptians will wrestle with many a plague, by thinking the "magicians" can do so;[2] and the Philistines will try to the utmost whether it be his hand, or a chance that happened to them.[3] "LORD," saith the prophet, "when thy hand is lifted up, they will not see," Isa. xxvi. 11. Yea, oftentimes (especially when judicial blindness is gone forth upon them),[4] though they cannot but see his arm awaked as of old, and made bare, they will not rest in his sovereign disposal of things, but rise up against the works of his revenge and holiness; like wild beasts that are pursued, when all ways of escape and turning are shut up, they fly in the face of him that follows them. They repent not of their evil deeds, but bite their tongues for anger, and blaspheme the God of heaven, Rev. xvi. 10, 11. Yea, such is the power of deceivable lusts, that many will admire at the blindness of others in former generations who considered not the works of God (as the Jews in the wilderness), when themselves are under actual contempt of no less glorious dispensations; like the Pharisees, who

[1] Ps. xix. 1, 2; Rom. i. 20; Acts xiv. 16, 17.
[2] Exod. vii. 11, 12.
[3] 1 Sam. vi. 9.
[4] Isa. vi. 9, 10.

bewailed the folly of their fathers in persecuting the prophets, when themselves were endeavouring to kill the Son of God, Matt. xxiii. 29, 30. To bring, then, upon the spirits of men a conviction of the works of God, and his righteousness therein, so as to prevail with them to rest in his determination of things, is a task meet only for him who knows all their hearts within them, and can carry on the issues of his providence until to a man they shall say, "Verily there is a reward for the righteous: verily he is a God who judgeth in the earth," Ps. lviii. 11. And this is that which the Lord here undertakes to accomplish, "And," saith he, "all the trees," &c.

In the preaching and prophesying of Ezekiel, this one thing among others is eminent, that he was "artifex parabolarum,"—a wonderful "framer of similitudes and parables;"[1] a way of teaching attended with much evidence, clearness, and power.

In particular, he frequently compares the world to a field, or a forest, and the inhabitants of it to the trees therein;—an allusion exceedingly proper, considering the great variety and difference of condition both of the one and the other. The trees of the field are some high, some low; some green, some dry; some strong, some weak; some lofty, some contemptible; some fruitful, some barren; some useful, some altogether useless: so that you have all sorts of persons, high and low, of what condition, relation, or interest soever, clearly represented by the trees of the field; and these are the trees in my text.

This chapter, unto verse 22, is taken up in a riddle, a parable, with the exposition of it.[2] The time being come that God would destroy the outward, visible monarchy of the Jews, for their false worship, tyranny, persecution, and oppression, he employs the king of Babylon in that work,[3] who subdues the nation, takes away two kings, one after another, and appoints Zedekiah a titulary governor under him.[4] But the wrath of God being to come upon them to the uttermost, he also closes with Egypt, rebels against him[5] by whose appointment alone he had any right to be a ruler, verse 16; so way is made, by his ruin, to put an end to the kingly reign of the house of David in Jerusalem, Jer. xxix. 16, 17. The Lord had of old erected a kingly government in the house of David, 1 Sam. xvi. 1; 2 Sam. xii. 7;—not for any eminency in the government itself, or for the civil advantage of that people,—for he had long before chosen and established another, consisting of "seventy elders of the people," Numb. xi. 24, to whom he added prophets and judges, extraordinarily raised up in several generations, according to his promise, Deut. xviii. 18, (which when the people rejected, he said they rejected him, or his institution, 1 Sam.

[1] Ezek. xx. 49. [2] xvii. 2. [3] 2 Chron. xxxvi. 17.
[4] 2 Kings xxiv. 1–3. [5] Jer. xxxvii. 1; 2 Kings xxiv. 17; 2 Chron. xxxvi. 10.

viii. 7),—but that it might be a *type* of the spiritual dominion of their Messiah;[1] and so was a part of their pedagogy and bondage, as were the residue of their types, every one of them;—yea, the most glorious enjoyments whatsoever which were granted them (which did yet represent something that was afterward to be brought in), was part of that servile estate wherein God kept that people, that without us they should not be made perfect. But now this carnal people, beholding the outward beauty, lustre, and glory of the type, began to rest in it, to the neglect of the spiritual kingdom of Christ represented thereby.[2] And thus did they with the rest of their types, until the Lord destroyed all their outward pomp and glory, Isa. i. 11, 12; Jer. vii. 4, 14, 15. So, in particular, dealt he with their kingly government, when once they began to account their bondage their glory, and to embrace the shadow instead of the substance. And this did he, to recall them to a serious consideration of the tendency of all typical institutions, and the design he was carrying on concerning the kingdom of Christ.

Hence, verse 22 of this chapter, he calls them from their thoughtfulness about the destructions, desolations, and contentions that were amongst them in reference to their civil rule, to the consideration of that design which he was secretly and silently carrying on under all these dispensations. "I will also take of the highest branch of the high cedar, and will set it; I will crop off from the top of his young twigs a tender one, and will plant it upon an high mountain and eminent: in the mountain of the height of Israel will I plant it; and it shall bring forth boughs, and bear fruit, and be a goodly cedar: and under it shall dwell all fowl of every wing; in the shadow of the branches thereof shall they dwell." As if the Lord should say, There is a great noise in the world about setting up and plucking down of kings, in this their carnal rule; and many of you see nothing else,—you will look no farther: but I also have my work in hand; my design is not bounded within these limits and outward appearances; I am setting up a King that shall have another manner of dominion and rule than these worms of the earth. He shall stand;—as Mic. v. 4.

The setting up, then, of this kingdom of Christ, who is "the highest branch of the high cedar," and planting it in the church, the "mountain of Israel," with the prosperity thereof, and safety of him that shall dwell therein, is the subject of verses 22, 23. This being *that* to the consideration whereof God here calls his people at such a season, I shall name one or two observations from this connection of the words.

[1] Ps. xlv. 6; Hos. iii. 5; Isa. ix. 7, xvi. 5, xxii. 22; Jer. xxiii. 5; Amos ix. 11; Ezek. xxxiv. 23, 24, xxxvii. 24, 25.

[2] 1 Cor. x. 11; Acts xv. 10; Gal. iii. 4.

Observation 1. *In the midst of all the tumults and embroilments of the nations, that which the Lord takes peculiarly as his own design, into his own management, is the carrying on of the kingdom of the Lord Jesus.*

You are about your work, saith the Lord,—I also am about mine; you have your branches and cedars,—I also have one to plant, that shall flourish. Dan. ii. 44, "In the days of these kings shall the God of heaven set up a kingdom, which shall never be destroyed," &c. Were not those kings and kingdoms also of his setting up, that it is said, In their days he shall set up one of his own? Yea, doubtless; "He changeth the times and the seasons; he removeth kings, and setteth up kings," chap. ii. 21. He "ruleth in the kingdom of men, and giveth it to whomsoever he will," chap. iv. 25. There is not a persecuting Pharaoh, but he raises him up for his own purpose, Exod. ix. 16. But yet, in respect of the kingdom of his Son, he speaks of them as if he had nothing to do with them: In their days I will do my own work,—advance the kingdom of the Lord Christ.

There are great and mighty works in hand in this nation; tyrants are punished,—the jaws of oppressors are broken,—bloody, revengeful persecutors disappointed,—and, we hope, governors set up that may be "just, ruling in the fear of God, that they may be as the light of the morning," etc., 2 Sam. xxiii. 3, 4. The hand of the Lord hath been wonderfully exalted in all these things; but yet, should we rest in them,—should they not be brought into an immediate subserviency to the kingdom of the Lord Jesus,—the Lord will quickly distinguish between them and his own peculiar design, and say, In the days of these changes I will do so and so;—speak of them as if he had nothing to do with them. The carrying on of the interest of Christ is his peculiar aim; he, of his goodness, make it ours also!

Observation 2. *Among all the designs that are on foot in the world, there is none that hath either stability, fixedness, or final success, but only the design of God concerning the kingdom of Christ.*

Other branches may be set, but the branch of the Lord only prospers.[1] The likeliest appearances of other undertakings are but as the glorious rising of the sun in the morning,—quickly clouded. The interest of Christ is like Joseph, Gen. xlix. 23, 24. Ofttimes the archers shoot at it, and grieve it; but in the close the bow thereof abides in strength; and therefore this is the issue of all these dispensations, that the kingdoms and nations are at length to be possessed by the Lord Christ,[2] his sheaf standing up, and all others bowing thereunto.

[1] Hag. ii. 6, 7; Heb. xii. 26, 27; Isa. viii. 9, 10, ix. 7, xlvi. 10, liii. 10; Ps. xxxiii. 11; Prov. xix. 21, xxi. 30; Job xxiii. 13.

[2] Isa. lx. 12, 13; Rev. xi. 15.

And unto the consideration of these things, in the midst of all the tumults in the world, doth God effectually recall his people, and withal tells them how he will carry it on, in the words of my text, "And all the trees," &c.

In the words three things are to be observed,—First, The *work that God ascribes to himself.* And that he sets down under a twofold similitude: of pulling down the "high tree," and setting up the "low tree;" and of drying up the "green tree," and making the "dry tree" to flourish; and both these similitudes are coincident, serving only in this redoubling for the clearer illustration of that which they shadow out. Secondly, There *is the issue that God will carry this out unto in respect of others:* "All the trees of the field shall know." Thirdly, *A particular assurance that the Lord gives for the accomplishment of all this, from the engagement of his name:* "I the LORD," &c.

First, For the first, the expression of the work of the Lord may be taken two ways: 1. *Strictly and properly;* 2. *Largely,* and by the way of analogy and proportion.

1. In the first way you may consider,—

(1.) The tree that is to be cast down and withered, and that is the "high tree," and the "green tree,"—a tree that in their eyes had both beauty and vigour, high and green; this was the Judaical kingdom, admired and delighted in by the Jews. This, says God, I will reject; as also he will many a tall Eliab, that even some Samuels may think to be his anointed.

(2.) The tree that is to be exalted and made to flourish, and that is the "low tree," the "dry tree," contemptible for growth;—it is low, useless for fruit, it is dry. And this is the spiritual kingdom of the Messiah, contemned, despised. This, says God, I will exalt, carry on, and make glorious; for though the interest of Christ and the gospel may seem low and dry for a season, in comparison of the glory of other flourishing interests, yet, in the issue, it shall be exalted above them all.

2. As taken more *largely,* and by the way of analogy; and so,—

(1.) The high and the green tree are the things of the most glorious appearance in the world,—persons and states that seem to be exceedingly suited for the work that God hath to do, that are in the greatest probability to be eminently instrumental in his hand: but, alas! says God, These will I pull down, and cause to wither. Perhaps you will think it strange, that a mighty monarchy, a triumphing prelacy, a thriving conformity, should all be brought down; but so it shall be, "Every mountain shall be made a plain."

(2.) The "low tree," and the "dry tree," are things, persons, assemblies, outwardly weak and contemptible,—such as wise men do verily believe that God will never use; they will not understand that such Moseses shall be deliverers, but cry, Who made them judges and rulers?[1] But even these will God exalt and cause to flourish: "Every valley shall be exalted."

Two observations flow from hence, which I shall insist upon:—

I. *In the carrying on of the interest of Christ and the gospel, God will work wonderful providential alterations.*

II. *The actings of God's providence in carrying on the interest of Christ, shall be exceedingly unsuited to the reasonings and expectations of the most of the sons of men.*

Some trees must be plucked down, and some raised up; yea, high trees thrown down, and the low caused to flourish. There is the issue of God's thus dealing in respect of others, "All the trees of the field," &c. By the "trees of the field" are meant men of all sorts that are concerned in these transactions.

And herein you may observe two things:—something *intimated;* and that is, an unwillingness in men to own these dispensations of God; hence the Lord undertakes himself to set on a conviction upon them, as a thing of great difficulty;—and something *expressed;* which is the conviction itself that shall in the issue fall upon them, notwithstanding all their reluctancy. Hence also are these two observations:—

Observation 1. *Men are exceeding unwilling to see and own the hand of God in those works of his providence which answer not their reasonings, interests, and expectations.*

Observation 2. *The Lord will not cease walking contrary to the carnal reasonings of men, in his mighty works for the carrying on the interest of the Lord Jesus, until his hand be seen, owned, and confessed.*

For what remains concerning the *assurance* of the accomplishment of all this from the engagement of his name, I shall only add, that *the power and faithfulness of God are engaged in the carrying on the things of the kingdom of Christ, to the conviction of the most stubborn opposers.*

I begin with the first,—

I. *In the carrying on the interest of Christ and the gospel, God will work wonderful providential alterations,*—alterations among the trees of the field, nations, states, and men on earth.

When the beginning of the saints' departure from under the dominion of Antichrist was followed with wars, tumults, and destructions, it was objected to Luther, that that doctrine could not be of God which was attended with such desolations: he replied, according to the vigour of his spirit, "Ego nisi tumultus istos viderem, Christum in mundo esse non crederem;"—"Did he not see those tumults, he

[1] Exod. ii. 14; Acts vii. 27.

would not believe that Christ was come forth into the world." The Lord tells you how he will bring on his kingdom, Hag. ii. 6, 7, "I will shake the heavens, and the earth, and the sea, and the dry land; and I will shake all nations, and the Desire of all nations shall come," &c. The "Desire of the nations," is to be brought in by the "shaking of the nations." They are to be civilly moved, that they may be spiritually established. Neither are they only to be shaken, but also to undergo great alterations in their shakings, Heb. xii. 27, "This word, Yet once more, signifies the removing of those things that are shaken, as of things that are made, that those things that cannot be shaken may remain." They must have a removal as well as a shaking;—μετάθεσιν, "a change," a translation. Most nations in their civil constitution lie out of order for the bringing in of the interest of Christ;—they must be shaken up and new disposed of, that all obstacles may be taken away. The day of the gospel is not only terrible in its discovering light, and as it is a trying furnace, Mal. iii. 2, but also in its devouring fury, as it is a consuming oven, chap. iv. 1.

There are three principal seasons of the Lord's eminent appearance to carry on the kingdom of Christ and the gospel, and all attended with dreadful providential alterations: and unto one of these heads may all particular actings be reduced.

1. The first is, the promulgation of the gospel among the Jews by the Lord Christ himself and his apostles. What this was attended withal is graphically described, Matt. xxiv. 6, 7, "And ye shall hear of wars, and rumours of wars; for nation shall rise against nation, and kingdom against kingdom, and there shall be famines, and pestilences, and earthquakes in divers places." And the close of it you have, verse 29, "Immediately after the tribulation of those days shall the sun be darkened, and the moon shall not give her light, and the stars shall fall from heaven, and the powers of heaven shall be shaken." The Judaical state, in all the height and glory of it, was utterly consumed; so that all flesh, all the Jews, were in danger of utter destruction, verse 22; their own historian, himself a Jew, affirming, that from the foundation of the world never was there such destruction and desolation brought upon any nation. Which words of his are a comment on that prediction of our Saviour, Matt. xxiv. 21. And the reason of this eminent desolation you have, Isa. ix. 5, 6.

2. The second is, in the farther carrying on of the gospel, after the destruction of Jerusalem, throughout the world of the Gentiles, subject then in a great proportion to the Roman empire. And what is the issue hereof? The opening of the six seals immediately follows thereon, Rev. vi; which, after manifold and various alterations, end in that dreadful dissolution of the Pagan empire which you have described from verse 14 to the end.

3. The most signal is the coming of the Lord Christ to recover his people from antichristian idolatry and oppression: which, of all others, is, and shall be, attended with the most astonishing alterations and desolations,—pulling down of high trees, and exalting them that are low. Thence is that war described Rev. xvii. 14, and that mighty vengeance poured out by the Lord Christ on the nations, their kings and captains, chap. xix. 11 to the end; which the Holy Ghost describes by a collection of all the most dreadful expressions which are any where used to set out great devastations in the Old Testament.

And this is the head whereunto the present actings of Providence in this nation are to be referred; they all tend to the accomplishment of his main design therein. He that thinks Babylon is confined to Rome and its open idolatry, knows nothing of Babylon, nor of the new Jerusalem. The depth of subtle mystery doth not lie in gross, visible folly. It hath been insinuating itself into all the nations for sixteen hundred years, and to most of them is now become as the marrow in their bones. Before it be wholly shaken out, these heavens must be dissolved, and the earth shaken; their tall trees hewed down, and set a howling, Rev. xviii., and the residue of them transplanted from one end of the earth to another. This, I say, then, is the work that the Lord hath now in hand; and this is a day of thankfulness in reference to what he hath done for us in this nation. I know no better way of praising God for any work, than the finding out of his design therein, and closing with him in it. God hath gone with you, I hope, now to the end of your work; leave him not until he comes to the end of his. He hath compelled you "to go with him one mile" for your own good,—go with him two for his glory. The two tribes and a half sat not down in their own possessions until the whole work of the Lord was done. I speak not with respect to any engagements of war with foreign nations;—what have I to do with things that are above me? You will find work enough for your zeal to the kingdom of Christ at home; and this is the work of thankfulness which you are called unto.

Now, the reasons of this are,—

(1.) Because amongst all men, where the kingdom of Christ is to be set up, there is something or other possessed that he alone must and will have; and, therefore, the Lord giving Jesus Christ but his own inheritance, it must needs be attended with great alterations. I dare say, until of late (whatever now is) there was not any state or nation in the world, where the name of Christ is known, but that there was an intrenchment upon that which is the pure portion and inheritance of the Lord Christ, and that detained with falsehood and force. Yea, such is the folly and blindness of the most of men, that they think their greatest interest lies in holding that fast which Christ will take from them;—Pharaoh-like, that thought it the great advantage of his kingdom not to let the people go, when it proved the ruin of him and his land. This, I dare say, will, in the issue, be the ruin of all or most of the tall trees of Europe; they have grasped much of the power of Christ, and endeavour to impose on the consciences of his in the worship of God, or otherwise oppress them in what he hath purchased for them: and, by a dreadful mistake, they suppose their own interest lies therein; which makes them hold fast until Christ hath shaken them all to pieces, and taken away even that also which was their own. The late king had learned a saying from his predecessor, "No bishop, no king." Hence he supposes his main interest to lie in holding fast Prelacy; whatever he seems to part withal, that he will not let go,—that is his main interest. And what is this Prelacy? A mere antichristian encroachment upon the inheritance of Christ. Christ coming to take his own, shakes the other to pieces. Those who would have been our oppressors in Scotland, but that God hath crushed the cockatrice in the shell, and filled the pit with their dead bodies which they had digged for us,—they also had prepared a Procrustes' bed, a heavy yoke, a beast that, had it grown to perfection, would have had horns and hoofs; and in maintaining this they think their great interest to lie. And in holding this fast, are they, after all their associations, broken in pieces. And this is one cause.

(2.) The works that God hath to do in such a season require it. God hath three great works to do, in the day of his carrying on the interest of Christ and the gospel:—[1.] *He hath great revenges to take;* [2.] *He hath great deliverances to work;* [3.] *He hath great discoveries to make.* I shall but touch on each.

[1.] He *hath great revenges* to take, and that on three sorts of persons.

1*st. On oppressing Babylonians,*—false worshippers and persecutors. Whilst the bride is preparing for the Lord Christ, he goes forth, with the armies of heaven following him, to take vengeance on these his enemies, Rev. xix. 11. These are the Absaloms, the usurpers of his throne,—the Hamans, the forcers of his spouse, the chiefest adversaries of his kingdom.[1] "He shall fill the places with dead bodies" of these; and upon this account "wound the heads over many countries," Ps. cx. 6. The axe is laid to the root of many a tall tree on this score, even in this nation, where he is reckoning for blood and imposition of yokes; and he hath found out men inheriting this spirit from one generation to another.

2*dly. Scoffing Edomites.*—There is a twofold quarrel that God hath with that generation of men;—their rejoicing at Zion's distress, and desiring its increase, Ps. cxxxvii. 7; and their endeavour to destroy

[1] Isa. xliii. 14; Jer. xxv. 12, li. 35; Rev. xvi. 19.

the residue, when at any time straitened, Obad. 14. How many in the late trial rejoiced in the straits of Zion, that sat expecting our destruction, that they might have risen to stand in the cross ways to have cut off them that escaped! Wherewith should they have reconciled themselves to their master, but with the heads of the servants of Christ? God hath vengeance in such a day as this for Edom also.

3dly. Lukewarm Laodiceans,—neutralists, that "drink wine in bowls," and are no way moved at the "suffering of Joseph,"—Gallios, that care for none of these things. There is not a generation in the world with whom the Lord is more provoked than with this Meroz generation. When God is jealous for Zion, he is displeased with them that are at ease, Zech. i. 14, 15. Now, consider how many persons of all these sorts are fixed in the nation, and you will see that vengeance cannot be taken on them without great alterations.

[2.] He *hath deliverances to work.* It is the time of "visiting the prisoners of hope:" the prey must be taken out of the jaws of the terrible,—every "staff of the oppressor broken in pieces;" yea, he delivers his saints, not only from all that they have suffered, but from all that was in the contrivance of their enemies to bring upon them,—which is greater than they can execute; and this will cost something, before the Pharaohs of the nation will let his people go.

[3.] *He hath great trials to make;—1st. Of his own, that they may be purged; 2dly. Of hypocrites, that they way be discovered.*

1*st.* The day of carrying on the interest of Christ is a day of purifying and purging, Dan. xii. 10, "Many shall be purified, and made white, and tried;" that is, a day like a furnace, Mal. iii. 3, that will consume dross and tin. The remainder of the people must be brought through the fire, Zech. xiii. 9. Joshua's garments are defiled by dwelling in Babylon;[1] many of Christ's own have contracted rust and soil, have got carnal interests and engagements, that must be scoured from them.

2*dly.* Of the discovery of hypocrites. It is emphatically said of the saints, that they "follow the Lamb whithersoever he goeth."[2] All sorts of professors will follow him in some paths; in such as are consistent with their power, dominion, and advantages, they are even ready to run before him: but he hath some paths that are unpleasing to flesh and blood,—paths that he gives no loaves in; here men that say they are Jews, and are not, but lie, give quite out from him. Now, upon all these several accounts, must that day of the gospel of necessity be attended with great providential alteration.

Use 1. To discover where dwells that spirit that actuates all the great alterations that have been in these nations. Such things have been brought to pass as have filled the world with amazement;—

[1] Zech. iii. 3. [2] Rev. xiv. 4; John vi. 26.

a monarchy of some hundred years' continuance, always affecting and at length wholly degenerated into tyranny, destroyed, pulled down, swallowed up;—a great and mighty potentate, that had caused "terror in the land of the living," and laid his sword under his head, brought to punishment for blood;—hypocrites and selfish men abundantly discovered, wise men made fools, and the strong as water;—a nation (that of Scotland) engaging for and against the same cause, backward and forward twice or thrice, always seeking where to find their own gain and interest in it, at length totally broken, in opposition to that cause wherewith at first they closed;—multitudes of professors, one year praying, fasting, mightily rejoicing upon the least success, bearing it out as a sign of the presence of God; another year, whilst the same work is carried on, cursing, repining, slighting the marvellous appearance of God in answer unto prayers and most solemn appeals, being very angry at the deliverances of Zion:—on the other side, all the mighty successes that God hath followed poor despised ones withal, being with them as with those in days of old, Heb. xi. 33, "Who through faith subdued kingdoms, wrought righteousness, obtained promises, stopped the mouths of lions, quenched the violence of fire, escaped the edge of the sword, out of weakness were made strong, waxed valiant in fight, turned to flight the armies of the aliens." He, I say, that shall consider all this, may well inquire after that principle which, being regularly carried on, yet meeting with the corruption and lusts of men, should so wheel them about, and work so many mighty alterations. Now, what is this but the most effectual design of the Lord to carry on the interest of Christ and the gospel, whatever stands in the way? This bears down all before it,—wraps up some in blood, some in hardness, and is most eminently straight and holy in all these transactions. Isa. xiv. 32, "What shall one then answer the messengers of the nation? That the LORD hath founded Zion, and the poor of his people shall trust in it."

Use 2. To magnify the goodness of God, who unto us hath sweetened and seasoned all his dreadful dispensations, and all the alterations in those nations, with this his gracious design running through them all: this is that which puts all their beauty and lustre on them, being outwardly dreadful and horrible. The carrying on of this (which is hidden from the men of the world, who have therefore no joy) is the only thing we have to rejoice at in this day; our victories have no glory but what they receive from hence, Isa. iv. 2. That blood which is an acceptable sacrifice to the Lord is the blood of the enemies of this design of his; the vengeance that is to be delighted in is the vengeance of the temple; heaven, and all that is in it, is called to rejoice, when Babylon "is destroyed with violence and fury," Rev. xviii. 21,—when those who would not have the King of saints reign are brought forth and slain before his face: and in this God makes distinguishing work, and calls to rejoicing, Isa. lxv. 13, 14, "Therefore thus saith the Lord God, Behold, my servants shall eat, but ye shall be hungry: behold, my servants shall drink, but ye shall be thirsty: behold, my servants shall rejoice, but ye shall be ashamed: behold, my servants shall sing for joy of heart, but ye shall cry for sorrow of heart, and shall howl for vexation of spirit."

Thus the saints are called to sing "the song of Moses the servant of God, and the song of the Lamb," Rev. xv. 3. The deliverance by Moses was a temporal deliverance from outward yokes and bondage; —the deliverance of the Lamb was a spiritual deliverance from spiritual bondage: the deliverance that God will give his saints from this oppression shall be mixed; as their bondage partakes of both, so shall their deliverance be; and therefore they shall sing the song of Moses and the Lamb. If ever any persons in the world had cause to sing the song of Moses and the Lamb, we have this day. The bondage prepared for us was both in spirituals and temporals;—about a tyrant full of revenge, and a discipline full of persecution, hath been our contest: whether the yoke of the one and the other should by the sword and violence be put upon our necks and consciences, is our controversy. There was both Egypt and Babel in the bondage prepared,—and both these enraged. Pharaoh doubled the task of the Israelites when they did speak of liberty; what would he have done had he recovered them under his hand after they were escaped? What would the thoughts of that man of blood have been, and his ways, had he prevailed, after so many provocations? "Cæde ac sanguine, quisquis ab exilio." And what would their ways have been who thought to sit on his right hand and his left in his kingdom? But of this afterward. Now, God having broken both the one snare and the other, surely we have cause to sing the song of Moses and of the Lamb this day, when others are in the condition mentioned Isa. viii. 21, 22.

It is true, all things are not clear to all perhaps that serve the Lord. Some cannot rejoice in the works of our God; but they are not the first on whom that sin hath been charged. Nothing more frequent in the Scripture than the laying this sin at the door of professors, that they set not their hearts to the work of the Lord. If they are of the armies in heaven, they will at length learn to follow the Lamb; and for the present, music with some discords may make melody for the Lord. The song of Deborah is full of complaint,[1]—divisions of Reuben,—Gilead, Dan, and Asher, slow in their helps,—Meroz wholly neutral:—though we have of all these sorts, yet may we make a song to the Lord, that in Jesus Christ may be acceptable

[1] Isa. xliii. 18; Ps. lxxviii. 42-44; Judges v. 15, 17, 23.

this day. And the Lord, I hope, will open the eyes of them amongst us, and give them to cry for mercy when his righteous judgments have driven them from all their holds. When the mighty army was destroyed in the north about three years ago, many would see nothing in it, but that they had not the blessing of the church. Hence they began to think of it as Balak did of Balaam;—"whom he blessed, they were blessed; and whom he cursed, they were cursed."[1] God could not bear the robbing him of his glory, and giving it unto selfish men. They shall bless, and bless again, and be no more heard than the Baalists' cry:—even to the Lord shall they cry, but he will not regard them: the Lord, I say, will drive them from such holds as these, that they may acknowledge his hand. Let, then, the great work of the Lord be owned, be rejoiced in, for it will certainly bear down all that stand in the way of it: neither is there the least true consolation in any of these alterations, but what arises from a closing with it.

Come we to the second observation.

II. *The actings of God's providence, in carrying on the interest of Christ, are and shall be exceedingly unsuited to the reasonings and expectations of the most of men.*

He hath a glorious work here to be accomplished. Of whom should he now make use? Surely the "high tree," the "green tree" will be employed. If one be to be anointed in the family of Jesse, will it not be goodly Eliab? if the king will honour any, who should it be but I, says Haman? But all on the contrary, the low, dry tree is taken;—David from the flock, and Mordecai from the gate. The thoughts of God are not as our thoughts, neither doth he look on outward appearances.

To give some instances in his most signal actings in this kind.

The Jews knew that God had a great work to do in giving of a Messiah, the Saviour of the world. They are raised up to expectation of it; upon every considerable appearance, they cry, Is this he? And what withal did they expect?—*Outward glory*, beauty, deliverance, carnal power and dominion. God at length comes to do his work, and bringeth forth a poor man, that had not where to lay his head, followed by a few fishermen and simple women,—that had "neither form nor comeliness that he should be desired;" persecuted, despised, crucified from the beginning to the end;—quite another thing than what they looked for.[2] Thus lays he the foundation of the gospel in the person of his Son, by frustrating the expectations of the most of men: "The stone which the builders refused," &c. Again, seeing salvation is of the Jews, the rod of Christ's strength being

[1] Numb. xxii. 6; 1 Kings xviii. 26.

[2] Luke iii. 15; John i. 19, 20; Acts i. 6; Matt. xx. 21, 22, xiii. 55, viii. 19; John iv. 28, 29; Isa. liii. 2, 3; Phil. ii. 7, 8, &c.

to be sent out of Zion, and that living waters were to flow forth from Jerusalem,—the gospel being from thence to be published through the world,—whom should the Lord choose to do it? Surely the great, the wise, the learned of that nation; the high priests, learned scribes, devout Pharisees, that might have won their message some repute and credit in the world.[1] But, contrary to all the wisdom of the flesh, he takes a few ignorant, weak, unlearned fishermen, despised upon all accounts, and commits this great work unto them; and accordingly out they go, friendless, helpless, harbourless, unto their great employment. The like instruments, for the most part, did he employ to make an entrance upon the great work of casting down false worship and idolatry. Moreover, in that great work for the Lord Christ which is to be accomplished in the ruin and destruction of Babel, when it must be done with might, power, and strength, with armies and blood, will not now the Lord use the "high and green tree?" Many kings and potentates having in profession embraced the doctrine of the gospel, nobles and great ones having given up their names in appearance unto Christ,—who but they shall now be used in this work of the Lord? But yet plainly the Lord tells them the contrary, Rev. xviii. 9;—all these persons bewail the judgments of God that are executed on Babel, which shall be done by low, dry trees.

To give one instance in the mighty works which God hath lately wrought in these nations:—A work of reformation and carrying on the interest of Christ is here undertaken. What, upon this, are the thoughts of the most of men? whither were their eyes turned? Tall trees, green trees are pitched on. This and that great lord, popular with the multitude, Eliabs in their eyes, they must do it;—the Scots shall certainly effect it;—the king shall be taken from his evil counsel, he shall be active in it. A church government shall be set up, and no man suffered to live in the nation that will not submit unto it. Some, like the sons of Zebedee, shall sit on the right and left hand of Christ, in the kingdom they were setting up for him;—these and those, sound good men, shall be next the king: then all will be great and glorious indeed. What now, I pray? Do all things indeed suit and answer these expectations and reasonings of men? doth God accomplish the thoughts of their hearts? Alas! the high trees rested on proved, for the most part, broken reeds, that ran into our hands, and let out our blood in abundance to no purpose;—the top bough, hoped for, fallen as an abominable branch;—the Scots shaken and broken with unparalleled destruction, in the maintenance of the interest and cause which at first they prosperously opposed;—the iron yoke, pretended to be that of Christ (though it be fleshly, carnal, and cruel,

[1] John iv. 22; Ps. cx. 2; Ezek. xlvii. 1; Zech. xiv. 8; Acts iv. 13; 1 Cor. i. 20, 26–28.

suited to the wisdom of a man, and his rule be spiritual, meek, and gentle), cast off and thrown away:—low trees, dry trees, despised ones, contemned ones, without form or comeliness, exalted, used, employed, and the hand of the Lord evidently lifted up in all these transactions.

Some reasons of this may be given, and,—

1. The first is taken from the *corruptions of the hearts* of men squaring the works of God to their fleshly reasonings, corrupt interests and principles. They are bold with the wisdom of God, and conclude thus and thus things ought to be,—ordering their thoughts for the most part according to their corrupt and carnal advantages. I shall instance both as to carnal advantages and principles.

(1.) *Carnal power and glory* seem excellent to the Jews: hence think they, When God gives us our Messiah, all this must be accomplished. Their affections are disordered by corrupt lusts and desires, and that enslaves their minds to strange apprehensions:—God comes in his own way, and how cross do things run to their expectations. What was the corrupt design of many in Scotland? That they might set up a son of Tabeal in England, and themselves be great under him; that they and their partakers might impose on the residue of the nation, especially in the things of God. Their great desire that things should be thus, corrupts their minds to think that it ought to be so, and shall be so. Hence ambition to rule and to have all under their power, even in conscience, is quickly mistaken for zeal to the kingdom of Christ,—re-enthroning of tyranny is loyalty; and all according to covenant. As if men had sworn to be good to themselves, and to be true to their own interests all their days; which surely few need to be sworn to. Thus men's minds and judgments are distempered by their lusts and interests, which makes them frame a way for God to proceed in; which, when he doth not, how are they surprised!

(2.) *For principles.* Men take up principles that they will adhere unto:—wise principles, forsooth, yea, and very righteous too! All things whatever that fall out must be squared unto their principles. They expect that nothing must be done but what suits unto them; and if any thing contrary be wrought, even of God himself, how deceived, how disappointed are they! The most tremendous judgment of God in this world is the hardening of the hearts of men;—this seals them up for the most part to destruction:—a thing it is often mentioned in the Scripture, and many subtle disputes there are, how it should come forth from Him who is most holy, seeing it is the greatest sin of the creature.

I shall give you my thoughts, in a most eminent instance or two, as to one particular of it. Look on Pharaoh, of whom it is most signally spoken, that God "hardened his heart." How did the Lord accomplish this? Pharaoh settles himself upon as righteous principles as ever any of the sons of men could do: one is, "That it belongs to the chief ruler of a nation to see to the profit and glory of the nation." What more righteous principle is there in the world? You that talk of your principles, give me one more righteous than this. Hence he concludes, that if it be incumbent on him to see that the realm receive no detriment, he must not let the people go by whom they received so many great advantages. God confirms his heart in these principles, *which are good in themselves*, but abominable when taken up against the mind and providence of God. Hence he and his perished in their principles, acting against the appearance of God. It is also said of Sihon, the king of the Amorites, that "his heart was hardened that he would not let the people go through his land." How, I pray? Even by adhering to that wise principle, "That it is not meet to let a potent enemy into the bowels of a people." And this made way for his ruin.

Thus is it with many; they fix on principles, good in general, and in their season. Old bounds must not be broken up;—order must not be disturbed:—let God appear never so eminently, so mightily, they will keep to their principles. What is this but judicial hardness? And this, I say, is one reason why the actings of God in such a day as this are so unsuited to the expectations of men;—they square his work to the interests and principles which it will not answer.

2. God chooseth thus to do things above and beside the expectations of men, that his *presence* and the *presence* of the Lord Christ may be the more conspicuous in the world. Did the Lord always walk in paths that men had rationally—that is, foolishly (for such is our wisdom in the ways of God)—allotted to him, the appearances of his glory would be exceedingly eclipsed. It is hard for men to have a clear and naked view of the power of God[1] in effecting any thing, when there is great help of means to do it; but it is much harder to discern the wisdom of God in an affair, when men's own wisdom and designing is all accomplished. But now, when the way of God is "like the way of an eagle in the air,"—when "his paths are in the deep, and his footsteps are not known,"—then is he glorious in his goings. Men think all things would be very glorious, if they might be done according to their mind: perhaps, indeed, they would;—but with their glory, not the glory of God.

3. God will do it for the hardening of many false, empty professors and others in the world, that the judgments appointed may come upon them to the uttermost.[2] The hardening of men to their de-

[1] Judges vii. 4.

[2] Rom. ix. 18; Deut. ii. 30; Ps. lxxxi. 12, lxix. 22; Josh. xi. 20; Isa. vi. 9–12; John xii. 40–43; Deut. xxxii. 15.

struction, being a close and inward work, is one of the most eminent acts of the providence of God in governing the world:—by this he accomplisheth most of the judgments that he hath threatened. Now, there is not any dispensation of God towards man but he can, and doth sometimes, cause it to be so managed and ordered, that it shall be a way and means of hardening such as he hath appointed thereunto:—some are hardened by the word, some by mercies, some by judgments. Amongst other ways that he useth for this purpose, this is one,—the disposal of the works of his providence contrary to the reasonings of men,—doing things unlikely and unfitly in the eyes of flesh and blood, that so they may despise those ways of his, and be broken in opposition unto them. Take an instance in Pharaoh's last hardening for destruction: When he brought the people out of Egypt, he did not lead them the direct way to Canaan, but carries them into the wilderness, and shuts them up between the mountains and the sea. Pharaoh justly concludes that they are entangled beyond escape, and that he shall surely overtake them and destroy them. This draws him out to his ruin. Had God led them in the straight path, probably he had not pursued after them; but the Lord lays this as a plot for his destruction. God will harden Jeroboam, and therefore a lion shall slay the prophet that preached against his idolatry. So was it with the Jews. They expect all glory to attend the coming of the Messiah; and after the coming of him indeed, God follows them with judgments to a total desolation;—which being so unsuited unto the dispensation they expected, hardness thereby is come upon them to the uttermost. Tertullian says, he dares say that "the Scriptures were on purpose framed in many things to give occasion to proud and curious unhumbled wits to stumble and fall." And I dare say that the Lord doth order many of his works in the world in "ways past finding out," on purpose to give occasion to many to stumble and fall. God fulfilleth many mighty works, that could not otherwise be brought about, by hardening the hearts of men. The hardening of the late king's heart was an engine whereby he wrought mighty things and alterations. Had not God laid obdurateness and stubbornness upon his spirit, we had long since, in all probability, been ruined. To accomplish this end, then, God will so order the works of his providence, that men shall reason themselves into unreasonable and brutish hardness and stupidity. Thus God hath done in the days wherein we live. His mighty acts that he hath wrought, both for the matter of the things done and the manner of their doing, have been so contrary to men's principles, interest, expectations, and reasons, that they have slighted them to such a degree of hardening that they seem to have no reason left at all;—and when it comes to that, God will fall judicially upon the very faculties of their souls; he will blind their eyes, deprive them of their judgment and insight into things, that they shall be as incapable of [understanding] God's mind as fools; and give them up to vile affections, to do the things that are not seemly;—as it hath fallen out with too many amongst us.

Let us now make some use of this point.

Use. It serves, then, to discover the vanity of those men who, because the works of God have not been carried on in ways *suitable to their reasonings and expectations,* do utterly reject them, disown them, and oppose him in them. Can these men give any one instance of any one eminent work of God that he hath brought about by such ways and means as men would rationally allot thereunto, especially in things that are in immediate subserviency to the kingdom of the Lord Christ? Can they instance that they have been so managed? nay, hath not this been a means to harden multitudes to their destruction that have limited the Holy One, and chalked out paths for him to walk in? I cannot but fear that it was a great provocation of the eyes of God's glory, that at the beginning, and in the carrying on of the great alterations that have been wrought by his providence among us, we did speak of confirming and continuing, under any condition whatsoever, any things or persons which it was in his design to evert:—we must be promising to keep up the high tree, and to keep down the low tree; which was not at all in his thoughts, neither ever came it into his heart. I hope he hath taught us (though with thorns) to follow him sometimes, like Abraham, not knowing whither we go. Now, the Lord convince them who are yet under this darkness;—that think the ways of God not equal, because not measured by their line;—that bring their crooked rules unto that which is really straight, and cast it away as abominable. The children of Israel had got a proverb against the ways of God;[1] it was so taken for granted that the ways of his providence were not right and straight, that it was grown into a common by-word. A little discovery of the pride and hypocrisy of their own hearts undeceived them at last.

I shall not say to our brethren that they have showed this day, that if Absalom had lived, and all we had been slain, it would have been well-pleasing to them; but this I shall say, that it is a sad sign that our ways please not God, when his ways please not us at all.

There being not space for handling the two remaining propositions contained in the text, I shall go forth to one general use, and so conclude.

Use. Now, this I shall take from that of the prophet Amos, chap. iv. 12;—the generality of the people being exercised with various judgments, the residue of them are said to be saved "as a firebrand

[1] Ezek. xviii. 2.

out of the burning;" that is, powerfully, effectually, from a very terrible and a very near destruction. After all the Lord's great dispensation of providence, in carrying on his own design, this being the condition of the people of this nation, many being destroyed by foregoing judgments, and the residue now saved like a firebrand out of the burning, God having given us this issue of his mighty works in pulling down the high tree, and exalting the low tree, it cannot but be our wisdom to close with the counsel which God gives in such a condition; and that you have, I say, Amos iv. 12, "Because I will do this unto thee, prepare to meet thy God, O Israel." Seeing that all this is done, prepare to meet thy God, O England: prepare to meet thy God, O parliament: prepare to meet thy God, O army.

To lead you a little towards the performance of this duty, it being that, and that alone, which is incumbent on you, I shall show you these two things:—1. *What it is wherein we are to meet our God.* 2. *How we must meet him therein.*

1. For the first, there are three ways wherein we must meet the Lord, if we desire to answer his mind in any of these dispensations:—(1.) *In the way of his providence;* (2.) *In the way of his worship;* (3.) *In the way of his holiness.*

(1.) The *eminent ways of the providence* of God in these days may be referred unto three heads.

[1.] *His general design, to pull down all those high oppositions to the kingdom of his Son which I have mentioned.*

[2.] *His peculiar aim, to stain the glory of all flesh, to pull down high trees, that no flesh may glory.*

[3.] *His shaking of all endearments and enjoyments here below, that the hearts of his may be fixed only on the things that cannot be shaken.*

And these, upon all accounts and considerations whatever, appear to be the main tendencies of the actings of providence in these our days.

(2.) There is the *way of his worship;* wherein also he will be met. It is most remote from my thoughts to enter into contests concerning that peculiar way of gospel worship which Christ hath appointed. It sufficeth me, that seeing God hath promised that in these days he will have his tabernacle with men, and that barrenness and drought shall be on every soul that comes not up to his feast of tabernacles, it is bottom sufficient to press men to meet him in that way, according as he shall graciously make out light unto them.

(3.) *There is the way of his holiness.* As he is holy, so are all his ways holy,—so he will be met and walked with in all ways of holiness and obedience to Jesus Christ. And these are the ways wherein God will be met by his remnant, his delivered remnant.

2. What, then, is it *to meet* the Lord in any of these ways? what is it to meet him in the way of his providence, his worship, his holiness? To meet one in any thing, is to close with him in that thing: —we say, Herein I meet you, when we are of one mind. To meet the Lord in these things, is to close with the will and mind of God in them. This is that which I would exhort you unto, yea, lay the charge of God upon you this day, even on you and your companions, who are as a brand snatched out of the burning,—

(1.) To meet God in the way of his providence.

[1.] Meet him in his general design of casting down all combined opposition to the kingdom of his Son; that God in his appointed time will bring forth the kingdom of the Lord Christ unto more glory and power than in former days, I presume you are persuaded. Whatever will be more, these six things are clearly promised:—

1*st*. *Fulness of peace* unto the gospel and the professors thereof, Isa. xi. 6, 7, liv. 13, xxxiii. 20, 21; Rev. xxi. 25.

2*dly*. *Purity and beauty of ordinances* and gospel worship, Rev. xi. 2, xxi. 3. The tabernacle was wholly made by appointment, Mal. iii. 3, 4; Zech. xiv. 16; Rev. xxi. 27; Zech. xiv. 20; Isa. xxxv. 8.

3*dly*. *Multitudes of converts*, many persons, yea, nations, Isa. lx. 7, 8, lxvi. 8, xlix. 18–22; Rev. vii. 9.

4*thly*. *The full casting out and rejecting of all will-worship*, and their attendant abominations, Rev. xi. 2.

5*thly*. *Professed subjection of the nations* throughout the whole world unto the Lord Christ, Dan. ii. 44, vii. 26, 27; Isa. lx. 6–9;—the kingdoms become the kingdoms of our Lord and his Christ, [Rev. xi. 15,] amongst whom his appearance shall be so glorious, that David himself shall be said to reign.

6*thly*. *A most glorious and dreadful breaking of all that rise in opposition unto him*, Isa. lx. 12,—never such desolations, Rev. xvi. 17–19.

Now, in order to the bringing in of this his rule and kingdom, with its attendances, the Lord Christ goes forth, in the first place, to cast down the things that stand in his way, dashing his enemies "in pieces like a potter's vessel." This is a part of the design of Providence, wherein we are to meet him in these days.

I shall speak a word,—(1*st*.) Unto them who are enabled to look through the clouds and darkness whereby his paths are encompassed; (2*dly*.) Unto them who cannot.

(1*st*.) For the former, be you persuaded to meet the Lord in this his design,—yet to continue steadfast in helping him against the mighty. I speak not only to you who are in authority, nor unto you to whom the sword is girded, but unto all that wish well to Zion. We have every one our mite that we may cast into this treasury: we may be all princes in this case, all Israels,—prevailers with God and men. There be three things whereby even you, who are but as the number, the common soldiers of Christ, may meet the Lord in this design.

[1*st.*] *By faith.* Believe the promises, close with them, act faith upon them, and you will believe the beast unto destruction, antichrist into the pit, and Magog to ruin. Believe that[1] the enemies of Christ shall be made his footstool, that the nations shall be his inheritance, that he shall reign gloriously in beauty, that he shall smite in pieces the heads over divers nations;—live in the faith of these things, and as it will give you the sweetness of them before they come, so it will hasten their coming beyond the endeavours of thousands, yea, millions of armed men.

[2*dly.*] *Meet him with your supplications.* Cry unto him, as Ps. xlv. 3–5, "Gird thy sword upon thy thigh, O most Mighty, with thy glory and thy majesty. And in thy majesty ride prosperously, because of truth, and meekness, and righteousness; and thy right hand shall teach thee terrible things. Thine arrows are sharp in the heart of the King's enemies; whereby the people fall under thee." This will make you be the armies of heaven, that follow him in his great undertakings, Rev. xix. 14. It is his praying people that are his conquering armies that follow him. Now you find it coming, leave not pulling with all your strength, lest it roll back again. Shoot not two or three arrows, and so give over; but never leave shooting until the enemies of the Lord be all destroyed. Seeing it is his gospel whose advancement the Lord Jesus aimeth at in all these dispensations, and whose quarrel alone he revengeth (whatever men may do), help on to the advancement of that gospel of his; which, as formerly it was oppressed by the height and tyranny of the tower of Babel, so for the present is exceedingly defiled and cumbered by the rubbish of it being in some measure cast down.

[3*dly.*] Whereas in these dispensations it is most eminently and frequently, in the praise of Christ, said that he is just and righteous in all his ways,—as you may see in all the acclamations of the saints upon the execution of his judgments on his enemies ("Just and righteous art thou"); which is signally done on this account, because the ways whereby he doth it are counted most unrighteous in the world,—in this, then, also is he to be met, *even in the administration of justice and judgment:* you will otherwise certainly be found in a cross path unto him, and be borne down before him. This is that wisdom which he calls for among the judges of the earth, when he is set to reign on his holy hill, Ps. ii. 10, 11.

(2*dly.*) I shall add one word or two unto them who, either from the darkness of the things themselves, or from the prejudices and

[1] Ps. cx. 1, 4, ii. 7, 8; Micah v. 3, 4; Isa. lx. 12.

temptations of their own spirits, are not able to discern the righteousness of the ways of God, but rather lift up themselves against him.

First, then, Consider the constant *appearing of God* against every party that, under any colour or pretence whatever, have lifted up themselves for the reinforcement of things as in former days:—what colour or pretence soever they have put on, or which way soever they have turned themselves, God hath still appeared against them. Can you not discern his leavening their counsels with folly and madness, weakening their hearts and hands,—making the strong become as tow, and the successful a reproach? Though they have gone from mountain to mountain to seek for divination, and changed their pretences as often as Laban did Jacob's wages, yet they find neither fraud nor enchantment that will prevail: and doth not this proclaim that the design which God had in hand is as yet marvellously above you?

Secondly, Consider the constant *answer of prayers* which those which have waited on God in these dispensations, to their unspeakable consolation, have received,—finding God to be nigh unto them in all that they call upon him for. If in this thing they regarded iniquity in their hearts, surely God would not have heard them. Others also cry, even to the Lord do they cry; but he will not bear witness to the abomination of their hearts. Oh, that upon these and the like considerations you would at last take the counsel of the psalmist, Ps. xlvi. 10, Be still, and know that he is God. Be silent before him, for he is risen out of his holy habitation. Say, God hath done great things for these; who hath hardened himself against him and prospered? And this is the first particular.

[2.] The second design of Providence in these dispensations, is evidently *to stain the glory of all flesh;* so Isa. xxiii. 9. Never did the Lord any work more eminently. What sort of men is there amongst us whose glory God hath not stained? I had rather leave this unto a silent thought, than give you particular instances of it; otherwise, it were very easy to make it as clear as the sun, that God hath left neither self-honour nor glory to any of the sons of men. Meet him, then, in this also:—

1*st*, Cease putting *confidence* in man; say, He is a worm, and the son of man is but a worm; his breath is in his nostrils, and wherein is he to be accounted of? This use doth the church make of mercies, Ps. xx. 6, 7, "Some trust in horses, and some in chariots; but we will remember the name of the LORD:" we will not trust in parliaments or armies. "All flesh is grass," Isa. xl; let it have its withering time, and away. See no wisdom, but the wisdom of God,—no strength, but the strength of God,—no glory but his.

2*dly*, Have any of us any glory, any *crowns*, any gifts, any graces, any wisdom or valour, any useful endowments?—let us cast them all down at the feet of Jesus Christ. If we look on them, if we keep them as our own, God withers all their beauty and their glory. Thus do the elders who worship the Lamb for ever, Rev. iv. 10, 11, say to him, Lord Jesus, thine is the glory,—thine are all the mighty works which have been wrought in our days;—thine are all the means whereby they have been accomplished:—we are nothing, we can do nothing; thou art all, and in all. And this is the second.

[3.] He aims at the *shaking* of all these things here below. He is taking down the rate and price of all things here below; on that which was worth a thousand pounds, he takes his bill and writes down scarce the thousandth part. He hath laid his hand upon the nests of the nation, and hath fitted wings unto all their treasures, and so eminently written vanity and uncertainty on them all as must needs lessen their esteem, were not men blinded by the god of this world. In this also are we to meet the Lord,—

1*st.* By getting a *low esteem* of the things that God is thus shaking, and that upon this account, that he shakes them for this very end and purpose, that we should find neither rest nor peace in them. Perhaps thou hast had a desire to be somebody in the world;—thou seest thyself come short of what thou aimest at; say now, with Mephibosheth upon the return of David, Not only half, but let all go, seeing that the Lord Jesus shall reign with glory. A man may sometimes beat a servant for the instruction of his son; God hath shaken the enjoyments of his enemies to lead his friends to disesteem them. God forbid the quite contrary should be found upon any of us.

2*dly.* By labouring to find all riches and treasures in the Lord Christ. The earth staggers like a drunken man;—the princes of it are reduced to a morsel of bread;—all that is seen is of no value: doth not God direct us to the hidden paths,—to the treasures that cannot be destroyed? Many say, "Who will show us any good? Lord, lift thou up the light of thy countenance upon us."

(2.) We are to meet the Lord in the *way of his ordinances*,—in the way of gospel worship. The exalting of the Lord Christ herein is the issue of all the mighty works of God: this is given in as the end of all, Rev. xxi. 3, "The tabernacle of God," &c. After great shakings, the promise still is of a new heaven and earth, Isa. lxv. 17; Rev. xxi. 1; and this is that the people of God put themselves upon in the days wherein Babylon is to be destroyed, Jer. i. 4–8; that is the work they then take in hand. The end of all is the building of the temple, Ezek. xlvii.; and this is the conclusion that the people of God do make, Isa. ii. 3, 4; and if this be neglected, the Lord will say of us, as David of Nabal, "Surely in vain have I kept these men, and all that they have." To meet the Lord in this also,—

[1.] *Inquire diligently into his mind and will*, that you may know his paths, and be acquainted with his statutes. I dare say, no temptation in the world presses with more colour and violence upon men under mercies, than that [temptation] to a neglect of walking and holding communion with God in his ordinances. The devil thinks thus to revenge himself of the Lord Jesus;—his own yoke being broken, he thinks to prevail to the casting away of his. Christ hath a yoke, though it be gentle and easy.

[2.] You that do *enjoy holy ordinances*, labour to have holy hearts answerable thereunto. You have heavenly institutions, labour to have heavenly conversations. If we be like the world in our *walking*, it is no great *matter* if we be like the world in our *worship*. It is sad, walking contrary to God in his own paths. Show out the power and efficacy of all gospel institutions in a frame of spirit, course of life, and equability of spiritual temper, all your days.

[3.] Keep up the power of *private worship*, both personal and family. I have seen many good laws for the Sabbath, and hope I shall see some good examples! Look what the roots are in the family; such will the fruit be in the church and commonwealth. If your spirits are not well manured there, you will be utterly barren elsewhere. That is done most clearly to God which is done within doors.

(3.) *Meet him in the way of his holiness.* In the cry of the saints unto the Lord for the execution of his judgments and vengeance, they in an especial manner invocate his holiness, Rev. vi. 10, "How long, O Lord, holy and true, dost thou not judge and avenge our blood on them that dwell on the earth?" And in their rendering praises to him, they still make mention of his holiness and righteousness in all his ways. Though the ways of God are commonly traduced as unequal and unholy ways, yet in the close there is no property of his that he will more vindicate in all his works than that of his holiness; in this, then, we are also to meet the Lord in this day of our deliverance,—the day wherein he hath wrought such great and wonderful alterations.

This use the Holy Ghost maketh upon such like dispensations, 2 Pet. iii. 11, "Seeing that all these things," &c.; and so also, Heb. xii. 27, 28, "And this word, Yet once more, signifieth the removing of those things that are shaken, as of things that are made, that those things which cannot be shaken may remain. Wherefore, we receiving a kingdom which cannot be moved, let us have grace, whereby we may serve God acceptably with reverence and godly fear." All things opposing removed, a freedom established,—therefore let us have grace. God is the thrice holy one,—holy in his nature, holy in his word, and holy in all his works; and he requires that his people be a holy people. To this he still urged his ancient people, from the argument of his presence amongst them. Oh, that the Spirit of the Lord would bring forth this one fruit of all his dealing with us, that we might be a holy people! If we put God's pure and clean mercies into impure and unclean vessels, they will to us be defiled. Let us take heed of prostituting the mighty works of God to the service of our lusts. Should we now make such conclusions to ourselves as the rich fool in the gospel, and say, Well, we have now peace and prosperity laid up for some years;—soul, take thy ease, eat, drink, and be merry; grow rich and great; follow after vanity, pride, folly, uncleanness; enjoy with delight the things which we have, and heap up thereto:—why, as this is to labour to draw the Lord God into a partnership with our abominations, and to enforce his mighty works to bear witness to our lusts, so certainly it is such a frame as he will surely and speedily revenge. The end why God delivers us from all our enemies is, not that we may serve our lusts and ourselves without fear; but that we may serve him without fear, in righteousness and holiness, all the days of our lives. Let, then, this be the issue upon our hearts of all the victories, and successes, and returns of prayers that we have received,—that we give up ourselves to the Lord in all manner of holiness: this is that which the Lord's voice calls us unto. Let not now him that is filthy be filthy still; let not him that is worldly be worldly still; let not him that is loose, and hath cast off the yoke of Christ, be so still; let not him that hath sought himself do so still; let not him who hath contemned the institutions of Christ do so still; let not him that hath been lifted up above his brethren be so still;—but let every one forsake his evil way, and the iniquity that is in his hand, that we who were not a people at all may be a people to the praise of the God of all; that you who rule over men may be just, ruling in the fear of the Lord, that you may be as the light of the morning when the sun is risen, even as a morning without clouds, as the tender grass springing out of the earth by clear shining after rain;—that we who are under rule may sit under our vines and fig-trees, speaking well of the name of God, and labouring to carry on the kingdom of the Prince of Peace, even every one as we are called, and abiding therein with God;—that as, when you sought this mercy of God which we rejoice in, in solemn humbling of yourselves before the Lord, I made it appear unto you that it was the remnant of Jacob, God's secret and holy ones, lying in the bowels of the nation, that must be the rise of all our deliverances, so we would now every one strive to be of that number,—for they alone enjoy the sweetness of this and every mercy.

SERMON VIII.

THE LABOURING SAINT'S DISMISSION TO REST:

A SERMON PREACHED AT

THE FUNERAL OF THE RIGHT HON. HENRY IRETON,

LORD-DEPUTY OF IRELAND.

PREFATORY NOTE.

This sermon on the death of Ireton, though printed, as we are told in the dedication, from the first notes which the author took, contains some beautiful and interesting thoughts, and is pervaded by a strain of peculiar tenderness and solemnity. Henry Ireton was the eldest son of German Ireton of Attenton, Nottinghamshire. He was born in 1610; entered Trinity College, Oxford, in 1626; and having graduated as bachelor of arts, devoted himself to the study of law at the Middle Temple. He entered the parliamentary army when the civil war commenced, and gave proof of singular courage and capacity. In 1646 he married Bridget, the eldest daughter of Cromwell; and by the powerful interest which he thus secured, as well as his own abilities, he obtained rapid promotion in the army. At the battle of Naseby he commanded the left wing of the parliamentary army, and was defeated by the impetuous charge of Prince Rupert. Led in the ardour of the struggle beyond his own rank, he was himself wounded and taken prisoner, but contrived soon afterwards to make his escape. It was at his suggestion that the secret council of officers was held, to consider what course should be taken in disposing of the king's person. He was one of the judges on the king's trial, and signed the warrant for his execution. In 1649 he was second in command to Cromwell in Ireland, was made president of Munster, and afterwards was left as lord deputy when Cromwell returned to England. In the midst of a successful career, he was seized, after having taken Limerick, with an inflammatory fever, on the 16th of November, and died on the 26th, 1651. His memory was honoured by a public funeral, and his remains were interred in Henry the Seventh's Chapel in Westminster Abbey. His widow and his children, consisting of one son (Henry) and four daughters, had a grant of £2000 settled on them by Parliament out of the confiscated estates of the Duke of Buckingham. After the Restoration, his body was disinterred, gibbeted along with that of Cromwell, and buried at Tyburn.

Various testimonies might be adduced in proof of the high esteem in which he was held by his party. Burnet affirms, that "he had the principles and temper of a Cassius;"—Hume, that "he was a memorable personage, much celebrated for his vigilance and capacity;"—Noble ("Memoir of the Cromwell Family," vol. ii. p. 298), that "he was the most artful, dark, deliberate man of all the Republicans, by whom he was much beloved;"—Heath ("Flagellum," p. 124), that "he was absolutely the best prayer-maker and preacher in the army; for which he may thank his education at Oxford;"—Ludlow ("Memoir," vol. i. p. 33), that "he erected for himself a more glorious monument in the hearts of good men, by his affection to his country, his abilities of mind, his impartial justice, his diligence in the public service, and his other virtues; which were a far greater honour to his memory than a dormitory among the ashes of kings;"—and Carlyle ("Cromwell's Letters and Speeches," vol. ii. p. 167) thus closes a reference to his death,—"One brave and subtle-working brain has ended; to the regret of all the brave. A man, able with his pen and his sword; 'very stiff in his ways.'"—Ed.

TO

THE HONOURABLE AND MY VERY WORTHY FRIEND,

COLONEL HENRY CROMWELL.

SIR,

THE ensuing sermon was preached upon as sad an occasion as on any particular account hath been given to this nation in this our generation. It is now published, as at the desire of very many who love the savour of that perfume which is diffused with the memory of the noble person peculiarly mentioned therein, so also upon the requests of such others as enables me justly to entitle the doing of it, *obedience*. Being come abroad, it was in my thoughts to have directed it immediately, in the first place, to her who, of *any individual person*, was most nearly concerned in him. But having observed how near she hath been to be swallowed up of sorrow, and what slow progress *He* who took care to seal up instruction to her soul by all dispensations, hath given her hitherto towards a conquest thereof, I was not willing to offer directly a new occasion unto the multitude of her perplexed thoughts about this thing. No doubt, her loss being as great as it could be, upon the account of one subject to the law of mortality, as many grains of grief and sorrow are to be allowed her in the balance of the sanctuary as God doth permit to be laid out and dispended about any of the sons of men. He who is able to make sweet the bitterest waters, and to give a gracious issue to the most grievous trial, will certainly, in due time, eminently bring forth that good upon her spirit which he is causing all these things to work together for. In the meantime, sir, these lines are to you: your near relation to that rare example of righteousness, faith, holiness, zeal, courage, self-denial, love to his country, wisdom, and industry, mentioned in the ensuing sermon;—the mutual tender affection between you whilst he was living;—your presence with him in his last trial and conflict;—the deserved regard you bear to his worth and memory;—your design of looking into and following after his steps and purpose in the work of God in his generation, as such an accomplished pattern as few ages have produced the like,—with many other reasons of the like nature, did easily induce me hereunto. That which is here printed is but the notes which I first took, not having had leisure since to give them a serious perusal; and upon that account must beg a candid interpretation unto any thing that may appear not so well digested therein as might be expected. I have not any thing to express concerning yourself, but only my desire that your heart may be fixed to the Lord God of your fathers; and that, in the midst of all your temptations and oppositions wherewith your pilgrimage will be attended, you may be carried on and established in your inward subjection unto, and outward contending for, the kingdom of the Dearly Beloved of our souls, not fainting or waxing weary until you receive your dismission to rest for your lot in the end of the days.

SIR,

Your most humble and affectionate Servant,

J. OWEN.

OXON, CHR. CH., *April* 2.

SERMON VIII.

THE LABOURING SAINT'S DISMISSION TO REST.

"But go thou thy way till the end be: for thou shalt rest, and stand in thy lot at the end of the days."—DAN. xii. 13.

THE words of my text having no dependence (as to their sense and meaning, but only as to the occasion of them) on the verses foregoing, I shall not at all look backward into the chapter, but fall immediately upon them, that I be not hindered from my principal intendment;—being unwilling to detain you long, though willing to speak a word from the Lord to such a congregation, gathered together by such an eminent act of the providence of God.

The words are the Lord's dismission given to a most eminent servant, from a most eminent employment, wherein these four things are observable:—

First, The *dismission* itself in the first words: "Go thou thy ways."

Secondly, The *term* allotted for his continuance under that dismission: "Until the end be."

Thirdly, His *state* and condition under that dismission: "For thou shalt rest."

Fourthly, The utmost *issue* of all this dispensation, both as to his foregoing labour, his dismission, and rest following: "Stand in thy lot at the end of the days."

I. In the first I shall consider two things:—1. The *person dismissed:* "Thou;" 2. The *dismission* itself: "Go thou thy ways."

1. The person dismissed is Daniel, the writer of this prophecy, who received all the great visions of God mentioned therein; and I desire to observe concerning him, as to our purpose in hand, two things:—(1.) His *qualifications;* (2.) His *employment.*

(1.) For the first, I shall only name some of them that were most eminent in him, and they are three:—[1.] Wisdom; [2.] Love to his people; [3.] Uprightness and righteousness in the discharge of that high place whereunto he was advanced.

[1.] For the *first,* the Holy Ghost beareth ample testimony thereunto, Dan. i. 17, 20, "As for these four children, God gave them knowledge and skill in all learning and wisdom: and Daniel had understanding in all visions and dreams. And in all matters of wisdom and understanding, that the king inquired of them, he found them ten times better than all the magicians and astrologers that were in all his realm." In all matters of wisdom and understanding, none in the whole Babylonian empire, full of wise men and artists, were to be compared unto Daniel and his companions; and Ezekiel, chap. xxviii. 3, rebuking the pride and arrogancy of Tyrus, with a bitter scorn he says, "Behold, thou art wiser than Daniel," or thou thinkest thyself so,—intimating that none in wisdom was to be compared unto him.

[2.] *Love to his people.* On this account was his most diligent inquiry into the time of their deliverance, and his earnest contending with God, upon the discovery of the season when it was to be accomplished, chap. ix. 1–4. Hence he is reckoned amongst them who in their generation stood in the gap in the behalf of others,—"Noah, Daniel, and Job." Hence God calls the people of the Jews, his people, chap. ix. 24, "Seventy weeks are determined on thy people;" —the people of thy affections and desires, the people of whom thou art, and who are so dear unto thee.

[3.] For his *righteousness* in discharging of his trust and office, you have the joint testimony of God and man:—his high place and preferment you have, chap. vi. 2. He was the first of the three presidents who were set over the hundred and twenty other princes of the provinces; and the Holy Ghost tells you, that, in the discharge of this high trust and great employment, he was faithful to the utmost, verse 4, "Then the presidents and princes sought to find occasion against Daniel concerning the kingdom; but they could find none occasion nor fault; forasmuch as he was faithful, neither was there any error or fault found in him." Which also his enemies confessed, verse 5, "Then said these men, We shall not find any occasion against this Daniel, except we find it against him concerning the law of his God."

These qualifications, I say, amongst others, were most eminent in this person who here received his dismission from his employment.

(2.) There is his *employment* itself, from which he is dismissed; and herein I shall observe these two things:—[1.] The *nature* of the employment itself; [2.] *Some considerable circumstances* of it.

[1.] For the first, it consisted in receiving from God, and holding out to others, clear and express visions concerning God's wonderful providential alterations in kingdoms and nations, which were to be accomplished from the days wherein he lived to the end of the world. All the prophets together had not so many clear discoveries as this one Daniel concerning these things.

[2.] For the latter, this is observable, that all his visions still close with some eminent exaltation of the kingdom of Christ;—that is the centre where all the lines of his visions do meet, as is to be seen in the close almost of every chapter; and this was the great intendment of the Spirit in all those glorious revelations unto Daniel, to manifest the subserviency of all civil revolutions unto the interest of the kingdom of the Lord Christ.

This, then, is the person concerning whom these words were used, and this was his employment.

2. There is his dismission itself: "Go thou thy ways." Now this may be considered two ways:—(1.) Singly, relating to his employment only; (2.) In reference to his life also.

(1.) In the first sense, the Lord dischargeth Daniel from his farther attendance on him, in this way of receiving visions and revelations concerning things that were shortly to come to pass, although haply his portion might yet be continued in the land of the living: as if the Lord should say, Thou art an inquiring man; thou art still seeking for farther acquaintance with my mind in these things;—but content thyself, thou shalt receive no more visions; I will now employ Haggai, Zechariah, and others; thou shalt receive no more. But I cannot close with this sense, for,—

[1.] This is not the manner of God, to lay aside those whom he hath found faithful in his service. *Men, indeed, do so;* but God changeth not: whom he hath begun to honour with any employment, he continueth them in it whilst they are faithful to him.

[2.] Daniel was now above a hundred years old, as may be easily demonstrated by comparing the time of his captivity, which was in the third year of the reign of Jehoiakim, chap. i. 1, with the time of his writing this prophecy, which is expressly said to be in the reign of Cyrus, the king of Persia, chap. x. 1; and, therefore, probably his end was very nigh. And after this you hear of him no more; who, had he lived many days, it had been his sin not to have gone up to Jerusalem, the decree of Cyrus, giving liberty for a return, being passed.

(2.) It is not, then, God's laying him aside from his office simply, but also his intimation that he must shortly lay down his mortality, and so come into the condition wherein he was to "rest" until the end. This, then, is his dismission. He died in his work;—life and employment go together. "Go thou thy ways."

Observation I. *There is an appointed season, wherein the saints of the most eminent abilities, in the most useful employments, must receive their dismission:*—be their work of never so great importance, be their abilities never so choice and eminent, they must in their season receive their dismission.

Before I handle this proposition, or proceed to open the following words, I shall crave leave to bring the work of God and the word of God a little close together, and lay the parallel between the persons dismissed,—the one in our text, the other in a present providence, which is very near, only that the one lived not out half the days of the other.

1. Three personal qualifications we observed in Daniel, all which were very eminent in the person of our desires.

(1.) *Wisdom.* There is a manifold wisdom which God imparteth to the sons of men. There is *spiritual* wisdom, that, by the way of eminency, is said to be "from above," James iii. 17; which is nothing but the gracious acquaintance of the soul with the hidden wisdom of God in Christ, 1 Cor. ii. 7. And there is a *civil* wisdom, or a sound ability of mind for the management of the affairs of men, in subordination to the providence and righteousness of God. Though both these were in Daniel, yet it is in respect of the latter that his wisdom is so peculiarly extolled. And though I am very far from assuming to myself the skill of judging of the abilities of men, and would be far from holding forth things of mere common report; yet, upon assured grounds, I suppose this gift of God,—ability of mind, and dexterous industry for the management of human affairs,—may be ascribed to our departed friend.

There are sundry things that distinguish this wisdom from that policy which God abhors; which is "carnal, sensual, and devilish," James iii. 15, though it be the great darling of the men of the world. I shall name one or two of them.

[1.] A gracious discerning of the mind of God, according to his appearance in the affairs wherein men are employed, Mic. vi. 9, "The LORD'S voice crieth unto the city, and the man of wisdom shall see thy name: hear ye the rod, and who hath appointed it." It is *the wisdom of a man*, to see the name of God, to be acquainted with his will, his mind, his aim in things, when his providential voice crieth to the city. All the works of God have their voice,—have their instruction;—those of signal providences speak aloud; they cry to the city, Here is the wisdom of a man: he is a man of substance,[1] a substantial man, that can see his name in such dispensations. This carnal policy inquires not into, but is wholly swallowed up in the concatenation of things among themselves; applying secondary causes unto events, without once looking to the name of God,—like swine following acorns under the tree, not at all looking up to the tree from whence they fall.

[2.] Such acquaintance with the seasons of providence as to know

[1] The Hebrew word translated "wisdom" stands alone in the text, without "man;" תּוּשִׁיָּה, derived from יָשָׁה or יֵשׁ; Sanscrit, *as*; Pers., *ess*; Latin, *esse*, *essentia*, *opes*,—substance. See Fürst's Concordance.—ED.

the duty of the people of God in them, 1 Chron. xii. 32, "The children of Issachar, men that had understanding of the times, to know what Israel ought to do." This it is indeed to be a man of understanding,—to know in any season the duty of Israel, that they may walk up to acceptation with God in the performance thereof;—a thing which is neither prescribed in the rules nor followed in the practice of men wise only with that cursed policy which God abhors. To have a mind suited unto all seasons and tempers, so as to compass their own selfish ends, is the utmost of their aim.

Now, in both these did this gift of God shine in this deceased saint.

1*st*, He ever counted it *his wisdom* to look after the name of God, and the testification of his will, in every dispensation of providence wherein he was called to serve. For *this* were his wakings, watchings, inquiries. When that was made out, he counted not his business half done, but even accomplished, and that the issue was ready at the door: not, What saith this man? or, What saith that man?—but, What saith the Lord?—that being evident. He consulted not with flesh and blood, and the wisdom of it; whereof, perhaps, would he have leaned to it, he was as little destitute as any in his generation,—I mean, the whole wisdom of a man. The name of God was as land in every storm;—in the discovery whereof he had as happy an eye, at the greatest seeming distance, when the clouds were blackest and the waves highest, as any.

2*d*, Neither did he rest here. "What Israel ought to do" in every season, was also his inquiry. Some men have a wisdom to know things, but not seasons, in any measure. Surely a thing in season is no less beautiful than a word in season;—"as apples of gold in pictures of silver." There are few things that belong to civil affairs but are alterable upon the incomprehensible variety of circumstances. These alter and change the very nature of them, and make them good or bad; that is, useful or destructive. He that will have the garment that was made for him one year serve and fit him the next, must be sure that he neither increase nor wane. Importune insisting on the most useful things, without respect to alterations of seasons, is a sad sign of a narrow heart. He of whom we speak was wise to "discern the seasons," and performed things when both themselves and the ways of carrying them on were excellently suited unto all coincidences of their season. And, indeed, what is most wisely proposed in one season may be most foolishly pursued in another. It had been wisdom in Joshua not to have made any compact, but to have slain all the Gibeonites; but it was a folly sorely revenged in Saul, who attempted to do the same. He who thinks the most righteous and suitable proposals or principles that ever were in the world (setting aside general rules of unchangeable righteousness and equity, compassing all times, places, ways, and forms of government), must be performed, as desirable, because once they were so, is certainly a stranger to the affairs of human kind.

Some things are universally unchangeable and indispensable amongst men, supposing them to live answerable to the general principles of their kind:—as, that a government must be; without which every one is the enemy of every one, and all tend to mutual destruction, which are appointed of God for mutual preservation;—that in government some do rule, and some be in subjection;—that all rule be for the good of them that are ruled; and the like principles, that flow necessarily from the very nature of political society.

Some things, again, are alterable and dispensable merely upon the account of preserving the former principles, or the like. If any of them are out of course, it is a *vacuum* in *nature politic*, for which all particular elements instantly dislodge and transpose themselves to supply. And such are all forms of governments amongst men; which, if either they so degenerate of themselves that they become directly opposite, or are so shattered by providential revolutions as to become useless, to their proper end, may and ought to be changed, and not upon other accounts. But now for other things in government,—as the particular way whereby persons shall be designed unto it,—the continuance of the same persons in it for a less or greater proportion of time,—the exercise of more or less power by some sorts, or the whole body of them that are ruled,—the uniting of men for some particular end by bonds and engagements, and the like occasional emergencies, —the universal disposal of them is rolled on prudence to act according to present circumstances.

(2.) *Love to his people.* This was the *second qualification* wherein Daniel was so eminent. And our deceased friend—not to enter into comparison with them that went before—had clearly such a proportion as we may heartily desire that those who follow after may drink but equal draughts of the same cup. That his pains, labour, travail, jeopards of his life and all that was dear to him, relinquishment of relations and contentments, had sweetness and life from this motive, even intenseness of affection to his people, the people of whom he was, and whose prosperity he did desire, needs no farther demonstration than the great neglect of self and all self-concernments which dwelt upon him in all his tremendous undertakings. "Vicit amor patriæ," or certainly he who had upon his breast and all his undertakings self-contempt so eminently engraven, could not have persisted wrestling with so many difficulties to the end of his days. It was Jerusalem and the prosperity thereof which was preferred to his chief joy. Neither,—

(3.) Did he come short in *righteousness* in the administration of that high place whereto he was called; nay, than this there was not a more eminent stone in that diadem which he had on the earth. If he lay not at the bottom, yet at least he had a signal concurrence in such acts of justice as antiquity hath not known, and posterity will admire. Neither was it this or that particular act that did in this bespeak his praise, but a constant will and purpose of rendering to every one his due.

I shall not insist upon particulars: in these and sundry other personal qualifications, between the persons mentioned a parallel may lie.

2. As to employment, that of Daniel was mentioned before: it was the receiving and holding out from God visions of providential alterations, disposing and transposing of states, nations, kingdoms, and dominions. What he had in *speculation* was this man's part to follow in *action.* He was an eminent instrument in the hand of God in as tremendous providential alterations as such a spot of the world hath at any time received, since Daniel foresaw in general them all: and this, not as many have been, carried along with the stream, or led by outward motives and considerations far above their own principles and desires, but seeingly and knowingly he closed with the mind of God, with full purpose of heart to serve the will of the Lord in his generation. And on this account did he see every mountain made a plain beforehand by the Spirit of the Lord, and "staggered not at the greatest difficulties through unbelief; but being steadfast in faith, he gave glory to God." And to complete the parallel,—as Daniel's visions were still terminated in the kingdom of Christ, so all his actions had the same aim and intendment. This was that which gave life and sweetness to all the most dismal and black engagements that at any time he was called out unto. All made way to the coming in of the promised glory. It was all the "vengeance of the Lord and his temple,"—a Davidical preparation of his paths in blood, that He might for ever reign in righteousness and peace. But be he so or so, the truth of our proposition is confirmed towards him, *That there is an appointed season, when the saints of the most eminent abilities, in the most useful employments, shall receive their dismission,* etc.

I shall briefly open the rest of the words, and so take up the proposition again which was first laid down.

II. Then, there is the term allotted to him in this state of his dismission: "Until the end be."

Three things may be here intended in this word, "end."

1. *The end of his life:* "Go thou thy ways to the end of thy life and days." But this we before disallowed, not consenting that Daniel received a dismission from his employment before the end of his life and pilgrimage.

2. *The end of the world:* "Go thy ways to the end of the world: till then thou shalt rest in thy grave." But neither yet doth this seem to be particularly intended in these words. The words in the close of the text do expressly mention that, calling it "the end of days;" and in so few words, the same thing is not needlessly repeated: besides, had this expression held out the whole time of his abode in the state of rest here signified, it must have been, "Go thou thy ways, for thou shalt rest until the end be." So that,—

3. The "end" here is to be accommodated unto the things whereof the Holy Ghost is peculiarly dealing with Daniel; and that is, the accomplishment of the great visions which he had received, in breaking the kingdoms of the world, and setting up the kingdom of the Holy One of God. Daniel is dismissed from farther attendance in this service; he shall not see the actual accomplishment of the things mentioned, but is dismissed, and laid aside unto the end of them. The word "until," in the Scripture, is not such a limitation of time as to assert the contrary to what is excepted, upon its accomplishment "Until the end," doth not signify that he should not rest after the end of the things intimated; no more than it is affirmed that Michal had children after her death, because it is said that until her death she had none, 2 Sam. vi. 23. This, then, is that end that he is dismissed unto,—*The appointed season for the accomplishment of those glorious things which he had foreshown.*

Observation II. *God oftentimes suffers not his choicest servants to see the issue and accomplishment of those glorious things wherein themselves have been most eminently engaged.*

III. The third thing (that we may make haste) is his state and condition during the time which he lies under this dismission, in these words, "For thou shalt rest."

There is nothing of difficulty in these words, but what will naturally fall under consideration in the opening of the proposition which they hold out: which is,—

Observation III. *The condition of a dismissed saint is a condition of rest:* "Thou shalt rest until the end be."

What this rest is, and from what, with wherein it consists, shall be afterward explained.

IV. The last thing in the text is the utmost issue of all these dispensations, both as to his *foregoing labour* and his *present dismission*, and *following rest:* "Thou shalt stand in thy lot," &c.

Here are two things considerable in these words.

1. *The season of the accomplishment of what is here foretold and promised unto Daniel;* and that is, "in the end of the days;" that is, when time shall be no more, when a period shall be put to the days of the world:—called "the last day, the great day, the day of

judgment;"—that is, the season of the accomplishment of this promise, "The day wherein God will judge the world by the man whom he hath ordained."

Observation IV. *There is an appointed, determinate season, wherein all things and persons, according to the will of God, will run into their utmost issue and everlasting condition.*

2. The thing foretold and promised; that is, that he should "stand in his lot."

Observation V. *There is an appointed lot for every one to stand in, and measured portion, which in the end they shall receive.*

Observation VI. *There is an eminent lot hereafter, for men of eminent employment for God here.*

I shall not be able to handle all these several truths which lie in the words; those only which are of most importance, and most suitable, may briefly be handled unto you. And the first is,—

Observation I. *There is an appointed season wherein the saints of the most eminent abilities, in the most useful employments, must receive their dismission.*

Zech. i. 5, "Your fathers, where are they? and the prophets, do they live for ever?" Fathers and prophets have but their season, and they are not: they have their dismission. So old Simeon professeth, "Nunc Dimittis," Luke ii. 29;—Now, thou givest me a dismission. They are placed of God in their station, as a sentinel in his watch-tower; and they have their appointed season, and are then dismissed from their watch. The great Captain of their salvation comes, and saith, Go thou thy ways: thou hast faithfully discharged thy duty; go now unto thy rest. Some have harder service,—some have harder duty than others. Some keep guard in the winter,—a time of storms and temptations, trials and great pressures; others in the sunshine, the summer of a more flourishing estate and condition. Yet duty they all do;—all attend in the service,—all endure some hardship, and have their appointed season for their dismission: and be they never so excellent at the discharging of their duty, they shall not abide one moment beyond the bounds which he hath set them, who saith to all his creatures, Thus far shall you go, and no farther. Oftentimes this dismission is in the midst of their work for which they seem to be most eminently qualified.

The three most eminent works of God, in and about his children, in the days of old, were his giving his people the law, and settling them in the land of Canaan;—his recovering them from the Babylonish captivity;—and his promulgation of the gospel unto them. In these three works he employed three most eminent persons;—Moses in the first, Daniel in the second, and John Baptist in the third; and none of them saw the work accomplished wherein they were so eminently employed. Moses died the year before the people entered Canaan: Daniel, some few years before the foundation of the temple; and John Baptist in the first year of the baptism of our Saviour, when the gospel which he began to preach was to be published in its beauty and glory. They had all but their appointed seasons. Though their abilities were eminent,—who like unto them! and their employment excellent,—what like it in the earth! yet, at their seasons, they must go their ways to rest, and lie down, till they stand in their lot at the end of the days. The reasons of which are,—

1. The general condition of their mortality doth require that it should be so: "It is appointed to all men once to die," Heb. ix. 27. There is a stable law fixed concerning the sons of men, that is not upon the account of any usefulness here to be dispensed withal. The number of our months is with God; he hath fixed our bounds, which we shall not pass. Our days are as the days of an hireling, that have a certain, prefixed, and determinate end. Their strength is not the strength of stones, neither is their flesh of brass, that they should endure for ever. See Job xiv. 10–12. This, I say, requires that there should be an appointed season for their employment, for it is so for their lives. And yet there is more in it than this; for in the course of five thousand years, God hath exempted two persons by his sovereignty from the condition of mortality, who walked with him in their generations: so that the bounds fixed to them were not upon the account of their lives, but merely of the work they had in hand.

2. God doth it, that he may be the more *eminently seen* in the carrying on his own works, which in their season he commits to them. Should he leave his work always on one hand, it would seem at length to be the work of the instrument only. Though the people opposed Moses at the first, yet it is thought they would have worshipped him at the last: and therefore God buried him where his body could not be found. Yet, indeed, he had but the lot of most who faithfully serve God in their generations;—despised whilst they are present,—idolized when they are gone. I do not know of any great work that the Lord carried out the same persons to be the beginners and enders of. He gave them all their seasons, that his power and wisdom might the more evidently appear in carrying it from one hand to another.

3. God makes room, as it were, in his vineyard for the budding, flourishing, and fruit-bearing of other plants which he hath planted. Great employments call for great exercise of graces. Even in employments in and about providential things, there is the exercise of spiritual grace;—as much faith and prayer, as much communion with God, walking before him, and wrestling with him, may be used in casting down of armies, as in setting up of churches. God exerciseth all the graces of his in the work he calleth them out unto. He principles

them by faith and fellowship with himself for their employment; and therefore he gives each individual but his appointed season, that others, in whose hearts he hath lodged the same spirit wherewith they are endued, may come forth and show the fruits thereof. Daniel lieth down in the dust in rest and peace. And why so? The spirit of prophecy is poured out on Haggai and Zechariah, &c.; they must also carry on this work, and bear my name before my people. Consider the use of this.

Use 1. Of exhortation unto all that are employed in the work of God, especially such as with *eminent abilities* are engaged in eminent employments. You have but your allotted season for your work;—your day hath its close, its evening; your night cometh, wherein none can work. The grave cannot praise the Lord; death cannot celebrate him: it is the living, the living that are fitted for that work, Isa. xxxviii. 18, 19. It is true, men may allot you your season, and all in vain; but your times are in the hand of God,—that which he hath appointed out unto you shall stand. Be you never so excellent, never so useful, yet the days of your service "are as the days of an hireling," that will expire at the appointed season. Be wise, then, to improve the time that is in your hands. This is the praise of a man, the only praise whereof in this world he is partaker, that he doth the will of God before he fall asleep; that he faithfully serves his generation, until he be no more. For a dying man to wrestle with the rebukes of God and the complaints of his own conscience, for meeting with the *end* of his *days* before he hath attained the *midst* of his *duty*, is a sad condition. You have your *season*, and you have *but* your season; neither can you lie down in peace, until you have some persuasion that your *work* as well as your *life* is at an end. Whatever, then, you find to do, do it with all your strength; for there is neither wisdom nor power in the grave, whither you are going, Eccles. ix. 10.

Some particular rules may direct you herein.

(1.) Compare yourselves with the saints of God, who were faithful in their generations, and are now fallen asleep. What a deal of work did Josiah do in a short season! what a light did John set up in a few years! with what unwearied pains and industry did our deceased friend serve his generation! It is said of Cæsar, that he was ashamed of his own sloth, when he found that Alexander had conquered the eastern world at the age wherein he had done nothing. Behold here one receiving his dismission about the age of forty years; and what a world of work for God and the interest of the Lord Christ did he in that season! and how well, in the close, hath he parted with a *temporal* life for Him who, by his death, procured for him an eternal life! And now rest is sweet unto this labouring man. Provoke one another by examples.

(2.) Be diligent to *pass through your work*, and let it not too long hang upon your hands; your appointed season may come before you bring it to the close;—yea, search out work for God. You that are intrusted in power, trifle not away your season. Is there no oppressed person that with diligence you might relieve?—is there no poor distressed widow or orphan whose righteous requests you might expedite and despatch?—are there no stout offenders against God and man that might be chastised?—are there no slack and slow counties and cities in the execution of justice, that might be quickened by your example?—no places destitute of the gospel that might be furnished and supplied by your industry and wisdom? Can you not find out something of this or the like nature to be despatched with vigour and diligence? nay, do not innumerable particulars in each kind lie upon your hands? and is not your non-performance of them such a sacrifice as wherewith God is not well pleased? Your time is limited and appointed; you know not how soon you may be overtaken with it; and would it not be desirable unto you, that you had done these things? will it be bitterness in the end, that you so laid out your endeavours?

Use 2. All *men have but their seasons in any work;* only God abideth in it for ever: in every undertaking let your eye still be on him, with whom is the fulness and the residue of the Spirit. Jeremiah's great bewailing of Josiah's death was doubtless made upon the account of his discerning that none would come after him to carry on the work which he had begun, but the wickedness of that people was to come to its height;—else God can raise up yet more Josiahs. Let him be eyed as the principal and only abiding agent in any great undertaking.

In the residue of the observations I shall be very brief. The next is,—

Observation II. *God oftentimes suffers not the choicest of his servants to see the accomplishment of those glorious things wherein themselves have been most eminently engaged.*

The case of Moses is most eminently known. He had a large share in suffering the persecutions which were allotted to the people:—forty years' banishment he endured in the wilderness, under the reproach of Christ;—forty years more spent in wrestling with innumerable difficulties, dangerous perils, mutinies, wars, and contentions. At the close, when he comes to look upon the land,—when the end of all that dispensation was to be wound up, and the rest and reward of all his toil and labour to be had, which formerly he had undergone for twice forty years,—"Go thou thy ways," saith the Lord; "thou shalt rest;"—take thy dismission; thou shalt not enter into the good land; lie down here in the wilderness in peace.

John Baptist goes and preaches the drawing nigh of the kingdom of God, but lived only to point out Christ with his finger; cries, "Behold the Lamb of God; I must decrease,"—and is cut off. David makes the great preparation for the temple; but he shall not see so much as the foundation laid. Men must take their appointed lot. God will send by the hand of him whom he will send. Daniel must rest until the end be. It is said of some, they began to deliver Israel. The case of Zerubbabel was very rare, who saw the foundation and also the top-stone of the temple laid; and yet the work of Jerusalem was not half finished in his days, as you may see, Zech. i. And this because,—

1. God oftentimes receives secret provocations from the choicest of his servants, which move him to take them short of their desires. Those of his own whom he employs in great works, have great and close communion with him. God usually exercises their spirits in near acts of fellowship with himself: they receive much from him, and are constrained to unburden themselves frequently upon him. Now, when men are brought into an intimacy with God, and have received great engagements from him, the Lord takes notice of every working and acting of their souls in an especial manner, and is oftentimes grieved and provoked with that in them which others can take no notice of. Let a man read the story of that action of Moses upon which the Lord told him directly he should not see the finishing of the work he had in hand, nor enter into Canaan, Numb. xx. 7, 8, 11. It will be a hard matter to find out wherein the failing was. He smote the rock with the rod, with some words of impatience, when he should only have spoken to it,—and this with some secret unbelief as to the thing he had in hand. God deals with others visibly, according to their outward actions; but in his own he takes notice of all their unbelief, fears, withdrawings, as proceeding from a frame in no measure answering those gracious discoveries of himself which he hath made unto them; and on this account it is that some are taken off in the midst of their work.

2. To manifest that he hath better things in store for his saints than the *best* and *utmost* of what they can desire or aim at here below, he had a heaven for Moses; and therefore might in love and mercy deny him Canaan. He employeth some eminently;—their work is great,—their end glorious: at the very last step almost of their journey he takes off one and another,—lets them not see the things aimed at. This may be thought hard measure, strict severity, exact justice,—yea, as Job complains, "taking advantages against them;" but see what he calls them to, in calling them off from their greatest glories and excellencies on the earth, and all this will appear to be love, tenderness, and favour in the highest. Whilst you are labouring for a handful of *first-fruits*, he gives you the *full*

harvest; whilst you are labouring for the *figure* here below, he gives you the *substance above.* Should you see the greatest work wherein any of you were ever engaged brought to perfection, yet all were but a few drops, compared with that fulness which he hath prepared for you. The Lord, then, doth it to witness to the children of men that the things which are seen—the best of them—are not to be compared with the things that are not seen, yea, the least of them; inasmuch as he takes them whom he will honour from the very door of the one, to bear them into the other. The meanest enjoyment in heaven is to be preferred before the richest on earth, even then when the kingdom of Christ shall come in most beauty and glory.

Use 1. You that are engaged in the work of God, seek for a reward of your service in the service itself. Few of you may live to see that beauty and glory which perhaps you aim at as the end of all your great undertakings for God whereunto you have been engaged. God will proceed at his own pace, and calls on us to go along with him; and in the meantime, until the determinate end come, to wait in faith, and not make haste. Those whose minds are so fixed on, and swallowed up with, some end (though good) which they have proposed to themselves, do seldom see good days and serene in their own souls. They have bitterness, wrath, and trouble all their days,—are still pressing to the end proposed, and commonly are dismissed from their station before it be attained. There is a sweetness, there is wages to be found in the work of God itself. Men who have learned to hold communion with God in every work he calls them out unto, though they never see the main harvest they aim at in general, yet such will rest satisfied, and submit to the Lord's limitation of their time:—they bear their own sheaves in their bosoms. Seeing God oftentimes dismisses his choicest servants before they see or taste of the main fruits of their endeavours, I see not upon what account consolation can be had in following the Lord in difficult dispensations, but only in that reward which every duty bringeth along with it, by communion with God in its performance. Make, then, this your aim, that in sincerity of heart you do the work of God in your generation. Find his presence with you, his Spirit guiding you, his love accepting you in the Lord Christ; and, whenever you receive your dismission, it will be rest and peace,—in the meantime, you will not make haste.

Use 2. See a bottom and ground of consolation when such eminent instruments as this departed worthy are called off from their station, when ready to enter upon the harvest of all their labours, watchings, toilings, and expense of blood. God hath better things for them in store, abiding things, that they shall not enjoy for a day or two,—which is the best of what they could hope for here, had they lived to see all their desires accomplished,—but such as in the fulness whereof they may lie down in peace to eternity. Why do we complain?—for our own loss? is not the residue and fulness of the Spirit with Him who gave him his dismission?—for his loss? he lived not to see Ireland in peace, but enjoys the glory of that eternal kingdom that was prepared for him before the foundation of the world; which is the condition held out in the third observation.

Observation III. *The condition of a dismissed saint is a condition of rest:* "Go thy way until the end be; for thou shalt rest."

The apostle gives it in as the issue of a discourse from a passage in the Psalms, "There remaineth therefore a rest for the people of God," Heb. iv. 9;—it remains and is reserved for them; this the Lord hath solemnly proclaimed from heaven, Rev. xiv. 13, "Blessed are the dead which die in the Lord from henceforth: yea, saith the Spirit, that they may rest from their labours; and their works do follow them." They go into a blessed condition of rest. There is not any notion under which the state of a dismissed saint is so frequently described as this of "rest,"—which, indeed, is the proper end and tendency of all things. Their happiness is their rest; their rest is all the happiness they can be partakers of: "Fecisti nos ad te, Domine, et inquietum est cor nostrum, donec veniat ad te."[1]

Now, "rest" holds out two things unto us:—A freedom from what is opposite thereunto, wherein those that are at rest have been exercised, in reference whereunto they are said to be at rest; and something which suits them and satisfies their nature in the condition wherein they are; and, therefore, they are at rest: which they could not be were it not so with them; for nothing can rest but in the full fruition and enjoyment of that which satiates the whole nature of it in all its extent and capacity. We must briefly inquire,—1. What it is that the saints are at rest from; and, 2. What it is that they are at rest in. Which I shall do very speedily.

1. The many particulars which they are at rest from may be referred unto two general heads:—(1.) Sin; (2.) Labour and travail.

(1.) Sin. This, on all considerations whatever, is the main disquietness of the soul. Temptations to it, actings in it, troubles for it,—they are the very Egypt of the soul, its house and place of bondage and vexation;—either the power of it indwelling, or the guilt of it pressing, are here still disquieting the soul. For the first, how doth Paul complain, lament, yea, cry out concerning it, Rom. vii. 24, "O wretched man that I am!" and what a sad, restless, and tumultuating condition upon this account doth he describe in the verses foregoing! *The best, the wisest, the holiest* of the saints on this account are in a restless condition. Suppose a man a *conqueror* in every battle, in every combat that he is engaged in; yet whilst he hath any

[1] [August. Confes., lib. i. c. 1.]

fighting, though he be never foiled, he hath not peace. Though the saints should have success in every engagement against sin, yet because it will still be rebelling, still be fighting, it will disturb their peace. So also doth the guilt of it;—our Saviour testifieth, that a sense of it will make a man to be "weary and heavy laden," Matt. xi. 28. This oftentimes makes the inhabitants of Zion say they are sick; for though an end be made of sin, as to the guilt of it, in the blood of Christ, yet, by reason of our darkness, folly, and unbelief, and the hiding of the countenance of God, the conscience is oftentimes pressed with it, no less than if it lay indeed under the whole weight and burden of it.

I shall not instance in more particulars concerning this cause of want of rest and disquietness;—the perplexity of temptations, buffetings and winnowings of Satan, allurements and affrightments of the world, darkness and sorrows of unbelief, and the like, do all set in against us upon this account.

This, in general, is the first thing that the dismissed saints are at rest from: They sin no more, they wound the Lord Jesus no more, they trouble their own souls no more, they grieve the Spirit no more, they dishonour the gospel no more,—they are troubled no more with Satan's temptations without, no more with their own corruption within; but lie down in a constant enjoyment of one everlasting victory over sin, with all its attendants: saith the Spirit, "They rest from their labours," Rev. xiv.,—those labours which make them faint and weary, their contending with sin to the uttermost. They are no more cold in communion; they have not one thought that wanders off from God to eternity. They lose him no more, but always lie down in his bosom, without the least possibility of disturbance. Even the very remembrance of sin is sweet unto them, when they see God infinitely exalted and admired in the pardon thereof. They are free from trouble, and that both as to doing and suffering. Few of the saints but are called out, in one kind or another, to both these. Every one is either *doing* for God or *suffering* for God;—some both do and suffer great things for him. In either of them there is pain, weariness, travail, labour, trouble, sorrow, and anxiety of spirit; neither is there any eminent doing or working for God but is carried on with much suffering to the outward man.

What a life of labour and trouble did our deceased friend lead for many years in the flesh! how were his days consumed in travail! God calling him to his foot, and exercising him to understand the sweetness of that promise, that they that die in him shall have rest. Many spend their days deliciously,—with so much contentment to the flesh that it is impossible they should have any foretaste and sweet relish of their rest that is to come.

The apostle tells us that "there remaineth a rest for the people of God;" and yet withal, that they who believe are entered into that rest;—those who in their labours, in their travails, do take in the sweetness of that promise of rest, do even in their labour make an entrance thereinto.

(2.) They rest from all trouble and anxiety that attend them in their pilgrimage, either in doing or suffering for God, Heb. iv. 10. They enter into rest, and cease from their works. God wipes all tears from their eyes. There is no more watching, no more fasting, no more wrestling, no more fighting, no more blood, no more sorrow; the ransomed of the Lord do return with everlasting joy on their heads, and sorrow and sighing flee away. There, tyrants pretend no more title to their kingdom; rebels lie not in wait for their blood; they are no more awakened by the sound of the trumpet, nor the noise of the instruments of death:—they fear not for their relations, they weep not for their friends; the Lamb is their temple, and God is all in all unto them. Yet,—

2. This will not complete their rest; something farther is required thereto,—even something to satisfy, everlastingly content, and fill them in the state and condition wherein they are. Free them in your thoughts from what you please, without this they are not at rest. This, then, you have in the second place, God is the rest of their souls, Ps. cxvi., "Return to thy rest, O my soul." Dismissed saints rest in the bosom of God, because in the fruition and enjoyment of him they are everlastingly satisfied, as having attained the utmost end whereto they were created, all the blessedness whereof they are capable. I could almost beg for liberty a little to expatiate in this meditation of the sweet, gracious, glorious, satisfied condition of a dismissed saint. But the time is spent, and therefore,—without holding out one drop of water to quench the feigned fire of purgatory; or drawing forth any thing to discover the vanity of their assertion who affirm the soul to sleep, or to be nothing until the resurrection, or theirs who, assigning to them a state of subsistence and perception, do yet exclude them from the fruition of God, without which there is no rest, until the end of all; with such other by-persuasions as would disquiet the condition or abridge the glory of those blessed souls; which yet were a facile undertaking,—I shall draw towards a close.

There are three points yet remaining. I shall speak only to the first of them, and that as an use of the doctrine last proposed, and I have done.

Observation IV. *There is an appointed determinate season, wherein all things and persons, according to the will of God, will run into their utmost issue and everlasting condition.*

Thou art going, whoever thou art, into an abiding condition and there is a lot appointed for thee, wherein lies an estate everlastingly unchangeable. It is the utmost end whereunto thou art designed, and when once thou art entered into that lot, thou art everlastingly engaged: no more change, no more alteration; if it be well with thee, it will abide; if otherwise, expect not any relief. In our few days we live for eternity; in our mutable estate we deal for an unchangeable condition. It is not thus only in respect of particulars, but God hath "appointed a day, wherein he will judge all the world by the man whom he hath ordained." An end is coming unto all that whole dispensation under which we are;—to you who, by the riches of free grace, have obtained union and communion with the Lord Jesus, rest and peace, when God shall everlastingly rain snares, fire and brimstone, upon the workers of iniquity. Some mock, indeed, and say, "Where is the promise of his coming?" But we know "the Lord is not slack, as some men count slackness," but exerciseth patience until the appointed season for the bringing about of his own glorious ends, which he hath determined concerning his creatures. Why should we, then, complain, when any one, perhaps before our expectation, but yet according to God's determination, makes an entrance into the end of all? All things work to that season. This state of things is not for continuance. That which is incumbent is in this uncertain space of time allotted to us, to give all diligence to make our calling and election sure, as also to serve the Lord faithfully in our generations, wherein we cannot be surprised. We have an example in him who is gone before. It is true, the Lord Jesus is our primitive pattern and example; but those also who have followed him, wherein they have followed him, are to be eyed and marked as provocations to the same labour of faith and love wherein they were exercised. And, that this use may be made by this assembly, I shall add one word concerning him from whom is the occasion thereof.

Every man stands in a threefold capacity,—natural, civil, religious. And there are distinct qualifications that are suited unto these several capacities.

1. To the first, as the ornaments and perfections of nature, are suited some seeds of those *heroical* virtues, as courage, permanency in business, etc.; which being in themselves morally indifferent, have their foundations eminently laid in the natures of some persons, which yet hinders not but that their good improvement is of grace.

2. To the second, or man's civil capacity, there are many eminencies relating as peculiar endowments, which may be referred unto the three heads of *ability, faithfulness,* and *industry;* that through them neither by weakness, treachery, nor sloth, the works and employments incumbent on men in their civil state and condition may suffer.

3. Men's peculiar ornament and improvement, in their *religious capacity,* lies in those fruits of the Spirit which we call Christian graces. Of these, in respect of usefulness, there are three most eminent, viz., *faith, love,* and *self-denial.* I speak of them upon another account than the apostle doth, where he placeth hope amongst the *first three* of Christian graces. Now, all these, in their several kinds, were as eminent in the person deceased, in his several capacities, as perhaps is usually found in any one in a generation. My business is not to make a funeral oration, only I suppose that without offence I may desire, that in courage and permanency in business (which I name in opposition to that unsettled, pragmatical, shuffling disposition which is in some men),—in ability for wisdom and counsel,—in faithfulness to his trust and in his trust,—in indefatigable industry in the pursuit of the work committed to him,—in faith on the promises of God, and acquaintance with his mind in his mighty works of providence,—in love to the Lord Jesus and all his saints,—in a tender regard to their interest, delight in their society, contempt of himself and all his for the gospel's sake, with eminent self-denial in all his concernments,—in impartiality and sincerity in the execution of justice,—that in these and the like things we may have many raised up in the power and spirit wherein he walked before the Lord and the inhabitants of this nation. This (I say) I hope I may speak without offence here upon such an occasion as this. My business being occasionally to preach the word, not to carry on a part of a funeral ceremony, I shall add no more, but commit you to Him who is able to prepare you for your eternal condition.

SERMON IX.

CHRIST'S KINGDOM

AND THE

MAGISTRATE'S POWER.

PREFATORY NOTE.

THE complete title of the earlier editions of the following sermon indicates the design of the author,—"Concerning the Kingdom of Christ, and the Power of the Civil Magistrate *about the things of the Worship of God*." It was preached to the Parliament on October 13, 1652, "a day of solemn humiliation." It was the time of the naval war with the Dutch. The bill for a New Representative, or, in other words, the question whether the Long Parliament should now be dissolved, was keenly agitated. The weightier question, as to the settlement of the Constitution, burdened and perplexed the nation. During the month in which the sermon was preached, numerous private conferences on the former point took place between the leaders of the Parliament and the officers of the Army. These circumstances may account for the appointment of a day of humiliation. What determined Owen to make choice of the delicate and important subject of which he treats in this sermon, might be the prevalence of a desire in many quarters for a proper adjustment of ecclesiastical affairs. A petition from the Army (see "Whitelocke's Memorials," p. 516) had been presented to the Parliament on the 13th of August 1652, "reciting that they had often sought the Lord, and desire these particulars to be considered." Then follows a list of twelve "particulars;" the first of which is, "That speedy and effectual means be used for promoting the gospel, profane and scandalous ministers be outed, good preachers encouraged, maintenance for them provided, and tithes taken away."

The sermon breathes a spirit weary of the lengthened confusion which had distracted the land. The principles contained in it raise questions as important in themselves, and as fresh in interest now, as in the days when Owen lived and preached. Whatever may be thought of his views on the relation of the magistrate to the church, this sermon, in which his judgment is declared on this topic of paramount and engrossing moment, has evidently been prepared with unusual care.—ED.

SERMON IX.

CHRIST'S KINGDOM AND THE MAGISTRATE'S POWER.

"I Daniel was grieved in my spirit in the midst of my body, and the visions of my head troubled me. I came near unto one of them that stood by, and asked him the truth of all this. So he told me, and made me know the interpretation of the things."—DAN. vii. 15, 16.

WHAT there is of concernment for the right understanding of these words in that part of the chapter which goes before, may be considered in the opening of the words themselves; and therefore I shall immediately attend thereunto.

There are in them four things considerable:—I. The state and condition which Daniel, the penman of this prophecy, expresseth himself to be in,—wherein he hath companions in the days wherein we live: "He was grieved in his spirit in the midst of his body." II. The cause and means whereby he was brought into this perplexed frame of spirit: "The visions of his head troubled him." III. The remedy he used for his delivery from that entangled condition of spirit wherein he was: "He went nigh to one of them that stood by, and asked him the truth of all this." IV. The issue of that application he made to that one that stood by for redress: "He told him, and made him know the interpretation of the things."—All these I shall briefly open unto you, that I may lay a foundation for the truth which the Lord hath furnished me with to hold out unto you this day.

I. In the first, the person spoken of is Daniel himself: "I Daniel." He bears this testimony concerning himself, and his condition was,—"He was grieved in his spirit."

The person himself was a man highly favoured of God above all in his generation; so richly furnished with gifts and graces that he is once and again brought forth as an example, and instanced in by God himself upon the account of eminence in *wisdom* and *piety*. Yet all this preserves him not from falling into this perplexed condition, Dan. i. 17–20; Ezek. xiv. 14, xxviii. 3. Now, as the principal work of all the holy prophets, which have been since the world began,

Luke i. 70; 1 Pet. i. 10–12, was to preach, set forth, and declare the Lord Jesus Christ, the Messiah who was for to come; so some especial concernments of his person, righteousness, and kingdom, were in especial manner committed unto them respectively;—his passion and righteousness to Isaiah; the covenant of grace in him to Jeremiah; and to this Daniel, most eminently, the great works of the providence of God in the shaking and overturning of kingdoms and nations in a subserviency to his kingdom. With the revelation hereof, for the consolation of the church in all ages, did the Lord honour him of whom we speak.

For the present he describes himself in a somewhat perplexed condition. His spirit (mind and soul) was grieved, sick, troubled, or disquieted in the midst of his body; that is, deeply, nearly, closely:—it sets out the greatness of his trouble, the anxiety of his thoughts within him. Like David, when he expostulated with his soul about it,—"Why art thou so sad, my soul? and why art thou so disquieted within me?" Ps. xliii. 5,—he knew not what to say, what to do, nor wherewith to relieve himself. He was filled with sad thoughts, sad apprehensions of what was to come to pass, and what might be the issue of the things that had been discovered unto him. This, I say, is the frame and temper he describes himself to be in,—a man under sad apprehensions of the issues and events of things and the dispensations of God (as many are at this day); and upon that account closely and nearly perplexed.

II. The cause of this perturbation of mind and spirit was from the visions of his head: "The visions of his head troubled him."

He calls them "visions of the head," because that is the seat of the internal senses and fantasy, whereby visions are received. So he calls them "a dream," verse 1, "and visions of his head upon his bed." Yet such visions, such a dream it was, as, being immediately from God, and containing a no less certain discovery of his will and mind than if the things mentioned in them had been spoken face to face, he writes them by the inspiration of the Holy Ghost, verse 2, for the use of the church.

I shall not take the advantage of going forth unto any discourse of dreams, visions, oracles, and those other divers ways and manners (Heb. i. 1) of revealing his mind and will, which God was pleased to use with his prophets of old, Numb. xii. 6–8. My aim lies another way:—it sufficeth only to take notice, that God gave him in his sleep a representation of the things here expressed, which he was to give over for the use of the church in following ages. The matter of these visions, which did so much trouble him, falls more directly under our consideration. Now,—

1. The subject of these perplexing visions is a representation of the

four great empires of the world, which had, and were to have, dominion in and over the places of the church's greatest concernments, and were all to receive their period and destruction by the Lord Christ and his revenging hand.

And these three things he mentions of them therein:—(1.) *Their rise;* (2.) *Nature;* (3.) *Destruction.*

(1.) In verse 2 he describes their rise and original: it was "from the strivings of the four winds of the heavens upon the great sea;" he compares them to the most violent, uncontrollable, and tumultuating things in the whole creation. Winds and seas!—what waves, what horrible storms, what mixing of heaven and earth, what confusion and destruction must needs ensue the fierce contest of all contrary winds upon the great sea! Such are the springs of empires and governments for the most part amongst men,—such their entrances and advancements. In particular, such were the beginnings of the four empires here spoken of. Wars, tumults, confusions, blood, destruction, desolation, were the seeds of their greatness: "Ubi solitudinem faciunt, pacem adpellant," Galgac. apud Tacit. [Agr., 30.] Seas and great waters do, in the Scripture, represent people and nations, Rev. xvii. 15, "The waters which thou sawest, where the whore sitteth, are peoples, and multitudes, and nations, and tongues." As "waters," they are unstable, fierce, restless, tumultuating; and when God mingleth his judgments amongst them, they are as "a sea of glass mingled with fire,"—brittle, uncertain, devouring, and implacable. It is a demonstration of the sovereignty of God, that he is above them, Ps. xciii. 3, 4, "The floods have lifted up, O LORD, the floods have lifted up their voice; the floods lift up their waves. The LORD on high is mightier than the noise of many waters, yea, than the mighty waves of the sea." Now, from these, tossed with the winds of commotions, seditions, oppressions, passions, do flow the governments of the world, the Spirit of God moving upon the face of those waters, to bring forth those forms and frames of rule which he will make use of.

(2.) Unto verse 9 he describes them *in order as to their nature and kind;*—one of them being then ready to be destroyed, and the other to succeed, until the utter desolation of them all, and all power rising in their spirit and principle.

I shall not pass through their particular description, nor stay to prove that the *fourth beast*, without name or special form, is the Roman empire; which I have elsewhere[1] demonstrated, and it is something else which at this time I aim at. This is that which troubles and grieves the spirit of Daniel in the midst of his body. He saw what worldly powers should arise,—by what horrible tumults, shakings, confusions, and violence they should spring up,—with what

[1] Sermon on Heb. xii. 27.

fierceness, cruelty, and persecution, they should rule in the world, and stamp all under their feet.

(3.) *Their end and destruction* is revealed unto him, from verse 10 unto verses 12, 13; and this by the appearance of "the Ancient of days" (the eternal God) in judgment against them; which he sets out with that solemnity and glory, as if it were the great judgment of the last day;—God, indeed, thereby giving a pledge unto the world of that universal judgment he will one day exercise towards all, "by the man whom he hath ordained," Acts xvii. 31. And this increaseth the terror of the vision, to have such a representation of the glory of God as no creature is able to bear. God also manifests hereby his immediate actings in the setting up and pulling down the powers of this world; which he doth as fully and effectually as if he sat upon a throne of judgment, calling them all by name to appear in his presence, and, upon the evidence of their ways, cruelties, and oppression, pronouncing sentence against them. "Be wise, therefore, O ye kings; be instructed, ye judges of the earth. Serve the LORD with fear, and rejoice with trembling," Ps. ii. 11, 12. "He changeth the times and seasons," Dan. ii. 21. "He ruleth in the kingdom of men, and setteth over it whom he pleaseth," chap. v. 21.

And this is the first thing in this vision at which the prophet was perplexed.

2. There is the approach of the Lord Christ unto the Father, with his entrance into his kingdom and dominion, which is everlasting, and passeth not away, verse 14.

This being the end of the vision, I must a little insist upon it; not that I intend purposely to handle the kingdom of Christ as mediator, but only a little to consider it as it lies here in the vision, and is needful for the right bottoming of the truth in our intendment.

Various have been the thoughts of men about the kingdom of Christ in all ages. That the Messiah was to be a King, a Prince, a Ruler,—that he was to have a kingdom, and that the government was to be on his shoulder,—is evident from the Old Testament; that all this was and is accomplished in Jesus of Nazareth, whom God exalted, made a Prince and a Saviour, is no less evident in the New;—but about the nature of this kingdom, its rise and manner of government, have been, and are, the contests of men.

The Jews to this very day expect it as a thing carnal and temporal, visible, outwardly glorious, wherein, in all manner of pleasure, they shall bear rule over the nations at their will;—such another thing, of all the world, as the popedom, which the Gentile or idolatrous worshippers of Christ set up for his kingdom: and of some such thing it may be supposed the apostles themselves were not without thoughts, until they had conversed with the Lord after the resurrection, Luke ix. 46; Acts i. 6. Neither are all amongst us free from them at this day.

Those who with any simplicity profess the name of Christ, do generally agree that there are three parts of it.

(1.) First, and principally, in that which is *internal and spiritual*, in and over the souls of men, over spirits both good and bad, in reference unto the ends which he hath to accomplish upon them. Of that which is direct and immediate upon the hearts and souls of men, there are two parts.

[1.] That which he exerciseth towards his elect, who are given unto him of his Father, *converting, ruling, preserving* them, under and through great variety of dispensations, internal and external, until he brings them unto himself: "He stands and feeds them in the strength of the LORD, in the majesty of the name of the LORD his God," Mic. v. 4;—even he who is the "Ruler in Israel," verse 2. He is exalted and made "a Prince and a Saviour, to give repentance to Israel, and the forgiveness of sins," Acts v. 31. He makes his people "a willing people in the day of his power," Ps. cx. 3,—sending out his Holy Spirit to lead them into all truth, and making his word and ordinances "mighty through God to the pulling down of strongholds" in their hearts, "casting down imaginations, and every high thing that exalts itself against the knowledge of God; and bringing into captivity every thought to the obedience of himself," 2 Cor. x. 4, 5. He takes possession of their hearts by his power, dwelling in them by his Spirit, making them kings in his kingdom, and bringing them infallibly into glory. Oh, that this rule, this kingdom of his, might be carried on in our hearts! We busy ourselves about many things; we shall find at length this one thing necessary. This is that part of the kingdom of Christ which we are principally to aim at in the preaching of the gospel: "We preach Christ Jesus the Lord," 2 Cor. iv. 5,—him to be Lord and King, though others have had dominion over us. They are the grains of Israel which the Lord seeks for in his sifting the nations by his word, as well as by his providence: and we are, in the work of the gospel, to "endure all things for the elect's sakes," 2 Tim. ii. 10.

[2.] In the power which he exerciseth towards others, to whom the word of the gospel doth come, *calling, convincing, enlightening, hardening* many, whom yet, being not his sheep, nor of his fold, he will never take to himself; but leaves to themselves, under aggravations of condemnation, which they pull upon themselves by the contempt of the gospel, 2 Cor. ii. 16; Heb. x. 29. He sends his Spirit to convince even the perishing "world of sin, righteousness, and judgment," John xvi. 8. He sendeth sharp arrows into the very hearts of his enemies, Ps. xlv. 5,—making them stoop, bow, and fall under him; so bounding their rage, overbearing their lusts, leaving them without excuse in themselves, and his people oftentimes not without profit from them:—with some dealing even in this life more severely; causing the witnesses of the gospel to torment them by the preaching of the word, Rev. xi. 10, yet giving them up to "strong delusions, that they may believe lies, and be damned," 2 Thess. ii. 11, 12, &c.

[3.] In carrying on of this work towards the one and the other, he puts forth the power, rule, and dominion, which he hath of his Father *over spirits*, both good and bad.

1*st*. Being made head of principalities and powers, and exalted far above every name in heaven or earth, being made the "first-born of every creature," and all the angels of God being commanded to worship him, Heb. i. 6, and put in subjection under his feet;—he sends them forth, and uses them as ministering spirits for them who shall be heirs of salvation, verse 14,—appointing them to behold the face of his Father, ready for his commands on their behalf, Matt. xviii. 10,—attending in their assemblies, 1 Cor. xi. 10, and to give them their assistance in the time of danger and trouble, Acts xii. 9, destroying their adversaries, verse 23, with innumerable other advantageous administrations, which he hath not thought good to acquaint us withal in particular, that our dependence might be on our King himself, and not on any of our fellow-servants, though never so glorious and excellent, Rev. xxii. 9.

2*dly*. For Satan, as he came to bind the strong man armed, and to spoil his goods, Matt. xii. 29,—to destroy him that had the power of death, Heb. ii. 14; and being made manifest to this end, that he might destroy his works (1 John iii. 8) in the souls of men in this world, 2 Cor. x. 4, 5; so, having in his own person conquered these principalities and powers of darkness, making an open show of them in his cross, and triumphing over them, Col. ii. 15, he continues overruling and judging him and them, in their opposition to his church, and will do so until he bring them to a full conquest and subjection, that they shall be judged and sentenced by the poor creatures whom in this world they continually pursue with all manner of enmity, 1 Cor. vi. 3.

And this looketh to the inward substance of the kingdom of Christ, which is given him of his Father, and is not of this world, though he exercise it in the world to the last day;—a kingdom which can never be shaken nor removed. "The government of it is upon his shoulder, and of the increase of it there shall be no end."

(2.) That *rule* or *government* which in his word he hath appointed and ordained for all his saints and chosen ones to walk in, to testify their inward subjection to him, and to be fitted for usefulness one to another. Now, of this part the administration is wrapped up in the laws, ordinances, institutions, and appointments of the gospel,—and it is frequently called "The kingdom of God." That Jesus Christ doth not rule in these things, and is not to be obeyed as a king in them, is but a late darkness, which, though it should spread as a cloud over the face of the heavens, and pour forth some showers and tempests, yet it would be as a cloud still, which will speedily scatter and vanish into nothing.

And this is that whose propagation, as the means of carrying on the former spiritual ends of Christ, you desire strength and direction for this day. Men may gather together unto Christ, and say, with heads full of hopes, poor souls, and eyes fixed on the right hand and left, "Lord, wilt thou at this time restore the kingdom to Israel?" Take you his answer, and be contented with it, "It is not for you to know the times or the seasons, which the Father hath put in his own power," Acts i. 6, 7,—but do your work faithfully. I know in this thing, it is far easier to complain of you for not doing, than to direct you what to do. The Lord be your guide, and give you straw wherever bricks are required of you!

(3.) In the *universal judgment*, which the Father hath committed to him over all, which he will most eminently exercise at the last day;—rewarding, crowning, receiving some to himself; judging, condemning, casting others into utter darkness, John v. 22–27; Acts ii. 36; Rom. xiv. 9; Acts xvii. 31. And of this universal, righteous judgment he giveth many warnings unto the world, by pouring forth sundry vials of his wrath upon great Nimrods and oppressors, Ps. cx. 6; Mic. iv. 3; Rev. xix. 11–13. And in the holding forth these three parts of the kingdom of the Lord Jesus doth the Scripture abound.

But now, whether over and beyond all these the Lord Christ shall not bear an outward, visible, glorious rule, setting up a kingdom like those of the world, to be ruled by strength and power; and if so, when or how it shall be brought in,—into whose hands the administration of it shall be committed, and upon what account,—whether he will personally walk therein or no,—whether it shall be clearly distinct from the rule he now bears in the world, or only differenced by more glorious degrees and manifestations of his power,—endless and irreconcilable are the contests of those that profess his name. This we find, by woful experience, that all who, from the spirituality of the rule of Christ, and delight therein, have degenerated into carnal apprehensions of the beauty and glory of it, have, for the most part, been given up to carnal actings, suited to such apprehensions; and have been so dazzled with gazing after temporal glory, that the kingdom which comes not by observation hath been vile in their eyes.

3. Now, because it is here fallen in my way, and is part of the

vision at which the prophet was so much troubled, I shall give you some brief observations of what is clear and certain from Scripture relating hereunto, and so pass on. It is, then, certain,—

(1.) That the interest of particular men, as to this kingdom of Christ, is to look wherein the universal concernment of all saints, in all ages, doth lie. This, undoubtedly, they may attain, and it doth belong to them. Now, certainly, this is in that part of it which comes not by observation, Luke xvii. 20, but is within us, which "is righteousness, and peace, and joy in the Holy Ghost," Rom. xiv. 17. This may be possessed in a dungeon as well as on a throne. What outward glory soever may be brought in, it is but a shadow of this;—this is the kingdom that cannot be moved, which requires grace in us to "serve God acceptably with reverence and godly fear," Heb. xii. 28. Many have failed in grasping after outward appearances: never any failed of blessedness who made this their portion. Oh, that this were more pursued and followed after! Let not any think to set up the kingdom of Christ in the world, while they pull it down in their own hearts by sin and folly. In this let the lines fall to me, and let my inheritance be among those that are sanctified. Yet,—

(2.) This is certain, that all nations whatever, which in their present state and government have given their power to the dragon and the beast to oppose the Lord Christ withal, shall be shaken, broken, translated, and turned off their old foundations and constitutions, into which the antichristian interest hath been woven for a long season. God will shake the heavens and the earth of the nations round about, until all the Babylonish rubbish, all their original engagements to the man of sin, be taken away.

This I have fully demonstrated elsewhere.[1] All those great wars which you have foretold, wherein the saints of God shall be eminently engaged, are upon this account.

(3.) That the civil powers of the world, after fearful shakings and desolations, shall be disposed of into a useful subserviency to the interest, power, and kingdom of Jesus Christ. Hence they are said to be his kingdoms, Rev. xi. 15; that is, to be disposed of for the behoof of his interest, rule, and dominion. Of this you have plentiful promises, Isa. lx., and elsewhere. When the nations are broken in opposition to Zion, their gain must be consecrated to the Lord, and their substance to the Lord of the whole earth, Mic. iv. 13. Even judges and rulers, as such, must kiss the Son, and own his sceptre, and advance his ways. Some think, if you were well settled, you ought not in any thing, as rulers of the nations, to put forth your power for the interest of Christ: the good Lord keep your hearts from that apprehension! Have you ever in your affairs received any en-

[1] Sermon on Heb. xii. 27.

couragement from the promises of God? have you in times of greatest distress been refreshed with the testimony of a good conscience, that in godly simplicity you have sought the advancement of the Lord Christ? do you believe that he ever owned the cause as the head of his church? Do not now profess you have nothing to do with him:—had he so professed of you and your affairs, what had been your portion long since!

(4.) Look, what *kingdom* soever the Lord Christ will advance in the world, and exercise amongst his holy ones, the beginning of it must be with the Jews; they are to be "caput imperii." The head and seat of this empire must be amongst them; these are the "saints of the Most High," mentioned by Daniel: and, therefore, in that part of his prophecy which he wrote in the Chaldean tongue,—then commonly known and spoken in the east, being the language of the Babylonish empire,—he speaketh of them obscurely, and under borrowed expressions; but coming to those visions which he wrote in Hebrew, for the sole use of the church, he is much more express concerning the people of whom he spake. The rod of Christ's strength goes out of Zion, and thence he proceeds to rule those that were his enemies, Ps. cx. 2. All the promises of the glorious kingdom of Christ are to be accomplished in the gathering of the Gentiles, with the glory of the Jews. The Redeemer comes to Zion, and to them that turn from transgression (that great transgression of unbelief) in Jacob, Isa. lix. 20. Then shall the Lord rise upon them, and his glory shall be seen upon them. The Gentiles shall come to their light, and kings to the brightness of their rising, Isa. lx. 2, 3. I dare say there is not any promise anywhere of raising up a kingdom unto the Lord Christ in this world, but it is either expressed or clearly intimated that the beginning of it must be with the Jews, and that in contradistinction to the nations: so eminently in that glorious description of it, Mic. iv. 7, 8, "I will make her that halted a remnant, and her that was cast far off a strong nation; and the LORD shall reign over them in mount Zion from henceforth, even for ever. And thou, O tower of the flock, the strong hold of the daughter of Zion, unto thee shall it come, even the first dominion; the kingdom shall come to the daughter of Jerusalem." When the great hunter, Nimrod, set up a kingdom, the beginning of it was Babel, Gen. x. 10; and when the great Shepherd sets up his kingdom, the beginning of it shall be Zion: so farther it is at large expressed, Mic. v. 7, 8. Nothing is more clear to any, who, being not carried away with weak, carnal apprehensions of things present, have once seriously weighed the promises of God to this purpose. What the Lord Christ will do with them, and by them, is not so clear; this is certain, that their return shall be marvellous, glorious,—as life from the dead. When, then, Euphrates shall be dried up, Turkish power and Popish idolatry be taken out of the world, and these "kings of the east" are come,—when the seed of Abraham, being multiplied like the stars of heaven and the sands of the sea-shore, shall possess the gates of their enemies, and shall have peace in their borders,—we may lift up our heads towards the fulness of our redemption; but whilst these things are, or may be, for any thing we know, afar off, to dream of setting up an outward, glorious, visible kingdom of Christ, which he must bear rule in, and over the world, be it in Germany or in England, is but an ungrounded presumption. The Jews not called, Antichrist not destroyed, the nations of the world generally wrapped up in idolatry and false worship, little dreaming of their deliverance,—will the Lord Christ leave the world in this state, and set up his kingdom here on a molehill?

(5.) This is a perpetual *antithesis* and opposition that is put between the kingdoms of the world and the kingdom of Christ,—that they rise out of the strivings of the winds upon the sea; he comes with the clouds of heaven;—they are brought in by commotions, tumults, wars, desolations (and so shall all the shakings of the nations be, to punish them for their old opposition, and to translate them into a subserviency to his interest); the coming in of the kingdom of Christ shall not be by the arm of flesh, nor shall it be the product of the strifes and contests of men which are in the world,—it is not to be done by might or power, but by the Spirit of the Lord of hosts, Zech. iv. 6. Great wars, desolations, alterations, shall precede it; but it is not the sons of men that, by outward force, shall build the new Jerusalem:—that comes down from heaven adorned as a bride for Christ, fitted and prepared by himself. Certainly the strivings of men about this business shall have no influence into it. It shall be by the glorious manifestation of his own power, and that by his Spirit subduing the souls of men unto it;—not by the sword of man setting up a few to rule over others. Hence, it is everywhere called a creating of "new heavens, and a new earth," Isa. lxv. 17,—a work, doubtless, too difficult for the worms of the earth to undertake. There is nothing more opposite to the spirit of the gospel, than to suppose that Jesus Christ will take to himself a kingdom by the carnal sword and bow of the sons of men. The raising of the tabernacle of David, which is fallen down, and the setting up the decayed places of it, Acts xv. 16, is done by his visiting the people with his Spirit and word, verse 14. It is by the pouring out of his Spirit in a covenant of mercy, Isa. lix. 21. Thus the Lord sets up one shepherd of his people, "and he shall feed them, even," saith he, "my servant David; he shall feed them, and he shall be their shepherd, and I the LORD will be their God, and my servant David a prince among them," Ezek. xxxiv. 23, 24. He brings in the kingdom of his Son by making the children of Israel "seek the LORD their God, and David their king, and to fear the Lord and his goodness," Hos. iii. 5. Who, now, can fathom the counsels of the Almighty?—who hath searched his bosom, and can by computation tell us when he shall pour out his Spirit for the accomplishment of these things?

This, then, is the last thing in this vision, whose consideration brought the prophet into so great perplexity and distress of spirit.

III. There is the means that Daniel used for redress in that sad condition whereunto he was brought by the consideration of this vision: "He drew near to one of them that stood by, and asked him the truth of all this."

This also was done in vision. There is no mention of his waking before his making this address; but the vision continuing, he draws nigh in the same manner to one of them that stood by,—one of those angels, or holy ones, that stood ministering before the throne of God, who was commissionated to acquaint him with the mind and will of God in the things represented to them. This, then, is the remedy he applies himself unto;—he labours to know the mind and will of God in the things that were to be done. This, it seems, he pitched on as the only way for quieting his grieved and troubled spirit; and hereupon,—

IV. He is told and made to know the interpretation of the things, so far, at least, as might quiet his spirit in the will of God.

Not that he is clearly instructed in every particular; for he tells them, in the close of the chapter, that he had troublesome thoughts about the whole;—"his cogitations troubled him, and his countenance changed," verse 28; but having received what light God was willing to communicate to him, he inquires no farther, but addresses himself to his own duty.

Take, then, from the words thus opened in these propositions (some whereof I shall do little more than name unto you),—

Observation I. *In the consideration of God's marvellous actings in the world, in order to the carrying on of the gospel and the interest of the Lord Jesus Christ, the hearts of his saints are oftentimes filled with perplexity and trouble.*

They know not what will be the issue, nor sometimes what well to do. Daniel receives a vision of the things which in part we live under: and if they fill his heart with astonishment, is it any wonder if they come close to us, and fill us with anxious, perplexing thoughts, upon whom the things themselves are fallen?

Observation II. *The only way to deliver and extricate our spirits from under such perplexities and entanglements, is to draw nigh to God in Christ, for discovery of his will.*

So did Daniel here; he went to one of them that ministered before the Lord, to be acquainted with his will. Otherwise thoughts and contrivances will but farther perplex you. Like men in the mire, whilst they pluck one leg out, the other sticketh faster in,—whilst you relieve yourselves in one thing, you will be more hampered in another. Yea, he that increaseth wisdom, increaseth sorrow;—the larger the visions are, the greater will be their troubles; until, being consumed in your own fears, cares, and contrivances, you grow useless in your generation. Those who see only the outside of your affairs sleep securely; those who come nigher, to look into the spirits of men, rest is taken from them; and many are not quiet, because they will not. The great healing of all is in God.

Observation III. *When God makes known the interpretations of things, it will quiet your spirits, in your walking before him, and actings with him.*

This was that which brought the spirit of Daniel into a settlement. How God reveals his mind in these things,—by what means,—how it may be known by individual persons, for their quiet and settlement, —how all God's revelations are quieting, and tend to the calming of men's spirits, not making them foam like the waves of the sea,— should be handled on this observation.

But I begin with the first observation.

Observation I. *In the consideration of God's marvellous actings in the world, in order to the carrying on of the gospel, the hearts of his saints are oftentimes filled with perplexity and trouble.*

When John received his book of visions in reference to the great things that were to be done, and the alterations that were to be brought about, though it were sweet in his mouth, and he rejoiced in his employment, yet it made his "belly bitter," Rev. x. 9, 10. It filled him with perplexity, as our prophet speaks, in the midst of his body. He saw blood and confusion, strife and violence; it made his very belly bitter.

Poor Jeremiah, upon the same account, is so oppressed, that it makes him break out of all bounds of faith and patience, to curse the day of his birth, to wax quite weary of his employment, chap. xv.

Our Saviour, describing such a season, Luke xxi. 26, tells us, that "men's hearts shall fail them for fear, and for looking after those things that are coming upon the earth." They will be thinking what will become of them, and what will be the issue of God's dispensations; fearing that the whole frame of things will be wrapped up in darkness and confusion. Hence our Saviour bids his disciples not be troubled when they hear of these things, Matt. xxiv. 6, intimating that they will be very apt so to be.

Now, the causes and occasions (which are the reasons of the point) arise,—

1. From the greatness and astonishableness of the things themselves which God will do; even great and terrible things, which men looked not for, Isa. lxiv. 2, 3. When he comes to make his name known to the nations, that his adversaries may tremble at his presence, and doth terrible things, quite above and beyond the expectation of men, which they never once looked for,—no wonder if their hearts be surprised with amazement. It hath of late been so with this nation. All professors at the beginning of these days joined earnestly in that prayer, Isa. lxiii. 17–19, lxiv. 1. God, in answer hereunto, comes down and rends the heavens, and the mountains flow down at his presence, according to the desire of their souls; yet withal he doth terrible things,—things that we looked not for. How many poor creatures are turned back with astonishment, and know not how to abide with him! When our Saviour Christ came in the flesh, who had been the desire of all nations for four thousand years, and most importunately sought after by the men of that generation wherein he came, yet doing great and unexpected things at his coming, who was able to abide it? This, says Simeon, will be the issue of it, "He shall be for the fall and rise of many; and the thoughts of many hearts shall be revealed," Luke ii. 34, 35. Hence is that exclamation, Mal. iii. 2, "Who may abide the day of his coming, and who shall stand when he appeareth?" His coming is desired indeed, but few can bear it. His day will "burn as an oven," as a furnace, chap. iv. 1: some are overheated by it, some consume in it;—blessed are they that abide. This is one cause of the perplexing of the spirits of men;—the consideration of the things themselves that are done, being above and beyond their expectations; and this even many of the saints of God are borne down under at this day. They little looked for the blood and banishment of kings, change of government, alteration of nations, such shakings of heaven and earth as have ensued; not considering that he who doth these things weighs all the nations in a balance, and the rulers of them are as the dust thereof before him.

2. From the manner whereby God will do these things. Many perplexing, killing circumstances attend his dispensations. I shall instance only in one,—and that is, darkness and obscurity, whereby he holds the minds of men in uncertainty and suspense, for his own glorious ends. Such, he tells us, shall his day and the works thereof be: "And it shall come to pass in that day, that the light shall not be clear, nor dark: but it shall be one day which shall be known to the LORD, not day nor night: but it shall come to pass, that at evening-time it shall be light," Zech. xiv. 6, 7. Men shall not know what to make of it, nor what to judge. He brings not forth his work all at once, but by degrees; and sometimes sets it backward, and leads

it up and down, as he did his people of old in the wilderness, that none might know where they should fall or settle; and he that believeth will not make haste. When God is doing great things, he delights to wrap them up in the clouds; to keep the minds of men in uncertainties, that he may set on work all that is in them; and try them to the utmost, whether they can live upon his care and wisdom, when they see their own care and wisdom will do no good. Men would fain come to some certainty; and commonly, by the thoughts and ways whereby they press unto it, they put all things into more uncertainty than ever, and so promote the design of God, which they so studiously endeavour to decline. Hence is that description of the presence of the Lord in his mighty works, Ps. xviii. 9, 11, "Darkness was under his feet;" men could not see his paths, &c. He hath ends of surprisal, hardening, and destruction towards some, for which they must be left unto their own spirits, and led into many snares and by-paths, for their trial, and the exercise of others; which could not be accomplished did he not come in the clouds, and were not darkness his pavilion and his secret place. On this account is that cry of men of profane and hardened spirits, Isa. v. 19, "Let him make speed, and hasten his work, that we may see it: and let the counsel of the Holy One of Israel draw nigh and come, that we may know it!" They know not what to make of what they see,—of all that is yet done or accomplished. They would have the whole work out, that they might once see the end of it, and so know what to judge; they would be at a point with him, and not always kept at those perplexing uncertainties. And this is another cause of the trouble of men's spirits, in consideration of the dispensations of God. God still keeps a cloud hanging over, and they know not when it will fall, nor what will be done in the issue of things. This makes some weary of waiting on him, and, with the profane king of Israel, to cry, This evil is of the Lord; there is no end; confusion will be the issue of all;—why should I abide any longer?

3. The *lusts of men* do commonly, under such dispensations, fearfully and desperately tumultuate, to the disturbance of the most settled and weighed spirits. Satan takes advantage to draw them out in such a season to the utmost, both in spirituals and civils. What will be the constant deportment of men of corrupt minds in such a time our Saviour sets forth, Matt. xxiv. 5. They shall come in the name of Christ to deceive; and shall deceive many, and cause iniquity to abound. In such a day Edom will appear an enemy,[1] and Ephraim with the son of Remaliah will join with Syria for the vexing of Judah: hence are perplexities, and swords piercing through the very souls of men. Take an instance in the days wherein we live. From

[1] Obad. 12, 13; Isa. vii.

the beginning of the contests in this nation, when God had caused your spirits to resolve that the liberties, privileges, and rights of this nation, wherewith you were intrusted, should not, by his assistance, be wrested out of your hands by violence, oppression, and injustice; this he also put upon your hearts, to vindicate and assert the gospel of Jesus Christ, his ways, and his ordinances, against all opposition, though you were but inquiring the way to Zion, with your faces thitherward. God secretly entwining the interest of Christ with yours, wrapped up with you the whole generation of them that seek his face, and prospered your affairs on that account: so that, whereas causes of as clear a righteousness among the sons of men as yours have come to nothing, yet your undertaking hath been like the sheaf of Joseph in the midst of the nations, which hath stood up when all the others have bowed to the ground. Being, then, convinced that your affairs have fallen under his promises, and have come up to an acceptance before him, solely upon the account of their subserviency to the interest of Christ, God hath put it into your hearts to seek the propagation of his gospel. What now, by the lusts of men, is the state of things? Say some, There is no gospel at all; say others, If there be, you have nothing to do with it;—some say, Lo, here is Christ; others, Lo, there:—some make religion a colour for one thing; some for another;—say some, The magistrate must not support the gospel; say others, The gospel must subvert the magistrate;—say some, Your rule is only for men as men, you have nothing to do with the interest of Christ and the church; say others, You have nothing to do to rule men but upon the account of being saints. If you will have the gospel, say some, down with the ministers of it, chemarims,[1] locusts, etc.; and if you will have light, take care that you may have ignorance and darkness:—things being carried on as if it were the care of men that there might be no trouble in the world but what the name of religion might lie in the bottom of. Now, those that ponder these things, their spirits are grieved in the midst of their bodies;—the visions of their heads trouble them. They looked for other things from them that professed Christ; but the summer is ended, and the harvest is past, and we are not refreshed. Again, God had so stated your affairs, that you were the mark of the antichristian world to shoot at in the beginning, and their terror in the close: and when you thought only to have pursued Sheba the son of Bichri, the man of your first warfare, behold one Abel after another undertakes the quarrel against you; yea, such Abels as Scotland and Holland, of whom we said in old times, We will inquire of them, and so ended the mat-

[1] כְּמָרִים, a contemptuous appellation of idolatrous priests. It occurs 2 Kings xxiii. 5; Hos. x. 5; Zeph. i. 4; and is derived from a Syriac word, *blackness;* in the concrete, *one in black attire, an ascetic, a priest.*—Ed.

ter: and there is not a wise man or woman amongst them that can dissuade them. Strange! that Ephraim should join with Syria to vex Judah their brother,—that the Netherlands, whose being is founded merely upon the interest you have undertaken, should join with the great antichristian interest, which cannot possibly be set up again without their inevitable ruin. Hence also are deep thoughts of heart; men are perplexed, disquieted, and know not what to do.

I could mention other lusts, and tumultuatings of the spirits of men, that have an influence into the disturbance of the hearts of the most precious in this nation, but I forbear.

4. Men's own lusts disquiet their spirits in such a season as this. I could instance in many; I shall name only four:—(1.) *Unstableness of mind;* (2.) *Carnal fears;* (3.) *Love of the world;* (4.) *Desire of pre-eminence.*

(1.) Unstableness of mind, which makes men like the waves of the sea, that *cannot rest.* The Scripture calls it ἀκαταστασίαν, "tumultuatingness" of spirit. There is something of that which Jude speaks of, in better persons than those he describes,—"raging like waves of the sea, and foaming out their own shame," verse 13. If God give men up to a *restless* spirit, no condition imaginable can quiet them; still they think they see something beyond it that is desirable. Hannibal said of Marcellus, that he could never be quiet,—conqueror nor conquered. Some men's desires are so enlarged, that nothing can satiate them. Wise men, that look upon sundry godly persons in this nation, and beholding how every yoke of the oppressor is broken from off their necks, that no man makes them afraid, that they are looked on as the head, not as the tail,—enjoying the ordinances of God according to the light of their minds and desires of their hearts, no man forbidding them,—are ready to wonder (I speak of private persons) what they can find to do in their several places and callings, but to serve the Lord in righteousness and holiness, being without fear, all the days of their lives. But, alas! when poor creatures are given up to the power of an unquiet and unstable mind, they think scarce any thing vile, but being wise unto sobriety,—nothing desirable, but what is without their proper bounds, and what leads to that confusion which themselves, in the issue, are least able of many to undergo. It is impossible but that men's hearts should be pierced with disquietness and trouble, that are given up to this frame.

(2.) *Carnal fears.*—These even devour and eat up the hearts of men. What shall we do? what shall become of us? Ephraim is confederate with Syria, and the hearts of men are shaken as the trees of the wood that are moved with the wind. What! new troubles still! new unsettlements! This storm will not be avoided; this will be worse than all that hath befallen us from the youth of our undertakings. God hath not yet won upon men's spirits to trust him in shakings, perplexities, alterations; they remember not the manifestations of his wisdom, power, and goodness in former days, and how tender hitherto he hath been of the interest of Christ, that their hearts might be established. Could we but do our duty, and trust the Lord with the performance of his promises, what quietness, what sweetness might we have!

I shall not instance in the other two particulars. It is too manifest that many of our piercing and perplexing thoughts are from the tumultuating and disorder of our own lusts. So that what remains of the time allotted to me I shall spend only in the use of this point, and proceed no farther.

Use. Of instruction, to direct you into ways and means of quietness, in reference unto all these causes and occasions of piercing, dividing thoughts in such a season as this. The good Lord seal up instruction to your souls, that you may know the things that belong to your peace, and what Israel ought to do at this, even at this time. For my brethren's and companions' sake, I wish you prosperity. Though my own portion should be in the dust, for the *true, spiritual,* not *imaginary, carnal* interest of the church of God in this nation, and the nations about, I wish you prosperity.

(1.) First, then, in reference to *the things that God is doing,* both as to their *greatness and their manner of doing;* whose consideration fills men with thoughts that grieve their spirits in the midst of their bodies. Would you have your hearts quieted in this respect?—take my second *observation* for your direction;—The only way to extricate and deliver our spirits from under such perplexities and entanglements, is to draw nigh to God in Christ for the discovery of his will. So did Daniel here in my text. I fear this is too much neglected. You take counsel with your own hearts, you advise with one another, —hearken unto men under a repute of wisdom; and all this doth but increase your trouble,—you do but more and more entangle and disquiet your own spirits. God stands by and says, "I am wise also;" and little notice is taken of him. We think we are grown wise ourselves, and do not remember we never prospered but only when we went unto God, and told him plainly we knew not what to do. Public fastings are neglected, despised, spoken against; and when appointed, practised according as men's hearts are principled to such a duty,—coldly, deadly, unacceptably. Life, heat, warmth is gone; and shall not blood and all go after? The Lord prevent it! Private meetings are used to show ourselves wise in the debate of things, with a form of godly words; sometimes for strife, tumult, division, disorder. And shall we think there is much closet inquiring after God, when all other actings of that principle which should carry out thereunto are opposed and slighted? When we do sometimes wait upon God, do not many seem to ask amiss, to spend it on their lusts;—not waiting on him poor, hungry, empty, to know his will, to receive direction from him; but rather going full, fixed, resolved, settled on thoughts, perhaps prejudices, of our own,—almost taking upon us to prescribe unto the Almighty, and to impose our poor, low, carnal thoughts upon his wisdom and care of his church? Oh, where is that holy and that humble frame wherewith at first we followed our God into the wilderness, where we have been fed and clothed, preserved and protected for so many years? Hence is it that the works of God are become strange, and terrible, and dark unto us; and of necessity some of us, many of us, must shut up all with disappointment and sorrow. We fill our souls boldly, confidently, with cross and contrary apprehensions of the intendments of God, and of the mediums whereby he will accomplish his ends; and do not consider that this is not a frame of men who had given up themselves to the *all-sufficiency* of God. Some, perhaps, will say, this belongs not unto them; they have waited upon God, and they do know his mind, and what are the things he will do, and are not blind also, nor in the dark, as other men. But if it be so, "what means this bleating of sheep and oxen in mine ears?" yea, what means that roaring and foaming of unquiet waves which we hear and see;—hard speeches, passionate reproaches, sharp revilings of their brethren, in boundless confidence, endless enmity, causing evil surmises, biting, tearing, devouring terms and expressions, casting out the names of men upright in their generations, saying, The Lord be praised? When the Lord discovers his mind and will, it settleth the heart, composeth the mind, fills the soul with reverence and godly fear, conforms the heart unto itself,—fills it with peace, love, meekness, gentleness. And shall we be thought to have received the mind, the will of God, when our hearts, words, ways, are full of contrary qualities? Let it be called what it will, I shall not desire to share in that which would bring my heart into such a frame. Well, then, beloved, take this for your first direction: Be more abundant with God in faith and prayer, deal with him in public and private, take counsel of him, bend your hearts through his grace to your old frame, when it was your joy to meet in this place,—which now, I fear, to many is their burden. Seek the Lord and his face, " seek him while he may be found." And hereby,—

[1.] You will empty your hearts of many perplexing contrivances of your own, and you will find faith in this communion with God, by little and little, working out, killing, slaying these prejudices and presumptions which you may be strong in, that are not according to the will of God; so you be sure to come not to have your own lusts and carnal conceptions answered, but to have the will of God fulfilled. When men come unto the Lord to have their own *visions fulfilled*, it is righteous with God to answer them according to those visions, and confirm them in them, to their own disturbance, and the disturbance of others.

[2.] You shall certainly have *peace in your own hearts in the all-sufficiency of God.* This he will give in upon your spirits, that whatever he doth, all his ways shall be to you mercy, truth, faithfulness, and peace;—yea, the discoveries which you shall have of his own fulness, sweetness, suitableness, and the excellency of things which are not seen, will work your hearts to such a frame, that you shall attend to the things here below, merely upon the account of duty, with the greatest calmness and quietness of mind imaginable.

[3.] You shall surely know your own particular paths, wherein you ought to walk in serving God in your generation. Those that wait upon him, he will guide in judgment; he will not leave them in the dark, nor to distracted, divided, piercing thoughts. But whatever others do, you shall be guided into ways of peace. This you shall have when the lusts of men will neither let themselves nor others be at quiet. Oh, then, return to your rest; look to Him from whom you have gone astray. Take no more disturbing counsel with yourselves, or others; renew your old frame of humble dependence on God, and earnest seeking his face. You have certainly backslidden in this thing. Is the Lord not the God of counsel and wisdom, as well as the God of force and power, that you run to him when in a strait in your actions, but when your counsels seem sometimes to be mixed with a spirit of difficulty and trouble, he is neglected? Only come with humble, depending hearts;—not every one to bring the devices, imaginations, opinions, prejudices, and lusts of their own hearts, before him.

(2.) For the troubles that arise from the *lusts of other men*, and that about the *gospel* and the *propagation thereof* (the tumultuating of the lusts of men in reference whereunto I gave you an account of formerly), there are many piercing thoughts of heart. What *extremes*, I had almost said *extravagances*, men have in this matter run out into, I shall now not insist upon; only I shall give you a few directions for your own practice.

If once it comes to that, that you shall say you have nothing to do with *religion as rulers of the nation*, God will quickly manifest that he hath nothing to do with you as rulers of the nation. The great promise of Christ is, that in these latter days of the world he will lay the nations in a subserviency to him,—the kingdoms of the world shall become his; that is, act as kingdoms and governments no longer against him, but for him. Surely those promises will scarcely be accomplished in bringing commonwealths of men professing his name to be of Gallio's frame,—to take care for none of those things: or as the Turk,—in an absolute indifferency what any profess; I mean, that are not his own, for in respect of them he changes not his God. Not that I would you should go and set up forms of government to compel men to come under the line of them, or to thrust in your sword to cut the lesser differences of brethren; not that I think truth ever the more the truth, or to have any thing the more of authority upon the conscience, for having the stamp of your authority annexed to it, for its allowance to pass in these nations. Nor do I speak a word of what is, may, or may not be incumbent on you in respect of the most profligate opposers of the truths of the gospel, but only this, that, not being such as are always learning, never coming to the knowledge of the truth, but being fully persuaded in your own minds, certainly it is incumbent on you to take care that the faith which you have received, which was once delivered to the saints, in all the necessary concernments of it, may be protected, preserved, propagated to and among the people which God hath set you over. If a father, as a father, is bound to do what answers this in his family unto his children; a master, as a master, to his servants; if you will justify yourselves as fathers or rulers of your country, you will find in your account this to be incumbent on you. Take heed of them that would temper clay and iron, things that will not mingle,—that would compound carnal and fleshly things with heavenly things and spiritual,—that they may not entangle your spirits. *The great design of grasping temporal power upon a spiritual account, will prove at last to be the greatest badge of Antichrist.* Hitherto God hath appeared against it; and will, no doubt, to the end. If either you, by the authority God hath given you in the world, shall take upon you to rule the house of God, as formally such, as his house, though you rule the persons whereof it is made up; or those who are, or pretend to be, of that house, to rule the world on that account,—your day and theirs will be nigh at hand.

Now, because you wait on God for direction in reference to the propagation of the gospel, and the preventing that which is contrary to sound doctrine and godliness, I shall,—[1.] Show you very briefly what God has promised concerning magistrates to this end; [2.] Give you some principles whereon you may rest in your actings; and, [3.] Lay down some rules for your direction: and so draw to a close.

[1.] Take, in the first place, what God hath *promised* concerning magistrates, kings, rulers, judges, and nations, and their subserviency to the church. What God hath promised they shall do, that is their duty to do; he hath not measured out an inheritance for his people out of the sins of other men. Let us a little view some of these promises, and then consider their application to the truth we have in hand, and what is cleared out unto us by them. There are many; I shall instance in the most obvious and eminent. "I will restore thy judges as at the first, and thy counsellors as at the beginning," Isa. i. 26. It is to Zion redeemed, purged, washed in the blood of Christ, that this promise is made. Isa. xlix. 7, "Kings shall see and arise, and princes shall bow down themselves." [Heb.] The Jews being, for the greatest part of them, rejected upon the coming of Christ, this promise is made unto him upon his pouring out of the Spirit for the bringing in of the Gentiles; as it is farther enlarged, verses 22, 23, "Kings shall be thy nursing-fathers, and their queens thy nursing-mothers." Isa. lx. looks wholly this way. Taste of the nature and intendment of the whole: "And the Gentiles shall come to thy light, and kings to the brightness of thy rising. Therefore thy gates shall be open continually; they shall not be shut day nor night; that men may bring unto thee the forces of the Gentiles, and that their kings may be brought. Thou shalt also suck the milk of the Gentiles, and shalt suck the breast of kings: and thou shalt know that I the LORD am thy Saviour and thy Redeemer, the mighty one of Jacob. For brass I will bring gold, and for iron I will bring silver, and for wood brass, and for stones iron: I will also make thy officers peace, and thine exactors righteousness," verses 3, 11, 16, 17. To which add the accomplishment of all those promises mentioned, Rev. xi. 15, xxi. 24.

You see here are glorious promises, in the literal expression, looking directly to what we assert concerning the subserviency of rulers to the gospel, and the duty of magistrates in supporting the interest of the church. Let us, concerning them, observe these three things; as,—1*st*, *To whom they are made;* 2*dly*, *On what occasion they are given;* 3*dly*, *What is the subject or matter of them in general.*

1*st*, Then, they are all given and made to the church of Christ after his coming in the flesh, and his putting an end to all *ceremonial, typical, carnal* institutions. For,—

(1*st.*) They are every way attended with the circumstances of *calling the Gentiles*, and their flowing into the church; which were not accomplished till after the destruction of the Jewish church. So is the case in that which you have, Isa. xlix. 20, "The children which thou shalt have, after thou hast lost the other, shall say again in thine ears, The place is too strait for me: give place to me that I may dwell." It shall be when the church shall have received the new children of the Gentiles, having lost the other of the Jews; which he expresseth more at large, verse 22, "Thus saith the Lord GOD, Behold, I will lift up mine hand to the Gentiles, and set up my standard to the people: and they shall bring thy sons in their arms, and thy daughters shall be carried upon their shoulders." So also are the rest. When God gives the nations to be the inheritance of Christ, the Holy Ghost cautions rulers and judges to kiss the Son, and pay the homage due to him in his kingdom, Ps. ii. 10, 11.

(2*dly.*) Because these promises are pointed unto as accomplished to the Christian Church in that place of the Revelation before mentioned: "And the seventh angel sounded; and there were great voices in heaven, saying, The kingdoms of this world are become the kingdoms of our Lord, and of his Christ; and he shall reign for ever and ever," chap. xi. 15. "And the nations of them which are saved shall walk in the light of it: and the kings of the earth do bring their glory and honour into it," chap. xxi. 24. So that there are plainly promises of kings and princes, judges and rulers, to be given to the church, and to be made useful thereunto; and kingdoms and nations, people in their rules and governments, to be instrumental in the good thereof: so that these promises belong directly to us and our rulers, if, under any notion, we belong to the Church of Christ.

2*dly.* For the *occasion* of these promises;—it is well known what a trust, by God's own appointment, there was invested in the rulers, judges, kings, and magistrates, of the judicial state and church under the Old Testament, in reference unto the ways and worship of God, —the prosecution and the execution of the laws of God concerning his house and service being committed to them. Farther, when they faithfully discharged their trust,—promoting the worship of God according to his institutions,—encouraging, supporting, directing, reproving others, to whom the immediate and peculiar administration of things sacred was committed,—destroying, removing whatever was an abomination unto the Lord,—it was well with the whole people and church; they flourished in peace, and the Lord delighted in them, and rejoiced over them to do them good. And, on the other side, their neglect in the discharge of their duty was then commonly attended with the *apostasy of the church,* and great breakings forth of the indignation of the Lord. This the church found in those days, and bewailed. To hold out, therefore, the happy state of his people that he would bring in, he promises them such rulers and judges as he gave at first, who faithfully discharged the trust committed to them:—not that I suppose them bound to the Mosaical rules of penalties in reference to transgressions and offences against gospel institutions, but only that a duty in general is incumbent on them, in reference to the church and truth of God, which they should faithfully discharge;—of which afterward.

This, then, being the occasion of those promises, and their accomplishment being, as before, in a peculiar manner pointed at, upon the shaking, calling, and new-moulding of the kingdoms and nations of the world which had given their power to the beast, and thereupon framed anew into a due subserviency to the interest of Christ, there is not the least shadow or colour left for the turning off and rejecting the sweetness of all these promises, upon account of their being merely metaphorical, and shadowing out spiritual glories:—neither their beginning nor ending, neither their rise nor fall, will bear any such gloss or corrupting interpretation.

3dly. As to the *matter* of these promises, I shall only assert this in general,—that the Lord engageth that judges, rulers, magistrates, and such like, shall put forth their power, and act clearly for the good, welfare, and prosperity of the church. This is plainly held out in every one of them. Hence kingdoms are said to serve the church; that is, all kingdoms. They must do so, or be broken in pieces, and cease to be kingdoms. And how can a kingdom, as a kingdom (for it is taken formally, and not materially, merely for the individuals of it, as appears by the threatening of its being broken in pieces) serve the church, but by putting forth its power and strength in her behalf? Isa. lx. 12. And therefore, upon the accomplishment of that promise, they are said to become the kingdoms of the Lord Christ, Rev. xi. 15, because, as kingdoms, they serve him with their power and authority; having before, as such, and by their power, opposed him to the utmost. They must nurse the church, not with dry breasts, nor feed it with stones and scorpions, but with the good things committed to them. Their power and substance, in protection and supportment, are to be engaged in the behalf thereof: hence God is said to give these judges, rulers, princes, kings, queens to the church; not setting them in the church, as officers thereof, but ordering their state in the world (Rev. xi. 15) to its behoof. In sum, there is not any one of the promises recited but holds forth the utmost of what I intend to assert from them all; viz., that the Lord hath promised that the magistrates whom he will give, own, and bless, shall put forth their power, and act in that capacity wherein he hath placed them in the world, for the good, furtherance, and prosperity of the truth and church of Christ. They shall protect them with their power, feed them with their substance, adorn them with their favour and the privileges wherewith they are intrusted; they shall break their forcibly oppressing adversaries, and take care that those who walk in the truth of the Lord may lead a peaceable life, in all godliness and honesty. If, then, you are such magistrates as God hath promised, (as woe be unto you if you are not!) know that he hath undertaken for you, that you shall perform this part of your duty; and I pray that you may rule with him therein, and be found faithful.

[2.] *The second ground* that I would point unto, as a bottom of your actings in this thing, ariseth from sundry undoubted principles, which I shall briefly mention. And the first is,—

1*st*. *That the gospel of Jesus Christ hath a right to be preached and propagated in every nation, and to every creature under heaven.* Jesus Christ is the "Lord of lords, and King of kings," Rev. xvii. 14. The nations are given to be his inheritance, and the utmost parts of the earth to be his possession, Ps. ii. 8, 9. He is appointed the "heir of all things," Heb. i. 2. God hath set him over the works of his hands, and put all things in subjection under his feet, Ps. viii. 6. And upon this account he gives commission to his messengers to preach the gospel to all nations, Matt. xxviii. 19, or, to every creature under heaven, Mark xvi. 15. The nations of the world being of the Father given to him, he may deal with them as he pleaseth, and either bruise them with a rod of iron, and break them in pieces as a potter's vessel, Ps. ii. 9,—he may fill the places of the earth with their dead bodies, and strike in pieces the heads of the countries, Ps. cx. 6,—or, he may make them his own, and bring them into subjection unto himself;—which towards some of them he will effect, Rev. xi. 15. Now, the gospel being the rod of his power, and the sceptre of his kingdom,—the grand instrument whereby he accomplisheth all his designs in the world, whether they be for life or for death, 2 Cor. ii. 16,—he hath given *that* a right to take possession, in his name and authority, of all that he will own in any nation under heaven. And, indeed, he hath in all of them some that are his peculiar purchase, Rev. v. 9; whom, in despite of all the world, he will bring in unto himself. To have free passage into all nations is the undoubted right of the gospel; and the persons of Christ's good-will have such a right to it and interest in it, that, look, from whomsoever they may claim protection in reference unto any other of their most undoubted concernments amongst men, of them may they claim protection in respect of their quiet enjoyment and possession of the gospel.

2*dly*. *That wherever the gospel is by any nation owned, received, embraced, it is the blessing, benefit, prosperity, and advantage of that nation.* They that love Zion shall prosper, Ps. cxxii. 6. Godliness hath the promise of this life, and is profitable unto all things, 1 Tim. iv. 8. The reception of the word of truth, and subjection to Christ therein, causing a people to become willing in the day of his power, entitle that people to all the promises that ever God made to his church. They shall be established in righteousness; they shall be far from oppression; and for fear and terror, they shall not draw nigh unto them: whosoever contends against such a people, shall fall thereby. No weapon that is formed against them shall prosper; every tongue that shall rise against them in judgment, they shall condemn.

For this is the inheritance of the servants of the Lord, Isa. liv. 14, 15, 17.

To the prosperity of a nation two things are required:—(1*st.*) That they be freed from oppression, injustice, cruelty, disorder, confusion, in themselves, from their rulers, or others; (2*dly.*) That they be protected from the sword and violence of them that seek their ruin from without. And both these do a people receive by receiving the gospel.

(1*st.*) For the first, they have the promise of God that they shall have "judges as at the first," Isa. i. 26,—such in justice and judgment shall bear rule over them and among them, as the first judges whom he stirred up and gave to his ancient people; their officers shall be peace, and their exactors righteousness, Isa. lx. 17. Even the very gospel which they do receive is only able to instruct them to be just, ruling in the fear of the Lord; for that only effectually teacheth the sons of men to live righteously, soberly, and godly in this present world, Tit. ii. 12.

(2*dly.*) And for the second, innumerable are the promises that are given to such a people; whence the psalmist concludes, upon the consideration of the mercies they do and shall enjoy, "Happy is the people whose God is the LORD," Ps. cxliv. 15. The glorious LORD will be to them a place of broad rivers and waters, in which no galley with oars, nor gallant ship shall pass by; the LORD will be their redeemer, lawgiver, king, and saviour, Isa. xxxiii. 21. It will interest any people in all the promises that are made for the using of the church to thrash, break, destroy, burden, fire, consume, and slay the enemies thereof;—so far shall a people be from suffering under the hands of oppressors, that the Lord will use them for the breaking and destruction of the Nimrods of the earth: and this blessing of the nations do they receive by the faith of Abraham.

3dly. The rejection of the gospel by any people or nation to whom it is tendered, is always attended with the certain and inevitable destruction of that people or nation; which, sooner or later, shall, without any help or deliverance, be brought upon them by the revenging hand of Christ.

When the word of grace was rejected and despised by the Jews, the messengers of it professedly turning to the Gentiles, Acts xiii. 46, xxviii. 28,—God removing it from them, unto a nation that would bring forth fruit, Matt. xxi. 43, as it did in all the world, or among all nations, for a season, Col. i. 6,—with what a fearful and tremendous desolation he quickly wasted that people, is known to all;—he quickly slew and destroyed those husbandmen that spoiled his vineyard, and let it forth unto others, that might bring him his fruit in due season. Hence, when Christ is tendered in the gospel, the judges and rulers of the nations are exhorted to obedience to him, upon pain of being destroyed upon the refusal thereof, Ps. ii. 12. And we have the experience of all ages, ever since the day that the gospel began to be propagated in the world. The quarrel of it was revenged on the Jews by the Romans,—upon the Romans by the Goths, Vandals, and innumerable barbarous nations; and the vengeance due to the antichristian world is at hand, even at the door. The Lord will certainly make good his promise to the utmost, that the kingdom and nations which will not serve the church, even that kingdom and those nations shall utterly perish, Isa. lx. 12.

4thly. That it is the duty of magistrates to seek the good, peace, and prosperity of the people committed to their charge, and to prevent, obviate, remove, take away every thing that will bring confusion, destruction, desolation upon them; as Mordecai procured good things for his people, and prosperity to his kindred, Esther x. 3. And David describes himself with all earnestness pursuing the same design, Ps. ci. Magistrates are the ministers of God for the good, universal good, of them to whom they are given, Rom. xiii. 1–4; and they are to watch and apply themselves to this very thing, verse 6. And the reason the apostle gives to stir up the saints of God to pray, amongst all sorts of men, in special for kings and those that are in authority,—to wit, that they may, in general, come to the knowledge of the faith, and be saved; and, in particular, discharge the duty and trust committed to them (for on that account are they to pray for them as kings and men in authority),—is, "that we may lead a quiet and peaceable life, in all godliness and honesty," 1 Tim. ii. 1–4. It being incumbent on them to act even as kings and men in authority, that we may so do; they are to feed the people committed to their charge with all their might, unto universal peace and welfare.

Now, the things that are opposite to the good of any nation or people are of two sorts:—(1*st.*) Such as are really, directly, and immediately opposed to that state and condition wherein they close together, and find prosperity. In general, seditions, tumults, disorders; in particular, violent or fradulent breakings in upon the respective designed bounds, privileges, and enjoyments of singular persons, without any consideration of Him who ruleth all things, are of this kind. If nations and rulers might be supposed to be Atheists, yet such evils as these, tending to their dissolution and not-being, they would, with all their strength, labour to prevent, either by watching against their commission, or inflicting vengeance on them that commit them, that others may hear, and fear, and do so no more. (2*dly.*) Such as are morally and meritoriously opposed to their good and welfare; in that they will certainly pluck down the judgments and wrath of God upon that nation or people where they are practised and allowed. There are sins for which the wrath of God will be assuredly revealed from heaven against the children of disobedience. Sodom and Gomorrah are set forth as examples of his righteous judgment in this kind. And shall he be thought a magistrate, to bear out the name, authority, and presence of God to men, that so he and his people have present peace, [who,] like a herd of swine, cares not though such things as will certainly first eat and devour their strength, and then utterly consume them, do pass for current? Seeing that they that rule over men must be just, ruling in the fear of the Lord, the sole reason why they sheathe the sword of justice in the bowels of thieves, murderers, adulterers, is, not because their outward peace is actually disturbed by them,—and therefore they must give example of terror to others, who being like minded, are not yet actually given up to the practice of the like abomination,—but also, yea, principally, because He in whose stead they stand and minister to the world is provoked by such wickedness to destroy both the one and the other. And if there be the same reason to be evidenced concerning other things, they also call for the same procedure.

To gather up, now, what hath been spoken:—considering the gospel's right and title to be propagated, with all its concernments, in every nation under heaven; the blessing, peace, prosperity, and protection wherewith it is attended when and where received; and the certain destruction and desolation which accompanies the rejection and contempt thereof;—considering the duty that, by God's appointment, is incumbent on them that rule over men,—that in the fear of the Lord they ought to seek the good, peace, and welfare and prosperity of them committed to their charge; to prevent, obviate, remove, revenge, that which tends to their hurt, perturbation, dissolution, destruction, immediate from heaven, or from the hand of men; and in the whole administration to take care that the worshippers of God in Christ may lead a quiet and peaceable life, in all godliness and honesty;—let any one, who hath the least sense upon his spirit, of the account which he must one day make to the great King and Judge of all the world, of the authority and power wherewith he was intrusted, determine whether it be not incumbent on him—by all the *protection* he can afford, by all the *privileges* he can indulge, the *supportment* that he can grant, by all that *encouragement* which, upon the highest account imaginable, he is required or allowed to give to any person whatsoever—to further the propagation of the gospel; which upon the matter is the only thing of concernment, as well unto this life as that which is to come. And if any thing be allowed in a nation, which in God's esteem may amount to a contempt and despising thereof, men may be taught by sad experience what will be the issue of such allowance.

5thly. I shall only propose one thing more to your consideration. *Although the institutions and examples of the Old Testament, of the duty of magistrates in the things and about the worship of God, are not, in their whole latitude and extent, to be drawn into rules* that should be obligatory to all magistrates now, under the administration of the gospel,—and that because the magistrate then was "custos, vindex, et administrator legis judicialis, et politiæ Mosaicæ," from which, as most think, we are freed;—yet, doubtless, there is something moral in those institutions, which, being unclothed of their Judaical form, is still binding to all in the like kind, as to some analogy and proportion. Subduct from those administrations what was proper to, and lies upon the account of, the church and nation of the Jews, and what remains upon the general notion of a church and nation must be everlastingly binding. And this amounts thus far, at least, that judges, rulers, and magistrates, which are promised under the New Testament to be given in mercy, and to be of singular usefulness, as the judges were under the Old, are to take care that the gospel church may, in its concernment as such, be supported and promoted, and the truth propagated wherewith they are intrusted; as the others took care that it might be well with the Judaical church as such. And on these, and such like principles as these are, may you safely bottom yourselves in that undertaking wherein you seek for direction from God this day.

[3.] For the rules which I intimated, I shall but name them, having some years since delivered my thoughts to the world at large on this subject;[1] and I see no cause as yet to recede from any thing then so delivered. Take, then, only, for the present, these brief directions following:—

1*st.* *Labour to be fully persuaded in your own minds, that you be not carried up and down with every wind of doctrine,* and be tempted to hearken after every spirit, as though you had received no truth as it is in Jesus. It is a sad condition, when men have no zeal for truth, nor against that which is opposite to it, whatever they seem to profess; because, indeed, having not taken in any truth in the power and principle of it, they are upon sad thoughts, wholly at a loss whether there be any truth or no. This is an unhappy frame indeed;—the proper condition of them whom God will spue out of his mouth.

2*dly.* Know that error and falsehood have no right or title, either from God or man, unto any privilege, protection, advantage, liberty, or any good thing you are intrusted withal. To dispose that unto a lie, which is the right of and due to truth, is to deal treacherously with Him by whom you are employed. All the tenderness and forbearance unto such persons as are infected with such abominations is

[1] Discourse on Toleration.

solely upon a civil account, and that plea which they have for tranquillity whilst neither directly nor morally they are a disturbance unto others.

3dly. Know that in things of practice, so of persuasion, that are impious and wicked, either in themselves or in their natural and unconstrained consequences, the plea of *conscience* is an aggravation of the crime. If men's consciences are seared, and themselves given up to a reprobate mind, to do those things that are not convenient, there is no doubt but they ought to suffer such things as to such practices are assigned and appointed.

Should I now descend unto particulars in all the things mentioned, and insist on them, time would wholly fail me,—neither is it a work for a single sermon; and, therefore, in one word I shall wind up the whole matter, and end.

Know them, then, that are faithful and quiet in the land; regard the truth of the gospel; remember the days of old,—what hath done you good, quieted your heart in distress, crowned your undertakings with sweetness; lose not your first love; draw not out your own thoughts for the counsel of God; seek not great things for yourselves; be not moved at the lusts of men; keep peace what in you lieth with all that fear the Lord; let the glory of Christ be the end of all your undertakings, etc.

SERMON X.

GOD'S WORK IN FOUNDING ZION,

AND

HIS PEOPLE'S DUTY THEREUPON.

PREFATORY NOTE.

An English Parliament was summoned by Cromwell, as Lord Protector, to meet at Westminster on the 17th September 1656. At this time Admiral Blake was pursuing his victorious career, and combating on the ocean the inveterate enemy of England and English Protestantism,—Spain. In order to obtain the supplies requisite for the maintenance of the war, the Parliament was convened, and Dr Owen preached on the occasion. The Parliament agreed to support the Protector in the war, and voted him for the purpose £400,000. The sermon of Owen is remarkable for the tone of cheerful gratitude pervading it, for the peace and freedom which the nation now enjoyed. While contrasting present advantages with the evils from which the country had been delivered, he warns his audience against any course that might expose them, under the judgment of God, to the loss of privileges so dearly won, and against indulging in the strife and animosities which would "turn judgment into wormwood, and truth into hemlock."—Ed.

Wednesday, 17th of September 1656.

Ordered by the Parliament, That Mr Maidstone and the Lieutenant of the Tower do give the hearty thanks of the House to Dr Owen, Dean of Christ Church and Vice-Chancellor of the University of Oxford, for his great pains taken in his sermon preached this day in the Abbey Church at Westminster, before his Highness the Lord Protector and the members elected to sit this present Parliament; and that he be desired to print his sermon; and that no man presume to print it without his leave.

Hen. Scobell, *Clerk of the Parliament.*

TO HIS HIGHNESS,

THE LORD PROTECTOR,

AND TO

THE PARLIAMENT OF THE COMMONWEALTH OF ENGLAND, SCOTLAND, AND IRELAND, &c.

ALTHOUGH I need plead no other reason for the publishing of the ensuing discourse but your order and command for my so doing; yet, because I know that your peculiar interest, as governors of this commonwealth, in the several stations wherein you are placed of God, is truly stated therein,—in the pursuit whereof your peace and the peace of these nations will be found to lie,—I crave leave to add that consideration also. Being fully acquainted in and with what weakness it was composed and delivered, I cannot but conclude that it was merely for the truth's sake therein contained, which is of God, and its suitableness, through his wise providence, to the present state of things in these nations, that it found acceptance and entertainment with you; which also makes me willing to be therein your remembrancer a second time. From the day wherein I received a command and call unto the service of preaching unto you, unto this issue of it, wherein it is clothed anew with obedience to your order, I found mercy with God to have that caution of the great apostle abiding in my heart and thoughts, "If I yet please men, I am not a servant of God." Hence I can with boldness profess, that, influenced in some measure with the power of that direction, I studiously avoided whatever might be suggested with the least unsuitableness thereunto, with respect either to myself or others.

It was for Zion's sake that I was willing to undertake this duty and service, rejoicing that I had once more an opportunity to give public testimony to the great concernment of the great God and our dear Lord Jesus Christ in all the concussions of the nations in the world, and peculiarly in his wonderful providential dispensations in these wherein we live. And here, as the sum of all, to use plainness and liberty of speech, I say, if there be any thing, in any person whatever in these nations, that cannot stand with, that can stand without, the general interest of the people of God pleaded for, let it fall, and rise no more; and the Lord, I know, will send his blessing out of Zion on whatever, in singleness of heart, is done in a tendency to the establishment thereof.

Farther, I shall not need to suggest any thing of the ensuing discourse:—they who take themselves to be concerned therein will acquaint themselves with it by its perusal. I shall only add, if the general principles asserted therein be in your hearts; if, in pursuit thereof, you endeavour that in no corner of the nation it may be said, This is Zion, that no man careth for; but that those who love the Lord Jesus Christ in sincerity, and are, by faith and obedience, separated from the perishing world, following the Lamb, according to the light which he is graciously pleased to impart unto them, and engaged, by the providence of God, in that work which he hath undertaken to accomplish amongst us, be not overborne by a spirit of profaneness and contempt of the power of godliness raging in the earth; that they may be preserved and secured from the return of a hand of violence, and encouraged in the testimony they have to bear to the kingdom of Christ, in opposition to the world, and all the ways which the men thereof have received by tradition from their fathers, that are not according to his mind;—you will, undoubtedly, in your several conditions, receive blessing from God. Which also that you may, in all your concernments, is the daily prayer of

Your humble Servant

In the work of our dear Lord Jesus,

JOHN OWEN.

SERMON X.

GOD'S WORK IN FOUNDING ZION, AND HIS PEOPLE'S DUTY THEREUPON.

"What shall one then answer the messengers of the nation? That the LORD hath founded Zion, and the poor of his people shall trust in it."—ISA. xiv. 32.

THE head of the prophecy whereof these words are the close, lies in verse 28, "In the year that king Ahaz died was this burden;" which gives us the season and just time of its revelation and delivery. The kingdom of Judah was at that season low and broken;—foreign invasions and intestine divisions had made it so. An account hereof is given us, 2 Chron. xxviii. throughout, as it is especially summed up, verse 19 of that chapter, "For the LORD brought Judah low because of Ahaz king of Israel; for he made Judah naked, and transgressed sore against the LORD." Amongst their oppressing neighbours that took advantage of their low and divided condition, their old enemies the Philistines, the posterity of Ham in Canaan, had no small share, as verse 18 of that chapter, "The Philistines also had invaded the cities of the low country, and of the south of Judah, and had taken Beth-shemesh, and Ajalon, and Gederoth, and Shocho with the villages thereof, and Timnah with the villages thereof, Gimzo also and the villages thereof: and they dwelt there."

In this state of things, God takes notice of the joy and triumphing of the whole land of Palestina,—that is, the country of the Philistines,—in that the rod of him that smote them was broken; that is, the power of the kings and kingdom of Judah, which, for many generations, had prevailed against them,—especially in the days of David, 2 Sam. v., and of Uzziah, 2 Chron. xxvi. 6,—and kept them under, was made weak and insufficient for that purpose, verse 29, "Rejoice not thou, whole land of Palestina, because the rod of him that smote thee is broken."

It is no wonder if Palestina, that was to be smitten and broken by the rod of God among his people, rejoice at their perplexities and distresses when we have seen men so to do who pretend to dwell in Judah.

To take them off from their pride and boasting, their triumph and rejoicing, the Lord lets them know that, from the people whom they despised, and that broken rod they trampled upon, their desolation was at hand, though they seem to be perplexed and forsaken for a season, verses 29–31, " Rejoice not thou, whole Palestina, because the rod of him that smote thee is broken: for out of the serpent's root shall come forth a cockatrice, and his fruit shall be a fiery flying serpent. And the first-born of the poor shall feed, and the needy shall lie down in safety; and I will kill thy root with famine, and he shall slay thy remnant. Howl, O gate; cry, O city; thou, whole Palestina, art dissolved: for there shall come from the north a smoke, and none shall be alone in his appointed times." That it is Hezekiah who is principally intended in these lofty allegorical expressions, that was then rising up from the broken rod of Judah, is evident. He is termed a "cockatrice," and a " fiery flying serpent," not from his own nature, which was tender, meek, and gentle, wherein the comparison doth not at all lie nor hold; but in respect of the mischief that he should do unto, the irrecoverable destruction that he should bring on, the land of Palestina: which, accordingly, he performed, 2 Kings xviii. 8, " He smote the Philistines, even unto Gaza, and the borders thereof, from the tower of the watchmen to the fenced city;" that is, he wasted and destroyed the whole land, from one end even to the other.

It is, it seems, no *new* thing, that the season of the enemies' *rejoicing*, built upon the *outward appearance* and state of things among the people of God, is the *beginning* of their disappointment and desolation. The Lord make it so in this day of England's expectation, that the rod of it may be strengthened again, yet to smite the whole land of Palestina!

The words of my text are the result of things upon God's dealings and dispensations before mentioned. Uncertain it is, whether they ought to be restrained to the immediate prophecy before-going concerning Palestina, or whether they relate not also to that in the beginning of the chapter, concerning the destruction of the Assyrian, which is summed up, verses 24, 25, " The LORD of hosts hath sworn, saying, Surely as I have thought, so shall it come to pass; and as I have purposed, so shall it stand: that I will break the Assyrian in my land, and upon my mountains tread him under foot: then shall his yoke depart from off them, and his burden depart from off their shoulders." It is the ruining of Sennacherib and his army in the days of Hezekiah that is foretold. Yea, and this seems to claim a peculiar share and influence into this ἐπινίκιον, or triumphant close;

because, eminently and signally, not long after, messengers were thus sent from Babylon to inquire of the health and congratulate the good success of Hezekiah. And well had it been for him and his posterity had he given those messengers the return to their inquiry which was here prepared for him some years before. His mistake herein was the fatal ruin of Judah's prosperity. Let not, then, that consideration be excluded, though the other insisted on be principally intended.

The words, you see, have in them an inquiry, and a resolution thereof. I shall open them briefly as they lie in the text.

FIRST, There is an inquiry.

1. "*What* SHALL *one;*"—what shall, or what ought,—what is it their duty to do, or to say? or, what shall they, upon the evidence of the things done, so do or say? Either their *duty* or the *event* is denoted, or *both;* as, in such predictions, it often falls out.

2. "*What shall* ONE;"—that is, any one, or every one. The answer spoken of is either the duty of every one to give, or it will be so evident, that any one shall be able to give it. The word *one,* I confess, is not expressly in the original, but is evidently included in the verb וּמַה־יַּעֲנֶה,—what shall be answered? that is, by any one whatever. There is no more in the *translation* than is eminently infolded in the *original expression* of this thing.

3. "*What shall one* THEN;"—that is, in the season when God hath disappointed the hopes and expectations of the enemies of his people, and hath strengthened their rod to bruise them again more than ever. That is a *season* wherein great inquiry will be made about those things. "What shall one then answer?" This word also is included in the interrogation; and much of the emphasis of it consists therein.

4. "*Answer the messengers;*"—that is, men coming on set purpose to make inquiry after the state of affairs among God's people,—ambassadors, agents, spies, messengers,—inquirers of any sort; or the word may be taken more largely, for any stranger that came to Jerusalem. The Septuagint render these words, βασιλεῖς ἐθνῶν, "the kings of the nations." What shall they say in this case? Τί ἀποκριθήσονται; "what shall they answer," or "say?"—So that word is sometimes used. Some think that for מַלְאֲכֵי, which they should have rendered ἄγγελοι, or "messengers," they read מַלְכֵי, or "kings," by an evident mistake; but all things are clear in the original.

5. "*Of the* NATIONS;"—that is, of this or that nation, of any nation that shall send to make inquiry: גּוֹי, "of the heathen," say some. Those commonly so called, or "the nations estranged from God," are usually denoted by this word in the plural number; yet not always under that consideration: so that there may be an enallagy of number, the nation for the nations; which is usual.

"What shall one answer" them? They come to make inquiry

after the work of God among his people, and it is fit that an answer be given to them.

Two things are observable in this interrogation:—

I. *The nations about will be diligently inquiring after God's dispensations among his people.*

Besides what reports they receive at home, they will have messengers, agents, or spies, to make inquiry.

II. *The issues of God's dispensations amongst his people shall be so evident and glorious, that every one, any one, though never so weak, if not blinded by prejudice, shall be able to give a convincing answer concerning them to the inquiries of men.*

Something shall be spoken to these propositions in the process of our discourse.

SECONDLY, There is the resolution given of the inquiry made in this interrogation. Hereof are two parts:—1. *What God hath done.* 2. *What his people shall or ought to do.*

Wrap up at any time the work of God and the duty of his people together, and they will be a sufficient answer to any man's inquiry after the state of things among them. As to our wisdom in reference unto providential dispensations, this is the whole of man.

1. The first thing in the answer to be given in is the *work* of God. "The LORD hath founded *Zion;*"—Zion, that is, his *church,* his people, his chosen ones, called Zion from the place of their solemn worship in the days of David, the figure and type of the gospel church, Heb. xii. 22, "Ye are come unto mount Zion, and unto the city of the living God, the heavenly Jerusalem." It is generally used, not for the whole body of that people, unless as they were typically considered, in which respect they were all holy; but for the secret covenanted ones of that people,—as is evident from all the promises made thereunto,—yet with special regard to the ordinances of worship.

This God "hath *founded;*"—founded, or established, strengthened, that it shall not be removed. Ps. lxxxvii. is a comment on these words. He "hath founded" it; that is, in faithful promises and powerful performances, sufficient for its preservation and establishment.

Now this expression, "The LORD hath founded Zion," as it is an *answer* to the inquiries of "the messengers of the nation," may be taken two ways.

(1.) As giving an account of the *work itself done,* or what it is that God hath done in and amongst his people. What is the work that is so famed abroad, and spoken of throughout the world, that, being attempted in many places, and proving abortive, is here accomplished? This is it, shall one say: God hath established his people and their interest. It is no such thing as you suppose,—that some are set up, and some pulled down;—that new fabrics of government or ruling are erected for their own sakes, or their sakes who are interested in them. But this is the thing that God hath done, he "hath founded Zion;"—established his people and their interest, in despite of all opposition.

(2.) As giving a *reason* of the work done. Whence is it that the Lord hath wrought so mightily for you, amongst you, in your behalf,—preserved you, recovered you, supported you, given you success and victory,—when all nations conspired your ruin? Why, this is the reason of it, "God hath founded Zion;"—he bore it good-will, hath taken care of the interest of his church and people.

The words may be taken in *either* sense; the issue of their intendment, as to our instruction, will be the same. This is the answer to be given to "the messengers of the nation," who perhaps expected to have heard of their strength and policy, of their counsellors and armies, of their wealth and their riches, of their triumphs and enjoyments. No: "God hath founded Zion." And well had it been for Hezekiah had he given his answer, prepared for him so long before, to the messengers of Babylon.

III. *The great design of God, in his mighty works, and dispensations in the world, is the establishment of his people, and their proper interest, in their several generations.*

Give me leave to say, it is not for this or that *form of government*, or civil administration of human affairs,—it is not for these or those *governors*,—much less for the advantage of one or other sort of men, for the enthroning of any one or other persuasion, gainful or helpful to some, few or more,—that God hath wrought his mighty works amongst us; but it is *that Zion may be founded*, and the general interest of all the sons and daughters of Zion be preserved;—and so far as any thing lies in a subserviency thereunto, so far, and no farther, is it with him accepted. And whatever, on what account soever, sets up against it, shall be broken in pieces.

What answer, then, should we give to inquirers? "That the LORD hath founded Zion." This is that, and that alone, which we should insist upon, and take notice of, as the *peculiar* work of God amongst us. Let the reports of other nations be what they will,—let them acquaint the messengers of one another with their glory, triumphs, enlarging of their empires and dominions,—when it is inquired what he hath done in England, let us say, "He hath founded Zion." And he will not leave until every man concerned in the work shall be able to say, We have busied ourselves about things of no moment, and consumed our days and strength in setting up sheaves that must bow hereunto. This is the main of God's intendment; and whilst it is safe, he hath the glory and end of his dispensations.

2. The other part of the answer relates to the people: "The poor of his people shall trust in it."

The words contain either their *duty*,—they *ought* to do so; or the *event*,—they *shall* do so; or both jointly.

(1.) "The poor of his people," verse 30, they are called, "The first-born of the poor and needy;" that is, those who are very poor. Now, this expression may denote either the people in general, who had been poor and afflicted,—and so "the poor of his people" is as much as "his poor people,"—or some in particular, that, partly upon the account of their low outward condition, partly on the account of their lowliness of mind, are called "The poor of his people;" and so the words are excellently paraphrased, Zeph. iii. 12, 13, "I will also leave in the midst of thee an afflicted and poor people, and they shall trust in the name of the LORD. The remnant of Israel shall not do iniquity, nor speak lies; neither shall a deceitful tongue be found in their mouth; . . . . and none shall make them afraid." We may take the words in a sense comprising both these; namely, for the poor preserved remnant, carried through the fiery trial, and preserved to see some comfortable issue of God's dealing with them, though yet wrestling with difficulties and perplexities.

(2.) What shall they do? They "shall trust in it;" וּבָהּ יֶחֱסוּ, "and in it they shall trust;"—that is, being "in it, they shall trust," confide, acquiesce, namely, in the Lord, who hath wrought this work; or, "in it," that is, either in the work of God, or in Zion so established by God.

The word here used for "trusting," is sometimes taken for to "repair" or to retreat to any thing, and not properly to put trust, affiance, or confidence; and so it is rendered in the margin of your books, "They shall betake themselves to it." So is the word used, Judges ix. 15; Ps. xxxvi. 7. So the intendment is,—that the poor, preserved people of God, seeing his design to found Zion, and to establish the interest of his chosen, shall leave off all other designs, aims, and contrivances, and wind up all on the same bottom:—they shall not, at least they ought not (for I told you the words might denote either their duty, what they ought to do; or the event, what they shall do), set up designs and aims of their own, and contend about other things; but betake their hopes to that which is the main intendment of God, the establishment of the interest of his people, and cast all other things in a subserviency thereunto. The sum is,—

IV. *It is the duty of God's poor preserved remnant, laying aside all other aims and contrivances, to betake themselves to the work of God, founding Zion, and preserving the common interest of his people.*

Of the propositions thus drawn from the words, I shall treat severally, so far as they may be foundations of the inferences intended. And,—

I. *The nations about will be diligently inquiring concerning God's dispensations among his people;*—their eyes are upon them, and they will be inquiring after them.

In the handling of this, and all that follows, I humbly desire that you would consider in what capacity, as to the discharge of this work, I look upon myself and you. As you are hearers of the word of God (in which state alone at present, though with reference to your designed employment, I look upon you), you are not at all distinguished from others or among yourselves, but as you are believers or not,—regenerate persons, or coming short thereof. And on this account, as I shall not speak of my *rulers* without *reverence*, so I shall endeavour to speak to my *hearers* with *authority*.

I say, then, there are certain affections and principles, that are active in the nations, that will make them restless, and always put them upon this inquiry. The people of God, on one account or other, shall be, in all seasons, a separated people, Numb. xxiii. 9, "Lo, the people shall dwell alone, and shall not be reckoned among the nations;" yea, they are separated from them, whilst they are in their bowels, and dwell in the midst of them, Mic. v. 7, 8. Whether they are amongst them as the spring of their mercies or the rise of their destruction (one of which they will always be), yet they are not of them. No sooner, then, is any people, or portion of them, thus dedicated to God, but all the nations about, and those amongst them not engaged in the same way with them, instantly look on them as utterly severed from them. Having other ways, ends, and interests than they,—being built up wholly on another account and foundation,—they reckon not of them as a people and a nation. The conclusion they make concerning them is that of Haman, Esther iii. 8, "There is a certain people scattered abroad, and dispersed among the people in all the provinces of thy kingdom; and their laws are diverse from all people." Not their moral and judicial laws, which were the sum of that perfection which all nations aimed at,—on which account they said of them, "Surely this great nation is a wise and understanding people," Deut. iv. 6; and the keeping of those laws was their wisdom and understanding among all nations;—nor yet merely the laws of their religious worship; but the whole way, interest, design, profession of that people, is comprised in this expression, —they "are diverse from all people." Looking on them in this state, they have principles, as I said, that will carry them out to an inquiry into their state and condition.

1. They are full of *envy* against them: "They shall be ashamed for their envy at the people," Isa. xxvi. 11. Looking on them as *wholly separated from them*, and standing on another account than they do, they are full of envy at them. *Envy* is a restless passion, full of

inquiries and jealousies; the more it finds of *poison*, the more it swells and feeds. It will search into the bottom of that which its eye is fixed on. The transaction of the whole business between Nehemiah and Sanballat gives light to this consideration. See Neh. iv. 1–6. And ever the *nearer* any nation is to this people, the greater is their envy. It was Edom, and Moab, and Ammon, the nations round about, that were most filled with wrath and envy against Israel. Yea, when that people was divided among themselves, and the true worship of God remained with Judah, and they became the *separated* people, Ephraim was instantly filled with envy against them, Isa. xi. 13, "The envy also of Ephraim shall depart, and the adversaries of Judah shall be cut off: Ephraim shall not envy Judah;" for there must be a desire of the same thing, or something answering it (which befalls in proximity of habitation), that a man is *envied* for in him that *envies* him. This is one fountain of the nations' inquiry after your affairs.

Through the providence of God you dwell alone; that is, as to your main design and interest. You are not reckoned among the nations, as to the state of being the people of God. So far, and under that consideration, they count you not worthy to be reckoned or esteemed a nation. They envy to see the men of their contempt exalted, blessed. The same is the condition of Ephraim amongst us; men not engaged in the same cause and way with you, they are full of envy. Wherefore do they inquire of your welfare,—of your state and condition,—of your affairs? Is it that they love you,—that they desire your prosperity,—that they would have you an established nation? No; only their envy makes them restless. And, as it is in general, so no sooner doth any man, upon *a private account*, separate himself from the public interest of the people of God, but he is instantly filled with envy against the managers of it. And, notwithstanding all our animosities, if this hath not befallen us in our differences and divisions, I no way doubt a peaceable composure and blessed issue of the whole. If *envy* be not at work, we shall have *establishment.*

2. A second *principle* whereby they are put upon their inquiries, is *fear*. They fear them, and therefore will know how things stand with them, and what are the works of God amongst them, Hab. iii. 7, "I saw the tents of Cushan in affliction, and the curtains of the land of Midian did tremble." "I saw" it: when God was doing the great work, described in that chapter with many lofty allegorical expressions, of bringing his people out of bondage, to settle them in a new state and condition, the nations round about, that looked on them, were filled with affliction, fear, and trembling. They were afraid whither these things would grow. Ps. xlviii. 1–6, "Great is the

LORD, and greatly to be praised in the city of our God, in the mountain of his holiness. Beautiful for situation, the joy of the whole earth, is mount Zion, on the sides of the north, the city of the great King. God is known in her palaces for a refuge. For, lo, the kings were assembled, they passed by together. They saw it, and so they marvelled; they were troubled, and hasted away. For fear took hold upon them there, and pain, as of a woman in travail." The close of all the considerations of these kings and their attendants is, that fear took hold upon them. Fear is solicitous and inquiring; it will leave nothing unsearched, unlooked into; it would find the inside and bottom of every thing wherein it is concerned. Though the more it finds, the more it is increased; yet the greater still are its inquiries, fearing more what it knows not, than what it knows,—what is behind, than what appears. This puts the nations upon their inquiry; they are afraid what these things will grow to. Ps. cxxvi. 2, "Then was our mouth filled with laughter, and our tongue with singing: then said they among the heathen, The LORD hath done great things for them;"—they are the words of men pondering their affairs, and filled with fear at the issue. If God do such things as these for them, what think you will be the issue? I dare say of the proudest adversaries of the people of God at this day, notwithstanding all their anger, they are more afraid than angry. The like also may be said concerning their wrath, revenge, and curiosity,—all pressing them to such inquiries.

This is the *issue* of this proposal: If we are not a separated people unto God;—if our portion be as the portion of the men of the world, and we are also as they, reckoned among the nations;—if we have had only national works, in the execution of wrath on men fitted thereunto amongst us;—woe unto us that we were ever engaged in the whole affair that for some years we have been interested in! It will be bitterness and disappointment in the latter end. If we be the Lord's peculiar lot, separate unto him; the nations about, and many amongst ourselves, on the manifold accounts before mentioned, will be inquiring into our state and condition and the work of God amongst us. Let us consider what we shall answer them,—what we shall say unto them. What is the account we give of God's dealings with us, and of his mighty works amongst us?—what is the profession we make? If we seek ourselves,—if we are full of complaints and repinings one against another,—if every one hath his own aims, his own designs (for what we do, not what we say, is the answer we make),—if we measure the work of God by its suitableness to our private interests; —if this be the issue of all the dealings of God amongst us, we shall not have wherein to rejoice. But of these things afterward. The second proposition is,—

II. *The issue of God's dealing with and dispensations among his people, shall be so perspicuous and glorious, that one, any one, every one, shall be able to give an answer to them that make inquiries about them.*

"What shall *one* then say?" Whether it be for judgment or mercy, all is one;—he will make the event to be evident and glorious. He "is our rock, and his work is perfect;" and he will have his works so known as that they may all praise him. Be it in judgment, see what issue he will bring his work unto, Deut. xxix. 24, 25, "Even all nations shall say, Wherefore hath the LORD done thus unto this land? what meaneth the heat of this great anger? Then men shall say, Because they have forsaken the covenant of the LORD God of their fathers, which he made with them, when he brought them forth out of the land of Egypt." "*Men* shall say,"—ordinary men shall be able to give this sad account of the reason of the works of God, and his dealings with his people. So also as to his dispensations in mercy, Isa. xxvi. 11, "LORD, when thy hand is lifted up, they will not see: but they shall see, and be ashamed for their envy at the people; yea, the fire of thine enemies shall devour them." He will not leave the work of his favour towards his people, until those who are willing to shut their eyes against it do see and acknowledge his hand and counsel therein.

I do not say this will hold in every dispensation of God, in all seasons, from the beginning to the ending of them. In many works of his power and righteousness he will have us bow our souls to the law of his providence, and his sovereignty, wisdom, and goodness therein, when his footsteps are in the deep, and his paths are not known;—which is the reasonablest thing in the world. But this, generally, is the way of his proceedings, especially in the common concernments of his people, and in the disposal of their public interests;—his works, his will and counsels therein, shall be eminent and glorious. It is chiefly from ourselves and our own follies that we come short of such an acquaintance with the works of God as to be able to give an answer to every one that shall demand an account of them. When David was staggered at the works of God, he gives this reason of it, "I was foolish, and as a beast before him," Ps. lxxiii. 22. That thoughtfulness and *wisdom* which keeps us in darkness, is our *folly*.

There are sundry things that are apt to cloud our apprehensions as to the mind of God in his dealing with his people. As,—

1. *Self-fulness* of our own private apprehensions and designs. A private design and aim in the works of Providence, is like a private, by-opinion in matters of religion. You seldom see a man take up a by-opinion (if I may so speak), but he instantly lays more weight upon it than upon all religion besides. If that be not enthroned, be

it a matter of never so small importance, he scarce cares what becomes of all other truths which he doth embrace. When men have fixed to themselves that this or that particular must be the product of God's providential dispensations, that alone fills their aims and desires, and leaves no room for any other apprehension. Have we not seen persons, in the days wherein we live, so fixed on a reign, a kingdom,—I know not what, that they would scarce allow God himself to be wise if their minds were not satisfied? "Give me this child, or I die!" Now, is it probable, that, when men's whole souls are possessed with a design and desire of their own, so fully that they are cast into the mould of it, are transformed into the image and likeness of it,—they can see, hear, think, talk, dream nothing else, —they shall be able to discern aright, and acquiesce in the general issue of God's dispensations, or be able to "answer the messengers of the nations," making inquiry concerning them? Fear, hope, wrath, anger, discontentment, with a rabble of the like mind-darkening affections, are the attendants of such a frame. He who knows any thing of the power of prejudices in diverting the minds of men from passing a right judgment on things proposed to them, and the efficacy of disordered affections for the creating and confirming of such prejudices, will discern the power of this darkening disturbance.

2. Private *enmities*, private *disappointments*, private *prejudices*, are things of the same consideration. Let a man of a free and large heart and spirit abstract his thoughts from the differences that are among the people of God in this nation, and keep himself from an engagement into any particular design and desire;—it is almost impossible that he should wink so hard but that the issue and reason of God's dealing with us will shine in upon his understanding, so that he shall be able to give an account of them to them that shall make inquiry. Will he not be able to "say to the messengers of the nations," and all other observers of the providential alterations of the late times that have passed over us, The people of God in this nation were despised, but are now in esteem: they were under subjection to cruel task-masters,—some in prisons, some banished to the ends of the earth, merely on the account of the worship of their God; the consciences of all inthralled, and of many defiled and broken on the scandals laid before them; whilst iniquity and superstition were established by law;—but this is that which God hath now done and accomplished,—the *imprisoned* are set at liberty, the *banished* are recalled; they that have *lain among the pots* have got doves' wings; conscience is no more inthralled; their sacrifices are not mixed with their blood, nor do they meet with trembling in the worship of God? O ye "messengers of the nations," this is that which the Lord hath done! Who, I say, not entangled with one prejudicate engagement

or other, may not see this with half an eye? But such is our state and condition, such our frame and temper, so full are we of our own desires, and so perplexed with our own disappointments, that we can see nothing, know nothing, nor are able to give any word of account that may tend to the glory of our God to them that inquire of us; but every one vents his own discontentments, his own fears, his own perplexities. The Lord look down in mercy, and let us not be found despisers of the work of his power and goodness! Ah! how many glorious appearances have I seen, of which I said, Under the shadow hereof shall we live among the heathen! but in a short space they have passed away. Shall we, therefore, choose us a *captain*, and go down again into Egypt? The third proposition ensues.

III. *The great design of God, in his mighty works and dispensations, is the establishment of his people, and their proper interest, in their several generations.*

To make this clear, some few things are previously to be considered; as,—

1. The proper *interest* of the people of God is to glorify him in their several places, stations, and generations: none of us are to live unto ourselves. It is for this end that God hath taken a peculiar people to himself in this world, that his name may be borne forth by them,—that he might be glorified by them and upon them. This is the great end whereunto they are designed, and that which they ought to aim at only, even to glorify God. If this be not done, they fall off from, and are beside their proper interest. Besides innumerable testimonies to this purpose, I might give evidence to this assertion from God's eternal, electing love towards them, with his intendment therein;—from their redemption out of every kindred, tribe, and family under heaven, by the blood of Christ;—from their separation from the world, by their effectual calling, and the like considerations. But I have the consenting voice of them all in general, and of every individual in particular, crying out, This is our, this is my proper interest, that we may glorify God; fail we and come short in this, we come short and fail in the whole: so that I shall not need farther to confirm it.

2. God is the only proper and *infallible judge*, in what state and condition his people will best and most glorify his name in their several generations. I think I need not insist on the proof of this assertion. "Should it be according to thy mind," saith he, in Job xxxiv. 33; or according to the mind of God? Should the disposal of things be according to his will, or ours? Whose end is to be obtained in the issue of all? is it not his glory? Who hath the most wisdom to order things aright,—he or we? Who hath the chiefest interest in, and right unto, the things contended about? Who sees

what will be the event of all things,—he or we? Might men be judges, would they not universally practically conclude, that the condition wherein they might best glorify God would be, that they might have peace and rest from their enemies, union and a good understanding among themselves,—that they might dwell peaceably in the world, without control, and have the necks of their adversaries under their feet? This in general:—in particular, that this or that persuasion, that they are peculiarly engaged in, might be always enthroned; that their proper sheaf might stand upright, and all others bow thereunto; and that nothing is contrary to the glory of God but what disturbs this condition of affairs? I know not what may be accomplished before the end of the world; from the beginning of it hitherto, for the most part, the thoughts of God have not been as these thoughts of ours. He hath judged otherwise as to the condition wherein his people should glorify him. God is judge himself; let us, I pray you, leave the determination of this difference to him. And if it be so as to our general condition, much more is it so as to our peculiar designs and aims, wherein we are divided.

3. *Providential dispensations*, are discoveries of the wisdom of God in disposing of the condition of his people, so as they may best glorify him. To dispute against the condition wherein at any time we are cast by his providence, is to rise up against his wisdom in disposing of things to his own glory.

These things being premised, it is easy to give light and evidence to the assertion laid down.

I might go through the stories of God's dealings with the nations of the world, and his own people amongst them, and manifest in each particular that still his design was the establishment of his people's proper interest. But, instead of instances, take two or three testimonies that occur. Deut. xxxii. 8, "When the Most High divided to the nations their inheritance, when he separated the sons of Adam, he set the bounds of the people according to the number of the children of Israel." From the beginning, God hath so ordered all the nations of the world, that they may bear a *proportion* to what he hath to do with his people; that he may so order and dispose of them, as that his design towards his own may be accomplished. Amos ix. 9, "For, lo, I will command, and I will sift the house of Israel among all nations, like as corn is sifted in a sieve, yet shall not the least grain fall upon the earth." All the stirs and commotions that are in the world, are but God's siftings of all the nations, that his chosen ones may be fitted for himself, and not lost in the chaff and rubbish. Heb. xii. 26, 27, "Whose voice then shook the earth: but now he hath promised, saying, Yet once more I shake not the earth only, but also heaven. And this word, Yet once more, signifieth the removing of those things that are shaken, as of things that are made, that those things which cannot be shaken may remain." All the shakings of the nations are, that the unshaken interest of the saints may be established. Isa. li. 15, 16, "But I am the LORD thy God, that divided the sea, whose waves roared: The LORD of hosts is his name. And I have put my words in thy mouth, and I have covered thee in the shadow of mine hand, that I may plant the heavens, and lay the foundations of the earth, and say unto Zion, Thou art my people." Heaven and earth, and all things therein, are disposed of, that Zion may be built and established. All God's works in this world lie in a subserviency to this end and purpose. Doth God at any time prosper an evil or a wicked nation?—an antichristian nation? Is it for their own sakes? Doth God take care for oxen?—hath he delight in the prosperity of his enemies? No; it is only that they may be a rod in his hand for a little moment, and a staff for his indignation against the miscarriages of his people, Isa. x. 5, "O Assyrian, the rod of mine anger, and the staff in their hand is mine indignation." This, in such a season, is their proper interest,—to glorify God in distress. Doth he break, ruin, and destroy them, as sooner or later he will leave them neither root nor branch? All that he doth to them is a recompense for the controversy of Zion, Isa. xxxiv. 8, "For it is the day of the LORD'S vengeance, and the year of recompenses for the controversy of Zion."

We see not, perhaps, at this day, wherein the concernment of the remnant of God's people doth lie, in the great concussions of the nations in the world; we know not what design in reference to them may lie therein. Alas! we are poor, short-sighted creatures; we know nothing that is before us,—much less can we make a judgment of the work of God, in the midst of the darkness and confusion that is in the world, until he hath brought it to perfection. All lies open and naked to his eye, and the beauty of all his works will one day appear. The true and proper interest of his people, so as they may best glorify him in the world, is that which he is pursuing in all these dispensations.

The grounds, reasons, and foundations of this truth, in the counsel, from the love and attributes of God, the redemption in the blood of Jesus, I must not now pursue. This one thing I shall only offer:—The state of Zion, of the people of God, being much to depend upon the disposals of them whom God, by his providence, raiseth up to rule and government among the nations; though sometimes he sets up men whose hearts and minds are upright with himself, yet he will not trust his own to their mercy and the variableness of their wills in general; but will so dispose, alter, weaken and strengthen them, to set them up, and pull down, that it shall be their interest (to which they will always abide faithful) so to deal with his people as he will have them dealt with, that they may best glorify him in their generations.

If it be in the infinite, wise counsel of God, to give his saints in this nation peace and tranquillity, they shall not have it precariously upon the wills of men; for he will not leave moulding and disposing of the affairs of the nation, until it find that it is its proper interest to give and measure out unto them what is to the mind of God. All that hath been done amongst us, all that we are in expectation of, turns on this hinge alone. But lastly,—

IV. *It is the duty of God's preserved remnant, laying aside all other aims and contrivances, to betake themselves to the work of God, founding Zion, and preserving the common interest of his people.*

"God hath founded Zion, and the poor of the people shall trust therein," or betake themselves unto it. We are apt to wander on hills and mountains, every one walking in the imagination of his own heart, forgetting our resting-place. When God was bringing the power of the Babylonian upon his people, the prophet Jeremiah could neither persuade the whole nation to submit to his government, nor many individuals among them to fall to him in particular. And when the time of their deliverance from that captivity was accomplished, how hardly were they persuaded to embrace the liberty tendered! Notwithstanding all encouragements and advantages, the greatest part of them abide in that place of their bondage to this day. So hardly are we brought to close with God's peculiar work, and our own proper interest, although his glory and our own safety lie therein. The reasons of this frame I have in part touched before; I shall add but two more.

1. *Discontentment* with our peculiar lot and portion in the work of the Lord and common interest of his people. It is with us, in our civil affairs, as the apostle saith it is not in the natural body, nor ought to be in the spiritual or church body. The foot doth not say, Because I am not the head, I am not of the body; no, it doth not, but is content with its own place and usefulness. It is so with the rest of the members, that are more noble, and yet are not the head neither. It is otherwise with us. I interpose not my thoughts as to your present constitution, and the order of things amongst us. I speak no more than I have sundry years since, sundry times complained of to a parliament of this commonwealth. Every one, if not personally, yet in association with them of some peculiar persuasion with himself, would be the head; and because they are not, they conclude they are not of the body, nor will care for the body, but rather endeavour its ruin. Because their peculiar interest doth not reign, the common interest shall be despised. And this hath been the

temper, or rather distemper, of the people of God in this nation now for sundry years; and what it may yet produce I know not. Only, for the present, the work of God in founding Zion, in pursuing his people's common interest, is despised, thought light of, and all the pleasant things thereof trodden under foot. Unless God end this frame, my expectations, I confess, of a happy issue of the great work of God amongst us will wither day by day.

2. The suffering of our *wills* and *judgments*, as to the products of providence, to run before the will of God. This the experience of these days hath taught us. Those who have a forwardness in prescribing to God what he should do, as to the "modus" or manner of the work which at any time he hath to accomplish, are stubbornly backward in closing with what he doth actually produce. These, and the like things, which might be in large *catalogues* reckoned up, one after another, detain the minds of men from acquiescing in the common interest of Zion, whose preservation is the whole peculiar design of the great work of God in any place or season.—These foundations being laid in the words of the text, let us now see what inferences from them may be made for our advantage and instruction.

Use 1. Let us, then, consider diligently what we shall "answer the messengers of the nations." Some think that by the "nation" is peculiarly intended the nation of the Jews themselves, whose messengers from all parts came to Jerusalem to inquire of the work of God, and to advise about the affairs of the whole. In this sense you are the messengers of this nation, to whom an answer is to be returned. And because the text saith, *one* shall do it,—that is, any one,—I shall make bold, before we close, to give an answer to your inquiries, and endeavour to satisfy your expectations. In the meantime, as the words seem more directly to respect the inquiries of other nations; so it is in a special manner incumbent on you, who will be especially inquired of, to return an answer to them. Be provided, then, I pray, in your own hearts, to give an answer in this business. And, oh, that you could do it with one heart and lip,—with one consent and judgment! On whom are the eyes of this nation, and of those round about? from whom are the expectations of men? to whom should we go to inquire what God hath done in this nation, what he is doing, what are the effects of his power, if not of you? Some of you have been engaged in this work with the Lord from the beginning. And I hope none of you have been engaged in heart or hand against it; and you speak still with living affections to the old and common cause. If you will be able to steer your course aright, if you would take one straight step, have in a readiness an acquaintance with the work of God, what it is that he aims at, by which you may be guided in all your undertakings. Suppose, now, a man, or men, should come and ask of you what God hath done in these nations,—what he hath wrought and effected,—what is brought forth? Have you an answer in readiness? Certainly God hath done so much, as that he expects you should be able to give an account of it. Take heed that every one of you be not ready to speak the disquietness of your own spirits, and so cast contempt on the work of God. Something else is required of you. I have sometimes, in darkness and under temptations, myself begun to think, that what hath been, is the thing that is, and there is no new thing under the sun;—as it hath been among the heathen of old, so it hath been amongst us; or as it was with Israel, 1 Kings xvi. 21, 22, "Then were the people of Israel divided into two parts: half of the people followed Tibni the son of Ginath to make him king, and half followed Omri; but the people that followed Omri prevailed against the people that followed Tibni the son of Ginath: so Tibni died, and Omri reigned:"—that a *common* thing, and frequent in the world, had befallen us, wherein God had no hand but that of common providence, in dashing one sort of men against another. So foolish have I been, and as a beast, so ready to condemn the generation of the righteous,—so unbelieving and ready to cast away the faith and prayer of ten thousand saints, one of whose sighs shall not be lost. But such fearful effects, sometimes trouble, disquietment, disappointment, and carnal fear will produce. But certain it is, none of the many cries of the people of God shall be lost, nor their faith be disappointed. God hath a peculiar design in hand, and we are to find it out, that we may be able to answer them that make inquiries. If you lay not this foundation of your procedures, I shall not wonder if you err in your ways. It is your pole-star, and will be so, by which your whole course is to be steered;—your shield, which whilst it is safe, though you die, your glory abides.

But you will say, What, then, is this great design of God among his people? Let the Holy One of Israel bring nigh his work, that we may know it. What is that true and general interest of Zion that he hath founded? Let us know it, that we may be able to give an answer to them that inquire after it. Ask themselves,—those who have *prayed* for it, *waited* for it, *expected* it, are made *partakers* of it, do enjoy it, live upon it,—probably they will be able to give you an account what is their peculiar and only interest as to these providential dispensations;—surely they cannot but know that which they enjoy and live upon.

But you will say, Of all others this is the most unlikely and irrational course,—a way to perplex and entangle, not to inform us at all. Is it not clear that they are divided among themselves? Is not their language, is not their voice, like that of the Jews at the building of the second temple? Some shouted for joy, and some wept at the remembrance of the former temple? Are not their desires rather like that, and those of theirs who built Babel, than of those who cry Grace, grace, whilst God is founding Zion? Do not many of them utterly deny any work or design of God (I mean that is peculiar) in the affairs of this nation, and utterly fall away from the society of them who are otherwise persuaded? And is it likely that we can gather any resolution from them? Doth not the greatest danger of our own miscarriage lie in this, that we may be apt to attend to their peculiar desires, and so to divide amongst ourselves as they are divided?

And is this the return that indeed is to be made? Oh, that mine eyes might run down with water day and night on this account,—that my heart might be moved within me, for the folly of my people! "O foolish people and unwise, do ye thus requite the LORD?" It is true, many at all times have desired the day of the Lord, who, when it hath come, have not been able to abide it;—it hath consumed them, and all the principles whereon they have acted, and upon which they did desire it. But that those who have their share in it indeed, should be thus broken among themselves, should bite one another, devour one another, and scarce allow one another to be sharers in the common interest of the saints in that day,—this is a lamentation, and shall be for a lamentation. But yet something may be farther pressed on them in this business. When one went to demand of the philosophers of the several sects which was the best of them, every one named his own sect and party in the first place; but all of them, in the second place, granted that of Plato to be the most eminent. The inquirer knew quickly what to conclude: setting aside prejudicate affections, self-love, and by-interests, he saw that the judgment of all ran on that of Plato, as the best and most eminent sect; and which thereupon he preferred before the rest.

May not some inquiry of the like nature be made of the people of God amongst us? Ask them, What is the common interest of Zion, that God takes care of, that he hath founded in the days wherein we live, in the great transactions of providence that have passed over us? Say some, That such a form of church worship and discipline be established, such a rule of doctrine confirmed, and all men whatever compelled to submit unto them; herein lies that kingdom of Christ which he takes care of,—this is that which God will have founded and established: and what this *form*, what this *rule* is, *we* are to declare.—That that *discipline* be eradicated, the ministers' *provision* destroyed, and the men of such a persuasion enthroned, to rule all the rest at their pleasure; seeing that, notwithstanding all their pretended reformation, they are yet antichristian, say others.—Say some, That a kingdom and rule be set up in our hands, to be exercised in the name and authority of Jesus Christ, taking away all law and magistracy already established, to bring forth the law of righteousness conceived in our minds, and therein to be preserved;—all uniting only in this, that a sovereignty as unto administration of the things of God is to be theirs.—Say others, lastly, That the *people* of God be delivered from the hands of their cruel enemies, that they may serve the Lord without fear all the days of their lives, in righteousness and holiness;—that, notwithstanding their present differences, they may live peaceably one with, or, at least, one by another, enjoying rule and promotion as they are fitted for employments, and as he gives promotion in whose hand it is;—that godliness and the love of the Lord Jesus Christ be preserved, protected, and secured, from a return of the hand of violence upon it. Herein, say some, lies the common interest of the people of God; this he hath wrought out for them,—herein he hath founded Zion. Ask, now, the people of God in this nation, I say, or any of them, one or more, at any time, what he or they look upon as the chief thing aimed at in the mighty dispensations of God amongst us. Will they not every one answer, in the first place, That is aimed at, that is to be *enthroned*, that so doing is the will of God, the end of his works among them, wherein their or his particular engagement and interest lies? But ask them now again, in the second place, Which of the remaining persuasions, concerning the work of God and the common interest of his people, they would prefer next to their own? Will they not all unanimously fix on that mentioned in the last place, rather than any of the others? Is it not, then, evident, that, setting aside *prejudicate affections*, and such determinations as may reasonably be supposed to arise from them,—laying away all *private animosities*, and desire of rule and pre-eminence, with other worldly and selfish designs,—the universality of the people of God do answer to them that inquire, that in the last persuasion lies the aim and work of God in our generation? For my own part, on this and other considerations hereafter to be mentioned, I shall dare freely to give this answer to the messengers of this or any nation in the world who shall make inquisition after the work of God amongst us, and his design in reference to his people; and it is no other than my heart hath been fixed upon for many years, and which I have several times, on one account or other, intimated or pressed unto the parliament, which first undertook to manage, and successfully carried on, that cause in whose protection you are now engaged.

This, I say, then, "God hath founded Zion;" he hath taken care of the generation of the righteous, the children of Zion, however differenced among themselves;—hath broken the yoke of their oppressors, given them peace, ordered the affairs of this nation so, that they do or may all of them enjoy quietness, one not envying the other, nor they vexing them, but, serving God according to the light which he is graciously pleased to afford them, they wait for farther manifestation of the glorious gospel; and that God hath broken, and will break, every design that, either openly and professedly, or under specious pretences of crying, "Lo, here is Christ, or, Lo, there," hath sought, or shall seek and endeavour, to subvert this his work, to the preservation whereof he will certainly mould the government and interest of this nation; ordering its affairs in a peculiar manner on that account only, and not that he delighteth in one way or form whereinto it hath been cast more than another. And whatever high-minded men, full of their own apprehensions and wisdom, may do, to this "work of God the poor of his people shall repair." And for my insisting on this answer, and this only, I have these farther reasons to add for my justification:—

(1.) This is an *interest comprehensive of all the sons of Zion*, whose founding God intends;—it excludes none that can claim a share in the city of the living God. God takes equal care of all the dwelling-places of Zion. Every dwelling-place of Zion hath its beauty, hath its glory, Isa. iv. 5. The glory of one may be as the glory of the sun; of another, as the moon; of others, as the stars; and those differing from one another in glory;—yet each hath its glory; "and upon it there shall be a defence,"—a covering, a protection. This is the promise; this hath been the work of God.

(2.) This compriseth all them who have lived by faith, and abode in supplications in reference to God's late dispensations amongst us. Who dare despise any one of those little ones, and say, God hath heard me, not you; regarded me, not you; you have no share or portion in the returns of supplications which we enjoy?

(3.) This alone preserveth the dwellers of Zion from offering violence one to another,—from taking the work of Babylon out of its hands, and devouring one another. Let any other apprehension whatever of the work of God be embraced, and the first work that thereby men will be engaged in is the oppressing, persecuting, ruining of their brethren; which, whether it be the founding of Zion or no, the day of judgment shall determine.

(4.) This is that which the common enemy seeks to destroy. It is not this or that party that he would devour; it is not this or that persuasion he would cast down; his hatred is πρὸς τὸ γένος, "against the whole race" and kind. This is that which he would accomplish, that all the children of God, however differenced among themselves, might be ruined, destroyed, cast down, and rooted out for ever,—that the name of Israel might no more be had in remembrance. This, then, is that which God, in their disappointment, aims to establish.

(5.) Because the founding of Zion doth not consist in this or that form of the civil administration of human affairs, there being nothing promised nor designed concerning them, but that they be laid in an orderly subserviency to the common interest of the saints; which, let men do what they will, yea, what they can, all governments shall at last be brought unto. And who is there amongst us that, in singleness of heart, dares make such an "answer to the messengers of the nations," inquiring after the peculiar work of God amongst us,—namely, that it consists in the establishment of this or that form of civil administration, though much of the work of God lies therein, in relation to this general end? This, then, is the answer which I "shall give to the messengers of the nations;" and of it there are these three parts:—

[1.] God hath broken, destroyed, ruined them and their contrivances, who made it their business to overthrow Zion, and to root out the generation of the righteous, not under this or that way or form, whereby they are differenced among themselves, but as such, as the saints of the Holy One; and will continue so to do.

[2.] He hath given to them—to "the poor of his people"—peace, liberty, freedom, from impositions on their consciences, with much glorious light in several degrees in his worship and service.

[3.] He hath cast (as he hath promised) the power of the nation into a subserviency to this common interest of Christ and his people in this world; and hath made, or will make, them to understand, that as the peace of Zion lies in their peace, so their peace lies in the peace of Zion. And what to say more "to the messengers of the nations," I know not.

Use 2. If this, then, be the work of God, let us *repair* to it. The poor of the people shall trust therein, or join themselves thereunto. That you may do this in judgment, be pleased to take these directions, which, with all humility, I offer to you, and I hope from the Lord:—

(1.) Engage in no *way*, no counsels, be the reasonings and pretences for them never so *specious*, which have an inconsistency with this *common interest* of Zion in this generation. If, instead of repairing to the work of God, you should be found contending against it, and setting up your own wisdom in the place of the wisdom of God, it would not be to your advantage. I know many things will be suggested unto you;—*settling* of religion, establishing a *discipline* in the church, not to *tolerate* errors, and the like. From which discourses I know what conclusions some men are apt to draw, if no otherwise, yet from what they have been doing for many years. Do we, then, plead for errors and unsettlement? God forbid! God hath undertaken to found and establish Zion, to settle it, and he will do it; and I pray God you may be instrumental therein, according to his mind. He will also give his people one heart and one way; and I pray that you, by your example of union in love, and by all other good means, may be instrumental towards the accomplishment of that promise amongst us. It is only the liberty and protection of the people of God as such that is pleaded for; and he that shall set up any thing inconsistent therewith, as so set up, will lay the foundation of his building in the first-born of his peace, and set up the gate of it in the utmost and last of his welfare. In a word, the people of God may possibly, in this nation, devour one another, and wash their hands in the blood of one another, by widening the breaches that are among them,—and woe be to them that shall be instrumental therein! but if ever they come to a coalescency in love and truth, it must be by their mutual forbearance of one another, until the Spirit be poured down from on high, and the fruits of peace be brought forth thereby. And herein the Lord make you as the mountains that bring forth righteousness, and the little hills that bring forth peace unto his people!

There are some things that I am afraid of, that lie contrary to what I am exhorting you unto. I wish the event may manifest that I am afraid without cause. However, give me leave to caution you of them, because I cannot be faithful to my call if I do not.

[1.] Take heed lest that evil be still abiding upon any of our spirits, that we should *be crying out and calling for reformation without a due consideration of what it is, and how it is to be brought about.* I wish one of many of them who have prayed for it, and complained for want of it, had endeavoured to carry it on as they might. Would you have a reformation? Be you more humble, more holy, more zealous; delight more in the ways, worship, ordinances of God; reform your persons in your lives, relations, families, parishes, as to gospel obedience, and you will see a glorious reformation indeed. What mean you by a reformation? Is it the hurting of others, or doing good to ourselves? Is it a power over other men's persons, or our own lusts? God hath now, for sundry years, tried us, whether indeed we love reformation or no. Have any provoked us or compelled us to defile the worship of God with ceremonies or superstitions, and our own consciences therewithal? Have we been imposed on in the ways of God by men ignorant of them? Hath not God said to us, You that have prayed under persecution for reformation,—you that have fought in the high places of the field for reformation,—you that have covenanted and sworn for reformation,—go now, reform yourselves:—you ministers, preach as often as you will, as freely as you please, no man shall control you; live as holily as you can,—pray as often, fast as often as you will,—be full of bounty and good works, giving examples to your flock, none shall trouble you; be instant in season, out of season, preach the whole counsel of God without control:—you people, be holy, serve God in holiness,—keep close to his worship and ordinances, love them, delight in them, bring forth such fruits as men may glorify God on your account; condemn the world, justify the cause of God by a gospel conversation, take seven years' peace and plenty, and see what you can do?—If, after all this, we still cry out, Give us a reformation, and complain not of our own negligence, folly, hatred of personal reformation, to be the only cause of that want, it is easy to judge what we would have, had we our desires.

[2.] Take heed lest any who have formerly desired the day of the Lord, considering the purity and holiness wherewith it will be attended, grow weary of it and its work, as not being able to abide it, and so lay aside all thoughts of growing up with it in the will of God;—lest any say, Is this the day of the Lord, that holiness, godliness, exact obedience, should be prized, exalted, esteemed; that profaneness, pride, selfishness, formality should be despised, consumed, devoured?—we will have none of this day.

[3.] Take heed that there rise not up a *generation that know not Joseph;*—that knew us not in the days of our distress and contending with those who would have destroyed us;—who were not engaged with us in praying, fasting, fighting, in England, Scotland, and Ireland, but were unconcerned in all our affairs;—who know nothing of the cries, tears, trembling, and fears, wherewith this cause hath been managed. Can we expect that they should be acted by the spirit of it, or have a due sense of what they must be engaged in? What know they of the communion we have had with God in this business all along, what answers he hath given us, what obligations he hath put upon us thereby? The whole business is to them as a story only of that which is past, wherein *they* are not *concerned.* There are such abiding impressions left on the souls of as many as have been engaged in the work of God in this nation, from the beginning to the end, as will never be blotted out. If a spirit not sensible of former ways should arise amongst us and prevail, it would be sad with the interest of Christ and his people in this nation. To return to my directions:—

(2.) Make this work of God your *pole-star*, that you may steer and guide your course by it. In all your consultations and actions, whatever is proposed, whatever is to be done, let this consideration attend it—*But how will it suit the design of God in establishing Zion?* Men speaking of a thing of manifest evidence, say that it is written with the beams of the sun. Give me leave to tell you of a thing that is written in the *prayers* of the saints, the *fears* of your enemies, the *condition* of this nation, the *counsels* of princes of the earth, the *affairs* of the nations abroad in the world,—all the issues of the providence of God in these days; all which concurring, I suppose, will give as good an evidence as any thing in the like kind is capable of. What is this, you will say? It is, in brief, Let the work of God as stated be your guide in all your consultations, and it will direct you to aim at these ends:—

[1.] To preserve *peace*, to compose differences, to make up breaches, to avoid all occasions of divisions at home.

[2.] To *make up, unite*, gather into one common interest, the Protestant nations abroad in the world, that we may stand or fall together, and not be devoured one after another. That these are the things which God calls you to mind, and do, if you will bear any regard to his present work is, I say, written with all the beams of Providence before mentioned. If the Lord should suffer you to be *regardless* either to the one or the other, know you not that it would be bitterness in the latter end? Ask your friends what they desire, your enemies what they fear, the nations abroad what they are doing,—consider Babylon, consider Zion; and if one and the same voice come from them all, not to attend unto it, would be not to attend to the voice of God. It is, indeed, an easy thing for you to gratify Satan, satiate the desire of your enemies, lay a foundation of troubles;—it is but attending to the clamours of men without, and the tumultuating of lusts and carnal wisdom within, and the whole work is done. But to carry on the work of God in the particulars mentioned,—this is not so easy a task;—self must be denied, many glorious pretences laid aside, contrary reasonings answered, men's weaknesses, miscarriages, failings borne withal, because they are men; and, which is more than all, our own particular darling desires, it may be, let go unsatisfied, though moulded into contrivances for many years. The truth is, the combinations of the antichristian party in the world are so evident, their successes so notorious, their designs so fixed, their advantages to carry them on so many, that to persuade with them who have power for that end and purpose to make it their business to keep union amongst ourselves, on all good and honest terms, and to endeavour the union of all that call on the name of the Lord Jesus Christ, their Lord and ours, in the world, were to cast a reproach upon their wisdom, foresight, and zeal. So that it sufficeth me to have mentioned these things.

Use 3. Encourage all things that lie *in a tendency and subserviency* to the work of God, unfolded and insisted on. For instance,—

(1.) Wherever you see any work of *real reformation*, tending to the advancement of the gospel, discarding of old useless forms received by tradition from our fathers, separating the precious from the vile, according to the several measures of light which God, in his infinite wisdom, hath graciously imparted, let not needless objections and hinderances lie in the way, but give in all due encouragements to the men of such engagements. Perhaps the business of carrying on reformation is grievous to some, who, in their anger and wrath, revenge and disappointment, may make complaints of it to you, in private or in public. The Lord give you wisdom, that you may never weaken the hands or sadden the hearts of men who are willing to join hearts and hands with you to save a poor nation, and to keep life in the work of God in the midst thereof!

(2.) What you find established already in this *kind*, encourage, preserve, improve, that the work fail not.

(3.) Find out what is *wanting*, and pursue it as God gives you advantage and opportunity.

(4.) Where men, under pretence of religion, make it their business to defile themselves, or disturb the civil peace and quiet of others, let them know that the sword is not borne in vain. I can but name these things.

HONOURABLE!—My heart's desire and prayer to God for you is, that you may be the repairers of breaches, and the restorers of paths for men to walk in; that you may be the preservers of *the good old cause of England*, according to the growth it received in and under several providential dispensations. Many particulars lie in my heart to propose unto you; but, on very many considerations, I shall name none at present of them, but close all with some few general directions.

[1.] Secure your spirits, that in sincerity you seek the *public good* of the nations, and the prosperity of the good people therein, who have adhered to the good cause of liberty and religion. If this be in your eye as that which is principally intended, as you may pray in faith for the presence of God with you, and have a comfortable expectation of his protection and favour; so if, in the pursuit of it, through human frailty you should err, or mistake in the choice of means, paths, ways, tending to that end, God will guide you, and lead you, and not leave you until he hath made straight paths for your feet. But if at the bottom there lie secret animosities, self-will, desire of obtaining greatness or power, on the one hand or other,—if every such thing be not on all hands subdued unto public good,—prayers will be weakened, carnal wisdom increased, the counsel of God rejected, and you will wander in all your ways without success.

[2.] Keep alive this principle (which whether any will hear, or whether any will forbear, I know not; but this I am sure of, in the latter end it will be found to be true), according as you regard, cleave to, promote, protect, on the one side, or despise, contemn, and oppose, on the other, the common interest of Zion, the people of God, before laid down; so will your affairs either flourish, prosper, and succeed, on the one hand, or wither, decay, and be fruitless, on the other. In all other things that shall fall under your consideration, that relate to the civil government of the nations, prudence, conjecture, probability, consideration of circumstances, and the present posture of things, may take place;—this is capable of no framing to the one hand or other, upon any pretence whatever.

[3.] If it be possible, keep up a spirit of love and forbearance among yourselves; "love thinketh no evil." Do not impose designs on one another, and then interpret every thing that is spoken, though in never so much sincerity and simplicity of spirit, in a proportion to that design;—this will *turn judgment into wormwood, and truth into hemlock.*

SERMON XI.

GOD'S PRESENCE WITH A PEOPLE THE SPRING OF THEIR PROSPERITY;

WITH

THEIR SPECIAL INTEREST IN ABIDING WITH HIM.

PREFATORY NOTE.

Before the same Parliament to which the last discourse was delivered, Dr Owen made a similar appearance on October 30, 1656. The close of the sermon gives a vivid picture of the religious state of Wales. We have seen that, in the first sermon he ever preached before Parliament, he took the opportunity of urging the necessity of some measures for promoting education and religion in that part of Britain. The circumstance that he was descended from a Welsh family, may account for the special interest which he evinced in the religious welfare of Wales. Great religious destitution prevailed in it. The Welsh at this time had neither Bibles nor Catechisms, and had scarcely sermon four times in the year. In 1649 an act was passed for the better propagation of the gospel, and the ejection of scandalous clergymen, in Wales. From the report of the commissioners in 1652, one hundred and seventy-five ministers had been ejected since 1645. Through the exertions of Parliament, one hundred and fifty preachers were appointed to officiate in thirteen Welsh counties; whose zeal in their duties may be judged of from the fact, that most of them preached three or four days every week. A schoolmaster was appointed for every market-town; and two of superior qualifications, educated at the university, were supported in all the larger towns. In addition to all this agency, six itinerant preachers were appointed for each county, at an allowance of £100; these were aided by the services of thirty-two ministers; and as all these arrangements were insufficient to meet the necessities of the case, pious laymen travelled through the counties, and conducted public devotion in the presence of the people. The first sermon of Owen had, accordingly, borne ample fruit. Whitelocke tells us, that in 1649 every Friday was devoted by Parliament to the purpose of consulting in regard to the spread and maintenance of religion. These facts deserve to be known to their credit, as evincing a lively and zealous interest in the highest welfare of the people, whatever view may be taken of the duty or competency of the state to make such provision for the support of the gospel and the spiritual enlightenment of a nation. For full details on these points, the reader may be referred to Neal, vol. iv. pp. 14 and 104, and the publications of the Rev. Vavasor Powell, one of the commissioners, in defence of their proceedings.—Ed.

Friday, the 31*st October* 1656.

Ordered by the Parliament, That the thanks of this House be given unto Dr Owen, Dean of Christ Church and Vice-Chancellor of the University of Oxon, for his great pains taken in his sermon before this House yesterday, in Margaret's Church, Westminster, being a day set apart for solemn fasting and humiliation; and that he be desired to print his sermon; and that he have the like privilege in printing thereof as hath been formerly allowed to others in like cases. And Major-General Kelsey is desired to give him the thanks of this House accordingly.

Hen. Scobell, *Clerk of the Parliament.*

TO THE

PARLIAMENT OF THE COMMONWEALTH

OF

ENGLAND, IRELAND, AND SCOTLAND, WITH THE DOMINIONS THEREUNTO BELONGING.

SIRS,

MY hope that some impression may possibly remain upon your hearts and spirits of and from the things delivered unto you in the ensuing sermon, makes me willing unto the obedience of presenting it unto you, upon your command, in this manner. Were I not persuaded that your peace, interest, and concernment are expressed therein, and knew not with what simplicity of heart you were minded thereof, I should have chosen, on many accounts, to have waived this duty. But having now performed what is incumbent on me to render this service useful, recommending it yet farther to the grace of God, I humbly beg that it may not, in this return unto you, be looked on as a thing of course, and so laid aside; but be reviewed with that intension of spirit which is necessary in duties of this importance; whereby you may manifest that your command unto this service was grounded on a sense of some advantage to be made by that performance of it. Sundry things, I confess, that were spoken unto you are gone beyond my recovery, having had their rise from the present assistance which God was pleased to afford in the management of the work itself. The sum of what was provided beforehand, and no otherwise, without the least addition, is here presented unto you, with hearty desires that the vision of the truth herein considered may be to them that love you, and the accomplishment thereof be found in the midst of you. So prays

Your humblest Servant

In our dear Lord Jesus,

JOHN OWEN.

Nov. 17, 1656.

SERMON XI.

GOD'S PRESENCE WITH A PEOPLE THE SPRING OF THEIR PROSPERITY.

"And he went out to meet Asa, and said unto him, Hear ye me, Asa, and all Judah and Benjamin; The LORD is with you, while ye be with him; and if ye seek him, he will be found of you; but if ye forsake him, he will forsake you."—2 CHRON. xv. 2.

IT will not, I am sure, seem strange to any, that I have taken a text to preach on, in a day of humiliation, out of a thanksgiving sermon, such as this discourse of Azariah seems to be; if they shall but consider the suitableness of the instruction given therein to any great and solemn *occasion*, whether of *humiliation* or *rejoicing*. The words, indeed, are the *sum* of all directions that in such cases can be given,—the *standard* of all rules and exhortations wherein any nation or people, in any condition, are or may be concerned;—so plainly measuring out our fate and *lot*, the event and *issue* of our affairs, with all the great undertakings of the people of God in this nation, that of themselves I hope they will make some passage to the hearts of them to whom the inferences from them shall this day be applied.

In the foregoing chapter we have an account of a great victory that Asa and the people of Judah, fighting in faith and with prayer, obtained against the huge host of the Ethiopians, with the abundant spoils which they took and carried away thereupon. In their triumphant return to Jerusalem the Spirit of God stirs up a prophet to go out and meet them, to give them an account of the rise and cause of their success, and direction for their future deportment under the enjoyment of such mercies and deliverances. The Lord knows how apt even the best of men are to forget *the spring of their mercies*,—how negligent in making suitable returns, by a due improvement of the advantages put into their hands, unto the Lord of all mercies; therefore are they in all seasons to be minded of their proper interest and duty.

This is done in my text to Asa and Judah by Oded; and I desire in my sermon that it may with the same spirit and the same success be done by me unto you. The words I intend principally to insist on, having the same thing for substance three times repeated in them, the opening of the first clause, with the general tendency of the whole, will suffice as to their exposition, and the grounding of that general proposition which I shall improve. Two things are, then, principally to be inquired into:—

First. What it is for God *to be with any people.*

Secondly. What it is for a people *to be or abide with God.*

And according to the analogy of these two, the following assertions, of seeking the Lord, and forsaking him, will be easily understood. For though the words differ in expression, yet they are all of the same way of assertion. They are three hypothetical propositions, or promissory assertions on supposition:—"If you abide with the Lord, he will be with you;" "If you seek the Lord, he will be found of you;" "If you forsake the Lord, he will forsake you." The same matter is trebled, for the fuller and surer confirmation of the thing asserted;—only, whereas the last proposition supposeth a thing possible,—namely, that they might forsake the Lord,—the first supposes a thing present; and therefore it is so expressed,—"whilst you are with him,"—because they had abode with God in their late war and trial.

Before I enter upon the opening of the words themselves, I cannot pass by the *earnest preface* of the prophet, "Hear ye me, O Asa." He saw the people, upon their success, taken up with many thoughts, thinking of many businesses, full of many contrivances,—one imagining one thing, another another; all of them, it may be, how they should use and improve their peace and success to their advantage, interest, profit, or security. Or the princes and rulers, as it is probable and usual in such cases, might be considering how to carry on their victory, how to make the best advantage of it, in their dealing with neighbouring princes and nations, in making peace or war. In the midst of these thoughts the prophet meets them, and diverts them, with all earnestness, to things quite of another nature, and of unspeakably greater importance and concernment to them. "Hear ye me," saith he; it is not your own counsel nor your own valour that hath brought about this great work, this mighty victory; the Lord himself hath done it, by his presence with you. It is not of any concernment unto you what other nations do, or may do; but the presence of God concerns you alone to look after.

Observation. *The great concernment of any people or nation is, to know that all their prosperity is from the presence of God amongst them, and to attend to that which will give continuance thereunto.*

You may tire yourselves in the imaginations and contrivances of your own hearts, and lay out your thoughts and time about things that will not profit nor advantage you;—this is your interest, this is your concernment, "Hear ye me, Asa, and all Judah and Benjamin." Of this proposition afterwards.

For the words *themselves*, the first thing proposed to be inquired into for their explanation is this,—

FIRST, What is it for God to be with a people?

God may be said to be with men, or present with them, in sundry respects.

1. He may be said to be with them in respect of the *omnipresence* of his essence. So he is naturally and necessarily present with all creatures,—indistant from them, present with them. The ubiquity and immensity of his essence will not allow that he should be distant from any thing to which he hath given a being. "The heaven, even the heaven of heavens, cannot contain him," 1 Kings viii. 27. Doth he not fill heaven and earth? Is he a God at hand only, and not afar off, as to the ends of the earth? This presence of God with all things David *emphatically* declares, Ps. cxxxix. 7–12. But it is not that that is here intended;—that is universal, to all creatures, —natural and necessary; this, especial, to some,—voluntary, and of mercy;—that, of nature and essence; this, of will and operation.

2. God may be said to be with one in respect of *personal union*. So he was with, and only with, the man Jesus Christ, Acts x. 38, Θεὸς ἦν μετ' αὐτοῦ, "God was with him;" that is, in personal union, the human nature being taken into subsistence with the Son of God.

3. God is present or with any in respect of *the covenant of grace*. He is with them to be their God in covenant;—the tenor whereof is, that he will not leave them, nor shall they forsake him; he will be for them, and they shall be for him, and not for another. He is with them for all the ends of *mercy, love, kindness, pardon, salvation*, that are proposed and exhibited in it. But neither is this the presence of God here intended, though this be something that flows from it and does attend it. For,—

(1.) That presence of God with his people hath not such a *conditional* establishment as this here mentioned. It stands on other terms and better security than that here proposed; it hath received an eternal ratification in the blood of Christ, is founded in the *immutable purpose* of grace, and is not left to the *conditionality* here expressed, as we shall see afterward.

(2.) The presence here mentioned respects the whole *body* of the people, all Judah and Benjamin, in their *national state* and consideration, unto whom, as such, the effectual covenant of grace was never extended; for they were not all Israel who were of Israel.

(3.) The presence here promised respects immediately the peculiar end, of blessing the *whole people* with success in their wars and undertakings;—so the occasion of the words and the context, with regard to the following discourse, do undeniably evince. It is not, then, this presence of God only that is intended; though, as it will afterward appear, it is not to be separated from it.

4. There is a presence of God in respect of *providential dispensations.* And this is twofold:—

(1.) *General;*—ordering, disposing, guiding, ruling all things, according to his own wisdom, by his own power, unto his own glory. Thus he is also present with all the world; he disposes of all the affairs of all the sons of men as he pleaseth;—sets up one, and pulls down another; changes times, seasons, kingdoms, bounds of nations, as seems good to him. The help that is given to any, he doth it himself. The shields of the earth belong unto God; he works deliverance in the earth, even among them that know him not. And the evils, desolations, and destruction, that the earth is full of, are but the effects of his wrath and indignation, revealing itself against the ungodliness of men. He is thus present with every person in the world; holds his breath and all his ways in his hand; disposes of his life, death, and all his concernments, as he pleaseth. He is present in all nations, to set them up, pluck them down, alter, turn, change, weaken, establish, strengthen, enlarge their bounds, as he sees good; and the day is coming when all his works will praise him. Neither is this here intended;—it is necessary, and belongs to God, as God, and cannot be promised to any; it is a branch of God's natural dominion, that every creature be ruled and disposed of, agreeably to its nature, unto the end whereunto it is appointed.

(2.) *Special;*—attended with peculiar love, favour, good-will, special care towards them with whom he is so present. So Abimelech observed that he was with Abraham, Gen. xxi. 22, "God is with thee in all that thou doest,"—with thee to guide thee, bless thee, preserve thee, as we shall see afterward. So he promised to be with Joshua, "I will be with thee," chap. i. 5; and so he was with Gideon, "The LORD is with thee," Judges vi. 12,—to bless him in his great undertaking; and so with Jeremiah, "I am with thee," chap. xv. 20. This is fully expressed, Isa. xliii. 1, 2, "I have redeemed thee, I have called thee by thy name; thou art mine. When thou passest through the waters, I will be with thee; and through the rivers, they shall not overflow thee."

And *this is the presence of God here intimated,*—his presence with the people as to special providential dispensations, as is manifest from the whole discourse of the prophet; and wherein this consists, shall be afterward at large declared.

SECONDLY, What is a people's *abiding* with God?

There is a twofold abiding with God,—

1. In *personal obedience*, according to the tenor of the covenant. This is not here intended, but supposed. There is no abiding in any thing with God where there is not an abiding in this thing; yet this, as I said, is not here principally intended, but supposed;—something farther is intended; for, as hath been declared, it is *national work* and *national abiding* that is intended. So that,—

2. There is an abiding with God in *national administrations;*— this is a fruit of the other, in those who are called to them. And that this is principally here intended is evident from that use that Asa made of this information and exhortation of the prophet. He did not only look to his personal walking thereupon, but also immediately set upon the work of ordering the whole affairs of the kingdom so as God might be glorified thereby. How this may be effected, shall at large afterward be declared. What hath already been spoken may suffice for a foundation of that proposition which I shall this day insist upon; and it is this,—

Observation. *The presence of God with a people, in special providential dispensations for their good, depends on their obediential presence with him in national administrations to his glory:* "The LORD is with you, while ye be with him."

For the explication of this proposition some few things are to be premised:—

1. The presence of God with his people as to *special grace* in the covenant, and his presence with them as to *special assistance* in providence, proceed on very different accounts.

(1.) They have a very different *rise.* The foundation and principal law of special grace, dispensed in the covenant, is this,—that some sinned, and another was punished. So it is laid down expressly, Isa. liii. 6, "All we like sheep have gone astray; we have turned every one to his own way; and the LORD hath laid on him the iniquity of us all;"—2 Cor. v. 21, "He was made sin for us, that we might be made the righteousness of God in him;"—Gal. iii. 13, 14, "a curse for us," that the blessing of faithful Abraham might come on them that believe. 1 Pet. ii. 24, This is the great and sovereign principle of the covenant of grace, that a commutation should be made of persons, as to punishments and rewards; that sinners should be provided of a substitute,—one that should undergo the punishment due to them, that they might go free, and procure a reward for them who could procure none for themselves.

Now, the supreme and sovereign *law* of providential dispensations is utterly diverse and alien from this of the covenant of grace. This you have asserted, Ezek. xviii. 20, "The soul that sinneth, it shall die:" one shall not bear the iniquity of another: "the righteousness of the righteous shall be upon him, and the wickedness of the wicked shall be upon him." Take this for a law of universal right, and indispensable, extend it to the covenant of grace, and it is absolutely exclusive of the substitution and satisfaction of Christ. But it is the ground, rule, and law of providential dispensations that God is there treating about, and vindicating his dealing with any people as to his presence with them and acting towards them therein; which is diverse, as you see, from the foundation of the covenant before mentioned.

(2.) As the foundations are diverse, so is the rule of their *continuance*. What is the rule and measure of God's continuance with his people in the covenant of grace? Plainly this,—that he will never forsake them; and, on that account, will take care that they shall never forsake him, but abide with him for ever. It is not whilst they do so and so, he will abide with them; and when they cease so to do, he will forsake them, as to his federal and covenant presence;—there is not such a sandy foundation left us of our abiding with God in Christ. See the tenor of the covenant, Jer. xxxi. 33, xxxii. 38–40. The sum is, that God will be with them, and take care that they always abide with him; and therefore hath he provided for all interveniences imaginable, that nothing shall violate this union. God lays his unchangeableness as the foundation of the covenant, Mal. iii. 6, and he therein makes us unchangeable;—not absolutely so, for we change every moment; but with respect to the terms and bounds of the covenant, he hath undertaken that we shall never leave him. The law of God's presence in respect of providential dispensations, and all special privileges attending it, is quite of another importance: it is purely conditional, as you may see in my text. The tenor of it is expressed to the height, 1 Sam. ii. 30, "I said indeed that thy house, and the house of thy father, should walk before me for ever: but now the LORD saith, Be it far from me; for them that honour me I will honour, and they that despise me shall be lightly esteemed." Here is no alteration of *counsel or purpose* in God; but merely an explanation of the rule, law, and tenor of *providential dispensations;*—no interpretation of the covenant of grace (Eli held not the priesthood by that covenant); but an explication of the tenor of a privilege given in special providence, Ps. lxxxix. 32, 33. Hence is that variety of God's dealings with men mentioned in the Scripture; which yet are always righteous, according to one or other of these rules and laws. Isa. xliii. 22–24, says God of his people, "Thou hast not called upon me, O Jacob; but thou hast been weary of me, O Israel. Thou hast not brought me the small cattle of thy burnt-offerings; neither hast thou honoured me with thy sacrifices."—"Thou hast bought me no sweet cane with money, neither hast thou filled me with the fat of thy sacrifices: but thou hast made me to serve with thy sins, thou hast wearied me with thine iniquities." What, then, shall be done with this people?—depart from them, destroy them, let them die? No, verse 25, "I, even I, am he that blotteth out thy transgressions for mine own sake, and will not remember thy sins." So also, chap. lvii. 17, "For the iniquity of his covetousness was I wroth, and smote him: I hid me, and was wroth, and he went on frowardly in the way of his heart." Surely now God will utterly consume them, root and branch, as persons incorrigible and irrecoverable. No; the case is quite otherwise, verses 18, 19, "I have seen his ways, and will heal him; I will lead him also, and restore comforts unto him:" I will pity him, pardon him, save, sanctify him, and fill him with consolation. Go now to Ezekiel, chap. xxxiii. 18, "When the righteous turneth from his righteousness,"—what then? God will heal him, and restore comforts unto him, as it was in the places before mentioned? No, no; "He shall die,"—he shall be cut off. What is the reason of this diversity? Why, in the first place, God speaks of his dealings unto their souls as to *his covenant of grace*, and all the mercies of it;—in this last, as to his dealings with their persons, and their *outward concernments* in the dispensations of his providence. And the not heeding hereof hath made some pronounce, inconsiderately, the covenant of grace to be merely conditional, because they find many mercies and privileges spoken of under such a notion;—not considering that all those proposals belong to the law of outward providence, and not to the nature of the covenant of promise established in the blood of Christ. And unless this be allowed, nothing can be more contrary to my text than that promise, and such as that which we have, Isa. liv. 9, where provision is made for God's abiding with his people, notwithstanding all their backslidings and provocations; which he will so far heal as that he may not forsake them. And this is first to be observed, that we do not, in the consideration of God's presence and withdrawings as to providential dispensations, cast any reflection on the stability and unchangeableness of the covenant of grace. David hath fully stated this business, 2 Sam. xxiii. 5; saith he, "Although my house be not so with God; yet he hath made with me an everlasting covenant, ordered in all things, and sure: for this is all my salvation, and all my desire, although he make it not to grow." David had a promise for the prosperity of his house; he had also an engagement of the sure mercies of the covenant. The different tenor of these engagements, as to their success and establishment, he gives us this account of:—the covenant is absolute and unchangeable; that is, ordered in all things, and sure;—the prosperity of his house depends on another law and rule, that is subject to alteration.

2. Observe the *nature* of this dependence of God's presence on

our abiding with him. It doth not depend upon it, as the *effect* upon its proper *cause*, as though it were procured by it, *merited* by it;—we enjoy not the least morsel of bread on any such account, much less such eminent privileges as attend God's special providential presence. We deserve nothing at the hand of God; and, therefore, if he should take us in the midst of the choicest obedience, and fill us with the fiercest of miseries, he does us no wrong;—and, therefore, the Lord does so deal sometimes with his; and that not only with particular persons, as in the case of Job, but also with his people in general, as Ps. xliv. 17–19, "All this is come upon us; yet have we not forgotten thee, neither have we dealt falsely in thy covenant. Our heart is not turned back, neither have our steps declined from thy way; though thou hast sore broken us in the place of dragons, and covered us with the shadow of death." Though he requires our *duty* at our hands, yet he is not tied to any such *present reward*. This is all,—it ordinarily depends upon it as a consequent upon an antecedent, which allows an interposition of grace and mercy; as Neh. ix. 17, Nevertheless, thou being merciful, "forsookest them not." So, elsewhere, that good man prays, "Remember me for good, and spare me, according to the multitude of thy mercies." For the glory of his righteousness, and of his ways in the world, God hath ordered that his people shall walk with him, when he abides eminently and conspicuously in a special manner with them.

3. Observe, that our abiding with God, even in national administrations, is the proper *effect of his presence with us* in covenant dispensations; so that all, in the issue, is of mere mercy and grace: though the condition seems to be imposed on us, yet it is from him alone that we have strength for its performance. It is in this, and such like cases, as David said it was with them at their dedicating their silver and gold for the building of the temple: Τὰ σὰ, ἐκ τῶν σῶν,—"Of thine own, Lord, have we given unto thee." We do but return him his own, we give him but the fruits of his own grace; and without it we can make no return whatever.

These things being premised, I shall give the proposition some confirmation, and so descend to the due improvement of it.

I suppose I need not go for proof beyond the observation of the constant tenor of God's proceedings with his people of old. When did he not deal thus with them? What instance can be given of transgressing this rule? Is the whole story of the nation of the Jews any thing but the illustration of this proposition? Some ruled well, and sought the Lord; and the Lord was with them, and prospered them in all their ways;—some fell from him, and walked according to their own imaginations; and the Lord cut them short on that account;—yea, sometimes the same man, as Solomon, Asa, Uzziah, experienced both these states and conditions. Hath not the state of all nations, since they came into the power of men professing the knowledge of him, been the same? Look on the Roman empire; did it not flourish under the hand of men who ruled with God, and were faithful with the saints? Is not the present distraction of it, under the fury and cruelty of Turk and Pope, the issue of the violence, unrighteousness, idolatry, luxury, and persecution of ill governors? Doth not the demonstration of all God's people in the world—the consideration whereof, in particular, might be insisted on as the ground and reason of the truth insisted on—require that it should be thus? Lev. xxvi., and almost the whole book of Deuteronomy, are sermons on this text; and every verse, almost, in them would afford a new confirmation of the truth in hand. I shall need rather, then, to caution from mistakes, than farther to confirm the proposition. For this end, take these ensuing observations:—

1. All outward flourishing or *prosperity* of a people doth not always argue the special presence of God with them. There are sundry things required to make success and prosperity an evidence of the presence of God:—

(1.) That the people themselves prospered be *his people*,—his peculiar. How many wicked nations are there in the world, that for a long season have received blessings (as it were) and success in their undertakings! Is the Lord amongst them by his *special presence?* Not at all. He is using them, indeed, for his own end and purposes,—to break others, or fill up the measure of their own iniquities, that their destruction may be an evident demonstration of his vengeance and righteous judgment to all the world; but present with them in the sense contended about, he is not. The case is stated, Hab. i., ii., as you may see in those chapters at large. It is the same case with the Antichristian and Mohammedan nations in the world at this day. Their prosperity is no evidence of God's presence, because themselves are his enemies. Other bottoms, reasons, and grounds there are of their successes;—God's owning of them is none of them.

(2.) That the whole *work* be good, and have a tendency to *God's glory,* wherein they are engaged. David's counsel for the killing of Uriah prospered and took effect; yet was not God with him therein. The work engaged in must be according to his mind. And,—

(3.) Made useful and *subservient* to his glory. When the hearts of a people can secure themselves in these things, then may they rejoice in their prosperity, as a pledge of God's presence with them.

2. Even *great afflictions*, eminent distresses, long perplexities, may have a consistency with God's special presence. Though the *wheel* goes on, yet it may have a *cross wheel* in it, that may cause rubs and disturbances. The rule of God's acting in his presence, is his own

wisdom, and our good in the issue,—not our partial, self-destroying desires. Had the best people in the world all their own desires, they would be every way ruined. When God is nigh to us, he knows what is best for us. Security from destroying evils, not [from] trying evils, he gives to *them* with whom he is.

And this is all that I shall offer for the explication, confirmation, and cautioning of the proposition insisted on; what remains farther to be opened will fall in under the uses of it, which now ensue.

Use 1. This special presence of God being, as you have heard, the great and only *concernment* of any people,—the tenure or condition thereof being our abiding with him,—let our first use be to instruct us particularly,—(1.) What this *special presence* of God is, and wherein it doth consist; (2.) What it *is for us* to abide with God, so as we may enjoy it.

(1.) For the full discovery of the first, I shall consider it in that eminent instance wherein of old he did grant his presence to his people. The bottom of that stupendous undertaking of the Israelites in leaving Egypt, and journeying through the wilderness into Canaan, lay in the promise of the presence of God with them, Exod. iii. 10–12. On this one consideration their whole undertaking and affair turned; to this issue it is put by Moses, Exod. xxxiii. 15, "If thy presence go not [with us,] carry us not up hence;"—they will not move one step without him; and with him they care not whither they go.

Now, this presence of God with them symbolically did consist in, or rather was represented by, two things:—[1.] The *pillar of the cloud* and *fire*, which was with them ordinarily; [2.] The *appearance of his glory*, which they enjoyed on extraordinary occasions.

[1.] The first, with the first use of it, is mentioned, Exod. xiii. 21, 22, "And the LORD went before them by day in a pillar of a cloud, to lead them the way; and by night in a pillar of fire, to give them light, to go by day and night. He took not away the pillar of the cloud by day, nor the pillar of fire by night, from before the people." There is mention here as if it were of two pillars, one by day, and another by night; but it seems to have been the same pillar with several properties. For, chap. xiv. 19, 20, the same pillar, at the same time, performs both these offices in respect of several persons;—to some it was, on the one side, a cloud and darkness; to others, bright and shining as fire: "The pillar of the cloud went from before their face, and stood behind them. And it came between the camp of the Egyptians and the camp of Israel; and it was a cloud and darkness to them, but it gave light by night to these." After this, when the ark was made, and the tabernacle erected, this cloud, which until then went before the camp, came and covered the tabernacle night and day, as it stood in the midst of the camp, or the congregation;

as a cloud it was by day, and as a pillar of fire by night, Exod. xl. 34–38; and there it continued with the people all the while they were in the wilderness, Neh. ix. 19. This being the first eminent pledge of the presence of God with that people, let us consider what was indulged or granted to them thereby.

1*st.* They had hereby *constant direction* in all their journeyings and undertakings: they were by this pillar directed in their way; so at large it is expressed, Numb. x. 33, as also Exod. xl. God, by this pledge of his presence, was the beginning of all their rest and motion, the guide and director of all their undertakings; so that they moved, acted, rested, proceeded, according to his will and counsel. He guided them by his eye, and led them by his counsel. Sometimes, perhaps, they would be forward,—they would be up, acting, doing,—their hearts are full of desires, and they are impatient of delay. If it be not according to his mind, he will cause a cloud to abide on their tabernacle, or their assemblies and meetings,—a cloud that shall darken them, and distract them in their consultations, that they shall not be able to take one step forward. Though their desires be great, their intentions good, yet the cloud shall be upon them, and they shall not know their way. Sometimes, perhaps, they are heavy, fearful, slothful;—there is a lion in the way,—giants are in the land; difficulties and perplexities lie in the way before them in such and such undertakings,—they have no heart to them; the way is long and perilous,—better return than go forward. Would God now have them pass on and engage?—the cloud shall break up and go before them,—they shall see so far on their way as to go forth with cheerfulness. Only, observe this, that when the cloud was taken up, they knew they were to go on in the way wherein they were, and journeyed accordingly; yet they knew not whither they should go, nor what would be the end of their journey. And therefore it is said, that when they journeyed the ark went before them, to seek out a resting-place for them, Numb. x. 33. It was carried on, to see where the pillar or cloud of direction would stay, and there they rested, wherever it was. When God gives a people so much direction as that they see it is their duty to go on, and to trust him in so doing, though they see not the end, nor know what their resting-place will be, yet it is a pledge of God's presence with them. I suppose in your assembly you have had the cloud taken off, as to your engagements in some undertakings, concerning which you are to trust that the Ark of God's presence, the Lord Jesus Christ, will find you out a resting-place, which as yet appears not unto you.

What a full experience have we had of this kind of proceeding among us! In the last assembly of parliament, how many had no less real intentions to be at work for God than now! God saw that it would not be for the advantage of the people that they should proceed; hence the cloud rested on that assembly, that they could not see how to take one step forward. He was still present with us; but it was by a darkening cloud, that we could not journey towards our rest. Nor is it the will or counsel of man, but of God, that is to be looked to in these things. We now hope the cloud is up, and we are journeying towards our rest. The great Angel of his presence will find a rest for us in the good providence of God. This, then, lies in God's special presence,—he is with us to give us direction in all our undertakings;—to take away darkness, perplexities, difficulties from our counsels; or to cause us to rest and cease from whatever may come into our hearts that is not according to his mind. The Lord give us evermore of this his presence!

I cannot stay to show you the several ways whereby God now communicates direction to a people;—how he inclines their hearts insensibly, yet powerfully; fixes the bent of their spirits effectually, their hearts being in his hand as the rivers of water, which he turns as he pleaseth; supplies them with reasonings and consultations beyond the verge of their own wisdom; proposes occasions, invitations, provocations; gives them spirit and courage beyond their natural frames and tempers; enlarges them in prayer, or shuts them up; makes walls on the one hand, and open paths on the other; with innumerable such ways and means as, in his infinite wisdom, he is pleased to make effectual for their guidance. It suffices that, in the use of means, through patience and waiting upon him, they shall be directed to that which is pleasing to him. So is he with them.

2dly. The second use of this pillar was, to give them *protection and defence* in their ways; so Exod. xiv. 19, 20, 24. This protected them from the Egyptians;—and from thence God troubled their enemies out of the pillar; that is, from his especial presence. This use of it is insisted on, Isa. iv. 5, 6. The cloud, that was as smoke by day, and as fire by night, was also a shadow, a place of refuge, and a covert; in one word, a protection or a defence.

And this is a *second* thing which is in God's special presence,—he will protect or defend them with whom he is so present. He is their dwelling-place, Ps. xc. 1, then, when in this world they have none; their refuge in the time of trouble: so Isa. xxv. 4, xxvi. 1, xxxi. 4. Promises and instances to make this good abound;—they are known to all; the time would fail me to insist upon them. I might go over all the causes, means, and ways of the fears, dangers, ruin of such a people, and show you how a defence is provided against them all. Are their fears from themselves, because of their folly, weakness, and division? or from pretended friends, because of their envy and desertion? or from open enemies, because of their power, cruelty, malice, and revenge? A defence is provided on every account. Heat, rain, tempests, storms, adversity, prosperity,—all are provided against, where God is present, Isa. xxxii. 1, 2.

And if any people in the world have experience of this truth, we have it this day. Had not the Lord been with us, who had not destroyed us? Enemies, friends, abroad, at home, our own follies,—all, any of them, had done the work, had not the Lord himself been with us.

Only observe, that the presence of God, as to these effects, may sometimes, in some particulars, be eclipsed, and the *effects* themselves for some season be entangled, though there be not an utter breach between him and his people. How often did the Israelites attempt things without his direction! how often did he break in upon them, to their woe and sorrow! yet, for the main, he forsook them not, until the great work intended by them was accomplished, Neh. ix. 19. It is not every entanglement, every disappointment, every defeat, that argues God's departure, as to his special presence. It may be good for us sometimes to be in such a condition; and then that desertion that carries into it, is from the presence of God. We are now grown to that, that if every thing immediately surmount not our imagination, say some, *God is gone from them;*—not because it is so, but because they would have it so. But he is merciful with whom we have to do, and will not cast off his people for ever.

[2.] The people with whom God was, had *the glory of Jehovah* as a pledge of his *presence* with them. This appeared only at extraordinary seasons;—so it did at the giving of the law, Exod. xxiv. 16; so also at the setting up of the tabernacle. It differed from the cloud; for when the cloud was upon the tabernacle, the glory of the Lord filled it. It appeared again to all the people, Lev. ix. 23. I shall not now inquire what was this visible representation of the majesty of God;—it sufficeth, as to the purpose in hand, that when God gives his presence to a people at extraordinary seasons, he affords them extraordinary manifestations of his glory. So in Ezekiel's vision of those dreadful wheels of providence, the glory of the Lord is said to appear in the temple; and as his especial presence departed from the temple and the city, so the glory, by several degrees, departed also, chap. x. 10, 18, 19, xi. 23.

Eminent and glorious appearances with and for a people in extraordinary seasons is, then, another thing that accompanies God's special providential presence with them. When they are at an utter loss in their counsels, at a stand in their motions, disappointed in their undertakings, deserted in their enterprises, pressed on every side above measure, or called to some extraordinary work, so that their ordinary direction and protection will not carry them on nor bear them up,—

then will God relieve them by some especial appearance of his glory. "In the mount will the LORD be seen." This will give a relief when all is at a loss. And in this lies the most *discriminating* evidence of special providence. Glorious appearances in great straits are eminent testimonies of God's regard.

Could I now insist on some of the instances that might be given of this kind of dealing with us in England, in the pursuit of the cause we have in hand, it would make us ashamed of all our unworthiness, carnal fears, and unbelief.

This is the second evidence of God's presence:—he is with a people to direct them, to protect, to manifest his glory amongst them,—his glory in balancing the issues of providence one in respect of another,—so that all shall acknowledge that of a truth the Lord is amongst them. "Blessed is the people that is in such a case; yea, blessed is the people whose God is the LORD." What would you have more? Here is ease of all cares, a remedy for all sores, security in the midst of troubles,—rest, and peace, and assured dwelling-places, though the Assyrian should be in the land.

Thus you see what is this great concernment of any people.

(2.) Let us now consider the *tenure* of this blessedness,—on what account it is to be obtained or enjoyed. Now this is, *our abiding with God*. This, then, is next to be considered: What it is for a people,—what it is for you and us, so to abide with God, as that we may in all our affairs enjoy his presence in the ways before described.

Now, something is hereunto previously required,—something it consists in.

[1.] That we may abide with God, this is indispensably required,—that we may have *peace with him in Jesus Christ*. If we are *never* with him, we cannot *abide* with him; no man can abide where he never comes. The acceptance of our *persons* lies at the bottom of the acceptance of our *duties*. As the special presence of God with any, is in and by Christ, and no otherwise, so is our abiding with God in and through him. "God with us" is the name of Christ: our being with God is in him who is our peace. Two cannot walk together, unless they be agreed, Amos iii. 3.

Now, because this is not to be expected from all the individuals of a nation, yet this thing is to be endeavoured,—*that the rulers of it be such as have this interest*. I do not divest of a share in government, those who have no share in Christ, if lawfully called thereunto; but I say, when God gives governors whom he intends to make a blessing unto a people, they shall be such as are blessed of him in Christ. And if ever the government of this nation, in this present constitution,—suppose it the most exactly framed and balanced, in the several parts of it, for the furtherance of public good,—be devolved into the hands of men not interested in God by Christ, though the constitution may be absolutely good, yet the government will not be blessed, and the nation will be ruined; for God and his glory will depart, Mic. v. 5, 6. It is Christ that is our peace, even in outward troubles. They are "seven shepherds under him," and "eight principal men" accepted with him, that are to be our relief.

It is true, for some particular actions or works a wicked man may be anointed particularly,—as Jehu, and Jeroboam the son of Joash; but you have no instance that ever God was with a people, to bless them indeed in a course of special providence, when wicked men, by their own consent, were their rulers,—where the union and relation between them and the people is considerable. I confess unto you, I never think of the state of England, but my heart trembles at this thing,—namely, that those who have, and it is fit should have, so great a share in the government of this commonwealth, should have their rise from the body of the people, that is dark and profane, and full of enmity against the remnant. Did not God overrule men, contrary to their own inward principles and lusts, how soon would ruin and desolation break in upon that hand! And give me leave to say, that God, in his sovereign providence, having called so many at this time to the place of rule and authority, who indeed (as we believe) love the Lord Jesus in sincerity, it seems to me to look as your duty, to consider all ways and means, whereby the power of these nations may be, in succeeding seasons, devolved on men of the like spirit and condition.

I shall not interpose in that which by some is so much spoken of, —*the reign of the saints.* I am sure the means used and attempted by some, to set upon and to set up such a rule and dominion, have not become sober men, much less saints of Christ. Yet this I must say, and in the saying of it, I dare say, "Hear ye me, Asa, and all Judah and Benjamin," If ever God cease to call saints—that is, men interested *personally* in Christ—to places of chief authority in this nation, or commit the power of it into other hands,—and when those called to power, cease to exert it in a subserviency to the kingdom of Christ, for the true spiritual advantage of his people,—there will be an end of England's glory and happiness. I say, Hear ye this, all ye people! This I have delivered long ago, and many times in this place; —this I say still, and in this persuasion hope to live and die. The Lord guide you in this thing; however, we shall live on the good providence of our God, who hath hitherto taken care for us.

This, then, I say, is pre-required, as a qualification of any person to the performance of this duty of abiding with God. It is the psalmist's advice, Ps. ii. 11, 12. Let this principle be always owned amongst you; by it honour Christ in the world. Give him the pre-eminence; it is the Father's will he should have it in all things. Expect not the presence of God, but upon this account. Bear testimony herein against the world of profane men, who despise these things. Seeing, then, it cannot be expected to have this qualification diffused universally, as yet, through the body of the people, let the rulers take care that they be not the cause of God's departure from us.

[2.] What is it, now, for such persons to abide with God, so as they may expect comfortably the continuance of his presence with them? —which is their all that they need or desire. I shall name some few things that are signally required thereunto.

1*st.* That they *inquire* of God, *ask* counsel at his hand,—look to him for *direction* in all their affairs. He is present with them to give them direction:—not to seek for it at his hand, is exceedingly to despise him. It must arise from one of these two apprehensions;—either he cares not for us, or he knows not how to direct us. When he gave direction by the cloud on the tabernacle, the people being reproved for their carnal fears and unbelief upon the return of the spies, some of them would needs instantly into the mountain, and fight with the Canaanites; but, says the Holy Ghost, the "ark abode in the camp." They went without God's direction, and prospered accordingly. With what contempt doth God speak of the wisdom and counsels of the sons of men, when they will adhere unto them! How does he make it his glory, to turn all their consultations into folly, and to make them err in their ways like a drunken man! How doth he bid them take counsel together, when he intends to destroy them! What instances may be given of all good and prosperous rulers of old, of their seeking direction from God! What promises of a success, and a blessed issue in so doing, are there! The words of my text will suffice as an instance in every kind.

But you will say, How shall we inquire of God?

The nations had their oracles, whereby they deluded themselves. The people of God had their Urim and Thummim, their prophets and oracle. "Bring hither the ephod, and inquire of God," was the word with them. But, alas! what is all this to the advantage we have of seeking counsel of God, and taking direction from him? We have a High Priest always present with us, by whom we may inquire. Our high priest is the angel of God's presence, the mighty counsellor, the power and eternal wisdom of God himself. And where is he? He appears in the presence of God for us, in the holy place not made with hands, having made a new and living way for us to come within the vail, to inquire of the oracle. What would we have more? He is our captain, our leader, our high priest, urim and thummim, our oracle, our ark, on whom the cloud of direction rests and abides for ever. Would you, then, be with God? Take direction from him by

Christ in all your undertakings; so do in deed, and not in word or profession only.

I hope I need not stay to give you directions how this duty is to be performed. The "unction" will teach it you, and your "fellowship," I hope, "is with the Father, and with his Son Jesus Christ." Only now take these few words with you:—

(1st.) *Captivate* all your desires to his glory. Set your hearts on nothing, but with this express reserve,—If it is consistent with and expedient unto the glory of Christ and his kingdom. Be not sick of your own violent desires; but lay all your aims and designs at his feet always, becoming as weaned children before him.

(2dly.) Bear before him a *real sense* of your own weakness and folly, both severally and jointly, if not directed by him, that in his pity and compassion he may relieve you.

(3dly.) Keep your *hearts* in that integrity, that you may always press and urge him with his own concernment in all your affairs. This is a thing that none but upright hearts can do uprightly.

(4thly.) Actually inquire by *faith and prayer*, what is his will and mind;—do it severally and jointly;—do it privately, publicly;—do it every day, and in days set apart for that purpose. He will assuredly be found of you. You know how easy it were to exemplify all these things by testimonies and instances; but time will not permit.

If, instead of these things, you bear yourselves up on the wings of your own wisdom and contrivances,—though you may seem for a season to have attained a fair pitch and flight, you will be entangled, and brought down in the midst of your course with shame and sorrow: for the Lord will not be with you.

2*dly.* Another thing wherein we are to be with God, is by trusting in him for *protection.* "O trust in the LORD for ever, for in the Lord Jehovah there is everlasting strength. This man made the LORD his refuge. He that trusteth in the LORD shall be as mount Zion, that shall never be removed. Commit your ways to the LORD, roll your burden on him; stand still and see his salvation." What glorious things are spoken of this trusting to the Lord for protection you all know. It were endless to insist on commands and promises to this purpose; and to single out one or two were but to weaken the cause in hand, seeing hereunto the whole Scriptures bear witness. I shall only show you what it is so to do, in some few particulars.

(1*st.*) It is to *strengthen* and *encourage* your hearts in difficult affairs, a comfortable issue whereof you cannot on visible causes conjecture, on the account of God's engagement for your good. To omit the instances of Asa, Jehoshaphat, and many others, take that signal one of David in his great distress at Ziklag, 1 Sam. xxx. You know the story:—his habitation was burnt and spoiled, his wives and children captived, his people consulting to stone him, so that he was greatly distressed; the enemy numerous and without his reach;—all means of relieving his condition, and bringing it to a comfortable issue, far removed. But what course did he now take? did he despond? did he give over? did he rest on his own counsel and strength? No, saith the Holy Ghost; "but David encouraged himself in the LORD his God." Have you any affair that lies before you that is good and honest, but yet dreadful, difficult, entangled? Your hearts are ready to faint whenever you think of it;—it is almost beyond your imaginations to contrive a comfortable issue. In such a season, if you will be with God, he will be with you;—if you so trust him as to encourage your hearts on the account of his wisdom, goodness, power, that he can find out and bring about a comfortable, glorious end,—this is to trust him for protection. Ps. xlvi. is this doctrine delivered to the full.

(2*dly.*) To trust God for protection, is to wait under discouragements and disappointments for a desired issue of the affairs we commit to him. "He that believeth will not make haste," Isa. xxviii. 16. This the Lord pleads for, Hab. ii. 3, 4. Men will have their desires precisely accomplished this year, this month, this week, or they will wait no longer. These, says God, are proud men; their hearts are lifted up in them; they trust not to me for protection. Men love to trust God (as they profess) for what they have in their hands, in possession, or what lies in an easy view; place their desires afar off, carry their accomplishment behind the clouds out of their sight, interpose difficulties and perplexities,—their hearts are instantly sick,—they cannot wait for God; they do not trust him,—nor ever did. Would you have the presence of God with you? Learn to wait quietly for the salvation you expect from him. Then, indeed, is he glorified, when he is trusted in a storm, when he is waited for under long perplexities and distresses. Want of this ruined the Israelites in the wilderness. Their work was long, their difficulties and entanglements many;—they would have had an immediate end of their troubles. What! more difficulties! more hardships! nay, then, let us choose a captain, and go down again into Egypt. We know the worst of that; where this will end we know not. This laid their carcases in the wilderness, and deprived them of enjoying the good land.

(3*dly.*) It is to *commit your affairs* to the Lord with *submission* to his will, as to their issue and accomplishment. Trust respects protection, but it prescribes not as to particular events. It is to commit our affairs to God with thoughts of his infinite wisdom, sovereignty, and goodness, with resolutions thereupon that the product of his will is that which will be good, be best for us, though it should not at all fall in with our present desires. It is true, the Psalmist says, "Commit thy way unto the LORD; trust also in him, and he shall bring it to pass," Ps. xxxvii. 5. And so he shall and will, in all such cases as that there particularly insisted on by the Psalmist, wherein his own glory is particularly engaged. But this prescribes not, as to all cases, that we should cry, "Give me this child, or I die." The rule is known; abide in this frame, and we shall have that we desire, or that which is better for us. But I must not abide in these things. See Ps. xxxvii. 3–5, lxxiii. 23–26.

And these are some of those ways wherewith we abide with God, as to our trusting of him in reference to special protection.

3dly. A third thing I should fix upon is, *a people's universal owning of God's concernments in the world.* His presence with them is, his owning their concernments; and certainly he expects that they abide with him in the owning of his. God's concernment in the world is his people, as invested with the privileges purchased for them by Christ. Deut. xxxii. 9, "The LORD's portion is his people." This is that which the Lord has particularly kept to himself; the vineyard that he has chosen out of all the forests of the world; the handful that he hath taken to himself,—his sons and daughters,—his family. These he expects that you should abide by, if you would have him abide by you; yea, it is most certain, as your respect and regard shall be to them and their interest as his people, so will his respect and regard be to you and your interest as the people of this nation. But I have formerly spoken hereof unto you, and therefore, though it be a matter of the greatest importance, I shall not farther insist upon it.

And these are some of the conditions of God's special presence with you. Pleasant conditions! their performance is your glory, your rest, your blessedness;—not your bondage, not your burden. Not one duty doth God on this account require of you, but it is also your reward. O blessed terms of peace and agreement! Blessed be the great Peacemaker! cursed be the breakers of this blessed agreement! Is this all, indeed, that is required, that we may have the special presence of God with us for ever? O how inexcusable shall we be if we neglect these terms!—how just will be our ruin! Behold, I have set before you life and death this day; the life or death of these nations. O choose life! seeing it may be had on such easy, such blessed terms; terms wherein, in doing good to others, you will also do good to your own souls; you will give peace to the nation, and have peace and rest in your own souls.

Use 2. Look on this presence of God as your *main concernment.* This is that which the prophet calls for in the words of the text. So the psalmist, "There are many that say, Who will show us any good? LORD, lift thou up the light of thy countenance upon us," Ps. iv. Let other men make what inquiries they please,—look for good, for rest, for peace in what they best fancy; acquiesce you in this, that the light of God's countenance, a pledge of his presence with you, is that alone which you are to inquire after. I remember, since the beginning of these last wonderful days, how often we have thought ourselves utterly ruined:—If such alterations come, we are undone; if such men die, fall off, oppose, there is little hope of carrying on the work wherein we are engaged; if such shakings, such divisions befall us, our ruin is at hand; if we break with such and such foreign nations, what hope remaineth? But, alas! we have found by experience, that our affairs have turned on none of these things; our prosperity hath been built on none of those principles. Such desertions as we feared, have happened; such alterations, such divisions have befallen us,—we have been sometimes almost reduced to Gideon's number; such breaches with foreign nations have ensued: one party that was with us hath gone off, and asked, What will ye now do? and then another party hath gone off, and asked us, What will ye do now? And no sooner do any fall off, but instantly they expect, and foretell destruction to them that do abide; as though they were God, and not man; or as though God were bound to follow them with his presence in all their passions, in all their wanderings. It would, I confess, be more desirable unto me than life itself, to see all those at least, who stuck to the cause of God in its greatest difficulties and trials, and then when it ceased to be carried on in the ordinary paths of nations, united again in the same common interest,—to see their passions and prejudices cured, and their persons returned to their former usefulness. But this is that which is the result of all this discourse;—it is not this or that thing, or any thing whatever, but the presence of God alone with a people, that is their life, their preservation, their protection, and prosperity. If our strength had lain in any thing else in this world, our light had gone out long ago, and it had departed from us: but hence it is that we are not consumed. Now, if you are so careful not to lose these and those friends, this and that party of the nation,—not to provoke this or that people causelessly; oh, what weight ought it to have upon your hearts and souls, that you provoke not the Lord to depart from you! that you take care for the continuance of his presence with you! This is your life, your safety, your success, —your peace. Learn to prize it, value it.

Use 3. Whilst you have any pledge of the presence of God with you, be not greatly moved nor troubled by any *difficulties* that you may meet withal; be not moved with any terror, but sanctify the Lord of hosts in your hearts, and make him your dread and your fear, and he shall be a refuge and a hiding-place unto you.

Some pretend to *visions* of God, and they prophesy your ruin and destruction; yea, they have limited times thereof, to the shame of their prognostications. Some are *full of revenge,* and they threaten your ruin, and talk what a catholic interest is complicating, and rising up against you. Some are *troubled at your proceedings,*—that they are not in such equal paths as might be desired; as though that were a work and way of yesterday; as though we had not been turned and driven out of *old tracks* and paths above ten years ago; and as though the old paths were not so worn to the interest of a profane multitude, that it is yet impossible to keep the burden upright in them whose guidance you are intrusted with. Some say you will never be able to go through with the *charge* of your undertakings; as though God had never said, "The gold and silver are mine." Should these things busy or distract you? Doth the issue of the business in hand depend on the thoughts of these men? Will the end be according to their contrivances? Have these things, indeed, any influence at all into the determination of this controversy? Will not this one consideration guide your hearts and spirits, when all these waves roll all together upon you? Yea, but the whole of this affair must be ordered, and will fall out, according as the presence of God is with us, or otherwise. "If God be with us, who can be against us?" How may you on this account triumph against all oppositions whatsoever!

Use 4. *Fix,* then, your thoughts on the things which lie in a tendency towards the *confirming* of God's special providential presence with you. You have heard of the tenure of it, the means whereby it is procured and retained: these things I have spoken to in general before. Besides your own dependence on God, and comportment with his providence, the things incumbent on you are such as respect either persons or things.

(1.) For *persons,* it is that which I have minded you of before, and which I shall do whilst I have life and opportunity to speak to you, or any concerned in the government of this nation, in public or private; because I know it is your life, your peace, your duty;—and that is, that the end and aim of all your consultations be the protection, encouragement, liberty of the seed of Jacob, the remnant, the hidden people,—those whom God hath owned, accepted, blessed, given his presence unto and amongst them. I plead not for their exaltation, promotion, preferment,—I know not what; but charge it as your duty, to take care that they be not trodden under foot, nor swallowed up, nor exposed to the rage and contempt of the men of the earth. It is not this or that party of them that I speak of, but the generation of them that seek the face of God; whose cause alone it is ,and not [that] of any other men, or frame of things, that is, through the mighty power of God, triumphant in these nations. They are to God as the apple of his eye; and let their safety be so also to you, and you will not fail of the presence of God.

(2.) For *things*, they are either, [1.] The things of *God;* or, [2.] *Men:* of each a word.

[1.] For the things of God, or the *public profession* of religion in the land, my time is too far spent for me to enter into a serious discourse on the subject. Some things have of late been done, which, when envy, and anger, and disappointment shall cease to operate, the whole people of God in this nation will have cause to rejoice in.

Let it not be thought amiss, if I mind you of one part of the nation in especial: the example of the saints allows us a special regard to those of our own nation, our kinsfolks in the flesh. It is for Wales I speak, where the unhappiness of almost all men running into extremes, hath disadvantaged the advancement of the gospel and the progress of it, when we had great ground for the expectation of better things. Some are still zealous of the traditions of their fathers; and nothing, almost, will satisfy them, but their old road of beggarly readers in every parish. Others, again, perhaps out of a good zeal, have hurried the people with violence beyond their principles,—and sometimes, it may be, beyond the truth; and, as Jacob said, over-driving the cattle and young ones has almost destroyed the whole flock. Between complaints on one side and the other, I fear—between misguided zeal and formality—the whole work is almost cast to the ground;—the business of Zion, as such, is scarce by any cared for. The good Lord guide you to somewhat for its relief, that those who are godly may be encouraged, and those that need instruction may not be neglected.

[2.] The things of man, or righteous *administrations of justice* in things relating to this present pilgrimage. These wheels, also, are you to set going. Many particulars lie before you, more will present themselves;—troublesome times have always produced good laws;—your wisdom will be, to provide for good execution, that not only the generations to come, but the present, may eat of the fruit of your labours and travail.

SERMON XII.

THE GLORY AND INTEREST OF NATIONS PROFESSING THE GOSPEL.

PREFATORY NOTE.

A GREAT event has occurred since the last two sermons, comparatively cheerful and buoyant in their tone, were preached. Oliver Cromwell is dead. His son Richard is in his place; but cannot fill it. The Parliament has been convened on the 27th of January 1659; and on the 4th of February Dr Owen is called to preach before it. It is most interesting to gather the spirit of the day from the scope and character of this discourse. In the last discourses, complacency in the peace prevailing in the country, and jealousy lest unseemly contention should renew the distraction and turmoil from which the nation has made its escape, are predominant characteristics. In the discourse that follows, it is easy to mark a spirit of anxiety as to the future developments of Providence. One emphatic sentence lays bare the very heart of the nation, heaving and throbbing with painful uncertainty in regard to the issue of public events ;—" We have peace now, outward peace; but, alas! we have not *quietness:* and if any thing may be done that may give us *quietness*, yet perhaps we may not have *assurance*." The preacher, however, has not abated his confidence in God,—insists upon His presence and aid as the true source of hope to the nation, and of preservation from ruin,—shows that, from the multitude of the godly in the land, God's presence is still with the nation, and rejoices in the belief that they will prove to it " as the ark in the house of Obed-edom, as Joseph in the house of Potiphar." Whatever reasons might exist for the prevailing anxiety, Owen " encouraged himself in God;" and sought in this discourse to infuse into the minds of his hearers his own unshaken steadfastness of faith.

It appears, from the dedication, that some exception had been taken to certain views which he had expressed in the sermon about civil government. The only passage in it which bears on civil government will be found at the foot of p. 466; in which he mentions, that although he does not think a man may not be lawfully called to magistracy who is not a believer, yet he had "no great expectation from them whom God loves not." In the dedication he affirms that he had advanced nothing which could "really interfere with any form of civil government in the world, administered according to righteousness and equity."—ED.

TO THE RIGHT HONOURABLE,

THE COMMONS OF ENGLAND,

ASSEMBLED IN PARLIAMENT.

I NEED not give any other account of my publishing this ensuing short discourse, than that which was also the ground and reason of its preaching,—namely, your *command.* Those who are not satisfied therewith, I shall not endeavour to tender farther grounds of satisfaction unto, as not having any persuasion of prevailing if I should attempt it. Prejudice so far oftentimes prevails, even on good soils, that satisfaction will not speedily thrive and grow in them. That which exempts me from *solicitousness* about the frame and temper of men's minds and spirits, in the entertainment of discourses of this nature, is the annexing of that injunction unto our commission in delivering the word of God: it must be done, "whether men will hear, or whether they will forbear." Without, therefore, any plea or apology for whatever may seem most to need it in this sermon, I devolve the whole account of the rise and issue it had, or may have, on the providence of God in my call and your command. Only I shall crave leave to add, that, in my waiting for a little leisure to recollect what I delivered out of my own short notes and others' (that I might not preach one sermon and print another), there were some considerations that fell in exciting me to the obedience I had purposed. The desire I had to make more public, at this time and season, the testimony given in simplicity of spirit to the interest of Christ in these nations, and therein to the true, real interest of these nations themselves,—which was my naked design, openly managed, and pursued with all plainness of speech (as the small portion of time allotted to this exercise would allow),—was the chief of them. Solicitations of some particular friends gave also warmth unto that consideration. I must farther confess, that I was a little moved by some mistakes that were delivered into the hands of report, to be managed to the discountenance of the honest and plain truth contended for, especially when I found them, without due consideration, exposed in print unto public view. That is the manner of these days wherein we live. I know full well that there is not any thing, from the beginning to the ending of this short discourse, that doth really interfere with any form of civil government in the world, administered according to righteousness and equity,—as there is not in the gospel of Christ, or in any of the concernments of it. And I am assured, also, that the truth proposed in it inwraps the whole ground of any just expectation of the continuance of the presence of God amongst us, and his acceptation of our endeavours about the allotment and just disposal of our civil affairs. Let others lay what weight they will or please, upon the lesser differences that are amongst us on any account whatever; if this shield be safe,—this principle maintained and established, that is here laid down,—and the just rights of the nation laid in a way of administration, suited unto its preservation and furtherance, I shall not easily be cast down from my hopes, that amongst us—poor, unprofitable, unthankful creatures as we are—we may yet see the fruit of righteousness to be peace, and the effect of righteousness quietness and assurance for evermore. For those, then, who shall cast their eye on this paper, I would beg of them to lay aside all those prejudices against persons or things, which their various contexture in our public affairs may possibly have raised in them. I know how vain, for the most part, expectations of prevailing in such a desire by naked requests are; but sick men must be groaning, though they look for no relief thereby. Wherefore, committing it into that hand wherein lie also your hearts and mine, I shall commend it, for your use, unto the sovereign grace of Him, who is able to work all your present works for you, and, which is more, to give you an inheritance among them that are sanctified. So prays

Your Servant in the work of

Our Lord Jesus Christ and his Gospel,

JOHN OWEN.

SERMON XII.

THE GLORY AND INTEREST OF NATIONS PROFESSING THE GOSPEL.

"Upon all the glory shall be a defence."—ISA. iv. 5.

THE design of this chapter is to give in relief against *outward* perplexing extremities, from gospel promises, and the presence of Christ with his people in those extremities. The next intendment of the words in the *type* seems to relate to the deliverance of the people of the Jews from the Babylonish captivity, and the presence of God amongst them upon their return;—God frequently taking occasion from thence to mind them of the covenant of grace, with the full ratification and publication of it by Christ, as is evident from Jer. xxxi. and xxxii., and sundry other places.

As to our purpose, we have considerable in the chapter,—the *persons* to whom these promises are given; the *condition* wherein they were; and the *promises* themselves that are made to them, for their supportment and consolation.

First. The *persons* intended are the remnant, the escaping, the "evasion of Israel," as the word signifies, verse 2,—they that are left, that remain, verse 3,—who escape the great desolation that was to come on the body of the people, the furnace they were to pass through. Only, in the close of that verse they have a farther description added of them, from the purpose of God concerning their grace and glory; they are written among the living, or rather, written unto life;—"Every one that is written," that is, designed, unto life in Jerusalem.

As to the persons, in themselves considered, the application is easy unto this assembly. Are you not the remnant,—the escaping of England? Is not this a brand plucked out of the fire? Are you not they that are left,—they that remain from great trials and desolations? The Lord grant that the application may hold out, and abide to the end of the prophecy!

Secondly. The *condition* that this *remnant*, or escaping, had been in, is laid down in some figurative expressions concerning the smallness of this remnant, or the paucity of them that should escape, and the greatness of the extremities they should be exercised withal. I cannot insist on particulars. It may suffice, that great distresses and calamities are intimated therein; and such have the days of our former trials and troubles been to some of us.

Thirdly. The *promises* here made to this people, thus escaped from great distresses, are of two sorts:—*Original* or fundamental; and then *consequential* thereon.

1. There is the great spring, or *fountain-promise*, from which all others, as lesser streams, do flow; and that is the promise of Christ himself unto them, and amongst them, verse 2. He is that "branch of Jehovah" and that "fruit of the earth" which is there promised. He is the bottom and foundation, the spring and fountain, of all the good that is or shall be communicated unto us; all other promises are but rivulets from that unsearchable ocean of grace and love that is in the promise of Christ;—of which afterward.

2. The promises that are derived and flow from hence may be referred unto three heads:—(1.) Of *beauty and glory*, verse 2; (2.) Of *holiness and purity*, verses 3, 4; (3.) Of *preservation and safety*, verses 5, 6.

My text lies among the last sort; and not intending long to detain you, I shall pass over the others, and immediately close with that of our present concernment.

Now, this promise of verse 5 is of a comprehensive nature, and relates to spiritual and temporal safety or preservation. Godliness, though it be not much believed, yet indeed hath the promise of this life and that which is to come.

I shall a little open the words of the verse, and thereby give light to those which I have chosen peculiarly to insist upon. It is, as I have said, safety and preservation, both spiritual and temporal, that is here engaged for; and concerning it we have considerable,—

[1.] The *manner of its production*.—I will create it, saith God. There is a creating power needful to be exerted for the preservation of Zion's remnant. Their preservation must be of God's creation. It is not only, not to be educed out of any other principle, or to be wrought by any other means; but it must, as it were, by the almighty power of God, be brought out of nothing;—God must create it. At least, as there were two sorts of God's creatures at the beginning,—that *dark body of matter*, whose rise was merely from nothing; and those things which from that dark, confused heap, he made to be *other things* than what they were therein,—it is of the last sort of creatures, if not of the first. If the preservation of this remnant be not out of nothing, without any means at all, yet it is for the most part from that darkness and confusion of things which contribute very little or nothing towards it. I will create it, saith God; and whilst he continues possessed of his creating power, it shall be well with his Israel.

[2.] For the *nature of* it;—it is here set out under the terms of that eminent pledge of the presence of God with his people in the wilderness, for their guidance and protection in the midst of all their difficulties and hazards, by a pillar of cloud and a flaming fire. This guided them through the sea, and continued with them after the setting up of the tabernacle in the wilderness forty years. The use and efficacy of that pillar, the intendment of God in it, the advantage of the people by it, I cannot stay to unfold:—it may suffice, in general, that it was a great and signal pledge of God's presence with them, for their guidance and preservation; that they might act according to his will, and enjoy safety in so doing. Only, whereas this promise here respects gospel times, the nature of the mercy promised is enlarged, and thereby somewhat changed. In the wilderness there was but one tabernacle; and so, consequently, one cloud by day, and one pillar of fire by night, was a sufficient pledge of the presence of God with the whole people. There are now many dwelling-places, many assemblies of mount Zion; and in the enlargement of mercy and grace under the gospel, the same pledge of God's presence and favour is promised to every one of them as was before to the whole. The word we have translated "a dwelling-place," denotes not a common habitation, but a place prepared for God; and is the same with the assemblies and congregations in the expression following. The sum of all is, God, by his creating power, in despite of all opposition, will bring forth preservation for his people; guiding them in paths wherein they shall find peace and safety.

Only ye may observe the order and dependence of these promises; the promise of holiness, verse 4, lies in order before that of safety, verse 5. Unless our filth and our blood be purged away by a spirit of judgment and a spirit of burning, it is in vain for us to look for the pillar and the cloud. If we are not interested in holiness, we shall not be interested in safety;—I mean as it lies in the promise, and is a mercy washed in the blood of Jesus; for as for the peace of the world, I regard it not. Let not men of polluted hearts and defiled hands once imagine, that God cares for them in an especial manner. If our filth and our blood, our sin and our corruption, abide upon us, and we are delivered, it will be for a greater ruin; the way unto the cloud and pillar is by the spirit of judgment and burning.

The words of my text are a recapitulation of the whole verse, and are a gospel promise given out in law terms; or a New Testament *mercy* under Old Testament *expressions.*

I shall, then, briefly show you these two things:—1*st.* What is here expressed as to the *type and figure;* 2*dly.* What is here intended as to *the substance* of the mercy promised.

1*st.* For the *figure;* by the "glory" and "defence," a double consort, or two pairs of things seem to be intended;—the *ark* and the *mercy-seat;* the *tabernacle* and the *pillar of fire.*

For the *first,*—the *ark* is oftentimes called the "glory" of God, Ps. lxxviii. 61, "He delivered his strength into captivity, and his glory into the enemy's hand;"—where he speaks of the surprisal of the ark by the Philistines; which when it was accomplished, Phinehas's wife called her son Ichabod, and said, "The glory is departed," 1 Sam. iv. 21. The word which we have rendered "a defence," properly signifies "a covering;" as was the mercy-seat, the covering of the ark. So that, "Upon the glory shall be a defence," is as much as, Unto you the mercy-seat shall be on the ark; or, You shall have the mercy represented and intimated thereby.

The *tabernacle* and *cloud,* or *pillar of fire,* are also called to mind. So the words are expressive of that figure of God's gracious presence with his people which we have recounted, Exod. xl. 34, "Then a cloud covered the tent of the congregation, and the glory of the LORD filled the tabernacle." So it continued: the glory of God was in the tabernacle, and the cloud upon it, or over it, as the word here is; and so "upon all the glory there was a defence."

2*dly.* I need not stay to prove that all those things were typical of Christ. He was the "end of the law," represented by the ark, which did contain it, Rom. x. 3, 4. He was "the mercy-seat," as he is called, and said to be, Rom. iii. 25; 1 John ii. 2,—covering the law from the eye of justice, as to those that are interested in him. He was the tabernacle and temple, wherein dwelt the glory of God, and which was replenished with all pledges of his gracious presence.

Apply, then, this promise to gospel times, and the substance of it is comprehended in these two propositions:—I. *The presence of Christ with any people, is the glory of any people.* This is the glory here spoken of; as is evident to any one that will but read over the second verse, and consider its influence unto these words: "The branch of the LORD shall be to them beautiful and glorious;" and, "Upon all the glory shall be a defence." II. *The presence of God in special providence over a people, attends the presence of Christ in grace with a people.* If Christ, the glory, be with them, a defence shall be upon them; what lies else in allusion to the mercy-seat, not drawn forth in these propositions, may be afterward insisted on.

I. For the first: What, I pray, else should be so? This is their glory, or they have none. Is it in their *number,* that they are great, many, and populous? God thinks not so, nor did he when he gave an account of his thoughts of his people of old: "The LORD did not set his love upon you, nor choose you, because ye were more in number than any people; for ye were the fewest of all people," Deut. vii. 7. God made no reckoning of numbers; he chose that people that was fewest of all. He esteemed well of them, when they were but "a few men in number; yea, very few, and strangers," Ps. cv. 12. You know what it cost David in being seduced by Satan into the contrary opinion. He thought the glory of his people had been in their number, and caused them to be reckoned; but God taught him his error, by taking off with a dreadful judgment no small portion of the number he sought after. There is nothing more common in the Scripture, than for the Lord to speak contempt of the multitude of any people, as a thing of nought; and he takes pleasure to confound them by weak and despised means. Is it in their *wisdom and counsel*, their understanding for the ordering of their affairs? Is *that* their glory? Why, see how God derides the prince of Tyrus, who was lifted up with an apprehension hereof, and counted himself as God upon that account, Ezek. xxvii. 3–6, &c. The issue of all is, "Thou shalt be a man, and no God, in the hand of him that slays thee." God will let him see, in his ruin and destruction, what a vain thing that was which he thought his glory. Might I dwell upon it, I could evince unto you these two things:—

1. That whereas the end of all *human wisdom* in nations, or the rulers of them, is to preserve human society in peace and quietness, within the several bounds and allotments that are given unto them by the providence of God, it so comes to pass, for the most part, through the righteous judgment and wise disposal of God, that it hath a contrary end, and bringeth forth contrary effects throughout the world. Do not the inhabitants of the earth generally owe all their disturbance, sorrow, and blood to the wise contrivance of a few men, not knowing how to take the law of their proceedings from the mouth of God, but laying their deep counsels and politic contrivances in a subserviency to their lusts and ambition? And what glory is there in that, which almost constantly brings forth contrary effects to its own proper end and intendment?

2. That God delights to mix a *spirit of giddiness*, error, and folly in the counsels of the wise men of the world; making them reel and stagger in their way like a drunken man, that they shall not know what to do, but commonly, in their greatest concernments, fix upon things as devoid of true reason and sound wisdom as any children or fools could close withal. "He taketh the wise in their own craftiness; and the counsel of the froward is carried headlong," Job v. 13, 14;—so at large, Isa. xix. 11–14. And now where is their glory? I could give instances of both these, and that plentifully, in the days

and seasons that have passed over our own heads. The like also may be said of the strength, the power, the armies of any people,—if their number and wisdom be vain, be no glory; their strength, which is but the result or exurgency of their number and wisdom, must needs be so also. But you have all this summed up together, Jer. ix. 23, 24, "Thus saith the LORD, Let not the wise man glory in his wisdom, neither let the mighty man glory in his might, let not the rich man glory in his riches: but let him that glorieth glory in this, that he understandeth and knoweth me, that I am the LORD." It is neither wisdom, nor might, nor riches, that is our glory; but our interest in Jehovah only.

This, I say, is in the presence of Christ only.

Now, Christ may be said to be present with a people two ways.

(1.) In respect of the dispensation of his gospel amongst them, the profession of it, and subjection to the ordinances thereof. The gospel of Christ is a blessed gospel,—a glorious gospel in itself, and unto them that embrace it. But yet this profession, separated from the root from which it ought to spring, is not the glory of any people; *Christ is not their glory who are his shame.* Empty profession is the shame of Christ in the world, and shall not be others' glory. The apostle tells us that this may consist with a litter of unclean lusts; making them in whom it is abominable to God and man, 2 Tim. iii. 4, 5. If the bare profession of the truth would render a nation glorious, oh, how glorious were this nation! So would have been the people of old, who cried, "The temple of the Lord! the temple of the Lord!" But when men profess the truth of Christ, but in their hearts and ways maintain and manifest an enmity to the power of that truth, and to all of Christ that is in reality in the world,—this is no glory.

(2.) Christ is present with a people in and by his Spirit,—dwelling in their hearts by his Spirit and faith, uniting them to himself. I do not distinguish this from the former, as inconsistent with it; for though the former may be without this, yet where this is there will be the former also. *Profession* may be without *union;* but *union* will bring forth *profession.* There may be a form of godliness without power; but where the power is, there will be the appearance also. Now, when Christ is thus present with a people,—that is, [when] they are united to him by his Spirit,—they are members of his mystical body;—that is their glory. Be they few or many in a nation that are so, they are the glory of that nation, and nothing else: and where there is the most of them, there is the most glory; and where they are diminished, there the glory is eclipsed. Christ mystical, the head and his body, is all the glory that is in the world. If any nation be glorious and honourable above others, it is because of this presence of

Christ in that nation. Christ is the glory of his saints, Isa. iv. 2,—in him they glory, Isa. xlv. 25; and the saints are Christ's glory, 2 Cor. viii. 23. They are the glory of Christ, and he glories in them; as God of Job, to Satan: "Hast thou considered my servant Job?" chap. i. 8. He doth, as it were, glory in him against the wickedness of the world; and Christ in them, and they in him, are all the glory of this world. So Zech. ii. 8, Christ was in the pursuit of the collection of his people from their dispersion. What seeks he after,—what looks he for? He goes "after the glory;" even to find out them who are God's glory in the world.

Now this is the glory of any people, upon a threefold account.

[1.] This alone makes them *honourable and precious before God.* So says God of them, Isa. xliii. 1, "I have redeemed thee, I have called thee by thy name; thou art mine;"—those are they of whom I spake. What then? Verse 4, "Thou art precious in my sight, thou art honourable, and I have loved thee." How doth God manifest his valuation of them? Verse 3, Why, he will give all the world,—the greatest, mightiest, wealthiest nations, for them; verse 5, all is as nothing in comparison of them who are his portion, and the lot of his inheritance. The Lord keep this alive upon your hearts, that that may be in your eyes the glory of this nation, on the account whereof it is precious to God, and honourable in his sight.

[2.] Because this presence of Christ makes men *comely and excellent in themselves*, with what eye soever the world may look upon them. The whole world, out of Christ, lies in evil,—under the curse of God and defilement of sin. In all the glittering shows of their wealth and riches, in the state and magnificence of their governments, the beauty of their laws and order (as they relate to their persons), they are, in the eye of God, a filthy and an abominable thing,—a thing that his soul loatheth. Curse and sin will make any thing to be so. But now Christ is to them, and in them, beautiful and glorious, Isa. iv. 2. Christ is so in himself, and he is so unto them, and makes them to be so. There is through him beauty, and excellency, and comeliness,—every thing that may make them lovely and acceptable. That the world looks not on them as such, is not their fault, but the world's misery. It looked on their master—Christ himself, the brightness of his Father's glory, who is altogether lovely, the chiefest of ten thousand—with no other eye, Isa. liii. 2. They are so in themselves, and are so to Christ. Being exposed, indeed, to many temptations, oftentimes they are made black and sully [sullied] by them; but yet they are comely still, Cant. i. 5. The ways whereby they are made black, for the most part we have expressed, verse 6; when the sun shines on them, and they are made keepers of the vineyard, it comes upon them. Prosperity and public employment oftentimes so sully them, that they are made black to the reproach of the world; but yet to Christ, who forgives and washes them, they are comely. Yea, this is all the excellency that is in the world. Sin, with honour, with wealth, with power, with wisdom, is a deformed and contemptible thing:—it is grace only that is beautiful and glorious; it is the gracious only that are excellent in the earth, Ps. xvi. 3.

[3.] This alone makes any truly useful unto others; and that either for *preservation* or *prosperity.*

1*st.* Here lies the preservation of any nation from ruin. Isa. lxv. 8, "Thus saith the LORD, As the new wine is found in the cluster, and one saith, Destroy it not; for a blessing is in it: so will I do for my servants' sakes, that I may not destroy them all." This is the blessing in the cluster, the hidden and secret blessing, for the sake whereof the whole is not destroyed. The "remnant" left by the Lord of hosts, Isa. i. 9,—that keeps the whole from being as Sodom or Gomorrah. If Elisha, a servant of the Lord, told the king of Israel, in his distress, that if he had not regarded the presence of Jehoshaphat, the king of Judah, he would not so much as have spoken to him; how much more will the Lord himself let a people know, in their distress, that were it not for the regard he hath to his secret ones, he would not take the least notice as to relief of them, or their concernments! Sodom could not be destroyed until Lot was delivered. The whole world owes its preservation and being to them, whom they make it their business to root out of it. They are as the foolish woman, that pulls down her own house with both her hands. It is not your *councils,*—you know how they have been divided, entangled, ensnared; it is not your *armies,* as such,—what have they been, to oppose against the mighty floods that have risen up in this nation? and they also have been as a reed driven to and fro with the wind (mankind is no better; John the Baptist says it of himself);—but it is this presence of Christ in and with his, that hath been the preservation of England, in the midst of all the changes and revolutions that we have been exercised withal, Mic. v. 5.

2*dly.* Not only preservation, but prosperity is from hence also. Mic. v. 7, "And the remnant of Jacob shall be in the midst of many people as a dew from the LORD, as the showers upon the grass, that tarrieth not for man, nor waiteth for the sons of men." It is the remnant of Jacob of whom he speaks; that is, this people of Christ, with whom he is so present, as hath been manifested. And where are they? They are in the midst of many people, in their inside,—in their bowels. They are woven, by their relations and employments, into the bowels of the nations; and on that account, there is neither this nor any nation about us, but shall spin out their mercies or their misery from their own bowels. Their providential fates lie in them; as is their deportment towards this remnant, such will their issue be. But what shall this remnant do? Why, it shall be "as dew from the LORD," and "as showers on the grass." It shall be that alone which makes them fruitful, flourishing, and prosperous. It may be, it will be so, provided there be good assistance, counsel, and strength, to carry on their affairs: yea, blessed be God for councils, and for armies; he hath made them useful to us. But the truth is, the blessing of this dew depends not on them; it tarrieth not for man; it waiteth not for the sons of men. It will be a blessing, let men do what they will; it depends not on their uncertain and unstable counsel,—on their weak and feeble strength. This remnant is as the ark in the house of Obed-edom, as Joseph in the house of Potiphar,—all is blessed and prospered for their sakes. It is not the glorious battlements, the painted windows, the crouching antics that support a building, but the stones that lie unseen in or upon the earth. It is often those who are despised and trampled on that bear up the weight of a whole nation. All the fresh springs of our blessings are in Zion.

It were easy to manifest, that in all our late *revolutions* we have turned on this hinge. According as the presence of Christ with his people, in the power of his Spirit, hath received entertainment in these nations, so hath our state and condition been. For many years before the beginning of these troubles, the land had been full of oppression; I mean, in respect to the people of God. Poverty, imprisonment, dangers, banishment, reproaches, were their portion. God was long patient. At length the height of their adversaries came to this, that they set not themselves so much against their persons or ways, as against the Spirit of Christ in and with them: that was made their reproach, that the by-word wherewith they were despised in the mouths of their adversaries, and the profane multitude. When things were come to this, that the very presence of Christ with his people was made the direct object of the hatred of men, the Lord could bear it no longer; but sware by himself that time should be given them no more. In this very house he raised up saviours and deliverers on mount Zion, to judge the mount of Edom. And how did he carry on this work? Not by might, nor by power, but by the Spirit of the Lord of hosts, as Zech. iv. 6; even by that very Spirit which had been reviled and despised. Give me leave to say, the work of judging this nation was carried on by the presence of the Spirit of Christ with his in faith and prayer. It was not by prudence of councils, or strength of armies above that of our enemies, that we prevailed; but by faith and prayer: and if any one be otherwise minded, I leave him for his resolution to the judgment of the great day, when all transactions shall be called over again. The adversaries themselves, I am sure, acknowledged it, when they openly professed that there was nothing left for them to overcome, or to overcome them, but the prayers of the *fanatic crew.*

After some years' contending, when the Lord had begun to give us deliverance, by breaking the power of the enemy, at least in this nation, besides those *bitter divisions* that fell out among the people of God themselves, and the backsliding of some to the cause and principles they had opposed, this evil was also found rising again amongst us;—slighting, blaspheming, contemning, under several pretences, of the Spirit and presence of Christ in and with his saints. You know what ensued;—what shakings, what revolutions, with new wars, bloodshed, and desolation, over the three nations. And give me leave to remember you, as one that had opportunity to make observations of the passages of Providence in those days, in all the three nations, in the times of our greatest hazards;—give me leave, I say, to remember you, that the public declarations, of those employed in the affairs of this nation, in the face of the enemies,—their addresses unto God among themselves, their prayers night and day, their private discourses one with another,—were, that the preservation of the interest of Christ in and with his people was the great thing that lay in their eyes; and that if it were not so, they desired that God would stop them in their way; yea, rather cause their carcases to fall in the high places of the field, than to prosper them in that which should be contrary thereunto: and we know what ensued. How we have used our mercies is another matter: this was the principle that prevailed with God and man.

Use 1. If you desire *the glory of these nations,* labour to promote the interest of Christ in these nations. I am not speaking unto you about disputable things,—differences among the people of God themselves; nor am I interposing my advice in your civil affairs; but I speak in general about those with whom Christ is present by his Spirit, his chosen ones, against whom there is an old enmity in Satan and the world. The glory of these nations is, that there is a people in them that have Christ in the midst of them; let it be your business to take care for that glory. But how shall we do it?

(1.) Labour *personally,* every one of you, to get Christ in your own hearts. I am very far from thinking that a man may not be lawfully called to magistracy, if he be not a believer; or that, being called, he should be impeded in the execution of his trust and place because he is not so. I shall not suspend my obedience whilst I inquire after my lawful governor's conversion; but yet this I say, considering that I cannot much value any good, but what comes in by the way of promise, I confess I can have no great expectation from them whom God loves not, delights not in. If any be otherwise minded, I shall not contend with him; but for this I will contend with all the world, that it is your duty to labour to assure Christ in your own hearts, even that you may be the better fitted for the work of God in the world. It is the promise of God to Zion, that "her officers shall be peace, and her exactors righteousness," Isa. lx. 17; and then shall she call her "walls Salvation, and her gates Praise," verse 18. It will be little advantage to any, to have the work of God raised in the world, and not to have the foundation-stone laid in their hearts. If there should be in any of you an enmity unto Christ and the power of godliness,—a hatred and contempt of the people of God,—an evil heart of unbelief,—an evil course of life, worldliness, oppression, vanity of mind, etc.,—would it advantage you to be intrusted with power in these nations? Would it not hasten your destruction, and increase your account? It is a noble promise that we have, Isa. xxxii. 17, "And the work of righteousness shall be peace; and the effect of righteousness, quietness and assurance for ever." It is a gospel righteousness that is spoken of; and that not of the cause as such only, but of the persons. The persons being righteous, and that with the righteousness of Christ, the effects mentioned shall follow their righteous undertakings. We have peace now, outward peace; but, alas! we have not *quietness;* and if any thing may be done that may give us *quietness,* yet, perhaps, we may not have *assurance.* We may be quickly shaken again; but when the righteousness of the *persons* and *cause* meet, all the rest will follow.

(2.) Set yourselves to oppose that *overflowing flood of profaneness,* and opposition to the power of godliness, that is spreading itself over this nation. Know you not that the nation begins to be overwhelmed by the pourings out of a profane, wicked, carnal spirit, full of rage, and contempt of all the work of reformation that has been attempted amongst us? Do you not know that if the former profane principle should prove predominant in this nation, that it will quickly return to its former station and condition, and that with the price of your dearest blood? And yet, is there not already such a visible prevalency of it, that in many places the very profession of religion is become a scorn; and in others, those old forms and ways taken up with greediness, which are a badge of apostasy from all former engagements and actings? And are not these sad evidences of the Lord's departing from us? If I should lay before you a comparison between the degrees of the appearances of the glory of God in this nation, the steps whereby it came forth, and those whereby it seems almost to be departing, it would be a matter of admiration and lamentation. I pray God we lose not our ground faster than we won it. Were our hearts kept up to our good old principles on which we first engaged, it would not be so with us; but innumerable evils have laid hold upon us; and the temptations of these days have made us a woful prey. *Gray hairs are here and there,* and it will be no wonder if our ruin should come with more speed than did our deliverance. Oh, then, set yourselves in the gap! by all ways and means oppose the growth of an evil, profane, common, malignant spirit amongst us. But I haste.

(3.) *Value,* encourage, and close with them *in and with whom* is this presence of Christ. They are the glory of the nation; its peace, safety, and prosperity will be found wrapped up in them. I know there lie divers considerable objections against the practice of this duty. I shall name some few of them, and leave the exhortation unto your consideration:—

[1.] Who are *those* persons in whom is this presence of Christ? Are they such as profess indeed religion, but neglect all rules of righteousness?—that would be accounted *godly,* but care not to be *honest,*—the marks of whose miscarriages are written on their foreheads? Are not these so far from being the glory, that they are the shame of any nation? I pray give me leave to endeavour the rolling away of this great stone of offence, in these few ensuing considerations:—

1*st,* Then, I shall willingly lay this down for a principle, that he is not religious who is not also righteous; as also, I shall not much value his righteousness who is not religious. He that is righteous doth righteousness; he doth so, in the bent of his spirit, and course of his ways and walkings. *If a man be froward, heady, high-minded, sensual, unjust, oppressive, worldly, self-seeking, a hater of good men, false, treacherous,* let him pretend to what he will, that man's religion is in vain; he may have a form of godliness, but he hath not the power of it. This principle we shall agree upon.

2*dly,* There have been, in the days wherein we live, many *false professors, hypocrites,* that have thought gain to be godliness; by reason of whose wicked lives, ways, and walking, the name of God hath been evil spoken of. And woe to them by whom these offences are come!—but yet, also, woe to the world because of offences! If these offences turn off men from an esteem of the remnant of Christ, in whom is his presence, woe to them also! I acknowledge, these days have abounded with offences; but woe to them who are turned aside by them from owning the portion and inheritance of Christ!

3*dly,* It cannot be denied, but that many of them who do belong unto Christ have wofully miscarried in these days. "O tell it not in Gath, publish it not in Askelon!" O that our souls could mourn in secret on that account! that we could go backward, and cover the nakedness and folly of one another! But, alas! this hath been far from being our frame of spirit! We have every one spread the failings of his brother before the face of men and devils. But yet, notwithstanding these miscarriages, those that are the people of Christ are his people still; and he loves them still, whether we will or no;—and commonly, those who are least able to bear with the miscarriages of others, have most of their own.

4*thly,* That differences of *judgments,* in civil affairs or *church matters,* ought not presently to be made arguments of men not being *righteous.* Some men think that none are righteous that are not of their principles; than which principle there is nothing more unrighteous. Let men that differ from them walk never so holily, profess never so strictly, yet, if they are not of their mind, they are not righteous! If men are offended on such accounts, it is because they will be so.

5*thly,* This hath ever been the way of the men of the world; that when any have been unblamable and zealous upon the account of religion, they will attempt their reputation, though without any ground or colour, upon the account of righteousness. So suffered the Christians of old; and so the Puritans of former days;—unjustly and falsely, as God will judge and declare. The world, then, in this matter, is not to be believed; the common reports of it are from the devil, the accuser of the brethren, who accuses them in the same manner before God night and day. These are but pretences, whereby men, ignorant of the mystery of the gospel and the power of grace, harden themselves to their ruin.

6*thly,* This *remnant* of Christ, with whom his presence is, who are the glory of a nation, is to be found only amongst the professors of a nation. For, although of those who are professors there may be many bad, yet of those that are not professors there is not one good. Where there is faith there will be a profession. If I should not know well where to find them, I am sure I know where I cannot find them. I cannot find them in the ways of the world, and conformity to it; in darkness, ignorance, neglect of duty, and utter unacquaintedness with gospel truths,—the gifts and graces of the Spirit. There I cannot find them. I shall not say of them, "Behold the Lord's anointed!" let their outward, worldly appearance be what it will. Now, by the help of these considerations, those who have in themselves principles of life and light in Christ, will, or may be (setting aside their temptations), enabled to discover this generation of the Lord's delight; and for others, I cannot take down the enmity that God hath set up. So then, notwithstanding this objection, I shall certainly esteem this remnant of Christ to lie among those who, having received gospel light and gospel gifts, evidently do make also profession of gospel grace, union and communion with Christ, separation from the world and the ways of it, in a conversation acceptable unto God in Christ. And to this portion shall I say, as Ruth to Naomi, let what will be glorious or uppermost in the world, "Whither thou goest, I will go; and where thou lodgest, I will lodge: thy people shall be my people, and thy God my God. The LORD do so to me, and more also, if ought but death part thee and me." With them let my portion be, and the portion of my family, whatever their lot and condition in this world should be; and the Lord say, Amen.

[2.] But it will be said, secondly, We are still at a loss; for what woful divisions are there amongst this generation of professors! Some are for one way, and some for another; some say one sort are the people of God, some another; some say the Prelatists are so, some the Presbyterians; some the Independents, some the Anabaptists; some the Fifth-monarchy-men, some others;—and on whom should the valuation pleaded for be cast?

To this I answer,—

1*st*. Some do say so, and plead thus, it cannot be denied; but the truth is, the greater is their weakness and folly. It is impossible men acquainted with the Spirit of Christ and the gospel should say so, unless they were under the power of one temptation or other. But it is no party, but the party of Christ in the world, and against the world—the seed of the woman against the seed of the serpent—that I am pleading for. That men, as to their interest in Christ, should be judged from such denominations as, though they make a great noise in the world, yet, indeed, signify very little things in themselves, is most unrighteous and unequal; nor will men find peace in such rash and precipitate judgments.

2*dly*. There may be many divisions amongst the people of God, and yet none of them be divided from Christ, the head. The branches of a tree may be entangled by strong winds, and stricken against one another, and yet none of them be broken off from the tree itself; and when the storm is over, every one possesses its own place in quietness, beauty, and fruitfulness. Whilst the strong winds of temptations are upon the followers of Christ, they may be tossed and entangled; but not being broken off from the root, when he shall say to the winds, "Peace, be still," they will flourish again in peace and beauty.

3*dly*. Let not Satan cheat you of your duty by this trivial objection. If he can keep you from duty whilst he can make divisions, he hath you sure enough. They of whom I speak, be they under what reproach or obloquies soever, they are all true men, all the children of one Father, though they are unhappily fallen out by the way.

Use 2. Of encouragement to those that have the presence of Christ with them in the manner declared;—they shall be safe. In vain it is for all the world to attempt their security; either they shall not prevail, or they shall mischief themselves by their own prevalency, Mic. v. 8. As they shall be a dew where they are appointed for a blessing; so, as a lion where they are oppressed. Destruction will come forth on their account, and that terribly, like the destruction of a lion; speedily in passing through it shall be done. And whence is it that this feeble generation shall be as a lion? It is from the presence of Christ among them, who is "the lion of the tribe of Judah;" and, to honour them, he assigns that to them which is his own proper work. Let men take heed how they provoke this lion. For the present, Gen. xlix. 9, he is "gone up from the prey: he stoopeth down, he coucheth as a lion, and as an old lion; who shall rouse him up?" He hath taken his prey in these nations, in the destruction of many of his enemies; he seemeth now to take his rest, to couch down, his indignation being overpast;—but who shall rouse him up? Why! what if he be provoked? what if he be stirred up? Why, he will not lie down, "until he eat of the prey, and drink the blood of the slain," Numb. xxiii. 24. There is no delivery from him. No; but what if there be a strong combination of many against him; will he not cease and give over? Isa. xxxi. 4. Be they who they will,—the shepherds of the people; be they never so many,—a multitude of them; let them lift up their voice and rage never so much,—all is one; he will perform his work and accomplish it, until you have him in the condition mentioned, Isa. lxiii. 1–6. Blessed are the people that are under his care and conduct; yea, blessed are the people whose God is the LORD!

SERMON XIII.

HOW WE MAY BRING OUR HEARTS TO BEAR REPROOFS.

PREFATORY NOTE TO THE THREE FOLLOWING DISCOURSES.

In the year 1672, the government of Charles II. began to abate its severity against Dissent. Penal laws against the Nonconformists and Popish recusants were suspended. They were allowed to meet for public worship, on the condition of taking out from government a licence to this effect. A large body of the Nonconformists availed themselves of the licence. Numerous congregations were formed; and, to illustrate the harmony between Presbyterians and Independents on the leading doctrines of the Christian system, a weekly lectureship was established, in which four Presbyterian and two Independent ministers officiated in rotation. The first lecturers were Dr Bates, Dr Manton, Dr Owen, Mr Baxter, Mr Collins, and Mr Jenkyn. The lectures were delivered in Pinner's Hall, an ancient and curious building in Old Broad Street. This lectureship was supported by considerable sums, which were bequeathed for the purpose. A division among the lecturers took place in 1694, occasioned by disputes in regard to the soundness of some opinions of Dr Crisp, whose works had been reprinted in 1690. The one party held these opinions to be Antinomian; the other party, who were called Neonomians, vehemently resented a work by Dr Williams, in refutation of Crisp's views. In the end, Dr Bates, Mr Howe, Mr Alsop, and Dr Williams withdrew, and established a separate lecture at Salter's Hall.

These lectures at Pinner's Hall were only the revival of a similar course of public instruction which had been instituted several years previously, and dropped at the Restoration. Neal, in his History of the Puritans, gives the following account of its origin:—"Most of the citizens of London having some relative or friend in the army of the Earl of Essex, so many bills were sent up to the pulpit every Lord's day for their preservation, that the ministers had not time to notice them in prayer, or even to read them. It was therefore agreed to set apart an hour at seven o'clock every morning, half of it to be spent in prayer for the welfare of the public, as well as particular cases, and the other in exhortations to the people. Mr Case began it in his church in Milk Street, from whence it was removed to the other distant churches in rotation,—a month at each. A number of the most eminent ministers conducted this service in town, and it was attended by great crowds of people. After the heat of the war was over, it became what was called a Casuistical Lecture, and continued till the Restoration." According to Palmer's Nonconformists' Memorial, most of the lectures were delivered at Cripplegate Church, and some at St Giles', whilst the lectures in the series against Popery were delivered at Southwark.

The lectures were published in successive volumes, and are very valuable. The first volume was edited by Case, who had been chiefly instrumental in the erection of the lectureship,—it is entitled, "The Morning Exercise Methodized; or, certain chief heads and points of the Christian religion opened and improved, in divers sermons," etc. The volume bears date 1660. Other four volumes successively appeared in 1661, 1674, 1683, and 1690. To each of the volumes there was a preface by Samuel Annesley, LL.D., who had also given one of the lectures in each course. In 1675, there was published, under the editorial superintendence of the Rev. Nathaniel Vincent, A.M., "The Morning Exercise against Popery; or, the principal errors of the Church of Rome detected and confuted, in a morning lecture preached lately at Southwark."

It is not so generally known, that, besides the works enumerated above, there were volumes of the same character published at still earlier dates. The titles of them may be given:—"The Morning Exercise at Giles-in-the-Fields, May 1655, printed for Richard Gibbs, in Chancery Lane, near Sergeants' Inn;" and "The Word of Faith, at Martin's-in-the-Fields, February 1655, printed for Fran. Tyton, at the Three Daggers, in Fleet Street."

Dr Owen contributed three sermons to these "Morning Exercises;"—one entitled, "How we may Bring our Hearts to Bear Reproofs," published in the Supplement to "The Morning Exercise" at Cripplegate, 1674; a second, "The Chamber of Imagery," etc., in "The Morning Exercise" in 1683; and a third,—which seems to have escaped the notice of Mr Orme, and is not included in Russell's edition of Owen's works,—entitled, "The Testimony of the Church is not the Only, nor the Chief Reason of our Believing the Scripture to be the Word of God," and published in "The Morning Exercise against Popery," 1675.—Ed.

SERMON XIII.

HOW WE MAY BRING OUR HEARTS TO BEAR REPROOFS.

"Let the righteous smite me, it shall be a kindness; and let him reprove me, it shall be an excellent oil, which shall not break my head: for yet my prayer also shall be in their calamities."—Ps. cxli. 5.

IT is generally agreed by expositors that this psalm, as that foregoing, with two of those that follow, was composed by David in the time of his banishment, or flight, from the court of Saul. The state wherein he describeth himself to have been, the matter of his pleas and prayers contained in them, with sundry express circumstances regarding that season, and his condition therein, do manifest *that* to have been the time of their composure.

That the psalmist was now in some distress, whereof he was deeply sensible, is evident from that vehemency of his spirit which he expresseth in the reiteration of his request or supplication, verse 1; and by his desire that his prayer might come before the LORD as incense; and the lifting up of his hands as the evening sacrifice, verse 2. The Jewish expositors guess, not improbably, that in that allusion he had regard unto his present exclusion from the holy services of the tabernacle; which in other places he deeply complains of.

For the matter of his prayer, in this beginning of the psalm (for I shall not look beyond the text), it respecteth himself, and his deportment under his present condition; which he desireth may be harmless and holy,—becoming himself, and useful unto others. And whereas he was two ways liable to miscarry,—first, By too high an exasperation of spirit against his oppressors and persecutors; and, secondly, By a fraudulent and pusillanimous compliance with them in their wicked courses; which are the two extremes that men are apt sinfully to run into in such conditions,—he prays earnestly to be delivered from them both. The first he hath respect unto, verse 3, "Set a watch, O LORD, before my mouth; keep the door of my lips;"—namely, that he might not, under those great provocations which were given him, break forth into an unseemly intemperance of speech against his unjust oppressors;

which sometimes fierce and unreasonable cruelties will wrest from very sedate and moderate spirits. But it was the desire of this holy psalmist, as, in like cases, it should be ours, that his heart might be always preserved in such a frame, under the conduct of the Spirit of God, as not to be surprised into an expression of distempered passion in any of his words or sayings. The other he regards in his earnest supplication to be delivered from it, verse 4, "Incline not my heart to any evil thing, to practise wicked works with men that work iniquity; and let me not eat of their dainties." There are two parts of his request unto the purpose intended. First, That, by the power of God's grace influencing his mind and soul, his heart might not be inclined unto any communion or society with his wicked adversaries in their wickedness. Secondly, That he might be preserved from a liking of, or a longing after, those things which are the baits and allurements whereby men are apt to be drawn into societies and conspiracies with the workers of iniquity: "And let me not eat of their dainties." See Prov. i. 10–14. For he here describeth the condition of men prospering for a season in a course of wickedness;—they first jointly give up themselves unto the practice of iniquity, and then together solace themselves in those satisfactions of their lusts which their power and interest in the world do furnish them withal. These are the "dainties" of which an impotent longing and desire do betray the minds of unstable persons unto a compliance with ways of sin and folly; for I look on these "dainties" to comprise whatever "the lust of the eyes, the lust of the flesh," or "the pride of life," can afford. All these David prays to be delivered from any inclination unto, especially when they are made the allurements of a course of sin. In the enjoyment of these dainties, it is the common practice of wicked men to soothe up, approve of, and mutually encourage one another in the way and course wherein they are engaged. And this completes that goodly felicity which in this world so many aspire unto, and whereof alone they are capable. The whole of it is but a society in perishing sensual enjoyments, without control, and with mutual applauses from one another.

This the psalmist had a special regard unto; who, casting his eye towards another communion and society, which he longed after, verse 5, that, in the first place, presents itself unto him, which is most opposite unto those mutual applauses and rejoicings in one another which are the salt and cement of all evil societies,—namely, rebukes and reproofs for the least miscarriages that shall be observed. Now, whereas the dainties, which some enjoy in a course of prosperous wickedness, are that alone which seems to have any thing in it amongst them that is desirable; and, on the other side, rebukes and reproofs are those alone which seem to have any sharpness, or matter of uneasiness and dislike, in the society of the godly; David balanceth that which seemeth to be sharpest in the one society against that which seems to be sweetest in the other, and, without respect unto other advantages, prefers the one above the other. Hence some read the beginning of the words, "Let the righteous rather smite me," with respect unto this comparison and balance.

"Let the righteous smite me, *it shall be* a kindness; and let him reprove me, *it shall be* an excellent oil, *which* shall not break my head: for yet my prayer also *shall be* in their calamities." The view of our translation will evidence the words to be elliptical in the original, by the various supplements which we make to fill up the sense of them, and render them coherent; and this hath put some difficulty on the interpretation of the text, and caused some variety of apprehensions in sober and learned expositors.

It is not unto my present purpose to engage into a discussion of all the difficulties of the text, seeing I design to found no other doctrine thereon, than what all will acknowledge to be contained in the words and their coherence. I shall only, therefore, briefly open them with respect unto our present purpose, and its concernment in them.

יֶהֶלְמֵנִי צַדִּיק חֶסֶד—צַדִּיק, "the righteous," is any one opposed to the workers of iniquity, verse 4,—any righteous person whatever,—any one who is of the society and communion of the righteous ones: for all the world falls under this distribution, as it will one day appear. "Let him smite me:" the word הָלַם is seldom used in the Scripture but to signify "a severe stroke," which shakes the subject smitten, and causeth it to tremble. See Prov. xxiii. 35; 1 Sam. xiv. 16; Ps. lxxiv. 6. And it is used for "the stroke of the hammer on the anvil," in fashioning of the iron, Isa. xli. 7. Wherefore the word חֶסֶד following may be taken adverbially, as a lenitive of that severity which this word importeth: "Let him smite me;" but "leniter, benignè, misericorditer,"—"gently, kindly, friendly, mercifully." And so some translations read the words, "Let the righteous smite me friendly," or kindly.

But there is no need to wrest the word to such an unusual sense; for the psalmist intends to show, that so he may be delivered from the society of ungodly men, and enjoy the communion of the righteous, he would not deprecate the greatest severities which, according to rule, might be exercised in rebuking or reproving him. And this he doth with so full a satisfaction of mind,—with such a high valuation of the advantage he should have thereby,—that he says not, he would bear it patiently and quietly, but חֶסֶד; it will be unto me "a benignity, a mercy, a kindness,"—as the word imports. And as it seems that some reproofs, at least,—some regular dealings of righteous persons with us,—may come as a stroke that makes us shake and tremble; so it is a good advance in spiritual wisdom, to find out kindness and mercy in those that are so grievous unto our natural spirits,—unto flesh and blood.

וְיוֹכִיחֵנִי, "And let him reprove me." This manifests what he intends by smiting, in the foregoing words. It is reproofs that he intends; and these he calls smiting, in opposition unto the flattering compliance of wicked men with one another in the enjoyment of their dainties, and with respect unto that smart unto the mind and affections wherewith some of them are sometimes accompanied. But this word, directly expressing that subject-matter whereof I intend to treat, must be again spoken unto.

שֶׁמֶן רֹאשׁ אַל־יָנִי רֹאשִׁי. These words have a double interpretation; for they may be either deprecatory of an evil implied, or declaratory of the psalmist's sense of the good he desired. Kimchi on the place observes, that his father Joseph divided the words of the text, and began here a new sense, wherein the psalmist returns unto the close of the fourth verse, "Let me not eat of their dainties," and, "Let not their precious oil"—that is, their flatteries and soothings in sin—"break my head;" but let the reproofs of the righteous preserve me. And this sense is followed by the Vulgar Latin, "Oleum autem peccatorum non impingat caput meum;" but the other construction and sense of the words is more natural. שֶׁמֶן רֹאשׁ, "Oleum capitis," the "oil of the head," we render, an "excellent oil;" and countenance may be given unto that interpretation from Exod. xxx. 23, where בְּשָׂמִים רֹאשׁ, "spices of the head," is well rendered, "principal spices." But I rather think that שֶׁמֶן עַל רֹאשׁ, "oil poured on the head"—which was the manner of all solemn unctions—is intended. This being a great privilege, and the token of the communication of great mercy, the psalmist compares the rebukes of the righteous thereunto; and therefore he adds, אַל־יָנִי רֹאשִׁי, "it shall not break my head." Considering reproofs in their own nature, he calls them "smitings;"—some of them being very sharp, as it is needful they should be where we are obliged to rebuke ἀποτόμως, "in a piercing and cutting manner," 2 Cor. xiii. 10; Tit. i. 13. But with respect unto their use, benefit, and advantage, they are like unto that anointing oil which, being poured on the head, was both gentle and pleasant, and a pledge of the communication of spiritual privileges, whence no inconveniences would ensue.

The last clause of the words belonging not unto our present design, I shall not insist on their explication.

Some few things must be farther premised unto our principal intention concerning the nature of those reproofs, which are proposed as a matter of such advantage in the text. And,—

1. The word יָכַח, here used, signifieth, "to argue, to dispute, to

contend in judgment," as well as "to reprove, rebuke, or reprehend." Its first signification is "to argue," or "to plead a cause with arguments." Hence it is used as a common term between God and man, denoting the reasons, real, or pretended only, on the one side and the other. So God himself speaks unto his people, לְכוּ־נָא וְנִוָּכְחָה, Isa. i. 18, "Go to, now, and let us plead," reason or argue, "together;" and Job calls his pleas or arguments in prayer unto God, תוֹכָחוֹת, chap. xxiii. 4, "I would fill my mouth with arguments." Wherefore, that only hath the true nature of a reproof, which is accompanied with reasons and arguments for the evincing of what it tends unto. Rash, groundless, wrathful, precipitate censures and rebukes, are evil in themselves, and, in our present case, of no consideration. Nor, indeed, ought any one to engage in the management of reproofs, who is not furnished with rule and argument to evince their necessity, and render them effectual. Sometimes things may be so circumstanced, as that a reproof shall so carry its own reason and efficacious conviction along with it, that there will be no need of arguing or pleas to make it useful. So the look of our blessed Saviour on Peter, under the circumstances of his case, was a sufficient reproof, though he spake not one word in its confirmation. But ordinarily, cogent reasons are the best conveyances of reproofs to the minds of men, be they of what sort they will.

2. *Reproofs do always respect a fault, an evil, a miscarriage, or a sin, in them that are reproved.* There may be mutual admonitions and exhortations among Christians, with respect unto sundry things in the course of their faith and obedience, without a regard unto any evil or miscarriage. The general nature of a reproof is an admonition or exhortation; but it hath its special nature from its regard unto a fault in course, or particular fact. And hence the word signifies also "to chastise;" wherein is a correction for, and the means of a recovery from, a miscarriage, 2 Sam. vii. 14, "I will reprove him with the rod of men;" that is, chastise him. This, therefore, is that reproof which we intend,—a warning, admonition, or exhortation, given unto any, whereby they are rebuked for, and with respect unto, some moral evil or sin in their course, way, practice, or any particular miscarriage, such as may render them obnoxious unto divine displeasure or chastisement; for it is essential unto a regular reproof, that, in him who gives it, it may be accompanied with, or do proceed from, an apprehension that the person reproved is, by the matter of the reproof, rendered obnoxious unto the displeasure of God.

3. *It may also be considered, that reproving is not left arbitrarily unto the wills of men.* Whatever seems to be so, it loseth its nature if it be not a duty in him who reproves, and will come short of its efficacy No wise man will reprove, but when it is his duty so

to do, unless he design the just reproach of a busy-body for his reward. The command is general, with respect unto brother and neighbour, Lev. xix. 17, "Thou shalt not hate thy brother in thine heart: thou shalt in any wise rebuke thy neighbour, and not suffer sin upon him." But as to the particular discharge of this work as a duty, there must be either an especial office or an especial relation, or a concurrence of circumstances for its warranty. God hath, in his wisdom and care, given rules and bounds unto our engagement unto duties; without a regulation whereby we shall wander in them with endless dissatisfactions unto ourselves, and unnecessary provocations unto others. But the duty of reproving, with the love, wisdom, tenderness, and compassion required in the discharge of it,—its motives, ends, and circumstances,—its proper rules and limitations,—fall not under my present consideration; but these things in general were necessary to be premised unto what do so.

That which the text instructs us in may be comprised in this general observation:—

Observation. *Reproofs, though accompanied with some sharpness, if rightly received and duly improved, are a mercy and advantage incomparably above all the satisfactions which a joint consent with others in sin and pleasures can afford.*

The latter part of the proposition I have mentioned only to express the balance that is proposed by the psalmist between the best and most desirable advantages of wicked society on the one hand, and the sharpest or most displeasing severities that accompany the communion of the righteous or godly. But I shall not at all handle the comparison, as designing only *some directions how men should behave themselves under reproofs,* that they may be a kindness, and an excellent oil unto them; or how they may by them obtain spiritual benefit and advantage unto their own souls. And this, however at present the matter may be managed, is of itself of great importance. For as, in the state of weakness and imperfection, of mistakes and miscarriages, wherein we are, there is no outward help or aid of more use and advantage unto us than seasonable reproofs; so in the right receiving and improving of them, as high a trial of the spirits of men, as to their interest in wisdom and folly, doth consist, as in any thing that doth befall them, or wherewith they may be exercised. For as scorners of reproofs, those that hear them unwillingly, that bear them haughtily and impatiently, with designs of revenge or disdainful retortions, have the characters of pride and folly indelibly fixed on them by the Holy Ghost; so their due admission and improvement is in the same infallible truth represented as an evident pledge of wisdom, and an effectual means of its increase. This is so much and so frequently insisted on in that great treasure of all wisdom, spiritual, natural, and political,—namely, the Book of Proverbs, that it is altogether needless to call over any particular testimonies unto that purpose.

Three things we are to inquire into, in compliance with our present design:—I. *How reproofs may be duly received.* II. *The reasons why they ought so to be.* III. *How they may be duly improved.*[1]

I. *That we may receive reproofs in a due manner*, three things are to be considered:—1. *The general qualification of the reprover;* 2. *The nature of the reproof;* and, 3. *The matter of it.*

1. *The Psalmist here desires that his reprover may be a righteous man:* "Let the righteous smite me,"—"Let him reprove me." To give and take reproofs, is a dictate of the law of nature, whereby every man is obliged to seek the good of others, and to promote it according to his ability and opportunity. The former is directed by that love which is due unto others; the latter, by that which is due unto ourselves: which two are the great rules, and give measure to the duties of all societies, whether civil or spiritual. Wherefore, it doth not evacuate a reproof, or discharge him who is reproved from the duty of attending unto it, that he by whom it is managed is not righteous, yea, is openly wicked; for the duty itself being an effect of the law of nature, it is the same, for the substance of it, by whomsoever it is performed. Yea, ofttimes such moral, or rather immoral, qualifications as render not only the reprover less considerable, but also the reproof itself, until thoroughly weighed and examined, obnoxious unto prejudicate conceptions, do occasion a greater and more signal exercise of grace and wisdom in him that is reproved than would have been stirred up had all things concurred unto the exact regularity of the reproof. However, it is desirable, on many accounts, that he who reproves us be himself a righteous person, and be of us esteemed so to be. For, as such a one alone will or can have a due sense of the evil reproved, with a right principle and end in the discharge of his own duty; so the minds of them that are reproved are, by their sense of his integrity, excluded from those insinuations of evasions, which prejudices and suggestions of just causes of reflections on their reprover will offer unto them. Especially, without the ex-

[1] This enunciation of the topics in the discourse differs slightly from what appears in "The Morning Exercises," where the order of the second and third heads is reversed. We prefer the arrangement adopted above, because it is consistent with the actual order of the topics in the discourse itself, and because it is given in the folio volume of Owen's Sermons published in 1721; for an account of which see the General Preface to this edition of his works. The editors of that volume state, "that, for the greater accuracy of the work, such original manuscripts as are yet remaining, even of those sermons which were formerly printed, have been consulted, which we chose rather to follow than the printed copies, where any thing had been altered and omitted; so that both the Sermons and other Tracts are free from those many gross faults that have hitherto sullied them."—ED.

ercise of singular wisdom and humility, will all the advantages of a just reproof be lost, where the allowed practice of greater sins and evils than that reproved is daily chargeable on the reprover. Hence is that reflection of our Saviour on the useless, hypocritical diligence of men in pulling the mote out of their brother's eyes whilst they have beams in their own, Matt. vii. 3–5. The rule in this case is:—*If the reprover be a righteous person, consider the reprover first, and then the reproof; if he be otherwise, consider the reproof, and the reprover not at all.*

2. *The nature of a reproof* is also to be considered. And this is threefold: for every reproof is either, (1.) *Authoritative;* or (2.) *Fraternal;* or (3.) Merely *friendly* and *occasional.*

(1.) *Authoritative* reproofs are either, [1.] *Ministerial;* or [2] *Parental;* or [3.] *Despotical.*

[1.] There is an especial authority accompanying *ministerial reproofs,* which we ought especially to consider and improve. Now, I understand not hereby those doctrinal reproofs when, in the dispensation of that word of grace and truth which is " profitable for correction and reproof," 2 Tim. iii. 16, they speak, and exhort, and " rebuke" the sins of men " with all authority," Tit. ii. 15; but the occasional application of the word unto individual persons, upon their unanswerableness in any thing unto the truth wherein they have been instructed. For every right reproof is but the orderly application of a rule of truth unto any person under his miscarriage, for his healing and recovery. Where, therefore, a minister of the gospel, in the preaching of the word, doth declare and teach the rule of holy obedience with ministerial authority, if any of the flock committed to his charge shall appear in any thing to walk contrary thereunto, or to have transgressed it in any offensive instance, as it is his duty, the discharge whereof will be required of him at the great day, particularly to apply the truth unto them in the way of private, personal reproof; so he is still therein accompanied with his ministerial authority: which makes his reproof to be of a peculiar nature, and as such to be accounted for. For as he is thus commanded, as a minister, to " exhort, rebuke, admonish," and " reprove" every one of his charge, as occasion shall require; so, in doing of it, he doth discharge and exercise his ministerial office and power. And he that is wise will forego no considerations that may give efficacy unto a just and due reproof; especially not such a one as, if it be neglected, will not only be an aggravation of the evil for which he is reproved, but will also accumulate his guilt with a contempt of the authority of Jesus Christ. Wherefore the rule here is,—*The more clear and evident the representation of the authority of Christ is in the reproof, the more diligent ought we to be in our attendance unto it and compliance with it.* He is the great reprover of his church, Rev. iii. 19. All the use, power, authority, and efficacy of *ecclesiastical* reproofs flow originally and are derived from him. In ministerial reproofs, there is the most express and immediate application of his authority made unto the minds of men; which, if it be carelessly slighted or proudly despised, or evacuated by perverse cavillings, as is the manner of some in such cases, it is an open evidence of a heart that never yet sincerely took upon it this law and yoke.

These things are spoken of the *personal* reproofs that are given by ministers, principally unto those of their respective flocks, as occasion doth require; wherein I shall pray that our Lord Jesus Christ, the great Shepherd of the sheep, would yet make us all more faithful and diligent, as the season wherein we live doth abundantly require it. But, moreover, church censures, in *admonition* and *excommunication*, have the nature and ends of ministerial reproofs. But the handling of their nature and use, with the duties of those persons who justly fall under them, and the benefit which they may reap thereby, is too long and large a subject to be here diverted unto.

[2.] Authoritative reproof is *parental.* Reproof is, indeed, one of the greatest and most principal duties of parents towards children, and without which all others, for the most part, do but pamper them unto slaughter and ruin. Neglect hereof is that which hath filled us with so many Hophnis, Phinehases, and Absaloms,—whose outrageous wickednesses are directly charged on the sinful lenity and neglect, in this matter, even of godly parents. And, indeed, whereas some parents are openly vicious and debauched, even in the sight of their children, in a sensual neglect and contempt of the light of nature, whereby they lose all their authority in reproving, as well as all care about it;—and whereas the most have so little regard unto sin as sin, whilst things are tolerably well in outward concerns, that they neglect the reproof of it as such; and many, through a foolish, contemptible prevalency of fond affection, will take no notice of the sinful follies, extravagances, and miscarriages of their children, until all things grow desperate with them; but soothe up and applaud them in such effects of pride, vanity, and wantonness, as ought to be most severely reproved in them;—the woful and dreadful degeneracy of the age wherein we live owes itself much unto the horrible neglect of parents in this duty. That parental reproof is a duty taught by the law of nature, confirmed in the Scripture, enjoined under severe threatenings and penalties, exemplified in instances of blessings and vengeance on its performance or neglect, rendered indispensably necessary by that depravation of our natures which works in children from the womb, and grows up in strength and efficacy together with them,—I should not need to prove, if it lay directly before me, it being a matter of universal acknowledgment. I shall only say, that whereas there is, on many accounts, an immediate impress of divine authority on parental reproofs, that which children ought to consider and know for themselves is, that a continuance in the neglect or contempt of them is a token that seldom fails of approaching temporal and eternal destruction, Prov. xxx. 17.

[3.] Authoritative reproof is *despotical;* namely, that of governors, rulers, and masters of families. This also partakes of the nature of those foregoing, and being a duty founded in the law of nature, as well as enforced by positive divine commands, casts a peculiar obligation to obedience on them that are so reproved. And where servants regard not sober and Christian reproofs, as the ordinance of God for their good, they lose the advantages of their condition, and may be looked upon as unsanctified sufferers in a state of bondage; which hath an especial character of the first curse upon it.

(2.) Reproof is *fraternal,* or such as is mutual between the members of the same church, by virtue of that especial relation wherein they stand, and the obligation thence arising unto mutual watchfulness over each other, with admonitions, exhortations, and reproofs. As this is peculiarly appointed by our Saviour, Matt. xviii. 15, in confirmation of the ordinance in the church of the Jews to that purpose, Lev. xix. 17, and confirmed by many precepts and directions in the New Testament, Rom. xv. 14; 1 Thess. v. 14; Heb. iii. 12, 13, xii. 15, 16; so the neglect of it is that which hath lost us not only the benefit, but also the very nature of church-societies. Wherefore, our improvement of rebukes in this kind, depends much on a due consideration of that duty and love from whence they do proceed: for this we are, by the royal law of charity, obliged unto the belief of, where there is not open evidence unto the contrary. And whereas, it may be, those things for which we may be thus reproved are not of the greatest importance in themselves, who that is wise will, by the neglect of the reproof itself, contract the open guilt of contemning the wisdom, love, and care of Christ in the institution of this ordinance?

(3.) Lastly, Reproofs are *friendly* or *occasional,* such as may be administered and managed by any persons, as reasons and opportunities require, from the common principle of universal love unto mankind, especially towards them that are of the household of faith. These also, having in them the entire nature of reproofs, will fall under all the ensuing directions, which have a general respect thereunto.

If, then, we would duly make use of, and improve unto our advantage, the reproofs that may be given us, we are seriously to consider the nature of them, with respect unto those by whom they are managed; for all the things we have mentioned are suited to influence our minds unto a regard of them, and compliance with them.

3. *The matter of a reproof* is duly to be weighed by him who designs any benefit thereby. And the first consideration of it is, whether it be true or false. I shall not carry them unto a more minute distribution of the substance and circumstances of the matter intended, of the whole or part of it; but do suppose, that, from some principal consideration of it, every reproof, as to its matter, may be denominated and esteemed true or false. And here our own consciences, with due application unto the rule, are the proper judge and umpire. Conscience, if any way enlightened from the word, will give an impartial sentence concerning the guilt or innocence of the person, with respect unto the matter of a reproof. And there can be no more infallible evidence of a miscarriage in such a condition, than when pride, or passion, or prejudice, or any corrupt affection, can either outbrave or stifle that compliance with a just reproof which conscience will assuredly tender, Rom. ii. 14, 15.

(1.) If a reproof, as to the matter of it, be *false* or unjust, and so judged in an unbiassed conscience, it may be considered in matter of *right* and of *fact*. In the first case, the matter may be true, and yet the reproof formally false and evil; in the latter, the matter may be false, and yet the reproof an acceptable duty.

[1.] *A reproof is false in matter of right, or formally, when we are reproved for that as evil which is indeed our duty to perform.* So David was fiercely reproved by his brother Eliab for coming unto the battle against the Philistines, ascribing it to his pride, and the naughtiness of his heart. Whereunto he only replied, "What have I done? Is there not a cause?" 1 Sam. xvii. 28, 29. And Peter rebuked our Lord Jesus Christ himself for declaring the doctrine of the cross, Mark viii. 32. And so we may be reproved for the principal duties that God requireth of us. And if men were as free in reproving as they are in reproaching, we should not escape from daily rebukes for whatever we do in the worship of God. Now, though such reproofs generally may be looked on as temptations, and so to be immediately rejected, as they were in the cases instanced in; yet may they sometimes, where they proceed from love, and are managed with moderation, be considered as necessary cautions to look heedfully unto the grounds and reasons we proceed upon in the duties opposed, at which others do take offence.

[2.] If the reproof be *false in matter of fact*, wherein that is charged on us, and reproved in us, whereof we are no ways guilty, three things are to be considered, that it may not be unuseful unto us:—

1*st*. The *circumstances* of the reprover; as, first, Whether he do proceed on *some probable mistake;* or, secondly, *Credulity and easiness in taking up reports;* or, thirdly, *On evil, groundless surmises* *of his own;* or, fourthly, From *a real godly jealousy, which hath been imposed on, as easily it will be, by some appearances of truth.* Without a due consideration of these things, we shall never know how to carry it aright, towards them by whom we are reproved for that whereof we are not guilty.

2dly. Consider aright the *difference between a reproof and a reproach;* for they may be both false alike, and that whereof we are reproved have no more truth in it than that wherewith we are reproached. Yea, we may be honestly reproved for that which is false, and wickedly reproached with that which is true. So Augustine calls the language of the maid unto her mother about drinking wine, "durum convicium," though the matter of it were true enough. But a reproach is the acting of a mind designing of, and rejoicing in, evil. Unto a reproof it is essential that it spring from love. "Whom I love I rebuke," is the absolute rule of these things. Let a man rebuke another, though for that which indeed is false, if it be in love, it is a *reproof;* but let him rebuke another, though for that which is true, if it be from a mind delighting in evil, it is a *reproach;* and if it be false, it is, moreover, a *calumny.*

3dly. Where a man, in such cases, is fully justified by the testimony of his own conscience, bearing witness unto his integrity and innocency; yet may he greatly miscarry under the occasion, if he attend not diligently unto his own spirit; which most men judge to be set at the utmost liberty under such injurious provocations, as they esteem them. Wherefore, to keep our minds *unto sedate, Christian moderation in such cases,* and that we may not lose the advantage of what is befallen us, we ought immediately to apply them unto such other duties as the present occasion doth require; as,—

First. *To search our own hearts and ways, whether we have not indeed upon us the guilt of some greater evils than that which is falsely charged on us, or for which we are reproved on mistake.* And if it appear so, upon examination, we shall quickly see what little reason we have to tumultuate, and rise up with indignation against the charge we suffer under. And may we not thence see much of the wisdom and goodness of God, who suffereth us to be exercised with what we can bear off with the impenetrable shield of a good conscience, whilst he graciously hides and covers those greater evils of our hearts, with respect whereunto we cannot but condemn ourselves?

Secondly. *To consider that it is not of ourselves that we are not guilty of the evil suspected and charged.* No man of sobriety can, on any mistake, reprove us for any thing, be it never so false, but that it is merely of sovereign grace that we have not indeed contracted the guilt of it; and humble thankfulness unto God on this occasion, for his real preserving grace, will abate the edge and take off the fierceness of our indignation against men for their supposed injurious dealings with us.

Thirdly. *Such reproofs, if there be not open malice and continued wickedness manifest in them, are to be looked on as gracious providential warnings, to take heed lest at any time we should be truly overtaken with that which at present we are falsely charged withal.* We little know the dangers that continually attend us, the temptations wherewith we may be surprised at unawares, nor how near on their account we may be unto any sin or evil which we judge ourselves most remote from, and least obnoxious unto. Neither, on the other hand, can we readily understand the ways and means whereby the holy, wise God issueth forth those hidden provisions of preventing grace which are continually administered for our preservation; and no wise man, who understands any thing of the deceitfulness of his own heart, with the numberless numbers of invisible occasions of sin wherewith he is encompassed continually, but will readily embrace such reproofs, as providential warnings unto watchfulness in those things whereof before he was not aware.

Fourthly. When the mind, by these considerations, is rendered sedate, and weighed unto Christian moderation, *then ought a man, in such cases, patiently and peaceably to undertake the defence of his innocency, and his own vindication.* And herein, also, there is need of much wisdom and circumspection; it being a matter of no small difficulty for a man duly to manage self and innocency, both which are apt to influence us unto some more than ordinary vehemency of spirit. But the directions which might, and indeed ought to be given under all these particular heads, could by no means be confined unto the limits fixed to this discourse.

(2.) If *the matter of the reproof be true in fact*, then it is duly to be considered, whether the offence for which any one is reproved be *private* or *public*, attended with scandal.

[1.] If it be *private*, then it is to be weighed, whether it was known unto, and observed in and by, the person himself reproved or no, before he was reproved. If it were *not so known* (as we may justly be reproved for many things which, through ignorance or inadvertency, or compliance with the customs of the world, we may have taken no notice of), and if the reproof bring along light and conviction with it, the first especial improvement of such a peculiar reproof is thankfulness to God for it, as a means of deliverance from any way, or work, or path, that was unacceptable in his sight. And hence a great prospect may be taken of the following deportment of the mind under other reproofs. For, a readiness to take in light and conviction, with respect unto any evil that we are ignorant of, is an evidence of a readiness to submit to the authority of God in any other rebukes that have their convictions going before them: so the heart that is prone to fortify itself, by any pleas or *pretences, against convictions of sin in what it doth not yet own so to be, will be as prone unto obstinacy under reproofs in what it cannot but acknowledge to be evil.* If it were *known before* to the person reproved, but not supposed by him to be observed by others,—under the covert of which imagination sin often countenanceth itself,—that soul will never make a due improvement of a reproof, who is not first sensible of the care and kindness of God in driving him from that retreat and hold where the interest of sin had placed its chiefest reserve.

[2.] Sins so far *public* as to give matter of offence or scandal, are the ordinary subject of all orderly reproofs; and therefore need not in particular to be spoken unto.

Having showed the nature of reproofs in general, with such considerations of the matter of them as have afforded occasion unto sundry particular directions relating unto the duty under discussion, it remains that we explain and confirm the other two generals comprised in the observation deduced from the text; namely, II. *Why we ought to receive reproofs, orderly or regularly given unto us, esteeming of them as a singular privilege;* and, III. *How we may duly improve them unto their proper end,*—the glory of God, and the spiritual advantage of our own souls.

II. As to the first of these, we may observe,—

1. That *mutual reproofs, for the curing of evil and preventing of danger in one another, are prime dictates of the law of nature, and [of] that obligation to seek the good of each other which our participation in the same being, offspring, original, and end, doth lay upon us.* This God designed in our creation, and this the rational constitution of our natures directs us unto. To seek and endeavour for each other, all that good whereof we are capable in time, or unto eternity, was indelibly implanted upon our natures, and indispensably necessary unto that society among ourselves, with the great end of our joint living unto God, for which we were made. All the mutual evils of mankind, whether of persons or of nations, designed or perpetrated against one another, are effects of our fatal prevarication from the law of our creation. Hence Cain, the first open violent transgressor of the rules and bounds of human society, thought to justify or excuse himself by a renunciation of that principle, which God in nature had made the foundation of a political or sociable life, with respect unto temporal and eternal ends. "Am I," saith he, "my brother's keeper?" Gen. iv. 9. Yea, God hath made every man the keeper of his brother so far as that they should in all things, in their opportunities, and unto their power, seek their good, and de-

liverance from evil. In those things which are good unto us, those which are spiritual and eternal have the pre-eminence. These nothing can prejudice but sin and moral evils; whose prevention, therefore, in one another, so far as we are able, is a duty of the law of nature, and the prime effect of that love which we owe unto the whole offspring of that "one blood" whereof God hath made all nations. And one of the most effectual means for that end are the reproofs whereof we treat; and the obligation is the same on those that give them and those to whom they are given, with respect unto their several interests in this duty. Wherefore, to neglect, to despise, not thankfully to receive, such reproofs as are justly and regularly given unto us at any time, is to contemn the law of our creation, and to trample on the prime effect of fraternal love. Yea, to despise reproofs, and to discountenance the discharge of that duty, is to open a door unto that mutual hatred and dislike which, in the sight of God, is murder. See Lev. xix. 17, with 1 John iii. 15. Let us, therefore, look to ourselves; for there is no greater sign of a degeneracy from the law and all the ends of our creation, than an unwillingness to receive reproofs, justly deserved and regularly administered, or not to esteem of them as a blessed effect of the wisdom and goodness of God towards us.

2. *Whereas the light of nature is variously obscured, and its directive power debilitated in us, God hath renewed on us an obligation unto this duty by particular institutions, both under the Old Testament and the New.* The truth is, the efficacy of the law of creation, as unto moral duties, being exceedingly impaired by the entrance of sin; and the exercise of original, native love towards mankind being impeded and obstructed by that confusion and disorder whereinto the whole state of mankind was cast by sin,—every one thereby being made the enemy of another, as the apostle declares, Tit. iii. 3,—[and that disorder] not being cured by that coalescency into civil societies, which respects only *political* and temporal ends; the discharge of this duty was utterly lost, at least beyond that which was merely *parental.* Wherefore God, in the institution of his church, both under the Old Testament and the New, did mould men into such peculiar societies and relations, as wherein they might be made meet again for the exercise thereof. He hath so disposed of us, that every one may know every one whom he is obliged to reprove, and every one may know every one whom he is obliged to hear. And as he hath hereby cured that confusion we were cast into, which was obstructive of the exercise of this duty; so, by the renovation of positive commands, attended with instructions, directions, promises, and threatenings, enforcing the giving and receiving of reproofs with respect unto moral and spiritual ends, he hath relieved us against

that obscurity of natural light which we before laboured under. Should I go to express the commands, directions, exhortations, promises, and threatenings, which are given in the Scripture to this purpose, it would be a work as endless as I suppose it needless, to all that are conversant in the holy writings. It may suffice unto our present purpose that,—there being an express institution of God for the giving and taking of reproofs, and that an effect of infinite goodness, benignity, and love towards us,—not thankfully to receive reproofs, when it is our lot to deserve them and to have them, is to despise the authority of God over us, and his gracious care for us. When, therefore, it befalleth any to be justly and orderly reproved, let him call to mind the authority and love of God therein; which will quickly give him that sense of their worth and excellency as will make him thankful for them: which is the first step unto their due improvement.

3. *A due consideration of the use, benefit, and advantage of them, will give them a ready admission into our minds and affections.* Who knows how many souls, that are now at rest with God, have been prevented by reproofs, as the outward means, from going down into the pit! Unto how many have they been an occasion of conversion, and sincere turning unto God! How many have been recovered by them from a state of backsliding, and awakened from a secure sleep in sin! How many great and bloody sins hath the perpetration of been obviated by them! How many snares of temptations have they been the means to break and cancel! What revivings have they been to grace, what disappointments unto the snares of Satan, who can declare! The advantage which the souls of men do or might receive every day by them, is more to be valued than all earthly treasures whatever; and shall any of us, when it comes to be our concern, through a predominancy of pride, passion, and prejudice, or through cursed sloth and security,—the usual means of the defeatment of these advantages,—manifest ourselves to have no interest in, or valuation of, these things, by an unreadiness or unwillingness to receive reproofs, when tendered unto us in the way and according to the mind of God?

III. But now, suppose we are willing to receive them, it will be inquired, in the last place, What considerations may further us in their due improvement, and what directions may be given thereunto?

An answer to this inquiry shall shut up this discourse: and I shall say hereunto,—

1. *If there be not open evidence unto the contrary, it is our duty to judge that every reproof is given us in a way of duty.* This will take off offence with respect unto the reprover, which unjustly taken, is an assured entrance into a way of losing all benefit and advantage

by the reproof. The reason why any man doth regularly reprove another, is because God requireth him so to do, and by his command hath made it his duty towards him that is reproved. And do we judge it reasonable, that one should neglect his duty towards God and us, and in some degree or other make himself guilty of our sins, for no other cause but lest we should be displeased that we are not suffered to sin securely, and, it may be, to perish eternally? And if we are convinced that it is the duty of another to reprove us, we cannot but be convinced that it is our duty to hearken and attend thereunto; and this will fix the mind unto a due consideration of the present duty that lies before us, and what is our just concernment in the reproof. Besides, if it be done in a way of duty, it is done in love; for all orderly rebukes are effects of love. And if we are convinced of any one, that he doth reprove in a way of duty, we must be satisfied that what he doth proceedeth from love, without by-ends or dissimulation. For what doth not so, be it what it will, belongs not to rebuking in a way of duty. And this will remove all obstructing prejudices, in all who have the least gracious ingenuity. Ahab despised the warning of Micaiah, because he thought they mutually hated one another; he knew how it was with himself, and falsely so judged of the prophet, by his necessary sharpness towards him. But where there are such surmises, all advantages of reproofs will be assuredly lost. Where, therefore, our minds are satisfied that any reproof is an effect of love, and given in a way of duty, "dimidium facti, [qui cœpit, habet,]"—we are half way in the discharge of the duty directed unto.

2. *Take heed of cherishing habitually such disorders, vices, and distempers of mind, as are contrary unto this duty and will frustrate the design of it.* Such are,—(1.) *Hastiness of spirit.* Some men's minds do with such fury apply themselves unto their first apprehension of things, that they cast the whole soul into disorder, and render it incapable of farther rational consideration. There may be, it is possible, some failures and mistakes in useful and necessary reproofs, in matter, manner, circumstance, some way or other. This immediately is seized on by men of hasty spirits (a vice and folly sufficiently condemned in Scripture), turned unto a provocation, made a matter of strife and dispute, until the whole advantage of the reproof is utterly lost and vanisheth. A quiet, gentle, considerative, sedate frame of spirit is required unto this duty. (2.) *Pride* and *haughtiness of mind*, self-conceit, elation of spirit,—which will be inseparably accompanied with the contempt of others, and a scorn, that any should think themselves either so much wiser or so much better than ourselves as to reprove us in any kind,—are a fenced wall against any benefit or advantage by reproofs; yea, things that will turn

judgment into hemlock, and the most sovereign antidote into poison. No wild beast in a toil doth more rave, and tear, and rend, than a proud man when he is reproved. And therefore, he who manifests himself so to be, hath secured himself from being any more troubled by serious reproofs from any wise man whatever. See Prov. ix. 7, 8. (3.) *Prejudices*, which are so variously occasioned, as it were endless to recount. If, now, we make it not our constant business to purge our minds from these depraved affections, they will never fail effectually to exert themselves on all occasions, to the utter defeatment of all use in, or benefit by, the most necessary and regular reproofs.

3. *Reckon assuredly, that a fault, a miscarriage, which any one is duly reproved for, if the reproof be not received and improved as it ought, is not only aggravated, but accumulated with a new crime, and marked with a dangerous token of an incurable evil.*—See Prov. xxix. 1. Let men do what they can, bear themselves high in their expressions, grow angry, passionate, excuse or palliate; unless they are seared and profligately obstinate, their own consciences will take part with a just and regular reproof. If hereupon they come not up to amendment, their guilt is increased by the occasional excitation of the light of conscience, to give it an especial charge. And there is an additional sin, in the contempt of the reproof itself. But that which principally should make men careful, and even tremble, in this case, is, that they are put on a trial, whether ever they will forsake the evil of their ways and doings, or no: for he who is orderly reproved for any fault, and neglects or despiseth the rebuke, can have no assurance that he shall ever be delivered from the evil rebuked; but hath just cause to fear that he is entering into a course of hardness and impenitency.

4. *It is useful unto the same end, immediately to compare the reproof with the word of truth.*—This is the measure, standard, and directory of all duties, whereunto, in all dubious cases, we should immediately retreat for advice and counsel. And whereas there are two things considerable in a reproof,—first, the matter of it, that it be true, and a just cause or reason of a rebuke; and, secondly, the right which the reprover hath unto this duty, with the rule which he walked by therein,—if both these, for the substance of them, prove to be justified by the Scripture, then have we, in such a case, no more to do with the reprover, nor any of his circumstances, but immediately and directly with God himself; for where he gives express warranty and direction for a duty in his word, his own authority is as directly exerted thereby as if he spoke unto us from heaven. Hereby will the mind be prevented from many wanderings and vain reliefs, which foolish imagination will suggest, and be bound up unto its present duty. Let our unwillingness to be reproved be what it will, as also our

prejudices against our reprover, if we are not, at least, free to bring the consideration and examination of the one and the other unto the word of truth, it is because our deeds are evil, and therefore we love darkness more than light. No milder nor more gentle censure can be passed on any, who is not free to bring any reproof that may be given him unto an impartial trial by the word, whether it be according to the mind of God or no. If this be done, and conviction of its truth and necessity do then appear; then let the soul know it hath to do with God himself, and wisely consider what answer he will return, what account he will give unto Him. Wherefore,—

5. *The best way to keep our souls in a readiness rightly to receive, and duly to improve, such reproofs as may regularly be given us by any, is to keep and preserve our souls and spirits, in a constant awe and reverence of the reproofs of God, which are recorded in his word.*—The neglect or contempt of these reproofs, is that which the generality of mankind do split themselves upon, and perish eternally. This is so fully and graphically expressed, Prov. i., that nothing can be added thereunto. And the great means whereby much hardness comes upon others, through the deceitfulness of sin, is want of keeping up a due sense or reverence of divine reproofs and threatenings on their souls. When this is done,—when our hearts are kept up unto an awful regard of them, exercised with a continual meditation on them, made tender, careful, watchful by them,—any just reproof from any, that falls in compliance with them, will be conscientiously observed, and carefully improved.

6. *We shall fail in this duty unless we are always accompanied with a deep sense of our frailty, weakness, readiness to halt or miscarry, and thereon a necessity of all the ordinances and visitations of God, which are designed to preserve our souls.*—Unless we have due apprehensions of our own state and condition here, we shall never kindly receive warnings beforehand to avoid approaching dangers, nor duly improve rebukes for being overtaken with them. It is the humble soul—that feareth always, and that from a sense of its own weakness, yea, the treacheries and deceitfulness of its heart, with the power of those temptations whereunto it is continually exposed—that is ever likely to make work of the duty here directed unto.

SERMON XIV.

THE TESTIMONY OF THE CHURCH IS NOT THE ONLY NOR THE CHIEF REASON OF OUR BELIEVING THE SCRIPTURE TO BE THE WORD OF GOD.

SERMON XIV.

THE TESTIMONY OF THE CHURCH IS NOT THE ONLY NOR THE CHIEF REASON OF OUR BELIEVING THE SCRIPTURE TO BE THE WORD OF GOD.

"They have Moses and the prophets; let them hear them."—LUKE xvi. 29.

As everlasting blessedness—men's greatest and most desirable good—is that which God only can bestow, and the way to it, that which he only can discover (who knows the Lord's mind like himself? who is so sure a guide in the way, as he who is himself the end?—nature can neither direct us to, nor fit us for, a supernatural happiness); so it is not only our interest to seek it, but likewise to see whether what pretends to be the rule of our walking, in order to our obtaining of it, be indeed the right one: which we can no otherwise be assured of, than by seeing that it be such an one as is given us by Him to whom alone it belongs to prescribe us the way, and who, being infinitely good, as well as infinitely wise, will no more deceive us than he can be himself deceived. Now, the holy scripture of the Old and New Testament, is that which we profess to own as the rule of our faith and life, in relation to our future glory. It is, then, the wisdom of every Christian to inquire upon what account he receives this rule;—why he believes it, and submits to it;—whether he be persuaded that it is of God by God himself, or only by men. For if he can find indeed that he receives it upon the authority of God, he may be secure of the truth and sufficiency of it; but if only on that of men, they, being liable to mistakes, may lead him into error; and so he can never be sure that what he owns as his rule is indeed the right one, and of God's own prescribing. Or admit [that] it really be so, yet if it be not received on right grounds, he will be exposed to innumerable fears and fluctuations, and never walk comfortably nor constantly in his way, when he doubts whether it be the right or a wrong one. The superstructure cannot be better than the foundation; and a well-ordered and comfortable conversation will never be the effect of an ill-grounded belief. It is good, therefore, in the beginning of our course, to be secure of our way,—to see both what we believe, and why; lest, otherwise, we be either forced to go back, or else upon as light grounds swerve from the way as we were at first persuaded to engage in it. Our great inquiry, then, in this discourse, will be,—

Upon what account we believe the Scripture to be the word of God; whether upon the authority of God, or the church? which I ground upon these words, "They have Moses and the prophets; let them hear them."

In this parable, whereof these words are a part, we have an account of the different estates of a wicked man, Dives, and a good man, Lazarus, both in this life and the other. In this life, Dives had his "good things," the whole of his happiness, all the portion he was ever to enjoy; and Lazarus had his "evil things," all the sorrow and misery he was ever to endure. And in the other life, we have Lazarus in Abraham's bosom, a place and state of rest, "entered into peace," Isa. lvii. 1, 2; and Dives in hell, a state of misery, and place of torments; where, finding so great a change, and being deeply affected with his now woful condition, he is (though in vain) desirous, if not of release, as despairing of that, yet at least of a little ease; and therefore, addressing himself to Abraham, he entreats him that Lazarus might be sent to "dip" but even "the tip of his finger in water, and cool his tongue," verse 24; but this is denied him as impossible, verse 26. Seeing that would not do, he desires, however, [that] his torments might not be increased by his brethren's coming to him; whom we may suppose to have been his fellow-sinners, and partakers with him in his riot and luxury. Or, if you will believe so much charity to be among the damned, his request is, that Lazarus might be sent to them, to admonish them for their good, that so they might be brought to a timely repentance, ere they came to an untimely end, and then to endless torments. But this is denied him too, as altogether needless and unprofitable, verse 31; and he is told, that God had made sufficient provision for them,—given them the most effectual means whereby they might be brought to repentance, in that he had given them his written word, "Moses and the prophets;" by whose writings if they were not persuaded to repent, a miracle would not persuade them. Lazarus rising from the dead would no more be believed than "Moses and the prophets," whose writings were among them; and therefore to them Abraham sends them, as a means sufficient for the end pretended, at least, by Dives to be aimed at: "They have Moses and the prophets; let them hear them." As if he had said, "The will of God concerning thy brethren's duty, and the truth of God concerning future rewards as the great motives to it, are clearly enough laid down in the Scripture; and if they believe not these things, and are not persuaded to repentance upon the authority of God in his word, much less will they be moved by the testimony of one coming from the dead." Hence I infer, *that the holy Scripture, or written word of God, is sufficient in itself, and most effectually able, to convince men of the truth of those things which are contained in it.* It was so then; why not now? "Moses and the prophets" were so; why are not the apostles and evangelists? Is all the whole Scripture grown *Old* Testament, and so old as to be decayed? When and by what means did it lose that life and power, that authority and efficacy, it sometimes had? It had formerly more virtue to convince men than a miracle itself; and now, belike, it hath less than a council! It could have done more than a man "from the dead;" and now it can do less than a dead man, a sinful pope! For his Holiness of Rome may be very wicked, the Papists themselves being judges.

From the former proposition it will undeniably follow, *that the Scripture is sufficient in itself to convince men of its own divineness, or its being itself the word of God, that being one truth it doth so often assert.* The general must comprehend the particular; and therefore, if the Scripture be sufficient to satisfy the minds of men as to all that it affirms to be truth, it must needs be able to satisfy them as to this too,—that the whole of it is the word of God.

But this our adversaries will not allow; and therefore, instead of taking it for granted, or resting on this single proof, we must here put it to the question, from whence the Scripture hath its authority, or upon what grounds we are to believe it to be the word of God. If you will give the Papists leave to answer, they will presently tell you, "Upon the sole authority of the church;" or, "Because the church declares it to be the word of God;" and that "without the determination of the church, it hath very little authority or weight in it," and you are "no more bound to believe the gospel of Matthew, than the history of Livy." Nay, one says plainly,[1] that "but for the church, you are no more bound to believe the Scripture than Æsop's Fables." And you may be sure the man was in earnest, when you do but consider how many incredible things another of them (alleged at large by our learned Whitaker) musters up out of the Scripture, which he would fain persuade the world would never be believed if the church did not interpose her testimony; and yet, as broad as the blasphemy mentioned is, another of the same party minceth the matter, and says [that] the words might be "piously spoken." And if a private doctor of the Church of Rome may thus transubstantiate blasphemy into piety, or make that pass for pious which is really blas-

[1] Surdis. *apud* Chamierum.

phemous, I see no reason why a pope might not add his authority, and make it canonical too. But, that we may give the best account of the controversy before us,—I. *Some things must be premised by way of explication, for the better understanding of terms.* II. *The state of the question must be laid down.* III. *The truth confirmed.* IV. *Popish objections answered.* V. *Some application made.*

I. For *explication of terms,* let us see,—

1. What we mean by the *Scripture.* By that, therefore, is understood "the word of God," declaring his mind concerning men's happiness and duty, or teaching us what we are to believe concerning God, and how we are to obey him; as it was at first revealed by himself to the apostles and prophets, and by them delivered by word of mouth; and afterward, for the perpetuity and usefulness of it, committed to writing, as we now have it, in the books of the Old and New Testament. So that "the word of God" and "the Scripture" are the same materially, and differ only in this, that "the word of God" doth not in itself imply its being written, nor exclude it, but may be considered indifferently as to either; whereas "the Scripture" signifies the same word, only with the addition of its being committed to writing.

2. What is meant by *authority,* when we inquire whence the Scripture hath its authority.[1] Authority in this business is a power of commanding or persuading, or, as some phrase it, "convincing," arising from some excellency in the thing or person vested with such authority. Whatever hath authority *de facto,* so far forth hath esteem and honour, or reverence, yielded to it; as whatever hath authority *de jure,* hath such esteem or honour of due belonging to it, and answering it as its correlate. And both the one and the other are founded on some excellency:—sometimes of nature, both in persons and things; sometimes of office and dignity; sometimes of knowledge; sometimes of virtue and manners; sometimes of prudence, as in persons: according to each of which, a suitable respect and honour is due to the authority therefrom arising. And as any man excels in any of these, so he hath authority in that, though he may not in other things. Thus, he that excels in the knowledge of the law may have authority in that, though he may have none in physic or divinity, in which he may not excel; and an honest man, that excels in morality, may on that account have the authority of a witness, though not of a judge. Now, when we speak of the authority of the Scripture, and ask from whence it hath it, we do but inquire whence it is that the Scripture persuades, convinces, or binds us to believe it, or commands us to assent to it, as the word of God; or whereon its power of so doing is founded,—whether it be

[1] Camero De Verbo Dei.

not some excellency inherent in itself, or whether it be only something foreign and extrinsical to it.

3. What we mean by *faith*, when it is demanded why we believe the Scripture to be the word of God. Faith, so far as it concerns the understanding (for in some acts of faith the will bears part), is an assent yielded to something proposed under the appearance, at least, of truth, built upon the testimony of another; and therefore, according as the testimony is, for the sake of which we believe any thing, accordingly will our faith be:—if it be the testimony of a man or men, our faith will be a human faith; but if the testimony be divine, or we believe a thing because God himself asserts it, we call it "a divine faith." Only we must remember, that a truly divine faith hath always God for its author; so that three things concur to the producing the act of such a faith:—(1.) The truth believed; which is *objectum materiale*, "the object of it." (2.) The testimony of God concerning that truth; which is *objectum formale*, "the formal reason and ground" of this faith. (3.) The efficiency of God producing it or working it in the mind. Now, when we speak of believing the Scripture to be the word of God, we speak of a divine faith. A man may, upon the credit of his parents, of his minister, of a particular church, or of the church catholic, if such a testimony can be had, believe the Scripture to be the word of God; but the question will be, what kind of faith that is, whether such an one as God requires him to receive the Scripture with.

4. What we understand by the *church* in the question. "The church" may be taken either for the universality of believers in all places of the world, so as to comprehend private saints as well as public officers, people as well as pastors, and those of former ages as well as the present,—prophets themselves, and apostles, and penmen of the Scripture. Or we may take it for that part of the catholic church which lives together in the same age, (call it, if you please, "the present catholic church,") comprehending in it all the believers, people as well as pastors, alive at the same time in the several parts of the whole world. Or else we may understand "the church" in the popish sense, only for the present church; and that, too, for the Church of Rome, which they call "Catholic;" and that, again, only for the pastors of it, excluding the people; and they, again, may be considered either separately or in conjunction, as meeting together in a general council; and that, either by themselves without the pope, or together with him; or, lastly, as represented by him, or virtually contained in him: for this great name, "The Church," dwindles at last into one only man. But, sure, he is no small one that contains so many in him; for, if we believe the Papists (not only, though especially, the Jesuits), the pope, in this controversy, is nothing else but

the church catholic compacted, and thrust into a single person, in whom all those several excellencies which are scattered among the members do, as in the head, collectively reside. And so the catholicness they vaunt so much of, is crowded into a narrow compass; for those, whether pastors or members of the church, that lived formerly, are first cut off, and the church is reduced to the present age; then the people, as excrescences, are pared away too, and the bulkiness of the church thereby lessened, the officers or pastors only remaining; and yet these, too, must be contracted into a council; and that at last epitomized into a pope, who is but the epitome of an epitome, and scarcely so much as a small synopsis of that voluminous thing "the church," they talk so largely of.

II. For *the state of the question*, these things being premised, take it thus:—1. *In some things we agree with them;* 2. *In some we differ from them.*

1. *In some we agree.*

(1.) That the scripture of the Old and New Testament, which we own (who yet exclude the apocryphal books of one sort or other) is the word of God, is acknowledged by them as well as by us.

(2.) Consequently, that it is in itself true and of divine authority, and that it doth not depend upon the church, as to that authority and truth which in itself it hath,—or that the testimony of the church doth not make it to be true, or to be the word of God,—the Papists themselves (at least the most wary among them) will (be sure, in words) grant. And therefore they have coined a distinction for the nonce: they tell us that the Scripture hath a twofold authority; one in itself, as it is true, and comes from God; the other in relation to us, as it binds us to receive and believe it. The former of these they own to be in the Scripture antecedently to the testimony of the church. The distinction is vain, when all authority is in relation to another, over whom either *de facto* it is, or *de jure* it ought to be, exercised. But let it pass.

(3.) That every Christian is bound, with a divine faith to receive the Scripture as the word of God, they grant as well as we do.

(4.) That the Holy Spirit hath a hand in men's believing the Scripture to be the word of God, allow the Papists their sense, and they will likewise yield no less than we. That the faith whereby men own the Scriptures (if it be a divine one, as they say it is) is wrought in the hearts of men by the Spirit of God, they do grant, and must, unless they will avow themselves to be Pelagians.

(5.) And, lastly, that the church (allow us our sense) may be a help to us, and furtherance to our faith, in receiving the Scripture as the word of God, we will grant as well as they. That the universal concurrence of all believers in receiving the Scripture, and [that] the testimony they do, and in all ages have, in their way and capacity, given to it, is a strong argument to persuade dissenters to submit to the divine authority of it, we easily yield; and that it is the duty of the present church, during its time, to labour to preserve the Scripture pure and entire, and to hold it forth to others, and endeavour to persuade them of its divineness, and so to perform the part of a teacher, we are willing likewise to yield. And so, in a word, we acknowledge the usefulness of the church's testimony, as an external help, and that by which some benefit may be reaped by men at the beginning of their faith. For it is the foundation of a human faith, and sufficient for the producing of that. And when a man hath so far yielded, as to receive the Scripture as God's word, though only on the credit of men, yet coming afterward to peruse and study it, and look more narrowly into it, he may then come to see better and more solid grounds for his belief; and, God working on his heart by the word, he may come to receive it with a divine faith, which at first he did only with a human; as, in John iv., the men of Samaria, who first believed Christ for the woman's words, did afterwards believe him because they heard himself. Thus far, therefore, there is some agreement between them and us. So that the question is not concerning the object of our faith, the thing to be believed; for both acknowledge it, in this business, to be the divineness of the Scripture: nor concerning the efficient cause of that faith; for both will own it to be the Spirit which works this faith in the heart: but concerning the medium or argument whereby the Spirit works it, and so the ground and foundation of our faith, that which is the formal reason why we believe the Scripture to be the word of God.

2. This, therefore, is *the thing wherein we and they differ:* something they affirm which we deny, and something we affirm which they deny.

(1.) They affirm *the testimony of the present church* (and that must be of Rome only now, for they count that only the catholic one)—that is, of the pastors of it convened in a general council, either with the pope, as some of them say, or without him, as others, or virtually in him, as others—to be *the only sufficient ground* of men's believing the Scripture to be the word of God; and so tell us that the Spirit bears witness to the divinity of the Scripture by the testimony of the church, and makes use of that as the medium or argument by which he persuades men to receive the Scripture as the word of God; and that without that testimony, or antecedently to it, men cannot know, nor are bound to believe, the Scripture so to be. This we deny.

(2.) We affirm, on the other side, that *the testimony of the Spirit of God in the word itself*—witnessing it to be of God, by that stamp and impress, or, which comes to the same, by those notes and marks of divinity which everywhere appear in it—is *the immediate and principal, and a sufficient, reason* of our believing it to be the word of God, and the medium the Spirit useth in working faith in us, or making us assent to the divinity of the Scripture. So that, as the Spirit, working inwardly in our hearts, moves as the efficient of our faith, so the Scripture itself, in its own intrinsical beauty, lustre, power, and excellency, is that which moves us, in the way of an object or medium, to yield our assent to its being of God. By this the Spirit of God, as the author of the Scripture, witnesseth it to be of God; and, by an internal application of this to our minds, induceth us to assent to its so being. The testimony of the Spirit in the word is open, public, general, to all, if they have but eyes to see it; whereas the inward application of it by the efficiency of the Spirit is only to believers.

This they deny; and this we shall first, though more briefly, prove; and then disprove—as well as we deny—what they assert.

Argument I. *The Holy Ghost, in Scripture, calls us to the Scripture itself, and God's authority only in it, and not to the church, for the settling of our belief of its divinity; and therefore in the Scripture itself we have a sufficient argument to move us to believe its coming from God.* In Isa. viii. 20, we are sent "to the law and to the testimony." The prophets generally propound what they deliver merely in the name and on the authority of God: their usual style is, "Thus saith the LORD," and, "The word of the LORD." They do nowhere send us to the church to know whether it be so or not; but leave it with us, as being of itself (that is, without the testimony of the church) sufficient to convince us; and if we will not believe it, at our own peril be it. So, in the text, Abraham (that is indeed Christ, whose mind Abraham in this parable is brought in speaking) sends Dives' brethren to "Moses and the prophets:" and our Saviour Christ sends the Jews to the Scriptures,—bids them "search" them, John v. 39; and so verses 46, 47. And Luke commends the Bereans, not that they sent up to Jerusalem to the church there, or waited for a general council, to assure them of the divineness of what was preached to them; but that "they daily searched the Scriptures, to see if those things were so," Acts xvii. 11. But all this would be in vain, our labour would be lost in searching the Scriptures, and looking into them for the confirmation of themselves, if there were not something in them sufficient to persuade us of their having God for their author, but at last we must have recourse to the church to assure us of it. Why are we sent thus far about, if a nearer way be at hand?

Arg. II. *Those properties which the Holy Ghost in the Scripture attributes to the Scripture will prove the same.* It is light: "The commandment is a lamp, and the law is light," Prov. vi. 23; "A lamp to my feet, and a light to my path," Ps. cxix. 105; "A light shining in a dark place," 2 Pet. i. 19. And, surely, that which is light may discover itself. He that needs another to tell him what is light, wants eyes. It "is quick, and powerful, and sharper than a two-edged sword," Heb. iv. 12; it enters into the soul: and therefore by its own power and efficacy discovers itself to us as well as us to ourselves. It is "like as a fire, and like a hammer that breaketh the rock in pieces," Jer. xxiii. 29. So likewise, 1 Cor. xiv. 24, 25; and Ps. xix. 7, 8: from both which we may argue, That word which convinceth men, judgeth them, makes manifest the secrets of their hearts; that, again, which converts the soul, makes wise the simple, rejoiceth the heart, enlightens the eyes; is sufficiently able to discover itself to be of God, though the church should not give in her testimony; but such a word is the Scripture: therefore, etc. And, farther, why may not God's word discover its author as well as his works do? If "the heavens declare the glory of God, and the firmament shows his handy-work," Ps. xix. 1; if "even the least creatures preach God to us,"[1] they that bear not his image on them, yet have some *vestigia*, some "footsteps" of him; and much more [if] his greater and more noble works, the glorious fabric of heaven and earth, and man, the most excellent of his creatures on earth, show forth that excellency in them which manifests itself to be from none but God; and [if] he hath, in a word, left such an impress of himself upon his works, as that they generally proclaim themselves to be his; why should it be thought incredible that God should leave the like notices of himself upon his word, and stamp that upon it which might plainly evidence it to be his? Nay, if men do commonly make themselves known by their works,—writers by their skill, artists by their curious pieces; if Apelles could have drawn such a picture, Phidias have cut such a statue, Cicero have penned such an oration, that any who had judgment in such things might have said [that] such a man, and no other, was the author of such a work; surely, then, much more may God in so lively a manner express himself in his word as clearly to notify to us that it is his. And if any should say, God could have done it, but would not, I desire to know a good reason why God, who hath left us so plain and conspicuous evidences of his wisdom, power, and goodness on his creatures, would not leave the print of himself in the like manner upon his word.

Arg. III. *God's revealing himself to us in the Scripture is the first and highest revelation upon which our faith is built; and therefore that revelation is sufficient to manifest itself to us, even without the church's testimony.*[2] The reason of the consequence is, because faith

[1] Præsentem clamat quælibet herba Deum.
[2] *Vide* Rob. Baron., Contra Turnebul.

(a divine one, such as we speak of) being always built upon revelation, whatever it be which is the first revelation, whereon our faith is built, must be sufficient to notify itself to us; otherwise, our faith is not founded upon any revelation at all, if that revelation needs something else, which is not revelation, to give credit to it, or if that which is the first revelation yet needs another to make it manifest to us it is not itself the first;—which is a palpable contradiction. And for the antecedent, I thus make it appear:—In the business of faith, either we must come to some first revelation, or we must go on from one to another without any end; for either the faith whereby I believe this revelation—that "the Scripture is the word of God"—to be divine, is founded upon this very revelation itself,—namely, the Scripture, which so many times tells me it is of God,—or upon some other revelation. If upon this itself, then I have what I would,—that this is the first revelation whereon my faith is built; but if on another, I ask again, Must I believe that for itself, or for some other? If for itself, then that must be the first; if for some other, I shall ask again, Am I to believe that for itself, or for another? And so there will be no end, no first revelation on which my faith is founded, but I must go higher, and higher, even *in infinitum.*

Other arguments might be produced to confirm what we assert, and are by our divines; but I intended brevity in these;—and the truth we maintain will be more confirmed by what I am in the next place to say against the Papists' assertion.

III. *That, therefore, the testimony of the church is not the only sufficient ground* (nor indeed a sufficient one at all) *of our believing the divinity of the Scripture,* I shall prove by several arguments.

Arg. I. I argue from Eph. ii. 20, And we "are built upon the foundation of the apostles and prophets." *The Scripture is the foundation of the church, and therefore hath not its authority,* even in respect of us, *from the church; but, on the contrary, the church hath its authority from the Scripture, upon which it depends in its very being, and without which it is not the church, nor if built upon any other foundation; it hath no authority but from the Scripture,—none in itself, but as thence it derives it, and we know none* [*that*] *it hath but as there we find it.* And this is spoken of the true church, and not merely the church in the popish sense. If ever we would find out the nature and definition of the church, we must seek it in the Scripture, where alone it is that we see it to be God's will to have a church upon earth, and by what means it is called, and of whom it is constituted, and with what power and privileges it is endowed. He that will question whether the Scripture be the word of God, will as easily question whether the church be the church of God, or whether God have any church or not. Now, if the church have all its authority from the Scripture, by which alone it is a church, and known to be so, how can it be with any reason said that the Scripture hath its authority, even as to us, from the church? For if the church have no authority but from the Scripture, then the authority of the church must suppose that of the Scripture, and the Scripture must be owned, or the church cannot be owned. For who knows what or which the church is, but as the Scripture describes it to us? And so the Scripture hath not its authority, as to us, from the church. For can the Scripture both give authority to the church, and yet receive its own authority from it? Can it authorize the church, before it be itself authorized by it? Can it give the church a power to communicate authority to it, and yet have no authority hitherto itself? Nay, can it be consistent with common sense, that the Scripture should give the church a power to bind men to the belief of it, and yet have no power in itself to bind the church to the belief of it?

Again: when they say the Scripture hath its authority from the church, I ask, How shall I know that there is a church? For if I be one that own no such thing as the Scripture (which the church is persuading me to believe), withal I own no such society as the church; and how will they prove there is such an one, but by the Scripture? For I, who am supposed to acknowledge no church, do acknowledge no authority it hath, and shall not take its own word. And yet if I grant there be a church, how shall I know that such a company of men as pretend to be the church are really so? I shall not take their own testimony; I am not satisfied in their being witnesses to themselves. And if they will prove themselves to be the church by the Scripture, then either the Scripture must have authority, as to me, before the church, or else they prove one obscure thing by another. If they say there be certain signs and marks of the church inherent in it, by which it may be known, —alas! I know not those marks but by the Scripture, which describes the church. If they say the Spirit witnesseth by those marks that this is the church, why may not I say the same of the Scripture; and so, that be known without the testimony of the church to be the word of God, as well as the church to be the church of God? And yet, after all this, granting this society of men to be the church, how shall I know that this church is infallible? And if I know it not to be so, I am not so mad as to build my faith upon its authority. If they say, "Because it is governed by the Holy Ghost," how shall I know that? for it is not obvious to me that it is. If they say, "Because Christ hath promised that it should," I ask, Where? where can it be but in the Scripture? Sure, then, the Scripture must be owned, and have its authority, as to me, or their proof is invalid, and they do but trifle instead of arguing.

Before I proceed to another argument, let us examine what is excepted against this. To this text, Eph. ii. 20, it is replied by some of the Papists,—

Exception I. That "by 'foundation' is not meant the *Scripture* written by the apostles and prophets, but their *preaching*."

Answer. But, 1. If that were granted, it would not prejudice our cause. What they wrote and preached is the same truth, and differs not essentially, but only in the way of delivery; one being delivered to their present hearers *viva voce*, and the other by writing, transmitted likewise to posterity: "Witnessing both to small and great, saying none other things than those which the prophets and Moses did say should come," Acts xxvi. 22. So Acts xvii.

2. The preaching of the apostles and prophets did last but a while; whereas Paul speaks of the lasting, perpetual foundation of the church.

3. If he speaks only of the preaching of the apostles and prophets, how comes he to join these two together? For the prophets were long since dead; and their preaching, if that only were the foundation of the church, could be the foundation of that church only which lived with them, and heard them.

Except. II. "He meant, therefore," say some of our adversaries, "the *New Testament* prophets, who preached at the same time with the apostles."

Answer. But that is not so easily proved as said: for though such prophets are mentioned in some places of the New Testament, it doth not follow that they must needs be understood here. For why doth the apostle mention them only, and not evangelists too, nay, pastors and teachers likewise, whom he joins all together in Eph. iv. 11, and who did at the same time preach the same truth which the apostles did? Beside that, we find, by the doctrine of "the prophets" mentioned in the New Testament, the truth preached and written by the prophets under the Old commonly understood. So, 2 Pet. i. 19, "A more sure word of prophecy." Heb. i. 1, "God spake to the fathers by the prophets." So also, Rom. i. 2, and Luke i. 70. The apostles under the New Testament were the chief that taught, though New Testament prophets, as likewise evangelists, pastors, and teachers, did preach the same doctrine; as formerly, under the Old Testament, the prophets that then lived were the chief, though others beside, as the Levites, did teach "the good knowledge of the Lord," 2 Chron. xxx. 22.

Except. III. "But," say they again, "the Ephesians were not built upon Paul's writings, which were not then extant, but on his preaching; and therefore these other kind of prophets must be understood, on whose preaching, together with the apostles', they were built.

Ans. The preaching [of] the truth, or writing it, makes no difference; but still it is the same truth, which is the foundation of the church, whether it be written or preached. And though the Ephesians were built on the word *as preached* by Paul, yet what hinders but they might likewise be built on the word *as written* by former prophets; whom, though they could not now hear, yet they might read? And Paul himself proves what he preached, by what the prophets had written; that so both the word preached and written might be propounded to the Ephesians as one and the same foundation of their faith.

Except. IV. They say that "by 'the church' in this place is understood, not the pastors, but the people; because the pastors were they that preached; and therefore, if they were meant, it would follow that they should be built upon themselves."

Ans. 1. It is most absurd to say, that the pastors and doctors of the church are not built upon the doctrine of the apostles and prophets. Who ever heard of one foundation for the faith of the teachers, and another for the faith of the people? It seems, then, by their own confession, [that] the pope and his clergy are not built upon the foundation of the apostles and prophets; and if they have not this foundation, I am sure they have no better. The faith of pastors and people is the same; and why is not the foundation the same too? Are *they* fit to build up others in the faith of the Scriptures, *who* are not themselves built upon the Scriptures? And it is idle to say, [that] they are built on the Holy Spirit: for will they separate the Spirit from the Scripture? What doth the Spirit teach, but out of, and according to, the Scripture? To be led by the Spirit, and yet built on the Scriptures, are very well consistent.

Ans. 2. It is not absurd to say, that the teachers of the church are built on the doctrine they teach; though *not as they teach it*, yet *as they have* BEFORE *received and believed it.* Indeed, they ought to offer nothing to others, as the foundation of their faith, but what is the foundation of their own; nor to hazard the souls of their hearers upon any worse bottom than they would venture their own souls. And it doth not follow from hence that they are taught by themselves, or are a foundation to themselves; but only, that the doctrine they have themselves believed and are built upon,—they deliver to others, that they too may believe it, and be built upon it.

Arg. II. *The doctrine delivered in the Scripture doth not, as to our receiving it, depend upon the church; and therefore neither doth the Scripture itself: the doctrine of the Scripture and the Scripture itself are really the same, and differ but in an accident of being written, or not written.* The same doctrines we have in the Scripture, were published and known before they were written; and they did not then depend upon the authority of the church; and why should they now? Doth the writing of them make them of less authority, or less credible, or less able to convince men's minds, than they formerly were? Upon the authority of what church did Adam, Seth, Enoch, Abraham, etc., receive the word of God, when it was yet unwritten? What council was there, what pope to persuade them of it? And how come the same truths to have less power and efficacy to persuade us than them? Will our adversaries say, the patriarchs received the word immediately from God himself? True, some of them did; but what is that to the church and her authority? Or will they say, those patriarchs from whom others received the word were infallible? They will hardly be able to prove it. How came Abraham to persuade his wife to tell a lie, and expose her chastity thereby, for the saving of his life, if he were infallible? And how came other patriarchs to allow polygamy, if they were infallible? And do not the Papists themselves tell us that the church of the Jews was not infallible; and that infallibility is the peculiar privilege of the gospel church, the promise of it being made only to that?[1]

And, to come down lower, Moses received many things of the Lord which were immediately received by the people,—as the law of the passover, Exod. xii.,—and where the people presently answer that all the words which the Lord had said, they would do, Exod. xxiv. 3. Did the people themselves ("the church in the wilderness," Acts vii. 38) give authority to these laws, or did the council of the elders do it? We find nothing of their being convened together upon any such account as to consider whether God's laws should be received or not. Or did they receive them on the authority of any other church? If so, which was it, where was it? Or, lastly, was Moses an Old Testament pope, and the virtual church of Israel? Then, belike, that church was infallible as well as the gospel, contrary to their own doctrine. That Moses was infallibly inspired in all that he commanded the people from God, is sure; but that ever he pressed them to receive the word of God on his own authority, or any but God's, can never be proved. If they say that the people received the word on the account of the miracles wrought by Moses, that is more to our purpose than theirs. And what shall we say of the law written in men's hearts? on whose authority is that received? It is the same for substance with the law written in the word; and must there be the testimony of the church to assure men that even this law too is of God? or, if it be acknowledged for its own light and power, whereby it manifests itself to be of God, why may not the law written in the word be so acknowledged too?

But come we farther down. On whose authority were the sermons

[1] Becani Man. Controv., lib. i. cap. 3.

of the prophets, after Moses' time, received? When they spoke to the people in the name of the Lord, did they ever cite the testimony of the church, to vouch what they said to be indeed from the Lord? or, did they ever seek the suffrages of the high priests and governors of the church, to establish their doctrine as divine? Their ordinary style is, "Thus saith the LORD;" not, "Thus saith the church," or, "The church says, that the LORD saith thus."

Lastly. If we descend to the times of the New Testament, we shall find the same there. When our Saviour Christ himself preached, what he spoke was as much the word of God when he spake it as now that it is written; but neither did he refer himself, as to the divinity of his doctrine, to the authority of the church, nor did any believe it on that account. He did not refer it to the church; for he did not receive testimony from men, John v. 34,—no, not from John Baptist himself, though of no small authority in the Jewish church, and generally taken to be a prophet. Though John, as his duty was, did bear witness to Christ, and point to him,—"Behold the Lamb of God, which taketh away the sin of the world," John i. 29, 36;—yet Christ had no need of this testimony to make himself be received as the Messiah, or what he preached as the word of God; as if the one or the other could not have been received without it. He therefore tells the Jews that he had "greater witness than that of John," John v. 36;—first his works; then his Father himself, verse 37; then the written word: "Search the Scriptures; for in them ye think ye have eternal life; and they are they which testify of me," verse 39. All this while, here is not one tittle of the church and its testimony; and if that be the only means whereby men can be assured of the divineness of the word, how comes Christ to overlook it? And that they who believed Christ's doctrine did not believe it on the authority of the church is clear; for the church of the Jews was generally corrupt, erred in many things, and therefore was unfit. And it was, especially as to its guides and officers, generally against Christ; and therefore unwilling to give testimony to him. It neither owned him nor his doctrine; so that they who received and believed Christ's preaching, did it on some other account than the testimony of the then present church. If the Papists shall say, they received his doctrine on the account of Christ's own divine authority, I would inquire, how they came to know he had any such authority; for that Christ was the Messiah, and, consequently, had this divine authority, were some of the truths he preached. If they say, that Christ's doctrine was received either upon the account of his miracles, or of its agreement with the scripture of the Old Testament, they say more for us than for themselves, and, either way, desert their cause.

And if we look to the apostles that followed Christ, and preached the same doctrine, we shall see that it was not received on the account of the church, no more than commanded to the hearers thereon. In Acts ii. 41, upon Peter's preaching, three thousand believed: "They gladly received the word;" they did not, it seems, expect the testimony of the church to tell them whether it were the word or not. In Acts iv. 4, we read of either five thousand more, or so many as made up the whole five thousand. And in Acts viii. the Samaritans receive the gospel on Philip's preaching; and afterward, the eunuch. And, to pass by others, the Bereans and Thessalonians receive the word, in Acts xvii. Of the former it is said, that "they received the word with all readiness of mind, and searched the Scriptures daily, whether those things were so," verse 11. Of the latter, Paul testifies that "they received the word, not as the word of man, but as it is in truth, the word of God," 1 Thess. ii. 13. All this while, here is no church interposing its authority, or asserting the divineness of what Peter, or Philip, or Paul preached. On what account, then, did these people believe the word preached by the apostles? "On the authority of the church," say the Papists. But what church? "Why," says a great one among them,[1] speaking of the Thessalonians, "the voice of Paul was the voice of the church, when he preached to the Thessalonians; and so they, in receiving the word on Paul's authority, received it on the authority of the church." Say the same of Peter and Philip.

Paul, it seems, then, was the church; or else how could Paul's preaching be the voice of the church? What kind of church, then, was Paul? Was he the church virtual? Was he a pope, and was Peter, and Philip, and the rest of the apostles and evangelists, so too? A blessed church, sure, that had so many popes! or rather, a miserable one, that either had no visible head or had so many! If they say, Paul's voice was the voice of the church, because he was an officer of it, by whom the church published the doctrine she believed and was to propagate;—Paul was indeed an officer of the church; but yet made so by Jesus Christ himself,—not an apostle of men, nor by man, Gal. i. 1. And the doctrine he preached was no otherwise the doctrine of the church, than as it was the same which the church believed, but never taught it him; for he "received it not of men, neither was taught it, but by the revelation of Jesus Christ," verse 12. And, therefore, they might more reasonably have said, that the voice of Paul was the voice of Christ; the word he preached being more properly the word of Christ, who was the author of it, than the word of the church, who only received it of Christ. But what will become of this fine invention of our Jesuit, if the Thessalonians did not receive the word on the authority of Paul himself, whether in his single or representative capacity, or call it as you please? And, surely, they

[1] Stapleton.

did not; for then his authority must be owned, ere, on the account of that, his preaching could be believed. But both Paul and his authority, whatever it were, were unknown to the Thessalonians when he first preached among them; and therefore could not induce them to believe what he taught. The same we may say of the other apostles, in their first planting the gospel when they came to the Gentiles; they were unknown till they made themselves and their authority known by their preaching. And when they came to the Jews, where they were known, yet they were not trusted, nor their apostolical authority acknowledged. And so it could prevail neither with the one nor with the other, till their doctrine was first believed.

Arg. III. *The Scripture hath its authority*, in relation to us, *before the church pass its judgment concerning it; and therefore it hath not that authority from the church.* This will appear,—

1. By the concession of the Papists themselves, who acknowledge that the church only declares the Scripture to be authentic, but doth not make it so. Surely, then, it was authentic in itself before that declaration of the church, which is only a pronouncing that to be which was before. And if it be in itself authentic, it is so to us too; that is, it hath in itself a power of binding us to the belief of it, so soon as we come to hear of it, whether the church hath declared its authenticness or not.

2. If the Scripture hath not its authority as to us, before the judgment of the church, then either it must be a private or public judgment of the church which gives it that authority. A private one it cannot be: for when we speak of the authority of the Scripture *as to us*, it is understood of all Christians everywhere; and it is not fit that a private judgment of the church, or, which is the same, the judgment of a private church, should give laws to all the rest. Nor can it be the public testimony, or that of the catholic church; for none such can be produced by the Papists from whence the Scripture hath its authority. Let them, if they can, show us the first general council that ever declared the Scripture to be the word of God. The council of Jerusalem, in Acts xv., if it were a general one, is the first we read of; and that toucheth not the point in hand,—doth not declare the Scripture to be authentic, but takes it for granted. They that were there met cite the scripture of the Old Testament, and thereby own its authority, but do not then first establish it. And Peter and the rest do the like in their preaching, Acts ii., iii. And dare the Papists say, then, that the Old Testament was not authentic before this council? Had the church hitherto no certain canon, nor authentic Scripture, to be the rule of its faith? After this council we find no general one till that of Nice. And was the church of God all this while too (for three hundred years) without the canon of the Scripture? to say

nothing that the Council of Nice itself did never define which it was; but acknowledged it as already received.

3. If a council meets to declare the divine authority of the Scripture, we would know by what authority it meets. If the several pastors of the church come together on the authority and by the command of the Scripture itself, then it hath its authority before they meet; else it could not make it their duty so to do. If by some revelation or impulse of the Spirit without the Scripture, what kind of spirit is that which acts in separation from the Scripture? And if the Papists will affirm this, let them no more call themselves good Catholics, but even the worst of fanatics.

Arg. IV. *The authority of the church is not more certain or clear,* as to us, *than that of the Scripture; and therefore the Scripture cannot have its authority from it.* That which proves another thing, must itself be more clear and better known. But that the authority of the church is not better known to us than that of the Scripture will soon appear; for whatever authority the church hath, she must prove it either from herself, or from something else.

If from any thing else, it must either be from the testimony of those that are out of the church; but they know not the church, nor any authority it hath: or from the Scripture; but then the authority of the Scripture must be more known than that of the church: or from the Spirit; but how will they make it out that they have the testimony of the Spirit for them, otherwise than by the Scripture, in and by which he is wont to bear witness? If they say the Spirit witnesseth to the authority of the church inwardly, so as to persuade the minds of dissenters that the church is the church of God; this is merely begged, and not proved, and yet will not satisfy neither. For we ask not, "What is the efficient cause of men's believing the authority of the church?" but, "What is the argument whereon that belief is grounded, and whereby the church persuades men of its own authority?"

Or else, on the other side, if the church prove its authority from itself, then the same thing shall be proved by itself. But yet, I ask, What judgment of the church is it whereby its authority is proved? They say, "Both the testimony of the ancient and of the present church." But how can the testimony of the ancient church be known but by the writings of those that formerly lived, the books of fathers, and decrees of councils? But we would know how we shall have greater assurance that those books were written by those fathers whose names they bear, and those decrees made by those councils to which they are ascribed, than that the Scripture is the word of God. How came we to be more certain that Cyprian's or Austin's works were written by them, than that the four Gospels were written by the four evangelists, or Paul's Epistles by him? And if the present church prove its authority by the ancient church, it must prove it but to very few; for they are but few that ever saw, and yet fewer that ever read, the writings of the ancients; and many, perhaps, have never heard of them. And besides, the ancient church was some time the present church; and when it was so, from whence might it prove its authority? From some more ancient, no doubt; according to our adversaries' discourse, it must be. But from whence did the first church prove its authority (for we must come to a first), when there was none before it to prove it by?

Lastly. The authority of the present church cannot be proved by the testimony of the present church. For then it must be either by a part of it; but that cannot be, for a part of the present church is inferior to the whole of it, and he that questions the authority of the whole will no less question that of a part: or else by the whole church; and then the authority of the whole church must be proved by the authority of the whole church,—we must believe she is the church, because she says she is the church.

Arg. V. *If we are to believe the divinity of the Scripture merely on the church's authority, then that faith can be but a human faith, because founded on no better than the authority of men.* Our faith can be no better than its foundation; a divine faith cannot be built upon human testimony. But the Papists themselves are ashamed to own a thing so grossly absurd, as that the faith whereby we believe one main article of religion—the divineness of the Scripture—should be but a human faith.

Except. To this, therefore, they say, that "the faith whereby we believe the Scripture to be the word of God is a divine faith, and built on the testimony of God; and that testimony is no other than the testimony of the church."[1] We easily reply,

Ans. 1. That the church's testimony is no otherwise the testimony of God than as it agrees with the word of God; and when it doth so, we are to believe what the church says, not merely because the church says it, but because God says it. And if the church holds forth to me any divine truth, and I yield my assent to it merely because the church declares it to me, though what I believe be a divine truth, yet the faith with which I receive it will be but a human faith; the truth is of God, but my faith is in man. Whereas, if I believe any truth because God speaks it, though not by the church, nor any officer of it, but some private person, yet my faith is a divine faith, and the testimony of a private person, speaking what the Scripture speaks, is as really the voice of God as the testimony of the church.

[1] "Deus per ecclesiam loquens non aliter loquitur, quàm si immediatè per visiones et somnia, aut quovis alio supernaturali modo revelandi, nobis loqueretur." —Stapletonus.

2. Some of the most learned of the Papists themselves[1] make a great difference between the testimony of God and of the church. The former they grant to be altogether divine; the latter, *modo quodam*, "after a sort" divine. The former they reckon to be the primary foundation of faith; the latter, but the secondary. Nay, some of them acknowledge that faith which rests only on the authority of the church not to be divine; and some, the church's testimony to be but the *conditio sine qua non*, "the condition without which we cannot" believe the divinity of the Scriptures;—which surely they would scarcely do, if they thought the testimony of the church to be the testimony of God. And if the testimony of the church be but "in some sort" a divine testimony, the faith which is built upon it can be but "in some sort" a divine faith. And if the testimony of the church be but the secondary foundation of faith, how comes it to be (according to Stapleton) the testimony of God himself, which surely they will allow to be the primary foundation of faith?

3. Before they can evince the testimony of the church to be the testimony of God, they must first prove the church to be absolutely infallible, and see they agree among themselves about it; lest we be still at a loss how to know what is that church whose testimony is the voice of God himself. And,—

4. If I do but deny the testimony of the church to be the testimony of God (as we do), how will they prove it? "By the testimony of the church." I shall not take its word. Or will they say it hath such notes of its being the voice of God in it, as thereby to manifest itself to be his voice? They will get nothing by that; for I am ready to say the same of the Scripture. Or, lastly, will they prove it by the Scripture? Then they plainly give away their cause, and own the authority of the Scripture to be before the testimony of the church.

Arg. VI. *If we must believe the Scripture to be the word of God only because the church determines it to be so, then we must believe all things in it to be of God for the same reason only.* That "Christ came into the world to save sinners," 1 Tim. i. 15; that "whosoever believeth in him shall have everlasting life," etc., John iii. 16; and all the promises of the gospel, must be believed to be made to us by God, only because the church tells us they were; and the truth of them, as to us, depends merely on the church's authority: and so all the comfort of our hearts, and the hopes we have of heaven, must be primarily derived from the authority of the church, and ultimately resolved into it. What a case had we been in, if it had not pleased the church to receive these promises into the canon! And if the Papists say true, she might not have received them: for, as we shall

[1] Bellarminus; Becanus apud Rob. Baron.; Melchior Canus, lib. ii. cap. 8.

see by-and-by,[1] it depends wholly upon the church what books shall be canonical, and what not; and, by the same reason, what parts of those books; and, consequently, whether all the promises of the gospel shall be canonical or not. And so we owe all our hope to the church's charity; and must count her a good-natured mother for not cutting off these "breasts of consolations," Isa. lxvi. 11; but leaving something for her poor children to hang upon, to keep them from perishing. Belike it is the church's favour that all the world is not damned. I am sure the best promises in the Scripture, if the popish doctrine take place, can afford but cold comfort. For if I be asked what ground I have for my hopes of salvation, I answer, The promises of God. If I be asked again, "Are these promises true?" I answer, Yes. "But how doth that appear?" Why, because God made them. "But how do I know God made them?" Well enough; for the church says he did. Here the authority of the church is the first foundation of all my hopes: and poor ones, God knows, they are, if no better grounded, and little comfort I am like to have in them. It is to little purpose to tell me the testimony of the church is not merely human; for is it merely divine? If it be not, it cannot found a faith which is merely divine. And when my soul and the everlasting salvation of it lie at stake, I think I am concerned to see that my faith and hopes have a sure foundation; and *that*, I am sure, none can be which is not merely divine.

Arg. VII. *If the testimony of the church is necessary, and the only sufficient reason of our believing the divineness of the Scripture, then it will certainly follow, that no man who is out of the church can be called into the church by the Scripture;*—which is pretty strange doctrine, and yet I see not how possibly the Papists can evade it. For they that are called into the church by the Scripture are persuaded by the Scripture, and convinced by it, that it is their duty to join themselves to the church; but this can never be if the Scripture be of no authority with them.[2] Whatever convinceth or persuades a man, must certainly have some authority with him; and if, therefore, the church persuades men by the Scripture, that Scripture must needs be received and owned ere they be joined to the church, the Scripture being the very reason and argument whereby they are persuaded. The conclusion will not be yielded to, if the medium from whence it is inferred be not first granted; and in this case the Scripture is the medium the church makes use of, in persuading men to embrace her society. Thus it was in the beginning of the gospel church; Peter disproves the conceit some of the Jews had of him and the rest of the apostles, that they were "full of new wine," Acts ii. 13, by the

[1] See the Papists' Objections, under head IV. of this discourse, pages 522–532. —Ed.
[2] *Vide* Chamieri Panstratia, de Can., lib. vi. c. 18.

testimony of Scripture, prophesying concerning the pouring out of the Holy Ghost in the latter days, Joel ii. 28–32. Then he proves the resurrection of Christ by Ps. xvi. 8, etc.; and his ascension into heaven by Ps. cx. 1; and his being the Christ promised to David to be of the fruit of his loins, by Ps. cxxxii. 11. And hereupon follows the bringing into the church three thousand of the hearers, who, "when they heard these things, were pricked in their hearts," Acts ii. 37. And so, in Acts iii., how often doth Peter cite the prophets, particularly Moses! verse 22. And Philip thus preacheth to the eunuch out of the prophet Isaiah, Acts viii. 27–39; and Peter again to Cornelius out of the prophets, Acts x. 43; and Paul, in Acts xiii., where we find some, both Jews and Gentiles, wrought on by his preaching, and brought into the church. And was it the authority of these apostles (that is, in the Papists' style, the church) that persuaded thus many? Alas! they that heard them did not once dream of their being the church; and therefore did not believe on that account.

Arg. VIII. *No law receives its authority of binding men to subjection to it from those that are merely subject to it, and did not make it; therefore the Scripture hath not its authority from the church, which is merely subject to it as a law, and is not the author of it.* The whole church is so, and not only pastors, but people; and if the pope himself be not under the Scripture, as the law by which he is to be ruled, well may he pass for ὁ ἄνομος, "that wicked or lawless one," spoken of in 2 Thess. ii. 8. True, indeed, a law may be made known by a herald that proclaims it; but who can say it receives its authority of binding the subjects from him, when he himself is one of them, and as much bound to it as any else? Allow the church to be the herald which proclaims and publisheth this law, must she therefore give authority to it? Put [a] case: a subject hears of a law, though not by a herald;—is he not bound to submit to it, because he did not hear it proclaimed? Suppose a man come to the knowledge of the Scripture some other way than by the ministry of the church, in the popish sense,—that is, the pastors of it (as it is storied the Indians and the Iberians did, by the help of private persons),—is he not bound to submit to it? Must he suspend his belief till he have the testimony of the church to assure him that the Scripture is of God?

If it be said, that "a law doth not bind till it be promulged, and the promulgation of it is the church's business;" I answer, God hath published his law sufficiently in the Scripture, and to it all must be subject to whom the Scripture comes, whether the church farther tells them that it is the word of God or not; as in the case mentioned, it was received and submitted to. I wonder how the church was the herald that proclaimed the law of God to the Iberians, when they received it from a poor captive woman. Stapleton (before) tells us, that when Paul preached to the Thessalonians, his voice was the voice of the church; and, I pray, was this poor woman's voice the voice of the church too? By my consent, let her even be the church itself, virtual, infallible,—a mere pope Joan I. But, farther: if the church publish this law we speak of, and it doth not bind till published by her, upon what account did she herself believe it when she first published it? (Let the question be concerning the herald himself, why he believes the law which himself proclaims.) Doth the church believe the Scripture to be the word of God at all, antecedently to her own publishing and propounding it to others, or not? Is her faith wrought in her by the testimony she herself gives to the Scripture, or by something before? I suppose the Papists will scarce be so mad as to say the former; for what kind of faith must that be, when a man believes merely upon his own testimony? And how can the church be the church before she believes? If they say the church's faith in the Scripture was wrought in her before her own testimony concerning its divineness, I would fain know what that is by which it is wrought. If it be any thing in the word itself, or be the testimony of the Spirit, why may not I, or any man else, believe the Scripture, before the church give in her testimony concerning it, upon the same account that she herself doth? But if she believe the divinity of the Scripture upon the testimony of the former church, I would know, again, what better assurance she hath of the testimony of the former church than of the Scripture itself, seeing she can know it only out of the writings of the ancients; and whoever questions the authority of the Scripture, may, upon much better grounds, question the writings of fathers, and decrees of councils, as was said before.

Arg. IX. *They that believe not the Scripture to be the word of God, when propounded to them as such, though they have not the testimony of the church to confirm them in it, yet sin in their not believing it; and are therefore bound to believe it antecedently to the church's testimony (for if they were not bound to believe it, they should not sin in disbelieving it): and consequently the Scripture hath its authority in itself, and before the testimony of the church, and therefore not from it.* That men sin in not believing the Scripture even without the church's testimony, is proved from Acts xiii. 46, 51, where Paul shakes off the dust of his feet against the unbelieving Jews, and tells them they "judge themselves unworthy of eternal life." See Acts xxviii. 24, etc., where he declares their actual unbelief to be the effect of their hard-heartedness; which, though it might be judicial, they being left of God to themselves and their own lusts, yet withal it was sinful too, and contracted by themselves. And will any man say that these Jews, in refusing the gospel, did not sin? I suppose the Papists themselves scarcely will. If they say, as formerly, that Paul's testimony was the testimony of the church; I answer, those Jews owned no such thing as a gospel church, nor any authority it had to bind them to the belief of the gospel; and consequently could not own Paul as an officer of that church, his apostleship being merely a gospel office; which a man could not submit to who did not first receive the gospel by which he was constituted an apostle. If they say, they might know him to be an apostle by the miracles he wrought; I answer again, that when he preached at Antioch in Pisidia, we have no mention of any miracle he there wrought; yet some, both Jews and Gentiles, believed, Acts xiii. 42, 43: and therefore they neither received himself nor his preaching upon the account of his miracles; nor could miracles make it the duty of the unbelieving Jews to submit to Paul as an officer of the gospel church, when no miracle was wrought by him. If it be said that he was known by the fame of his miracles elsewhere wrought, which gave credit to him; then it will follow that Paul was to be believed for his miracles' sake, as well as the gospel for his sake; and thence, again, that the gospel was not to be believed merely for Paul's own authority, but principally for his miracles, it being for their sake that he himself was owned as having any authority. And if so, either Paul's authority was not the authority of the church, or the authority of Paul as the church was not supreme; for that of his miracles was above it,—that which procured credit to him was of greater authority than himself. Upon the whole, it seems, by this reply of the Papists, that miracles were the great thing which procured credit to Paul's preaching; and if they did, the authority of the church did not,—unless, as before they made Paul and the church the same, so here they will make miracles and the church the same.

Arg. x. *It cannot be certainly known, by the testimony of the church, that the Scripture is the word of God; and therefore it hath not*, as to us, *its authority from the church.* If it may be certainly known that the Scripture is the word of God by the testimony of the church, then either it must be by the testimony of the universality of believers, or of the pastors. Not the former: for (beside that the Papists themselves exclude them, and say that the Scripture is to have authority *with* them, but not *from* them,[1]) either we speak of the multitude of believers separately and disjunctively; and so they cannot give credit to the Scripture, when they are all of them fallible and liable to error: or else all together and in conjunction; but so likewise they cannot certify us of the divineness of the Scripture, because they never did, never will, meet together to do it. And we may stay long enough ere we believe the divinity of the Scripture, if

[1] *Vide* Syntagma Thesium in Acad. Salmurien.

we tarry till all the believers in the world meet together to give in their verdict concerning it. If we speak of the church merely in the popish sense, for the pastors of it, there will be as much uncertainty as in the other; for either we must consider them separately too, or in conjunction. If separately, they are all liable to error; and, according to the Papists themselves, they do all believe the Scripture on the authority of the church; and therefore cannot give authority to it. If we consider them all together, when did, or when will, the pastors of all the churches in the world meet together, to give their joint testimony to the Scripture? And if they should, why are we bound to believe them? They were not infallible singly, nor can they be any more so conjunctly. If all the several parts of the integral—the church—be liable to error or corruption, why is not the whole? But suppose the pastors meet by their delegates in a general council, will that mend the matter? Not at all, that I see; for it is not yet determined by the Papists themselves, where the supreme authority, which should give testimony to the Scripture, doth reside,—whether in pope, council, or both. And so we are left at uncertainties, and know not to whom to go,—whose word to take; but must suspend our belief of the divineness of the Scripture, till it be agreed upon among our adversaries whose authority is indeed supreme, and to be relied upon.

Yet put [the] case, [that] a general council be the chief which gives testimony to the Scripture: how shall we know that this council hath not erred, in determining the Scripture to be the word of God? Shall we know it by the Scripture? It is supposed we doubt concerning that; and so its testimony is not valid. Or by the testimony of the church? Why, this council is the church itself, which determines in its own case; and so we must believe this council hath not erred, because it says it hath not erred. If the pope be the church virtual, and we must receive the Scripture on his credit, the same objection will be against him; for how shall we know he doth not err? By the Scripture? But it is yet in question. Or by the testimony of the church? The pope himself is this church; and then we must believe he hath not erred, only because he saith he hath not erred. Lastly, let pope and council both together be this church: how shall we know they both together do not err? Not by the Scripture, for that is not yet owned; nor by the testimony of the church, for pope and council together, are this church, and their testimony concerning themselves is not to be received. And, to conclude, how shall we know that pope and council are the church? Not because they themselves say so, nor because the Scripture doth; for that is not yet believed. Not by the testimony of the Spirit; for why shall that bear witness any more to the church, that it is the church, than to the Scripture, that it is the word of God? Nor yet by notes or marks inherent in the church; for why may not the same be allowed to the Scripture? And how shall we know these marks to be true, but by the Scripture; by which alone we can judge of the nature and properties of the church? And yet still it is supposed that the Scripture is not believed.

IV. This may suffice, to show the absurdity of the popish doctrine. Let us, in the next place, see *what grounds they have for it, and how they oppose the truth.* I shall only speak to the chief of their arguments, and reduce them to as few heads as I well can. Any that would see them more largely handled, may consult several of our protestant divines, who speak more fully to this point than the shortness of a sermon will permit.

Object. I. "Either," say they, "the authority of the Scripture must be known by the church, or by the Scripture itself, or by the testimony of the Spirit; but it cannot be known either of the two latter ways: and therefore can only [be known by] the first."

First. That it cannot be known *by the Scripture itself* they prove, because "neither the whole Scripture can be proved by the whole, nor one part of it by another. For if a man deny the whole Scripture, it will be in vain to attempt the proof of one part by another, when such an one doth no more receive the authority of one part than of another. And the whole cannot be proved by the whole; for then the same thing should be proved by itself: and whereas that which is brought to prove another thing should itself be more clear than that which it is to prove, in this case one obscure thing should prove another; or rather, an obscure thing be brought to prove itself, for the whole Scripture cannot be said to be more clear or better known than itself."

Before I propound the other part of their proof, I shall answer to this.

Ans. The divine authority of the Scripture may be known by the Scripture itself. For,—

1. *The authority of one part of it may be proved by another part, to those that do not deny the whole.* Some there have been, and still may be, who have received some part of the Scriptures, and not others; to such we may prove that part which they deny by that which they allow. The Sadducees acknowledged the Five Books of Moses, but not "the Prophets;" our Saviour Christ, therefore, when he had to do with them, did not cite the prophecy of Daniel to prove the resurrection of the dead, but Moses' writings, Matt. xxii. But when he dealt with others of the Jews who received the whole Old Testament, he proved what he spake out of other parts of it,—out of the prophets themselves; and so bids them, more generally, "search the Scriptures," John v. 39. Why may not we do likewise? We shall see how the Old and New Testament prove each other; so that

we may argue with men that acknowledge the one, so as, by that they allow, to prove that which they deny:—

(1.) *The Old Testament is proved by the New.* Christ divides the whole Old Testament into Moses, the Prophets, and the Psalms; and thereby declares them all to be canonical, Luke xxiv. 44. That was then the usual way by which the Jews did divide the Old Testament. And here in the text Abraham sends Dives' brethren to Moses and the Prophets. And Christ, mentioning a place out of the Psalms, bears witness to the whole Old Testament under the name of "The Scripture:" "The Scripture cannot be broken," John x. 34, 35. And we find particular parts of the Old Testament proved in the New. In Matt v., Christ confirms the Law of Moses, as to its divine authority, when he explains it; beside other places, in which he speaks of some particular laws. In Matt. xii. 38–42, and Luke iv. 25–27, and especially Heb. xi., the historical part of the Scripture is confirmed. And how many testimonies have we out of the Psalms and Prophets everywhere which do the same! The twelve lesser prophets are at once proved by Stephen's alleging them, in Acts vii. 42, where the testimony cited is out of Amos: but Stephen mentions the "book of the prophets;" that is, that volume of the smaller prophets which, among the Jews, was reckoned as one book.

(2.) *The New Testament is confirmed by the Old.* For how often do Christ and his apostles prove their doctrine out of the Old Testament! When they quote the Old Testament, it is a good proof of its authority to any that own the New; and when by those quotations they prove their own doctrine, it is a good argument for the proof of the New Testament to them that believe the Old, as the case was of the Jews at that time. And therefore our Saviour Christ refers them to the Old Testament, particularly Moses, John v. 45, 46, for the proof of the great doctrine he held forth to them,—that he was the Messiah that should come into the world. So Peter, in Acts iii. 22, 23, refers to Deut. xviii. 18, 19, to prove what he was preaching: "A prophet shall the Lord your God raise up to you," etc. The same we may say of the types of the Old Testament,—that they confirm the New, in which we find them fulfilled. If any say, "We find no particular confirmation of Ezra, Nehemiah, and Esther in the New Testament;" I answer, They are confirmed by our Saviour Christ in his general division of the Old Testament, according to the Jewish account, into the Law, the Prophets, and the Psalms, under which these books were contained, the whole volume of the Hagiographa going under the name of "The Psalms."

2. "But now, what if we have to do with *those that deny the whole Scripture,—admit no part of it?* how shall we convince them that it is the word of God?" I answer,—

(1.) Not by the church, be sure; for if they have no reverence for any part of the Scripture, they will have as little for the church, which hath no being, as a church, but from the Scripture. And therefore it will be a most vain thing to attempt a proof of the Scripture, either in part or in the whole, by the church, which is as unknown, in the nature of a church, to them that question the Scripture, as the Scripture itself is.

(2.) *We would prove the whole Scripture by the whole,* as well as one part of it by another. For as the whole system of God's works in the creation proves itself to be of God, and to have him for its author, Ps. xix. 1, etc., by all those eminent signs and effects of God's goodness, power, and wisdom, which are to be seen in the whole; so likewise doth the whole Scripture prove God to be the author of it, by all those signs and evidences of his wisdom, goodness, power, and holiness, which appear in the whole, and manifest it to be of God. Nor doth it follow from hence, that if the whole Scripture prove itself, it is, as the Papists say, more known than itself, simply and absolutely, though in some respects it certainly may be so; as a man in one respect, may be more known than himself in another. A man, when he hath given some eminent proofs of his learning, is thereby more known than without them he is; so the Scripture, too, considered with all those evidences of God's goodness, wisdom, holiness, etc., which appear in it, is more known than itself, when these are not considered. How do we prove the sun to be the sun, but by the glory of its light, which so far excels the light of other stars? And is not the sun, considered with its light, more known to us than considered in itself. How do we come to the knowledge of the nature of things in the world, but by considering their properties, qualities, effects, etc.; which plainly declare what their nature is, seeing such properties, etc., could not be but where such a nature is? So likewise here, there are those properties in the Scripture, those excellencies, which could be from none but God; and, therefore, make it appear that that writing, which hath those excellencies in it, is of God. To speak of these distinctly is not my present business, not having to do with them that deny the Scripture.

Secondly. "We cannot," say the Papists again, "know the Scripture to be the word of God *by the testimony of the Spirit.* For either it is by the public testimony, which is that of the church" (and if this be granted, they have enough); "or it is private testimony. But then," they say, "it will follow,—1. That our faith in the Scripture is enthusiasm. 2. That if the private testimony of the Spirit be questioned, it cannot be proved but by the Scripture; and so the Scripture being proved by the Spirit, and the Spirit again by the Scripture, we shall run in a round, which is no lawful way of arguing."

Ans. To this I answer, that we know the Scripture to be of God by the public testimony of the Spirit; but I deny his public testimony to be his witnessing by the church. It is indeed his witnessing by the Scripture itself, when he witnesseth it to be of God, by those excellencies of it which evidence it so to be; and this he witnesseth to all that have their eyes open to see it: and in that respect it may be called "public." And when he witnesseth the same thing, by the same means, in the hearts of particular believers, and so applies his public testimony to private consciences, enlightening and enabling men to believe upon his public testimony, you may, if you please, call that "his private testimony." This clearly cuts off all that the adversaries object; and no such things will follow, as they pretend, upon what we maintain. We know no other private testimony of the Spirit, but this particular application of his public one; and then, I am sure, there is no danger of enthusiasm. For that is properly enthusiasm, when God reveals any thing to men's minds immediately and in an extraordinary way, and without the intervention of the usual means whereby he is wont to make himself known to men; as in former times he did to the patriarchs, prophets, and apostles (and the enthusiasm both the Papists and we find fault with is, when men pretend to this, which yet they have not): but when God makes known his will in an ordinary way, by the use of instruments and means for the conveying of spiritual knowledge to them, this is not enthusiasm; as when "faith comes by hearing," Rom. x. 17. And so it is in the case before us: when the Spirit witnesseth to the hearts of private believers that the Scripture is the word of God, he doth it in an ordinary way,—working in them a faith of the Scripture by those arguments of divinity which are in the Scripture itself; and makes use of them as means to induce them to believe. As the light and brightness of the sun is the medium whereby it is known to be the sun; so that divine light and power which is in the word, is the very medium and argument whereby the Spirit, enabling us to perceive it, persuades us that that word is the word of God. And I would ask our adversaries, Can a private man believe the divinity of the Scripture merely on the authority of the church, without the Spirit's witnessing it to him by that authority? If they say, "Yes," then they must acknowledge that faith to be merely human, because not wrought by God. If they say, "No," (as they must if they be constant to themselves, in holding that the Spirit witnesseth by the church,) then, when the Spirit witnesseth to the conscience of a private believer by the church, why is not that enthusiasm too? For when he witnesseth to a private conscience by this application of his public testimony, here is as much a private spirit, and a private testimony, as any we speak of. The only difference is in the medium the Spirit useth in this private work; which they say is the testimony of the church, and we say is the Scripture itself. Both of us agree that it is the Spirit's public testimony; but they call one thing so, and we another. If they say that yet this is not enthusiasm, because here is no immediate revelation, but means are made use of; I say the same of the Spirit's witnessing to the divinity of the Scripture in the heart of a private believer by the Scripture itself, or those notes of divinity which are apparent in the word. This is no more immediate than the other, nor any less [so], by the intervention of means.

And for the other consequent they would infer from the private testimony of the Spirit,—that then "we shall run in a round, and prove the Scripture to be the word of God by the testimony of the Spirit, and prove the Spirit again by the Scripture,"[1]—there is as little fear of this as of the other For we bring not the private testimony of the Spirit in our consciences (against which only this objection is made), or his applying his public testimony to us in a way of illumination and conviction of our minds, as the argument inducing us to believe; but that, we say, is his public testimony in the word, when he witnesseth its divinity to us by that excellency, light, and power which is in the word itself, and makes use of that to persuade us to believe. The Spirit, indeed, is the efficient of our faith, or the agent which causeth us to believe, enlightening our minds, and drawing our hearts to consent to the truth; but the evidences of divinity we see in the Scripture, through the Spirit's enlightening us, is the reason or motive of our believing: they move us to believe objectively, but the Spirit effectively. So that here is no danger of a circle in our discourse, or proving *idem per idem*. For if I be asked, how I know the Scripture to be the word of God; this question may have a double sense: for either it is meant of the power and virtue whereby I believe; and then I answer, By the power and efficiency of the Spirit of God, opening the eyes of my understanding, and enabling me to believe;—or it is meant of the medium or argument made use of, and by which, as a motive, I am drawn to believe; and then I answer, Those impressions of divinity the Spirit hath left on the word, and by which he witnesseth it to be of God, are the argument or motive persuading me to believe. Now, when they ask how I know the Spirit, who witnesseth in my conscience to the divinity of the Scripture, to be the Spirit of God, the question is plainly, by what means or argument I am persuaded that it is the Spirit of God; and then I answer, By those properties of the Spirit which the Scripture mentions. And so the question, how I know the Scripture to be the word of God, either is concerning the *efficient* of my belief of the Scrip-

[1] *Vide* R. Baron., Contra Turneb.; Cameronem De Verbo Dei; et Turretinum De Cr. Pontif.

ture, or else it is not to the purpose (for I do not allege the efficiency or inward operating of the Spirit as the *motive* of my faith); and the latter is concerning the *objective cause* or *argument* inducing me to believe the Spirit to be the Spirit of God. The mistake is this,—they would fasten upon us, that we make the Spirit in his inward work upon our hearts to be the motive to our faith; whereas we only make it to be the efficient of our faith.

To conclude this answer to their first argument:—let us see if it may not be retorted upon themselves. If the church's testimony give authority to the Scripture, as Papists say, then if a man deny the authority of the church, how will they prove it? For neither one part of the church can give credit to the other, when the whole is questioned; nor can the whole church give credit to itself; for then the whole church will be more known than itself. Or if we ask, How comes the church to believe the Scripture? is it by its own testimony? But surely it must believe it ere it can give testimony to it. Or is it by the testimony of the Spirit? If so, is it by the public testimony of the Spirit? That cannot be; for, according to them, that is no other than the testimony of the church itself, the absurdity of which hath been already shown. Or if it be the private testimony of the Spirit; then they, by their own arguing, will run into enthusiasm, as well as we. And, indeed, they do plainly run into a circle, in their proving the Scripture by the authority of the church, and the authority of the church again by the Scripture; for with them the authority of the church is the motive or argument, whereby they prove the divine authority of the Scripture, and that again is the motive or argument, by which they prove the authority of the church. And so both the church and the Scripture are more known than each other, and yet less, too: more known, because they prove each other; and less known, because they are proved by each other. Here they are themselves in a noose. But it is no matter; the pope's omnipotency can easily break it, or the church's authority make her logic canonical, though all the Aristotles in the world should make it apocryphal!

Object. II. "It is necessary for us, in religion, to have the canon of Scripture certain: but this we cannot have, otherwise than by the church; because its authority is most certain, and the only one which is sufficient, to remove all doubts concerning the divineness of the Scripture out of our minds; both because God speaks by the church, and because the church best knows the Scripture. She is Christ's bride, and therefore best knows the voice of the Bridegroom; she hath the Spirit of Christ, and therefore can best judge of his word and the style of it."

Ans. We deny that the canon of the Scripture cannot be known but by the church, and the contrary hath been already proved: the

Scripture hath been owned and received where no such judgment of the church hath been. And it is as false, that the authority of the church is the greatest and most certain; for that of the Scripture, upon which the church and her authority depend, is above it. God speaks in the Scripture, and by it teacheth the church herself; and therefore his authority in the Scripture is greater,—the authority of him that teacheth, than of those by whom he teacheth: as the authority of a king in his laws, is greater than that of an officer that proclaims them. A king may, by his council or judges, acquaint his subjects with his laws; but will it therefore follow, because he speaks his mind, which is in those laws, by such officers, that their authority is greater than that of those laws themselves? God speaks by the church (the true church, we mean); but he speaks nothing by her but what he speaks in the Scripture, which she doth only ministerially declare to us: and therefore the authority of God and his law is above hers, who, though she publish, yet did not make it, but is herself subject to it, and by that law only stands obliged to publish it to others. And for what they say of the church's ability to judge of the Scripture, we answer, that she cannot judge of the style of the Scripture otherwise than by the help of the Spirit, and by the same private Christians may judge too; and there be no means whereby the church can know the Scripture to be the word of God, but particular believers may know it by the same. And if the church's authority be so great, in our adversaries' opinion, because she can so well judge of the style of the Scripture, how much greater is that of the Scripture, which is able, by its style, to manifest itself to the church!

Except. "But," say they, "we do not know the voice of Christ in the Scripture but by the church; therefore her authority is greater."

Ans. This is both false and inconsequent: *false*, for it hath been sufficiently evinced that the voice of Christ may be otherwise known, and hath been, too; *inconsequent*, in that it follows not that the authority of the church is therefore greater than that of the Scripture. John Baptist directed many to Christ: and suppose, without his direction of them and witnessing to Christ, they had never come to him, will it thence follow that John's authority was greater than Christ's? The church, we grant, may be a mean whereby many are brought to the belief of the Scripture, who yet, afterward, do believe upon better grounds, as being persuaded by the word itself.

Object. III. "We can no otherwise know the Scripture to be the word of God, than as we know what books are canonical, and what not—what were written by inspired men, and what were not; but this we can know only by the authority of the church. This is proved, because some books which at first were not received as canonical, the church did afterwards receive, as Ecclesiasticus, Tobit, Susanna, the books of Maccabees, etc.; the Epistle to the Hebrews, the second of Peter, second and third of John, and the Revelation. And books which are not canonical, are therefore not canonical because the church would not allow them as such; namely, the Revelation of Paul, the Gospel of Peter, Thomas, Matthias, etc. And, lastly, some books written by prophets and apostles are not canonical, because the church hath not determined that they are so."

Ans. To let pass what a learned Protestant[1] largely proves,—namely, that it is possible to know the Scripture to be the word of God, and yet not know which books are particularly canonical and written by inspired penmen,—that it may be known that the doctrine contained in those books is of God, though it be not known whether it were written by such as were immediately inspired themselves, or had it from those that were,—in the primitive times, some not only good men, but churches too, did deny some of those books to be canonical which we now generally receive; and yet they did receive the word of God, and the doctrine contained in those books, though they questioned whether those books themselves were written by such as were immediately inspired or not. And do not the Papists themselves tell us, that the canon of the Scripture was not established for a long time after the apostles' days, till it might be done by general councils? And yet, surely the church did in the meantime own the word of God, and know the voice of Christ.

We say, then, that it may be known which books are canonical, and which are not, otherwise than by the church; for the church herself knows them otherwise than by herself, or her own authority. When she declares them to be canonical, she believes them to be canonical; and her believing them to be canonical is antecedent to her declaring them to be so. She must learn herself, before she can teach others: she believes them, therefore, to be canonical, because she sees the stamp of God upon them, and that they are such as can be of none but God. The same way, likewise, private believers may know them. And when the church sees this stamp of God upon a book, she thence concludes it to be divine, and then declares it to be so.

Except. "But how, then, comes it to pass, that some books of canonical Scripture were not so soon received as others, if all have such an impress of divinity upon them?"

Ans. I answer, that these notes of divinity, which are sufficient in all the several books of Scripture to demonstrate them to be of God, yet may be more clear and illustrious in some than in others; as God's power and wisdom may be more apparent and conspicuous in

[1] Camero.

some of his works than in others of them. Or else it may be from the different degrees of illumination afforded to different persons, and in different ages. When some doubted of some books of Scripture, all did not; and they that did not, had a greater measure of the Spirit, as to that at least, than others had.

Now, to their particular proofs of the minor proposition in their arguments, we answer particularly,—

1. That those books annexed by the Papists to the Old Testament, and called by them "deutero-canonical," and by us no better still than "apocryphal," such as the books of Maccabees, Esdras, Tobit, etc., never were received into the canon by the ancient church, nor can they produce the decree of any one ancient council wherein they were owned; as for modern councils, we matter them not. They say that these books were doubted of at first, and afterward received. Belike, then, the church at first did not know them to be the word of God; and if she be the bride of Christ, who best of all knows the Bridegroom's voice, how came she for so long time not to know it? Here, certainly, in spite of infallibility, the church must be in an error; for if she doubted of the divinity of these books, when yet they were really divine, she erred in so doubting; and if she did know them to be of God, and yet did not receive them, she was more than erroneous; that is, she was plainly rebellious. As for the Epistle to the Hebrews, the second of Peter, and those others which we all own as canonical, though some particular persons or churches might doubt of their authenticness, yet it doth not appear that all ever did. Some of the Papists themselves confess that the Epistle to the Hebrews was generally acknowledged, unless by two or three of the Latin fathers; and Jerome reckons both that and the Revelation as generally acknowledged for canonical.[1] However, when these books were owned as canonical, it was not on the bare authority of the church. For how came the church herself to acknowledge them? How came she to know that they were written by inspiration? Did she believe it on her own credit? or did she not rather receive them as canonical because she found them canonical, perceiving the stamp of God upon them? And surely the same reason might make us receive them, though the church had not testified concerning them.

2. To the second thing they allege concerning the Revelation of Paul, the Gospel of Peter, etc., or any book written by philosophers or by heretics, I answer, that if the church did reject them, she did do but her duty; and it will not follow from her rejecting them, that

[1] Speaking of both: "Et tamen nos utramque suscipimus, nequaquam hujus temporis consuetudinem, sed veterum Scriptorum authoritatem sequentes, qui plerumque utriusque utuntur testimoniis, non ut interdum de apocryphis facere solent," etc.—Epist. ad. Dardan.

there was no other way of knowing them not to be canonical, beside the church's disowning them. For upon what grounds did the church disown them? upon her own authority? Then she rejected them, because she rejected them!—judged them not to be canonical, because she judged them not to be canonical! If she did disown them, because she saw not that dignity and excellency in them which she saw in the books of the Old and New Testament, and which might persuade that they were of God; surely, then, it was not merely the church's authority which made them not to be canonical;—and on the same grounds that the church rejected those books we likewise may do it. Sure I am, Eusebius reckons those books not only "as forged," but as something worse,—that is, "absurd and impious."[1]

3. When they say that "some writings of the prophets and apostles themselves are not canonical,—and *therefore* not so, because not acknowledged by the church to be so,—I answer, that some things the prophets and apostles might write as private men, and not by the inspiration and special direction of the Holy Ghost; and such never were to be received into the canon of the Scripture, nor were written with any intent that they should. But those things which they wrote as prophets and as apostles, by the immediate inspiration and special direction of the Spirit, and for this end, that they might be the rule of the saints' faith, were all received into the canon. If they deny this, let them produce any such writing of prophets or apostles not yet received as canonical. For what they say, out of 1 Chron. xxix. 29, of the writings of Samuel, Nathan, and Gad, how will they ever make it evident that they were other than the books of Samuel, written partly by himself while he lived, and partly by Gad and Nathan after his death? And so, likewise, 2 Chron. ix. 29, the writing of Nathan, Ahijah, and Iddo; and 2 Chron. xiii. 22, Iddo again; 2 Chron. xx. 34, Jehu: how will they ever prove them to be other than what we have in the books of Kings? It is true, too, that mention is made of some writings of Solomon which are not in the canon; but how will it appear that they ever ought to be there, or were ever written for that purpose? As for any writings of the apostles which are not in the Scripture, the chief insisted on is the Epistle (as they would have it) of Paul to the Laodiceans, mentioned Col. iv. 16; which we deny to have been written by Paul, nor will the words enforce any such thing: "the epistle *from* Laodicea" is one thing, and "*to* Laodicea" another.[2] It is most likely to have been some letter written by the Laodiceans to Paul, in which there being some things that concerned the Colossians, the apostle adviseth them to read that epistle. Jerome saith

[1] Ὅθεν οὐδ᾽ ἐν νόθοις αὐτὰ κατακτέον, ἀλλ᾽ ὡς ἄτοπα πάντη καὶ δυσσεβῆ παραιτητέον.—Lib. iii. cap. 25.

[2] It is in the Greek, ἐκ Λαοδικείας, not πρὸς Λαοδικείαν.

of this epistle, that "some do read it as one of Paul's; but *it is generally rejected*.[1] And for other books which they mention, they have been, as generally, disowned by the church as fictitious, and not written by the authors whose names they bear. The same father cashiers several of them together that went under the name of Peter, "as being all apocryphal."[2]

Object. IV. "We cannot confute heretics who deny the Scripture, or part of it, but by the authority of the Catholic Church, which receives it."

Ans. Those heretics that will acknowledge the church, may be confuted by its authority, but not have faith wrought in them: they may have their mouths stopped, but not their minds enlightened, by it. And though we may make use of the authority of the church with such, yet not as the chief, and much less only, argument to persuade them of the divinity of the Scripture. But even by the same way whereby believers are persuaded of it, may heretics be persuaded too. And if we meet with such heretics as pay no more reverence to the church than to the Scripture, we are in a fine case if we have no other way of dealing with them but by urging the authority of the church: surely they that deny the divinity of the one will not stick to deride the testimony of the other.

Object. V. To pass by other testimonies [which] they cite out of the ancients, one they mainly triumph in,—that saying of Austin, that he had not believed the gospel had not the authority of the church moved him to it.[3]

Ans. Austin speaks, when converted and orthodox, of himself as formerly a Manichee; and shows that he had *then* been moved by the authority of the church to receive the gospel. When he was a Manichee he was a heretic, not a heathen, and so might have some esteem for the church; or if he had no respect for the church as the church, yet he might—even by the confession of Papists themselves, so far as he saw the consent of so many nations, and the prescription of so long time, and other like arguments in the church, to induce him—reverence it.

V. *Application:*—

Use I. From what hath been spoken, we may conclude,—

1. *The mischief and danger of Popery as to this particular doctrine.* How dishonourable and injurious to God is this doctrine of the Papists, and how destructive to religion!

[1] Παρὰ πάντων ἐκβάλλεται.—De Script. Eccles.

[2] Ὡς ἀπόκρυφα ὄντα ἀποδοκιμάζεται.—Ibid.

[3] "Ego non crederem evangelio, nisi me ecclesiæ catholicæ commoveret authoritas." "Crederem et commoveret," for "credidissem, et commovisset," as is a frequent way of speaking with that father.—See Chamieri Panstr., lib. ii. cap. 11, at large.

(1.) *How dishonourable to God, for the credit of his word to depend upon the testimony of men, and not to be able of itself to discover its author!*

1*st. A dishonour it is to his wisdom,* if he could not otherwise assure men of the divine original of the Scripture, than by having men bear witness to it; if he knew no other way of certifying us of his will, and making known his laws to us, but by the help of our fellow-creatures, who, as well as we, are subject to those laws. Can God make "the heavens declare his glory," and cannot he make the Scripture do it? Ps. xix. 1. Can he make himself "known by the judgments which he executes," and not by the statutes he establisheth? Ps. ix. 16. Can he show forth his wisdom, power, and goodness by the things he doeth, and not by the things he speaks; and so make his works praise him, but not his word? Ps. cxlv. 10. Nay, can men so write, so speak, as thereby to discover themselves, and what wisdom, or knowledge, or skill they have; and cannot God do as much? Is God less wise and able than they are; or is he wise in some things, and not in others? How came "the Spirit of the Lord" to be thus "straitened," Mic. ii. 7, as to have but this one way of making known the word to us; and that such an one as he must be beholden to his creatures for it? It is certain that formerly he had other ways; and why hath he not now? How comes he to be less wise than he was? Surely, if there be "no variableness" in God, "nor shadow of turning," James i. 17, he must be as unchangeable in his wisdom as in any other attribute, and there can be no diminution of it.

2*d.* If God can otherwise make known the divineness of his word, than by the testimony of the church, and yet will not, *it looks* (to say no worse) *very like a reflection upon his goodness,* to leave men a more uncertain way of coming to the knowledge of his will and their duty, when he could give them a more sure one,—to leave his people no better helps against their weakness and doubtings, than the uncertain authority of a man, or a company of men, who may as easily be deceived in the testimony they give, as others may in the faith they yield to it. And if God did, formerly, give his people a better and more sure foundation for their faith than the authority of mere men, weak men, fallible men (as hath been proved), how comes his goodness to fail now, and to be less to saints under the gospel, than to those under the law, or the patriarchs before it?

3d. This doctrine of the Romanists greatly derogates from God's sovereignty. It degrades his authority, and lifts up the church into his place; it doth worse than make princes go on foot, and servants ride on horses, Eccles. x. 7. If what the Papists teach in this point be true, the Holy Ghost is in a worse condition than his apostle was, who needed not "letters of commendation" to or from the churches,

2 Cor. iii. 1; he must be fain to canvass for the votes of men, or seek their testimonials; God himself cannot establish his laws without the church's leave; Jesus Christ shall not be King of saints,—not sway his sceptre nor rule his house, without the good-liking of the pope and council. What is this but what was said of old?—"Nisi homini Deus placuerit, Deus non erit;"[1]—"God must be concerned to please men," at least the Papists: "for if he doth not, they know how to be quit with him; for then he shall not exercise his authority over them,"—not bind their consciences, not command their faith, not prescribe them their duty, not govern their lives: the church will not give their approbation to his laws, and so he shall not be their Sovereign, he shall not be their God. What can be more injurious to God's supremacy than this doctrine, which subjects the authority of God in his word to the pleasure of his creatures? What sovereign prince upon earth will endure to be so dealt with,—to have the authority of his laws suspended upon the testimony of those that publish them, of those that are themselves subject to them? I dare say, the pope scorns to have it said, that his decretals have their force from him that divulgeth them, or his bulls from him that posts them up. He would not endure, if he sent out his orders to a church or council, that they should sit upon them, and subject them to their judgment, and approve or disallow of them as they saw fit; he would expect, that they should be received and submitted to, upon the account of his stamp upon them, and seal annexed to them. Why may not the Scripture be allowed as much, which hath God's stamp so fairly impressed on it, and had the seal of so many miracles to confirm it?

(2.) *This doctrine of the Papists is prejudicial, indeed destructive, to Christian religion.* It leaves us only the name of Christianity, and no more. What is all religion, if God be not the author of it? and, if the Papists say true, we can never be sure, that God is the author of that which we call Christian. This one doctrine of the Romish synagogue puts us into a worse condition than the Jewish one is in; which hath some foundation for its faith and worship, whereas this leaves none at all for ours. It is, in a word, most perniciously contrary to, and destructive of, a Christian *faith*, and *comfort*, and *obedience*, all at once:—

1*st. It is destructive to our faith.* It leaves us no firm footing for it, when it must be first founded upon, and lastly resolved into, the authority of men; and we can never know the Scripture to be the word of God, without either the concurring votes of all the Christian world to assure us of it, or at least the definitive sentence of a pope or council, and have no better assurance of its being divine than their say-so. What can ruin our faith, if the undermining of it do not?

[1] Tertullianus.

and what is it to undermine it, if this be not? It takes away the very foundation of it; and, instead of the infallible veracity of the God of truth, puts us off with the uncertain testimony of, at least, a company of fallible men, who may every one of them be deceived; and therefore so may we too, for company, if we rely on their authority. Indeed, it leaves us little (if any at all) more certainty for our religion than the Turks have for theirs; for why may not they as well require us to believe, that God speaks to us in the Alkoran, because they say he doth, as the Papists require us to believe he speaks to us in the Scripture, merely because the pope or council says so? nay, how little difference doth this cursed doctrine make between the great mysteries of the gospel, the articles of our faith, and the ridiculous fables of the rabbins, or abominations of Mohammed! For if some writings are not canonical Scripture, merely because the church (that is, pope or council) hath not canonized them, and some are, because it hath,—the Acts of Peter and the Revelation of Paul are not the word of God, because the church would not so far dignify them; and the Epistles of Peter and Paul are therefore of divine authority, because it so seemed good to the church to determine,—why might not the same church, if she had been so pleased, have added the Talmud to the Scripture, ay, and the Alkoran too? And they cannot say, it is because these books contain not only innumerable fopperies, but notorious lies, unless they will eat their own words, and recede from one of their chiefest arguments; namely, that the apocryphal books they themselves do not receive are therefore only not canonical, because the church hath not received them, when the rest are, because she hath.

2*d*. *It is as destructive to our comfort.* When our great comfort proceeds from our faith, such as the one is, so will the other be too; an ill-grounded faith can never produce a well-grounded comfort: the foundation being shaken, the building must needs totter. What will become of that "comfort of the Scripture" the apostle speaks of, Rom. xv. 4,—that "joy and peace in believing," verse 13,—that hope in God's word David mentions, Ps. cxix. 81, cxxx. 5,—if we can no otherwise be sure that it is God's word, but only because men tell us it is so? How will our hope and comfort fail us, and our hearts fail us, when we come to consider, that that testimony of man, which is the ground of our faith, and therefore of our comfort, for aught we know, will (sure enough may) fail us! How should we stand, if our foundation sink under us? If the rain should descend, and the floods come, and the winds blow, and beat upon us, what shelter, what fence should we have? How great would our fall be! Matt. vii. 27. If temptations should arise, and assault and shake our faith, how should we maintain our comforts? Would it not be sad for us, or any of us, to say within ourselves, "I have ventured my soul and its eternal welfare upon the Scripture, and the promises I there find; but how do I know that this Scripture is the word of God? How do I know I am not mistaken? Am I as sure I am not deceived as I am certain of being miserable if I be? Here is, indeed, a company of men that call themselves "the church;" but that is a hard word; I never meet it anywhere but in their mouths, and in this book which they have put into my hands; and yet these are the only men that tell me it is the word of God. But what reason have I to believe them? They say, indeed, they are infallible, and cannot be deceived; but how shall I know that? They say the Scripture says so. Suppose it doth, what know I but they make it say so, and the Scripture and they are agreed together to gratify one another, and speak for one another? I see not that they are the church unless the Scripture makes them so; and yet they tell me, that the Scripture is not the word of God to me unless they make it so. I know no authority they have to bind me to believe them, but what this book gives them; and they know none it hath to bind me to believe it, but what they give it. And thus I am quite at a loss, if either this thing called "the church" be not honest, but will cheat me; or be not infallible, but may deceive me. How vain, then, and flattering have all my hopes been hitherto! how uncertain my faith, how deceitful my joys and comforts! Farewell "glory, and honour, and peace!" Farewell "life and immortality!" Farewell "the inheritance of the saints," and the "crown of righteousness!" Fine things, if I knew where to have them! Rom. ii. 10; 2 Tim. i. 10; Col. i. 12; 2 Tim. iv. 8. How would you like this, Christians? Do ye not even tremble at the thoughts of such dismal temptations? What think you, then, of the religion of the Papists, which exposeth all that embrace it to such uncertainties? It is no wonder they allow no certainty of salvation to believers, when they leave them at so great uncertainties for the very foundation of their faith.

3d. *It is as destructive to our obedience as to either of the other.* Gospel obedience is the fruit of faith; and therefore such as is the faith we have, such will be the obedience we yield. If our faith be not right, our obedience can be no better. A human faith is not sufficient to found our duty to God upon; and that obedience which proceeds only from such a faith, will neither be acceptable to God nor available to us. And yet such is the faith, and no higher, which causeth our obedience, if it be grounded only, or firstly, in the testimony of man, and resolved into it. "Without faith it is impossible to please God," Heb. xi. 6; and that faith, surely, is a divine faith, such as rests on God's own authority. But if we believe the Scripture to be of God only because men say it is, that faith cannot be divine; nor, therefore, the obedience which flows from it acceptable. In this case, the same testimony of the church, which would be the foundation of our faith, would likewise be the cause of our obedience. We should believe duty to be duty with the same kind of faith with which we believed the command of it to be of God, and that would be no other than men's telling us that it is; and so the result of all would be, that we must obey God, because they tell us he commands us to obey him; and so we first show a respect to men in believing, before we show any to God in obeying him. And then, not only we must be beholden to the church for the knowledge we have of our duty, but God must be beholden to her too for our performing of it.

2. *How much better a religion is ours than that of the Papists!* We are the veriest fools upon earth, if ever we change our own for theirs.

(1.) *We have more certainty in our way than they have, or ever can have, in their way.* Our faith is built upon no worse a bottom than the infinite veracity of Him who is the truth itself, revealing himself to us in the Scripture of truth, and not on the sandy foundation of any human testimony:—it leans upon God, not upon men; upon "Thus saith the LORD," not, "Thus saith the church." Though we despise not the true church, but pay reverence to all that authority wherewith God hath vested it, yet we dare not set it up in God's place. We are willing it should be a help to our faith, but not the foundation of it; and so should do its own office, but not invade God's seat, nor take his work out of his hands: that would neither be for his glory nor our own security. Our faith is a better than such an one would be: we receive it not from churches, from popes, from councils; but from God himself, that cannot lie to us, and will not deceive us. If we are beholden to men, parents, ministers, etc., for putting the Bible into our hands, and directing us to the Scripture; yet when we read it, hear it opened, and are enlightened by it, and see what a spirit there is in it; when the word enters into us, as the sunbeams into a dark room, and gives us light, Ps. cxix. 130; when we see its excellency, are ravished with its beauty, taste its sweetness, feel its power, admire its majesty; when we find it to be such a word as searcheth our hearts, judgeth our thoughts, tells us all that is within us, all that ever we did in our lives, John iv. 29, awakens our consciences, commands the most inward spiritual obedience, sets before us the noblest ends, and offers us the most glorious reward,—an unseen one,—an eternal one;—then we come to acknowledge that of a truth God is in it,—no mere creature could be the author of it. And so we believe it, not because men have ministerially led us to the knowledge of it, or have persuaded or commanded us to receive it, or told us it is of God; but because we ourselves have heard and felt him speaking in it. The Spirit shines into our minds by the light of this word, and speaks loudly to our hearts by the power of it, and plainly tells whose word it is; and so makes us yield to God's authority. Take a Christian whose faith is thus bottomed, and overturn it, if you can:—you must first beat him out of his senses,—persuade him he hath no eyes, no taste, no feeling, no understanding, no affections, no reflection upon himself, no knowledge of what is done in his own soul, and so, indeed, that he is not a man, but a brute or a stock,—ere ever you can persuade him that the Scripture is not the word of God. Whereas, on the other side, the Papists' religion is built merely on men, and their faith hath no more certainty than those men have infallibility. Ask them what is the great, nay, the only convincing reason why they believe the Scripture to be the word of God, and they will tell you, "The church's testimony concerning it." They believe it, because the church commands it; that is, the pope doth so, or a general council, or somebody,—they know not who.

And here they are at a loss already; for as much as they fill our ears with a great noise and din of "the church!" and can scarcely talk of any thing but "the church! the church!" yet they are not so much agreed among themselves what this very church is, upon whose authority they build their faith, and would have us build ours. In several countries they have several churches, several supremacies, several infallibleships: a council is the church, and supreme and infallible, in France; and the pope is the same in Italy. And so (amongst the Papists), if you do but change your climate, you must change your faith too;—if you but cross the Alps, you must translate your faith, and shift it from a council's shoulders to the pope's. A strange, variable thing you will find it, which must be calculated according to the meridian you are in, and will not serve indifferently for all places; so that you must be sure to fix your habitation, ere you can settle your belief. And yet, if this were agreed upon, you would still be at an uncertainty, as to the infallibility of whatsoever they call "the church:"—for you are likely to have nothing but their own word for it; and if you will take it so, you may; or if they prove it by the Scripture, they desert their cause, and own the Scripture as above them, and authentic without them; and so, while they would establish their infallibility, they lose their authority.

And so, to conclude, there is nothing certain, nothing solid, among them, nothing able to bear the weight of an immortal soul,—nothing upon which a man can venture his everlasting salvation. I see no such thing as a truly divine faith among them, unless it be therefore divine, because built upon the authority of their lord god, the pope. They call the pope *ecclesiæ catholicæ principem et sponsum.* In the mass at the election of him, they apply that to him which is said of the Holy Ghost: "I will pray the Father, and he will send you another Comforter," John xiv. 16. And in the time of Leo X. it was disputed in their schools, among other blasphemies, whether the pope were a mere man, or *quasi deus*, "as it were a god;" and whether he did not partake of both the natures of Christ, Mornæi Myster. Iniquit., p. 636.

(2.) *Our religion is more comfortable, as well as more certain.* Our faith being built upon the truth of God himself, and our comfort upon our faith, so long as our foundation remains immovable, we need not fear our superstructure. If our faith have good footing, our hopes and comforts will keep their standing. Faith in the promises is that from whence all the comfort of our hearts, and our "rejoicing in hope of the glory of God," doth proceed, Rom. v. 2. A Christian's joy, "is joy in believing;" and his peace, "the peace of God," Phil. iv. 7; and his comforts, the comforts of the Holy Ghost: but this can never be, if our faith be founded immediately on the testimony of men, and not of God; or if we believe the promises of the word to be made by God, because men tell us he made them. So long as we hold to the "sure word," 2 Pet. i. 19, we have sure hopes and sure comforts, and no longer; and therefore a Papist can never have any "strong consolation" by his faith, Heb. vi. 18, when his faith itself hath so weak a foundation. How can they ever rejoice in hopes of heaven, when they believe there is a heaven with no better a faith than they believe a pope or council to be infallible? It is to little purpose to say they believe there is a heaven (say the like of other articles), because God in the Scripture tells them so, when they would not have believed one tittle of that very Scripture, if a pope or a council had not bid them believe it: for then their hopes and comforts are all resolved into the authority of this church (whatever it be), as well as their faith is; and both the one and the other rest not on the real infallibility of the God of truth, but on the pretended infallibility of one single prelate at Rome, or a convention of them at Trent. From such a foundation for our faith, and such comforters of our consciences, the Lord deliver us!

By this you may gather what you must do, if you would be Papists. You must renounce your reason and faith too, if you would embrace their religion; you must enslave your consciences to the authority of men, and so put out your own eyes that you may see with other men's. You must not be "built upon the foundation of the apostles and prophets," Eph. ii. 20, but of popes and councils,—it may be, of a single pope; and so hazard your eternal peace and welfare on the credit of a man who may be himself a murderer, an adulterer, a sodomite, a necromancer, a blasphemer, a heretic; and may be so far from being saved himself, that he may, as some Papists acknowledge, carry whole cart-loads of souls to hell with him. Yet still he is infallible!—an infallible murderer, an infallible sodomite, an infallible sorcerer! etc. And you must believe him to be infallible all this while, by himself, or with a council, or you cannot be saved,—among them. The church, to be sure, you must believe and adore, whatever it be, either representative or virtual; you must not ask a reason for your faith neither, but tamely submit to its tyrannical dictates. And if it should ever come to this, would it not be as hard a chapter as the third of Daniel?—would not Smithfield be as hot a place as the plain of Dura, if every one that would not fall down and worship this great golden idol—Holy Church—should be cast into the burning fiery furnace?

Use II. And, therefore, to prevent this, and that your faith may be firm and immovable, as standing not in the authority or wisdom of men, but the power and truth of God; that your hearts may be full of comfort, your lives full of holiness, your deaths full of sweetness; and that you may be "more than conquerors" over all those temptations whereby the wicked one may at any time assault your faith,—*be sure to see that it have a good foundation,—see that you believe the Scripture upon solid and lasting grounds.* Trust the authority of no mere man, nor company of men, in the world, in a business on which the everlasting blessedness or misery of your soul doth depend. Hear Moses and the prophets; hear the apostles and evangelists. We are sure God spake by them; and they never err. As for popes and councils, we are sure they have erred, and so may do again. And so may your parents that first instructed you: masters, teachers, churches, all may err. And though, *de facto*, they do not err in this, when they tell you the Scripture is the word of God; yet, they being but men, and having no promise of absolute infallibility, and being liable to mistakes in other things,—when you find that, you may come to question whether they were not mistaken in this too; and so think you have been deluded all this while, and [have] taken that for the word of God and rule of your lives which is nothing less. And then you will either cast away your faith, or you must seek a new foundation for it. And if you come in a Papist's way, and hear talk of Peter's successors, Christ's vicars, catholic churches, general councils, infallibilities, long successions, apostolical traditions, you do not know what kind of spirit such conjuring words may raise up in you. You may be apt to think the major part (as you will be told, though falsely, it is) must carry it, and so determine your faith by the votes of men,—that is, not so much change the foundation of it, as enlarge it; and whereas, before, it was built upon the credit of a parent or a pastor, now build it upon the credit of a great many, or a great one in the name of all the rest; or if it rested before on a particular church, now it shall rely on that which you are told is the catholic one. For my part, I shall never wonder to see ill-grounded Protestants easily turn Papists: they are semi-Papists already, and they may soon be wholly such. They have a pope at home; and if they do not like him, they may easily exchange him for another abroad. He that pins his faith upon one man's sleeve may soon do it upon another's: he is already a church-Papist, and may soon be a Mass one.

And therefore, to conclude, whoever thou art, if thou have not formerly done it, search thyself now, ere Satan sift thee; try thy faith in the Scripture, that it may be approved; see whose image and superscription it bears, what foundation it hath, what answer thou canst give to any one that asks thee a reason of it; nay, what answer thou canst give thyself. Ask thyself, "Why do I believe the Bible to be the word of God? How do I know it was not the invention of man? By what arguments, by what authority, was I induced to give my assent to it? Do I take it merely on the credit of those of whom I was born, among whom I was bred,—with whom I have conversed? Is this a sufficient foundation for my faith? Dare I venture my soul upon such a bottom? Is this to build my house upon a rock? How near the Papists am I come, ere I was aware of it! I spit at them, and defy them, and yet act like them, if not below them, and can scarcely say so much for my faith as they can for theirs." If this be thy condition,—to work anew, for shame! and begin quickly too, and get thy faith well settled, and upon its right basis; or, I dare say, thou wilt never keep thy faith at the expense of thy life, but rather turn ten times than burn once. If thou hast, therefore, any regard to the constancy of thy faith, to the comfort of thy life, the honour of God, or the salvation of thy own soul, labour immediately to get thy belief of the word better founded: read the Scripture constantly, study it seriously, search it diligently, hear it explained and applied by others, meditate on it thyself, and beg of God an understanding of it, and a right faith in it; that he would give thee "an heart to perceive, and eyes to see, and ears to hear," Deut. xxix. 4; that he would "open thine eyes to behold wondrous things out of his law," Ps. cxix. 18; that he would give thee his Spirit, that thou mayest "search the deep things of God," 1 Cor. ii. 10;—that he would cause thee to hear his voice in that word which thou hast hitherto taken to be his, and direct thy heart into the surest grounds of believing it.

And, be sure hold on in such a way of painful endeavours for the getting thy faith settled till it be done, and what thou hast hitherto received on the account of man thou now believest for the sake of God himself. I deny thee not the testimony of the universal church of Christ in all ages, so far as thou art capable of knowing it, as well as of the present church, or any particular one to which thou art any way related, as a help to thee: make the best thou canst of it, only rest not on it. But especially take notice, if thou see not the stamp of God upon the word, characters of divinity imprinted on it, as well as external notes accompanying it, consider the antiquity of it, the continuance of it, the miracles that confirmed it, the condition of the men that penned it,—their aims, their carriage and conversation,—God's providence in keeping it and handing it down to thee through so many successive generations, when so many in all ages would have bereaved the world of it. And, farther, consider the majesty and gravity, and yet plainness and simplicity, of its style; the depth of the mysteries it discovers, the truth and divineness of the doctrine it teacheth, the spirituality of the duties its enjoins, the power and force of the arguments with which it persuades, the eternity of the rewards it promises and the punishments it threatens; the end and scope of the whole,—to reform the world, to discountenance and extirpate wickedness, and promote holiness and righteousness, and thereby advance God's glory, and lead man on to everlasting blessedness, etc.

And, be sure, leave not off till thou find thy faith raised from so low a bottom as the authority of men, and fixed on God's own testimony; till thou canst safely and boldly say, "I believe the Scripture now to be the word of God, not because I have heard men say so, but because I hear God himself in this very Scripture bearing witness to it: his Spirit hath given me new eyes, and enabled me to see the divineness of it. I know, and am sure, that this is the word of God: never mere man spake at such a rate; never did the word of man work such effects. The entrance of it hath given light to my soul, which was before in darkness, not knowing whither it went. How many glorious mysteries do I see in it! what purity, what spirituality, what holiness! etc.—all which speak the wisdom, and power, and goodness, and holiness, and truth of the Author of it. What sweetness have I tasted in it! It hath been as the 'honey and honeycomb" to me, Ps. xix. 10. What power, what life, what strange energy have I experienced in it! What a change hath it wrought in me! What lusts hath it discovered and mortified! What duties hath it convinced me of, and engaged me in! What strength hath it furnished me with! How hath it quickened me when I was dead in sin, revived my comforts when they were dying, actuated my graces when they were languishing, roused me up when I was sluggish, awaked me when I was dreaming, refreshed me when I was sorrowful, supported me when I was sinking, answered my doubts, conquered my temptations, scattered my fears, enlarged me with desires, and filled me "with joy unspeakable and full of glory!" 1 Pet. i. 8. And what word could ever have wrought such effects, but that of the eternal, all-wise, all-powerful God? And therefore upon his alone authority I receive it; him alone I adore in it, whose power I have so often found working by it. I durst venture a hundred souls, if I had them, and a hundred heavens, if there were so many, upon the truth and divine authority of this word; and should not stick, not only to give the lie to the 'most profound,' and 'most resolute,' and 'invincible,' and 'irrefragable,' and 'angelical,' and 'seraphical' doctors,[1] nay, and 'infallible' popes and councils too, but even to say 'Anathema' to angels themselves, and seraphims, if they should tell me the Scripture were not the word of God."

Christian! get but such a faith of the word as this into thy heart, and then thou mayest defy scoffers, atheists, Papists, and all their works. If they deride thee, let them mock on; thou wilt not easily be laughed out of thy senses, nor overcome by men's jeers to disbelieve what thou hast seen and felt. If they will not believe as thou dost, yet thou shalt never be brought to play the infidel as they do; no more than cease to behold and admire the glory of the sun, because birds of the night, owls and bats, care not for looking on it: thou wilt never deny what thou plainly seest, because others do not who have no eyes. Sure I am, if they see not what thou dost, it is either because they wink against the light, or look off from it; or God hath not yet in mercy opened their eyes, or hath in judgment closed them up: "If our gospel be hid, it is hid to them that are lost," 2 Cor. iv. 3.

[1] Such titles the Papists give their schoolmen.

SERMON XV.

THE CHAMBER OF IMAGERY IN THE CHURCH OF ROME LAID OPEN;

OR,

AN ANTIDOTE AGAINST POPERY.

SERMON XV.

THE CHAMBER OF IMAGERY IN THE CHURCH OF ROME LAID OPEN.

QUESTION: *How is the practical love of truth the best preservative against Popery?*

"If so be ye have tasted that the Lord is gracious."—1 PET. ii. 3.

WHEN false worship had prevailed in the church of old unto its ruin, God showed and represented it unto his prophet under the name and appearance of "a chamber of imagery," Ezek. viii. 11, 12. For therein were portrayed all the abominations wherewith the worship of God was defiled, and religion corrupted. Things relating unto divine truth and worship have had again the same event in the world, especially in the Church of Rome; and my present design is to take a view of the chambers of their imagery, and to show what was the occasion and what were the means of their erection: and in them we shall see all the abomination wherewith the divine worship of the gospel hath been corrupted, and Christian religion ruined. Unto this end it will be necessary to lay down some such principles of sacred truth as will demonstrate and evince the grounds and causes of that transformation of the substance and power of religion into a lifeless image, which shall be proved to have fallen out amongst them. And because I intend their benefit principally who resolve all their persuasion in religion into the word of God, I shall deduce these principles from that passage of it in 1 Pet. ii. 1–3.

The *first verse* contains an exhortation unto, or an injunction of, universal holiness, by the laying aside or casting out whatever is contrary thereunto: "Wherefore laying aside all malice, and all guile, and hypocrisies, and envies, and all evil speakings;" the rule whereof extends unto all other vicious habits of mind whatever.

And in the *second*, there is a profession of the *means* whereby this *end* may be attained; namely, how any one may be so strengthened in grace, as to cast out all such sinful inclinations and practices as are contrary unto the holiness required of us,—which is the divine word; compared therefore unto food, which is the means of preserving natural life, and of increasing its strength: "As new-born babes desire the sincere milk of the word, that ye may grow thereby."

Hereon the apostle proceeds, in verse *third*, to declare the *condition* whereon our profiting, growing, and thriving by the word doth depend; and this is an experience of its power, as it is the instrument of God whereby he conveys his grace unto us: "If so be that ye have tasted that the Lord is gracious." See 1 Thess. i. 5. Therein lies the first and chief principle of our ensuing demonstration, and it is this:—

Principle I. *All the benefit and advantage which any men do or may receive by the word, or the truths of the gospel, depend on an experience of its power and efficacy in communicating the grace of God unto their souls.*

This principle is evident in itself, and not to be questioned by any but such as never had the least real sense of religion on their own minds. Besides, it is evidently contained in the testimony of the apostle before laid down.

Hereunto three other principles of equal evidence with itself are supposed, and virtually contained in it.

Principle II. *There is a power and efficacy in the word, and the preaching of it,* Rom. i. 16, "I am not ashamed of the gospel of Christ, for it is the power of God unto salvation."

It hath a divine power, the power of God, accompanying it, and put forth in it, unto its proper ends: "For the word of God is quick and powerful," Heb. iv. 12.

Principle III. *The power that is in the word of God consists in its efficacy to communicate the grace of God unto the souls of men.*

In and by it they "taste that the Lord is gracious;" that is its efficacy unto its proper ends. These are salvation, with all things requisite thereunto; such as the illumination of our minds, the renovation of our natures, the justification of our persons, the life of God in holy worship and obedience,—all leading unto our eternal enjoyment of him. These are the ends whereunto the gospel is designed in the wisdom of God, whereunto its efficacy is confined.

Principle IV. *There is an experience to be obtained of the power and efficacy of the word.*

In that place of the apostle it is expressed by "tasting." But there is something antecedent unto their tasting, specially so called, and something consequent unto it, both inseparable from it; and therefore belonging unto the experience whereof we speak. Wherefore,—

1. The first thing required hereunto is light; that is, a spiritual, supernatural light, enabling us to discern the wisdom, will, and mind of God in the word, in a spiritual manner; without which we can

have no experience of its power. Hence the gospel is hid unto them that perish, though it be outwardly declared unto them, 2 Cor. iv. 3. This is the only means which lets into the mind and conscience a sense of this efficacy. This, in the increases of it, the apostle prays for on the behalf of believers, that they may have this experience, Eph. i. 16–19, iii. 16–19; and declares the nature of it, 2 Cor. iv. 6.

2. The taste intended follows hereon; wherein consists the life and substance of the experience pleaded for. And this taste is a spiritual sense of the goodness, power, and efficacy of the word and the things contained in it, in the conveyance of the grace of God unto our souls, in the instances mentioned, and others of a like nature; for in a taste, there is a sweetness unto the palate, and a satisfaction unto the appetite. By the one in this taste, our minds are refreshed; and by the other, our souls are nourished;—of both believers have an experience. And this is let into the mind by spiritual light, without which nothing of it is attainable. "God, who commanded light to shine out of darkness," shine into your hearts, to give the light of the knowledge of his glory "in the face of Jesus Christ," 2 Cor. iv. 6.

3. To complete the experience intended, there follows hereon a conformity in the whole soul and conversation unto the truth of the word, or the mind of God in it, wrought in us by its power and efficacy. So the apostle expresses it, Eph. iv. 20–24, "If so be that ye have heard him, and have been taught by him, as the truth is in Jesus: that ye put off concerning the former conversation, the old man, which is corrupt according to the deceitful lusts; and be renewed in the spirit of your mind; and that ye put on the new man, which after God is created in righteousness and true holiness."

Hereupon follows our last principle, which is the immediate foundation of the ensuing discourse, or that which is to be confirmed; and it is this:—

Principle V. *The loss of an experience of the power of religion hath been the cause of the loss of the truth of religion; or it hath been the cause of rejecting its substance, and setting up a shadow or image in the room of it.*

This transformation of all things in religion began and proceeded on these grounds. Those who had the conduct of it were always possessed of the general notions of truth, which they could not forego without a total renunciation of the gospel itself. But, having lost all experience of this power in themselves, they wrested them unto things quite of another nature,—destructive to the truth, as well as devoid of its power; hereon it came to pass that there was a dead image made and set up of religion in all the parts of it, called by the name of that which was true and living, but utterly lost. All experience, I say, of the power and efficacy of the mystery of the gospel, and the truth of it, in communicating the grace of God unto the souls of men, being lost, retaining the *general notion* of it, they contrived and framed an *outward image* or representation of them, suited unto their ignorance and superstition. Thus was the truth of religion once almost totally lost in the world, as we shall see; neither will it ever be lost any other way, or by any other means. When churches or nations are possessed of the truth and the profession of it, it is not laws, nor fines, nor imprisonments, nor gibbets, nor fires, that shall ever dispossess them or deprive them of it. Whilst an experience of the power of religion continued in the primitive times, all the bloody rage and cruelty of the world, all the craft of Satan, and the subtlety of seducers, who abounded, did utterly fail in attempting to deprive Christians of the truth, and the profession of it. But when this began to decay and be lost amongst them, they were quickly deceived, and drawn off from the simplicity of the gospel. Upon the reformation of religion in these parts of the world,—when the truth was received in the *love and power* of it, and multitudes had experience of the spiritual benefit and advantage which they received thereby, in liberty, holiness, and peace,—all the prisons, tortures, swords, and fires, that were applied unto its extirpation, did nothing but diffuse the profession of it, and root it more firmly in the minds of men. It cannot be lost but by another way, and other means. The Jesuits and their associates have been, for a hundred years, contriving methods and arts for the dispossessing nations and churches of the truth which they have received, and the introducing the Romish superstition. They have written books about it, and practised according to their principles, in every kingdom and state of Europe who own the Protestant religion. But the folly of most of their pretended arts and devices unto this end hath been ridiculous and unsuccessful; and what they have added hereunto of force hath been divinely defeated. There is but *one way*, one effectual engine to deprive any people of the profession of the truth which they have once received; and that is, by leading them into such profaneness and ignorance, as whereby they may lose all experience of its power and efficacy in communicating the grace of God unto their souls, and therein all sense of the advantage which they might have had by it. When this is done, men will as easily lay aside the profession of religion as burdensome clothes in summer.

There is much talk of a plot and conspiracy to destroy the Protestant religion, and introduce Popery again amongst us. *They* may do well to take care thereof who are concerned in public affairs: but as unto the event, there is but one conspiracy that is greatly to be feared in this matter; and that is, between *Satan* and the *lusts* of men. If they can prevail to deprive the generality of men of an experience in their own minds of the power and efficacy of the truth, with the spiritual advantage which they may have thereby, they will give them up to be an easy prey unto the other designers. And there are two engines that are applied unto this purpose;—the one is *ignorance*, the other is *profaneness*, or sensuality of life. Whenever either of these prevails, the experience intended must necessarily be lost and excluded; and the means of their prevailing are, *want of due instruction* by those who are the leaders of the people, and *the encouragement of sensuality* by impunity and great examples. This is the only formidable conspiracy against the profession of the truth in this nation; without whose aid all power and force will be frustrate in the issue. And as there is a great appearance of divine permission of such a state of things at present amongst us, so, if they be managed by counsel also, and that those ways of ignorance and sensuality are countenanced and promoted for this very end, that, the power of truth being lost, the profession of it may be given up on easy terms,—there is nothing but sovereign grace that can prevent the design. For the principle which we have laid down is uncontrollable in reason and experience,—namely, that the loss of an experience of the power of religion will issue, one way or other, in the loss of the truth of religion and the profession of it. Whence is it that so many corrupt opinions have made such an inroad on the Protestant religion and the profession of it? Is it not from hence, that many have lost an experience of the power and efficacy of the truth, and so have parted with it? Whence is it that profaneness and sensuality of life, with all manner of corrupt lusts of the flesh, have grown up, unto the shame of profession? Is it not from the same cause as the apostle expressly declares it comes by? 2 Tim. iv. 2–5. One way or other, the loss of experience of the power of truth will end in the loss of the profession of it.

But I proceed unto the instance which I do design in the Church of Rome; for the religion of it, at this day, is nothing but a dead image of the gospel, erected in the loss of an experience of its spiritual power, overthrowing its use, with all its ends, being suited to the taste of men, carnal, ignorant, and superstitious. This I shall make evident by all sorts of instances in *things relating to*,—I. *The person and offices of Christ;* II. *The state, order, and worship of the church; with,* III. *The graces and duties of obedience required in the gospel.* And in all my principal design is, to demonstrate what is the only way and means of securing our own souls,—any church or nation,—from being ensnared with, or prevailed against, by Popery.

I. *Section* I. It is a general notion of truth, that *the Lord Christ, in his person and grace, is to be proposed and represented unto men as the principal object of their faith and love.*

He himself, in his Divine Person, is absolutely invisible unto us;

and, as unto his human nature, absent from us; for the heaven must receive him "until the times of restitution of all things." There must, therefore, an image or representation of him be made unto our minds, or he cannot be the proper object of our faith, trust, love, and delight. This is done in the gospel, and the preaching of it; for therein he is "evidently set forth" before our eyes, as "crucified amongst us," Gal. iii. 1. So, also, are all the other concerns of his person and offices therein clearly proposed unto us; yea, this is the principal end of the gospel,—namely, to make a due representation of the person, offices, grace, and glory of Christ unto the souls of men, that they may believe in him, and "believing, have eternal life," John xx. 31. Upon this representation made of Christ and his glory in the gospel, and the preaching of it, believers have an experience of the power and efficacy of the divine truth contained therein, in the way before mentioned, as the apostle declares, 2 Cor. iii. 18, for "we all, with open face beholding as in a glass the glory of the Lord, are changed into the same image from glory to glory, even as by the Spirit of the Lord." Having a spiritual light to discern and behold the glory of Christ, as represented in the glass of the gospel, they have experience of its transforming power and efficacy, changing them into the likeness of the image represented unto them,—that is, of Christ himself; which is the saving effect of gospel power. But this *spiritual light* was lost among men, through the efficacy of their darkness and unbelief; they were not able to discover the glory of Christ, as revealed and proposed in the gospel, so as to make him the present object of their faith and love. And this light being lost, they could have no *experience* of the power of divine truth concerning him changing them into his image. They could make no *affecting* discovery of him in the Scripture. All things therein were dark and confused, or at least seemed an inaccessible mystery, which they could not reduce to practice. Hence, those who had got the public conduct of religion drove the people from reading the Scripture, as that which was of no use, but rather dangerous unto them. What shall these men, then, betake themselves unto? Shall they reject the notion in general, that there ought to be *such a representation made of Christ unto the minds of men*, as to inflame their devotion, to excite their faith, and stir up their affection to him? This cannot be done without an open renunciation of him, and of the gospel as a fable. Wherefore they will find out another way for it,—another means unto the same end;—and this is, by making *images of him* of wood and stone, or gold and silver, or painting on them. Hereby they supposed he would be made present unto his worshippers;—that he would be so represented unto them, as that they should be immediately stirred up unto the embraces of faith and love. And herein they found sensible effects, unto their great satisfaction; for their minds being dark, carnal, and prone to superstition,—as are the minds of all men by nature,—they could see nothing in the spiritual representation of him in the gospel that had any power on them, or did in any measure affect them. In these images, by the means of sight and imagination, they found that which did really work upon their affections, and, as they thought, did excite them unto the love of Christ.

And this was the true original of all the *imagery* in the Church of Rome, as something of the same nature, in general, was of all the image-worship in the world. So the Israelites in the wilderness, when they made the golden calf, did it to have a representation of a deity near unto them, in such a visible manner as that their souls might be affected with it: so they expressed themselves, Exod. xxxii. 1. Wherefore in this state, under a loss of spiritual light and experience, men of superstitious minds found themselves entangled. They knew it necessary that there should be such a representation made of Christ as might render him a present object of faith and love, wherewith they might be immediately affected. How this was done in the gospel they could not understand, nor obtain any experience of the power and efficacy of it unto this end. Yet the principle itself must be retained, as that without which there could be no religion; wherefore, to extricate themselves out of this difficulty, they brake through all God's commands to the contrary, and betook themselves to the making images of Christ, and their adoration. And from small beginnings, according as darkness and superstition increased in the minds of men, there was a progress in this practice, until these images took the whole work of representing Christ and his glory out of the hands, as it were, of the gospel, and appropriated it unto themselves. For I do not speak of them, now, so much as they are images of Christ, or objects of adoration, as of their being dead images of the gospel; that is, somewhat set up in the room of the gospel, and for the ends of it, as means of teaching and instruction. They shall do the work which the gospel was designed of God to do; for as unto this end, of the representation of Christ as the present object of the faith and love of man, with an efficacy to work upon their affections, there is in the Church of Rome a thousand times more ascribed unto them than unto the gospel itself. The whole matter is stated by the apostle, Rom. x. 6–8, "The righteousness which is of faith speaketh on this wise, Say not in thine heart, Who shall ascend into heaven? (that is, to bring Christ down from above:) or, Who shall descend into the deep? (that is, to bring up Christ again from the dead.) But what saith it? The word is nigh thee, in thy mouth, and in thy heart: that is, the word of faith, which we preach." The inquiry is, how we may be made partakers of Christ, and righteousness by him: or, how we may have an interest in him, or have him *present* with us. This, saith the apostle, is done by the *word of the gospel* which is preached, which is nigh unto us,—in our mouths, and in our hearts. "No," say these men, "we cannot understand how it should be so; we do not find that it is so,—that Christ is made nigh unto us, present with us, by this word. Wherefore we will ascend into heaven to bring down Christ from above; for we will make images of him in his glorious state in heaven, and thereby he will be present with us, or nigh unto us. And we will descend into the deep, to bring up Christ again from the dead; and we will do it, by making first crucifixes, and then images of his glorious resurrection, bringing him again unto us from the dead. This shall be in the place and room of that word of the gospel, which you pretend to be alone useful and effectual unto these ends."

This, therefore, is evident, that the introduction of this abomination, in principle and practice destructive unto the souls of men, took its rise from the loss of an experience of the representation of Christ in the gospel, and the transforming power in the minds of men which it is accompanied with, in them that believe. "Make us gods," say the Israelites, "to go before us; for as for this man Moses," who represented God unto us, "we know not what is become of him." What would you have men do? Would you have them live without all sense of the presence of Christ with them, or being nigh unto them? Shall they have no representation of him? No, no; make us gods that may go before us,—let us have images unto this end; for how else may it be done we cannot understand. And this is the reason of their obstinacy in this practice against all means of conviction; yea, they live hereon in a perpetual contradiction unto themselves. Their temples are full of graven images, like the house of Micah,—"houses of gods;" and yet in them are the Scriptures (though in a tongue unknown to the people), wherein *that practice is utterly condemned;* [so] that a man would think them distracted, to hear what their book says, and to see what they do in the same place. But nothing will reach unto their conviction, until the vail of blindness and ignorance be taken from their minds. Until they have spiritual light enabling them to discern the glory of Christ as represented in the gospel, and to let in an experience of the transforming power and efficacy of that revelation in their own souls, they will never part with that means for the same end, which they are sensible of to be useful unto it, and which is suited unto their inclination. Whatever be the issue, though it cost them their souls, they will not part with what they find, as they suppose, so *useful* unto their great end of making Christ nigh unto them, for that wherein they can see nothing of it, and of whose power they can have no experience.

But the principal design of this discourse is, to warn others of these abominations, and to direct unto their avoidance; for if they should be outwardly pressed unto the practice of this idolatry, whatever is of carnal affection, of blind devotion, or superstition in them, will quickly be won over unto a conspiracy against their convictions. Nothing will then secure them, but an experience of the efficacy of that representation which is made of Christ in the gospel. It is, therefore, the wisdom and duty of all those who desire a stability in the profession of the truth, continually to endeavour after this experience, and an increase in it. He who lives in the exercise of faith and love in the Lord Jesus Christ, as revealed in the gospel, as evidently crucified, and evidently exalted therein, and finds the fruit of his so doing in his own soul, will be preserved in the time of trial. Without this, men will, at last, begin to think that it is better to have a *false* Christ than *none at all;* they will suppose that something is to be found in *images*, when they can find nothing in the *gospel.*

Sect. II. It is a prevalent notion of truth, that *the worship of God ought to be beautiful and glorious.*

The very light of nature seems to direct unto conceptions hereof. What is not so may be justly rejected, as unbecoming the divine Majesty; and therefore, *the more holy and heavenly* any religion pretends to be, the more glorious is the worship prescribed in it, or ought so to be. Yea, the true worship of God is the height and excellency of all glory in this world: it is inferior unto nothing but that which is in heaven, which it is the beginning of, the way unto, and the best preparation for. Accordingly, even that worship is declared to be glorious, and that in an eminent manner, above all the outward worship of the Old Testament, in the tabernacle and temple, whose glory was great, and, as unto external pomp, inimitable. To this purpose the apostle disputes at large, 2 Cor. iii. 6–11. This, therefore, is agreed, that there ought to be *beauty and glory* in divine worship; and that they are most eminently in that which is directed and required in the gospel. But withal the apostle declares, in the same place, that this glory is spiritual, and not carnal: so did our Lord Jesus Christ foretell that it should be; and that, unto that end, all distinction of places, with all outward advantages and ornaments belonging unto them, should be taken away, John iv. 20–24.

It belongs, therefore, unto our present design, to give a brief account of its glory, and wherein it excels all other ways of divine worship that ever were in the world; even that under the Old Testament, which was of divine institution, wherein all things were ordered "for beauty and glory." And it may be given in the instances that ensue:—

1. The express *object* of it is God, not as absolutely considered, but

as existing in *three persons, of Father, Son, and Holy Spirit.* This is the principal glory of Christian religion and its worship. Under the Old Testament, the conceptions of the church about the existence of the divine nature in distinct persons were very dark and obscure; for the full revelation of it was not to be made, but in *the distinct actings* of each person in the works of redemption and salvation of the church; —that is, in the incarnation of the Son, and mission of the Spirit after he was glorified, John vii. 39. And in all the ways of *natural* worship, there was never the least shadow of any respect hereunto. But this is the foundation of all the glory of evangelical worship. The object of it, in the faith of the worshipper, is the holy Trinity; and it consists in an ascription of divine glory unto each person, in the same individual nature, by the same act of the mind. Where this is not, there is no glory in religious worship.

2. Its glory consists in that constant respect which it hath unto *each divine person,* as unto their peculiar work and actings for the salvation of the church. So it is described, Eph. ii. 18, "Through him"—that is, the Son as mediator—"we have access by one Spirit unto the Father." This is the immediate glory of evangelical worship, comprehensive of all the graces and privileges of the gospel; and to suppose that the glory of it doth consist in any thing but the light, graces, and privileges which it doth itself exhibit, is a vain imagination. It will not borrow glory from the invention of men. We shall therefore a little consider it as it is here represented by the apostle:—

(1.) The *ultimate object* of it, under this consideration, is God as THE FATHER: "We have access" therein "unto the Father." And this consideration, in our worship, of God as a Father—relating unto the whole dispensation of his love and grace by Jesus Christ, as he is his God and our God, his Father and our Father—is peculiar unto gospel worship, and contains a signal part of its glory. We do not only worship God as a Father,—so the very heathens had a notion that he was the Father of all things,—but we worship him *who is the Father;* and as he is so, both in relation to the eternal generation of the Son, and the communication of grace by him unto us, as our Father. So, "No man hath seen God at any time; the only begotten Son, who is in the bosom of the Father, he hath declared him," John i. 18. This access in our worship unto *the person of the Father,* as in heaven, the holy place above, as on a throne of grace, is the glory of the gospel. See Matt. vi. 9; Heb. iv. 16, x. 19–21.

(2.) The *Son* is here considered as a MEDIATOR;—through him we have this access unto the Father. This is the glory that was hidden from former ages, but brought to light and displayed by the gospel. So speaks our blessed Saviour himself unto his disciples: "Whatsoever ye shall ask the Father in my name, he will give it you. Hitherto have ye asked nothing in my name: ask, and ye shall receive," John xvi. 23, 24. To ask God expressly in the name of the Son, as mediator, belongs unto the glory of the gospel worship.

The especial instances of this glory are more than can be enumerated. The chief of them may be reduced to these three heads:—

1*st.* It is he who makes both the persons of the worshippers and their duties *accepted* of God. See Heb. ii. 17, 18, iv. 16, x. 19.

2*dly.* He is the administrator of all the worship of the church in the holy place above, as its great *High Priest* over the house of God, Heb. viii. 2; Rev. viii. 3.

3*dly.* His *presence* with and among gospel worshippers in their worship gives it glory. This he declares and promises, Matt. xviii. 19, 20, "If two of you shall agree on earth as touching any thing that they shall ask, it shall be done for them of my Father which is in heaven. For where two or three are gathered together in my name, there am I in the midst of them." All success of the prayers of the church dependeth on, and ariseth from, the presence of Christ amongst them: he is so present for their assistance and for their consolation. This presence of a *living Christ*, and not a *dead crucifix*, gives glory to divine worship. He who sees not the glory of this worship, from its relation unto Christ, is a stranger unto the gospel, with all the light, graces, and privileges of it.

(3.) It is in ONE SPIRIT that we have *access* unto God in his worship: and in his administration doth the apostle place the glory of it, in opposition unto all the glory of the Old Testament, as doth our Lord Jesus Christ also in the place before referred unto; for,—

1*st.* The whole *ability* for the observance and performance of it, according to the mind of God, is from him alone. His communication of grace and gifts unto the church is that alone which makes it to give glory to God in his divine service. If this should cease, all acceptable worship would cease in the world. To think to observe the worship of the gospel without the aid and assistance of the Spirit of the gospel, is a lewd imagination. But where he is, there is *liberty* and *glory*, 2 Cor. iii. 17, 18.

2*dly.* By him the sanctified minds of believers are made *temples of God*, and so the principal seal of evangelical worship, 1 Cor. iii. 16, vi. 19. This temple being of God's own framing, and of his own adorning by his Spirit, is a much more glorious fabric than any that the hands of men can erect.

3*dly.* By him is the church led into internal *communion* and converse with God in Christ, in light, love, and delight, with holy boldness; the glory whereof is expressed by the apostle, Heb. x. 19, 21, 22.

In these things, I say, doth the *true glory of evangelical worship* consist; and if it doth not, it hath no glory in comparison of that which did excel in the old legal worship. For the wit of man was never yet able to set it off with half the outward beauty and glory that was in the worship of the temple. But herein it is that it not only leaves no glory thereunto in comparison, but doth unspeakably excel whatever the wit and wealth of men can extend unto.

But there is a *spiritual light* required, that we may discern the glory of this worship, and have thereby an *experience* of its power and efficacy in reference unto the ends of its appointment. This the church of believers hath. They see it as it is a blessed means of giving glory unto God, and of receiving gracious communications from him; which are the ends of all the divine institutions of worship: and they have therein such an experience of its efficacy, as gives rest, and peace, and satisfaction, unto their souls. For they find, that as their worship directs them unto a blessed view, by faith, of God in his ineffable existence, with the glorious actings of each person in the dispensation of grace, which fills their hearts with joy unspeakable; so also, that all graces are exercised, increased, and strengthened in the observance of it, with love and delight.

But all light into, all perceptions of this glory, all experience of its power, was, amongst the most, lost in the world. I intend, in all these instances the time of the papal apostasy. Those who had the conduct of religion could discern no glory in these things, nor obtain any experience of their power. Be the worship what it will, they can see no glory in it, nor did it give any satisfaction to their minds; for having no light to discern its glory, they could have no experience of its power and efficacy. What, then, shall they do? The *notion* must be retained, that divine worship is to be beautiful and glorious. But in the spiritual worship of the gospel they could see nothing thereof; wherefore they thought necessary to make a glory for it, or to dismiss it out of the world, and set up such an image of it as might appear beautiful unto their fleshly minds, and give them satisfaction. To this end they set their inventions on work to find out *ceremonies, vestments, gestures, ornaments, music, altars, images, paintings, with prescriptions of great bodily veneration.* This pageantry they call the beauty, the order, the glory, of divine worship. This is that which they see and feel, and which, as they judge, doth dispose their minds unto devotion. Without it they know not how to pay any reverence unto God himself; and when it is wanting, whatever be the life, the power, the spirituality of the worship in the worshippers—whatever be its efficacy unto all the proper ends of it—however it be ordered according unto the prescription of the word,—it is unto them empty, indecent; they can neither see beauty nor glory in it. This light and experience being lost, the introduction of *beg-*

garly elements and carnal ceremonies in the worship of the church, with attempts to render it decorous and beautiful by superstitious rites and observances,—wherewith it hath been defiled and corrupted, as it was and is in the Church of Rome,—was nothing but the setting up a deformed image in the room of it. And this they are pleased withal. The beauty and glory which carving, and painting, and embroidered vestures, and musical incantations, and postures of veneration, do give unto divine service, they can see and feel; and, in their own imagination, are sensibly excited unto devotion by them. But hereby, instead of representing the true glory of the worship of the gospel, wherein it excels that under the Old Testament, they have rendered it altogether inglorious in comparison of it; for all the ceremonies and ornaments which they have invented for that end come unspeakably short, for beauty, order, and glory, of what was appointed by God himself in the temple,—scarce equalling what was among the Pagans.

It will be said, that the things whereunto we assign the glory of this worship are spiritual and invisible. Now, this is not that which is inquired after; but that whose beauty we may behold, and be affected with: and this may consist in the things which we decry, at least in some of them;—though I must say, if there be glory in any of them, the more they are multiplied the better it must needs be. But this is that which we plead:—men, being not able, by the light of faith, to discern the glory of things spiritual and invisible, do make images of them unto themselves, as gods that may go before them; and these they are affected withal: but the worship of the church is spiritual, and the glory of it is invisible unto eyes of flesh. So both our Saviour and the apostles do testify in the celebration of it: "We are come unto mount Zion, and unto the city of the living God, the heavenly Jerusalem, and to an innumerable company of angels, to the general assembly and church of the first-born, which are written in heaven, and to God the Judge of all, and to the spirits of just men made perfect, and to Jesus the mediator of the new covenant, and to the blood of sprinkling, that speaketh better things than that of Abel," Heb. xii. 22–24. The glory of this assembly, though certainly above that of organs, and pipes, and crucifixes, and vestments, yet doth not appear unto the sense or imaginations of men.

That which I design here is, to obviate *the meretricious allurements* of the Roman worship, and the pretences of its efficacy to excite devotion and veneration by its beauty and decency. The whole of it is but a deformed image of that glory which they cannot behold. To obtain, and preserve in our hearts, an experience of the power and efficacy of that worship of God which is in spirit and in truth, as unto all the real ends of divine worship, is that alone which will secure us.

Whilst we do retain right notions of the proper object of gospel worship, and of our immediate approach by it thereunto,—of the way and manner of that approach, through the mediation of Christ, and assistance of the Spirit; whilst we keep up faith and love unto their due exercise in it (wherein, on our part, the life of it doth consist), preserving an experience of the spiritual benefit and advantage which we receive thereby, we shall not easily be inveigled to relinquish them all, and give up ourselves unto the embraces of this *lifeless image.*

Sect. III. It is a *universal,* unimpeachable persuasion among all Christians, that there is a *near, intimate communion with Christ, and participation of him, in the supper of the Lord.*

He is no Christian who is otherwise minded. Hence, from the beginning, this was always esteemed the principal mystery in the *agenda* of the church; and that deservedly, for this persuasion is built on infallible divine testimonies. The communication of Christ herein, and our participation of him, are expressed in such a manner as to demonstrate them to be peculiar,—such as are not to be obtained in any other way or divine ordinance whatever; not in praying, not in preaching, not in any other exercise of faith on the word or promises. There is in it *an eating and drinking of the body and blood of Christ,* with a spiritual *incorporation* thence ensuing, which are peculiar unto this ordinance. But this especial and peculiar communion with Christ, and participation of him, is *spiritual* and *mystical,* by faith,—not carnal or fleshly. To imagine any other participation of Christ in this life but by faith, is to overthrow the gospel. To signify the real communication of himself and benefits of his mediation unto them that believe, whereby they should become the food of their souls, nourishing them unto eternal life, in the very beginning of his ministry, he himself expresseth it by eating of his flesh, and drinking of his blood; John vi. 53, "Except ye eat the flesh of the Son of man, and drink his blood, ye have no life in you." But hereon many were offended, as supposing that he had intended an oral, carnal eating of his flesh, and drinking of his blood; and so would have taught them to be *cannibals.* Wherefore, to instruct his disciples aright in this mystery, he gives an eternal rule of the interpretation of such expressions, verse 63, "It is the spirit that quickeneth; the flesh profiteth nothing: the words that I speak unto you, they are spirit, and they are life." To look for any other communication of Christ, or of his flesh and blood, but what is spiritual, is to contradict him in the interpretation which he gives of his own words.

Wherefore, this especial communion with Christ, and participation of him, is by *faith.* If it were not, unbelievers ought all to partake of Christ as well as those that believe,—which is a contradiction: for to believe in Christ, and to be made partakers of him, are one and the same. We must, therefore, find this peculiar participating of Christ in the special actings of faith, with respect unto the especial and peculiar exhibition of Christ unto us in this ordinance.

And these actings of faith are diverse and many, but may be referred unto four heads:—

1. It acts itself by *obedience* unto the authority of Christ in this institution. This is the foundation of all communion with Christ, or participation of him, in any ordinance of divine worship whatever, that is peculiarly of his own sovereign appointment; and that in and with such circumstances (as unto the time or season and manner of it) as require especial actings of faith with respect thereunto; for the institution of this ordinance was in the close of his ministry or prophetical office on the earth, and in the entrance of the exercise of his priestly office in offering himself a sacrifice unto God for the sins of the church. Between them both, and to render them both effectual unto us, he interposed an act of his kingly office, in the institution of this ordinance; and it was in "the same night in which he was betrayed," when his holy heart was in the highest exercise of zeal for the glory of God, and compassion for the souls of sinners. Faith hath herein an especial regard unto all these things. It doth not only act itself by a subjection of soul and conscience unto the authority of Christ in the institution, but respects also the exerting of his authority in the close of his prophetical, and entrance of the exercise of his sacerdotal office on the earth; with all those other circumstances of it which recommend it unto the souls and consciences of believers. This is peculiar unto this ordinance, and unto this way of the participation of Christ. And herein faith, in its due exercise, gives the soul an intimate converse with Christ.

2. There is in this divine ordinance *a peculiar representation of the love and grace of Christ in his death and sufferings*, with the way and manner of our reconciliation unto God thereby. The principal design of the gospel is, to declare unto us the love and grace of Christ, and our reconciliation unto God by his blood. Howbeit, herein there is such an eminent *representation* of them, as cannot be made by words alone. It is a *spiritual image* of Christ proposed unto us, intimately affecting our whole souls. These things,—namely, the ineffable love and grace of Christ, the bitterness of his sufferings and death in our stead, the sacrifice that he offered by his blood unto God, with the effect of it in atonement and reconciliation,—being herein contracted into one entire proposal unto our souls, faith is exercised thereon in a peculiar manner, and so as it is not in any [other] divine ordinance or way of the proposal of the same things unto us. All these things are, indeed, distinctly and in parts, set before us in the Scripture, for our instruction and edification: but as the light, which

was first made and diffused unto the whole creation, did suffice to enlighten it in a general way, yet was far more useful, glorious, and conspicuous, when it was reduced and contracted into the body of the sun;—so the truths concerning Christ, as they are diffused through the Scripture, are sufficient for the illumination and instruction of the church; but when, by divine wisdom and institution, they are contracted into this ordinance, their taste and efficacy is more eminent and communicative unto the eyes of our understandings,—that is, our faith,—than as merely proposed by parts and parcels in the word. Hereby faith leads the soul unto a peculiar communion with Christ; which is thereon made partaker of him in an especial manner.

3. Faith, herein, respects *the peculiar way of the communication and exhibition of Christ unto us, by symbols, or sensible outward signs of bread and wine.* It finds the divine wisdom and sovereignty of Christ in the choice of them, having no other foundation in reason or the light of nature: and the representation that is made herein of him, with the benefits of his death and oblation, is suited unto faith only, without any aid of sense or imagination; for although the symbols are visible, yet their relation unto the things signified is not discernible unto any sense or reason. Had he chosen for this end an *image* or a *crucifix*, or any such *actions* as did, by a kind of natural and sensible resemblance, show forth his passion, and what he did and suffered, there had been no need of faith in this matter; and therefore, as we shall see, such things are found out unto this end, by such as have lost the use and exercise of faith herein. Besides, it is faith alone that apprehends the *sacramental* union that is between the outward signs and the things signified, by virtue of divine institution; and hereby the one [latter] (that is, the body and blood of Christ) are really exhibited and communicated unto the souls of believers, as the outward signs are unto their bodily senses,—the signs becoming, thereby, *sacramentally*, unto us what the things signified are in themselves, and are therefore called by their names. Herein there is a peculiar exercise of faith, and a peculiar participation of Christ, such as are in no other ordinance whatever. Yea, the actings of faith with respect unto the sacramental union and relation between the signs and things signified, by virtue of divine institution and promise, is the principal use and exercise of it herein.

4. There is a peculiar exercise of faith in the *reception of Christ, as his body and blood are tendered and exhibited unto us in the outward signs of them;* for though they do not contain *carnally* the flesh and blood of Christ in them, nor are turned into them, yet they *really* exhibit Christ unto them that believe, in the participation of them. Faith is the grace that makes the soul to receive Christ, and whereby it doth actually receive him. To " as many as received him,

to them gave he power to become the sons of God, even to them that believe on his name," John i. 12. And it receives him according as he is proposed and exhibited unto us in the declaration and promise of the gospel, wherein he is proposed; it receives him by the gracious *assent* of the mind unto this truth, the *choice* of him, cleaving and trusting unto him with the will, heart, and affection, for all the ends of his person and offices, as the mediator between God and man: and in the sacramental mysterious proposal of him, his body and blood,—that is, in the efficacy of his death and sacrifice,—in this ordinance of worship, faith acts the whole soul in the reception of him unto all the especial ends for which he is exhibited unto us in this way and manner. What these ends are, which give force and efficacy unto the actings of faith herein, this is not a proper place to declare.

I have mentioned these things, because it is the great plea of the Papists at this day, in behalf of their transubstantiation, that, *if we reject their oral or carnal manducation of the flesh of Christ and drinking of his blood, there cannot be assigned a way of participation of Christ, in the receiving of him in this sacrament, distinct from that which is done in the preaching of the word.* But hereby, as we shall see, they only declare their ignorance of this heavenly mystery. But of this blessed, intimate communion with Christ, and participation of him in the divine institution of worship, believers have *experience* unto their satisfaction and ineffable joy. They find him to be the spiritual food of their souls, by which they are nourished unto eternal life by a spiritual incorporation with him. They discern the truth of this mystery, and have experience of its power. Howbeit, men growing carnal, and being destitute of *spiritual light*, with the wisdom of faith, utterly lost all experience of any communion with Christ, and participation of him in this sacrament. On the principles of gospel truth, they could find nothing in it; no *power*, no *efficacy*,—nothing that should answer the great and glorious things spoken of it: nor was it possible they should; for, indeed, there is nothing in it but unto faith,—as the light of the sun is nothing to them that have no eyes. A dog and a staff are of more use to a blind man than the sun; nor is the most melodious music any thing to them that are deaf. Yet, notwithstanding this loss of spiritual experience, they retained the *notion* of truth, that there must be a *peculiar participation* of Christ in this sacrament distinct from all other ways and means of the same grace.

Here the wits of men were hard put to it to find out an image of this spiritual communion, whereof in their minds they could have no experience; yet they fashioned one by *degrees*, and after they had greatened the mystery in words and expressions (whereof they knew nothing in its power), to answer unto what was to be set up in the room of it, until they brought forth the *horrid monster of transubstantiation*, and *the sacrifice of the mass.* For hereby they provided that all those things which are spiritual in this communion should be turned into and acted in things carnal: bread shall be the body of Christ carnally, the mouth shall be faith, the teeth shall be the exercise, the belly shall be the heart, and the priest shall offer Christ unto God. A *viler image* never was invented; and there is nothing of faith required herein;—it is all, but a fortifying of imagination against all sense and reason. Because there is a singular mystery in the sacramental union that is between the external signs and the things signified,—whence the one is called by the name of the other, as the bread is called the body of Christ,—which faith discerns in the exhibition and receiving of it, they have invented, for a representation hereof, such a prodigious imagination, of the real conversion or transubstantiation of the substance of the bread and wine into the substance of the body and blood of Christ, as overthrows all faith, reason, and sense also. And in the room of that *holy reverence* of Christ himself, in his institution of this ordinance, in the mystical exhibition of himself unto the souls of believers, in the demonstration of his love, grace, and sufferings for them, they have set up a wretched image of an idolatrous adoration and worship of the "*Host*," as they call it, to the ruin of the souls of men. And—whereas the Lord Jesus Christ, "by one offering, perfected for ever them that are sanctified," appointing this ordinance for the remembrance of it—having lost that spiritual light whereby they might discern the efficacy of that *one offering*, so long since accomplished, in the application of it by this ordinance unto the actual perfecting of the church, they have erected a *new image* of it, in a pretended *daily repetition of the same sacrifice;* wherein they profess to offer Christ again for the sins of the living and the dead, unto the overthrow of the principal foundation of faith and religion. All these abominations arose from the loss of an *experience* of that spiritual communion with Christ, and the participation of him by faith, which there is in this ordinance by divine institution. This cast the thoughts of men on invention of these images, to suit the general notion of truth unto the superstition of their carnal minds. Nor is it ordinarily possible to retrieve them from these infatuations, unless God be pleased to communicate unto them that *spiritual light* whereby they may discern the glory of this heavenly mystery, and have an experience of the exhibition of Christ unto the souls of believers therein without these. From innumerable prejudices and inflamed affections towards their idols, they will not only abide in their darkness against all means of conviction, but endeavour the temporal and eternal destruction of all that are otherwise minded.

This *image*, like that of Nebuchadnezzar, was once set up in this nation, with a law, that whoever would not bow down to it, and worship it, should be cast into the fiery furnace. God grant it to be so no more! But if it should, there is no preservation against the influence of force and fires, but a real experience of an *efficacious communication of Christ* unto our souls in this holy ordinance, administered according to his appointment. This, therefore, is that we ought with all diligence to endeavour; and this, not only as the only way and means of our edification in this ordinance, by an exercise in grace, the strengthening of our faith and present consolation, but as the effectual means of our preservation in the profession of the truth, and our deliverance from the snares of our adversaries. For whereas it is undeniable that this peculiar institution, distinct from all others, doth intend and design a distinct communication and exhibition of Christ; if it be pressed on us that these must be done by *transubstantiation* and *oral manducation* thereon, and can be no otherwise, nothing but an experience of the power and efficacy of the mystical communion with Christ in this ordinance, before described, will preserve us from being ensnared by their pretences. There is not, therefore, on all accounts of grace and truth, any one thing of more concernment unto believers, than the due exercise of spiritual light and faith unto a satisfactory experience of a peculiar participation of Christ in this holy institution.

II. The same is fallen out amongst them with reference unto the *church*, and all the principal concerns of it;—having lost or renounced the things which belong unto its primitive constitution, they have erected a *deformed image* in their stead; as I shall manifest in some instances.

Sect. IV. It is an unquestionable principle of truth, that the Church of Christ is in itself a *body*,—such a body as hath a *head*, whereon it depends, and without which it would immediately be dissolved.

A body without a head is but a carcase, or part of a carcase; and this head must be always present with it. A head distant from the body,—separated from it, not united unto it by such ways and means as are proper unto their nature,—is of no use. See Eph. iv. 15, 16; Col. ii. 19.

But there is a double notion of a *head*, as there is of a body also; for they both of them are either *natural* or *political*. There is a *natural* body, and there is a *political* body; and, in each sense, it must have a head of the same kind. A natural body must have a head of *vital influence*, and a political body must have a head of *rule* and *government*. The church is called a body,—compared to it,—is a body in both senses, or in both parts of the comparison; and in both must have a head. As it is a *spiritually living body*, compared to the natural, it must have a head of vital influence, without which it cannot subsist; and as it is an *orderly society* for the common ends of its institution, compared unto a political body, it must have a head of *rule* and *government,* without which neither its being nor its use can be preserved. But these are only distinct considerations of the church, which is every way one and the same. It is not two bodies; for then it must have two heads: but it is one body, under two distinct considerations, which divide not its essence, but declare its different respects unto its head.

And in general, all who are called Christians are thus far agreed,—nothing is of the church, nothing belongs unto it, which is not dependent on, which is not united to, the head. That which *holds the head* is the true church; that which doth not so, is no church at all. Herein we agree with our adversaries; namely, that all the privileges of the church, all the right and title of men thereunto, depend wholly on their *due relation to the head of it,* according to the distinct considerations of it. Be that head who or what it will, that which is not united unto the head, which depends not on it, which is separated from it, belongs not to the church. This head of the church is *Christ Jesus alone;* for the church is but one, although, on various considerations, it be likened unto two sorts of bodies. The *catholic church* is considered either as believing, or as professing; but the believing church is not *one,* and the professing *another.* If you suppose another catholic church besides this one, whoso will may be the head of it, we are not concerned therein; but unto this church Christ is *the only head.* He only answers all the properties and ends of such a head to the church. This the Scripture doth so positively and frequently affirm, without the least intimation, either directly or by consequence, of any other head, that it is wonderful how the imagination of it should befall the minds of any, who thought it not meet at the same time to cast away their Bibles.

But, whereas a head is to be present with the body, or it cannot subsist, the inquiry is, *How the Lord Christ is so present with his church?* And the Scripture hath left no pretence for any hesitation herein; for he is so *by his Spirit and his word,* by which he communicateth all the powers and virtues of a head unto it continually. His promises of this way and manner of his presence unto the church are multiplied; and thereon doth the being, life, use, and continuance of the church depend. Where Christ is not present by his Spirit and word, there is no church; and those who pretend so to be, are the synagogues of Satan. And they are inseparable and conjunct in their operation, as he is the head of influence unto the church, as also as he is a head of rule; for, in the former sense, the Spirit worketh by the word, and in the latter, the word is made effectual by the Spirit.

But the sense and apprehension hereof was for a long time lost in the world, amongst them that called themselves "the church." A head they did acknowledge the church must always have, without which it cannot subsist; and they confess that, in some sense, he was a head of influence unto it. They knew not how to have an image thereof; though by many other pernicious doctrines they overthrew the efficacy and benefit of it. But how he should be the only head of rule unto the church they could not understand; they saw not how he could act the wisdom and authority of such a head, and without which the church must be headless. They said, he was *absent* and *invisible*,—they must have one that they could see, and have access unto; he is in heaven, and they know not how to make address to him, as occasion did require: all things would go to disorder, notwithstanding such a headship. The church is visible, and it must, they thought, have a visible head. It was meet, also, that this head should have some such grandeur and pomp in the world as became the head of so great and glorious a society as the church is. How to apply these things unto Christ and his presence with the church, by his word and Spirit, they knew not. Shall they, then, forego the principle, that the church is to have such a head and supreme ruler? That must not be done, but be sacredly retained; not only because to deny it, in general, is to renounce the gospel, but because they had found out a way to turn it unto their own advantage. They would therefore make an image of Christ, as this head of the church, to possess the place and act all the powers of such a head; for the church, they say, is visible, and must have a visible head: as though the catholic church, as such, were any other way visible but as the head of it is,—that is, by faith. That there must be a head and centre of union, wherein all the members of the church may agree and be united, notwithstanding all their distinct capacities and circumstances, and how this should be Christ himself, they know not; that without a supreme ruler present in the church, to compose all differences, and determine all controversies, even those concerning himself, which they vainly pretend unto, they expressly affirm there never was a society so foolishly ordered as that of the church. And hereon they conclude the insufficiency of Christ to be this *sole head* of the church; another they must have for these ends. And this was their pope,—such an image as is one of the worst of idols that ever were in the world. Unto him they give all the titles of Christ, which relate unto the church; and ascribe all the powers of Christ in and over it, as unto its rule, to him also. But here they fell into a mistake; for, when they thought to give him *the power of Christ*, they gave him *the power of the dragon* to use against Christ, and those that are his. And when they thought to make an *image of Christ*, they made an *image of the first beast*, set up by the dragon, which had two horns like a lamb, but spake as a dragon; whose character and employ is at large described, Rev. xiii. 11–17.

This is the sum of what I shall offer on this head:—those who called themselves "*the* church," had lost all *spiritual light*, enabling them to discern the beauty and glory of the rule of Christ over the church, as its head; and hereon their minds became destitute of all *experience* of the power and efficacy of his Spirit and word, continually to order the affairs thereof, in the ways, and through the use of means, by himself appointed; they knew not how to acquiesce in these things, nor how the church could be maintained by them: wherefore, in this case, "they helped every one his neighbour, and every one said to his brother, Be of good comfort; so the carpenter encouraged the goldsmith, and he that smootheth with the hammer, him that smiteth the anvil." They set themselves, in their several capacities, to frame this idol, and set him up in the place and stead of Christ; so fixing him in the temple of God, that he might show himself from thence to be as God. Neither will this idol be ever cast out of the church, until the generality of Christians become spiritually sensible of the authority of Christ exerting itself, in the rule of the church, by his Spirit and his word, unto all the ends of unity, order, peace, and edification. Until that be done, a pope, or something like him, will be thought necessary unto these ends. But never was there a more horrid, deformed image made of so beautiful and glorious a head: all the craft of Satan, all the wits of men, cannot invent any thing more unlike Christ, as the head of the church, than this *Pope* is. A worse figure and representation of him cannot possibly be made.

This is he of whom nothing not great, nothing common, nothing not exceeding the ordinary state of mankind, on the one hand or the other, is thought or spoken. Some say he is "the head and husband of the church," "the vicar of Christ over the whole world," "God's vicegerent," "a vice-god," "Peter's successor," "the head and centre of unity" unto the whole catholic church, endued with a plenitude of power, with other ascriptions of the same nature innumerable; whereon it is necessary unto every soul, under pain of damnation, to be subject unto him;—others aver that he is "antichrist," "the man of sin," "the son of perdition," "the beast that came out of the earth with two horns like a lamb, and a voice like the dragon," "the false prophet," "the idol shepherd," "the evil servant that beateth his fellow-servants," "the adulterer of a meretricious and false church:" and there is no mean betwixt these;—he is undoubtedly the one or the other. The Lord Jesus Christ, who hath determined this controversy already in his word, will ere long give it its ultimate issue in his own glorious person, and by the brightness of his coming. And this is an eminent idol in the *Chamber of Imagery* in the *Roman Church.* But at present it is evident wherein lies the preservation of believers from being inveigled to bow down to this image, and to worship it. A due sense of the sole authority of Christ in and over his church, with an experience of the power of his word and Spirit unto all the ends of its rule and order, will keep them unto the truth herein; and nothing else will so do. And if once they decline from this in any instances, seem they never so small, so as to admit of any thing in the church or its worship which doth not derive immediately from his authority, they will be disposed to admit of another guide and head in all other things also.

Sect. V. Again: it is a notion of truth, that *the Church of Christ is beautiful and glorious.*

There are many prophecies and predictions concerning it, that so it should be; and there are sundry descriptions given of it as such. Its relation unto Christ, with his love unto it, and valuation of it, do require that it should be so glorious; yea, his great design towards it was to make it so to be, Eph. v. 25–27. This, therefore, all do agree in who profess Christian religion; but *what that glory is*, and wherein it doth consist,—whence it is, and is said to be glorious,—is not agreed upon. The Scripture, indeed, plainly declares this glory to be *spiritual and internal;*—that it consists in its union unto Christ, his presence with it, the communication of his quickening Spirit unto it, the clothing of it with his righteousness, in its sanctification and purification from the defilement of sin, with its fruitfulness in obedience, unto the praise of God. Add hereunto the celebration of divine worship in it, with its rule and order, according to the commandment of Christ, and we have the substance of this glory. And this glory believers do discern, so as to be satisfied with its excellency. They know that all the glories of the world are no way to be compared to it; for it consists in, and arises from, such things as they do value and prefer infinitely above all that this world can afford. They are a reflection of the glory of God or of Christ himself upon the church; yea, a communication of it thereunto. This they value in the whole, and in every member of it; neither the nature, use, nor end of the church, will admit that its glory should consist in things of any other nature. But the generality of mankind had lost that *spiritual light* wherein alone this glory might be discerned. They could see no form or beauty in the spouse of Christ, as only adorned with his graces. To talk of a glorious state of men, whilst they are poor and destitute, it may be, clothed with rags, and haled into prisons or to stakes, as hath been the lot of the church in most ages, was, in their judgment, a thing absurd and foolish. Wherefore, seeing it is certain that the Church of Christ is very glorious and illustrious in the sight of God, holy angels, and good men, a way must be found out to make it so, and so to appear in the world. Wherefore they agreed on a lying image of this glory,—namely, the *dignity, promotion, wealth, dominion, power, and splendour*, of all them that had got the rule of the church. And although it be evident unto all that these things belong unto the glories of this world, which the glory of the church is not only distinguished from, but opposed unto, yet it [they?] must be looked on as that wherein it is glorious; and it is so, though it have not one saving grace in it, as they expressly affirm. When these things are attained, then are all the predictions of its glory accomplished, and the description of it answered. This *corrupt image of the true spiritual glory* of the church,—arising from an ignorance of it, and want of a real experience of the worth and excellency of things internal, spiritual, and heavenly,—hath been attended with pernicious consequents in the world. Many have been infatuated by it, and enamoured of it, unto their own perdition. For, as a teacher of lies, it is suited only to divert the minds of men from a comprehension and valuation of that real glory, wherein if they have not an interest, they must perish for ever.

Look into foreign parts, as Italy and France, where these men pretend their church is in its greatest glory: what is it but the wealth, and pomp, and power of men, for the most part openly ambitious, sensual, and worldly? Is this the glory of the Church of Christ? Do these things belong unto his kingdom? [No;] but by the setting up of this image, by the advancement of this notion, all the true glory of the church hath been lost and despised. Yet these things, being suited unto the designs of the carnal minds of men, and satisfactory unto all their lusts,—having got this paint and gilding on them, that they render the Church of Christ glorious,—have been the means of filling this world with darkness, blood, and confusion. For this is that glory of the church which is contended for with rage and violence. And not a few do yet dote on these images, who are not sharers in the advantage it brings unto its principal worshippers, whose infatuation is to be bewailed.

The means of our preservation from the adoration of these images also is obvious, from the principles we proceed upon. It will not be done without light to discern *the glory of things spiritual and invisible;* wherein alone the church is glorious. And in the light of faith they appear to be what indeed they are in themselves,—of the same nature with the glory that is above. The present glory of the church, I say, is its initiation into the glory of heaven, and in general of the same nature with it. Here it is in its dawnings and entrances; there, in its fulness and perfection. To look for any thing that should be cognate, or of near alliance unto the glory of heaven, or any near resemblance of it, in the outward glories of this world, is a fond imagination. And when the mind is enabled to discern the true beauty and glory of spiritual things, with their alliance unto that which is above, it will be secured from seeking after the glory of the church in things of this world or putting any value on them unto that end.

That *self-denial* also, which is indispensably prescribed in the gospel unto all the disciples of Christ, is requisite hereunto; for the power and practice of it is utterly inconsistent with an apprehension that secular power, riches, and domination, do contribute any thing unto the church's glory. The mind being hereby crucified unto a value and estimation of these things, it can never apprehend them as any part of *that raiment of the church* wherein it is glorious. But where the minds of men, through their native darkness, are disenabled to discern the glory of spiritual things, and, through their carnal, unmortified affection, do cleave unto, and have the highest esteem of, worldly grandeur, it is no wonder if they suppose the beauty and glory of the church to consist in them.

Sect. VI. I shall add one instance more with reference unto the state of the church; and that is in its *rule* and *discipline.*

Here, also, hath been as fatal a miscarriage as ever fell out in Christian religion. For the truth herein being lost, as unto any sense and experience of its efficacy or power, a *bloody image,* destructive to the lives and souls of men, was set up in the stead thereof. And this also shall be briefly declared. There are certain principles of truth with respect hereunto that are acknowledged by all; as,—

1. That the Lord Christ hath appointed a *rule* and *discipline* in his church, for its good and preservation. No society can subsist without the power and exercise of some rule in itself; for rule is nothing but the preservation of order, without which there is nothing but confusion. The church is the most perfect society in the earth, as being united and compacted by the best and highest bonds which our nature is capable of, Eph. iv. 16; Col. ii. 19. It must, therefore, have a rule and discipline in itself; which, from the wisdom and authority of Him by whom it was instituted, must be supposed to be the most perfect.

2. That this discipline is *powerful and effectual unto all its proper ends.* It must be so esteemed, from the wisdom of Him by whom it is appointed; and it is so accordingly. To suppose that the Lord Christ should ordain a rule and discipline in his church, that in itself, and by its just administration, should not attain its ends, is to reflect the greatest dishonour upon him. Yea, if any church or society of professed Christians be fallen into that state and condition, wherein the discipline appointed by Christ cannot be effectual unto its proper

ends, Christ hath forsaken that church or society. Besides, the Holy Ghost affirms that the ministry of the church, in the administration of it, is "mighty, through God," unto all its ends, 2 Cor. x. 4, 5.

3. The ends of this discipline are the *order, peace, purity, and holiness of the church, with a representation of the love, care, and watchfulness of Christ over it, and a testimony unto his future judgment.* An imagination of any other ends of it hath been its ruin.

And thus far all who profess themselves Christians are agreed, at least in words. None dare deny any of these principles; no, not to secure their abuse of them, which is the interest of many.

4. But unto them all we must also add, and that with the same uncontrollable evidence of truth, that *the power and efficacy of this discipline, which it hath from the institution of Christ, is spiritual only,* and hath all its effects on the souls and consciences of those who profess subjection unto him, with respect unto the ends before mentioned. So the apostle expressly describes it, 2 Cor. x. 4, 5, "For the weapons of our warfare are not carnal, but mighty through God to the pulling down of strong holds; casting down imaginations, and every high thing that exalteth itself against the knowledge of God, and bringing into captivity every thought to the obedience of Christ." These are the ends, as of preaching of the gospel, so of the discipline of the church; and these are the ways and means of its efficacy:— it is spiritually mighty, through God, unto all these ends; and others it hath none. But we shall immediately see the total reverse of this order, in an image substituted in the room of it.

5. Of the power and efficacy of this *spiritual discipline* unto its proper end, *the primitive Christians,* at least, had experience. For three hundred years, the church had no other way or means for the preservation of its order, peace, purity, and holiness, but the spiritual efficacy of this discipline on the souls and consciences of professed Christians. Neither did it fail therein, nor were the churches any longer preserved in peace and purity, than whilst they had this discipline alone for their preservation, without the least contribution of assistance from secular power, or any thing that should operate on the outward concerns of mankind. And there can be no other reason given, why it should not be of the same use and efficacy still unto all churches, but only the loss of all those internal graces which are necessary to make any gospel institution effectual: wherefore, all sense and experience hereof—of the spiritual power and efficacy of this discipline—was utterly lost amongst the most of them that are called Christians. Neither those who had assumed a pretence of the administration of it, nor those towards whom it was administered, could find any thing in it that did affect the consciences of men, with respect unto its proper ends. They found it a thing altogether use-

less in the church, wherein none of any sort would be concerned. What shall they now do? what course shall they take? Shall they renounce all those principles of truth concerning it which we have laid down, and exclude it, both name and thing, out of the church? This probably would have been the end of it, had they not found out a way to wrest the pretence of it unto their unspeakable advantage. Wherefore they contrived and made a horrid image of the holy spiritual rule and discipline of the gospel: an image it was, consisting in outward force and tyranny over the persons, liberties, and lives of men; exercised with weapons mighty through the devil to cast men into prison, and to destroy them. Hereby that which was appointed for the *peace* and *edification* of the church being lost, an engine was framed, under its name and pretence, unto its ruin and destruction; and so it continues unto this day. It had never entered into the hearts of men to set up a discipline in the Church of Christ by law, courts, fines, mulcts, imprisonments, and burnings, but that they had utterly lost in themselves, and suffered to be lost in others concerned, all experience of the power and efficacy of the discipline of Christ towards the souls and consciences of men. But hereon they laid it aside, as a useless tool, that might do some service in the hands of the apostles and the primitive churches, whilst there was spiritual life and sense left amongst Christians; but as unto them, and what they aimed at, it was of no use at all. The deformity of this image in the several parts of it; its universal dissimilitude unto that whose name it bears, and which it pretends to be; the several degrees whereby it was forged, framed, and erected; with the occasions and advantages taken for its exaltation, would take up much time to declare: for it was subtly interwoven with other abominations, in the whole *Mystery of Iniquity*, until it became the very life or animating principle of Antichristianism. For, however men may set light by the rule and discipline of Christ in his church, and its spiritual power or efficacy towards the souls and consciences of men, the rejection of it, and the setting up of a horrid image of worldly power, domination, and force in the room of it, and under its name, is that which began, carried on, and yet maintains, the fatal apostasy in the Church of Rome.

I shall instance only in one particular. On the change of this rule of Christ, and, together with it, the setting up of Maüzzim, or an image, or "god of forces," [Dan. xi. 38,] in the stead of it; they were compelled to change all the ends of that discipline, and to make an image of them also. For this new instrument of outward force was of no use with respect unto them; for they are, as was declared, the spiritual peace, purity, love, and edification of the church. Outward force is no way meet to attain any of these ends. Wherefore, they must make an image of these also, or substitute some dead form in their room; and this was a universal subjection unto the pope, according unto all the rules, orders, and canons which they should invent. *Uniformity* herein, and *canonical obedience*, is all the end which they will allow unto their church discipline; and these things hang well together, for nothing but outward force by law and penalties is fit to attain this end. So was there an image composed and erected of the holy discipline of Christ, and its blessed ends, consisting of these two parts, *outward force* and *feigned subjection.* For hardly can an instance be given in the world of any man who ever bowed down to this image, or submitted unto any ecclesiastical censure, out of a conscientious respect unto it. Force and fear rule all.

This is that discipline in whose execution the blood of an innumerable company of *holy martyrs* hath been shed,—that wherein all the *vital spirits* of the Papacy do act themselves, and whereby it doth subsist; and although it be the image of jealousy, or the image of the first beast, set up by the dragon, yet it cannot be denied, but that it is very wisely accommodated unto the present state of the generality of them that are called Christians amongst them. For being both blind and carnal, and having thereby lost all sense and experience of the *spiritual power* of the *rule* of Christ in their consciences, they are become a herd not fit to be governed or ruled any other way. Under the bondage of it, therefore, they must abide, till the vail of blindness be taken away, and they are turned unto God by his word and Spirit; for "where the Spirit of the Lord is, there," and there alone, "is liberty."

Sect. VII. Unto the foregoing *particular* instances, with respect unto the church, I shall yet add one more *general;* which is indeed comprehensive of them all, or the root from whence they spring,—a root bearing gall and wormwood: and this is concerning *the catholic church.*

What belongs unto this catholic church, what is comprised in its communion, the apostle declares, Heb. xii. 22–24. It is the recapitulation of all things in heaven and earth in Christ Jesus, Eph. i. 10;—his body, his spouse or bride, the Lamb's wife, the glorious temple wherein God doth dwell by his Spirit;—a holy mystical society, purchased and purified by the blood of Christ, and united unto him by his Spirit, or the inhabitation of the same Spirit in him and those whereof it doth consist. Hence they with him, as the body with its head, are mystically called Christ, 1 Cor. xii. 12. And there are two parts of it, the one whereof is already *perfected* in heaven, as unto their spirits; and the other yet continued in the way of faith and obedience in this world. Both these constitute "one family in heaven and earth," Eph. iii. 15;—in conjunction with the holy angels, one mystical body, one catholic church. And although there is a great difference, in their present state and condition, between these two branches of the same family, yet are they both equally purchased by Christ, and united unto him as their head, having both of them effectually the same principle of the life of God in them. Of a *third part of this church*, neither in heaven nor in earth, in a temporary state, participant somewhat of heaven, and somewhat of hell, called purgatory, the Scripture knoweth nothing at all; neither is it consistent with the analogy of faith, or the promises of God unto them that do believe, as we shall see immediately. This church, even as unto that part of it which is in this world, as it is adorned with all the graces of the Holy Spirit, is the most beautiful and glorious effect,—next unto the forming and production of its Head, *in the incarnation of the Son of God*—which divine wisdom, power, and grace will extend themselves unto here below. But these things—the glory of this state—is visible only unto *the eye of faith;* yea, it is perfectly seen and known only to Christ himself. We see it obscurely in the light of faith and revelation, and are sensible of it according unto our participating of the graces and privileges wherein it doth consist.

But that spiritual light which is necessary to the discerning of this glory was lost among those of whom we treat. They could see no reality nor beauty in these things, nor any thing that should be of advantage unto them. For upon their principle, of the *utter uncertainty* of men's spiritual estate and condition in this world, it is evident that they could have no satisfactory persuasion of any concernment in it. But they had possessed themselves of the notion of a *catholic church;* which, with mysterious artifices, they have turned unto their own incredible secular advantage. This is that whereof they boast, appropriating it unto themselves, and making it a pretence of destroying others, what lies in them, both temporally and eternally. Unto this end they have formed the most deformed and detestable image of it that ever the world beheld; for the catholic church which they own, and which they boast that they are, instead of that of Christ, is a company or society of men, unto whom, in order unto the constitution of that whole society, there is *no one real Christian grace* required, nor spiritual union unto Christ, the head, but only an outside profession of these things, as they expressly contend;—a society united unto the Pope of Rome, as its head, by a subjection unto him and his rule, according to the laws and canons whereby he will guide them. This is the formal reason and cause constituting that catholic church which they are, which is compacted in itself by *horrid bonds and ligaments*, for the ends of ambition, worldly domination, and avarice;—a catholic church openly *wicked* in the generality of its rulers, and them that are ruled; and in its state *cruel*, oppressive, and dyed with the blood of saints, and martyrs innumerable. This, I say, is that image of the holy catholic church, the spouse of Christ, which they have set up. And it hath been as the image of Moloch, that hath devoured and consumed the children of the church; whose cries, when their cruel stepmother pitied them not, and when their pretended ghostly fathers cast them into the flames, came up unto the ears of the Lord of hosts; and their blood still cries for vengeance on this idolatrous generation. Yet is this pretence of the catholic church pressed, in the minds of many, with so many *sophistical* artifices, through the sleight of men and cunning craftiness, whereby they lie in wait to deceive, proposed with the allurements of so many secular advantages, and imposed ofttimes on Christians with so much force and cruelty, that nothing can secure us from the admission of it, unto the utter overthrow of religion, but the means before insisted on. A spiritual light is necessary hereunto, to discern the internal spiritual beauty and glory of the true catholic church of Christ. Where this is in its power, all the paintings and dresses of their deformed image will fall off from it, and its abominable filth will be made to appear. And this will be accompanied with an effectual experience of the glory and excellency of that grace in the souls of those that believe, derived from Christ, the sole head of this church, whereby they are changed "from glory to glory, as by the Spirit of the Lord." The power, life, and sweetness hereof, will give satisfaction unto their souls, to the contempt of the pretended order, or dependence on the pope as a head. By these means the true catholic church,—which is the body of Christ, the fulness of him that filleth all in all,—growing up unto him in all things who is the head, despiseth this *image*, and *Dagon* will fall to the ground when this *Ark* is brought in; yea, though it be in his own temple.

III. In the farther opening of this Chamber of Imagery, we shall yet, if it be possible, see greater abominations; at least, that which doth next ensue is scarce inferior unto any of them that went before.

Sect. VIII. It is a principle in Christian religion, an acknowledged verity, that *it is the duty of the disciples of Christ, especially as united in churches, to propagate the faith of the gospel*, and to make the doctrine of it known unto all as they have opportunity; yea, this is one principal end of the constitution of churches, and officers in them, Matt. v. 13–16; 1 Tim. iii. 15.

This our Lord Jesus Christ gave in special charge unto his apostles at the beginning, Matt. xxviii. 19, 20; Mark xvi. 15, 16. Hereby they were obliged unto the work of propagating the faith of the gospel, and the knowledge of him therein, in all places, and were justified in their so doing. And this they did with that efficacy and success, that, in a short time, like the light of the sun, "their sound went into all the earth, and their words unto the ends of the world," Rom. x. 18; and the gospel was said to be "preached to every creature which is under heaven," Col. i. 23. The way, therefore, whereby they propagated the faith, was by diligent, laborious preaching of the doctrine of the gospel unto all persons in all places, with patience and magnanimity in undergoing all sorts of sufferings on the account of it, and a declaration of its power in all those virtues and graces which are useful and exemplary unto mankind. It is true, their office and the discharge of it is long since ceased; howbeit it cannot be denied but that the work itself is incumbent, in a way of duty, on all churches, yea, on all believers, as they have providential calls unto it, and opportunities for it. For it is the principal way whereby they may glorify God and benefit men in their chiefest good; which, without doubt, they are obliged unto.

This notion of truth is retained in the Church of Rome: and the work itself is appropriated by them unto themselves alone. Unto *them*, and *them only*, as they suppose, it belongs to take care of the propagation of the faith of the gospel, with the conversion of infidels and *heretics*. Whatever is done unto this purpose by others, they condemn and abhor. What do they think of the primitive way of doing it,—by personal preaching, sufferings, and holiness? Will the pope, his cardinals and bishops, undertake this work or way of the discharge of it? Christ hath appointed no other; the apostles and their successors knew no other;—no other becomes the gospel, nor ever had success. No; they abhor and detest this way of it. What, then, is to be done? Shall the truth be denied? shall the work wholly and avowedly be laid aside? Neither will this please them; because it is not suited unto their honour: wherefore they have erected a dismal image of it, unto the horrible reproach of Christian religion. They have, indeed, provided a double painting for the image which they have set up. The first is the constant consult of some persons at Rome, which they call "Congregatio de Propagandâ Fide,"—a council for the propagation of the faith; under the effect of whose consultations Christendom hath long groaned: and the other is, the sending of missionaries, as they call them, or a surcharge of friars from their over-numerous fraternities, upon their errands into remote nations.

But the real image itself consists of these three parts:—1. *The sword;* 2. *The inquisition;* 3. *Plots and conspiracies.*

By these it is that they design to propagate the faith and promote Christian religion; and if hell itself can invent a more deformed image and representation of the sacred truth and work, which it is a counterfeit of, I am much mistaken.

1. Thus have they, in the *first way*, carried Christian religion into

the Indies, especially the western parts of the world so called. First the Pope, out of the plenitude of his power, gives unto the Spaniard all those countries and the inhabitants of them, that they may be made Christians. But Christ dealt not so with his apostles, though he were Lord of all, when he sent them to teach and baptize all nations. He dispossessed none of them of their temporal rights or enjoyments, nor gave to his apostles a foot-breadth of inheritance among them. But upon this grant, the Spanish Catholics propagated the faith, and brought in Christian religion amongst them. And they did it by killing and murdering many millions of innocent persons; as some of themselves say, more than are alive in Europe in any one age. And this savage cruelty hath made the name of Christians detestable amongst all that remained of them that had any exercise of reason; [only] some few slavish brutes being brought by force to submit unto this new kind of idolatry. And this we must think to be done in obedience unto that command of Christ, " Go ye into all the world, and preach the gospel to every creature. He that believeth and is baptized shall be saved; but he that believeth not shall be damned." This is the deformed image which they have set up of obedience unto his holy commands; whereunto they apply that voice to Peter with respect unto the eating of all sorts of creatures, " Rise, Peter; kill, and eat." So have they dealt with those poor nations whom they have devoured. But blood, murder, and unjust war (as all war is for the propagation of religion), with persecution, began in Cain, who derived it from the devil, that " murderer from the beginning;" for he " was of that wicked one, and slew his brother," [1 John iii. 12.] Jesus Christ, the Son of God, was manifested to " destroy the works of the devil," [1 John iii. 8.] And he doth it in this world by his word and doctrine, judging and condemning them. And he does it in his disciples by his Spirit, extirpating them out of their minds, hearts, and ways; so as that there is not a more assured character of a derivation from the evil spirit, than force and blood in religion for the propagating of it.

2. The next part of this image,—the next way used by them for the propagating of the faith, and the conversion of them they call heretics,—is the *Inquisition*. So much hath been declared and is known thereof, that it is needless here to give a portraiture of it. It may suffice, that it hath been long since opened, like Cacus's den, and discovered to be the greatest arsenal of cruelty, the most dreadful shambles of blood and slaughter, that ever was in the world. This is that engine which hath supplied the scarlet whore with the blood of saints, and the blood of the martyrs of Jesus, until she was drunk with it. And this is the *second way* or means whereby they propagate the faith of the gospel, and endeavour, as they say, the conversion

of the souls of men;—this is the second part of that image which they have set up instead of the holy appointment of Jesus Christ.

3. The *third way* they insist on unto this purpose,—the third part of this image,—consists in *plots and contrivances* to murder princes, to embroil nations in blood, to stir up sedition unto their ruin, inveigling and alluring all sorts of vicious, indigent, ambitious persons, into an association with them, so as to introduce the Catholic religion in the places which they design to subvert. This engine for the propagation of the faith hath been plied with various successes in many nations of Europe, and is still at work unto the same purpose. And hereunto belong all the arts which they use for the infatuation of the minds of princes and great men,—all the baits they lay for others of all sorts, to work them over into a compliance with their designs.

Of these parts, I say, is that dreadful image made up and composed, which they set up, embrace, and adore, in the room of the holy way for the propagation of the gospel appointed by Jesus Christ. *In his way* they can see no beauty,—they can expect no success;—they cannot believe that ever the world will be converted by it, or be brought in subjection unto the pope; and therefore betake themselves unto their own. Faith, prayer, holiness, preaching, suffering, all in expectation of the promised presence and assistance of Christ, are no ways, for efficacy, success, and advantage, to be compared unto the sword, inquisition, and underhand designings. And this also is that which they call zeal for the glory of God, and the honour of Christ!—another deformed image which they have brought into religion. For whereas that grace consists principally in *postponing self*, and all self-concerns, with an undervaluation of them, unto the glory of God, and the special duties whereby it may be promoted, this impious design to destroy mankind by all ways of subtlety and cruelty, unto their own advantage, is set up in the room of it. But the consideration of the *nature* and *spirit*, of the *use* and *end*, of the gospel,—of the design of Christ in it and by it,—is sufficient to preserve the souls of men, not utterly infatuated, in an abhorrency of this image of its propagation. It is that wherein "the god of this world," by the help of their blindness and lusts, hath put a cheat on mankind, and prevailed with them, under a pretence of doing Christ honour, to make the vilest representation of him to the world that can be conceived. If he hath appointed this way for the propagating of the gospel, he cannot well be distinguished from Mohammed; but there is nothing more contrary unto him,—nothing that his holy soul doth more abhor. And had not men lost all spiritual sense of the nature and ends of the gospel, they could never have given up themselves unto these abominations. For any to suppose that the faith of the gospel is to be propagated by such cruelty and blood,—by art and subtlety,—by plots, conspiracies, and contrivances,—any way but by the foolishness of preaching, which, unto that end, is the power and wisdom of God,—is to declare his own ignorance of it, and unconcernment in it. And had not men conceived and embraced another religion than what is taught therein, or abused a pretence thereof unto ends and advantages of their own, this imagination of the propagation of it had never taken place in their minds, it is so *diametrically* opposite unto the whole nature and all the ends of it.

Sect. IX. There is yet amongst them another image of a *general principle*, no less horrid than that before mentioned, and that with respect unto religious obedience. It is the great foundation of all religion, and in especial of Christian religion, that *God in all things is to be obeyed, absolutely and universally.*

Of all our obedience, there is no other reason, but that it is his will, and is known unto us so to be. This follows necessarily from the infinite perfections of the divine nature. As the first Essential Verity, he is to be believed in what he reveals, above and against all contradiction from pretended reasons, or any imaginations whatever; and as he is the only Absolute Independent Being, Essential Goodness, and the Sovereign Lord of all things, he is, without farther reason, motive, or inducement, to be absolutely obeyed in all his commands. An instance whereof we have in Abraham offering his only son without dispute or hesitation, in compliance with a divine revelation and command.

It will seem very difficult to frame an image hereof amongst men, with whom there is not the least shadow of these divine perfections,—namely, Essential Verity and Absolute Sovereignty in conjunction with Infinite Wisdom and Goodness; which alone render such an obedience lawful, useful, or suitable unto the principles of our rational natures. But those of whom we speak have not been wanting unto themselves herein, especially the principal craftsmen of this image-trade. The order of the Jesuits have made a bold attempt for the framing of it. Their *vow of blind obedience* (as they call it) unto their superiors, whereby they resign the whole conduct of their souls, in all the concernments of religion, in all duties toward God and man, unto their guidance and disposal, is a cursed image of this absolute obedience unto the commands of God which he requireth of us. Hence the founder of their order was not ashamed, in his Epistle *ad Fratres Lusitanos*, to urge and press this blind obedience from the example of Abraham yielding obedience unto God, without debate or consideration; as if the superiors of the order were good, and not evil and sinful men. Whilst this honour was reserved unto God, whilst this was judged to be *his prerogative* alone,—namely, that his commands are to be obeyed in all things, without reasonings and examinations as unto the matter, justice, and equity of them, merely because they are his, which absolutely and infallibly concludes them good, holy, and just,—the righteous government of the world, and the security of men in all their rights, were safely provided for; for he neither will nor can command any thing but what is holy, just, and good: but, since the ascription of such a god-like authority unto men, as to secure blind obedience unto all their commands, innumerable evils, in murders, seditions, and perjuries, have openly ensued thereon. But, besides those particular evils, in matter of fact, which have proceeded from this corrupt fountain, this persuasion at once takes away all grounds of peace and security from mankind; for who knows what a crew or sort of men called the Jesuits' superiors, known only by their restless ambition and evil practices in the world, may command their vassals, who are sworn to execute whatever they command, without any consideration whether it be right or wrong, good or evil?

Let princes, and other great men, flatter themselves whilst they please, that, on one consideration or other, they shall be the objects only of their kindness; if these men, according to their profession, be obliged in conscience to execute whatever their superiors shall command them,—no less than Abraham was, to sacrifice his son on the command of God,—they hold their lives at the mercy and on the good nature of these superiors, who are always safe out of the reach of revenge. It is marvellous, that mankind doth not agree to demolish this cursed image, or the ascription of a god-like power unto men to require blind obedience unto their commands, especially considering what effects it hath produced in the world. All men know by whose device it was first set up and erected;—by whom, by what means, and unto what end, it was confirmed and consecrated: and, at this day, it is maintained by a society of men of an uncertain extract and original, like that of the Janizaries in the Turkish empire,—their rise being generally out of obscurity, among the meanest and lowest of the people. Such they are, who, by the rules of their education, are taught to renounce all respect unto their native countries, and alliances therein, but so as to make them only the way and matter for the advancement of the interest of this new society. And this sort of men being nourished, from their very first entrance into the conduct of the society, unto hopes and expectations of wealth, honour, power, interest in the disposal of all public affairs of mankind, and the regulation of the consciences of men, it is no wonder if, with the utmost of their arts and industry, they endeavour to set up and preserve this image which they have erected, from whence they expect all the advantage which they do design. But hereof I may treat more fully when I come to speak of the image of Jealousy itself.

Sect. X. From these *generals* I shall proceed unto more particular instances; and those, for the most part, in important principles of religion, wherein Christian faith and practice are most concerned: and I shall begin with that which is of signal advantage unto the framers of these images,—as the other also are in their degree, for by this craft they have their livelihood and wealth,—and most pernicious to the souls of other men.

It is a principle of truth, and that such as wherein the whole course of Christian obedience is concerned, that *there is a spiritual defilement in sin.*

This the Scripture everywhere declares, representing the very nature of it by spiritual uncleanness. And this uncleanness is its contrariety unto the holiness of the divine nature, as represented unto us in the law. This defilement is in all men equally by nature;—all are alike born in sin, and the pollution of it: "Who can bring a clean thing out of an unclean?" And it is in all personally, in various degrees; some are more polluted with actual sins than others, but all are so in their degree and measure. This pollution of sin must be purged and taken away, before our entrance into heaven; for no unclean thing shall enter into the kingdom of God. Sin must be destroyed in its nature, practice, power, and effects, or we are not saved from it. This purification of sin is wrought in us, initially and gradually, in this life, and accomplished in death, when the spirits of just men are made perfect. In a compliance with this work of God's grace towards them, whereby they purify themselves, consists one principal part of the obedience of believers in this world, and of the exercise of their faith. The principal, internal, immediate, efficient cause of this purification of sins, is *the blood of Christ.* The blood of Jesus Christ, the Son of God, cleanseth us from all our sins, 1 John i. 7. The blood of Jesus purgeth our consciences from dead works, Heb. ix. 14. He washeth us in his own blood, Rev. i. 5. And there is an external helping cause thereof; which is trials and afflictions, made effectual by the word, and accomplished in death.

But this way of purging sins by the blood of Christ is *mysterious.* There is no discerning of its glory but by spiritual light,—no experience of its power but by faith. Hence it is despised and neglected by the most, that yet outwardly profess the doctrine of the gospel. Men generally think there are a thousand better ways for the purging of sin than this by the blood of Christ, which they cannot understand. See Mic. vi. 6, 7. It is mysterious in the application of it unto the souls and consciences of believers by the Holy Ghost. It is so, in the spring of its efficacy, which is the oblation of it for a propitiation; and in its relation unto the new covenant, which first it establisheth, and then makes effectual unto this end. The work of it is gradual and imperceptible unto any thing but the eyes of faith, and diligent spiritual experience.

Again; it is so ordered by divine wisdom, as strictly to require, to begin, excite, and encourage the utmost diligence of believers in a compliance with its efficacy unto the same end. What Christ did for us, he did without us, without our aid or concurrence. As God *made* us without ourselves, so Christ *redeemed* us; but what he doth *in us,* he doth also *by us;* what he works in a way of *grace,* we work in a way of *duty.* And our duty herein consists, as in the continual exercise of all gracious habits, renewing, changing, and transforming the soul into the likeness of Christ (for he who hopes to see him, "purifieth himself, as he is pure"); so also in universal, permanent, uninterrupted mortification unto the end;—whereof we shall speak afterward. This also renders the work both mysterious and difficult. The improvement of afflictions unto the same end is a principal part of the wisdom of faith; without which they can be of no spiritual use unto the souls of men.

This notion of the *defilement of sin,* and that of the *necessity of its purification,* were retained in the Church of Rome; for they could not be lost, without not only a rejection of the Scripture, but the stifling of natural conceptions about them, which are indelibly fixed in the consciences of men. But spiritual light into the glory of the thing itself, or the mystical purification of sin, with an experience of the power and efficacy of the blood of Christ, as applied unto the consciences of believers unto that end by the Holy Ghost, were lost amongst them. In vain shall we seek for any thing of this nature, either in their doctrine or their practice. Wherefore, having lost the substance of this truth, and all experience of its power, to retain the use of its name, they have made sundry little images of it,—creeping things,—whereunto they ascribe the power of purging sin; such as holy water, pilgrimages, disciplines, masses, and various commutations. But they quickly found, by experience, that these things would neither purify the heart, nor pacify the consciences of sinners, any more than the blood of bulls and of goats could do it under the law; yea, any more than the lustrations and expiations of sin amongst the heathen could effect it. Wherefore they have at length formed a more stated and specious image of it, to serve all the turns of convinced sinners. And this is a *purgatory* after this life; that is, a subterraneous place and various means, where and whereby the souls of men are purged from all their sins and made meet for heaven, when the Lord Christ thinks meet to send for them, or the pope judges it fit to send them to him. Hereunto, let them pretend what they please, the people under their conduct do trust a thousand times more for the purging of their sins than unto the blood of Christ; but it is only a cursed image of the virtue of it, set up to draw off the minds of poor sinners from seeking an interest in a participation of the efficacy of that blood for that end, which is to be obtained by faith alone, Rom. iii. 25. Only, they have placed this *image* behind the curtain of mortality, that the cheat of it might not be discovered. None, who find themselves deceived by it, can come back to complain or warn others to take care of themselves. And it was, in an especial manner, suited unto their delusion who lived in pleasures or in the pursuit of unjust gain, without exercise of afflictions in this world. From these two sorts of persons, by this engine, they raised a revenue unto themselves beyond that of kings or princes; for all the endowments of their religious houses and societies were but commutations for the abatement of *the fire of this purgatory.* But whereas in itself it was a *rotten post*, that could not stand or subsist, they were forced to prop it with many other imaginations. For unto this end, to secure work for this purgatory, they coined *the distinction of sins into mortal and venial;*—not as *unto their end*, with respect unto faith and repentance, nor as unto *the degrees of sin*, with respect unto the aggravations, but as unto *the nature of them;* some of them being such (namely, those that are venial) as were capable of a purging expiation after this life, though men die without any repentance of them. And when this was done, they have cast almost all the sins that can be named under this order; and hereon this image is become an engine to disappoint the whole doctrine of the gospel, and to precipitate secure sinners into eternal ruin. And to strengthen this deceiving security, they have added another invention, of *a certain storehouse of ecclesiastical merits*, the keys whereof are committed to the pope, to make application of them, as he sees good, unto the ease and relief of them that are in this purgatory. For, whereas many of their church and communion have, as they say, done more good works than were needful for their salvation (which they have received upon a due balance of commutative justice), the *surplusage* is committed to the pope, to commute with it for the punishment of their sins who are sent into purgatory to suffer for them;—than which they could have found out no engine more powerful to evacuate the efficacy of the blood of Christ, both as offered and as sprinkled, and therewith, the doctrine of the gospel concerning faith and repentance. Moreover, to give it farther countenance (as one lie must be thatched with another, or it will quickly rain through), they have fancied a separation to be made between *guilt and punishment*, so as that when the guilt is fully remitted and pardoned, yet there may punishment remain on the account of sin. For this is the case of them in purgatory;—their sins are pardoned, so as that the *guilt* of them shall not bind them over to eternal damnation, though "the wages of sin is death;" yet they must be variously *punished* for the sins that are forgiven. But as this is contradictory in itself, it being utterly impossible there should be any punishment properly so called but where there is guilt as the cause of it; so it is highly injurious both to the grace of God and blood of Christ, in procuring and giving out such a lame pardon of sins, as should leave room for punishment next to that which is eternal. These are some of the rotten props which they have fixed on the minds of persons credulous and superstitious, terrified with guilt and darkness, to support this tottering, *deformed image*, set up in the room of the efficacy of the blood of Christ, to purge the souls and consciences of believers from sin. But that whereby it is principally established and kept up is, *the darkness, ignorance, guilt, fear, terror of conscience*, accompanied with a love of sin, that the most among them are subject and obnoxious unto; being disquieted, perplexed, and tormented with these things, and utterly ignorant of the true and only way of their removal and deliverance from them, they greedily embrace this sorry provision for their present ease and relief, being accommodated unto the utmost that human or diabolical craft can extend unto, to abate their fear, ease their torments, and to give security unto their superstitious minds. And hereby it is become to be the life and soul of their religion, diffusing itself into all the parts and concerns of it,—more trusted unto than either God, or Christ, or the gospel.

Spiritual light and experience, with the consequents of them in *peace* with God, will safeguard the minds of believers from bowing down to this horrid image, though the acknowledgments of its divinity should be imposed on them with craft and force: otherwise it will not be done; for without this there will a strong inclination and disposition, arising from a mixture of superstitious fear and love of sin, possess the minds of men to close with this pretended relief and satisfaction. The foundation of our preservation herein lies in spiritual light, or an ability of mind, from supernatural illumination, to discern the beauty, glory, and efficacy of the purging of our sins by the blood of Christ. When the glory of the wisdom and grace of God, of the love and grace of Christ, of the power of the Holy Ghost herein, is made manifest unto us, we shall despise all the paintings of this invention,—Dagon will fall before the ark; and all these things do gloriously shine forth and manifest themselves unto believers in this mysterious way of purging all our sins by the blood of Christ. Hereon will ensue an experience of the efficacy of this heavenly truth in our own souls. There is no man whose heart and ways are cleansed by the blood of Christ, through the effectual application of it by the Holy Spirit, in the ordinance of the gospel, but he hath, or may have, a refreshing experience of it in his own soul; and, by the power which is communicated therewith, he is stirred up unto all that exercise of faith, and all those duties of obedience, whereby the work of purifying and cleansing the whole person may be carried on toward perfection. See 2 Cor. vii. 1; 1 Thess. v. 23; 1 John iii. 3. And he who is constantly engaged in that work with success, will see the folly and vanity of any other pretended way for the purging of sins, here or hereafter. The consequent of these things is, peace with God; for they are assured pledges of our justification and acceptance with him, and being justified by faith, we have peace with God. And where this is attained by the gospel, the whole fabric of purgatory falls to the ground; for it is built on these foundations, that no assurance of the love of God, or of a justified state, can be obtained in this life;—for if it may be so, there can be no use of purgatory. This, then, will assuredly keep the souls of believers in a contempt of that, which is nothing but a false relief for sinners, under disquietment of mind for want of peace with God.

Sect. XI. Some other instances of the same abomination I shall yet mention, but with more brevity, and sundry others must at present be passed over without a discovery. It is the known method of gospel faith and obedience,—the way of God's dealing with believers in the covenant of grace,—that, after their initiation and implantation into Christ, they *should labour to thrive and grow in grace, by its continual exercise, until they come to be strengthened and confirmed therein.*[1] And this, in the ordinary way of God's dealing with the church, they shall never fail of, unless it be through their own neglect: for there are many divine promises to this purpose, and it lies in the nature of the things themselves; for the seeds of grace are of that kind of habits which will be increased and strengthened by exercise. Wherefore, *this confirmation in grace* is that whereof believers have a blessed experience.

This truth, in general, of an implantation into Christ, and the ensuing confirmation in grace, is universally assented unto; none can deny it without denying the whole doctrine of the gospel. But the sense and experience of it was lost amongst them of whom we treat; yet would they not forego the profession of the principle itself,—which would have proclaimed them apostates from the grace of Christ. Wherefore they formed an image of it, or images of both its distinct parts, which they could manage unto their own ends, and such as the carnal minds of men could readily comply with and rest in. As in the other sacrament they turned the outward signs into the things signified, so in this of baptism, they make it to stand in the stead of the thing itself; which is to make it, if not an idol, yet an image of it. The outward participation of that ordinance with them is re-

[1] This section was first given in the folio edition of Owen's Sermons and Tracts, published in 1721. It does not appear in the sermon as printed in the "Morning Exercises."—ED.

generation and implantation into Christ, without any regard unto the internal grace that is signified thereby; so that which in itself is a sacred figure, is made an image to delude the souls of men.

And that which they would impose in the room of spiritual confirmation in grace is yet more strange. The image which they set up hereof is *episcopal imposition of hands.* When one that hath been baptized can answer some few questions out of a catechism, though he be very ignorant, and openly vicious in his conversation, by this laying on of hands he is confirmed in grace.

It may be some will say, there is no great matter, one way or other, in things of this sort; they may be suffered to pass at what rate they will in this world. I confess I am not so minded. If there be any thing in them but mere formality and custom,—if they are trusted unto as the things whose names they bear,—they are pernicious unto the souls of men. For if all that are outwardly baptized should thereon judge themselves implanted into Christ, without regard unto the internal washing of regeneration and renewing of the Holy Ghost; and all who have had this imposition of hands should, without more ado, suppose themselves confirmed in grace,—they are in the ready way to eternal ruin.

Sect. XII. It is granted among all Christians, that all *our helps, our relief, our deliverance from sin, Satan, and the world, are from Christ alone.*

This is included in all his relations unto the church,—in all his offices, and the discharge of them; and is the express doctrine of the gospel. It is no less generally acknowledged,—at least the Scripture is no less clear and positive on it,—that we receive and derive all our *supplies of relief from Christ by faith:* other ways of the participation of any thing from him, the Scripture knoweth not. Wherefore, it is our duty, on all occasions, to apply ourselves unto him by faith, for all supplies, reliefs, and deliverances: but these men can find no life nor power herein; at least, if they grant that somewhat might be done this way, yet they know not how to do it, being ignorant of the life of faith, and the due exercise of it. They must have a way more ready and easy, exposed to the capacities and abilities of all sorts of persons, good and bad; yea, that will serve the turn of the worst of men unto these ends. An image, therefore, must be set up for common use, instead of this spiritual application unto Christ for relief; and this is the making of the sign of the cross. *Let a man but make the sign of the cross on his forehead,* his breast, or the like,—which he may as easily do as take up or cast away a straw,—and there is no more required to engage Christ unto his assistance at any time. And the virtues which they ascribe hereunto are innumerable. But this also is an idol, a teacher of lies, invented and set up for no other end but to satisfy the carnal minds of men with a presumptuous supposition, in the neglect of the spiritually laborious exercise of faith. An experience ot the work of faith, in the derivation of all supplies of spiritual life, grace, and strength, with deliverance and supplies, from Jesus Christ, will secure believers from giving heed unto this trifling deceit.

Sect. XIII. One thing more, amongst many others of the same sort, may be mentioned. It is a notion of truth, which derives from the light of nature, that *those who approach unto God in divine worship should be careful that they be pure and clean, without any offensive defilements.*

This the heathens themselves give testimony unto, and God confirmed it in the institutions of the law. But what are these defilements and pollutions which make us unmeet to approach unto the presence of God,—how and by what means we may be purified and cleansed from them,—the gospel alone declares. And it doth, in opposition unto all other ways and means of it, plainly reveal, that it is by the sprinkling of the blood of Christ upon our consciences, so to purge them from dead works, that we may serve the living God. See Heb. ix. 14, x. 19–22. But this is a thing mysterious: nothing but spiritual light and saving faith can direct us herein. Men, destitute of them, could never attain an experience of purification in this way. Wherefore they retained the notion of truth itself, but made an image of it for their use, with a neglect of the thing itself. And this was the most ludicrous that could be imagined; namely, the *sprinkling of themselves and others with that they call holy water* when they go into the places of sacred worship; which yet also they borrowed from the Pagans. So stupid and sottish are the minds of men, so dark and ignorant of heavenly things, that they have suffered their souls to be deceived and ruined by such vain, superstitious trifles!

This discourse hath already proceeded unto a greater length than was at first intended; and would be so much more, should we look into all parts of this Chamber of Imagery, and expose to view all the abominations in it. I shall therefore put a close unto it, in one or two instances, wherein the Church of Rome doth boast itself as retaining the truth and power of the gospel in a peculiar manner, whereas in very deed they have destroyed them, and set up corrupt images of their own in their stead.

Sect. XIV. The first of these is, *the doctrine and grace of mortification.*

That this is not only an important evangelical duty, but also of indispensable necessity unto salvation, all who have any thing of Christian religion in themselves must acknowledge. It is also clearly determined in the Scripture, both what is *the nature of it*, with its causes, and in what acts and duties it doth consist; for it is frequently declared to be the crucifying of the body of sin, with all the lusts thereof. For mortification must be the bringing of something to death; and this is sin: and the dying of sin consists in the casting out of all vicious habits and inclinations, arising from the original depravation of nature. It is the weakening and graduate extirpation or destruction of them, in their roots, principles, and operations, whereby the soul is set at liberty to act universally from the contrary principle of spiritual life and grace. The means, on the part of Christ, whereby this is wrought and effected in believers, is the communication of his Spirit unto them, to make an effectual application of the virtue of his death unto the death of sin; for it is *by his Spirit* that we mortify the deeds of the flesh, and the flesh itself, and that, as we are implanted by him into the likeness of the death of Christ. By virtue thereof we are *crucified*, and made dead unto sin; in the declaration of which things the Scripture doth abound. The means of it, on the part of believers, is the exercise of faith in Christ, as crucified; whereby they derive virtue from him for the crucifying of the body of death: and this exercise of faith is always accompanied with diligence and perseverance in all holy duties of prayer, with fasting, godly sorrow, daily-renewed repentance, with a continual watch against all the advantages of sin. Herein consists, principally, that spiritual warfare and conflict that believers are called unto. This is all *the killing work* which the gospel requires. *That of killing other men for religion* is of a later date, and another original. And there is nothing, in the way of their obedience, wherein they have more experience of the necessity, power, and efficacy of the graces of the gospel.

This principle of truth, concerning the necessity of mortification, is retained in the Church of Rome; yea, she pretends highly unto it, above any other Christian society. *The mortification of their devotionists* is one of the principal arguments which they plead, to draw unwary souls over unto their superstition. Yet, in the height of their pretences unto it, they have lost all experience of its nature, with the power and efficacy of the grace of Christ therein; and have, therefore, framed an image of it unto themselves. For,—

1. They place the eminency and height of it in a *monastical life, and pretended retirement from the world.* But this may be, hath been, in all or the most, without the least real work of mortification in their souls; for there is nothing required in the strictest rules of these monastic votaries but may be complied withal, without the least effectual operation of the Holy Spirit in their minds, in the application of the virtue of the death of Christ unto them; besides, the whole course of life which they commend under this name, is neither ap-

pointed in, nor approved by, the gospel. And some of those who have been most renowned for their severities therein were men of blood, promoting the cruel slaughter of multitudes of Christians, upon the account of their profession of the gospel: in whom there could be no one evangelical grace; "*for no murderer hath eternal life abiding in him.*"

2. The ways and means which they prescribe and use for the attaining of it, are such as are no way directed by the divine wisdom of Christ in the Scripture;—such as multiplied *confessions* to priests, irregular, ridiculous *fastings, penances, self-macerations* of the body, unlawful *vows, self-devised rules of discipline and habits*, with the like trinkets innumerable. Hence, whatever their design be, they may say of it, in the issue, what Aaron said of his idol, "I cast the gold into the fire, and there came out this calf." They have brought forth only an image of mortification, diverting the minds of men from seeking after that which is really and spiritually so. And under this pretence they have formed a state and condition of life that hath filled the world with all manner of sins and wickedness; and many of those who have attained unto some of the highest degrees of this mortification, on their principles, and by the means designed unto that end, have been made ready thereby for all sorts of wickedness.

Wherefore, the mortification which they retain, and whereof they boast, is nothing but a wretched image of that which is truly so, substituted in its room, and embraced by such as had never attained any experience of the nature or power of gospel grace in the real mortification of sin.

Sect. XV. The same is to be said concerning *good works*,—the second evangelical duty whereof they boast.

The necessity of these good works unto salvation, according unto men's opportunities and abilities, is acknowledged by all; and the glory of our profession in this world consisteth in our abounding in them: but their principle, their nature, their motives, their use, their ends, are declared and limited in the Scripture; whereby they are distinguished from what may seem materially the same in those which may be wrought by unbelievers. In brief, they are the acts and duties of true believers only; and they are in them effects of divine grace, or the operation of the Holy Ghost; for they are "created in Christ Jesus unto good works, which God hath ordained that they should walk in them." But the principal mystery of their glory, which the Scripture insists upon, is, that although they are necessary, as a means unto the salvation of believers, yet are they utterly excluded from any influence unto the *justification of sinners;*—so there was never any work, evangelically good, performed by any who were not before freely justified.

Unto these *good works* those with whom we have to do lay a vehement claim, as though they were the only patrons of them, and pleaders for them; but they have also excluded them out of Christian religion, and set up a deformed image of them, in defiance of God, of Christ, and the gospel. For the works they plead for are such as so far proceed from their own *free will*, as to render them *meritorious* in the sight of God. They have confined them partly unto acts of superstitious devotion, partly unto those of charity, and principally unto those that are not so;—such are the building of monasteries, nunneries, and such pretended religious houses, for the maintenance of swarms of monks and friars, filling the world with superstition and debauchery. They make them meritorious, satisfactory; yea, some of them, which they call of *supererogation*, above all that God requireth of us, and the causes of our justification before God. They ascribe unto them a condignity of the heavenly reward, making it of works, and so not of grace; with many other defiling imaginations. But whatever is done from these principles, and for these ends, is utterly foreign unto those good works which the gospel enjoineth as a part of our new or evangelical obedience. But having, as in other cases, lost all sense and experience of the power and efficacy of the grace of Christ, in working believers unto this duty of obedience, unto the glory of God and benefit of mankind, they have set up the image of them, in defiance of Christ, his grace, and his gospel.

These are some of the *abominations* which are portrayed on the walls of the Chamber of Imagery in the Church of Rome; and more will be added in the consideration of the *image of Jealousy* itself; which, God willing, shall ensue in another way. These are the *shadows* which they betake themselves unto, in the loss of spiritual light to discern the truth and glory of the mystery of the gospel, and the want of an experience of their power and efficacy, unto all the ends of the life of God in their own minds and souls. And although they are all of them expressly condemned in the letter of the Scripture, which is sufficient to secure the minds of true believers from the admission of them, yet their establishment, against all pleas, pretences, and force, for a compliance with them, depends on *their experience of the power of every gospel truth unto its proper end*, in communicating unto us the grace of God, and transforming our minds into the image and likeness of Jesus Christ.

SERMON XVI.

AN HUMBLE TESTIMONY

UNTO THE GOODNESS AND SEVERITY OF GOD IN HIS DEALING WITH SINFUL CHURCHES AND NATIONS;

OR,

THE ONLY WAY TO DELIVER A SINFUL NATION FROM UTTER RUIN BY IMPENDENT JUDGMENTS:

IN A DISCOURSE ON THE WORDS OF OUR LORD JESUS CHRIST,
LUKE XIII. 1–5.

"Cry aloud, spare not; lift up thy voice like a trumpet, and show my people their transgression, and the house of Jacob their sins."—ISA. lviii. 1.

"In publico discrimine omnis homo miles est."

PREFATORY NOTE.

In his own preface to the reader Dr Owen very briefly alludes to the circumstances which had induced him to deliver to "a private congregation" several discourses on Luke xiii. 1–5, and afterwards to publish the substance of them in the following discourse. For obvious reasons, he evinces great caution in referring to passing events, which, about the time the discourse was published, excited "continual apprehensions of public calamities" in the minds of all the friends of liberty and order. The nation had been agitated with stormy discussions about the Exclusion Bill. The Whig party were bent on preventing the accession of James, the Duke of York, to the British throne on the demise of Charles II. In the agitation which shook the country in consequence of this attempt, "a whole year," says Macaulay, "elapsed,—an eventful year, which has left lasting traces in our manners and language. . . . On the one side, it was maintained that the constitution and religion of the state would never be secure under a Popish king;—on the other, that the right of James to wear the crown in his turn was derived from God, and could not be annulled, even by the consent of all the branches of the Legislature."

The bill had been several times introduced into the House of Commons,—in 1679, in November 1680, a third time in the following January, and finally, in the Parliament which met at Oxford in March 1681, when the Whig measures were defeated by the dissolution of the Parliament only seven days after it had met.

Whatever judgment be formed as to the expediency of the Exclusion Bill, the strenuous exertions which the Whigs and Nonconformists made to secure the success of that measure, enable us to estimate the alarm and forebodings which filled their minds, when the power of the Court had triumphed.

Apart, however, from this defeat, there were other causes of anxiety and apprehension. Dissenters were subjected to severe and increasing oppression; and while the friends of the popular cause were disconcerted and baffled, a manifest reaction was taking place throughout England in favour of the Court. It was this change of public sentiment, and decay of patriotic zeal—arising in some degree from growing indifference to religious principle—that led our author to entertain, at this juncture, gloomy views in regard to the prospects of the nation, and to issue a solemn and urgent warning to his countrymen.

The discourse of Dr Owen is extremely suitable to the crisis which had elicited it. While he makes no reference to the proceedings of the government, he dwells upon evangelical truths and duties, in a strain peculiarly fitted to elevate his readers above unworthy fears, and to make the danger to which they might feel themselves exposed a motive to repentance and godliness. "The 'Testimony,'" says Orme, "contains much of that practical wisdom which the Doctor had acquired from his long and deep study of the Word of God, and from his extensive experience in the ways of Providence." The discourse was published in the year 1681.—Ed.

TO THE READER.

THE ensuing discourse contains the substance of sundry sermons preached in a private congregation. Some who heard them, considering the subject-matter treated of, and the design in them with respect unto the present state of things in this nation, did judge that it might be convenient and seasonable to make them more public, for the use and benefit of others; but, knowing how remote I was from any such intention in their first composure, and how naked they were of all ornaments that might render them meet for public view, I was unwilling for a season to comply with their desires. Neither was it their importunity (which, as they did not use, so I should not in this case have valued), but their reasons, that prevailed with me, to consent that they might be published by any that had a mind thereunto; which is all my concernment therein. For they said, that whereas the land wherein we live is filled with sin, and various indications of God's displeasure thereon, yet there is an unexemplified neglect in calling the inhabitants of it unto *repentance*, for the diverting of *impendent judgments*. The very *heathen*, they said, upon less evidence of the approaches of divine vengeance than is now amongst us, did always solemnly apply themselves to their deities, for the turning it away. Wherefore, this *neglect* amongst us they supposed to be of such *ill abode*,[1] as that the weakest and meanest endeavour for relief under it might be of some use; and of that nature I cannot but esteem this discourse to be.

They added, moreover, that whereas, on various accounts, there are *continual apprehensions of public calamities*, all men's thoughts are exercised about the ways of *deliverance* from them; but whereas they fix themselves on various and opposite ways and means for this end, the conflict of their counsels and designs increaseth our danger, and is like to prove our ruin. And the great cause hereof is, a general ignorance and neglect of the only true way and means whereby this nation may be delivered from destruction under the displeasure of God. For if their thoughts did agree and centre therein, as it would insensibly work them off from their present *mutual destructive animosities*; so also it is of such a nature as would lead them into a *coalescency* in those counsels, whose fruit would be the establishment of truth, with righteousness and peace. Now, this way is no other but sincere *repentance*, and universal reformation in all sorts of persons throughout the nation.

That this is the only way for the saving of this nation from impending judgments and wasting desolations,—that this way will be effectual unto that end when all others shall fail,—is asserted and proved in this discourse, from the authority of our Lord Jesus Christ himself, to confront the wisdom of politicians, who are otherwise minded, with a plain word of truth and power.

It was hoped also by them, that some intimation of their duty might be hereby given unto those who, having *the ministerial oversight* of the generality of the people, do divert their minds unto the petty differences and contests, whilst the fire of God's displeasure for sin is ready to devour their habitations. And the truth is, if they persist in their negligence, if they give not a public evidence, at this season, of their zeal for repentance and reformation of life among all sorts of persons,—going

[1] *Abode* is an old English word signifying *omen* or *prognostic*,—from "bode," to portend.—ED.

before them in their example and endeavours unto the promotion of them,—I understand not how they will give an account of their trust and duty to God or men.

And therefore, were I worthy to give advice to any of my brethren in the ministry, who are in the same condition with myself as unto outward circumstances, it should be this only, namely, that whilst others do seek to obstruct them in the whole discharge of their duty, and to deprive the church of the benefit of their labours, they would, by their own personal example, by peculiar endeavours in their congregations, among all that hear them, and on every occasion, so press the present calls of God unto repentance, and so promote the work of a visible reformation, as eminently to help in saving of the nation from approaching judgments, and therein of them also who design their trouble;—and I doubt not but most of them are already engaged and forward herein.

This shall be our testimony, and our peace, in whatever may befall us in this world.

Let us not satisfy ourselves, that our congregations are in so good a posture as that they may continue for our lives; and so be like ill tenants, who care not if their houses fall upon the expiration of the term of their interest in them. That reparation is required of us which may make them serve for succeeding generations.

And when any church is so unobservant of its own decays as to be negligent of endeavours for proportionable reformation,—if, after a while, any will deliver their own souls, it must be by a departure from them that *hate to be reformed.*

It is a fond imagination, that churches may render their communion useless and dangerous only by *heresy, tyranny,* and *false worship;*—an evil, worldly, corrupt conversation in the generality of their members, contrary to the doctrine of the gospel, not opposed and contradicted by a constant endeavour for sincere reformation, is no less ruinous unto the being of churches than any of these other evils.

On these and such like considerations, I was not unwilling that this plain discourse should be exposed to public view, hoping that it might stir up others of greater abilities and opportunities more effectually to pursue the same design. I do not think it needful to make any apology for the plainness both of the matter and style in this small treatise.

The least endeavour to attire a discourse of this nature with the ornaments of speech or language, is even ridiculous; it is more fit to bear the furrows of sighs and tears, than to be smoothed and flourished with the oily colours of elegance and rhetoric.

And as for the obvious plainness of the matter contained in it, it is suited, as I judge, unto them whose good is principally designed therein. Plain men have sinned as well as others, though it may be not unto so high a degree, nor in such an outrage of excess. However, on many considerations, they are likely first to suffer, unless impendent judgments are diverted by repentance.

I do but a little plead with every man for himself and in his own cause. Neither, however wise or learned men may be, is it meet, in this case, to treat them otherwise. It is to no purpose to make a fine speech unto such as are falling into a lethargy, nor to discourse learnedly of the art of navigation unto them that are ready to perish in a storm; they must be plain words and plain things that are forcible in this case. And those by whom they are despised, from any principle of self-elation, give but an uncomfortable indication of what will be the issue of their dangers.

Let, therefore, the reader but candidly excuse and pass by the trouble which he will be put unto by the frequent mistakes of the press, especially in mispointings, rendering the sense sometimes obscure and unobvious; and I have, on the behalf of the treatise itself, no more to desire of his forbearance.

SERMON XVI.

AN HUMBLE TESTIMONY UNTO THE GOODNESS AND SEVERITY OF GOD IN HIS DEALING WITH SINFUL CHURCHES AND NATIONS.

"There were present at that season some that told him of the Galileans, whose blood Pilate had mingled with their sacrifices. And Jesus, answering, said unto them, Suppose ye that these Galileans were sinners above all the Galileans, because they suffered such things? I tell you, Nay: but, except ye repent, ye shall all likewise perish. Or those eighteen, upon whom the tower in Siloam fell, and slew them, think ye that they were sinners above all men that dwelt in Jerusalem? I tell you, Nay: but, except ye repent, ye shall all likewise perish."—LUKE xiii. 1–5.

IT is a part and duty of spiritual wisdom, as also an evidence of a due reverence of God, to take notice of *extraordinary occurrences* in the dispensations of his providence; for they are instructive warnings, and of great importance in his government of the world. In them the "voice of the LORD crieth unto the city, and the man of wisdom shall see his name." And there is a mark left on them,—as profligate persons,—who will not see when his hand is so lifted up. An example of this wisdom is given us here in our blessed Saviour, who, on the report that was made unto him of some severe providential accidents, then newly fallen out, gives an *exposition* of the mind of God in them, with an *application* of them unto the present duty of them that heard him, and *ours* therein.

Some things may be observed in general, to give light into the context, and the design of our Saviour in this holy discourse.

I. The *time* when the things mentioned did fall out, and wherein our Saviour passed his judgment on them.

1. It was a time of *great sin*,—of the abounding of all sorts of sins. The *nation* as such, in its rulers and rule; the *church* as such, in its officers, order, and worship; and the generality of the *people*, in their personal capacities, were all overwhelmed in provoking sins. Hypocrisy, oppression, cruelty, superstition, uncleanness, persecution,

impenitency, and security,—all proceeding from unbelief,—had filled the land, and defiled it. We have a sufficient account of this state of things in the story of the gospel, so as that it needs no other confirmation. Yea, so wicked were the people, and so corrupt the church-state, and so impenitent were the generality of them therein, that it suited the righteousness and holiness of God to revenge on that generation, not only their own sins, but the sins also of all wicked persecutors from the foundation of the world;—a thing which he doth not do but on high provocations. Luke xi. 50, 51, "That the blood of all the prophets, which was shed from the foundation of the world, may be required of this generation; from the blood of Abel, unto the blood of Zacharias, which perished between the altar and the temple: verily I say unto you, It shall be required of this generation."

There is in this *commination* an appearance of severity beyond the rule established, Exod. xx. 5. There, God declares that he is "a jealous God;" which title he assumes to himself with respect unto the highest provocations;—that he "will visit the iniquity of the fathers upon the children unto the *third* and *fourth* generation of them that hate him." But here, the vengeance and punishment due unto the sins of a *hundred* generations, is threatened to be inflicted on that which was present.

Something, in our passage, may be spoken for the vindication of divine justice herein, seeing we may be more concerned in that divine commination than the most are aware.

(1.) The *case* here is *particular*. That in the commandment respects the *common case* of all false worshippers and their posterity; but this respects persecution, unto blood and death, of the true worshippers of God. Now, though God be very much provoked with the sins of false worshippers, yet he can either bear with them, or pass over their sins with lesser punishments, or at least for a long season; but when they come to persecution, and the blood of them who worship him in spirit and in truth, in his appointed season he will not spare them;—their own, and the iniquities of their predecessors, shall be avenged on them; which will be the end of the antichristian church-state after all its present triumph.

(2.) All those who, from the beginning of the world, suffered unto blood on the account of religion, suffered *in the cause of Christ*, for their faith in him, and confession of him; namely, as he was promised unto the church. Unto him and his office did Abel, by faith, bear testimony in the bloody sacrifice that he offered. So it is said that Moses, in his danger for killing the Egyptian, bare "the reproach of Christ," because he did it in faith of the promised seed; which was Christ. They were, therefore, all slain in the cause of Christ. And whereas this generation was to *slay Christ himself*, and did so, they did, therein, approve of and justify all the blood that was shed in the same cause from the foundation of the world; and made themselves justly liable unto the punishment due unto it. Hence, our Saviour tells them, Matt. xxiii. 35, that they, the men of that generation, slew Zechariah, who was actually slain many hundred years before.

(3.) Our blessed Saviour mentions Abel and Zechariah particularly. This Zechariah, called the son of Barachias, was undoubtedly the Zechariah mentioned, 2 Chron. xxiv. 20–22. For concerning those two alone it is observed, that the one dead, and the other dying, "cried for vengeance." So God testifieth of the blood of Abel, Gen. iv. 10. And Zechariah, when he died, said, "The LORD look upon it, and require it." Hence the apostle affirms, that "Abel being dead, yet speaketh," Heb. xi. 4; that is, his blood did so,—it did so then, and it spake for vengeance, as he intimates, chap. xii. 24. It did so before and until the destruction of Jerusalem: for in the rejection and absolute destruction of that *apostatized church* and people, the blood of all that suffered under the Old Testament was expiated. Abel's blood cries no more; nor doth God look any more on the blood of Zechariah to require it.

But the same voice and cry is now continued by another sort of men; namely, those who have suffered in the cause of Christ since his coming, according to the promise, Rev. vi. 9, 10. And this cry shall be continued until the appointed time doth come for the utter destruction of the *antichristian, apostatized church-state.*

When a sinful church or people have passed the utmost bounds of divine patience and forbearance, they shall fall into such abominable, crying sins and provocations as shall render the utmost vengeance beneath their deserts. So Josephus affirms of this generation, after they had rejected and slain the Lord Christ, that they fell into such a hell of provoking abominations, that if the Romans had not come and destroyed them, God would have sent fire and brimstone upon them from heaven, as he did on Sodom.

And we may, by the way, observe from hence,—

It is a dangerous thing to live in the times of declining churches, when they are hastening unto their fatal period in judgments; such as will inevitably befall them all and every one.

And it is so for these three reasons:—

[1.] Because such times are *perilous* through temptations from *the abounding of the lusts of men* in all uncleanness and wickedness. So the apostle states it, 2 Tim. iii. 1–5. If any think they are free from danger, because as yet they feel no evil, whilst the lusts of men professing Christian religion visibly and openly abound and rage in the world, they will be mistaken.

[2.] Though destruction do not immediately befall them, yet, when they have passed the time of divine patience designing their reformation, they shall precipitate themselves into *bloody abominations*, as did the church of the Jews.

[3.] Judgment shall at length overtake them, and God will revenge on them the sins and provocations—especially the *persecutions and blood*—of them that went before them, and led them into their apostasy. So when he shall come to destroy mystical Babylon, or the antichristian church-state, it is said, that "in her was found the blood of the prophets, and of saints, and of all that were slain upon the earth," Rev. xviii. 24. Even the blood of saints that was shed by pagan Rome shall be avenged on antichristian Rome, after she hath espoused the cause and walked in the way of the other, justifying in her own practice what they had done.

2. It was *a time wherein judgments were near approaching;*—so our Saviour himself affirms it to have been, Luke xix. 42–44, "If thou hadst known, ... in this thy day." They had now but *a day*, and that now almost ready to expire, though they saw it not, nor would believe it. But the day of their desolation approached continually, and when the apostle wrote his Epistle to the Hebrews, was making its entrance upon them, chap. x. 25, "Ye see the day approaching." And we may hence learn,—

(1.) That *in the approaching of desolating judgments on a sinful, provoking church or nation, God is pleased to give previous intimations of his displeasure*, as well in the works of providence as by the rule of his word. Such were those here so interpreted by our Saviour in such a season.

This, I say, is the ordinary process of divine Providence; and, it may be, no nation, heathen or Christian, ever utterly perished without divine warnings of their approaching desolation. Some, indeed, seem to be taken away with a sudden surprisal, as God threateneth, Ps. lviii. 9–11.

But this is from their own security, and not for want of warnings. So the old world before the flood had warnings sufficient of their destruction, by the preaching of Noah, and the building of the ark, by which he "condemned the world," Heb. xi. 7, or left them inexcusable, to divine vengeance. Yet they took no notice of these things, but were surprised with the flood, as if they had never heard or seen any thing that should give them warning of it; as our Saviour declares, Matt. xxiv. 38, 39. And when the time comes of the destruction of mystical Babylon, she shall say, in that very day wherein her judgments come upon her, "I sit as a queen, and shall see no sorrow," notwithstanding all her warnings in the pouring out of the vials of previous judgments, Rev. xviii. 7, 8.

(2.) *It is the height of security, in such a time and season, either to neglect the consideration of extraordinary providences, or to misinterpret them, as any thing but tokens of approaching judgments, if not prevented.*

Nothing can be questioned herein without an arraignment of the divine wisdom of our Lord Jesus Christ, in the interpretation and application that he makes of these accidents. No doubt but they were neglected and despised by the most as common things;—to take any great notice of such occurrences is esteemed pusillanimity or superstition. So it is by many at this day, wherein all things, as we shall see afterward, are filled with tokens of divine displeasure; but things will come shortly unto another account. In the meantime, it is safe to follow this divine example, so as to find out sacred warnings in such providential occurrences.

II. The *providential accidents* spoken of are two, and of two sorts.

1. The first was that wherein *the bloody cruelty of men* had a hand,—"The Galileans, whose blood Pilate had mingled with their sacrifices." When this was done, on what occasion, and what was the number of the persons so slain, the Scripture is silent. However, it is certain that it was done at Jerusalem; for sacrifices might not be offered anywhere else. Thither came the Galileans with their sacrifices;—that is, either the beasts which they brought to the priests to offer for them, for they might not offer sacrifices themselves; or the paschal lamb, which they might slay themselves.

Whilst they were engaged in this work, Pilate, the bloody Roman governor (on what occasion or provocation is unknown), came upon them, and slew them in a cruel manner; intimated in that expression, that "he mingled their blood with their sacrifices." And this providence is the more remarkable, in that it fell out whilst they were engaged in their sacred worship;—which carries an indication of divine severity. And, it may be, there was, as it is in the ruin of mankind every day, occasion taken for it from the difference that was between two wicked governors, Pilate and Herod, unto whose jurisdiction these Galileans did belong, in whose blood Pilate thought to revenge himself on his enemy. However, they both combined at last in the killing of Christ,—as others use to do in the world; and so made themselves friends, leaving their example to their successors.

2. The other was *a mere effect of divine Providence;*—the death of eighteen men by the fall of a tower in Siloam; that is, a place of waters, and a running stream in Jerusalem itself. And our Lord Jesus Christ declares herein, not only that all such accidents are disposed by the providence of God, but that he speaks in them for our instruction.

Both these, as they were *warnings*, as we shall see, so they were *figures* of the approaching destruction of the city and people; for that, in the first place, is the perishing here intended, as is manifest in the ensuing parable, wherein the church-state of the Jews is compared unto a barren fig-tree, which was to be cut down and destroyed. And, accordingly, that destruction did befall them, partly by the bloody *cruelty of the Romans*, and partly by the *fall and ruin of the temple, towers, and walls of the city;* both included in the word, "likewise:" "Ye shall likewise perish," or in like manner. But although they were of various kinds, and men might evade the consideration of them on several pretences,—the one being nothing but the *tyrannical fury* of Pilate, the other only a somewhat *unusual accident,*—yet our Lord Jesus Christ finds out the hand and counsel of God in them both, and declares the same language to be spoken in them both. Signs of the same event are *doubled,* to show the certainty of it, like Pharaoh's dreams.

And we may observe,—

First. *That all sorts of unusual accidents, or effects of Providence, in a season of sin and approaching judgments, are of the same indication, and ought to have the same interpretation.*

So is the same application made of both these different signs and warnings by our Saviour;—they have, saith he, the same language, the same signification. There was nothing at this time [that] more hardened the Jews unto their utter ruin, than the false application they made of providential signs and warnings, which were all multiplied among them, as boding their good and deliverance, when they were all tokens of their approaching ruin. For when such things are rejected as warnings, calling to repentance and reformation, as they were by them, on a presumption that they were signs of God's appearance on their behalf, they became to be nothing but certain forerunners of greater judgments, and infallible tokens of destruction; and so they will be to them likewise by whom they are yet despised.

Secondly. *God is pleased sometimes to give warnings of approaching judgments, not only as unto the matter of them, that they shall be accompanied with severity, but also as unto the especial nature and manner of them.* So was it with these two signs, of *blood* by the sword, and *death* by the fall of the tower; representing as in a glass that common calamity which was to befall the city and nation. And I pray God that the prodigious appearance of fiery meteors, like swords, armies, and arms, with other things of the like nature, may not be sent to point out the very kind and nature of the judgments which are coming on England, if not diverted; for as unto these signs not only the Scripture, but all heathen stories are filled with an account of them. Before the approach of desolating judgments, nature, the common parent of mankind, did always put itself forth in *irregular, unusual actings,*—in fiery meteors, comets, earthquakes, strange appearances in the air, voices heard, and the like.

The brute elements tremble at the approaches of God in his judgment against the inhabitants of the earth. So the prophet expresseth it, Hab. iii. 10, " The mountains saw thee, and they trembled: the overflowings of the water passed by: the deep uttered his voice, and lifted up his hands on high."

They are, as it were, cast into a posture of trembling and supplication. And Æschylus, a heathen poet in Justin Martyr, [thus writes]:—

Τρέμει δ' ὄρη, καὶ γαῖα καὶ πελώριος
Βυθὸς θαλάσσης, κῶρέων ὕψος μέγα,
Ὅταν ἐπιβλέψῃ γοργὸν ὄμμα δεσπότου.

" When the dreadful eye of God (in his providence) is lifted up," all things tremble before it.

III. In the interpretation and application made of these severe accidents by our Saviour, in his divine wisdom, we may observe,—

1. *Especial judgments in such a season, befalling in any, do not prove an especial guilt or provocation in them.* This our Saviour expressly denies, and that with respect unto both the instances insisted on, and that distinctly, verses 2, 4. I do not hence absolutely establish a general rule as unto all times and persons. For,—First, The observation is here confined and limited unto such a season as that under consideration; namely, a time of provoking sins in the generality of the people, and approaching judgments. In such a season, no assignation of especial guilt ought to be made on especial calamitous sufferings. Secondly, Some persons may be guilty of such *daring, presumptuous sins*, that if they are overtaken with especial judgments in this world, it is the height of impiety not to own the especial revenging hand of God in their destruction. Such was the death of Herod, Acts xii. 22, 23.

2. *Judgments on private men in such a season are warnings to the public.* This is intimated by our Saviour in this place; namely, that God uses a sovereignty herein, by singling out whom he pleaseth, to make them examples unto others. This, saith he, was the sole reason, as far as you are concerned to judge or know, why God brought these sore destructions upon them; namely, that by these warnings he might call you to repentance. Yet, I judge, God doth not ordinarily exercise his sovereignty in this kind, unless it be when all have deserved to be destroyed: and then, as in the sedition and mutiny of military legions, they decimated them, or slew some for an example and terror unto others; so God calls out of a guilty multitude whom he pleaseth, to make previous instances of approaching judgments.

3. *Those who first fall under judgments are not always the worst that judgments shall befall; nor are the first judgments usually the most severe;*—so it is plain in these instances. And because we have

instances of this nature amongst us, we should consider how to make a right judgment concerning them. And these three things we may safely determine:—1. That those who suffered were sinners also, though they were not so only, or in an especial manner.[1] This is necessary unto the vindication of the justice of God. 2. That he who hath made them warnings unto us, might have made us warnings unto them. Herein his sovereignty and mercy towards us who escape is manifest. 3. That we also have a hand in that guilt, forerunning such providences so far as there is any thing penal in them. For such private previous judgments are the effect of public provocations.

IV. Here is a sure rule given us of the interpretation of *severe providences* in such a season as that here intended;—such, I mean, as we have had amongst us, in *plague*, and *fire*, and *blood;* and such as we have the signs and tokens of at this time in heaven and earth. For three things we are here taught safely to conclude concerning them:—First, That they are *warnings* from God. This our Saviour plainly declares in the interpretation and application of these two instances. Secondly, That their voice and language is a call to *repentance and reformation:* "Except ye repent," etc. Thirdly, When they are neglected as warnings, calling to repentance, they change their nature, and become certain *signs* of approaching destruction. And in the observation of these rules of interpretation of providential severities given us by our Saviour, we may be preserved from the excesses of neglecting, on the one hand, what is contained in them, and of rash judging of men or causes, on the other.

These things being premised for the opening of the words, the truth wherein we are instructed by them appears to be this:—

When a land, a nation, a city, a church, is filled with sin, so as that God gives them warnings or indications of his displeasure by previous judgments, or other extraordinary signs, if they are not as warnings complied withal by repentance and reformation, they are tokens of approaching judgments, that shall not be avoided.

This is the sacred truth which our Lord Jesus Christ doth here recommend to our observation. It is the great rule of divine Providence, with the especial seal of our Lord Christ annexed to it, "I tell you, Nay; but, unless ye repent, ye shall all likewise perish." When warnings for instruction are not received, they are tokens of destruction. This is a truth which none almost deny, and none almost believe. Had it been believed, many desolating judgments in former ages had been prevented; nations and cities should have abode in prosperity, which are now sunk into ruin, yea, into hell. See Luke xix. 41–44; Matt. xi. 23. And were it believed in the days wherein

[1] These things were spoken on the burning of several persons to death in one of the late fires in London.

we live, it would be the means of saving a poor nation from otherwise inevitable ruin. The state is so with us, that, unless we repent, we shall perish. I do not prescribe unto the sovereignty of God in his providential administrations. He can, if he please, suffer all his warnings to be despised, all his calls neglected, yea, scoffed at, and yet exercise forbearance towards us, as unto a speedy execution of judgment. But woe unto them with whom he so deals; for it hath only this end, that they may have a space to fill up the measure of their iniquities, and so be fitted for eternal destruction, Rom. ix. 22.

There is a threefold issue and event of the state we have described.

1. When a *sinful church or nation* so attend unto God's warnings in *previous judgments*, and other signs of his displeasure, as to comply with them by repentance and reformation. This is a blessed issue, which will certainly divert all impendent judgments; as shall be afterward declared.

2. When, by reason of the neglect of them, and want of compliance with them, God doth bring distress and calamities upon a people in general. This is a sad event. But, however, under it God doth often preserve a seed and remnant which, being brought through the fire, and thereby purged and purified, though but as a poor and afflicted people, yet they shall be preserved as a seed and reserve for a better state of the church. See Zech. xiii. 8, 9; Isa. vi. 11–13, xxiv. 6, 13; Zeph. iii. 12; Ezek. v. 2, 12.

3. When God utterly forsakes a people, he will regard them no more, but give them up unto *idolatry, false worship,* and all sorts of wickedness. When he says, "Why should ye be stricken any more? ye will revolt more and more,"—this is the sorest of judgments. "Woe also to them," saith the Lord, "when I depart from them!" Hos. ix. 12. Of such a people there shall be neither hope nor remnant, Ezek. xlvii. 11. Who would not rather see a nation suffering under some judgments, as the effects of God's displeasure for the neglect of his warnings, whereby it may be purged, and purified, and restored, than to be left under idolatry and all manner of wickedness for ever?

But the way is here proposed for the avoidance of these evils. And these things will be more fully spoken unto afterward.

I shall first give some evidences of the truth laid down, and then the reason of it; which will make way for what I principally intend.

I shall not insist on the *especial kind* of warnings or signs here mentioned, but only on the *general nature* of divine warnings, by the word or otherwise, in such a season as wherein an abounding of sin is accompanied with great evidences of approaching judgments.

1. According unto this rule was the dealing of God with the *old*

world; which is set forth unto us for an example. See 1 Pet. iii. 20; 2 Pet. ii. 5.

The men of the *old world* were a sinful, provoking generation. God gave them warning of his displeasure by the preaching of Noah, and other ways. During his ministry, the long-suffering of God waited for their repentance and reformation; for this was the end both of the season and of the ministry granted unto them therein: but when it was not complied withal, he brought the flood on those ungodly men.

2. So he dealt with *the church under the Old Testament.* A summary account is given of it, 2 Chron. xxxvi. 15–17. After a contempt of all God's previous warnings, with a neglect of repentance and reformation, the time came when there was no remedy, but the city and temple must be destroyed, and the people be partly slain, and partly carried into captivity. Accordingly, there is a general rule established for all times and seasons, Prov. xxix. 1.

3. Neither have his dealings been otherwise with the *churches of the New Testament.* All those of the first plantation have been ruined and destroyed by the sword of God's displeasure, for impenitency under divine calls and warnings.

4. God gave an eminent instance hereof in the *ministry of Jeremiah the prophet.* He gives him the law of his prophecy, chap. xviii. 7, 8, "At what instant I shall speak concerning a nation, and concerning a kingdom, to pluck up, and to pull down, and to destroy it; if that nation, against whom I have pronounced, turn from their evil, I will repent of the evil that I thought to do unto them." Here is the whole of the truth laid down represented unto us. The nation and kingdom especially intended was that of the people and church of the Jews. Concerning them it is supposed that they were evil, —that sin abounded amongst them. In this state God gave them warning by the ministry of Jeremiah, as he did otherwise also. The voice of these warnings was, that they should repent them of their evil, and reform their ways. On a supposition whereof he promises to remove the judgments which they had deserved, and which were impendent over them: upon their failure herein, he declares that fearful desolation should befall them; as it did afterward, verses 15–17. According to this rule, the prophet persisted in his ministry. The sum of his sermon was this: *It is a time of great sin and provocation;—these and these are your sins;—these are evident tokens of God's displeasure against you, and of the near approaching of desolating judgments. In this state, repent, return, and reform your ways, and you shall be delivered:—in case you do not, utter destruction shall come upon you.*

But the princes, the priests, and generally all the people, set themselves against him herein, and would not believe his word.

And by three things they countenanced themselves in their unbelief and impenitency, that they should be delivered; although they did not *repent* nor *reform* their ways.

First. By their *privileges;*—that they were the only church and people of God, who had the temple and his worship amongst them: as if he should say, *The best reformed church in the world.* This they directly confront his ministry withal, chap. vii. 3, 4. They fear none of his threatenings, they despise his counsel for their safety, approve their ways and their doings, because they were the church, and had the temple for their security.

Secondly. By their own *strength for war,* and their defence against all their enemies. They gloried in their wisdom, their might, and their riches; as he intimateth, chap. ix. 23.

Thirdly. By the help and aid which they expected *from others, especially from Egypt.* And herein they thought once that they had prevailed against him, and utterly disproved his rule of safety by reformation only; for when the Chaldeans besieged the city, by whom the judgments he had threatened them withal were to be executed, Pharaoh, the king of Egypt, coming up against them, they departed from Jerusalem for fear of his army, chap. xxxvii. 5, 11. Hereon, no doubt, they triumphed against him, and were satisfied that their own way for deliverance was better than that troublesome way of repentance and reformation which he prescribed unto them. But he knew from whom he had his message, and what would be the event of the false nopes and joys which they had entertained. So he tells them, verses 9, 10, " Deceive not yourselves, saying, The Chaldeans shall surely depart from us: for they shall not depart. For though ye had smitten the whole army of the Chaldeans that fight against you, and there remained but wounded men among them, yet should they rise up every man in his tent, and burn this city with fire." Which accordingly came to pass.

And so it will be with any other people, against all pleas and pretences to the contrary.

Let the case be stated according as it is laid down in the proposition, and explained in the instance of Jeremiah.

Suppose a church or people do abound *with provoking sins;* that, during the time of God's patience towards them, and warning of them, there are signs and tokens of his displeasure and of impendent judgments;—let them feed themselves so long as they please with hopes of deliverance and safety,—unless they comply with the calls of God unto repentance and reformation, they will fall under desolating judgments, or be utterly forsaken of God for ever.

The grounds and reasons of this rule and order in divine dispensations are many, plain and obvious; which I shall not at large insist upon.

I shall only at present mention some of them; because those of the most evidence and importance will accrue afterward unto our consideration:—

1. This rule of proceeding is suited unto *the righteousness of God in the government of the world*, in the inbred light of the minds of men. This notion, that *judgment or divine vengeance will overtake impenitent sinners, who have been previously warned of their sin*, is that which we are not taught, which we do not learn from one another,—which is not only the voice of divine revelation, but that which is born with us, which is inseparable from our nature; the light and conviction whereof, neither with respect unto ourselves or others, we can avoid. This is the voice of nature in mankind, *Impenitent sinners, incurable by warnings, are the proper objects of divine displeasure.* And the absolute impunity of such persons would be a great temptation unto atheism, as the suspension of deserved judgments on provoking sinners is with some at this day. But ordinarily and finally, God will not act contrary unto the *inbred notions* of his righteousness in the government of the world, which he himself hath implanted in the minds of men. But as for the times, seasons, and ways of the execution of his judgments, he hath reserved them unto his own sovereignty.

2. It is needful unto *the vindication of the faithfulness of God in his threatenings*, given out by divine revelation. By this he hath always, from the beginning of the world, testified unto his own holiness and righteousness, whereof they are the most proper expressions. Those first recorded of them are in the prophecy of Enoch, Jude 14, 15. And they have been since continued in all ages. But whereas the wisdom of God, acting in righteousness, hath been accompanied with patience and forbearance in the accomplishment of these threatenings, there have been, and yet are, mockers and scoffers at these divine threatenings, as though they were a mere noise, of no efficacy or signification. So the apostle declares the thoughts of the minds of men profane and ungodly, 2 Pet. iii. 3, 4. Wherefore, there is a condecency unto the divine excellencies, that God, in his own way and time, should vindicate his faithfulness in all his threatenings.

3. God hereby manifests himself to be a God hearing prayers, regarding the cries of his poor and distressed witnesses in the world. When the world abounds in provoking sins, especially in blood and persecution, there is a conjunct cry unto God of those that have suffered, and those that do suffer, in heaven and earth, for vengeance on obstinate, impenitent sinners. See Luke xviii. 7, 8; Rev. vi. 10. The voices of all those, I say, who have suffered unto death in foregoing ages, for the testimony of Jesus, and are now in heaven, in a

state of expectancy of complete glory, with all those of them whose sighs and groans under their oppressors do at present ascend unto the throne of God, have the sense in them, by divine interpretation, that *punishment be inflicted on impenitent sinners;* as is plainly expressed by our Saviour in that place of the gospel affirming that he will avenge his elect speedily, who cry unto him day and night. Herein God will vindicate his glory, as the God that hears prayers.

4. A sense of this divine truth is a great and effectual means of God's rule in the hearts of men in the world, setting bounds to their lusts, and restraining that superfluity of wickedness and villany which would otherwise take away the distinction, as to sin, between the earth and hell. If men can at any time free themselves from the terror and restraining power of this consideration, that *vengeance is always approaching towards impenitent sinners,* there is nothing so vile, so profane, so flagitious, as that they would not wholly give up themselves unto it, Eccles. viii. 11, "Because sentence against an evil work is not executed speedily, therefore the heart of the sons of men is fully set in them to do evil." And God knows, that if impunity in this world should always accompany provoking sinners, the temptation would be too strong and powerful for the faith of weak believers; which he will therefore relieve by frequent instances of his severity.

In a successive continuation of *previous judgments* on impenitent sinners, there is an uncontrollable evidence given of the certainty of that *final judgment* which all mankind shall be called unto. So the apostle proves it, and intimates that it is a foolish thing,—the effect of obstinacy in sin,—if men do not learn the certain determination and approach of the eternal judgment, from the drowning of the old world, the conflagration of Sodom, with the like instances of divine severity, 2 Pet. iii. 3.

My present inquiry hereon is, What is our own concernment in these things,—what are we, for our own good, to learn by the *blessed instruction* given us by our Lord Jesus Christ, in his interpretation of the providential occurrences mentioned in the text?

And this I shall manifest by an impartial inquiry into the things ensuing:—

I. When doth a church, a nation, a people, or city, so abound in sin, as to be immediately and directly concerned in his divine warning; and what, in particular, is the case of the nation wherein we live, and our own therein?

II. Of what sort are those desolating judgments, which, in one way and sense or another, are impendent with respect unto such a church or nation, and, consequently, unto ourselves, at this season?

III. What warnings, calls, and indications of divine displeasure, and the approach of calamitous distresses, doth God usually grant, and what he hath given, and is giving unto us at present?

IV. What is the equity, and wherein it doth consist, of the divine constitution here attested by our blessed Saviour, that in such a case repentance and reformation, and nothing else, shall save and deliver a church, a people, a nation, from ruin?

V. Whereas this rule is so holy, just, and equal, whence is it that all sorts of men are so unwilling to comply with it, even in the utmost extremity, when all other hopes do fail and perish; and whence is it so amongst ourselves at this day?

VI. What is required unto that reformation which may save any nation—this wherein we live—from desolating calamities when they are deserved?

VII. From what causes at present such a reformation may be expected, and by what means it may be begun and accomplished, so as to prevent our utter ruin?

VIII. What is the duty, what ought to be the frame of mind in true believers, what their walk and work, in such a season, that, in case all means of delivery do fail, they may be found of Christ in peace at his coming; for it is but "yet a little while, and he that shall come will come, and will not tarry?"

These things are necessary to be inquired into, that we may help to beat out the paths of truth and peace,—the only ways that lead unto our deliverance. The nation is filled with complaints and fears: *mutual charges* on one party and another, as unto the causes of our present troubles and approaching dangers,—various designs and contrivances, with vain hopes and vehement desires of this or that way or means of help and deliverance,—cruel hatred and animosities on differences in religion, designing no less than the extirpation of all that is good therein,—do abound in it, by all means rending itself in pieces, wearying itself in the *largeness of its ways;* and yet [it] says not that there is no hope. But for the most part, the true causes of all our troubles and dangers, with the only remedy of them, are utterly neglected. The world is filled, yea, the better sort of men in it, with other designs, other discourses;—we hear rarely of these things from the pulpits (which are filled with animosities about petty interests, and private difference in the approaches of public ruin), nor in the counsel of those who pretend to more wisdom. Some think they shall do great things by their wisdom and counsel, some by their authority and power, some by their number, some by owning the best cause, as they suppose; and with many such-like notions are the minds of men possessed. But the truth is, the land abounds in sin,—God is angry, and risen out of his holy place,—judgment lies at the door;

and in vain shall we seek for remedy or healing any other way than that proposed. This, therefore, we shall inquire into.

The first thing supposed in the proposition before laid down was taken from *the circumstance of the time* wherein, and with reference whereunto, our Lord Jesus Christ delivered the rule of *the necessity of repentance and reformation, unto an escape from total destruction;* and this was *a time when sin greatly abounded in the church and nation.* And this supposition is the foundation of the truth of the whole assertion; for in other cases it may not always hold.

I. Our first inquiry must, therefore, be,—"When is a people or nation so filled with sin, or when doth sin so abound among them, as, in conjunction with the things afterward to be insisted on, to render their salvation or deliverance impossible, without repentance and reformation?" And it doth so,—

First. When *all sorts of sin abound in it.* I do not judge that every particular sin, or kind of sinning, that may be named, or may not be named, is required hereunto; nor is it so, that there should be the same outrage in public sins—for instance, in blood and oppression—as there hath been at some times, and in some places of the world, the dark places of the earth being filled with habitations of cruelty; nor is it so, that sin doth reign at that height, and rage at that rate, as it did before the flood, or in Sodom, or before the final destruction of Jerusalem, or as it doth in the kingdom of Antichrist: for in that case there is no room or place either for repentance or reformation. God hides from them the things that concern their peace, that they may be utterly and irrecoverably destroyed. But this, I will grant, is required hereunto,—namely, that no *known sin* that is commonly passant in the world can be exempted from having a place in the public guilt of such a church or nation. If any such sin be omitted *in the roll of the indictment*, peace may yet dwell in the land. It would be too long, and not to my purpose, to draw up a catalogue of sins—from the highest *atheism*, through the vilest *uncleanness*, unto the lowest *oppression*—that are found amongst us. I shall only say, on the other hand, that I know *no provoking sin*, condemned as such in the book of God, whereof instances may not be found in this nation. Who dares make this a plea with God for it, namely, that yet it is free and innocent from such and such provoking sins? "Produce your cause, saith the LORD; bring forth your strong reasons, saith the King of Jacob;" let us stand up, if we can, and plead for ourselves herein. But the only way whereby we may come to plead with God in this matter is fully described, Isa. i. 16–20. It must be repentance and reformation, laying a ground for pleading and arguing with God for pardon and mercy, that must save this nation, if it be saved, and not a plea for exemption from judgments on the account of our innocency. This is that which, of all things, God most abhorred in the people of old, and which all the prophets testified against in them.

But yet, to speak somewhat more particularly unto the first part of the proposition, in reference unto ourselves,—There are four sins, or four sorts of sins, or ways in sinning, which, unless God prevent, will be the ruin of this nation.

1. The first is *atheism*,—an abomination that these parts of the world were unacquainted withal until these latter ages. I do not speak concerning *speculative or opinionative atheism*, in them that deny the being of God, or, which is all one, his righteous government of the world; for it will not avail any man to believe that God is, unless withal he believe that "he is the rewarder of them that diligently seek him;"—yet, of this sort it is to be feared that there are many amongst us; yea, some that make great advantages of religion, do live and talk as if they esteemed it all a fable. But I speak of that which is called *practical atheism*,—when men live and act as if they were influenced by prevalent thoughts that there is no God. Such the nation is replenished withal, and it exerts itself especially two ways:—

(1.) In *cursed oaths* and blasphemous execrations, whereby the highest contempt is cast on the divine name and being. The most excellent Thuanus,[1] giving an account of the Parisian massacre, with the horrible desolations that ensued thereon, ascribes it, in the first place, unto the anger of God revenging the horrid oaths and monstrous blasphemies which, from the court, had spread themselves over all the nation, Hist., lib. liii. Nor is it otherwise among us at present; though not generally amongst all, yet amongst many, and those unpunished.

(2.) *Boldness, confidence, and security in sinning.* Many are neither ashamed nor afraid to act, avow, yea, and boast of the vilest of sins. The awe that men have of the knowledge, conscience, and judgment of others, concerning their evil and filthy actions, is one means whereby God rules in the world for the restraint of sin. When the yoke hereof is utterly cast away, and men proclaim their sins like Sodom, it is the height of practical atheism. Nor, I think, did it ever more abound in any age than in that wherein we live.

2. *The loss of the power of that religion* whose outward form we do retain. We are all Protestants, and will abide to be of the Protestant religion. But wherein? In the *Confession*, and all the

[1] Jacques-Auguste de Thou, born at Paris in 1553, was made one of the presidents of the *Parlement de Paris* in 1594. The first eighteen books of his History were published in 1604. Though a Roman Catholic, he gives a candid and graphic description of the horrors of St Bartholomew's day; on which account, and for other similar reasons, his work was placed on the "Index Expurgatorius," in 1609.—Ed.

outward forms of the rule and worship of the church. But are men changed, renewed, converted to God, by the *doctrine of this religion?* are they made humble, holy, zealous, fruitful in good works by it? —have they experience of the power of it in their own souls, in its transforming of them into the image of God? Without these things, it is of very little avail what religion men profess. This is that which is of evil abode to the professors of the Protestant religion at this day through the world. The glory, the power, the efficacy of it, are, if not lost and dead, yet greatly decayed; and an outward *carcase* of it, in articles of faith and forms of worship, doth only abide. Hence have the Reformed Churches, most of them, "a name to live," but are dead; living only on a traditional knowledge, principles of education, advantages and interest; —in all which the Roman religion doth every way exceed them, and will carry the victory, when the contest is reduced unto such principles only. And unless God be pleased, by some renewed effusion of his blessed Spirit from above, to revive and reïntroduce a spirit of life, holiness, zeal, readiness for the cross, conformity unto Christ, and contempt of the world, in and among the churches which profess the Protestant religion, he will ere long take away the hedge of his protecting providence, which now for some ages he hath kept about them, and leave them for a spoil unto their enemies. So he threateneth to do in the like case, Isa. v. 5, 6. Such is the state described, 2 Tim. iii. 1–5.

3. *Open contempt and reproach of the Spirit of God, in all his divine operations,* is another sin of the same dreadful abode. Our Lord Jesus Christ tells us, that he who "speaketh against the Holy Ghost, it shall not be forgiven him, neither in this world, neither in the world to come," Matt. xii. 32;—that is, those who persist in opposing or reproaching the Holy Ghost, and his dispensation and operations under the New Testament, shall not escape vengeance and punishment even in this world; for so it befell that generation unto whom he spake. For continuing to do despite unto the Spirit of grace, wrath at length came upon them, even in this world, unto the utmost; which is the sense of the place. Now, scarcely, where the name of Christ was known, did this iniquity more abound than it doth at this day amongst us; for not only is *the divine person* of the Holy Spirit by some denied, and the substance of the preaching and writing of many is to oppose all his peculiar operations, but they are all made a scoff, a derision, and a reproach, openly and on all occasions, every day. Especially as he is a Spirit of *regeneration and supplication,* he is the object of multiplied sober blasphemies. This iniquity will be revenged.

4. *The abounding of uncleanness,* which, having broken forth from a corrupt fountain, hath overspread the land like a deluge. These

sins, I say, among others, have such a *predominancy* among us, as to threaten perishing, without repentance.

Secondly. It is required, *that all sorts and degrees of persons are concerned in the guilt of some of these provoking sins;* for destruction is threatened unto all: "Ye shall all likewise perish;"—all, not universally, "pro singulis generum;" but generally, "pro generibus singulorum." Therefore all must be, in some way, guilty of them. And this they may be three ways:—

1. *Personally,* in their own hearts, lives, and practices; which includes a great multitude.

2. By *not hindering* and preventing these sins in others, so far as their duty leads and their power enables them unto. What number of magistrates, of ministers, of parents, of masters of families are comprised herein, is evident unto all, especially ministers. See Mal. ii. 7, 8; Jer. xxiii. 14, 15.

3. By *not mourning for what they cannot help or remedy;* for it is such alone as shall be exempted from public calamities, Ezek. ix.: and this, in some measure, takes us all in. And the due consideration hereof is necessary upon a double account:—

(1.) It is so unto the manifestation of the glory of God in public calamities and desolations, when the sword slays suddenly, and destroys the righteous with the wicked. One way or other, in one degree or another, we have all of us an access unto the guilt of those things whereby such judgments are procured. Who can say he is innocent? who can complain of his share and interest in the calamities that are coming upon us? who can plead that he ought to be exempted? There will be at last an eternal discrimination of persons; but as unto temporal judgments, we must own the righteousness of God if we also fall under them. And,—

(2.) It is so, for the humbling of our souls under a sense of sin; which would better become some of us, than feeding on *the ashes of reserves* for exemption in the day of distress.

Some may suppose, that, by reason of their *personal freedom* from those public provoking sins which abound in the nation,—that on one account or other, by one means or other, they shall be safe, as in some high place, whence they may look down and behold others in distress and confusion. But it is to be feared their mistake will serve only to increase their surprisal and sorrow.

But yet farther; even the practice of provoking sins abounds among all sorts of persons. I do not say that all individuals amongst us are guilty of them; for were it so, our case were irreparable, like that of Sodom, when there were not ten righteous persons to be found in it,—that is, such as were free from the guilt of those sins whose cry came up to heaven; for then there would be no room for repentance or reformation. But whereas there are several sorts and degrees of persons, some high and some low, some rulers and some ruled, some rich and some poor,—there is no order, sort, or degree, in court, city, country, church, or commonwealth, that are free from provoking sins. Individuals of all sorts may be so, but no entire sort is so. And this farther entitles a nation unto the condition inquired after.

Thirdly. It is so when *the world is full of such sins as are its own,—as are proper to it; and the churches or professors, of such as are peculiar unto them.* If either of these were free from their several provocations, there might be yet room for patience and mercy. And these are distinct.

The sins of the world are, "the lust of the flesh, the lust of the eyes, and the pride of life,"—sensuality, luxury, uncleanness, covetousness, ambition, oppression, and the like, with security. In these things the nation is fertile towards its own ruin.

The sins peculiar unto churches and professors are intimated by our blessed Saviour in his charge on the Asian churches, Rev. ii. iii. —decays in grace, loss of faith and love, barrenness in good works, deadness, formality, coldness in profession, self-pleasing, pride, hypocrisy, want of zeal for God and delight in him, divisions among themselves, and conformity unto the world. And some of these things at present are so prevalent among us, that they can never be sufficiently bewailed.

It is no small evidence that the day of the Lord is nigh at hand, because *the virgins* are all slumbering. And it is not unlikely that judgment will begin at the house of God. All flesh hath corrupted its way; and therefore the end of all, as to its present condition, is at hand.

Fourthly. It is so when the sins of a people are *accompanied with the highest aggravations that they are capable of in this world;* and those arise from hence,—when they are committed against warnings, mercies, and patience. These comprise the ways and means which God in his goodness and wisdom useth to reclaim and recall men from their sins; and by whomsoever they are despised, they treasure up unto themselves "wrath against the day of wrath, and the revelation of the righteous judgment of God," Rom. ii. 4, 5. What can save a people, by whom the only remedies of their relief are despised? What warnings and previous judgments we have had in this nation shall be afterward spoken unto. That there hath been no effect, no fruit of them, is evident unto all. Their language is, "Except ye repent, ye shall perish." Who hath complied with the calls of God herein? what reformation hath been engaged in on this account? Have we not turned a deaf ear to the calls of God? Who hath mourned? who hath trembled? who hath sought for an entrance into the chambers of providence in the day of indignation? By some these warnings have been despised and scoffed at; by some, put off unto others, as their concernment,—not their own; by the most, neglected, or turned into matter of common discourse, without laying them to heart.

And as for mercies, the whole earth hath been turned into a stage for the consumption of them on the lusts of men. The nation hath been soaked with "showers of mercies," enough to have made it very fruitful unto God; but, through a vicious, malignant humour in the hearts of men, there have been truly brought forth nothing but pride, vanity, gallantry, luxury, and security, in city and country, everywhere. The pestilent, deceitful art of sin, hath turned the means of our conversion unto God into instruments of rebellion against God. How will England answer for abused mercies in the day of visitation? And in all these things hath the patience also of God been abused, which hath been extended unto us beyond all thoughts and expectations. And yet, men of all sorts please themselves; as if that, were they over this or that difficulty, all would be well again, without any return unto God.

Fifthly. These things render impendent judgments inevitable, without repentance and reformation, when they are *committed in a land of light and knowledge.* Such the land hath been; and wherein yet there is any defect therein, it is a part of the sin and punishment of the nation. See Isa. xxvi. 10. From the light that was in it, it might well be esteemed "a land of uprightness;" but how it hath been rebelled against, hated, opposed, maligned, and persecuted, in all the fruits of it, is rather (for the sake of some) to be bewailed than declared.

And thus much may suffice to be spoken unto the first supposition in our proposition concerning the sins of a church, nation, or people, which unavoidably expose them unto desolating judgments, when God gives indication of their approach, unless they are prevented by repentance; and we have seen a little, and but a little, of what is our concernment herein.

II. Our second inquiry is, "Of what sort those judgments are, which, in a time of great provocation, are to be looked on as impendent, and ready to seize on us?" And they are of three sorts:—

First. Such as are *absolute, decretory,* and *universal.*

There is mention in the Scripture of judgments threatened, which God hath, as it were, repented him of, and changed the actings of his providence, that they should not be inflicted. See Amos vii. 3, 6. And there are judgments threatened, which have been diverted by the repentance of men; as it was in the case of Nineveh. But in this case, neither *will God repent,* nor *shall man repent*; but those judgments shall be universal and unavoidable. And of this sort we have three instances recorded in Scripture;—two are past, and one is yet for to come:—

1. The first is that of *the old world* It is said that, upon their provocations, "God repented him that he had made man on the earth;" that is, he would deal with him as if he had done so,—which must be by a universal destruction. He would not repent of the evil he had determined; but positively declared that "the end of all flesh was come before him." Nor did man repent; for, as our Saviour testifies, they continued in their security "until the day that Noah entered into the ark," Matt. xxiv. 38. Yet it may be observed, that, after things were come to that pass that there was no possibility of turning away the judgment threatened, yet God exercised forbearance towards them, and gave them the outward means of repentance and reformation, 1 Pet. iii. 20. They had amongst them the ministry of Noah, a preacher of righteousness, and that continued for a long season, in the patience of God.

[And let none please themselves, that they have *the outward means of the ministry* continued unto them; for notwithstanding that fruit of God's patience, their destruction may be inevitable. For as God may grant it unto them to satisfy his own goodness, and glorify his patience; so unto them it may have no other end but the hardening of them in their sin, and the aggravation of their sins, Isa. vi. 9–12. And this example of the old world is frequently proposed, and that to Christians, to professors, to churches, to deliver them from security in a time of approaching judgments.][1]

2. The second instance hereof was in the *Judaical church-state;*—the people, nation, temple, worship, and all that was valuable among them. This judgment also, in its approach, was such as with respect whereunto God would not repent, and man could not repent, although a day, a time and space, of repentance was granted unto them. So it is declared by our Lord Jesus Christ, Luke xix. 41–44. They had a day,—it was theirs in a peculiar manner,—a day of patience and of the means of conversion, in the ministry of Christ and his apostles. Yet, saith he, the things of thy peace are now hid from thee;—so as that they must irrecoverably and eternally perish. So is their state described by the apostle, 1 Thess. ii. 14–16.

But it may be said, If their destruction was so absolutely determined that it was impossible it should be either longer suspended or diverted, unto what end did God grant them a day—such a day of grace and patience—which they could not make use of? I answer, He did it for the manifestation of the glory of his grace, righteousness, and severity; and that these two ways:—

[1] These brackets occur in the original edition, and are retained as they seem to indicate the digressive character of the remark contained in the paragraph.—ED.

(1.) In the calling, conversion, and gathering of his *elect* out of the perishing multitude of them that were hardened. During the continuance of that day of grace and patience among them, for about the space of forty years, all the elect of that generation were converted to God, and delivered from the curse that came upon the church and nation. For although I will not say but some of them might suffer, yea, fall, in the outward public calamities of that season; yet they were all delivered from the wrath of God in them, and saved eternally.

Hereof the apostle gives an account, Rom. xi. 5–10. It is therefore, in a time of great provocations, no certain evidence that inevitable public judgments are not approaching, because the word and other means of grace are effectual to the conversion of some amongst us; for God may hereby be gathering of his own unto himself, that way may be made for the pouring out of his indignation on them that are hardened.

(2.) He did it that it might be *an aggravation of their sin*, and a space to fill up the measure of their iniquity; to the glory of his severity in their destruction,—"Towards them that fell, severity." They had time to contract all the guilt mentioned by the apostle, 1 Thess. ii. 14–16; and were brought into the state and condition described by the same apostle, Heb. x. 26–30. See Isa. vi. 10–12.

Of this judgment and destruction, that of the old world was a precedent and token, which was despised by those obdurate sinners, 2 Pet. iii. 5–7.

3. The third instance of a judgment of this nature, which is yet to come, is in *the destruction of Antichrist*, and the idolatrous kingdom of the great adulteress and the persecuting beast. With respect hereunto, also, God will not repent, nor shall men do so; so that it is inevitable. So is it declared, Rev. xviii. 8. This God hath determined, and it shall be accomplished in its appointed season; "for strong is the Lord God who judgeth" them, and none shall deliver them out of his hand, because of the improbability of it, because of the great power of Babylon in itself, and in its allies, the kings and merchants of the earth. The omnipotency of God is engaged to secure the church of its destruction; "strong is the Lord God who judgeth her." She also hath her day, wherein she *will not*, wherein she *shall not*, repent. When God begins to execute his plagues against her, none that belong unto her will repent of any of their abominations, Rev. ix. 20, 21, xvi. 9, 11. Yet is there a day of patience continued unto this idolatrous, persecuting church;—partly that they may "fill up the measure of their iniquities;" and partly that God may, by the word and means of grace, gather out all his people from amongst them, according unto his call, Rev. xviii. 4. And our slowness in coming forth from them is probably one means of prolonging the day of her

desolation. And now the Lord Jesus Christ seems to say unto his people what the angel said unto Lot, when he led him out of Sodom, Make haste to escape, for I cannot do any thing until you are escaped, Gen. xix. 22. And I hope the time is approaching wherein he will deal with his people as the angel dealt with Lot, verse 16. They are apt to linger, and know not how to leave the outward accommodation of the Babylonish state, nor clear themselves of innumerable prejudices received therein; but he, being merciful unto them, will at length lay hold on them by the word of his power, and take them out of the city in a complete relinquishment of that cursed state.

Now, unto this sort of judgments there are two things concurring:—

1. That there is a *determinate decree* concerning them.

2. That there is a *judicial obduration* upon the people whom they are determined against, accompanying them;—that no calls to repentance or reformation shall be complied withal so as to divert them. I am satisfied, upon such evidence as I shall give afterward, that this is not the condition of England; howbeit we have cause enough to tremble at the severest of divine judgments.

Secondly. The second sort of judgments are such as are *deservedly threatened* and determined, yet so as that no judicial hardness doth go along with them, to make utterly void the preceding day of grace and patience, and all reformation impossible.

They cannot, they shall not, be utterly removed, by a total deliverance from them; but yet they may have many alleviations and mitigations, and be sanctified unto them whom they do befall. A full instance hereof we have in the Babylonish captivity, as an account is given us of it, 2 Kings xxiii. 25–27, "Like unto him was there no king before him, that turned to the LORD with all his heart, and with all his soul, and with all his might, according to all the law of Moses: neither after him arose there any like him. Notwithstanding the LORD turned not from the fierceness of his great wrath, wherewith his anger was kindled against Judah, because of all the provocations that Manasseh had provoked him withal. And the LORD said, I will remove Judah also out of my sight, as I have removed Israel, and will cast off this city Jerusalem, which I have chosen, and the house of which I said, My name shall be there."

God had decreed and determined to cast off Judah and Jerusalem for their sin,—to bring a wasting desolation upon them. When this judgment was approaching, Josiah endeavours a thorough reformation of all things in the land, religious, civil, and moral; yet would not God revoke his sentence of a great calamity on the whole nation. The secret reason hereof was, that the body of the people was hypocritical in that reformation, and quickly returned unto their former abominations, Jer. iii. 10, "Judah hath not turned unto me with her whole heart, but feignedly, saith the LORD." See chap. iv. 18. Howbeit, this reformation of Josiah was accepted with God, and had its influence into the mitigation or sanctification of the ensuing desolation.

And this sort of judgment is very different from that before insisted on. For,—

1. It is but *partial;* there is a remnant always left among a people, that shall escape it. So was there in those days; there was an *escape* of it, a *remnant* whom God delivered and preserved;—which were as a blessing in the cluster, on the account whereof the whole was not utterly destroyed. This the Scripture very much insists on, Isa. lxv. 6–8; Zech. xiii. 8, 9; Amos ix. 8, 9.

2. As it is not *total,* so it is not *final.* Even in the severity of his wrath, God designed the recovery of that people again in the appointed season,—giving promises thereof unto them that feared him. And so it came to pass, in the return of their captivity. See the history hereof, Jer. xxxi. 32. God may have, for our sins, determined a desolating calamity on this nation; yet if there be not a judiciary hardness upon us, it may only be partial, and recoverable;—not as it was with Israel, 1 Kings xiv. 10. See Jer. iv. 27, v. 18, xxx.–xxxii.

3. It was *sanctified and blessed* unto them who were upright and sincere, and who endeavoured the removal of it by reformation, though they suffered in the outward calamity. The good figs, or those typed by them, were carried into captivity; but the dealing of God with them therein was in mercy, Jer. xxiv. 6, 7, "I will," saith God, "set mine eyes upon them for good: and I will build them, and not pull them down; and I will give them an heart to know me, that I am the LORD: and they shall be my people, and I will be their God." Whatever was their outward condition, those internal, spiritual mercies and privileges made it sweet and useful unto them. The third part was brought through the fire, Zech. xiii. 8, 9.

4. God makes this sort of judgment a means fully *to reclaim and reform them,* as many of those who in general suffer under them. They are God's furnace, but not to burn;—they purify and cleanse as silver is tried, and do not burn up as stubble is consumed. So was that church by their captivity purged from their idols for ever. And many other differences of the like nature might be assigned.

And in the consideration of this sort of judgments lies our concernment. Who knows but that God, for our horrible neglect and contempt of the gospel, with all the cursed immoralities and abominations which have ensued thereon, and the cold, dead frame of professors under various means of instruction, hath determined to bring a wasting calamity on this nation, and that he will not turn away from the fierceness of his wrath, but it shall overtake us? If there be a *judicial hardness* upon the land, so as that there is no repentance, no reformation endeavoured in this day of patience and forbearance which we yet enjoy, our desolation will be total, unsanctified, irrevocable; and though another people may be raised up to profess the gospel in the land, yet shall we be unconcerned in the mercy. So hath it been before in this nation, and in all the Christian nations of Europe. Woe unto us, if we thus betray the land of our nativity,—if we thus give it up to be a hissing and astonishment! Hearken not unto vain words; this or that way we shall be delivered: it is the day of our trial, and who knows what will be the evening thereof? But, on the other hand, although a public calamity should be determined irrevocably against us, if we use the day of forbearance unto the ends of it,—in repentance and returning unto God,—we shall at length have all the advantages before mentioned. It will be but *partial;* it will be but *for a time;* it will be *sanctified;*—it will *purify* the church, and restore it unto a more glorious state than ever before.

Thirdly. There are judgments which are *deserved* and *threatened,* but not *decreed* and *determined,* which may be absolutely diverted and escaped. This sort of judgments is frequently mentioned in the Scripture; and so also are frequent deliverances from them, by the ways and means of God's appointment.

And concerning them we may observe,—

1. That *this threatening of approaching judgments,* which yet may be averted, *is a declaration of the ordinary rule of divine justice, according whereunto a nation or people, without an interposition of sovereign mercy, ought to be destroyed.*

God doth not threaten, he doth not give warnings, signs, or indications of approaching judgments, but when they are deserved, and may righteously be executed; nor is there any known rule of the word to give an assurance of the contrary. All that can be said is, "Who knows but that the LORD may repent, and turn from the fierceness of his wrath?"

2. *The threatening of them is an ordinance of God, to call us unto the use of such means as whereby they may be prevented.*

He foretells our destruction, that we may not be destroyed; as it was in the case of Nineveh. And this is the only symptom whereby we find out and discern the nature of threatened impendent judgments. If the consideration of them be an ordinance of God, stirring us up to the diligent use of the means whereby they may be prevented, the design of God is to give in deliverance in the issue. If it doth not, they are inevitable. God holds the balance yet in his hand, and we know not which way we incline. The best prognostication we can take, is from the frame of our own hearts under the threatenings of them.

Here lies the trial of this poor land and nation at this day; judgment is deserved, judgment is threatened, judgment is approaching, —the clouds are the dust of his feet. If all sorts of men turn not to God by repentance,—if we are not humbled for our contempt of the gospel and outrage against it,—if we leave not our provoking sins,—evil will overtake us, and we shall not escape. And yet, on the other hand, by a due application unto him who holds the balance in his hand, mercy may glory against justice, and we may have deliverance.

Those great men who suppose all things pervious unto their wisdom, and conquerable by their industry, who have a thousand flattering contrivances for the safety of a nation, cannot more despise these things than I do all their counsels without them. And when they shall be at a loss, and shall find one disappointment following on the neck of another, those who attend unto the advice of God in this case shall find rest and peace in their own souls. And as for them who scoff at these things, and say, "Where is the promise of his coming?" —that is, in the way of judgment,—"for since the fathers fell asleep, all things continue as they were from the creation;" there needs no regard unto God in these things; trouble us not with the fooleries of your repentance and reformation;—God will "laugh at their calamity," etc., Prov. i. 26, to the end.

This is the second thing we were to insist on, for the clearing and confirmation of the general proposition before laid down.

III. Our third inquiry is, "What evidences we have at present, or what warnings we have had, of approaching judgments?" for this also belongs unto the indispensable necessity of repentance and reformation, upon the approaching of troubles. And they are the ordinances of God unto that end; which when they are despised, desolating judgments will ensue.

And we may, unto this end, observe these things:—

First, *Ordinarily, God doth not bring wasting, desolating judgments on any people, church, or nation, but that he gives them warnings of their approach.*

I say, he doth not *ordinarily* do so; for he may, if he please, surprise a wicked, provoking generation of men with the most dreadful destructions; as he did Sodom and Gomorrah of old. And very many daily are so surprised, as unto their own apprehensions; though, really, God had given them signs of what was coming upon them, but they regarded them not, and so perished as in a moment. But ordinarily, before he executes great and severe judgments, he gives such indications, signs, and warnings of their coming, as that men should be forced to take notice of them, unless they be absolutely hardened and blinded. So he dealt with the old world, in the building of the ark, and the ministry of Noah; so he dealt with the church under the Old Testament, in and by the ministry of the prophets,—see Amos

iii. 6–8; and so he hath done with all others, who have had any knowledge of him or of his ways. They that are wise may discern these things, Hos. xiv. 9; Matt. xvi. 3; Mic. vi. 9; Dan. xii. 10. And in all heathen stories of the times that passed over them, we find remarks of strange indications of approaching desolations. And he doth it for two ends:—

1. For the satisfaction of his own *goodness and love to mankind* in the exercise of patience and forbearance unto the utmost, Hos. vi. 4; as also for the manifestation of the glory of his justice, when he comes to execute the severity of his wrath. When men are surprised with public calamities, they shall not be able to say, Would none tell us of their approach? would none give us warning of them?—had we been told of the terror of the Lord in his judgments, we would have turned from our iniquities, that we might have escaped. In this case, it is usual with God in the Scripture to call heaven and earth to witness against men, that he did warn them, by various means, of what would befall them in the end. This is our principal reason why this weak but sincere "Testimony for God" is published. And this shall be an aggravation of their misery in the day of their distress, when they shall seriously reflect upon themselves as unto their folly, guilt, and obstinacy, in despising the warnings which they had received;—which is a great part of the punishment of the damned in hell, Ezek. xxxix. 23, 24.

2. God doth it for the end under consideration; namely, that they may be *a means to call a poor guilty people unto* that repentance and reformation whereby impendent judgments may be diverted.

Secondly. There are five ways whereby God *giveth warning of the approach of desolating judgments* when a land is full of sin:—

1. He doth it by lesser *previous judgments and severities.* So was it in the instances in the text. The destruction of some by the sword and the fall of a tower, was a warning to the whole nation of the approach of a public calamity, unless they repented. As particular instances are given us hereof in the Scripture, so we have a general account of this method of divine Providence, Amos vii. 1–9. First, God sent the judgment of the *grasshoppers,* which eat up all the grass of the land, and so occasioned a famine. This judgment being not improved unto repentance, he "called to contend by *fire,* which devoured the great deep, and did eat up a part," or consumed their treasure, devouring a part of their substance. But when this also was neglected, then came the "plumb-line" of a levelling desolation.

2. He doth it by *extraordinary and preternatural* operations in the works of nature: such as are comets or blazing stars, fiery meteors, dreadful phantoms or appearances in the air, voices, predictions of uncertain original, mighty winds, earthquakes, stopping the course

of rivers, and the like. An account of these things, as they were to foretell and fore-signify the fatal destruction of Jerusalem, is given us by our Saviour, Luke xxi. 25, 26. And the story of the event in Josephus is an admirable exposition of this prophecy of our blessed Saviour. See Rev. vi. 13, 14. The frame of nature is, as it were, cast into a trembling disorder upon the approaches of God in his wrath and fury, and puts itself forth in extraordinary signs of its astonishment; trembling for the inhabitants of the earth, and calling on them to repent, before the wrath of the Terrible One do seize upon them. So in the Scripture, the seas and rivers, mountains and hills, are represented as mourning, shaking, trembling at the presence of God, when he comes to execute his judgments. See Hab. iii. 6, 8, 10, "He drove asunder the nations; and the everlasting mountains were scattered, the perpetual hills did bow. Was the LORD displeased against the rivers? was thine anger against the rivers? was thy wrath against the sea? The mountains saw thee, and they trembled: the overflowing of the water passed by: the deep uttered his voice, and lifted up his hands on high."

The mountains, hills, seas, rivers bowed, trembled, and lifted up their hands, as crying for compassion. See Ps. xcvii. 2–6. By these signs and tokens in heaven and earth doth God give warnings of his coming to judge the inhabitants of the earth. God doth not work these strange things in heaven above, and the earth beneath, that they should be gazed at only, and made a matter of talk; not that they should be subjects of some men's curiosity, and of the scorn of others. There is a voice in them all,—a voice of God; and it will be to their hurt by whom it is not heard and understood.

3. He doth the same constantly, *by the light of his word.* The general rule of God's ordinary dispensation of providence is fully laid down in the Scripture: "God hath magnified his word above all his name;" so as that no works of providence shall be unsuited to the rule of the word, much less contrary to it, or inconsistent with it. And if we were wise to make application of it unto present affairs and occasions, we should, in most instances, know in general what God is doing. Of old it was said, "Surely the Lord GOD will do nothing,"—that is, in the way of judgments, "but he revealeth his secret to his servants the prophets," Amos iii. 7. What they had by immediate revelation, we may have, in a measure, by the rule of the word, and the declaration which God hath made therein how he will deal with a sinful, provoking people. So, having threatened various sorts of judgments, the prophet adds, "Seek ye out of the book of the LORD, and read: no one of these shall fail," Isa. xxxiv. 16. That this great means of divine warnings may be useful unto us, we are to consider,—

(1.) What are the stable rules given in the Scripture concerning sin, repentance, impenitence, and judgments. Such rules abound in it: and no dispensations of Providence shall interfere with them. God will not give such a temptation unto faith that any of his works should be contradictions unto his word. And if we will learn our present condition from these rules, it will be an *antidote* against security.

(2.) Consider the instances recorded therein of God's dealings with sinful, provoking nations and churches. This God himself directed the people of old unto, when they boasted of their church privileges, sending them to Shiloh, which he had destroyed. And when we find a record in the book of God concerning his severity towards any nation in our circumstances, it is our duty to believe that he will deal so with us also in his time, unless we repent.

(3.) Always bear in mind our *infallible guidance* as unto God's final dealing with impenitent sinners. This the whole Scripture constantly, equally, universally witnesses unto, that it shall be eternal destruction; and this will preserve us from distracting surprisals, when we find things fall out beyond our expectation in a way of severity.

(4.) Consider those signs, marks, and tokens of approaching judgments which are set up in the world; which whoso doth wisely consider, he will not fail in his prognostication of future events. Among these, *abounding in sin with security,* in such persons, nations, cities, and churches, as God is pleased by the gospel to take near unto himself in a peculiar manner, is the most eminent. For those signs are buoys, fixed to show where we shall certainly make shipwreck if we approach unto them. When these rules are observed, when they are diligently attended unto and complied withal, so as that we receive instruction from them, I shall say with some confidence, that every believer shall know what God is doing in a way of judgment, so far as is necessary unto his guidance in his own duty, wherein he shall find acceptance, and not provoke God in the neglect of it.

4. God hath appointed *the ministry of the word* unto the same end. The principal end of the ministry under the gospel is the dispensation of the word of *reconciliation.* But neither is yet this work of giving *warning of approaching judgments* exempted from that office and duty. Christ himself in his ministry preacheth here on this subject. They are watchmen and overseers; and their duty herein is graphically expressed, Ezek. xxxiii. 2–9. When God placeth any as a watchman for a people, one part of his duty is to look diligently after the approach of dangers and evils,—such, I mean, as come on the account of sin; and thereon to awaken and stir up the people to take care of themselves that they be not destroyed. The shepherd is not only to provide good pasture for his sheep, but to keep them

from danger. The watchman " hearkened diligently with much heed, and he cried, A lion," Isa. xxi. 7, 8. Having made a discovery of approaching danger, he cries out to the people, to warn them of it. But if the watchmen are slothful and sleepy; if they are dumb dogs, and cannot bark when evil cometh; if they are light and treacherous persons, blind guides that have no vision; if they also are under a spirit of slumber and security, so as that the people are not warned by them of their danger,—this is one of the most severe tokens of wrath approaching. It is a great warning, when God takes away the means of warning;—when he says unto a people, " I will warn you no more," by giving them such watchmen as are neither faithful nor able to warn them, and by taking away those that are.

5. God gives warnings hereof, by bringing a people into such a posture, condition, and circumstances, as do in their own nature tend unto ruin. Such are cross interests among themselves, incurable divisions, contrary and unsteady counsels, weakness in spirit and courage, mutual distrusts, effeminacy through luxury, with one or other insuperable entanglement; which are the ways and means whereby nations precipitate themselves into a calamitous condition. In general, as unto this previous warning of approaching judgments, God threatens to send among a people who are tending towards ruin, a " moth," and a " hornet." The moth he threatens, Isa. li. 8; Hos. v. 12. Somewhat shall eat up and devour the strength and sinews of the counsels of a nation, as a moth devoureth a garment. Whilst it lies still, it seems, it may be, to be sound and firm;—hold it up to the light, and it appears full of holes, and is easily torn with the finger. So is it with a nation;—whatever outward peace it seems to enjoy, when it is decayed in the wisdom and strength of its counsels, it is easily torn in pieces. And in like manner he sends the hornet unto the same end, Exod. xxiii. 28; Deut. vii. 20;—that is, that which shall vex, disquiet, and torment them, that they shall be ready every one to strike himself, or the next that he meeteth withal. And many of these hornets are at present among us.

These are some of the ways whereby God warneth a people, church, or nation, of approaching judgments.

It concerneth us, now, to inquire how it is, how it hath been with us, with reference hereunto. And I say,—

1. It is *not necessary* that God should use all these ways of warning of a sinful people of approaching desolations, if not prevented by repentance. It is enough, unto the ends of this dispensation of divine wisdom and goodness, if he make use of some of them, or of any one of them in an eminent manner. Wherefore, if any of them have been wanting among us, yet if we have had others of them, it is sufficient to render us inexcusable if we repent not. But,—

2. The truth is, we have, upon the matter, *had them all,* and they have abounded amongst us.

We have had the *previous judgments* of plague, fire, and war.

Some may say they were *desolating judgments themselves;* and so indeed they were. But whereas sin still aboundeth, and no reformation ensued upon them in any places, among any sort of persons, they were but *warnings* of what is yet to come, if not prevented; and their language is, "Except ye repent, ye shall all likewise perish."

We have had *a multiplication of signs,* in the heaven above, and in the earth beneath; such as all mankind have ever esteemed forerunners of public calamities; and the more they are despised, the louder is their voice to the same purpose. God hath continued hitherto his word amongst us, wherein the ordinary rule of his providence in these things is openly declared. And if those unto whom the declaration of the word of God, in the dispensation of it, is committed, have not faithfully warned the people of their danger, their blood may be found at their door. Herein, at present, lies our greatest strait. The *efficacy* of all other calls of God unto repentance depends much on the application of them unto the souls and consciences of men in the *preaching of the word.* But whilst by some this work is despised, at least counted unnecessary, by some it is neglected utterly; and others, by reason of their private capacities, whereby they are disenabled to speak unto magistrates, cities, or the community of the people, think not themselves concerned therein, [and] it is almost wholly laid aside. For what, will some say, doth this speaking unto *a few* in a retirement signify, as unto a general reformation of the people of the land? But whereas we have all sinned in our measures,—churches, and all sorts of more strict professors of religion,—it is every one's duty to be pressing these warnings of God within his own bounds and precincts. And if each of us should prevail but with *one* to return effectually to God, it will be accepted with him, who, in such a season, seeks for a man to stand in the gap, to turn away his wrath, and will save a city for the *sake of ten,* if they be found therein. Let us not pretend that the repentance and reformation called for respect the public enormous sins of the nation, in atheism, profaneness, sensuality, luxury, pride, oppression, hatred of the truth, contempt of the ministry of the gospel, and the like. They do so, indeed, but not only;—they respect also the decays in faith, love, zeal, with love of the world, conformity unto it, lukewarmness, that are found amongst the most eminent professors of religion. This is our present wound; here lies our weakness,—namely, in the want of a quick, active, zealous ministry, to call and stir up magistrates and people to effectual repentance, and turning to God. Unless this be given unto us, I fear we cannot be saved. If it be otherwise,—if we have a ministry that really do attend unto their duty in this matter,—I beg their pardon for other apprehensions: but then I shall think it the most pregnant sign of approaching destruction; seeing it is apparent unto all that their endeavours have neither fruit nor success.

So far have we proceeded with our proposition,—namely, that *sin abounds amongst us;* that *judgments are approaching;* that *God hath given us manifold warnings of their so doing.*

IV. That which, in the next place, we are to speak unto is, "The equity of this divine constitution,—that, in the ordinary way of God's rule and dispensation of his providence, repentance and reformation shall turn away impendent judgments, and procure unto a people a blessed deliverance; and nothing else shall do it:" "Except ye repent, ye shall perish."

That upon repentance they shall be saved and delivered, is intended in the same rule. This is the unalterable law of divine Providence; this shall do it, and nothing else shall so do. The *wisdom and power of men* shall not do it; *fasting and prayer*, whilst we continue in our sins, shall not do it. *Repentance* alone is made the condition of deliverance in this state of things.

Upon this rule did God vindicate the equity of his ways against repining Israel, Ezek. xviii. 29–32: Can any thing be more just and equal? Ruin and utter desolation are ready to fall upon the whole people. This you have deserved by your iniquities and multiplied provocations. In strict justice, they ought immediately to come upon you. But "my ways are equal;" I will not deal with you in a way of strict justice; I will do it in equity, which is a meet temperature of justice and mercy. And this I make evident unto you herein, in that, whilst the execution of judgment is only threatened and suspended, if you make unto yourselves a new heart and a new spirit, in sincere repentance,—if you cast away all your transgressions by thorough reformation of your lives,—iniquity shall not be your ruin. What can be more just, righteous, and equal? Who can complain if, after all this, evil should overtake you, and you shall not escape? The same he pleads again, chap. xxxiii. 10, 11, as in many other places.

That this divine constitution (namely, that repentance and reformation shall save a church, people, or nation, in the state before described, and that nothing else shall do so, however men may please and pride themselves in their own imaginations) is equal, just, and good,—that it is meet it should be so,—that it hath a condecency unto the divine excellencies, and the rule of righteousness in government,—is evident; for,—

First. The *notion of this rule* is inbred in mankind by nature, as was mentioned before. There is no man, unless he be atheistically profligate, but, when he apprehends that evil and ruin, especially as unto his life, is ready to overtake him, and seize upon him, but he reflects on his sins, and comes to some resolutions of forsaking them for the future, so he may be at present delivered from his deplorable condition. Now, all this ariseth from these indelible notions ingrafted on the minds of men:—that all evil of punishment is from God; that it is for sin; that there is no way to avoid it but by repentance and reformation. And those who will not improve this natural light with respect unto the public, will be found, as it were, whether they will or no, to comply with it when it comes to be their own case in particular. Herein lies a thousand testimonies unto the equity of this divine constitution.

Secondly. When this rule is complied withal,—when repentance and reformation do ensue upon divine warnings, whereby peace with God is in some measure attained,—it will give men trust and confidence in him, with expectation of divine relief in their distress; which is the most effectual means for men to be instrumental unto their own deliverance: and, on the other side, when it is neglected, when evil approaches, guilt and terror will haunt the minds of men, and they shall not be able to entertain one thought of divine help; which will render them heartless, helpless, senseless, and betray them into cowardice and pusillanimity, however they may boast at present. If these two sorts are opposed, ten shall chase a hundred, and a hundred put a thousand to flight. And if any nation do openly refuse a compliance with this constitution, if God should send another to invade them, in a way of judgment, they would melt away before them as wax before the fire. When evils compass us about, and are ready to seize upon us, a reflection on the neglect of this rule will disturb our counsels, distract our thoughts, distress our minds, weaken our confidence in God, and dishearten the stoutest of the sons of men, giving them up a prey to their enemies.

Thirdly. This rule or constitution hath an impression of all divine excellencies upon it; namely, of the goodness, patience, wisdom, righteousness, and holiness of God.

If, when judgments are approaching and deserved, men could divert them by their wisdom, courage, or diligence, it would reflect dishonour on God in the government of the world. See Isa. xxii. 7–11. But in this way of the deliverance of any people, there is a salvo for the glory of all the divine excellencies, as is manifested unto all.

When, therefore, in this state, impendent judgments are not absolutely *determined*, yet so *deserved* as that, upon a supposition of continuance in those sins whereby they are deserved, the glory of divine justice cannot be vindicated in the absolute impunity; and whereas God hath now prepared all things, and made them ready for their execution, all means and instruments being girt unto the work, his sword is whetted, and his arrows are fixed in the bow, he will first give warning, then give space and time for repentance, and requires no more for the laying aside of all his preparations for destruction,—surely his ways are equal, kind, and full of mercy.

If men will look for, if they will expect deliverance, without a compliance with these good, holy, just, gracious, equal terms, they will find themselves, in the issue, wofully deceived. And if, after all this, we in this nation should be found in a neglect hereof,—if the nation should continue in its present frame, wherein, of all other means of safety, this seems to be least thought of or regarded,—what shall we plead for ourselves? who shall pity us in the day of distress? Most men now despise these things; but can their hearts endure, or can their hands be strong, in the day that the Lord shall deal with them? But,—

V. Whereas this way, this means of deliverance, is so just, so equal, so reasonable, manifesting itself to the consciences and reason of mankind, owned by the very heathens, and fully confirmed by divine revelation, our next inquiry must be, "Whence it is that there is such an unreadiness, such an unwillingness to comply with this duty as there is; that so many difficulties are esteemed to be in it,—so as that there is little hope it will be found among us in a prevalent degree?"

If men, especially such as are great, and esteem themselves to be wise, are told that this is the way to save and deliver the nation, they turn away in a wrath, as Naaman did when the prophet bid him wash and be clean, when he would have rather expected an injunction of some heroic exploits:—These are thoughts for weak and pusillanimous souls, who understand nothing of state affairs. But it will ere long appear who is wisest,—God or men. But a hard thing it is to prevail with any to think well of it, or to go about it, or to judge that it is the only balm for our wounds.

To find out the cause hereof, I shall briefly consider all sorts of persons who are concerned to plant this healing tree, whose root is repentance, and whose fruit is reformation of life. And they are of three sorts:—1. *Magistrates;* 2. *Ministers;* 3. *The people themselves.*

Unless there be a concurrence of the endeavours of them all, in their several places and duties, there will be no such public work of repentance and reformation wrought as is suited unto the turning away of public calamities. But yet, though it be the express duty of them all, though it be their interest, though it cannot be omitted but at their utmost peril, as unto temporal and eternal events, yet it is a marvellous hard and difficult work to prevail with any of them to engage vigorously in it. Some do not think it necessary;—some, after conviction of its necessity, either know not how to go about it, or linger in its undertaking, or are quickly wearied;—some wish it were done, so as that they may not be at the trouble of it.

Let us consider them distinctly,—

First. As unto *magistrates*. When Jehoshaphat set himself to reform the church, or his kingdom, to escape the judgment that was denounced against them, he appointed for magistrates and judges men fearing God and hating covetousness. And his charge unto them was, "Let the fear of the LORD be upon you; take heed and do it. Thus shall ye do in the fear of the LORD, faithfully, and with a perfect heart," 2 Chron. xix. 7, 9. Without this there will be no public reformation; and therefore the first difficulty of it ariseth from this sort of persons, and that upon two accounts:—

1. That magistrates themselves do live in sin, and love it, and hate to be personally reformed; yea, take delight in them that openly live in sin also,—which is the height of wickedness, Rom. i. 32. When magistrates are profane swearers, or scoffers at the power of religion, or drunkards, or unclean persons, or covetous oppressors, a great obstruction must needs be laid in the way of public repentance and reformation; neither doth this difficulty at present arise merely from their personal sins and miscarriages, but also from the want of conviction, and a sense of their duty in their places, with the account which they must give thereof. For,—

2. They seem not to believe that *the attempting of this work* is any part of their duty, or that they are concerned therein. Let it, therefore, be never so reasonable, so equal, so important, so necessary unto the deliverance and salvation of any people, if those who should further it in the first place do obstruct and hinder it, it will be attended with difficulties. Ill examples and negligence have ruined this nation.

Wherefore, we may lay it down as an assured truth, which the text will confirm,—

That unless magistrates, who have the visible conduct of the people, are convinced that it is their duty to promote the work of repentance and reformation at this time, by their own example, and in the discharge of their offices, the case of this nation is deplorable, and not to be relieved but by sovereign grace and mercy. For what shall the people do, when they see their guides, unto whose pattern they conform themselves, utterly regardless of any such thing? This is one means of the difficulty which is found among us, of affecting the minds of men with this equal constitution.

Secondly. Those who are principally concerned herein are *ministers*, or those who have the administration of the word and ordinances of the gospel committed unto them. Unto these is this work given in charge in an especial manner. They have the principal means of repentance and reformation committed to their management. From them is the beginning and carrying on of this work expected and required. Hereof, as unto their sincerity and diligence, they must give an account at the last day. And if this spring be stopped, whence should the refreshing waters of repentance and reformation arise? But yet herein the principal difficulty of the whole work doth consist. For,—

1. Some there are, pretending unto this office, in whom lies no small part of the *evil* that is to be reformed;—persons who labour among the most forward to fill up the measure of the iniquities of this nation; such as whose ignorance, negligence, profaneness, and debauchery, are, in all their effects, transfused and communicated unto all that are about them. Shall we expect that such persons will be instrumental in the reforming of others, who hate to be reformed themselves? Jer. xxiii. 15. It was so of old. But,—

2. There are very few of this sort of persons who will be at *the charge of carrying on this work.* They may quickly find what it will cost them; for unless they are *exemplary* in it themselves, it is in vain once to attempt the pressing of it upon others. They cannot go about it without great retrenchings of that which they have esteemed their liberty in the course of their conversations. All compliance with unreformed persons, for secular ends; all conformity unto the course of the world, in jollities and pride of life; all ostentation of riches, wealth, and power; all self-seeking and self-pleasing; all lightness and carnal confidences,—must utterly be cast away. And not only so, but unless, by incessant prayers and supplications, with earnestness and perseverance, they labour for fresh anointings with the Spirit of grace in their own souls, that faith, and love, and zeal for God, and compassion for the souls of men, and readiness for the cross, may revive and flourish in them,—they will not be useful, nor instrumental in this work. And is it any wonder that the most of them think it better to suffer things to go on at the present rate, than to venture at that which will cost them so dear in its pursuit? The truth is, I know very few, if any, who are meet and fit to engage in this work in a visible eminent manner;—those who have the best, almost the only, opportunities for it, seem to be asleep.

3. Besides the *charge* they must be at themselves, they perceive the *opposition* they shall meet withal from others. They find that they shall not only disoblige and provoke all sorts of persons, and lose many of their useful friends, but also expose themselves unto

obloquy, scorn, contempt, and reproach of all sorts. He is a lost man in this world, who, without respect of persons, will engage seriously in this work; every day he shall find one or other displeased, if not provoked. This neither they nor their families can well bear withal. Indeed, the hardest and most difficult service that ever God called any of his ministers unto, excepting only Jesus Christ and his apostles, hath been in the endeavouring the reformation of backsliding or spiritually-decayed churches. These are the two witnesses which, in all ages, have prophesied in sackcloth. Such was the ministry of Elijah, which brought him unto that conclusion, and an earnest longing to be delivered by death from his work and ministry, 1 Kings xix. 4. So was that of Jeremiah, in the like season, whereof he so complains, chap. xv. 10. John the Baptist, in the same work, lost first his liberty, then his life. And, in after ages, Chrysostom, for the same cause, was hated by the clergy, persecuted by the court, and at length driven into banishment, where he died. Most men care not how little a share they have in such a work as this, whose reward will reach them according to the proportion of their engagement in it. All churches, all persons almost, would willingly be let alone in the condition wherein they are;—they that would press them unto due reformation, ever were, and ever will be, looked on as their *troublers.*

Hence, then, it is that our wound is incurable:—Few of this sort are convinced of the present necessity of this duty; they hope things are indifferently well with them and their flocks,—that they may endure their time well enough. Few are willing to undergo the charge and trouble of it,—to put all their present circumstances into disorder. Few have received an anointing for the work; many are able to dispute against any attempts of it; and not a few have expectations of strange deliverances without it. What is left us in this case shall afterward be declared.

Thirdly. It is difficult also on the account of the *people* that are to be reformed. It is hard to convince them of its necessity,—hard to persuade them to endeavour it,—hard to get them to persevere in attempts for it.

Some of the reasons hereof we may briefly consider; as,—

1. That *self-justification* and approbation of themselves which all sorts of persons, both by nature and by incurable prejudices, are inclined unto, lie at the bottom of this fatal negligence. When they see all things amiss, they will grant that there is some reformation necessary; but that it is so for others, and not for them. Those that are worse than they (as there are but few who do not think, on one pretence or other, that there are many worse than themselves), they suppose this duty is necessary unto,—but not unto them. And if there are none visibly so, yet they will make them, and judge them

so to be. But whilst men have a form of godliness, though they deny the power thereof, they will justify themselves from all need of reformation. Churches will do so, and all sorts of professors of religion will do so,—especially if they have any peculiar notion or practice which they value themselves upon. So was it with the Jews of old, Jer. vii. 9, 10; and with the Pharisees in the days of our Saviour, John ix. 40. It is so at this day; and it is a rare thing to meet with any who will own themselves to stand in need of real laborious reformation.

Hence it is that *no churches* would *ever reform themselves;* which hath been the cause of all division and separation, whereby some have been saved from a general apostasy. They all approve themselves in their state and condition; which is come to that height in the papal church that they boast themselves infallible, and not *capable of reformation* in any thing. I pray God secure others from the like presumptions! It will be their ruin by whom they are entertained. Yet so it is at this day. Most churches think they need more *revenues*, more *honour*, more *freedom* from *opposition*, more *submission* of all men unto them; but they almost abhor the thought that they stand in need of any *reformation.*

2. The *nature of the work itself* renders it difficult; for it requires a general change of the course wherein men have been engaged;—a thing as difficult as to cause the streams of a mighty river to change their course and run backward. Vicious habits must be subdued,—inclinations rivetted in the mind by long practice and custom be cast out,—ways of conversation promoted and strengthened by all sorts of circumstances changed;—which render the work unto some men impossible. So the prophet declares it, Jer. xiii. 23, "Can the Ethiopian change his skin, or the leopard his spots? then may ye also do good, that are accustomed to do evil." Men cannot easily unlearn what they have been so taught or accustomed unto. The mighty power of God on the souls of men, both as unto individual persons and whole societies, is required unto this change. So it may be wrought, and not otherwise, Isa. xi. 6–9.

3. The advantage which many may make unto themselves by the present posture of things, and fear of alterations by reformation, is a mountain in the way,—a mighty obstacle against entertaining serious thoughts about it.

4. The Scripture most frequently casts the cause hereof on men's *security* in their earthly enjoyments. This keeps them safe from hearing God's calls, or taking notice of his warnings. And therefore it is laid down as the *cause* and *constant forerunner* of all desolating judgments. It is at large insisted upon by our Saviour himself, Matt. xxiv. 37–39; Luke xvii. 26–29.

Now, this security is like the disease in the body which is commonly called the scurvy;—it is not any single distemper or disease, but a complication or concurrence of many prevalent distempers. Security is not the name of any one vicious habit or inclination of the mind, but it is a concurrent complication of many;—spiritual stupidity and sloth, called a spirit of slumber, love of the world, carnal wisdom, groundless hopes of life, all proceeding from unbelief, do concur in its constitution. And if a practice in a course of sin have for some season ensued on these principles, whereby conscience comes to be *seared*, or is made senseless, the case of those in whom it is, is for the most part remediless. And not a few of this sort are amongst us.

And many other reasons there are rendering this work full of difficulty, though it be so necessary, so just and equal. As for those by whom all these things are despised, and even scoffed at, something shall be spoken afterward unto them, or concerning them.

But yet, this consideration ought not to deter any from endeavouring the discharge of their own duty herein. For, as we have seen it is indispensably necessary, that we and the nation may be saved from desolating judgments; so we shall see afterward how and by what means this difficulty may be surmounted, and those obstacles removed out of the way. However, happy will they be, be they never so few, never so poor, never so unknown to the world, whom God *shall find so doing*, when he ariseth out of his place to shake the earth terribly!

VI. I shall, therefore, in the next place, to bring all things nearer home, inquire, "What is the nature of that repentance and reformation which at this time God requires of us all, that we may not perish in his sore displeasure?"

After a devastation made of the treasure of the Roman empire by sundry tyrants successively, Vespasian coming to the government, acquainted the senate that there was need of so many millions of money, that the empire might stand;—not that it might flourish and grow vigorous, whereunto much more was required, but that it might be preserved from dissolution and ruin. And I shall propose, not what is requisite to render the church of God in this nation orderly, beautiful, and vigorous, but only what is necessary that it may stand and live, by a deliverance from desolating judgments. And,—

First. The repentance which, in any case, God requireth *absolutely*, is that which is internal and real, in sincere conversion unto himself, accompanied with fruits meet for such repentance. So is it declared, Ezek. xviii. 30, 31, "Therefore I will judge you, O house of Israel, every one according to his ways, saith the Lord GOD. Repent, and turn yourselves from all your transgressions; so iniquity shall not be your ruin. Cast away from you all your transgressions, whereby ye have transgressed; and make you a new heart and a new spirit, for why will ye die, O house of Israel?" A new heart and a new spirit, or real internal conversion unto God, by the grace of the covenant, is required in this repentance, as the renunciation and relinquishment of all iniquities must be the *fruit* of it. So also is it expressed, Isa. i. 16, 17. Internal purification of the heart, with the practice of universal obedience, and abstinence from all sin, is that which God requires.

This is that repentance which was the subject of the ministry of John the Baptist; on the neglect whereof he threatened the people with final excision; which, accordingly, not long after befell them, Matt. iii. 8–10. God doth not require a feigned repentance, or that which is merely outward and temporary. In this case, see Joel ii. 12, 13. But,—

Secondly. Where there is repentance and reformation that are *real* in the *root* or cause of them,—which is an effectual conviction of sin, and sense of ensuing, approaching judgments, giving testimony of sincerity in its fruits, by an abstinence from open provoking sins, and the performance of known duties (unto its sincerity in both which a sense and reverence of God is owned),—though it be not in many, in the most, it may be in few, *absolutely sincere and holy*, yet may it prevail to the turning away of threatened judgments, at least for a season.

These things, therefore, are required unto this repentance:—

1. A *real conviction of sin* in them that are called unto it, or do make profession of it. If this lie not in the foundation, no expression of repentance, no profession of reformation, is of any value in the sight of God;—yea, it is a mocking of him; which is the highest provocation. Men without this conviction may be driven to somewhat that *looks like repentance and reformation*, as the keeping of days of fasting or humiliation by outward force or compulsion of law; but there is nothing in what they do of what we inquire after. By such days and ways they shall never save the nation, Jer. iii. 10.

2. A *real sense of God's displeasure, and the approach of desolating judgments.* It is not enough that we have a conviction and sense of our own sins, but we must have them also of the sins of the nation, whereby God is provoked to anger; and apprehensions of his displeasure are to influence our minds in all that we go about herein. Unless these abide and dwell in our minds,—unless they accompany us continually in all our ways and occasions,—rise and lie down with us,—we shall not cordially engage in this duty.

3. Real reformation, in an *abstinence from all known sin*, and the avowed fruits of a reformed conversation, are required hereunto, Matt. iii. 10.

4. That it be *persisted in*, Heb. vi. 1.

On these suppositions, that this repentance is useful unto the end proposed is made fully evident in the instances of Nineveh and of Ahab, 1 Kings xxi. 27–29. Ahab, in his repentance and humiliation, manifested a deep sense of the guilt of sin and divine displeasure. "Seest thou," saith God to Elijah, "how he humbleth himself?" It might easily be known and taken notice of. There is a humiliation described by the prophet Isaiah, chap. lviii. 1–5, which God abhorreth, and which shall be profitable for nothing. Such have been the humiliations among us, for the most part. But although it be the duty of every man to endeavour that his repentance and reformation do consist in a sincere, internal, cordial conversion unto God,—which the divine calls do intend,—without which it will not be of advantage unto his own soul, as unto his eternal condition; yet as unto the turning away of *temporal calamities*, at least as to the suspension of them, such a public repentance and reformation as evidence themselves in their fruits to proceed from a real sense of sin and judgment, may be useful and prevalent. In brief, the repentance which God requireth with respect to his covenant,—that the souls of men may be saved, unto the glory of his grace by Jesus Christ,—is internal, spiritual, supernatural, whereby the whole soul is renewed, changed, and turned unto himself. But as God is the supreme governor of the world, in temporal things, with respect unto the dispensation of his providence in mercies and judgments, there may be a repentance and reformation wherein his glory is vindicated, in a visible compliance with his calls and warnings, and an acknowledgment of him in his righteous judgments, which may be of use unto the end proposed. Besides, wherever there is a general reformation of life sincerely attempted, it is to be believed that in many it is spiritual and saving.

5. The repentance and reformation required must be suited unto *the state and condition of those who are called thereunto.* All are to consider what is amiss in them, as unto their own state and condition, Isa. lv. 7, "Let the wicked forsake his way, and the unrighteous man his thoughts;"—every one his own way and thoughts in their present condition.

Wherefore the persons intended in this call are of two sorts:—

(1.) Such as are *wicked*, as unto their state and condition,—persons unconverted, unregenerate,—not born of God; and, (2.) Such as are *sincere believers*, really converted unto God.

The call of God is unto both sorts,—repentance and reformation are required of them both; and they are so in a suitableness unto their different conditions.

In each of these sorts there are *various degrees* of sin and provocation. Some of the first sort are openly flagitious,—public, habitual sinners,—such as whose sins "go beforehand unto judgment," as the apostle speaks, 1 Tim. v. 24; and some are more sober in their outward conversation. The call of God respects them in all their several degrees of sinning: "Let the wicked forsake his way, and the unrighteous man his thoughts;"—those which are his own, which are proper to him. None doubts, unless it be themselves, that the first sort ought to reform themselves;—the generality of men cry out against them, and fear that for their sins, especially if they be persons in high places, the judgments of God will come upon the land.

But if those of the other sort also, who are apt to justify themselves because they run not out unto the same excess of riot with them, do not apply themselves unto the repentance and reformation which are proper unto their state and condition, the will of God is not answered in his warnings. Yet it is the impenitency of this sort of men that is the most dangerous symptom at this day in the nation. Their unshaken security keeps all that truly fear God in a trembling posture.

Thirdly. It is so with churches peculiarly reformed, and true believers in them; as also all other true believers who walk more at large. They also are called unto repentance and reformation, and that according to their state and their respective degrees therein; for some are *more guilty* than others in decays of faith, love, zeal, holiness, and fruitfulness in obedience, with conformity to the world. And if there should be a public reformation in the nation as to outward *provoking sins*, yet if these of this sort do not reform themselves, according as their condition doth require, the desired deliverance would scarcely be obtained. And woe be to such persons, if, through their neglect of their duty, the whole nation should be exposed to ruin! Wherefore,—

Fourthly. The reformation called for, as the condition of escaping of impendent judgments, must be *universal*,—at least *general*,—amongst all sorts and degrees, all orders and estates of men. All sorts have sinned, all sorts are threatened; and therefore repentance is required of all, if we would not perish. It is so of magistrates and ministers, of nobles and common people, in city and country; and that to be evidenced by its fruits, so as that it may be said of us, See you not how they humble themselves?

But if this be so, some may be apt to say, It seems, if all do not set their hearts and hands unto this work, if all sorts do not engage in it, there is no good effect to be hoped or looked for; but when shall we see any such thing? when shall we see the generality of all sorts of men in this nation cordially to go about this work of repentance and reformation?—as good, therefore, let it alone as go about to attempt it.

I answer,—1. If you can be *content to perish* with the impenitent and unreformed, you may choose to do as they do. If you would avoid their punishment, you must avoid their sin, especially their refusal to turn on the call of God.

2. Some must *begin this work*, and be exemplary unto others;—and blessed are they of the Lord who shall receive the grace and honour so to do. Let us not, then, sit looking on others, to see what they will do, but immediately engage unto our own duty.

3. The duty herein of *no one private person*, much less of whole churches, shall be lost, though the nation should not be reformed in general. For,—

(1.) They *shall deliver their own souls;* and if they be not saved (as I believe they would be in an eminent manner) from somewhat of the outward part of a public calamity, yet they should be from all the wrath and displeasure of God in it.

(2.) A *few*—for aught I know, *one man*—may sometimes prevail with God for the suspending, at least, of judgments threatened unto a whole nation. And hereby,—

(3.) They shall give unto others a farther *season of repentance*, which God can bless and make effectual unto them.—There are, therefore, blessed encouragements unto all churches, unto all individual persons, to endeavour a compliance with the present calls of God, though the body of the people should not be gathered.

VII. Our next inquiry is, "Whence or from what causes such a reformation may be expected as may be useful unto the turning away of impendent judgments?" And these causes are either supreme or subordinate.

The *supreme* cause hereof must be the *sovereign grace of God*, in fresh effusions of his Spirit on the souls of men, to turn them unto himself. Without this, all other ways and means of attaining it will be in vain. This is everywhere in the Scripture attested unto as the only supreme, efficient cause of the conversion of men unto God. And unto that state are things come amongst us, that unless we are made partakers of it in a somewhat more than ordinary manner, our breaches cannot be healed. Whether we have grounds or no to expect any such thing, shall be afterward considered. At present there seems to be no other hopes of it, but only because it is a sovereign act of divine grace, which hath been exemplified in the church of old. There seems, indeed, rather, as yet, to be a withdrawing of the communications of the Holy Spirit in effectually prevalent grace on the part of God, and a contempt of them on the part of men; but sovereignty can conquer all obstacles. This way did God heal and recover his church of old, when all other means, all mercies, afflictions, and judgments, failed, Ezek. xxxvi. 22–28. And it may at present be for a lamentation, that this work of grace is so disregarded by the most, so despised by many, and so little cried for by the residue. But without it, in vain shall we use any other remedies; we shall not be healed. It is not the best projections of men for reformation by this or that order or state of things in church or state, that, without this, will be of advantage unto us.

The *subordinate* causes hereof must be the diligent discharge of their duty by magistrates and ministers.

I shall but name these things, that I give no place to complaints or indignation, though just, and almost necessary. And,—

First. As unto the furtherance of it by magistrates, it must consist in three things:—

1. By evidencing that the *promotion* of it is their interest. Unless it be understood so to be, whatever else they do in the countenance of it will be of no use nor advantage. For this is that which the generality will conform unto or comply withal. And if it be once understood that reformation is what they desire, what they design, what they place their chief interest in,—as it was with David, Hezekiah, Josiah, and others,—it will have an influence on the people, not inferior unto what the design of Jeroboam, in pursuit of his corrupt interest, had on the people of Israel to sin. All other means are dead, unless they are enlivened by an evidence of reality in the minds of magistrates, and a high concernment in the prosperity of their work. Let them make what laws and orders they please, appoint what outward means they can devise,—unless it be made uncontrollably evident that it is their *cordial design*, and what they place their *chief interest* in, they will not be available. Add hereunto,—

2. The due execution of laws against *flagitious immoralities*. And,—

3. An *encouraging example in their own persons;* without which all things will grow worse and worse, whatever else be done. Men seem to be weary, in some measure, of the dismal effects of sin; but they seem not to be weary of sin. Unto this weariness they yet want motives, encouragements, and examples. And it is strange unto me, that, in all our fears and dangers, —in the divisions of our councils and confusions amongst all sorts of men, under a high profession of zeal for the Protestant religion in the nation, and the preservation of it,—that this only expedient for our relief and safety lies wholly neglected.

As unto *ministers*, the faithful discharge of their duty, in preaching, prayer, and example, is required hereunto. Should I stay to show the necessity hereof at this season; as also what is required thereunto, —what care, what diligence, what watchfulness, what compassion, what zeal, what exercise of all gospel grace, with the over-neglect of these things among many,—it would take up a volume, rather than become a place in this present inquiry.

But I proceed unto that which is more our immediate concernment. Wherefore,—

VIII. "What if all these means do fail?—what if all expectations from them be in vain? what is incumbent on them in particular who are really sensible of these things,—namely, of the abounding of provoking sins, and the near approach of deserved judgments?"

That which I design herein is, to give some directions as unto what *frame of heart* ought to be found in us, and the *practice of what duties* we ought to be found in at such a season as this is. It is no common, no easy thing, to wait for the LORD in the way of his judgments, Isa. xxvi. 8, 9. There is inward soul-work night and day, as well as outward duties, required unto it. That God may be glorified in a due manner,—that we may be "found in peace," whatever be the event of things,—that we may be useful unto others, and in all serve the will of God in our generation,—are all expected from us in a way of duty.

Unto this end, the ensuing directions may be made use of:—

First. *Take heed of stout-heartedness, and a contempt or neglect thereby of divine warnings.* There is a generation who, either really or in pretence, are bold, fearless, stout-hearted, regardless of these things; they seem to provoke and dare God to do his utmost,—all that he seems to threaten. So they speak, Isa. v. 19, "Let him make speed, and hasten his work, that we may see it: and let the counsel of the Holy One of Israel draw nigh and come, that we may know it." Here is much talk, indeed, of the judgments of God, and of their near approach: When shall we see them? why do not they come? when shall he bring forth his work?

This hath been the great controversy between the church and the wicked world from the beginning of it. Those that truly feared God were always testifying that God would come, and take vengeance on them for their impieties and impenitency; but because these judgments were not speedily executed, the sinful world did always despise their warnings, and scoff at their message. So Enoch, the seventh from Adam, he preached and prophesied of these things,—namely, of the coming of God to take vengeance on ungodly men, Jude 14, 15. And this message was scoffed at, as is evident, because no reformation ensued thereon, until the flood took them all away. So was it with Noah and his preaching; and so it hath been with all that fear God, in their several generations. And this was one especial thing that the pagans laughed and mocked at the primitive Christians about,—as is plain in Lucian's "Philopatris."[1] So the apostle Peter

[1] The small piece entitled "Philopatris" has been ascribed to Lucian. It consists of a dialogue, in which Triepho and Critias discuss the respective merits of Paganism and Christianity, with a scoffing and sarcastic tone, indicating be-

gives us an account both of what was past, and what would afterward come to pass, 2 Pet. iii. 3 unto the end.

And such as these abound amongst us. All the *warnings* of God have been turned into ridicule, previous judgments despised, and sin itself made a scoff of. But, of all others, God most abhorreth this sort of men. They are said to be "far from righteousness," Isa. xlvi. 12. Unto such he speaks in his wrath, "Hear, ye despisers; wonder, and perish." Yea, the Scripture is full with the severest threatenings against this sort of men; nor shall any, in the appointed season, drink deeper of the cup of God's indignation. See Isa. xxviii. 14, 15; Deut. xxix. 19, 20. Such secure despisers, such scoffers at approaching judgments, such deriders of the signs and tokens of them, God will deal withal. And some there are who,—it may be, not from the same spirit of open profaneness, but out of prejudices, corrupt arguings, pretended observations of things past, disbelief of all they do not feel, and such like effects of long security,—do utterly scorn and scoff at all these things. They account it a matter of weakness, pusillanimity, or superstition, to concern themselves in these warnings of Providence, or the explication of them by the word. But their judgment sleepeth not. And it may be observed, and will be found true, that when judgments do really approach, of all sorts of men they are the most cowardly, distracted, fearful, and void of counsel. For when God begins to deal with them, their hearts cannot endure, nor their hands be strong. He smites through their loins, and filleth them with a spirit of horror and fear, that they shall tremble like the leaves of the forest. In that day you may say unto them, as Zebul did to boasting Gaal, upon the approach of Abimelech, his enemy, "Where is now thy mouth wherewith thou saidst, Who is Abimelech?" Where is now your mouth and your vauntings with respect unto these judgments of God? So Micaiah the prophet told Zedekiah the false prophet, in his boasting and confidence of success, 1 Kings xxii. 25, With all thy confidence and boasting, thou shalt be one of the first that shall endeavour to fly and hide thyself. Yea, this sort of persons are commonly the most ridiculous and contemptible, when real danger overtakes them, of any sort of men in the world.

That which God requires of us, in such a season, is called in Scrip-

lief in neither. Reference is made by Critias to some predictions he had heard among the Christians, that disaster and ruin were speedily to overtake the Roman empire. As if in ridicule and confutation of the prophecy, no sooner has he ended than Cleolaus makes his appearance, with the announcement of success and victory recently achieved by the Roman armies in the East. The dialogue concludes with a proposal to worship the unknown god of the Athenians. From the intimate knowledge evinced respecting the views and habits of the Christians, it has been inferred that Lucian must once have been a Christian himself; but, since the middle of last century, strong suspicions have been entertained that Lucian is not the author of this dialogue, but that it belongs to the time of Julian the apostate.—ED.

ture "trembling:" "They that tremble at my word." This he regards, this he accepts, this he approveth of, Isa. lxvi. 2, 5; Jer. v. 22. It is not a weakening, an astonishing, heartless consternation of spirit that is intended;—not such a dread and terror as should obstruct us in the cheerful performance of duty, and preparation to comply with the will of God; such is that mentioned, Deut. xxviii. 66, 67,—which is the most severe of judgments: but it is an awful reverence of the greatness and holiness of God, in the way of his judgments, casting out all carnal security, self-confidence, and contempt of divine warnings, so bringing the soul into a submissive compliance with the will of God in all things. But look well, in the first place, that this evil, on no pretences, do make any approach unto you.

If one evil seems to be diverted, do not say, with Agag, "Surely the bitterness of death is past" (which will prove an entrance into this evil frame), and so grow regardless of your duty. God expects other things from you. "The lion," saith he, "hath roared, who will not fear?" Amos iii. 8. There is the voice of a lion roaring for his prey in the present divine warnings: take heed that you despise not that which, when it comes to pass, you can neither abide nor avoid.

Secondly. Take heed of a frame of heart that is *regardless* of these things. We have a sort of men who, although they will not (they dare not) openly, as others, despise divine warnings, yet they see all things in such a light as suffers them not to take notice of any concernment of their own in them, Ps. xxviii. 5; Jer. xxxvi. 24. *The land is filled with sin;*—it is true, but they are the sins of other men, not theirs. *There are tokens and signs of God's displeasure, in heaven above, and the earth beneath;*—but men are not agreed whether these things be of any signification or no: some say Yea, and some Nay; but they are new and strange, and so are meet to be the subject of discourse. *Previous judgments have been upon us;*—they are but such accidents as fall out frequently in the world. But the *divisions among ourselves, and contrivances of our adversaries,* seem to threaten ruin to the nation;—it may be so, but these things belong unto our rulers; and men are divided about this also: some say one thing, and some another; some say there was a plot, and some say there was none. In the meantime they are filled with their own occasions, and will not be diverted from them unto any serious regard of God in his present dispensations; like the "wild ass in her occasion, who can turn her away?" Jer. ii. 24. Of this frame the prophet complains, as that which God will surely avenge, Isa. xxvi. 11, "LORD, when thy hand is lifted up, they will not see; but they shall see and be ashamed, for their envy at the people; yea, the fire of thine enemies shall devour them."

Others look on all things in another light, and under another notion; for whereas it is part of our sin and punishment in this nation, an evident fruit of the evil of our ways, that we are divided into designing parties, the one seeking the ruin of the other, they consider all providences as relating unto such differences. This gives them a zealous concernment in them, and continued talk about them; but the will, work, and design of God in them, are not laid to heart.

Some are so well pleased with their present advantages, in promotions, dignities, and wealth, as their interest, that they cannot endure to think of these things. Whatever warnings are portended of approaching judgments, they look on them as the threatenings of such as have ill-will against them, and would have these things to portend their trouble. Guilt makes them fearful and sensible, and they think it best to hide those things from themselves, which, if they are so, they cannot remedy.

To free us from this miscarriage also, this unanswerableness unto the mind of God in his present dispensation, we may consider,—

1. That a *deep consideration of, and inquiry into, the mind of God in such a season as we have described, is required of us in a way of duty.* It is our sin to neglect it, and that attended with many aggravations. It is not a thing that we may *attend* unto or *omit*, as it seems convenient; but it is required as a duty of us, without which we cannot glorify God in a due manner.

He that is not daily exercised with prevalent thoughts about the present ways of God in the approach of his judgments, lives in such a neglect of duty as will bring in a negligence and coldness in all other duties whatsoever; for this is certain, that when God calls unto any especial duty in an *extraordinary way* or manner, in any season, those by whom it is neglected are really cold, formal, and negligent in all other ordinary duties whatever. That grace which will not be excited unto especial duties on extraordinary occasions, is very lifeless in all other things. This is the best note to try, if not the truth, yet the power of grace. When it is in its vigour and due exercise, it makes the soul to be ready, inclinable, and disposed unto all intimations of the divine will and pleasure; as speaks the psalmist, "Thou shalt guide me by thine eye, and lead me with thy counsel." He attended to each look and guidance of divine Providence, to comply with it, when others must be forced with strong curbs and bridles, like the horse and mule.

2. It is such a duty as whereunto real wisdom and diligence are required. We think it needful to use our wisdom about other things, —our own affairs; but in this it is most necessary. "The LORD'S voice crieth unto the city, and the man of wisdom shall see thy name," Mic. vi. 9. Ordinary, slight, and transient thoughts will not answer this duty. Such all men that are sober cannot but have; and their

discourse is answerable thereunto. But consideration, with diligence and prudence, is required of us. Let these testimonies be consulted to this purpose, Ps. lxiv. 9; Deut. xii. 30; Hos. xiv. 9; Ps. cvii. 43. Prayer, study, and meditation, are all diligently to be engaged herein.

Thirdly. Take heed of *vain confidences.* Men are apt, in such seasons, to fix on one thing or other, wherewith they relieve and support themselves; and there is not any thing that is more effectual to keep them off from this duty and the frame of spirit which is required in them. If you speak with any man almost, you may, with a little heed, discover wherein his confidence doth lie, and what it is that he trusts unto. But, saith the prophet unto such persons, "The LORD hath rejected thy confidences, and thou shalt not prosper in them," Jer. ii. 37.

There are sundry sorts of vain confidences wherewith men are apt to relieve their minds in such a season, so as to countenance themselves in their security and a neglect of this especial duty. Two in particular I shall only mention, as I do only name the heads of things, which might be much enlarged:—

1. The first is some *certain privileges* whereon they trust for an exemption from common calamities;—they are the church,—they are the people of God,—they are separated from the world, and persecuted by it; and hence there is a secret reserve in their minds, that indeed they shall not be in trouble as other men. So was it with the Jews of old: when they were threatened with the judgments of God for their sins, and called thereon to repentance, they justified themselves in their ways, and despised all divine warnings, on a confidence they had in their church privileges. They cried against the prophet, "The temple of the LORD, The temple of the LORD, The temple of the LORD, are these," and no evil shall come nigh us, Jer. vii. 4. And in confidence hereof,—namely, that they were the church, and enjoyed the privileges belonging thereunto, and the solemn worship of God therein,—they gave themselves up unto all abominable immoralities, under an assurance of impunity by their privileges; as the prophet upbraids them, verses 8–10, "Behold, ye trust in lying words, that cannot profit. Will ye steal, murder, and commit adultery, and swear falsely, and burn incense unto Baal, and walk after other gods whom ye know not, and say you shall be delivered?"[1] At this day all sorts of men claim a refuge in their privileges. Those who design the ruin of the nation, and of all true religion therein, do it with confidence of success from hence, That they are the church,—that the temple of God is with them,—that all the privileges belonging unto the church

[1] The last clause is not according to the authorized version, but seems another translation of the words, to which Owen was inclined. Blayney renders it, "And say, Deliver us," etc.—ED.

are theirs, and so are the promises made unto it. And such is the infatuating efficacy of their prejudicate persuasion herein, that it hath had two marvellous effects;—the one against the light of nature, and the other against the fundamental principles of religion.

For, first, under the influence of this confidence they have engaged into as *vile immoralities* as ever were perpetrated under the sun;—murder, persecution, assassinations, dying in falsehoods, with a general design to pursue the same ways unto the utmost, in the destruction of multitudes of innocent persons, as they did formerly in Ireland. But what if they do all those abominations? yet they are *the church!* the promises and privileges of it are theirs! and all they do is accepted with God!—a principle tending directly to the vilest atheism.

Again; although God, in a marvellous, yea, a miraculous manner, hath discovered and frustrated their hellish designs, and brought many of them into the pit they digged for others, yet they will accept of no rebuke from God, but go on in an obstinate presumption that they are the church, and shall prevail at last. And *that church* which shall prevail by these means, no doubt they are. Some, indeed, pretend highly to be the church; but they lay claim, so far as I can find, to no other advantages thereby but dignities and promotions. And others also are apt to relieve themselves with this confidence, that they are *the people of God,* and shall have an especial interest in deliverance on that account. And I say, Far be it from me to weaken any persuasion of God's especial regard of those that are truly his. God hath a peculiar people in the world, let the world scoff at it whilst they please, unto whom all the promises of the Scripture and all the privileges of the church do belong. These promises they ought to mix with faith, and plead before God continually; and they shall be all accomplished towards them, in the way and time of God's appointment. Nor do any sort of dissenting professions, as they are called, that I know of, appropriate this right and privilege unto themselves, unto the exclusion of others; but extend it to all who are sincere believers. But this is that which I say concerning all sorts of men,—That if an apprehension or persuasion that they are the church or people of God do keep them off from that duty of repentance and reformation which God calls unto, it is a confidence which God rejecteth, and in which they will not prosper. I desire to ask of any, Hath not the church sinned? have not professors sinned? are there not sins amongst us against the Lord our God proper unto our state, and according to our measure? If it be so, our being the people of God, any of us, if we are so, unless we repent, doth only, as unto these providential dispensations, expose us unto his just severity; for judgment must begin at the house of God,—it must begin at us. Take heed of this failing reserve. I have observed much security to arise from hence, and great negligence of known duties. If you are the people of God, you had the more need to tremble at his judgments, and at the tokens of his displeasure. Especially ought it to be so with you at this day, when God seems in a peculiar manner to be "displeased with the rivers," as the prophet speaks, Hab. iii. 8,—those who should send forth streams of refreshment unto the nation. To me, at present, all things appear in that condition, that there is no reserve left, as unto public judgments, but only in sovereign grace and mercy, to be waited for in a way of repentance and reformation. As unto our privileges, God speaks unto us as he did to the people of old concerning their ornaments, Exod. xxxiii. 5, Put them off, "that I may know what to do unto thee." We are to lay aside our pleas and pretences, betaking ourselves to sovereign grace and mercy alone.

2. Another ground of vain confidence may be, *an unjust expectation of an accomplishment of such Scripture promises, prophecies, and predictions, as are not applicable unto our present condition.*

It is undeniable, that there are such promises, prophecies, and predictions concerning the deliverance of the church, the ruin of its adversaries, the glory and beauty of the kingdom of Christ, as those intended. For although the most of that kind in the Old Testament are of a *spiritual interpretation*, and have their accomplishment in all the elect in every age, whatever be their outward state and condition; yet that there are such also as concern the state of the church in this world, and the ruin of all its antichristian enemies, with peace and glory ensuing thereon, cannot be denied.

And concerning them we may observe sundry things, that we may not abuse them into vain and groundless confidences in such a season as this is:—

(1.) That we ought to have a *firm faith* of their accomplishment in their proper season. The rule of them all is that of the prophet, "I the LORD will hasten it in his time," Isa. lx. 22; as it is also Hab. ii. 2, 3. Though they seem to be prolonged, and tarry beyond their proper season, yet they have their fixed and determinate time, beyond which they shall not tarry. And two things I would offer on this occasion:—

[1.] That we are not only *to believe their accomplishment*, but to be in the actual exercise of faith about it; for without this, we shall want a great supportment of patient long-suffering in every time of trial. And by this faith do we take in the power and comfort of things promised, things not actually enjoyed; for "faith is the substance of things hoped for," Heb. xi. 1,—that which gives a previous subsistence in the mind and soul, as unto the benefit and comfort of them, of "the things hoped for." And those whose minds are exercised unto these things do know what benefit they have by such a perception of them. They are carried sometimes, by a way of believing, into communion with them who lived in the old world, as they had with us in the expectation of what we enjoy; and into the same kind of communion with those who hereafter shall enjoy the accomplishment of those promises which may yet be afar off.

[2.] This faith ought to be most firm when all things seem to conspire in rendering the accomplishment of such promises not only improbable, but also impossible, as unto present outward causes; as in the state of things at this day in the world. There are no visible or appearing means of the fulfilling any of them,—yea, the whole world is joined in a conspiracy to defeat them; but true faith riseth against those oppositions, and is prevalent against them all.

For, having God alone—his power, faithfulness, and truth—for its object, it values not the opposition that men can make against them. That shall be done in this kind which God is able to do, let men do what they please. God laughs all their proud attempts to scorn; and so may the virgin daughter of Zion also.

(2.) It is our duty *to pray for the accomplishment of all the promises and predictions* that are on record in the book of God concerning the kingdom of Christ and his church in this world. God will do these things; yet for all of them he will be sought unto by the house of Israel. This hath been the practice of believers in all ages, both under the Old Testament and the New. Prayer for the accomplishment of promises hath been the life-breath of the church in all ages; and faith hereby brings in great refreshment unto the soul. And the greatest evidence of its approach will be a plentiful effusion of the Holy Spirit in the hearts of believers, be they few or more at any time in the world, stirring them up and enabling them to pray effectually and fervently for their accomplishment; as in the example of Daniel, chap. ix. 1–3. Wherefore,—

(3.) There are three things considerable in such promises and predictions:—[1.] The *grace* and *mercy* that is in them; [2.] The *suitableness* of that grace and mercy unto the state of believers at any time; [3.] The *literal accomplishment* of them in their outward circumstances. The two former belong unto us at all times, and we may plead with God in faith for the effects of them in all our trials and distresses.

With respect hereunto it is that the people of God have faith in him against the world, with all their enemies and oppressors, which they have been so reproached withal, as the Lord Christ was with his faith unto the same purpose, Ps. xxii. 8. When things seem to go evil with them, when they are shut up in the hands of their enemies and oppressors, as the Lord Christ was upon the cross, the world is ready to reproach them with their confidence in God, and their owning themselves to be his people; but they faint not herein. However things may go for a season, they are secured of the grace and mercy which is in the promises; which are suited unto all their wants, all that they can desire absolutely, yea, their full deliverance, when it is best for them. But,—

(4.) Remember, that, as unto the *application* of the accomplishment of such promises and predictions, in their outward effects, unto certain times and seasons, many have been wofully mistaken; which hath been the ground and occasion of very scandalous miscarriages. The world hath scarce seen greater outrages of sin and wickedness than have been countenanced by this pretence, that such or such a time was now come, and that therein such and such things were to be done by those who made such interpretations and applications. For when such a conceit befalls the minds of men, it sets them loose from all rules but their own inclinations. And many have, from such apprehensions, fallen under sad and scandalous disappointments. Wherefore,—

(5.) *Such an expectation* or confidence of the events of promises, prophecies, and predictions, as hinders men from applying their minds thoroughly unto the present duties that God calls for, is heedfully to be watched against. I have heard many arguing and pleading for the strengthening of such confidences, but I never saw good effect of them. They please for the present; they profit not.

The story of the prophets Jeremiah and Hananiah is applicable in this case, Jer. xxviii. And it is certain that, before the final destruction of Jerusalem, that which principally hardened the people unto their utter ruin, so as they would hearken neither to the voice of God nor man for their safety, was a presumption they had, that at that time their Messiah would come and save them.

(6.) Few know of what sort that *day of the Lord* will be, which they desire, long for, and expect. We know how it proved unto the church of the Jews, Mal. iii. 1, 2. A day may be coming which, although it may be a glorious issue, yet it may consume all the hopes that men have treasured up in their expectation of it. But I will not touch farther on these things:—my design is only to take us all off from such vain confidences as may obstruct us in a diligent attendance unto those duties which God at this season calls us unto; which shall be declared immediately.

3. Some place their confidence in *secret reserves* which they have in themselves, that however it go with others, yet they shall escape well enough. They are rich, and they intend to be wise:—they intend not to be engaged in any thing, civil or religious, that should prejudice them in their possessions:—whilst things pass at the cheap rate of talking, they will be like unto others; but when trials come,

they will make a safe retreat. We have their character and their doom, Jer. xxviii. 15–17.

Fourthly. A fourth direction for our deportment in such a season is, that we diligently consider and search our own hearts and ways, to find out and understand how it is between God and our souls. This direction is given us, Lam. iii. 39, 40, " Wherefore doth a living man complain, a man for the punishment of his sins? Let us search and try our ways, and turn again to the LORD." When trials and punishments draw nigh, or are upon us, it is not our business nor duty to lie complaining under them, but so to search and try our ways as to turn unto the Lord. This is the first word of the voice of God in approaching judgments, " Search yourselves, try your hearts and your ways,—try how it is with you." At such a season, to pass by the consideration of ourselves, of our state, of our walk, of our actions, in an ordinary manner, or with slight or common thoughts, is to despise the voice of God. God speaks aloud: " The voice of God crieth unto the city." He doth so by the ways before mentioned;—he speaks articulately, distinctly, so as that a man of wisdom may see his name, and know his mind;—he speaks unto us, and says, Search now yourselves.

And in this search, respect is to be had unto the things ensuing:—

1. In general, search into your *state and condition*. Try whether it be built on a good foundation;—on the rock, by faith; or on the sand, by profession only;—whether it will hold His trial who will bring it to the refiner's fire: " He shall slay the hypocrite with the breath of his mouth." And many dreadful discoveries will be made of the false and rotten states of men when the Lord's day of trial shall come. This is one certain end of a fiery trial, namely, to discover and consume the profession of hypocrites; as hath been done in part already.

2. With respect unto those ways and sins which are the *peculiarly provoking sins* of churches and professors;—such as the Lord Christ testifieth his displeasure against in them, and which may have as great an influence into the procurement of temporal judgments as the more flagitious sins of open sinners: such are decays in love, zeal, and fruits of obedience; want of delight, warmth, and life in the ordinances of gospel worship; with pride, elation of mind, self-conceit, and barrenness in good works. If we would know what are the sins, in churches and professors, that the Lord Christ is so displeased with as to threaten his departing from them, we cannot better learn it than in the declaration of his mind which he makes unto the churches of Asia, Rev. ii. and iii. And these are the things which he chargeth on them. For persons under the capacities of church members and professors, to content themselves with such a search of their outward actions and duties of all sorts, religious, moral, and civil, as none

may justly cast blame upon them, it no way answers the search that God calls them unto. How is it as unto the inward frame of the heart? What is the vigour and power of faith and love in you? How do they act themselves? What is your real delight in the ways of God? Where is your fruitfulness in works of charity and mercy? Where is your readiness to forgive your enemies? Are there no failings, no decays in these things? Are there no indispositions, deadness, and coldness in duties grown upon you? How is it as unto constant meditation on spiritual things, and the fixing your affections on things that are above? With respect unto these things ought we to search ourselves diligently in such a day as this is; and if we find ourselves under decays in them, let us know of a truth that God calls us unto repentance, on pain of his highest displeasure.

For our parts, we cannot search into, we cannot judge, the hearts of others, any other way but by the *application* of the word unto their consciences; but I must needs say, that if men's outward actions be an indication of the inward frame of their minds, there is reason enough for the most of us to be jealous over ourselves herein.

3. With respect unto your *callings, circumstances*, and *inclinations*, and the sins that are peculiar unto them. There are sins which are very apt to insinuate themselves into the callings and circumstances of men, both of high and low degree, that do easily beset them; as, hardness, oppression, severity, and unmercifulness, in those that are great and have large possessions; and deceit, equivocations, over-reachings, in those of more ordinary employments. I speak not of these at present; they are of the number of those which "go beforehand unto judgment." But these things—namely, men's callings, circumstances, and inclinations—are apt to influence their mind with vicious habits, and to render their ways crooked. Pride of life, self-conceit, negligence in holy duties, distempered passions and lusts, devouring cares, carnal fears, with other hurtful evils, do spring from these things, if not watched against. In reference unto them, therefore, are we called to search ourselves in a day wherein God is pleading with us. With respect unto them ought we to be exceeding jealous over ourselves; for verily they have rendered the ways and walkings of the generality of professors a great provocation unto Christ Jesus.

4. In an especial manner with a respect unto *love of the world*, and conformity thereunto. This is that which the Lord Jesus Christ will not always bear withal in his churches; for it lies in opposition unto the whole work of faith and all the precepts of the gospel. It is not against this or that command only, but it is against the whole design of the gospel, and the grace administered therein.

Now, at present, concerning our outward conformity unto the world, there needs no great search to be made. It is open and evident unto all; so that, as unto attire, fashions, manner of ordinary converse, misspense of time, feastings of rich ones, and jollities, there is little difference left between professors and the world;—which God will not long bear with them in; especially not in those who have increased their wealth in, and grown into conformity with, the world, whilst others, under the same profession, have been harassed, imprisoned, impoverished, and ruined by the world. And as for inordinate love unto the world, I have spoken so often to it, treated so much of it, that I shall not here again insist upon it. I shall only say, that when men grow proud, high-minded, and value themselves according to the increase of their earthly enjoyments, and think themselves wronged if others do not also so value them, it is in vain for them to pretend that their hearts do not inordinately cleave unto the world and the things of it.

This *self-searching* is the first duty we are at this season called unto; and if we are negligent or overly herein, we shall not answer the mind and will of God in any one duty or instance of any other kind. We are, therefore, herein to call in God and men unto our aid and assistance, as also to stir up ourselves unto it with diligence and perseverance. So the psalmist, lest he should not be able to make a diligent, effectual examination of himself and his ways, cries unto God to search and try him, that he might be known unto himself, especially with respect unto any evil way of sin or wickedness, Ps. cxxxix. 23, 24. So we ought to cry for fresh communications of the Holy Spirit of God in his convincing efficacy, to acquaint us thoroughly with ourselves, and to deliver us from all self-deceivings in this matter. For when we go about this search, a thousand pretences and arguings will arise, to the concealment or countenance of self and sin against a discovery and pursuit. Nothing can remove and scatter them but the power of the Holy Spirit acting in his convincing efficacy. The whole deceit of the heart in such a season will be put forth, to hide, palliate, excuse, and countenance such frames and actings as ought to be seized on and brought to judgment. There is need of the "candle of the LORD, to search the inward parts of the belly," Prov. xx. 27;—of spiritual light, to look into the secret recesses of the mind and affections, to discover what is amiss in them. And there is need of spiritual strength, to cast down all the strongholds and fortifications of sin; which will be all set up at such a time, and will not be demolished or scattered without powerful actings of grace. This, therefore, in the first place, we are to apply ourselves unto, if we intend any success in this work of self-examination.

So also are we to pray that the word, in the preaching and dispensation of it, may be effectual unto the same end,—that we may find it quick and powerful, Heb. iv. 12,—that it may so judge the secrets of our hearts, 1 Cor. xiv. 25, that we may fall down and judge ourselves also. To hide ourselves at such a season from the power of the word, is an open evidence of a ruining security.

This work, in the use of these means, is to be called over and persisted in, if we design a compliance with the present calls of God, or an endeavour to be found of him in peace when he cometh.

Fifthly. To be deeply *humbled before the Lord* for our own sins, with a relinquishment of them all thereon, is the principal part of our duty in this season. This the whole Scripture testifieth unto, speaking of these things. Without this, all that we do, or can do, signifies nothing, as unto a compliance with the calls of God. This is the end of the search before insisted on. We are to find out, to know every one the plague, the stroke, the disease of his own heart, so as to be humbled before the Lord for it.

And unto this humiliation it is required,—

1. That it be *internal* and *sincere*. There is a humiliation commonly expressing itself in the observation of days of fasting and prayer; which oftentimes is but the hanging down of the head like a bulrush for a day. However, it may be so carried, sometimes, as to divert or prolong the execution of threatened judgments; but that which God requireth of us is to be in the fixed affections of the heart. When the Lord Christ comes to enjoin repentance and reformation, he gives himself that title, "I am he that searcheth the reins and hearts," Rev. ii. 23. It is an internal, hidden work which he looks after, in our humiliation for sin. So saith David in the same case, "Thou requirest truth in the inward parts," Ps. li. Truth or sincerity in the affections is that which God regards in our humiliation; which answers the charge in the prophet, "Rend your hearts, and not your garments;"—inward power, not outward signs, are accepted with God in this matter. Let us every one take it on our own souls, every one charge his own conscience in private, with the performance of this duty. God will bear no longer with pretences; no outward appearances or evanid affections, in a temporary humiliation for *a day*, though in the observation of the most solemn duties required on such a day, will answer the mind of God herein. For,—

2. It must be *extraordinary*. Humiliation for our own sins is a duty constantly incumbent on us. To walk humbly with God is the principal thing that he requires of us in this world, Mic. vi. 8. Hereof self-abasement, in a sense of sin, is the life and soul; the principle of all other acts and duties belonging thereunto. But when the calls of God are extraordinary, as they are at this day, it is necessary that we attend hereunto in an extraordinary manner. Failing in the necessary degrees of a duty renders it ineffectual and unacceptable. If, as unto times and seasons, ways, means, and manner, of this duty, we

do not apply ourselves unto it with more than ordinary diligence, and with great intention of mind, we fail in what is expected from us. To deal with God on extraordinary occasions in an ordinary frame of spirit, is to despise him; or argues, at least, no due reverence of him in his judgments, nor a due apprehension of our own concerns in them.

3. It is required that humiliation for sin be accompanied with a *relinquishment of sin:* "He that confesseth his sins, and forsaketh them, shall find mercy." Confession is grown a cheap and easy labour, whether it be read out of a book, or discharged by virtue of spiritual gifts. Humiliation may be pretended when it is not, and expressed when it is transitory;—no way answering the mind and will of God. But the real relinquishment of sinful frames, sinful ways, sinful neglects, can neither be pretended nor represented better than it is. He that thinks he hath nothing to forsake,—no evil way, no sinful negligence, no frame of heart,—will be awakened to a better knowledge of himself when it is too late. This we may, therefore, evidently try ourselves by:—What real change hath there been in us, in compliance with the calls of God? what have we relinquished in our ways, frames, or actings? what vain thoughts are utterly excluded, whereunto we have given entertainment? what passions or affections have been reduced into order, which have exceeded their due bounds and measures? what vain communication, formerly accustomed unto, hath been watched against and prevented? what dissimulation in love hath been cured or cast out? what irregular actings, in our persons, families, or occasions of life, have been forsaken? An inquiry into these things will give us real, sensible evidence whether our humiliation for our own sins be compliant with the present calls of God.

Sixthly. Another duty of the season is, that *we mourn for the sins of others,*—of those especially in whom we are providentially concerned; as relations, churches, the whole people of the land of our nativity, with whom we are engaged by manifold bonds and means of conjunction. It is well known that this sincere mourning for the sins of the places and times wherein we live, of the people and churches whereunto we do belong, is eminently approved of God, and a token unto themselves in whom that sense is of deliverance in a day of calamity, Ezek. ix. 4–6. To have minds careless and regardless of the sins of other men, is a great evidence of want of sincerity in our profession of the detestation of sin. Many pretences there are of it;—as, that they will not hear us;—we are not concerned in them;—that they are wicked enemies of God, and the worse they are, the more will their destruction be hastened. By such pretences do men deceive their souls into a neglect of this duty, yea, unto provoking sin, such as this is.

It is a matter of sorrow unto them that truly fear God, and have any concernment in his glory, or the honour of Christ, that the whole world, so far as we know, is filled with all abominable, provoking sins. It lies under a deluge of sin, as it lay of old under a flood of waters;—only here and there appeareth an ark, that is carried above it. Atheism, antiscripturism, disbelief of gospel mysteries, contempt of the religion which they themselves profess, amongst all sorts of Christians,—the loss of all public faith and trust, with a litter of unclean lusts,—ambition, pride, covetousness, in many who have the outward conduct of the church,—have spread themselves over the face of the earth. When God thus deals with the world, when he gives it up unto this open profligate excess which now abounds in it, it becomes, unto all that truly fear him, a place of darkness and sorrow, which calls for a mourning frame of heart.

It is so, much more as unto the *land of our nativity*. From a conjunction with this people in blood, language, manners, laws, civil interests, relations, arising from the common law of nativity, in a place limited and bounded by Providence unto especial ends, we cannot but have a great concernment in their good or evil. It is greater from hence, that the same true religion hath been professed in the whole nation, with innumerable privileges accompanying it.

On these and the like considerations, the whole nation is laid under the same law of providence for good or evil.

In the *sin*, therefore, of this people, we are in a peculiar manner concerned; and shall be so in their *sufferings*.

Whether sin abound in the land at present, we have already made inquiry; and nothing spoken before shall be repeated. If we have not a sense of these provocations,—if we endeavour not to affect our hearts with them, and mourn over them,—we are very remote from that frame which God calls unto.

And this mourning for the sins of others ariseth from a double spring:—1. *Zeal for the glory of God;* 2. *Compassion for the souls of men*,—yea, for the woful, *calamitous state and condition* which is coming upon them even in this world.

Surely, those who are true believers cannot but be concerned in all the concerns of the glory of God. If in all our afflictions he is afflicted, in all the sufferings of his glory we ought to suffer. In the blessed direction given us for our prayers, as unto what we ought to pray for, that which in the first place is prescribed, as that which principally and eminently we ought to insist on, is the glory of God in the sanctification of his name, the progressive coming of the kingdom of Christ, and the accomplishment of his will by the obedience of men in the world. If we are sincere herein, if we are fervent in these supplications, is it nothing unto us, when all these things are quite contrary amongst us? When the name of God is blasphemed, and all things whereon he hath placed his name are derided;—when the whole internal interest and kingdom of Christ are opposed, and the outward court of the temple given everywhere to be trodden down of the Gentiles;—when all manner of sins abound, in opposition unto the will and commands of God;—when the earth is almost as unlike unto heaven as hell itself;—is there nothing to be mourned for herein? We are for the most part selfish; and so it may go well with ourselves, according to the extent of our relations and circumstances, we are not greatly moved with what befalls others. There is evil enough herein; but shall we be, moreover, so minded towards Jesus Christ, that whilst we are in safety, we care not though his concernments are in the utmost hazard? Do we love the name of God, the ways of God, the glory of God in his kingdom and rule?—we cannot but be deeply affected with the suffering of them all in these days.

The other *spring of this mourning frame*, is compassion for the souls of sinners, and their persons also, in the approach of calamitous desolations.

I am hastening to an end, and cannot insist on these things: this only I shall say, he that can take a prospect of the eternally miserable condition of multitudes among whom we live, and the approaching miseries which, without repentance and reformation, will not be avoided, and not spend some tears on them, hath a heart like a flint or adamant, that is capable of no impression.

Seventhly. It is a season wherein we are called to a diligent, heedful attendance unto the *duties of our stations, places, and callings;*—duties in our church relations, duties in our families, duties in our callings and manner of conversation in the world. This is the advice given by the apostle, with respect unto such a season, 2 Pet. iii. 11, 14, "Seeing that all these things shall be dissolved, what manner of persons ought ye to be, in all holy conversation and godliness? Wherefore, be diligent that you may be found of him in peace, without spot, and blameless." Without a sacred diligence in all these duties, we cannot be found in peace of the Lord Christ when he comes to judge the world, and purify his church with a fiery trial.

Negligence, coldness, and sloth in these things, are tokens of approaching judgments. And of some of them at this day the generality of professors seem to be almost weary, and to attend unto them in a very indifferent and overly manner. But we may know assuredly, that if we thrive not in our diligence in these things, if the vigour of our spirits in watchfulness be not engaged in them, we are not compliant with the present calls of God.

Eighthly. It is required of us that we cry earnestly, continually, with perseverance, for *such an effusion of the Holy Spirit from above,* as may dispose and work the inhabitants of the land unto repentance and reformation.

That this is the only way, the only means of relief, of a sanctified deliverance from desolating judgments, hath been declared. And this is the only way which some of us have to help and assist the nation in its distress. Wherefore, by a constant continuance in supplication for such effusions of the Holy Spirit, we shall have a threefold advantage:—

1. We shall hereby *discharge the duty we owe unto the land of our nativity* in such a way as none can deny or hinder.

We owe a duty unto it on all good accounts,—moral, political, spiritual. We are, for the most of us, shut up from giving any other assistance unto it, by advice, counsel, or action. This is that which none can hinder,—wherein the poorest may be as useful and serviceable as the mighty. And if it be diligently attended unto, it will be far above whatever can be contributed by wisdom, wealth, or strength, unto the same end. For by this means we shall be saved, or perish.

2. It will preserve our own hearts in *the best frame* for what we ourselves may be called unto. He that is earnest and sincere in his supplications for the communication of the Spirit unto others, shall not want blessed supplies of him in his own soul. He will not withdraw from them, as unto themselves, who so esteem, prize, and value his work towards others.

3. We shall hereby give *testimony unto God* and his grace against the cursed profaneness of the world, who reject and despise this only means of relief and deliverance; for when all other remedies fail, if God will not utterly forsake a church or people, he doth constantly assign this as the only means of their safety. See Jer. xxxi. 31–33; Ezek. xi. 17–19, xxxvi. 25–27. This way the world despiseth, regardeth not; wherefore we can in nothing give a greater testimony unto God than by insisting on this way with faith and patience, contemning the reproaches of the world on the account of it.

Ninthly. Let us labour ourselves to be *exemplary in reformation*, thereby to promote it among others. Let us plead and exhort what we will, unless we give an evidence in our own persons of the necessity which we judge that there is of present reformation, we shall be of little use unto the promotion of it.

Many retrenchments of liberty in conversation may be made among the best of us; many duties may be attended with more diligence; many causes of offence avoided; many evidences given of a deep sense of deserved judgments, and of our reverence of the name of God therein;—much fruitfulness in charity and good works be declared.

I have heard that in the country, where a man is looked on to be a wise man and a *good husbandman* among his neighbours, they will note the times of his ploughing, sowing, and manuring his ground, and not undertake any thing until they find him going before them in it. And if men are looked on in a peculiar manner as professors of religion at such a time as this, under calls and warnings from God for repentance and reformation, the eyes of other men will be towards them, to see what they do on this occasion. And if they find them, as unto all outward appearance, careless and negligent, they will judge themselves unconcerned, and abide in their security. Wherefore, so far as I know, if such persons be not exemplary, not only in repentance, but also in the evidence and demonstration of it by its outward fruits, they may be, and are, the great obstructers of the reformation of the cities, towns, and places wherein they do inhabit; nor can any contract the guilt of a greater sin. And if God should bring an overflowing scourge on the inhabitants of this land, because they have not turned unto him at his calls, it is most righteous that they should share in the judgment also who were an occasion of their continuance in security,—a matter we have all just cause to tremble at.

END OF VOL. VIII.